LIBRARY OF NEW TESTAMENT STUDIES

454

formerly the Journal for the Study of the New Testament Supplement series

Editor
Mark Goodacre

Editorial Board
John M. G. Barclay, Craig Blomberg, R. Alan Culpepper,
James D. G. Dunn, Craig A. Evans, Stephen Fowl, Robert Fowler,
Simon J. Gathercole, John S. Kloppenborg, Michael Labahn,
Robert Wall, Steve Walton, Robert L. Webb, Catrin H. Williams

HOW TO KILL THINGS WITH WORDS

Ananias and Sapphira under the Prophetic Speech-Act
of Divine Judgement (Acts 4.32–5.11)

DAVID R. MCCABE

t&t clark

BS
2625.52
.M388
2011

Published by T&T Clark International
A Continuum Imprint
The Tower Building, 11 York Road, London SE1 7NX
80 Maiden Lane, Suite 704, New York, NY 10038

www.continuumbooks.com

All rights reserved. No part of this publication may be reproduced or transmitted in any form or by any means, electronic or mechanical, including photocopying, recording or any information storage or retrieval system, without permission in writing from the publishers.

© David R. McCabe, 2011

David R. McCabe has asserted his right under the Copyright, Designs and Patents Act, 1988, to be identified as the Author of this work.

British Library Cataloguing-in-Publication Data
A catalogue record for this book is available from the British Library

ISBN: HB: 978-0-567-52543-7

Typeset by Free Range Book Design & Production Limited
Printed and bound in Great Britain

For my sweetheart and best friend, Rashella.
This labour of love is evidence of your generous
support and saintly patience.

And for our two children, Sarina and Ezra,
who fill life with such joy and celebration.
Now, Daddy can come play with you …

CONTENTS

Acknowledgements	xi
Abbreviations	xiii
Abstract	xvii

1. Introduction: Reopening the Case of Ananias and Sapphira	1
1.1. Previous Questions and Approaches to the Text	2
1.2. The Contribution and Approach of this Study	4
1.2.1. Narrative Logic and Verbal Transaction	4
1.2.2. Reading Luke-Acts as a Coherent Narrative	4
1.2.3. Textual Transmission: Two Narratives?	6
1.3. The Trajectory of this Study	7
2. Ananias and Sapphira as an Episode in the Narrative of Acts	9
2.1. Divine Judgement Discourse Embedded in Community-of-Goods Discourse	9
2.2. Community-of-Goods Discourse Embedded in Community Interaction and Conflict Discourse	11
2.3. Internal Repetition and Echo Effect	14
2.3.1. Following the Plot of Acts	14
2.3.2. The Sanctity of the Community	20
2.3.3. Conflicting Leadership Appeals	23
2.3.4. Godly Obedience and Satanic Opposition	26
2.3.5. Building Suspense over the 'Enemies of God'	28
2.4. Summary and Conclusion for Literary Co-text	29
3. Introducing Prophetic Speech-Acts	30
3.1. Narrative as Dialogue and the Philosophy of Language	30
3.2. The 'Referential' View	31
3.3. The 'Magical' View	37
3.4. Peter's Language as 'Performative' Prophetic Utterance	39
3.5. Speech-Act Theory as a Socio-Pragmatic Tool for 'Thick' Description	43
3.5.1. Necessary Elements of Speech-Act Theory	45
3.5.1.1. Focusing on the Illocutionary Act	46
3.5.1.2. Dimensions of Illocutionary Acts	47
3.5.1.3. Accepted Conventions and the Fictive Context of Narrative	48

viii *Contents*

3.5.1.4. Deputized Agency and Superintendence	52
3.5.2. The Limits of Speech-Act Theory	53
4. Socio-Historical Repertoire I: The Jerusalem Church	56
4.1. Community-of-Goods and Friendship	56
4.1.1. 'Embedded' Economy	57
4.1.1.1. Symbolic Economic Transactions	57
4.1.1.2. Reciprocity and Exchange	58
4.1.2. Primary Social Structures	60
4.1.2.1. Honour/Shame and the Ancient Gift	60
4.1.2.2. Benefaction and Friendship	62
4.1.2.3. Friendship and (E)utopia	64
4.2. The Divine Economy in Luke-Acts	65
4.2.1. The Moral Universe of the Early Christian Community-of-Goods	67
4.2.2. Messianic (E)utopian Community-of-Goods	71
4.2.2.1. The Character of the Christian Community-of-Goods	72
4.2.2.2. Discipline and Extirpation	76
4.3. Summary and Looking Ahead	82
5. Socio-Historical Repertoire II: Pagan and Jewish Examples	84
5.1. The Divine Economy of the Pythagoreans	84
5.1.1. The Problems and Limitations of the Sources	85
5.1.2. The Moral Cosmos of the Pythagorean Community	88
5.1.3. The Pythagorean Community-of-Goods	91
5.1.4. Initiation and Excommunication	94
5.1.5. Summary and Connection with Acts	97
5.2. The Divine Economy of the Essenes	98
5.2.1. Josephus and Philo on Essene Communities-of-Goods	99
5.2.1.1. Virtuous (Common) Life and Honourable Reputation	101
5.2.1.2. Communal Solidarity and Hospitality	104
5.2.1.3. Moneyless Economy and General Reciprocity	104
5.2.1.4. Initiation Ritual and Discipline	105
5.2.1.5. Summary and Connection with Acts	106
5.3. The Communities of Khirbet Qumrân	107
5.3.1. The Moral Universe of the Renewed Covenant	108
5.3.2. The Community Rule	111
5.3.2.1. Introduction	111
5.3.2.2. Initiation and Discipline	112
5.3.2.3. Summary	115
5.3.3. The Damascus Document	116
5.3.3.1. Introduction	116
5.3.3.2. Economic Transactions as Community Boundary Markers	118

	5.3.3.3. Initiation and Discipline	120
	5.3.3.4. Summary	123
5.4.	Summary and Conclusions for Socio-Historical Context	123

6. Inscribed Conventions: Divine Deputation and the Pattern of Salvation and Judgement — 124
  6.1. External Literary Repertoire: Effective Prophetic Speech in the Scriptures of Israel — 125
    6.1.1. Accusing Questions and Assertions — 125
  6.2. Internal Repertoire: Effective Prophetic Speech in Luke-Acts — 127
    6.2.1. The Holy Spirit: The Divine Performance — 128
    6.2.2. Jesus as Prophet-King Pronouncing Salvation and Judgement — 132
      6.2.2.1. The Preparation and Anointing of the Messiah — 134
        6.2.2.1.1. The Birth of the Messiah — 134
        6.2.2.1.2. The Baptism and Testing of the Messiah — 135
      6.2.2.2. The Story of Lukan Messianic Prophecy: The Lineage of Rejected Prophets — 137
      6.2.2.3. The Shape of Lukan Messianic Prophecy: Jesus as a Prophet-King like Moses and David — 140
        6.2.2.3.1. The Prophet-King's Exodus to Jerusalem — 140
        6.2.2.3.2. Jesus' Prophetic Indictment of Jerusalem — 144
        6.2.2.3.3. The 'Raising-Up' of the Prophet-King in Jerusalem — 145
        6.2.2.3.4. Proclaiming the Risen Prophet-King — 146
    6.2.3. Further Examples Clarifying Performative Prophetic Speech — 148
      6.2.3.1. The Apostle-Prophet and the Magician (Acts 8.9-25) — 148
      6.2.3.2. The Missionary-Prophet and the False Prophet (Acts 13.1-12) — 154
      6.2.3.3. An Unsuccessful Speech-Act: The Sons of Sceva (Acts 19.8-20) — 158
  6.3. Summary and Conclusions — 161

7. Legitimate Authority: Apostolic-Prophetic Succession and the Characterization of Peter — 163
  7.1. Apostolic Commission and Prophetic Transference — 163
    7.1.1. Covenanting Jesus' Kingdom: The Twelve and Their Thrones to Judge Israel — 164
    7.1.2. Apostolic Commission: Witness as Identity — 168
    7.1.3. Ascension-Exaltation as Prerequisite for Prophetic Transference — 170

x   *Contents*

7.1.4. Pentecost: Prophetic Transference and Vocation	177
7.1.5. Summary: Commission and Transference Strategy	183
7.2. Peter: The Character of the Apostolic-Prophetic Successor Par Excellence	183
7.2.1. Peter: Characterization and Relational Interaction	184
7.2.1.1. Frame of Reference	185
7.2.1.2. Character Indicators	187
7.2.1.2.1. Direct Description	188
7.2.1.2.2. Indirect Presentation	190
7.2.1.2.3. Inter-Character Relationships	194
7.2.1.3. Narrative Sequence	197
7.2.1.4. Socio-Cultural Literacy	198
7.2.1.5. Summary for Peter's Characterization	199
8. Successful Execution: Ananias and Sapphira Under the Speech-Act of Divine Judgement	200
8.1. The Characterization of those Condemned to Die	200
8.1.1. Judas the Betrayer	200
8.1.2. Ananias and Sapphira and Divine Displeasure	208
8.2. Summary and Conclusion	218
9. Conclusion	219
9.1. Summary of Argument	219
9.2. Prospects for Further Research	222
Bibliography	225
Index of References	263
Index of Subjects	271

Acknowledgements

> Nobody would ever eat with her now. Nobody would walk with her. If she touched any Romani thing it would be destroyed, no matter what value: horse, table, dish. When she died, nobody would bury her. She would not have a funeral. She could not come back, even as a spirit. She could not haunt them. They would not talk of her, they could not even mention her: she had betrayed the life and she was beyond dead, not Gypsy, not gadži, nothing at all.
>
> McCann, *Zoli*[1]

A book that is about the dynamics of being invested in the life of close, intimate community demands that I take account of the many generous and abundant gifts I have received through the process of researching and writing it. First and foremost, my dearest wife deserves more credit than I can express here. She has been supportive and encouraging throughout the entirety of my educational career, kindness that is made all the more acute given to someone who did not even plan to attend college. Next, mention of my daughter, Sarina, and my son, Ezra, must be made for their heroic spirit of adventure. May it be that our travels around the globe have only begun!

This book began as a doctoral dissertation at New College, University of Edinburgh. I am grateful to my supervisor, Professor Larry Hurtado, who remained generous with his time. Thanks are due also to my examiners, Dr Helen Bond (University of Edinburgh) and Professor Loveday Alexander (University of Sheffield). Their comments and critiques have been beneficial. Other scholars and friends deserve mention for their sage advice and for reading drafts of some or all of the study. Joel B. Green has been a constant support offering generous and invaluable perspective on a variety of subjects. Jim VanderKam read the entire manuscript and graced me with insightful comments and expert feedback. John Mason read an entire draft with his keen editorial eye. I had the privilege of preparing for my examination through the support of friends from LCC International University who provided me with lively discussion. These friends include Marlene Wall, Rebecca Powell, Simona Mačukaitė, Sue Fry, and Steve Dintaman. I have also experienced the benefit and encouragement of e-mail correspondences throughout the process with Richard Briggs, Brian Capper, and Max Turner. Appreciation is also due to the anonymous reviewer who recommended the manuscript for publication. All of this input has made the study better than it could have been without

1. Colum McCann, *Zoli* (London: Weidenfeld & Nicolson, 2006).

it. It stands to reason that the responsibility for all deficiencies remain on my shoulders.

Thanks are also due to many who have offered support in a more personal nature. The Centre for the Study of Christian Origins (CSCO), and those who met for reading group, provided stimulation on many different subjects. Appreciation extends to Holly, Jeff, Chris, Dave, Dieter, Mike, Hon Lee, Jeromey, Judy, Siang and Will. My family also experienced remarkable hospitality from a number of friends. Thanks go to Helen, Laurence and Ann Wareing (who pointed me to the poignant citation from *Zoli*), Karen Forbes, Ian and Sandy Gordon, and to our meek hostess Nora Gustovska and her kind grandparents (who provided a quiet place for me to do the necessary editing). We will never forget the rich times we had with our friends Holly and Warren Carey, and we look forward to all of the good times yet to come. Special thanks are due to my aunt Yvonne and uncle Jerry, who provided invaluable assistance and helped us create rich holiday memories when we were oceans away from family. My mother, Linda McCabe, remained supportive and giving through unspeakably hard times in her own life. I am grateful to my nana, Mary Fuqua, who was also a voice of encouragement and constant prayer. Overflowing kindness and support came from our friends and mentors, Jim and Barbara Holsinger. Many more should be identified and I offer my gratitude to the many friends and family who have invested in this journey with us. Financial provisions were provided by scholarships from the University of Edinburgh, the Overseas Research (ORS) scholarship, and A Foundation for Theological Education. The substantial gift from the John Wesley Fellows is matched by the wealth in friendship and spiritual support.

Finally, I would like to express my gratitude to Dr Mark Goodacre, general editor for the Library of New Testament Studies monograph series, and Dominic Mattos at T&T Clark for accepting the manuscript for publication. Thanks to Holger Szesnat for bringing the manuscript to their attention.

ABBREVIATIONS

ABD	Anchor Bible Dictionary
AJPS	American Journal of Political Science
AJS	American Journal of Sociology
AnBib	Analecta biblica
ANF	Ante-Nicene Fathers
ANRW	Aufstieg und Niedergang der römischen Welt
ASR	American Sociological Review
AsTJ	Asbury Theological Journal
BBR	Bulletin for Biblical Research
BECNT	Baker Exegetical Commentary on the New Testament
BETL	Bibliotheca Ephemeridum Theologicarum Lovaniensium
Bib	Biblica
BibInt	Biblical Interpretation
BSL	Biblical Studies Library
BTB	Biblical Theology Bulletin
BWANT	Beiträge zur Wissenschaft vom Alten und Neuen Testament
BZ	Biblische Zeitschrift
CBQ	Catholic Biblical Quarterly
CI	Critical Inquiry
CP	Classical Philology
CQ	Classical Quarterly
CQS	Companion to the Qumran Scrolls
CTL	Cambridge Textbooks in Linguistics
CulAnth	Cultural Anthropology
CurBS	Currents in Research: Biblical Studies
DJD	Discoveries in the Judaean Desert
DRev	Downside Review
DSD	Dead Sea Discoveries
EKKNT	Evangelisch-katholischer Kommentar zum Neuentestament
ESEC	Emory Studies in Early Christianity
ETL	Ephemerides theologicae lovanienses
ETR	Etudes théologiques et religieuses
ExpTim	Expository Times
GSCC	Groningen Studies in Cultural Change
HTKNT	Herders theologischer Kommentar zum Neuen Testament
HTR	Harvard Theological Review
HvTSt	Hervormde teologiese studies

IBS	*Irish Biblical Studies*
IEJ	*Israel Exploration Journal*
IJPR	*International Journal for the Philosophy of Religion*
Interp	*Interpretation*
IVPNTCS	InterVarsity Press New Testament Commentary Series
JAAC	*The Journal of Aesthetics and Art Criticism*
JAAR	*Journal of the American Academy of Religion*
JBL	*Journal of Biblical Literature*
JECS	*Journal of Early Christian Studies*
JJS	*Journal of Jewish Studies*
JNES	*Journal of Near Eastern Studies*
JPT	*Journal for Pentecostal Theology*
JPTSup	*Journal of Pentecostal Theology: Supplement Series*
JRS	*Journal of Roman Studies*
JSJ	*Journal for the Study of Judaism*
JSNT	*Journal for the Study of the New Testament*
JSNTSup	*Journal for the Study of the New Testament: Supplement Series*
JSP	*Journal for the Study of the Pseudepigrapha*
JSPSup	*Journal for the Study of the Pseudepigrapha: Supplement Series*
JSS	*Journal of Semitic Studies*
JTS	*Journal of Theological Studies*
LCL	*Loeb Classical Library*
LumVie	*Lumiere et vie*
MLN	*Modern Language Notes*
Neot	*Neotestamentica*
NICNT	New International Commentary on the New Testament
NLH	*New Literary History*
NovT	*Novum Testamentum*
NovTSup	Supplements to Novum Testamentum
NPNF[1]	*Nicene and Post-Nicene Fathers*, Series 1.
NTS	*New Testament Studies*
NTTS	New Testament Tools and Studies
OBT	Overtures in Biblical Theology
Phil	*Philologus*
PIBA	*Proceedings of the Irish Biblical Association*
Pneuma	*Pneuma: Journal for the Society of Pentecostal Studies*
PRSt	*Perspectives in Religious Studies*
PT	*Poetics Today*
RB	*Revue biblique*
REG	*Revue des études grecques*
RevExp	*Review and Expositor*
RevQ	*Revue de Qumran*
RevScRel	*Revue de Sciences Religieuses*
RFCC	Religion in the First Christian Centuries
RHPR	*Revue d'histoire et de philosophie religieuses*
RM	*Rheinisches Museum*

RS	*Religious Studies*
RSR	*Recherches de science religieuse*
SANT	Studien zum Alten und Neuen Testaments
SBLDS	Society of Biblical Literature Dissertation Series
SBLMS	Society of Biblical Literature Monograph Series
SBLRBS	Society of Biblical Literature Resources for Biblical Study
SBLSP	*Society of Biblical Literature Seminar Papers*
SBLSymS	Society of Biblical Literature Symposium Series
SBT	Studies in Biblical Theology
SCL	Sather Classical Lectures
SDSSRL	Studies in the Dead Sea Scrolls and Related Literature
SE	*Studia Evangelica*
Semeia	Semeia
SJOT	*Scandinavian Journal of the Old Testament*
SJT	*Scottish Journal of Theology*
SHR	Studies in the History of Religions (Supplements to *Numen*)
SHS	Scripture and Hermeneutics Series
SNTSMS	Society for New Testament Studies Monograph Series
SNTU	Studien zum Neuen Testament und seiner Umwelt
SP	Sacra Pagina
STAC	Studien und Texte zu Antike und Christentum
STDJ	*Studies on the Texts of the Desert of Judah*
SubBi	*Subsidia biblica*
SUNT	Studien zur Umwelt des Neuen Testaments
TANZ	Texte und Arbeiten zum neutesamentlichen Zeitalter
TAPA	*Transactions and Proceedings of the American Philological Association*
TDNT	*Theological Dictionary of the New Testament*
TJ	*Trinity Journal*
TNTC	Tyndale New Testament Commentaries
TRu	*Theologische Rundschau*
TS	*Theological Studies*
TSoc	*Theory and Society*
TT	Texts and Translations
TynBul	*Tyndale Bulletin*
TZ	*Theologische Zeitschrift*
VoxEv	*Vox Evangelica*
VT	*Vetus Testamentum*
WUNT	Wissenschaftliche Untersuchungen zum Neuen Testament
WW	*Word and World*
ZAW	*Zeitschrift für alttestamentliche Wissenschaft*
ZNW	*Zeitschrift für die neutestamentliche Wissenschaft und die Kunde der älteren Kirche*
ZTK	*Zeitschrift für Theologie und Kirche*

Abstract

This study is an examination of the dynamics of the Ananias and Sapphira episode in Acts (5.1-11) and its role in the narrative of Luke-Acts. It begins by locating the passage within its literary context, emphasizing the framing of this divine judgement discourse by its literary surroundings, and the manner in which it is embedded in a discourse on the life of the Christian community expressed through shared goods. The study then moves on to examine the dynamics in the verbal encounter between Peter and the couple. Utilizing Speech-Act Theory, I argue that Peter's words, divinely sanctioned, directly execute the divine judgement upon Ananias and Sapphira. This claim is supported by appealing to the social processes and conventions of language use within the context of community-of-goods discourse as manifest in the Lukan narrative. Appeal is made to the socio-cultural repertoire of community-of-goods discourse in contemporary traditions sharing the socio-cultural milieu of Luke-Acts. I look at both a Hellenistic example (the Pythagoreans) and some Jewish examples (the Essenes and the Qumran covenanters). Next, I appeal to the conventions deployed in the narrative world of Luke-Acts which undergird the efficacy of prophetic speech to effect divine judgement. This includes the patterns established by prophetic figures in the Scriptures of Israel and Luke's own characterization of Jesus as Prophet-King. Attention is also given to Luke's strategy of preparing his audience to see the character of Peter as an apostolic-prophetic successor to Jesus, deputized to speak on behalf of God. Finally, there is an examination of the successful execution of the speech-act of divine judgement.

Chapter 1

INTRODUCTION:
REOPENING THE CASE OF ANANIAS AND SAPPHIRA

Divine wrath is a sensitive topic in an age that is legitimately concerned with abuses of religion and vicious wars executed in the name of God or the gods. The stakes are raised when divine violence is used to legitimate a certain group or leader. The story of Ananias and Sapphira in Acts (5.1-11) disturbs many contemporary readers because its terminal judgement is executed for what seems to be a trivial deception. Gail O'Day, who calls it 'perhaps the most infamous story in Acts', says that it 'offends modern sensibilities and defies any rational or psychological explanation'.[1] Some decades earlier, Foakes-Jackson quipped, 'The brief narrative is frankly repulsive.'[2] These modern interpreters are not alone in their disdain. It seems that this story was offensive to the ancient Hellenistic mind as well. John Cook notes that some pagan philosophers of the fourth and fifth centuries CE, like Porphyry, 'found the story to be morally repellent'.[3] Jerome found himself defending the character of the Apostle Peter, yet also conceded the severity of Peter's destroying the unfortunate couple.[4] Another pagan philosopher complains about the hypocrisy of Peter, who in judging the couple should have remembered that he was forgiven for his own deceit in denying Jesus (cf. Luke 22.31-34, 54-62).[5] Such negative reactions provoke the question, what is Luke's theological agenda in his narrative strategy? More specifically, what is the role of divine judgement in Luke's account of God's purposes as they come to fruition in Jesus of Nazareth and the early Jerusalem messianic community?

1. Gail R. O'Day, 'Acts', in *The Women's Bible Commentary* (eds Carol A. Newsom and Sharon H. Ringe; London: SPCK, 1992), 398 [394–403].
2. F. J. Foakes-Jackson, *The Acts of the Apostles* (MNTC; London: Hodder and Stoughton, 1931), 42.
3. John G. Cook, *The Interpretation of the New Testament in Greco-Roman Paganism* (Tübingen: Mohr Siebeck, 2000), 155.
4. Cook, *Interpretation*, 155, citing Jerome, *Ep.* 130.14.
5. Cook, *Interpretation*, 209–10. Cook writes, 'The problem is of inconsistency... The attack is an example of vituperative rhetoric since Peter's virtue is called into question' (210). Macarius, the Christian apologist, responds with recognition that Ananias' sin was against God, and so received divine judgement.

The above questions concern why Luke included such a story in an otherwise 'ideal' account of the early Christian community (Acts 4.32-37). Located where it is in the text, how does this story function in Luke's narrative logic? And what precisely is the dynamic between Peter and the condemned couple? These and related questions will be addressed in the course of this study.

1.1. Previous Questions and Approaches to the Text

In discussing this puzzling story, some studies have looked at the provenance of the narrative. Philippe-H. Menoud proposed that the story originally addressed anxiety about members who had passed away before the Parousia, and was later recast as a narrative about divine judgement.[6] Gerd Lüdemann suggested that a community member 'violated sacred law, was anathematized and ostracized by the leader of the community. Whether in the actual case the malefactor died is far from certain, but according to sacred law he should have.'[7]

An early tradition of exegesis concerning this passage has been to read the involvement of the Holy Spirit (Acts 5.3, [4], 9a) as evidence of the divine personhood of the Holy Spirit. The discussion is presented by Paul Brown in his 1969 ThD dissertation.[8] Brown demonstrates that Luke's text was certainly read as a remarkable precedent in the subsequent development of the Christian conception of God's Spirit leading to Trinitarian doctrinal formulation.

Most studies engaging this passage have focused on contextualizing the incident in a plausible socio-historical context, often folding mention of it into the wider discussion of community-of-goods. Brian Capper has utilized the Ananias and Sapphira episode as evidence of an actual, historical community-of-goods practiced by the early Jerusalem messianists. Peter's accusing questions to Ananias, according to Capper, are evidence of an initiation ritual, in this case gone awry.[9]

---

6. Philippe-H. Menoud, 'La mort d'Ananias et de Saphira (Actes 5. 1–11)', in *Aux de sources la tradition chrétienne Mélanges offerts à M. Maurice Goguel à l'occasion de son soixante-dixième anniversaire* (eds O. Cullman and P.-H. Menoud; Biblothéque Theologique; Neuchâtel: Delachaux et Niestlé, 1950), 146–54.

7. Gerd Lüdemann, *The Acts of the Apostles: What Really Happened in the Earliest Days of the Church* (Amherst, NY: Promethius Books, 2005), 81; see idem, *Early Christianity According to the Traditions in Acts: A Commentary* (London: SCM Press, 1987), 66.

8. Paul B. Brown, 'The Meaning and Function of Acts 5:1–11 in the Purpose of Luke-Acts' (ThD diss., Boston University School of Theology, 1969).

9. Brian J. Capper, 'The Interpretation of Acts 5.4', *JSNT* 19 (1983), 117–31; idem, '<<In der hand des Ananias...>> Erwagungen zu 1 QS VI, 20 und der Urchristlichen Gütergemeinschaft', *RevQ* 12 (1986), 223–36; idem, 'Community of Goods in the Early Jerusalem Church', *ANRW* II. 26.2 (1995): 1730–74; idem, 'The Palestinian Cultural Context of Earliest Christian Community of Goods', in *The Book of Acts in Its Palestinian Setting* (ed. Richard Bauckham; vol. 4 of *Acts in its First Century Setting*, ed. Bruce W. Winter; Grand Rapids: Eerdmans, 1995), 323–56.

Other studies try to identify the precise nature of the sin of the couple. J. Duncan M. Derrett reads the story through the lens of rabbinic law, arguing that the couple sold Sapphira's *ketubah*, her dowry and her financial security retained in the event the marriage was dissolved.[10] Derrett is followed by the more developed argument of Ivoni Richter Reimer, a feminist-liberation scholar. Richter Reimer distinguishes between Ananias' guilt of 'holding back' proceeds committed to the community, and Sapphira's guilt of complicity with her husband.[11] Richard Ascough looks to the Greco-Roman milieu of 'voluntary associations' to find a context for the sin of attempting to merit more honour through making a public gift than is actually earned.[12] Henriette Havelaar has offered an innovative form-critical study, arguing that the episode is a combination of the *form* of a 'rule miracle of punishment' with the *content* of an excommunication story, resulting in divine judgement for blasphemy.[13]

The most fertile contributions have come from those who have paid attention to the literary integrity of the passage within its narrative context. Luke Timothy Johnson furthered the conversation immensely by demonstrating the symbolic function of possessions within Luke-Acts. When Ananias and Sapphira withheld some of the proceeds of their sale, they were holding back a part of themselves from full commitment to Jesus, the Messiah, and the messianic ethic.[14] Robert O'Toole, in a wide-ranging study, explores the compositional logic of the passage within the Jerusalem community account in Acts 1–5 as well as the rich intertextuality of previous accounts and relationships within Luke-Acts.[15] Likewise, Daniel Marguerat provides a suggestive study, engaging previous scholarship and extending the discussion in new and helpful ways. He elucidates the narrative context which takes into consideration the motif of conflict, the invitational proclamation of the community's witness, and the Spirit's guarantee of the community's integrity.[16]

---

10. J. Duncan M. Derrett, 'Ananias, Sapphira, and the Right of Property', *DRev* 89 (1971), 225–32.

11. Ivoni Richter Reimer, 'Sapphira: A Women's Story for Mourning, or: The Deadly Guilt of the Co-Conspirator (5.1–11)', in *Women in the Acts of the Apostles: A Feminist Liberation Perspective* (trans. Linda M. Maloney; Minneapolis: Fortress, 1995), 1–29.

12. Richard Ascough, 'Benefaction Gone Wrong: The "Sin" of Ananias and Sapphira in Context', in *Text and Artifact in the Religions of Mediterranean Antiquity: Essays in Honour of Peter Richardson* (eds Stephen G. Wilson and Michael Desjardins; ESCJ 9; Waterloo, Ontario, Canada: Wilfrid Laurier University Press, 2000), 91–110.

13. Henriette Havelaar, 'Hellenistic Parallels to Acts 5.1–11 and the Problem of Conflicting Interpretations', *JSNT* 67 (1997), 63–82.

14. Luke Timothy Johnson, *The Literary Function of Possessions in Luke-Acts* (SBLDS 39; Missoula, MT: Scholars Press, 1977), esp. ch. 4; idem, *The Acts of the Apostles* (SP 5; Collegeville, MN: The Liturgical Press, 1992).

15. Robert F. O'Toole, '"You Did Not Lie to Us (Human Beings) but to God" (Acts 5,4c),' *Bib* 76 (1995): 182–209.

16. See, e.g., Daniel Marguerat, 'Ananias and Sapphira (Acts 5. 1–11): the Original Sin', in *The First Christian Historian: Writing the 'Acts of the Apostles'* (SNTSMS 121; trans. by K. McKinney, G. J. Laughery and R. Bauckham; Cambridge: Cambridge University Press, 2002), 155–78.

These and other proposals are discussed more fully in the body of this study. We should note at the outset that much has been achieved in the previously mentioned studies; yet, some of the most crucial questions regarding this passage have been either obscured or ignored by commentators. This book seeks to fill that lacuna.

1.2. The Contribution and Approach of this Study

1.2.1. Narrative Logic and Verbal Transaction

The method of the present investigation is primarily narrative-critical. It does not focus on the historical provenance of the event or redactional layers of the narrative. Historical questions are poised to serve the aim of expounding the literary presentation of a narrative episode. The purpose is to understand the passage within its existing discursive context. I ask, how does the surrounding material frame the episode? In the other direction, how does the episode contribute to the plot and drama of which it is a part?

Luke's discourse, like all language use, is situated and informed by particular social horizons. These horizons suggest parameters for considering what plausibly could have informed Luke's first century Mediterranean auditors as they received the episode couched in the utopian discourse of shared property.

One primary purpose of this study is to examine the nature of the verbal transaction between Ananias and Sapphira and Peter. What is the relationship between Peter's questions and indictments, and the couple's immediate deaths? Commentators often address this issue with brief, apparently dismissive comments, or assume certain claims without offering warrant. Some interpreters attempt to exonerate Peter, and ultimately God, from any complicity in Ananias' and Sapphira's death. By contrast, I argue that the couple does die as a direct consequence of divine judgement. The judgement is effected through the medium of Peter's utterances. Using the socio-pragmatic tools of Speech-Act Theory, I describe the encounter as an apostolic-prophetic indictment and condemnation unto death. Aside from the narrator's framing comments, the episode consists mainly of a verbal encounter between Peter and the couple. Action is expressed through an exchange of words and gestures. Therefore, this study takes up the task of addressing the primary elements of the story itself, taking into account both the socio-historical context and the narrative strategy of Luke-Acts.

1.2.2. Reading Luke-Acts as a Coherent Narrative

The analysis here proceeds on the assumption that one and the same author wrote both the Gospel of Luke and the Acts of the Apostles. For convenience, the author is referred to as 'Luke' without necessarily assuming any particular identification of a historical person. Following the narrative strategy of the two books together means that Luke 1.1 through Acts 4.31 is taken to have direct bearing on the way Acts 4.32–5.11 has an effect on its audience.[17] It also means reading narrative unity at the level of story, reading Luke-Acts as a theological history of salvific promise, tracing patterns from regional Judaean tradition and extending them toward universal significance.

The decision to read Luke and Acts together has not been made uncritically. It is well known that Mikeal Parsons and Richard Pervo, among others, sought to 'loosen the hyphen' of Luke-Acts.[18] Their most compelling arguments were their attacks on the generic and narrative unities of Luke and Acts. They garnered support from the church's historical reception of these documents. The extant manuscript tradition does not keep them together. In P[45], though Acts is included with the Gospels, Acts is separated from Luke by Mark.[19] In the same manner, Codex Bezae (D05) has the order Matthew, John, Luke, Mark, and Acts.[20] In the canonical tradition, Acts could also serve as an introduction to the catholic epistles.[21] With the weight of such traditions, why should Luke and Acts be read together?

The reason for doing this is that the text invites us to do so. The preface of Acts points Luke's model reader back to the Gospel, the 'former treatise' (πρῶτος λόγος, 1.1a). The context of Acts presupposes the Gospel. Acts is an account of the continuation of 'all that Jesus began to do and teach' (1.1b). The reading presented here is faithful to the *literary potential* formed in this narrative.[22] The validity of the approach will be demonstrated by its account of the 'narrative world' of the text.[23]

---

17. I use the term 'effect' (*Wirkung*) in the manner of Wolfgang Iser's reader-response criticism. See his *The Act of Reading: A Theory of Aesthetic Response* (Baltimore: Johns Hopkins, 1978), ix.

18. Mikeal C. Parsons and Richard I. Pervo, *Rethinking the Unity of Luke and Acts* (Minneapolis: Fortress, 1993).

19. See Frederic G. Kenyon, *The Chester Beatty Biblical Papyri, Fasciculus II, The Gospels and Acts* (London: Emery Walker Ltd, 1933), viii; T. C. Skeat, 'A Codicological Analysis of the Chester Beatty papyrus Codex of Gospels and Acts (P[45])', in *The Collected Biblical Writings of T. C. Skeat* (ed. J. K. Elliott; NovTSup 113; Leiden: Brill, 2004), 146–7.

20. Noted by Parsons and Pervo, *Rethinking*, 8.

21. P[74] (seventh century) and 0166 (fifth century). See David E. Smith, *The Canonical Function of Acts: A Comparative Analysis* (Collegeville, MN: The Liturgical Press, 2002); Robert W. Wall, 'The Acts of the Apostles in Canonical Context', in *The New Testament as Canon: A Reader in Canonical Criticism* (Robert W. Wall and Eugene E. Lemcio; JSNTSup 76; Sheffield: JSOT Press, 1992), 110–28.

22. See Andrew Gregory, 'The Reception of Luke and Acts and the Unity of Luke-Acts', *JSNT* 29 (2007), 459–72.

23. Joel B. Green (*The Theology of the Gospel of Luke* [Cambridge: Cambridge University Press, 1995], 4–6) distinguishes three 'worlds' associated with a historical-narrative text: (1) First, there is the world that the text assumes, the world it claims to represent. (2) But, since all history writing is necessarily selective, there is also, the world *actualized* in his text, the world as Luke portrays it. (3) Furthermore, '"the world of Luke" signifies the world as Luke wants it to be, the world which, according to his theological perspective, God purposes. Thus, Luke is not content to present the world "as it really is", but purposefully shapes the story in such a way that some of its facets are undermined, others legitimated' (5). In other words, this is the world according to Luke's theological agenda.

In this study I use the semiotic-literary strategy of Umberto Eco's 'model reader' to navigate the tension between responsible historical inquiry and a narrative-critical approach informed by literary sensibilities. Eco writes:

> To make his text communicative, the author has to assume that the ensemble of codes he relies upon is the same as that shared by his possible reader. The author has thus to foresee a model of the possible reader (hereafter Model Reader) supposedly able to deal interpretively with the expressions in the same way as the author deals generatively with them.[24]

This strategy provides the freedom to build a body of literary conventions from the socio-cultural context of Luke's texts as well as from within the text itself. For example, Luke had traditionally governed precedents in his characterization of prophetic figures, but his construction of the prophetic persona has a shape of its own. Thus, it is necessary to see the broad literary milieu of the ancient Mediterranean environment as well as to maintain a generative contribution from the reader in reading Luke-Acts. There is dialectic between tradition and convention informing Luke's narrative and the selection and arrangement of these elements in Luke's narrative world.[25] Throughout this study, 'reader' and 'auditor' or 'audience' will be used interchangeably to indicate awareness of the primarily oral transmission and aural access to texts in the ancient Mediterranean world.[26]

1.2.3. Textual Transmission: Two Narratives?

Regarding the two divergent textual traditions of Acts this study does not presuppose a priori the superiority of either the 'Alexandrian text' (ℵ, A,

---

24. Umberto Eco, *The Role of the Reader: Explorations in the Semiotics of Texts* (Bloomington: Indiana University Press, 1979), 7. See further Umberto Eco, *The Limits of Interpretation* (Bloomington: Indiana University Press, 1990), 52, 58–60, 128–9, 133–6.

25. Paul Ricœur ('Philosophical Hermeneutics and Biblical Hermeneutics', in *From Text to Action: Essays in Hermeneutics, II* [trans. Kathleen Blamey and John B. Thompson; Evanston, IL: Northwestern University Press, 1991], 94) writes: 'The very originality of the event requires that it be transmitted by means of an interpretation of preexisting signification – already inscribed – available within the cultural community.'

26. See William D. Shiell, *Reading Acts: The Lector and the Early Christian Audience* (BIS 70; Leiden: Brill Academic Publishers, Inc., 2004). Generally, see Richard A. Burridge, 'Who Writes, Why, and for Whom?', in *The Written Gospel* (eds Markus Bockmuehl and Donald Hagner; Cambridge: Cambridge University Press, 2005), 99–100, 108–10; Martin Hengel, 'Eye-Witness Memory and the Writing of the Gospels', in *Written Gospel* (eds, Bockmuehl and Hagner), 92–3; Harry Y. Gamble, *Books and Readers in the Early Church: A History of Early Christian Texts* (New Haven: Yale University Press, 1995), esp. 5, 203–41, 321–34; Bridget Gilfillan Upton, *Hearing Mark's Endings: Listening to Ancient Popular Texts Through Speech Act Theory* (BIS 79; Leiden: Brill, 2006). Stephen D. Moore (*Literary Criticism and the Gospels: The Theoretical Challenge* [New Haven: Yale University Press, 1989], 84–8) notes the parallels between narrative critical strategy and studies on aural reception in that both draw attention to the dynamic development of plot and linear development.

B, P⁴⁵, P⁷⁴) or the so-called 'Western text' (D, E, 614) of Acts. Different communities in the ancient world read both textual traditions as legitimate witnesses to Luke's work. As a result, the data of both traditions are considered as contributions to distinct narrative presentations where relevant.

1.3. The Trajectory of this Study

Chapter 2 situates the episode within its literary context. The chapter will examine the dynamics within the pericope itself and argue that the Ananias and Sapphira episode is the negative example of the community-of-goods discourse. In an ever-widening literary investigation it is argued that the primary drama in the Jerusalem section of Acts focuses on the messianic community as well as a subplot of conflict with the established Jerusalem hierocracy. These dynamics are explored both in the movement of context framing the episode and the movement of contribution from the specific passage to the wider plot of Acts. **Chapter 3** commences with the theoretical method of my approach, examining different approaches to answer the query about the relationship between Peter's utterances and the couple's immediate demise. After discussing recent suggestions of 'reference' (i.e., information and prediction) and 'magic' (i.e., formulaic imprecation), I suggest a fresh proposal to defend an ancient view, that is: Peter's words themselves 'performed' the execution of the deviant deceivers. Speech-Act Theory provides a linguistic apparatus which will allow a systematic description of both the socio-literary body of conventions and the compositional strategy of the Lukan narrative. Three elements of Speech-Act Theory inform the approach to reading the Lukan story: (1) social conventions and expectations, (2) appropriate authority, and (3) successful execution of the conventions.

Chapter 4 offers assessment of the socio-cultural background of the community-of-goods discourse. This chapter considers the specific character of the divine economy among the early Jerusalem messianists. **Chapter 5** canvasses examples of the community-of-goods discourse in contemporary traditions which are shared in the socio-cultural milieu of Luke-Acts, a Hellenistic example (the Pythagoreans) and some Jewish examples (the Essenes and the Qumran covenanters). The purpose is to demonstrate that community-of-goods discourse in the ancient world was associated with laudatory esteem of the community and its severe disciplinary practices. As a result, I suggest that the incident of Ananias and Sapphira in Acts 5.1-11 should be interpreted historically and literarily in a manner other than 'offensive' or 'repulsive'.

Chapter 6 examines the conventions that are reflected in Luke's 'narrative world' which undergird the efficacy of prophetic speech to effect divine judgement. The purpose is to show that there are precedents in the Scriptures of Israel and in the Gospel of Luke which demonstrate that prophetic speech performs the divine will, and that the same power resides in the narrative world of Acts. **Chapter 7** explores the Lukan strategy to indicate that Peter is in fact authorized as an apostolic-prophetic successor to Jesus, deputized to speak on behalf of God. Finally, in **Chapter 8**, the study brings together the strands to discuss the successful execution of divine judgement upon miscreants who threaten the integrity of the community. Peter's words, divinely sanctioned, directly execute the divine judgement upon Ananias and Sapphira.

Chapter 2

ANANIAS AND SAPPHIRA AS AN EPISODE
IN THE NARRATIVE OF ACTS

Ananias and Sapphira die as a consequence of divine displeasure incurred by their deceit in withholding proceeds pledged for communal use. The two are executed in an act of divine retribution for lying 'to the Holy Spirit' (Acts 5.4), that is, lying 'to God' (5.5), and testing 'the Spirit of the Lord' (5.9). This episode is an illustration of divine judgement discourse embedded in a narrative plot. More specifically, this discourse of divine judgement is embedded in a wider discourse of the collective life of a nascent messianic community in Jerusalem (1.1–8.3). This description in turn is embedded in the wider discourse of the early Jerusalem community life which three times results in conflict between leaders of the Christian community and an opposing group of Jerusalem elite (4.1-22; 5.17-42; 6.8–8.3). These aristocrats cooperated with the foreign rulers in the execution of Jesus (4.25-29; Luke 23.1-6, 10, 13-25). These conflicts form a pattern in which an agent of God divides Israel between those who accept God's word and those who reject it and are therefore heading for destruction.[1] The events are presented from the point of view of the Lukan narrator,[2] which is expressed through narrative discourse that generates a particular perspective with ideological evaluation and a theological agenda. This theological agenda frames the continuing description of the messianic community's public interaction with the Jerusalem populace and private associations of believers with one another.

*2.1. Divine Judgement Discourse Embedded in
Community-of-Goods Discourse*

It is important to see that the boundaries of the Ananias and Sapphira episode (Acts 5.1-11) extend back to Acts 4.32, and so include a summary

---

1. The pattern runs throughout Luke-Acts: Luke 2.34-35; 4.23-30; 6.1-11; 7.29-30; 11.14-54; 12.49–13.9; 13.10-17; 14.25-35; 15.1-2; 19.28-48; 20.1-47; Acts 2.12-13; 3.22-23; 4.3-4, 21; 5. 12-16, 26, 33, 38-39; 6.7-15; 7.54-58; 13.42-52; 14.1-7, 19; 16.19-34; 17.4-9, 32-34; 18.5-8, 12-17; 19.8-10; 21.27-36; 22.22-25; 23.12-15; 25.1-12; 28.17-31.
2. The 'Lukan narrator' here designates the textual voice of Luke and Acts which represents the perspective of the implied author.

of community life and the introduction of Barnabas. Luke has provided an idyllic summary of community life that would have evoked Greco-Roman utopian and friendship ideals[3] and Jewish eschatological hopes.[4] There are two illustrations of the communal ethos, one positive (Barnabas, 4.36-37) and one negative (Ananias and Sapphira, 5.1-11). The pericope is underscored by the action of bringing goods and proceeds and laying them 'at the apostles' feet' for distribution (4.35, 37; 5.2, [10]).[5] The boundary of the passage is then 4.32–5.11.[6] The significance of the Ananias and Sapphira episode depends on the ethical and theological implications of the early Christian community-of-goods. The meaning of the execution of divine judgement on this couple is informed by the framing discourse of the language expressing the shared property and the 'abundant grace' which touched them all (Acts 4.33).

The narrative of Ananias and Sapphira should not be separated from the summary of the messianists' communal life that included sharing their property and distributing to those in need. The couple transgresses this community ethos by their deceit, and so threaten the integrity of the community that belongs to the Holy Spirit. In these circumstances Peter confronts the husband and his wife. The surrounding discourse establishes the moral framework within which to understand the couple's crime and the severity of the divine sanction upon it.

---

3. With terms like καρδία καὶ ψυχὴ μία and ἅπαντα κοινά in 4.32.
4. Compare 4.34, οὐδὲ γὰρ ἐνδεής τις ἦν ἐν αὐτοῖς, with LXX Deut. 15.4, ὅτι οὐκ ἔσται ἐν σοὶ ἐνδεής.
5. 4.35 – παρὰ τοὺς πόδας τῶν ἀποστόλων.
    4.37 – παρὰ τοὺς πόδας τῶν ἀποστόλων.
    5.2 – παρὰ τοὺς πόδας τῶν ἀποστόλων.
    (5.10 – πρὸς τοὺς πόδας αὐτοῦ.)
6. See Sœur Anne-Etienne and Corina Combet-Galland, 'Actes 4/32–5/11', *ETR* 52 (1977): 548–53; Maria Anicia Co, 'The Major Summaries in Acts (Acts 2,42–47; 4,32–35; 5,12–16): Linguistic and Literary Relationship', *ETL* 68 (1992): 62–3 [49–85]. *Contra* Benjamin E. Williams, *Miracle Stories in the Biblical Book* Acts of the Apostles (Lewiston: Edwin Mellen Press, 2001), 61, who argues that the editorial bracketing of the surrounding summaries 'allows 5.1-11 to be isolated as a self-contained and independent unit'. Williams (*Miracle Stories*, 62, 63) contradicts himself in his sections on 'analysis' and 'redaction', where he recognizes the episodes of Barnabas and Ananias and Sapphira as examples of Acts 4.34-35.

Raymond M. Gen ('The Phenomena of Miracles and Divine Infliction in Luke-Acts: Their Theological Significance', *Pneuma* 11 [1989], 18 [3–19]) sets the limits as Acts 5.1 to 5.14, in order to show that the theological function of the miracle is to add believers to the Lord. These limits neglect the structural features linking the pericope to the summary in Acts 4.32-35. The proposal of S. J. Noorda ('Scene and Summary: A Proposal for Reading Acts 4,32–5,16', in *Les Actes des Apôtres: Traditions, redaction, théologie* [ed. J. Kremer; BETL 48; Leuven: Leuven University Press, 1979], 480–3 [475–83]), advances the discussion beyond the old *Sammelberichte* identification (Dibelius, Cadbury), but does not offer a persuasive argument for placing 5.12-16 with what comes before (4.32–5.11) rather than with what follows (5.17-42). The coordinating δέ (5.17) links the reaction of the high priest and the Sadducees to the gathering of the people (5.16).

In the same way the community-of-goods discourse is itself not a freestanding unit. It is embedded in a wider co-text[7] about the emergence of the messianic community and their conflict with the Jerusalem elite. Acts 4.32–5.11 is part of a larger section starting in 4.23 where the setting moves from the court of the Jerusalem Council (4.1-22) to the messianic community (4.23–5.11). This section is part of an account of escalating confrontation between the emerging messianic community and the established Jerusalem leaders in Acts 3–5, and ultimately 1.3–8.3.[8] The compositional pattern interlaces scenes and summaries, weaving the movement of the messianic community between public encounters with the Jerusalem populace and private interactions within the community itself.

2.2. Community-of-Goods Discourse Embedded in Community Interaction and Conflict Discourse

What does Acts 4.32–5.11 contribute to the narrative plot of Luke-Acts? Conversely, what would be lost if this pericope was not included? At first glance it might be seen that removing this pericope would not disrupt the unity of the narrative logic. Acts 4.31 could easily be followed by 5.12, with the prayer of the community and the subsequent filling of the Spirit resulting in many signs and wonders taking place at the hands of the apostles. Yet, it is worth inquiring further about the function and contribution of Acts 4.32–5.11 to the wider plot of Acts 1.3–5.42(–8.3).

As noted above, Acts 1–5 oscillates between the messianic community's public interaction with the Jerusalem populace on the one hand (2.5-40; 3.1–4.22; 5.17-42; 6.8–8.3) and their own private associations on the other (1.12–2.4; 2.41-47; 4.23–5.11; 6.1-7). In this narrative progression a subplot emerges of conflict between the emerging apostolic leadership and the Jerusalem elite. Both have claims vying for the attention and devotion of the Jerusalem populace. The apostles continually preach the word of God with boldness (2.14-40; 3.12-26; 4.8-12, 13, 19-20, 29, 31; 5.21, 29-32, 42), while the Jerusalem elite attempt to maintain the status quo (4.2-3, 16-18, 21; 5.17-18, 26-28, 33-40). The conflict divides the people in Jerusalem (2.41; 4.4, 21; 5.13-16, 26).

---

7. Gillian Brown and George Yule define the 'co-text' as the sentences and larger textual units surrounding a passage that constrain its interpretation (*Discourse Analysis* [CTL; Cambridge: Cambridge University Press, 1983], 46–50). 'Context' refers to the socio-historical setting of a text. They follow M. A. K. Halliday, *Language as Social Semiotic: The Social Interpretation of Language and Meaning* (London: Edward Arnold, 1978), 133.

8. This extension of the boundaries from Acts 3–5 to 1.3–8.3 is an attempt to mitigate Robert Tannehill's emphasis on 'conflict' as the primary motif subordinating all others. See Robert Tannehill 'The Composition of Acts 3–5: Narrative Development and Echo Effect', in *The Shape of Luke's Story: Essays in Luke-Acts* (Eugene, OR: Cascade Books, 2005), 185–219; idem, *The Narrative Unity of Luke-Acts: A Literary Interpretation* (2 vols; Minneapolis: Fortress, 1986, 1990), 2:59–79.

The narrative of Acts opens with the commission of the risen Christ to his chosen apostolic successors and then the narration of his ascension (Acts 1.3-11). This is followed by a time of communal prayer and discernment regarding a replacement for Judas to bring the apostolic number back to twelve. This symbolic number represents a restored Israel centred on God's vindicated Messiah (1.12-26). In this manner the church awaits the fulfilment of the 'promise of the Father' (Luke 24.49; Acts 1.4–5, 8).

In Acts the Holy Spirit is poured out on the messianic community, causing utterances spoken in many languages. Peter then addresses those visiting Jerusalem for the feast of Pentecost. Peter admonishes the people for their complicity in the death of God's Messiah (2.22-23) exhorting them to 'repent and be baptized' (2.38) and calling them to be separated from 'this perverted generation' (2.40). This results in a mass conversion and baptism (about three thousand persons). The community life is described as idyllic, they share their goods, their hearts are united, and they celebrate as companions (2.42-47).

In Acts 3.1-10, Peter and James approach the Temple at the hour of prayer. They encounter a lame beggar, who is healed (σέσωται, 4.9) and who becomes for Luke a paradigm of salvation (4.12, ἡ σωτηρία, σωθῆναι),[9] a making straight of 'the Way of the Lord' (Luke 3.4 [Isa. 40.3]; Acts 13.10).[10] It is precisely the healing of the lame beggar, and the attention it draws, that initiates Peter's second speech in the Temple precincts (3.12-26), a speech which provokes the Jerusalem elite (4.1-3). Peter and John are arrested, detained, questioned, and threatened (4.5-22). The presence of the healed beggar alongside Peter and John shows how the motif unites the entire section (4.9, 14, 22).

The apostles respond to the threat by returning to their companions and addressing God in prayer, associating the events with the messianic 'narrative'

---

9. For a detailed exposition of Acts 3.1–4.12 along these lines, see Dennis Hamm, 'Acts 3,1–10: The Healing of the Temple Beggar as Lucan Theology', *Bib* 67 (1986): 305–19; idem, 'Acts 3:12–26: Peter's Speech and the Healing of the Man Born Lame', *PRSt* 11 (1984): 199–217; idem, 'The Sign of Healing, Acts 3:1–10: A Study in Lucan Theology' (PhD diss., St. Louis University, 1975). Hamm ('Acts 3,1–10', 306) writes, 'This pun [on σῴζω] suggests that in Luke's mind the physical healing of the lame man is a sign of eschatological salvation – one word, *sōzō*, serving to name both kinds of restoration.' (cf. idem, 'Acts 3.12–26', 200).

10. Hamm ('Acts 3,1–10', 305) writes, 'In the Gospel of John, where believing is symbolized as a kind of seeing, it is clear why the fourth evangelist makes his elaborate healing story the cure of a man born blind (John 9). Similarly, in Acts, where the Christian enterprise is called The Road (or Way) and where much stress is given to journey narratives, it should come as no surprise that great emphasis falls upon the healing of a man born lame.'

See also Octavian D. Baban, *On the Road Encounters in Luke-Acts: Hellenistic Mimesis and Luke's Theology of the Way* (Milton Keynes: Paternoster, 2006), especially the literature review on pp. 27–71; Schuyler Brown, *Apostasy and Perseverance in the Theology of Luke* (Rome: Pontifical Biblical Institute, 1969), 82, 131–45; and Charles H. H. Scobie, 'A Canonical Approach to Interpreting Luke: The Journey Motif as a Hermeneutical Key', in *Reading Luke: Interpretation, Reflection, Formation* (eds Craig G. Bartholomew, Joel B. Green, and Anthony C. Thiselton; SHS 6; Grand Rapids: Zondervan, 2005), 327–49.

of Psalm 2. They ask for boldness to continue their favourable participation in the divine plan (4.24-30). The result is a divine response echoing the theophany of Pentecost.[11] It is from here that Luke extends the plot with a second summary of the communal life of the early messianists with its illustrations (4.32–5.11).

Following this summary with its illustrative examples there is a further summary incorporating the activity of the apostles in 'signs and wonders' (5.12-16). These events draw large crowds which are seeking healing, and this provokes jealousy among the Jerusalem high priest and his associates (5.17). Again, the apostles are arrested, but they are released through angelic intervention and they return to their preaching. The Temple guard seeks after the apostles, but after confusion at their absence, the guard is redirected to the Temple precincts where they arrest the apostles for a third time. Now, the confrontation between the apostles and the Jerusalem elite intensifies. Peter expresses the dichotomy of the divine will versus the human will (5.29-32; see 3.13-15; 4.10-11, 24-30) accusing the Temple leadership of opposing the servants of God. Recognizing the indictment, the high priest and his associates 'were enraged and desired to kill them' (5.33). At this point Gamaliel warns the Council against the possibility that they may be found 'fighting against God' (5.39, θεομάχοι). The Council heals the Pharisee's warning, but still increase their persecution of the apostles by beating them.

This pattern continues into Acts 6–7 with a final escalation leading to the death of Stephen, one of the messianists, a death recalling the righteous death of Jesus. Acts 6.1-7 returns to a setting within the private life of the community, where there is a conflict between the Greek-speaking and the Aramaic-speaking members of the community.[12] The conflict is resolved by appointing seven men of good repute, 'full of the Holy Spirit and of wisdom' who ensure provision for the widows of the Greek-speaking members. Stephen is a Greek speaker, whose story occupies the rest of the Jerusalem section of Acts. He has the longest speech in Acts recounting the story of Israel. He serves as the culmination of the persecution against the messianic community in Jerusalem, which resulted in his own death. Stephen's death and the explosion of persecution in Jerusalem is the catalyst that ejects the messianic community into wider areas (μὲν οὖν, 8.4). The final section of the Jerusalem narrative continues the plot alternating between the encounter with

---

11. See Earl Richard, 'Pentecost as a Recurrent Theme in Luke-Acts', in *New Views on Luke Acts* (ed. Earl Richard; Collegeville, MN: The Liturgical Press, 1990), 133–49.

12. See Martin Hengel, 'Between Jesus and Paul: The "Hellenists", the "Seven", and Stephen (Acts 6.1-15; 7.54–8.3)', in *Between Jesus and Paul: Studies in the Earliest History of Christianity* (trans. John Bowden; SCM Press, 1983), 1–29. See also Craig C. Hill, *Hellenists and Hebrews: Reappraising Division within the Early Church* (Minneapolis: Fortress, 1992), 5–101; idem, 'Acts 6.1–8.4: Division or Diversity?', in *History, Literature and Society in the Book of Acts* (ed. Ben Witherington III; Cambridge: Cambridge University Press, 1996), 129–53. Hill demonstrates that the division between 'Hebrews' and 'Hellenists' was a linguistic issue, and not one of ideologically or ethnically diverse groups in the early church.

the Jerusalem populace, specifically the conflict with the Jerusalem Council, and glimpses into the inner-life of the messianic community.

It was noted above that the prayer and divine response of Acts 4.24-31 could have been followed immediately by the summary of 'signs and wonders' in 5.12-16. In fact, the 'signs and wonders through the hands of the apostles' of v. 12 could be understood as an extension of the hand of God which heals, and of the 'signs and wonders' which take place through the Name of God's holy Servant Jesus (4.30). Without 4.32–5.11, the pattern of inside-outside movement structuring Acts 1.3–8.3 would not be disrupted. In fact, it could appear that the second communal summary (Acts 4.32-35) is gratuitous since Luke has already given an idyllic picture in 2.42-47. This unexplained appearance of the second portrayal of community life should cause us to pay close attention to the extended treatment of this discourse, which could potentially evoke a negative reaction from Luke's audience on account of the severe punishment of the couple. It has not been clear to many commentators how the section moves the plot forward. Therefore, the question remains: what does the second summary of communal life contribute to the ensuing plot? How do its illustrations of Barnabas and the couple add to the narrative?

2.3. Internal Repetition and Echo Effect

2.3.1. Following the Plot of Acts

The movement of the apostles Peter and John back to their companions (4.23) and the prayer that follows establish a dramatic interpretation of the preceding and subsequent events in the narrative. The prayer of the messianists effectively scripts the characters and events into a larger story including the story of Israel, Israel's God, Israel's Messiah and Israel's enemies, and it extends the dynamics of that plot to include the activity of the apostles. The messianists' prayer quotes Psalm 2.1-2 (LXX), making explicit the continuity of the conflict between Jesus and the Jerusalem elite on the one hand, and the apostles and the Jerusalem elite on the other. Herod possibly corresponds to the role of the 'kings' in the psalm[13] and Pilate stands in the role of the 'rulers' (Acts 4.26-27; Ps. 2.2 LXX). Commenting on the community's prayer, Tannehill writes, 'This recall of Jesus' passion is relevant because Jesus' situation, threatened by rulers and peoples, is viewed as essentially the same as the church's situation, faced with the threats of the Sanhedrin.'[14] From this Tannehill concludes, 'The opponents of Jesus and the opponents of the

---

13. Only in Luke's Gospel is a trial before Herod included (Luke 23:6-12, 15). See Beverly Roberts Gaventa, *Acts* (ANTC; Nashville: Abingdon, 2003), 96; Ernst Haenchen, *The Acts of the Apostles* (trans. R. McL. Wilson; Oxford: Basil Blackwell, 1971), 227; Luke Timothy Johnson, *The Acts of the Apostles* (SP 5; Collegeville, MN; The Liturgical Press, 1992), 84. Tannehill (*Narrative Unity* 2:71, n. 26) suggests rather that the 'kings' refer to political authorities and 'rulers' to religious authorities, comparing Acts 4.26 with 4.5.

14. Robert C. Tannehill, 'Composition', 211.

church are viewed as one continuous group, a simplification facilitated by the Sanhedrin's leading role in both situations.'[15] In other words, the enemies of Jesus and the apostles are the same – the Jerusalem leadership continues to reject God's agents of salvation. This 'internal repetition' of characters in conflict is one example of what Tannehill demonstrates as a complex intertextuality giving a multifaceted texture and rich depth of meaning to the development of the narrative. He explains, 'The prayer of the church (and later the speech and death of Stephen) reveals that there are actually two levels of echoes that may be heard by the passion story in Luke, and both are echoed by Scripture.'[16] In other words, the prayer of the community is a glimpse into what may be called Luke's triangular-dialectic hermeneutical pattern. There is a three-way network of significance generated through the echoes between the story of God's promises to Israel as read in the Scriptures, Jesus as the Prophet-King addressing Israel, and Jesus' prophetic successors continuing this same vocation. The three sides of the triangle are the Scriptures, the story of Jesus, and the story of the apostles.

This dialectic feature of Luke-Acts is illuminated by Joel Green who argues that Luke is motivated to build a story 'of the covenanting God who intervenes on behalf of humanity to accomplish his gracious aim'.[17] Green writes,

> Vis-à-vis the intertextual reverberations of the Lucan narrative with the LXX (i.e., external repetition), Luke inscribes himself in scriptural tradition, showing his debt to this previous story, and inviting his auditors to hear in this story the resounding continuation of that story. Vis-à-vis intertextual reverberations within Luke-Acts (i.e., internal repetition), Luke shows the great extent to which the story of the early church is inscribed into the story of Jesus, all as the continuation of the divine story of redemption.[18]

Tannehill demonstrates these parallels skilfully.[19] He argued at length for parallels between the passion account in Luke and the Jerusalem section in Acts (1.3–8.3), and parallels within Acts 1–7 itself. He also suggests that this pattern extends to the presentation of Paul's ministry. Tannehill asserts that 'the church's prayer in 4.23-31 relates not only to the specific situation of the apostles' arrest by the Sanhedrin and the previous situation of Jesus' rejection of death. It also anticipates the recurrent opposition from Jews and Gentiles encountered by the mission from this point on.'[20] He has suggested patterns of

---

15. Robert C. Tannehill, *The Narrative Unity of Luke-Acts: A Literary Interpretation* (2 vols; Minneapolis: Fortress, 1986, 1990), 2:71; idem, 'Composition', 211–12.
16. Tannehill, 'Composition', 212.
17. Joel B. Green, 'Internal Repetition in Luke Acts: Contemporary Narratology and Lucan Historiography', in *History, Literature, and Society* (ed. Witherington), 290.
18. Green, 'Internal Repetition', 290.
19. Tannehill, *Narrative Unity*, 2:48–101; idem, 'Composition'. Tannehill's work is evaluated by Douglas S. McComiskey (*Lukan Theology in the Light of the Gospel's Literary Structure* [Carlisle: Paternoster, 2004], 33–75) with eleven tests for evaluating the probability of authorial intention behind the proposed correspondences.
20. Tannehill, *Narrative Unity*, 2:73.

repetition between characters, events, settings, and sequences. Tannehill offers points of comparison between Luke's passion narrative and the apostles' conflicts in Jerusalem (noting the distinctives of Luke when compared with Matthew and Mark):

(1) Both Luke 22.52 and Acts 4.1 refer to 'captains of the temple' (στρατηγός).
(2) The temple officials 'laid hands on' (ἐπέβαλον τὰς χεῖρας, Acts 4.3; 5.18) the apostles, with a similar phrase used in the attempt 'to lay hands on' (ἐπιβαλεῖν ... τὰς χεῖρας, Luke 20.19) Jesus.
(3) Both Acts 4.5 and Luke 22.66 place examination on the morning after the arrest.
(4) Both Acts 4.5-6 and Luke 22.66 refer to the Sanhedrin being 'gathered together' (passive of συνάγω).
(5) The reference to 'rulers' (ἄρχοντες) in Acts 4.5 corresponds to Luke 23.13, 35; 24.20. It can be added to Tannehill's point that a similar entourage of 'elders' (πρεσβυτέροις), 'chief priests' (ἀρχιερεῖς), and 'scribes' (γραμματεῖς) are composite in the opposing leadership (Luke 20.1; 22.52; Acts 4.5-6, 23).
(6) A similar sequence of teaching before arrest and in the setting of the Temple correspond between Luke 20.1-37 and Acts 3.12–5.42.
(7) A similar interrogation is made to Jesus ('By what authority are you doing these things?', Luke 20.2) and to Peter ('By what power or what name do you do this?', Acts 4.7).
(8) Both Jesus (Luke 20.17) and Peter (Acts 4.11) make reference to 'the stone the builders rejected' (cf. Ps. 117.22 LXX) in their response to accusers.[21]
(9) Jesus' citation of Ps. 117.22 LXX is a veiled accusation of the leaders following the parable of the vineyard (Luke 20.9-16) which becomes explicit in Acts (4.11, ὁ ἐξουθενηθεὶς ὑφ' ὑμῶν; 5.30).
(10) In both Luke and Acts 'the people' (ὁ λαός) prevent the rulers from taking direct, violent action against Jesus or his followers (Luke 19.47-48; 20.19; 22.2; Acts 4.21; 5.26).[22]

Tannehill also argues for a 'reduplication pattern' within Acts 1–5. Comparing Acts 4.1-22 with 5.17-42, he notes the parallels between (1) the arrests of the apostles (4.1-3; 5.17-18, 26-27), (2) their appearance before the Council with short kerygmatic responses (4.10-12; 5.30-32), and (3) declarations that the apostles must obey God and keep speaking (4.19-20; 5.29). (4) In both cases the Council deliberates after sending the apostles out from the council

---

21. On this see the insightful essay by J. Ross Wagner, 'Psalm 118 in Luke-Acts: Tracing a Narrative Thread', in *Early Christian Interpretation of the Scriptures of Israel: Investigations and Proposals* (eds Craig A. Evans and James A. Sanders; JSNTSup 148; Sheffield: Sheffield Academic Press, 1997), 154–78.
22. Tannehill, 'Composition', 208–9; idem, *Narrative Unity*, 2:68–9.

chamber (4.15-17; 5.34-39), and (5) this results in the release of the apostles, with a prohibition of speaking in Jesus' Name (4.21; 5.40).[23]

Charles Talbert offers a still more extensive comparison of correspondences.[24] He sets Acts 1.12–4.23 alongside 4.24–5.42, noting that each passage starts with the messianic community in prayer (1.12-14, 15-26; 4.24-31a), and being filled with the Spirit (2.4; 4.31b), resulting in bold preaching (2.14-40; 4.31c). These scenes are followed by summaries of the communal life (2.41-47; 4.32–5.11) and 'signs and wonders' (2.43; 3.1-10; 5.12-16) leading to arrests (4.1-7; 5.17-28), Peter's defence (4.8-12, 19-20; 5.30-32), deliberation by the Council (4.13-17; 5.33-39), and release of the apostles (4.18, 21-23; 5.40-42). Talbert does not comment on the asymmetrical relationship of the communal summaries, with the extended examples in the second account. The patterns Talbert identifies usually work the other way around, with the longer set coming first. Thus, (1) 1.12-26; (2) 2.1-11; (3) 2.14-36; (7) 3.1-11 correspond to a second short set (1) 4.24-31a; (2) 4.31b; (3) 4.31c; (7) 5.13-16 (Talbert's numbering). In other words, what is a scene in the first set becomes a summary in the second set. Yet, in the second communal summary (4.32-35) there are scenic illustrations without a counter-part in the first communal summary (2.41-47).

Talbert suggests a general function for Acts 4.32–5.11: 'It serves to illustrate a threat to the church's unity, and it illustrates one way such a threat is resolved.'[25] Talbert's concluding statement in his commentary on Acts 4.24–5.42 reveals his understanding of the narrative logic of the progressing plot: 'If prayer leads to empowering and empowering to witness, the mission is not deterred by opposition, even imprisonment and flogging.'[26]

The readings of Tannehill and Talbert are narrative-oriented, but they do not leave much space for the contribution of Acts 4.32–5.11 to the plot of Luke-Acts.[27] Viewing the passage as just a 'minor theme', Tannehill explains its significance for the wider plot with one sentence: 'Thus the early church not only faced an external threat from the temple authorities but also an internal threat.'[28] Is the second communal summary with its scenic illustrations merely an anecdote to balance the idealized description of the community

---

23. Tannehill, 'Composition', 214–15.
24. Charles H. Talbert, *Literary Patterns, Theological Themes and the Genre of Luke-Acts* (SBLMS 20; Missoula MT: Scholars Press, 1974), 35–9; idem, *Reading Acts: A Literary and Theological Commentary on the Acts of the Apostles* (New York: The Crossroad Publishing Company, 1997), 51, 50–72. Talbert's proposals are evaluated by McComiskey, *Lukan Theology*, 76–161.
25. Talbert, *Reading Acts*, 66.
26. Talbert, *Reading Acts*, 72.
27. Acts 4.32–5.11 receives about two-and-a-half pages in Tannehill's commentary (*Narrative Unity*, 77–9), and no space in his shorter essay ('Composition'). Talbert affords more space (*Reading Acts*, 63–6), but offers little by way of integrating the summary into the narrative logic.
28. Tannehill, *Narrative Unity*, 2:79. Tannehill does rightfully set this crisis in the community in parallel with the next internal crisis mentioned in Acts 6.1-7 (77, 79, 80).

sharing goods?²⁹ Is a distinction between 'major' and 'minor' themes the best way to distinguish between the scenes of external and internal conflict? We should not overlook the larger theme of 'being or giving a witness' to Jesus' resurrection (Luke 24.48; Acts 1.8, 22; 2.32; 3.15; 4.33; 5.32; 10.39, 41; 13.31). Peter's preaching and the community-of-goods are manifestations of the themes of telling and modelling the message. It is also the catalyst for the external conflict.

Daniel Marguerat offers an exceptional literary and theological exploration of the Ananias and Sapphira episode. He notes how the pericope is located between two summaries, one devoted to the sharing of possessions (4.32-35) and the other to the miraculous activity of the apostles (5.12-16). Both reflect the significance of the Ananias and Sapphira episode (5.1-11). Marguerat suggests the following as the plot of the macro-narrative of Acts 2.42–5.42: 'It recounts *how the Spirit of Pentecost seized the first Christian community, grouped around the apostolic nucleus, in order to constitute and expand it in an open crisis with the Jewish religious authorities.*'³⁰ In other words, Acts 2–5 is about the territorial quarrel between the Christian group and the aristocratic leaders, both 'aiming to determine who possesses the theological authority at the centre of Israel's religion'.³¹ Marguerat suggests a recurring schema that governs this narrative section: (a) summary – (b) event (scene) – (c) interpretation (speech) – (d) contrasted effect.³² In this schema, Marguerat

---

29. Tannehill (*Narrative Unity*, 2:79) writes, 'The portrait is not so idealized as to deny the necessity of clearly facing problems in order to preserve and restore the life to which the church has been called.'

30 Daniel Marguerat, 'Ananias and Sapphira (Acts 5.1–11): The Original Sin', in *The First Christian Historian: Writing the 'Acts of the Apostles'* (SNTSMS 121; trans. Ken McKinney, Gregory J. Laughery and Richard Bauckham; Cambridge: Cambridge University Press, 2002), 161, emphasis his. This essay is a revised translation of Marguerat, 'La mort d'Ananias et Saphira (AC 5.1–11): dans la stratégie narrative de Luc', *NTS* (1993): 209–26 [215].

31. Marguerat, 'Ananias and Sapphira', 162.

32. Marguerat, 'Ananias and Sapphira', 158–61; idem, 'La mort', 211–15. He schematizes the narrative as follows (see his chart, 'Ananias and Sapphira', 160; 'La mort', 213):

(1) *First summary*: (a) 2:42–47 (unanimity of believers as a result of Pentecost) – (b) 3:1–10 (healing the lame man) – (c) 3:11–26 (Peter's speech about the efficacy of Jesus' death) – (d¹) 4:1–3 (Sadducees' negative response, imprisonment of Peter and John), (d²) 4:4 (crowd's positive response).

(2) (b) 4:5–7 (interrogation by Sanhedrin) – (c) 4:8–12 (Peter's speech about rejected prophet) – (d¹) 4:13–22 (Sanhedrin's deliberation and warning), (d²) 4:23–31 (communal prayer).

(3) *Second summary*: (a) 4:32–35 (idyllic summary) – (b) 4:36–37 (Barnabas), 5:1–11 (Ananias and Sapphira) – (c)-[*null*] – (d) 5:5b, 11 (effect: fear).

(4) *Third summary*: (a) 5:12–16 (intensification of miraculous activity of the Apostles) – (b) 5:17–21a (Apostles again imprisoned, delivered by an angel), 5:21b–26 (Apostles teaching in temple, pursuit by Sanhedrin) – (c) 5:27–32 (Peter's speech about the exalted Christ) – (d¹) 5:33 (wish to put apostles to death), (d²) 5:34–40 (Gamaliel's wise counsel).

(5) *Final summary*: 5:41–42.

writes that '4.32–5.11 *does not fit into the growth of Jewish hostility*'.[33] However, the effects of the episode, 'fear' (5.5b, 11) and the excess of the miraculous (5.12-16) attest to the role the passage plays in the success of the community.

Marguerat proposes to read the Ananias and Sapphira episode by noting how the narrative strategy of the surrounding co-text bears upon this passage. He notes four consequences of reading Acts 4.32–5.11 as centring upon the community.[34] First, in the macro-narrative dedicated to showing the marvellous growth of the community, the summary serves to contrast the unified Christian community with the hostile, helpless or divided Jewish authorities. Second, Acts 5.1-11 is distinctive in showing internal conflict of the Christian community. For Marguerat, the focus of the resolution of this conflict is the effect among the λαός. 'The community in 5.1-11 is then not considered from the angle of how it handles discipline, but from the perspective of its power of missionary expansion.'[35] Third, the first use of the term ἐκκλησία in Acts (5.11) 'designates the community of Jerusalem as a prototype of the eschatological community of salvation.[...] Acts 5.1-11 *recounts how the community of believers* [...] *acquire the status of the assembly of the people of God* (ἐκκλησία).'[36] Finally, for Marguerat, the 'decision of Ananias and Sapphira is thus oriented toward the needs of others and toward the construction of a loving community. The summary places their crime in *the ethical perspective of the sharing of possessions*, rather than in the register of a sacrilegious offence pertaining to holy possessions.'[37] Marguerat carries the discussion forward by suggesting the consequences of reading Acts 4.32–5.11 in light of its surrounding co-text.

33. Marguerat, 'Ananias and Sapphira', 162, emphasis his; 'La mort', 215.

34. Robert F. O'Toole ('"You Did Not Lie to Us [Human Beings] but to God" [Acts 5,4c]', *Bib* 76 [1995], 198) criticized the logical flow of Marguerat's earlier article, 'La mort', because it subordinated, as Tannehill had done, the communal focus to the motif of conflict ('La mort', 215 n. 12, 216 n. 13, referring to Tannehill, *Narrative Unity*, 2:48–50, 63–77 and 43–4, 77–9, respectively). Marguerat tried to alleviate this difficulty in the English version, removing the references to Tannehill ('Ananias and Sapphira', 162 n. 15, 163 n. 17), but leaving the structure of his argument intact and so remaining vulnerable to O'Toole's critique.

35. Marguerat, 'Ananias and Sapphira', 163; 'La mort', 216. However, it is possible to read the apprehension of some in Acts 5.13a to join or associate with the church as a direct response to the divine judgement.

36. Marguerat, 'Ananias and Sapphira', 163, 164, emphasis his; idem, 'La mort', 216, 217. It seems inconsistent to exclude the motif of communal discipline, on the one hand, but then to designate this pericope as ascribing the political status of ἐκκλησία to the Christian community, on the other hand. The two should go together. The problem is related to Marguerat's conception of the Jerusalem church as 'the archetype of all Christian communities' ('Ananias and Sapphira', 163; 'le modèle archétypique de toute communauté chrétienne', in 'La mort', 216).

37. Marguerat, 'Ananias and Sapphira', 164, emphasis his; 'La mort', 217. This is Marguerat's polemic against what he deems as the 'typological' reading of the passage correlating it with the Achan story of Joshua 7. However, this assertion seems to be in conflict with his polemic against what he deems 'Qumranian' communal-discipline parallels in his second point, where he denies this focus in contrast to the effect on the people.

In addition to these results, Marguerat's proposal invites an investigation of its other side: having read Acts 4.32–5.11 in its narrative co-text, how does this passage contribute to the narrative development of Acts 1.3–5.42?

What follows is my proposal for the contribution of Acts 4.32–5.11 to the narrative logic of Luke-Acts.[38] If in fact the Jerusalem section of Acts (2.1–8.3) is a crescendo of opposition to the apostolic mission echoing the passion narrative of Luke's Gospel, then it will be crucial to locate the second summary of communal life in the flow of the unfolding of the plan of God. The summary serves to legitimate the sanctity of the messianic community and the authority of the apostolic leadership. It also serves to assess the nature of the opposition to the apostles as diabolic and heightens the suspense with regard to the danger to the Jerusalem Temple leadership of rejecting the Messiah's emissaries.

2.3.2. The Sanctity of the Community

An immediate contribution Acts 4.32–5.11 makes to the narrative logic of Luke-Acts is to establish a radical view of the sanctity of the community. Already when the messianic community has been filled with the Holy Spirit (2.4) the group is distinguished as an eschatological community of restoration and divine mission.[39] In the first communal summary following the Pentecost event (2.41-47) the community is marked by congregational solidarity and a practical piety resulting from the filling of the Holy Spirit.[40]

---

38. My proposal is similar to O'Toole ('"You Did Not Lie"', 198–9). O'Toole appeals to Giuseppe Betori (*Perseguitati a causa del Nome: Strutture dei racconti di persecuzione in Atti 1,12–8,4* [AnBib 97; Rome: Pontifical Biblical Institute, 1981]), in seeing the overall structure of Acts 2.42–8.4 (1.12–8.3) as being about the life of the Jerusalem community, of which conflict is a subordinate theme.

39. See Max Turner, *Power from on High: The Spirit in Israel's Restoration and Witness in Luke-Acts* (JPTSup 9; Sheffield: Sheffield Academic Press, 1996), 266–315, 401–27; Matthias Wenk, *Community-Forming Power: The Socio-Ethical Role of the Spirit in Luke-Acts* (JPTSup 19; Sheffield: Sheffield Academic Press, 2000), 232–73.

40. I follow Turner and Wenk in their arguments regarding the relationship of the communal ethos and the Holy Spirit, in contrast to Robert P. Menzies (*The Development of Early Christian Pneumatology: With Special Reference to Luke-Acts* [JSNTSup 54; Sheffield: JSOT Press, 1991], 47–9, 205–35, 245–79, 316–18) and to Roger Stronstad (*The Prophethood of All Believers: A Study in Luke's Charismatic Theology* [JPTSup 16; Sheffield: Sheffield Academic Press, 1999], 10–11, 63 n. 7, 116–23). Turner (*Power*, 412–15) offers three reasons why the community life in Acts should be understood as a result of the Spirit's work, and Wenk (*Power*, 260–73) adds five more:

(1) The community depicted is a result of the restoration of the Messiah and his baptizing the community with the Spirit.

(2) The co-text of the first two summaries suggests that the community life follows the giving of the Spirit (note the 'mini Pentecost' in 4.31).

(3) Certain elements in the summaries suggest or require explanation in terms of the Spirit, like the power with which the apostles give witness (4.33) and the communal care.

The sacredness of the association formed by the Spirit is further marked in the second communal summary (4.32–5.11) by an ethical use of resources for the believers, the 'abundant grace' (4.33b), and the resultant eradication of need (4.34-35). Appellations such as οἱ δοῦλοι μοῦ/σοῦ (2.18;[41] 4.29) indicate that the messianists are located in the inviolable household of God, and the death of Ananias and Sapphira only serves to underscore the strength of God's guarantee upon the community's sacred character.[42]

The filling (πίμπλημι) of the community following the prayer of supplication (4.31), precisely by the *Holy* Spirit, is set in stark contrast to Peter's accusation of Ananias, where 'Satan has filled (πληρόω) your heart to lie to the Holy Spirit' (5.3) (as well as the Sadducees who are 'filled with jealousy', 5.17).[43] The descriptor 'holy' is used of Jesus (Luke 1.35; 4.34; Acts 2.27 [Ps. 15.10 LXX]; 3.14; 4.27, 30; 13.35)[44] and serves derivatively to mark the community.[45] Ju Hur notes how the Holy Spirit can be contrasted with evil or unclean spirits,[46] clearly visible in the contest between God's agent, Peter, and Satan's agent, Ananias. Here, the confrontation between Peter and the couple recalls the contrast between the Spirit and the devil in the account

(4) Compositional structures tend to encourage the relationship between Acts 2.1-41 and 42-47.

(5) The literary function of the summaries, according to Wenk, express the self-understanding of the messianic community and provide narrative linkages from what comes before to what follows.

(6) A comparison with the Qumran community's understanding as a 'congregation of the Holy Spirit' and Acts 2.42-47 expressed through sharing goods (cf. 1QS 1.11-13; 5.1-3; 6.15-25), adherence to the teaching of the community (cf. 1QS 5.2-12; 6.4-8; 1QSa 1.1-5; 1QM 10.10; CD 4.7-9; 1QH 12.22-27), and a ritual (proleptic) meal (cf. 1QS 5.8-12; 1QSa 2.17-22).

(7) The role of the Spirit in the summaries, Acts 2.42-47 mentioned above; Acts 4.32–5.11 with the offence by Ananias and Sapphira; Acts 5.12-16, linking the Spirit with the 'signs and wonders' and the advancement of the church's mission; and Acts 9.31, linking the Spirit to the encouragement of the church's walk with the Lord.

(8) The messianic community is signified as the arrival of the prophecy of Joel 3.1-5 LXX and the 'Year of the Lord's Favour' Proclaimed to the Poor (see Luke 4.18-19).

41. The possessive pronoun 'my' in Acts 2.18 (and not in Joel 3.2 LXX) indicates that the δοῦλοι and δοῦλαι are the servants of God, not of Israel, as in Joel. Robert L. Brawley, *Text to Text Pours Forth Speech: Voices of Scripture in Luke-Acts* (Indianapolis: Indiana University Press, 1995), 81.

42. Turner writes, 'The radical holiness and corporate unity of this community is actively promoted and vigilantly preserved by the Spirit (cf. Acts 5.1-10)' (*Power*, 445; cf. 129, esp. 406–7, 432). See also Wenk, *Power*, 48, 181 n. 19, 235, 264 n. 19, 270, 305–6.

43. On the language of 'filling' in Luke-Acts, see Turner, *Power*, 165–9; idem, 'Spirit Endowment in Luke-Acts: Some Linguistic Considerations', VoxEv 12 (1981): 45–63; Ju Hur, *A Dynamic Reading of the Holy Spirit in Luke-Acts* (London: T&T Clark International, 2001), 165–71.

44. See Hur, *Dynamic Reading*, 137–8.

45. See also the remarks about communal holiness by Rick Strelan, *Strange Acts: Studies in the Cultural World of the Acts of the Apostles* (BZNW 126; Berlin: Walter de Gruyter, 2004), 199–200, 208.

46. Hur, *Dynamic Reading*, 138, 175–8.

of Jesus' temptation in the wilderness (Luke 4.1-13).[47] O'Toole makes the connection in this way, 'Like Jesus at his temptation, the early church cannot be compromised or deceived by Satan because ultimately one is not lying *only* to human beings but to God and the Holy Spirit, who are present in the community and working through the apostles, especially Peter.'[48] These events help to explain the severity of the punishment executed on the couple, and in turn indicate the level of relentless fervour with which God guards the religio-economic practices of the community.[49] Jervell explains with reference to the fulfilment of eschatological Israel, 'For it [the life of the community] is indeed determined by the Spirit. The one who lives differently and sins is inevitably cut off from the people, [Acts] 3.23. If two community members are met by punishment, this shows that God acts through and for the community' (my translation).[50] As already noted, it may be no accident that the designation of ἐκκλησία for the messianic community is used immediately following these events.[51]

Another indication of the sanctity of the early messianic community is the polarity between the 'great grace' (4.33; cf. 2.43) and the 'great fear' (5.5, 11) that features in the descriptions of the community life and its distribution of goods. In 2.47 the community enjoys 'favour' with the people. By contrast, in 4.33 the 'grace' is a divine gift of favour and blessing.[52] This divine approval, coupled with the severe divine disapproval of the couple, results in a reaction from those who heard of reverential awe, even pious dread, at the prospect of offending the divine authority behind this community. This serves to heighten the irony of a suggestion from one of the Jerusalem Council's members of a possibility that 'this plan or this work' might be hallowed by God (5.38).

47. See Pesch, *Apostelgeschichte*, 204; O'Toole, '"You Did Not Lie"', 205–6. For O'Toole, the parallel between the Ananias and Sapphira episode and the temptation of Jesus 'best explains Luke's purpose in the former story' (205). He draws five parallels between the two stories: (1) the Holy Spirit and the devil/Satan play a significant role in each story which (2) occurs toward the beginning of each volume. (3) The same Greek root, πειράζειν, is used to express the temptation in each story (Luke 4.2, 12; Acts 5.9). (4) Each story touches on behaving with integrity before God, and (5) in the encounter between the divine and the anti-divine, the devil/Satan and its agents are overcome.

48. O'Toole, '"You Did Not Lie"', 182.

49. O'Toole ('"You Did Not Lie"', 196–7) writes, 'The message is more one of encouragement, for Christians know that God and the Holy Spirit (of Jesus?) are guarantors of the Church's integrity.'

50. Jacob Jervell, *Die Apostelgeschichte* (Göttingen: Vandenhoeck & Ruprecht, 1998), 198–9, 'Denn sie wird ja von dem Geist bestimmt. Wer anders lebt und sich versündigt, wird unweigerlich aus dem Volk ausgerottet, [Apg.] 3,23. Wenn die zwei Gemeindemitglieder von der Strafe getroffen werden, zeigt das, dass Gott durch und für die Gemeinde handelt'.

51. Those who see the initial use as significant include, William J. Larkin, *Acts* (Downers Grove: InterVarsity Press, 1995), 87; Marguerat, 'Ananias and Sapphira', 163–4; idem, 'La mort', 216–17; Ivoni Richter Reimer, *Women in the Acts of the Apostles: A Feminist Liberation Perspective* (trans. Linda M. Maloney; Minneapolis: Fortress, 1995), 21; Witherington, *Acts*, 219–20.

52. With Johnson, *Acts*, 86; and Haenchen (*Acts*, 231, n. 4) and Schneider (*Aposelgeschichte*, 1:366, n. 26). The latter two refer back to Luke 2.40.

2.3.3. Conflicting Leadership Appeals

A second contribution that Acts 4.32–5.11 makes to the plot of Luke-Acts is to demonstrate that the community's apostolic leadership is authorized by God. This divine legitimation is all the more apparent when the apostolic leadership is compared with the incompetent Jerusalem leadership headed by the high priest.[53] The summary of communal life in 4.32–5.11 points to the strengthening role of the apostles within this eschatologically marked community. The special authority of the apostles was already indicated when they were commissioned as witnesses (1.4-5, 8, 21-22). Other indications are the boldness of Peter's speeches, inspired by the Spirit (2.14 [ἀπεφθέγξατο; cf. 2.4]; 4.8, 13 [παρρησία], 31), and not least by the apostolic 'signs and wonders' (2.43; 4.16, 22; cf. 2.19, 22; 4.30; 5.12). All of these confirm the apostles as chosen for the specific mission of bearing witness to the resurrection of Messiah. Yet, the execution of divine judgement through the vehicle of Peter's words is the most dramatic example of the apostolic representative rule on behalf of the enthroned Christ over restored Israel.[54]

The rule of the apostles through Peter's execution of judgement on the miscreant couple should be compared with the incompetence of the Jerusalem elite. This group was unable to execute judgement on the apostles, to bring 'order' to their city (4.13-17; 5.19-28), or to influence the populace (4.21; 5.26b). On the other hand, the authority of the apostolic leadership is enhanced.[55] The impotence of the Judicial Council to control the actions of the apostles or execute justice as they saw fit is in sharp contrast with the competence of the apostolic witness and the high esteem in which the people held the apostles (2.47; 5.13b).

The one place where the Jerusalem Council takes direct action to control the outcome of an unfavourable public situation is in the confrontation with Stephen. Here the Council does not prove its claims to be worthy for ruling the people, but rather condemns itself through acts of violence akin to its rejection of Jesus. The crowd is portrayed as a violent, impulsive reaction to Stephen's message. More important than the impulsive behaviour of the crowd is its unanimity, joined in rage with the Council. Johnson suggests that

---

53. For Luke Timothy Johnson (*The Literary Function of Possessions in Luke-Acts* [SBLDS 39; Missoula, MT: Scholars Press, 1977], 198), 'the story *around* 4:32–5:11 is that of the progressive assertion of the authority of the Twelve over against threat from outside, and the steady erosion of the old leaders' authority over Israel'. See idem, *Acts*, 83, 89–93; and Marguerat, 'Ananias and Sapphira', 167. Similarly, O'Toole ('"You Did Not Lie"', 185, 190) writes that 'these rule miracles of punishment primarily demonstrate that God and the Holy Spirit are working through the apostles, especially Peter, in the community.[...] Luke portrays a radical connection between the apostles, especially Peter, and God.[...] The activity of God and of the Holy Spirit in and through the apostles makes them the true representatives of the divine and authority figures.'

54. On the apostolic rule, see §7.1 below.

55. See Marguerat, 'Ananias and Sapphira', 162; and Tannehill, *Narrative Unity*, 2:66.

there may be an ironic echo of the 'one mind and heart' of the messianists' fellowship (Acts 2.46; 4.24; 5.12; cf. 4.32).[56]

Steve Mason draws out the narrative progression of gathering antagonism to Stephen's message. Stephen at first is opposed by fellow Greek-speaking Jews from the Synagogue of the Freedmen (6.9). Then, they collect false witnesses (6.11, 13) who stir up the people, the elders, and the scribes. These witnesses drag him into the council chamber (6.12; see Luke 22.66). Finally, the high priest inquires whether the accusations are true (7.1). Thus, at the end of Stephen's speech, the 'they' who heard and became enraged (7.54) would seem to be the mass of all Jerusalem, as in the narrative of Jesus' condemnation (Luke 23.13, 18, 21, 23). Mason concludes:

> When Stephen is brought before the *synedrion*, the High Priest has broad support for his execution; there is no question of fearing the people or dealing with the Pharisees. Stephen accuses the whole people (7:51–53), and one of those who consents to Stephen's death is Saul (8:1), who turns out to be a Pharisee (26:5).[...] The Temple-based opposition to Christianity is now solidifying with the apparent inclusion of Pharisees and many of the people.[57]

Hence, the Judicial Council in Jerusalem, as the local ruling body, did use its power, legitimate or not, to proscribe and condemn. However, as a result of this action the Council and all the people stand condemned in the court of divine opinion.

In contrast, the divine retribution executed through Peter's indictment on Ananias and Sapphira demonstrates a *divine* legitimation and sanction of apostolic authority. Peter has merely to speak, and God executes final judgement through his word. It is through the hands of the apostles that 'signs and wonders' occur (5.12), which evoke jealousy from the high priest and his associates (5.17). When the pattern of the Council's inability to control the messianists is broken in the execution of Stephen, the narrative perspective remains consistent by condemning the action as the persecution of the righteous martyr, who dies like the innocent Christ. In other words, even when the Council provokes a capital retribution, it stands condemned as a people 'stiff-necked and uncircumcised in heart and ears [who] are always resisting the Holy Spirit', 'persecutors of the prophets', 'betrayers and murderers of the Righteous One', and as those 'who received the law

---

56. Johnson, *Acts*, 140.
57. Steve Mason, 'Chief Priests, Sadducees, Pharisees and Sanhedrin in Acts', in *The Book of Acts in its Palestinian Setting* (ed. Richard Bauckham; vol. 4 of *The Book of Acts in its First Century Setting*, ed. Bruce W. Winter; Grand Rapids: Eerdmans, 1995), 152. I do not find persuasive Mason's suggestion for the trajectory for Luke's overall plot: 'over against other Christian authors, Luke sees himself charting a *gradual development* of Christianity from Jewish roots' (130). Here I think Mason underplays Luke's continual inclusion of *some* Jews (note Mason's own recognition of this, pp. 152–3), and so the expansion of the people of God to include Gentiles as *Gentiles*, retaining Christianity's faithfulness to its roots in the story of the Scriptures that were from Israel and for Israel and Gentiles.

ordained by angels, and yet do not keep it' (7.51-53). From the perspective of the narrator, the one executed is the vindicated one, as seen by the divine reception of Stephen, and therefore the Council remains condemned as the one who killed the righteous martyr who died like God's Christ.[58] In Acts, the Jerusalem Supreme Judicial Council stands condemned by the indictments of God's prophetic envoys, reinforcing the prophetic indictments and dire predictions of Jesus against Jerusalem (Luke 13.35; 19.27, 41-46; 20.9-19; 21.6, 20-54; 23.31).

In summary, the incompetent Jerusalem elite, perplexed and divided, is contrasted to the unified messianists, led by the Spirit-filled, competent apostles.[59] The Jerusalem Council cannot manage their people. It is reduced to impulsive brutality when confronted by Stephen, who is 'full of grace and power' (6.8), and so reminded that it has been displaced by the Son of Man who receives Stephen, the righteous martyr (Acts 7.56; Luke 22.69). The apostles, represented by Peter, rule the nascent community with Spirit-enabled capability, and in 5.1-11 with divine legitimation of his indictment of Ananias and Sapphira. The Ananias and Sapphira episode contributes a balance of perspective regarding apostolic power and governance. If it were not for the dramatic events of the Ananias and Sapphira episode, the apostolic leadership would appear more as persistent victims of persecution than as powerful and endowed vice regents of the eschatological restored Israel.

---

58. Hill, *Hellenists*, 59, offers a summary of the parallels between the stories of Stephen's martyrdom and Jesus' passion (noting the redactional deferrals Luke makes in shifting from Mark various themes from his Gospel account to Acts):

(1) Trial before high priest Sanhedrin (Mark 14:53 and par. / Acts 6:12; 7:1)

(2) False witnesses (Mark 14:56–57; Matt. 26:60–61; *not* in Luke / Acts 6:13)

(3) Testimony concerning the destruction of the temple (Mark 14:58; Matt. 26:61; *not* in Luke / Acts 6:14)

(4) Temple 'made with hands' (Mark 14:58; *not* in Luke / Acts 7:48)

(5) Son of man saying (Mark 14:62; and par. / Acts 7:56)

(6) Charge of blasphemy (Mark 14:64; Matt. 26:65; *not* in Luke / Acts 6:11)

(7) High priest's question (Mark 14:61; Matt. 26:63; *not* in Luke [cf. 22:67, 'they'] / Acts 7:1)

(8) Committal of spirit (*only* in Luke / Acts 7:59)

(9) Cry out with a loud voice (Mark 15:34 = Matt. 27:46; Mark 15:37 and par. / Acts 7:60)

(10) Intercession for enemies' forgiveness (*only* in Luke 23:34 / Acts 7:60)

See also Helen K. Bond, *Caiaphas: Friend of Rome and Judge of Jesus?* (Louisville: Westminster / John Knox Press, 2004), 116–18, who recognizes the redactional deferral of elements from Mark's passion narrative to the Stephen story in Acts 7.

59. Bond (*Caiaphas*, 116) writes, 'It will be here [the trial of Stephen in Acts 7] that the high priest will reject the early Christian movement and, following this rejection, the traditional leaders of Jerusalem will show themselves to be no longer capable of guiding God's people – a people that will now be composed of both Jews and Gentiles.'

2.3.4. Godly Obedience and Satanic Opposition

A third contribution Acts 4.32–5.11 makes to its surrounding co-text is to add a cosmic orientation to the conflict theme. Peter's accusation against Ananias that Satan has filled his heart (Acts 5.3) has a converse in the messianic community, whose 'heart' has been filled by the Spirit (4.31).[60] The confrontation between Peter and the couple draws out the underlying cosmic struggle between God and Satan, between the divine agents and diabolical agents.[61] Jervell says, 'The question of Peter shows that the actors are not actually Peter and the couple, but Satan and the Holy Spirit' (my translation).[62]

Luke reveals the satanic character of the opposition to the divine mission at strategic points throughout the narrative of Luke-Acts. Beginning with the temptation of Jesus (Luke 4.1-13), through the mention of the fall of Satan as a result of the mission of the seventy(-two) (10.18), and to the entry of Satan into Judas (22.3), Satan is a haunting shadow who polarizes responses to Jesus and the divine mission.[63] Throughout Acts, the story remains the same. Satan is credited with the seduction of Ananias and Sapphira (Acts 5.3), and this oppressing devil also appears in Peter's kerygmatic summary of the gospel to Cornelius as a contrast to the Spirit-anointed Jesus who performs deeds of power and healing (10.38). Paul condemns the false prophet, Bar-Jesus, as the 'son of the devil' (13.10). In Paul's third recounting of his testimony, he asserts that the risen Christ commissioned him to go to the Gentiles 'to open their eyes so that they may turn from darkness to light and from the dominion of Satan to God' (26.18). Luke's continual reference to the devil and Satan throughout his narrative makes him out to be 'the personification of evil, a being who sums up all opposition to the good that comes in Jesus, his word, his disciples or their mission'.[64]

Robert Brawley reads the temptation narrative (Luke 4.1-13) as manifesting 'a basic antithesis between the divine and the satanic'.[65] The devil attempts to hijack the divine plan here by routing the Son of God down a diabolical path. From this point forward, argues Brawley, all opposition to Jesus is polarized between God and Satan. He writes,

---

60. See Marguerat, 'Ananias', 170–1; idem, 'La mort', 220–1. However, it is unclear why Marguerat says Ananias' crime is not 'ethical' because it is a crime toward God: 'The offence is not ethical; the lie is not denounced as hypocrisy, but as a fraud toward God' ('Le délit n'est pas éthique; le mensonge n'est pas dénoncé comme une hypocrise, mais comme une fraude envers Dieu') ('La mort', 221).

61. See Marguerat, 'Ananias', 167, 170–1; O'Toole, '"You Did Not Lie"', 197–8.

62. Jervell, *Apostelgeschichte*, 196, 'Die Frage des Petrus zeigt, dass die Akteure nicht eigentlich Petrus und das Ehepaar sind, sondern Satan und der Heilige Geist'.

63. See Susan R. Garrett, *The Demise of the Devil: Magic and the Demonic in Luke's Writings* (Minneapolis: Fortress, 1989), 37–60.

64. Joseph A. Fitzmyer, 'Satan and Demons in Luke-Acts', in *Luke the Theologian: Aspects of his Teaching* (New York: Paulist Press, 1989), 147.

65. Robert Brawley, *Centering on God: Method and Message in Luke-Acts* (Louisville: Westminster / John Knox Press, 1990), 75.

> [T]he satanic is the organizing force for the polemical axis throughout Luke-Acts. [...] The basic antithesis, therefore, is not between Jesus and opponents. Rather, the opposition to Jesus is a manifestation of a larger conflict between the divine and the satanic. The devil does not succeed in tempting Jesus but does succeed in organizing a potent antithesis to him.[66]

Joel Green offers a similar interpretation: 'Indeed, it is not too much to say that Luke regards any aim that opposes that of God as diabolically motivated.'[67] This has important implications for those who oppose Jesus in the narrative world of Luke-Acts, opponents such as the Pharisees and the Temple elite. It stereotypes opposition to Jesus as that which wars against God (cf. Acts 5.39). Indeed, when the scorned messianic community prays to God after Peter and John were arrested for preaching the resurrection of the dead (Acts 4.2),[68] their prayer links together Herod, Pilate, the Gentiles, and the peoples of Israel as the opponents of the Lord and his Christ (Acts 4.25-28; Ps. 2.1-2 LXX). Thus, the temptation of Jesus establishes polarizing of allegiances for either God or Satan. Brawley argues that the narrative agenda to gather the people of God that is established in John's prophetic word (Luke 3.17) includes a sifting aspect that excludes from the people of God those who reject Jesus. To reject Jesus, or his witnesses, is to reject the kingdom of God (Luke 10.16; 12.8-12), and therefore salvation itself.

Precisely in the midst of escalating persecution in Acts, the Ananias and Sapphira episode emphasizes that opposition to Jesus and his followers is 'diabolically motivated'. Peter's response to the Council's initial censorship subtly removes them from the sphere of the divine will (Acts 4.19). The division is made more explicit in the prayer recalling the cosmic battle of the nations against 'the Lord and his Christ' (4.25-28). When an angel releases the apostles from prison, the opposition of the high priest and his associates is proved futile.[69] Finally, in Gamaliel's admonition, the Jerusalem Council is identified as θεομάχοι – those who are at war with God (5.39). The Ananias and Sapphira episode, set in between the two trials of the apostles, expresses plainly that opposition to the divine community is satanic.

---

66. Brawley, *Centering*, 76. Brawley's discussion of 'the polemical axis' draws from structuralist hermeneutics contrasting as polar opposites 'principal programs' versus 'polemical programs' in narrative schema (see pp. 67–8).

67. Green, *Theology*, 31. See also idem, *Luke*, 195–6. Gaventa (*Acts*, 98–9), commenting on the community's prayer in Acts 4.24-30, and following John Calvin, states: 'In Luke-Acts those who oppose Jesus and the proclamation about him are identified with Satan.'

68. See John J. Kilgallen, 'What the Apostles Proclaimed at Acts 4,2', in *Resurrection in the New Testament: Festschrift J Lambrecht* (eds R. Bieringer, V. Koperski, and B. Lataire; Leuven: Leuven University Press, 2002), 233–48.

69. With O'Toole, '"You Did Not Lie"', 194; Tannehill, *Narrative Unity*, 2:65–6.

2.3.5. Building Suspense over the 'Enemies of God'

The previous three contributions of Acts 4.32–5.11 to its context can be brought together. First, the messianic community has been guaranteed to be sacred by God's Holy Spirit. Second, the apostolic leadership has a divine appointment to the task of ruling over the messianic community, bringing it inevitably into conflict with the Jerusalem elite. Third, this elite group is unveiled as a satanic opposition. In the narrative order suspense escalates from irritated threats to physical violence and ultimately to lethal brutality. Ironically this tragedy concerning Stephen becomes the catalyst for the expanding global mission. Paul, who is 'born' through this violence into this narrative (9.1-9), experiences the pattern of opposition and conflict throughout his ministry, driving him at last to Rome, where the narrative of Acts ends with a scathing indictment of those in Israel who persist in rejecting God's Messiah (Acts 28.25-28; cf. Isa. 6.9-10).

There are three cycles of hostility directed at the messianists: 4.1-22, which ends with a warning; 5.17-42, which ends with a beating; and 6.8–8.3, which ends with martyrdom and persecution. There are also three indications of the danger of opposing God and God's agents. In 4.24-28 those opposing the apostles are first presented as part of the cosmic warfare between God and the Lord's Anointed fighting against the raging nations with their 'kings' and 'rulers'. The potentially threatening military imagery from Exodus of God's 'extended right hand'[70] and 'signs and wonders'[71] is tempered by the transforming aim of 'healing' and the agency of the Name of Jesus, God's 'holy Servant'. This healing is contrasted with the 'hand of God' that strikes Ananias and Sapphira. In actuality, this episode raises the stakes. Gamaliel warns the Sanhedrin not to oppose the messianists 'lest you be found warring against God' (5.39). The Ananias and Sapphira episode is essential because without it Gamaliel's warning would not convey the height of danger posed to the enemies of Christ and his community.

In conclusion, Acts 4.32–5.11 is an integral passage in the Jerusalem section of Acts (1.12–8.3) which demonstrates the awesome sacredness of the community, the divinely legitimated authority of the apostolic leadership, the satanic character of the opposition, and the solemn danger posed to those who combat God and God's agents.

---

70. The 'stretching forth of the hand' often occurs in an Exodus or military context. Exod. 6.8; 7.5, 19; 8.1, 2, 12, 13; 9.22, 23; 10.12, 21, 22; 14.16, 21, 26, 27; 15.12; Num. 14.30; Josh. 8.18, 19; Judg. 3.21; 5.26; 6.21; 2 Kgdms 24.16; 1 Chron. 21.16; Pss. 137.7 LXX; Jer. 6.12; 15.6; 21.5; 28.25 LXX; Ezek. 6.14; 13.9; 14.9, 13; 16.17; 25.7, 13, 16; 30.25; 35.3; Dan. (TH) 11.42.

71. 'Signs and wonders' are associated with the Exodus. Exod. 4.8, 9, 17, 28, 30; 7.3; 11.9, 10; 15.11; Deut. 4.34; 6.22; 7.19; 11.3; 26.8; 24.11; Neh. 9.10; Pss. 78.43; 105.27; 135.9 LXX; Jer. 32.21 LXX; Sir. 36.5; Acts 7.36.

2.4. Summary and Conclusion for Literary Co-text

Interpretation of Acts 4.32–5.11 requires constant attention to the narrative logic of the whole of Luke-Acts, the progression of the plot and the development and interaction of the characters. Attention to the plot requires close reading of each passage. How does the Ananias and Sapphira episode fit into Acts' emplotment of the nascent messianic community in Jerusalem? In this section we have examined the way in which the Ananias and Sapphira episode is rooted in, and framed by, the summary of the messianists' communal life manifest through the sharing of goods and the eradication of need. Barnabas is the positive example of this ethos, whereas Ananias and Sapphira are the negative example. Spanning out through the broadening concentric circles of discourse, the auditor is led through the interweaving of the earlier messianists' encounters with the Jerusalem populace and their own intra-communal interactions. The pattern of conflict with the Jerusalem aristocracy propels the plot forward from initial inquisition and censorship to physical violence (flogging), and ultimately to a fatal brutality (Stephen) and open persecution that drives the messianic mission beyond Jerusalem.

How does the Ananias and Sapphira episode contribute to this plot? The communal summary, and specifically the encounter between Peter and the condemned couple, demonstrates the divine guarantee upon the messianic community and the divine sanction of the apostolic leadership. God is on the side of the messianists, and no longer (if ever!) on the side of the current Jerusalem hierocracy. In fact, the high priest and his associates, by their obstinate antagonism to the apostles' mission, have aligned themselves with the satanic in the cosmic war between the Lord's Christ and the enemies of God. The Ananias and Sapphira episode serves as a bridge between the community's prayer, which interprets the persecution in light of the ancient battle motif, and the ironic warning of Gamaliel that the Council may indeed be found to be warring with God. The suspense is heightened, for the hearer dramatically sees the dire consequences of opposing the community and its protection by God's Spirit. The Ananias and Sapphira episode contributes to the wider plot of Acts by developing the characterization of the community, and Peter specifically, and by adding to the dramatic suspense about the potential consequences of resisting compliance with God and the divinely legitimized communal ethos.

These observations invite a closer examination of the specific dynamics in the encounter between Peter, as the apostolic representative, and the offending couple. These dynamics primarily unfold through linguistic action that demands an adequate methodological approach to explain the complex logic of the verbal transaction.

Chapter 3

INTRODUCING PROPHETIC SPEECH-ACTS

3.1. Narrative as Dialogue and the Philosophy of Language

The primary action in Acts 5.1-11 between the characters occurs through linguistic exchange, and therefore a commentator's latent philosophy of language will frame the way she or he understands the dynamics of the narrative encounter between Peter and the couple. Is Peter's speech – his rhetorical questions and damning accusations – directly linked to the couple's death? What did Peter *accomplish* when he spoke to the couple? What did he *do*? Did Peter merely predict the couple's death? Did they die out of shock, Ananias from overwhelming guilt and Sapphira from the distress of hearing that her husband had died and was buried without her knowledge? Or, is it that Peter utters a magical curse upon the miscreants? Ernst Haenchen states the thesis, albeit more crassly and less nuanced, that I defend here. In comparing the narrative to the condemnation of Achan (Josh. 7), he writes, 'Peter's accusation causes him [Ananias] to fall dead. The end of his wife Sapphira resembles Achan's more closely: Peter *kills* her by announcing her husband's demise and her own imminent death.[...] Peter does not merely prophesy Sapphira's death but [...] wants to kill – and succeeds.'[1] I argue for the following claim: Peter's words utter an apostolic-prophetic indictment against the couple who has lied to the Holy Spirit (Acts 5.3) and tested the Spirit of the Lord (5.9), which brings them under divine judgement. His inquisition and indictment *perform* the judicial death sentence and the execution of divine judgement.

Generally speaking, modern commentators construe the function of Peter's utterances in one of two ways: either as 'referential' or as 'magical'. By 'referential' I mean they posit a static, abstract use of language which in itself does not cause the death. The 'magical' view posits a dynamic use of language where a kind of formulaic or ritual imprecation causes the death. These approaches fall short of what is needed to elucidate the dynamics of the encounter. What is needed is a philosophy of language that allows

---

1. Ernst Haenchen, *The Acts of the Apostles: A Commentary* (14th edn; trans. R. McL. Wilson; Oxford: Basil Blackwell, 1971), 239, emphasis his. Haenchen offers no defence of how this can be the case.

words to function performatively while not sacrificing the referential or representative function of the words. This 'performative' view recognizes a dynamic power that accomplishes the deaths of Ananias and Sapphira, like the 'magical' view, while following closely the propositional content, as does the 'referential' interpretation. The performative view interprets the speech as active engagement while disallowing the exclusiveness of the previous options. The 'performative' view is an application of Speech-Act Theory, proposed by J. L. Austin and his philosophical descendants. It posits that Peter's speech is to be understood as a social action embedded in a particular narrative world that is rooted in the historical discourse of early Christian origins.[2]

3.2. The 'Referential' View

A growing number of contemporary scholars read Peter's words in a manner that can be called a 'referential' view. This view reads Peter's words as merely referring to states of (future) affairs. On the one hand Peter merely *informs* the couple of crucial information. For Ananias, he informs him of the true nature of his crime ('You have not lied to humans, but to God'). For Sapphira, Peter informs her of her crime (indirectly through a rhetorical question, 'You have put the Spirit of the Lord to the test') and of her imminent fate ('The feet of those who have buried your husband...shall carry you out as well'). On the other hand, it is sometimes suggested that Peter merely *predicts* the future outcome, his words having no (direct or indirect) consequential relationship with the penalty.

J. Duncan M. Derrett takes the referential approach. Following the information given by Peter, Ananias and Sapphira die as a result of psychological means.[3] For Derrett, the psychosomatic causes are these: Ananias dies out of heart failure at the news that he offended the Holy Spirit. Sapphira dies from the grief upon realizing that her husband's death had not been mourned.[4] Derrett's psychological explanation for the deaths of the couple has not been widely accepted by scholars. While Derrett remains consistent in separating Peter's words from a directly causative relationship

---

2. The scope of this study is concerned solely with what can be stated about the narrative world within Luke-Acts, and is not a historical research project to get at 'what actually happened'. There is not enough comparative evidence to conduct a study with regard to the aspect of historical veracity of this narrative. Alternatively, denial of the possibility of the event can come only on grounds other than historical.

3. J. Duncan M. Derrett, 'Ananias, Sapphira, and the Right of Property', *DRev* 89 (1971), 225–32. He is followed in this suggestion by Ben Witherington III, *The Acts of the Apostles: A Socio-Rhetorical Commentary* (Grand Rapids: Eerdmans, 1998), 215–17.

4. Other commentators who suggest natural causes for the death of the couple include William M. Furneaux, *The Acts of the Apostles: A Commentary for English Readers* (Oxford: Clarendon Press, 1912), 69; Ronald R. Williams, *The Acts of the Apostles* (TBC; London: SCM Press, 1953), 161.

to the couple's death, he does not take into account the context of the community-of-goods discourse nor the dramatic movement of the episode from the scene with Ananias to the scene with Sapphira.[5]

The 'referential approach' is expressed negatively by others in statements about what Peter did not do. For example, Ivoni Richter Reimer does

> not think that Peter utters a 'condemnation.' Instead his statement uncovers the couple's sin. He does not pass sentence on them. His function is not that of a judge, but rather of a legal representative of the community of saints. He intends to uncover death-dealing actions; they must be made known. The judge is God alone. Not even the words Peter says to Sapphira in v. 9 need be understood as condemnation. The word ἰδού – 'see' – can be a word of judgment, but it is not carried out by Peter: Peter expresses his conviction that, now that Sapphira has tried to cover her sin with a lie, God's dealing with her will surely be similar to the fate of Ananias. As I understand it, Peter's words are anything but joyful; they are surely spoken in sorrow. There is no feeling of smug satisfaction; instead, we find a painful admission that sin continues its reign.[...] If we read Peter's words as 'condemnation,' we would have to draw the logical conclusion that, practically speaking, he sentences the couple to death, or at least to punishment.[6]

Here Richter Reimer is setting up a false dichotomy. Peter's words must be either smug, arrogant condemnation, or else sorrowful exposing of dangerous sin. Richter Reimer is reluctant to read Peter's words as 'condemnation'. However, we may wonder why Peter needs to be exonerated from sentencing the couple to death? I accept the premise that reading Peter's words as 'condemnation' logically implies that Peter sentenced the couple to death, but my conclusion is opposite to that of Richter Reimer. Richter Reimer makes Peter out to be merely a 'legal representative of the community of saints'. Yet Peter's position, as one of the apostles who receive the ritual presentation of the proceeds of property sales, makes him more than simply a legal representative. The effect of Richter Reimer's diminution of Peter's role is to distort the assessment of the relationship of the characters. Richter Reimer continues,

> It is not the words of Peter (as a sentence of punishment) that kill, but the sinful deed that is revealed to the community. Its consequence is a total, radical exclusion

---

5. Derrett ('Ananias', 231) also speculates on the couple's share in the life of the world to come, asserting that the couple, through their death, 'atoned for their sin, and retained their right to share with their fellow members of the earliest ecclesia in the eternal life'.

6. Ivoni Richter Reimer, *Women in the Acts of the Apostles: A Feminist Liberation Perspective* (trans. Linda M. Maloney; Minneapolis: Fortress, 1995), 17. Compare the statement of Aaron J. Kuecker ('The Spirit and the "Other," Satan and the "Self": Economic Ethics as a Consequence of Identity Transformation in Luke-Acts', in *Engaging Economics: New Testament Scenarios and Early Christian Reception* [eds Bruce W. Longenecker and Kelly D. Liebengood; Grand Rapids: Eerdmans, 2009], 99, n. 63) who perceives Peter's words as regretful, denying that Peter is responsible for the couple's death, but blaming it on 'something that is apparently an inherently *natural consequence* of self-separation from the community' (emphasis added).

from the community. The revelation of the sin merely brings to a conclusion the self-destruction that is already inherent within it.[7]

Appealing to Paul's conception of 'sin' as a malevolent agent, she qualifies her statement:

> Sin is the *ruler of the world*. In saying this, Paul was thinking of 'governance with the dimensions of the *imperium Romanum*.' Its rule appears like that of a *slaveholder*: people are its instruments. This rule can express itself as *demonic power*: those possessed are alienated from themselves. All three levels of domination belong together and cannot be sharply distinguished. Thus sin is a 'comprehensive reign of terror.'[8]

The 'ruler of the world' is a reference to Paul's letter to the Romans (e.g., Rom. 6.12-23), but the reference of this to Luke-Acts cannot be simply assumed. Not only does Richter Reimer lack justification for appealing to Paul's rhetoric in his epistle to the Romans to warrant her claims concerning Acts, but she also neglects the more obvious agency of Satan as the culprit threatening to invade the sacral messianic community. The Ananias and Sapphira pericope is 'over-read', filling in what seems to be appropriate 'feelings' for Peter ('pain', 'sorrow'). This approach also 'under-reads' the text by forcing the Lukan voice into a sort of Pauline ventriloquism. Richter Reimer's equivocation ultimately fails to persuade because she does not take the narrative of Acts on its own terms.

Luke Johnson also denies a direct causal power to Peter's utterances. He writes, 'Peter does not strike him [Ananias] dead. Nor does he pronounce a judgment of death. But on hearing his prophetic declaration, Ananias dies.'[9] Johnson only restates the problem when he says, 'The power of his [Peter's] prophetic presence is so palpable that when he states the truth to each of the conspirators, they die.'[10] The mechanism of this transaction is unexplained, and therefore remains a mystery.

Similar positions on the 'referential' function of Peter's language are presupposed by O'Toole and Marguerat. O'Toole, in an article that is otherwise instructive, states, 'Peter's statement [to Sapphira in Acts 5.9b] is more explanatory than condemnatory.'[11] That is to say, O'Toole sees the force exerted and the action conducted by Peter here as explanation rather than condemnation. However, in the immediate co-text of his article,

---

7. Richter Reimer, *Women*, 17–18.
8. Richter Reimer, *Women*, 20–1, emphasis hers. The quotations originate with Luise Schottroff, *Befreiungserfahrungen: Studien zur Sozialgeschichte des Neuen Testaments* (Munich: Kaiser Verlag, 1989), 60, 63.
9. Luke Timothy Johnson, *The Acts of the Apostles* (SP 5; Collegeville, MN: The Liturgical Press, 1992), 88.
10. Johnson, *Acts*, 92.
11. Robert F. O'Toole, '"You Did Not Lie to Us (Human Beings) but to God" (Acts 5,4c),' *Bib* 76 (1995): 194.

O'Toole affirms, 'Sapphira's death confirms Peter as a prophet like Jesus.'[12] This prophetic persona means more for O'Toole than the simple fact that a prophet could foresee events or see 'into one's heart'. Rather, for O'Toole the use of παραχρῆμα here 'underlines Peter's prophetic ability and the rapidity with which the Lord can act to defend his community'.[13] Therefore, it would seem O'Toole does in fact leave open the possibility that Peter's statement was more condemnatory than explanatory.

Daniel Marguerat asserts that 'the powerful word of the apostle is the work of the Spirit (4.8)', but at the same time insists that Peter 'does not pronounce any sentence (cf. Also 13.1) [sic].[14] He *predicts* the imminent end of Sapphira (v.9b), but does not sentence her to death. Peter's task [...] never goes beyond the status of a mediator indwelt by the Spirit (4.31).'[15] Apparently, for Marguerat, the powerful work of the Spirit in Acts precludes sentencing a person to death. Yet, Marguerat is willing to follow Theissen's designation of this episode as a 'rule miracle of punishment'[16] and Marguerat includes as other examples the cursing of the fig tree (Mark 11.12-14, 20-21), the 'punishing' (*sic*) of Simon the magician (Acts 8.18-24), and the blinding of Elymas (13.11-12) (!).[17] The final example causes one to think that Marguerat is wavering in his insistence of the type of actions presented by the Spirit-empowered word of God's agents. Furthermore, it is seen below that the case of Simon Magus does not comprise the force of a condemnation, but only a warning.[18]

The 1984 ThD dissertation of Robert Beyer presents another example of a predictive 'referential' reading of Peter's words.[19] Beyer's entire thesis seems anxious to 'set apart the primitive Christian mission from Jewish and philosophic missions'.[20] Beyer wants to argue that all the so-called 'punitive miracles' in Acts are in fact not 'punitive miracles' at all, nor even

---

12. O'Toole, '"You Did Not Lie "', 194.
13. O'Toole, '"You Did Not Lie"', 194.
14. The English version of Marguerat's article quoted here should probably reference Acts 13.11, where Paul curses Elymas. If so, this would seem to militate against Marguerat's proposal that Peter is merely predicting and not sentencing Sapphira. Unfortunately, there is no parallel to offer confirmation of the correct citation in the original French version of the essay, 'La mort d'Ananias et Saphira (AC 5.1–11): dans la stratégie narrative de Luc', *NTS* (1993): 209–26.
15. Daniel Marguerat, 'Ananias and Sapphira (Acts 5.1–11): The Original Sin', in *The First Christian Historian: Writing the 'Acts of the Apostles'* (SNTSMS 121; trans. Ken McKinney, Gregory J. Laughery and Richard Bauckham; Cambridge: Cambridge University Press, 2002), 167.
16. Gerd Theissen, *The Miracle Stories of the Early Christian Tradition* (ed. John Riches; trans. Francis McDonagh; Philadelphia: Fortress, 1983), 109.
17. Marguerat, 'Ananias', 168–9.
18. See §6.2.3.1. below.
19. Robert Beyer, 'The Challenge: Restoring the Seven So-Called "Punitive Miracles" in Acts to the Prophetic Genre' (ThD dissertation, Lutheran School of Theology, 1984).
20. Beyer, 'Challenge', 1.

apostolic miracles, 'but [examples] of prophecy and fulfillment'.[21] Beyer sets up an unfruitful, simplistic dichotomy in trying to distinguish between 'punitive miracles' and simple (referential) prophecy with its (corresponding) fulfilment. With reference to distinguishing between the utterance of blessings and prophetic utterance he writes, 'The critical difference is in the nature of the words used. Those of blessing are power-laden and those of prophecy are ordinary, but spiritually endowed.'[22] Underpinning this statement is precisely the type of philosophy of language which views words as determinate containers having one-to-one correspondence with the things to which they refer, disallowing a performative use for language. Furthermore, this does not even begin to address Beyer's ambiguous distinction between 'power-laden' and 'spiritually endowed'. When it comes to the deaths of Ananias and Sapphira, Beyer is content to fall back on the psychological explanation (appealing to Derrett in a footnote),

> A more plausible solution to the deaths is to focus, with Luke, [sic] on Peter as predictor of that shock which overwhelmed those whose hearts were already overloaded with Satan's influence.[...] It should be clear that we are not taking the smoking gun from Peter and placing it in God's hands; rather, Ananias and Sapphira played Russian roulette and lost, as the prophet Peter knew they would.[23]

Can this deferral to a heart 'overloaded' with Satan's influence or an unmanned 'smoking gun' explain the death of the couple? This attempt to exonerate Peter and God from performing a death sentence on the couple fails to convince just as Richter Reimer's approach failed. Beyer's array of metaphors does not answer the question, but merely circumvents the relationship between Peter's words and the subsequent death of the couple.

Charles Kingsley Barrett, in his commentary on Acts, also illustrates the idea of Peter's language as predictive. With a concern for the provenance of the narrative, he writes,

> What was the origin of the story? Did Peter in fact strike dead two unsatisfactory church members? Judas (1.18) and Herod (12.23) died unhappy deaths; Paul struck blind Elymas, the magus of the proconsul Sergius Paulus (13.11); and there is nothing more miraculous in striking dead than in raising the dead (e.g. 9.32–43). There are OT parallels, notably Lev. 10.1–5. The difference and the difficulty are moral as well as rational, but are mitigated by the fact that Peter is not actually said to have caused, or even to have willed, the two deaths...[I]n fact he *foretells* [emphasis added] her [Sapphira's] death, but foretelling is not willing, and with Ananias did not even go so far.[24]

---

21. Beyer, 'Challenge', 2. Beyer includes seven pericopae that he desires to recast as (referential) prophecy in Acts: Judas (1.15-20), Ananias and Sapphira (5.1-11), Simon Magus (8.9-24), the death of Herod (12.19-23), the blinding of Elymas (13.4-12), the Seven sons of Sceva (19.13-17), and Ananias, the high priest (23.2-5).
22. Beyer, 'Challenge', 42.
23. Beyer, 'Challenge', 103–4.
24. C. K. Barrett, *Acts* (2 vols; ICC; London: T&T Clark, 1994, 1998), 1:262.

Thus, for Barrett, foretelling prophecy in this instance is merely referential to some future events. His approach is more sophisticated than to attribute the couple's deaths to psychological misfortune, and he recognizes that 'supernatural and dangerous powers were at work.[...] The φόβος μέγας [experienced by those who heard of the incident] is fear of the supernatural.'[25]

However, in quoting the same passage from Barrett, Gerd Lüdemann offers two convincing rebuttals:

> [1] The specific manner of foretelling Sapphira's death is tantamount to a death sentence.[...] [2] As concerns Ananias's fate, Peter had no need to predict it since he in effect pronounced it: 'You lied to God!' Can we seriously imagine that Luke's [historical?] readers were the sorts who would understand such an imprecation to be merely an objective assessment of the situation[...]?[26]

It seems that Barrett's philosophy of language in this instance excludes the possibility that the speech of Spirit-filled, prophetic successors to Jesus could have performed the execution of the judgement of God. I argue a case that this is both possible and likely in Luke's narrative world. Perhaps the various assessments have been confined to the form of Peter's words. Peter does not in fact say, 'I hereby condemn you ...' or the like. However, we should not confuse the form of an utterance with its force. That is, people do things with words all the time without overtly identifying the action with an explicit first-person pronoun accompanying a present-indicative verb.

A question remains: what is the relationship between Peter's words of inquisition and indictment and the couple's death? Ascribing merely a 'referential' function to Peter's words avoids making Peter responsible for the deaths, but the result is a failure to take account of the narrative drama that ensues in the confrontation between God's apostolic-prophetic agent and the miscreant couple.[27] Some commentators evade the issue by appealing to the Pauline personification of 'sin' or else propose psychological causes for the couple's deaths. Yet, there is a suggestion that would link Peter's words directly to the couple's death, magic. Is this suggestion sufficient to explain the relationship?

---

25. Barrett, *Acts*, 1:268.
26. Gerd Lüdemann, *The Acts of the Apostles: What Really Happened in the Earliest Days of the Church* (Amherst, NY: Promethius Books, 2005), 81.
27. Some Lukan scholars waver between false alternatives, fumbling for appropriate language to use concerning the relationship between Peter's speech and the death of the couple. See Joseph A. Fitzmyer, *The Acts of the Apostles: A New Translation with Introduction and Commentary* (AB 31; New York: Doubleday, 1998), 323–4: 'Peter's words do not directly condemn Ananias to death, but they imply something similar, because Ananias's punitive death follows upon them as a result of God's judgment. It is God who strikes down the guilty.' My argument aligns Peter's and God's actions together: God strikes the couple; Peter is the deputized vehicle who speaks on God's behalf.

3.3. The 'Magical' View

Hans Conzelmann illustrates the 'magical' view in his brief statement: 'The story [of Acts 5.1-11] derives from conceptions of corporate and magical power.'[28] In his early work on Acts, Howard Clark Kee also attributed the death of Ananias and Sapphira to the residue of magical technique:

> In the Book of Acts [...] there is evidence of the influence of magical technique, even though the basic outlook of the writer is religious, and most of the miracles fit the religious pattern. Magical features are apparent in some healing stories but especially in accounts of divine punitive action, which is a typical feature of magic. In the story of Ananias and Sapphira, for example [...] both are struck dead as a consequence of their disobedience (Acts 4:32–5:11).[29]

Carsten Colpe suggests that Peter's 'magically effective power' is the means of causing the couple's death.[30] He writes,

> Peter raises the magical break to full reality in that he utters it. Ananias falls down dead. Peter has spoken no judgement and has caused no punishment-miracle, nor has he excommunicated or performed the first case of church discipline.[31] Also, the death of the wife, coming later, is caused by no such thing, but by a repetition of magic. (My translation)[32]

Are these explanations of 'magical power' or its residue sufficient to connect Peter's words with the couple's death in the narrative? Does the force of his

---

28. Hans Conzelmann, *Acts of the Apostles* (trans. J Limburg, A. T. Kraabel and D. H. Juel; Hermeneia; Philadelphia: Fortress Press, 1987), 38.

29. Howard C. Kee, *Medicine, Miracle and Magic in New Testament Times* (Cambridge: Cambridge University Press, 1986), 118. Kee maintains a distinction between the magical versus the religious worldview, attributing the latter to the New Testament documents as a whole. In Kee's later work, he focuses on the discourse of the community ethos represented by the common fund, and the deaths as a punitive miracle. See his *Good News to the Ends of the Earth: The Theology of Acts* (London: SCM Press / Philadelphia: Trinity Press International, 1990), 86–7; and idem, *To Every Nation Under Heaven: The Acts of the Apostles* (Harrisburg, PA: Trinity Press International, 1997), 74–6, cf. 160–1, 230–1, 314–15 n. 46, 324 n. 66, 332 n. 61. See the criticisms of Kee's early work by Susan R. Garrett, *The Demise of the Devil: Magic and the Demonic in Luke's Writings* (Minneapolis: Fortress Press, 1989), 29–30.

30. Carsten Colpe, 'Die erste urchristliche Generation', in *Die Anfänge des Christentums. Alte Welt und neue Hoffnung* (ed. Jürgen Becker, et al.; Stuttgart: Verlag W. Kohlhammer; 1987), 71, 'magisch wirksamer Macht'.

31. Richter Reimer (*Women*, 19) curiously quotes this statement as support of her reading. However, Colpe's reference to magic in the immediate co-text does not sit well with Richter Reimer's thesis.

32. Colpe, 'urchristliche Generation', 70, 'Petrus erhebt den damit eingetretenen magischen Bruch zu voller Realität, indem er ihn ausspricht. Ananias fällt tot um, Petrus hat kein Urteil gesprochen und kein Strafwunder herbeigeführt, er hat nicht exkommuniziert und keinen ersten Fall von Kirchenzucht exekutiert. Auch der Tod der später hinzukommenden Gattin Sapphira wird durch nichts dergleichen, sondern durch eine Art Wiederholungszauber bewirkt'.

words reside in magical power? Is Peter performing a magical incantation or an imprecatory curse which directly causes the deaths of Ananias and Sapphira?

Assessing claims about magic is difficult because 'magic' is notoriously resistant to definition. Frederick Cryer captures the problem well:

> All historical attempts to define magic have failed seriously, as being either too reductive to cover a significant portion of acknowledged cases, or else being so inclusive as to leave virtually nothing out. The difficulty is that, even within one and the same society, there is no unequivocal understanding of existence such that all phenomena are assigned to a single category by native believers.[33]

The problems with assessing whether the function of 'magic' can be attributed to Peter's utterances are both linguistic and ideological.

Those who suggest that 'magic' is at work here view Peter's words as containers of formulaic power able to manipulate and shape the extra-linguistic world.[34] John Hull describes three defining characteristics of miracles caused by magic: (1) they have 'no cause but the will of the miracle worker', (2) the connection between cause and effect is based on 'a theory of sympathetic bonds or *mana* or something similar', and (3) the wonders are believed to result from the performance of rituals that are 'efficacious in themselves [...] brought about by human effort acting through a ritual'.[35] While such an absolutist statement of the coercive nature of magic may need to be qualified in many cases, it is helpful to contrast such magic with the prophetic performance of signs and wonders in Acts, which is undergirded by the Holy Spirit and requires the personal divine authorization in relation to God's Messiah.

There are two basic problems with identifying Peter's utterances to Ananias and Sapphira as 'magical'. The first is that Peter nowhere utters a formulaic imprecation, a necessary feature of 'magical' curse. There is no curse formula, indicating that there is a different discursive framing involved for this episode. Second, a 'magical' proposal would contradict Luke's criticism and subversion of magic elsewhere in Acts. Luke opposes magic in the encounter between Peter and Simon Magus (Acts 8.9-25), in Paul's encounter with Bar-Jesus (13.1-12), and when Paul is in Ephesus and is contrasted with the Sons of Sceva (19.11-20). Peter does not control or manipulate the power of the

---

33. Frederick H. Cryer, 'Magic in Ancient Syria – Palestine – and in the Old Testament', in *Witchcraft and Magic in Europe: Biblical and Pagan Societies* (eds Bengt Ankarloo and Stuart Clark; Philadelphia: University of Pennsylvania Press, 2001), 114.

34. See Andy M. Reimer, *Miracle and Magic: A Study in the Acts of the Apostles and the Life of Apollonius of Tyana* (JSNTSup 235; Sheffield: Sheffield Academic Press, 2002), 107–11; Garrett, *Demise*, 3, 4.

35. John M. Hull, *Hellenistic Magic and the Synoptic Tradition* (SBT, 2.28; London: SCM Press, 1974), 54. See his discussion on pp. 54–61. See also Fritz Graf, *Magic in the Ancient World* (trans. Franklin Philip; Cambridge, MA: Harvard University Press, 1997), 205–7, 296. Cf. Garrett, *Demise*, 26–9, 142 n. 20, for assessment and critique of Hull.

Holy Spirit.[36] It is consistent with the ideological perspective of Luke-Acts that deviant 'magic' should be distinguished from divinely enabled 'miracle working'.[37] Designations of 'magic' were often polemical accusations against an opponent.[38] Rather than being imbued with magical power, Peter's words are apostolic-prophetic speech-acts directly undergirded by divine power.

3.4. Peter's Language as 'Performative' Prophetic Utterance

The idea that Peter's words had a direct causal link with the couple's death is not a new proposal. In the context of discussing the divine hardening of Pharaoh's heart, Origen wrote of Peter slaying Ananias and Sapphira 'with the sword of his mouth'.[39] Clement of Alexandria, in a telling passage about the life of Moses, compares the tradition of the 'mystics' who say that Moses slew the Egyptians by only a word, 'as, certainly, Peter in the Acts is related to have slain by speech those who appropriated part of the price of the field, and lied'.[40]

More recently Anthony Robinson and Robert Wall have declared, 'Peter's rebuke carries the weight of a death sentence (5:5) [...] The reader must presume that this is not an accidental or coincidental death: Peter's words

---

36. See Graf, *Magic*, 222–9, 299–301; Anitra Bingham Kolenkow, 'Persons of Power and their Communities', in *Magic and Divination in the Ancient World* (eds Leda Ciraolo and Jonathan Seidel; Leiden: Brill, 2002), 133–44.

37. With Garrett, *Demise*, 11–36, 37–46, 59, 60, 63, 66, 75, 77, 86, 94–5, 98–9, 101–9; Hans-Josef Klauck, *Magic and Paganism in Early Christianity: The World of the Acts of the Apostles* (trans. Brian McNeil; Minneapolis: Fortress Press, 2000), 120; Daniel Marguerat, 'Magic and Miracle in the Acts of the Apostles', in *Magic in the Biblical World: From the Rod of Aaron to the Ring of Solomon* (ed. Todd Klutz; JSNTSup 245; London: T&T Clark, 2003), 100–24 ('[T]he title of *magos* comprises all the necessary ingredients to become a classic weapon in religious polemic [...] all authors of antiquity, without exception (Greek authors, Latin authors, biblical authors, and Church Fathers), are not past using this sulphurous stamp' [116]); Stanley Porter, 'Magic in the Book of Acts', in *A Kind of Magic: Understanding Magic in the New Testament and its Religious Environment* (eds Michale Labahn and Bert Jan Lietaert Peerbilte; London: T&T Clark, 2007), 110–11, 114–21 [107–21]; Reimer, *Miracle*, 44–6, 89–95; Andy M. Reimer, 'Virtual Prison Breaks: Non-Escape Narratives and the Definition of "Magic"', in *Biblical World* (ed. Klutz), 125–39. Cf. Fritz Graf, 'Excluding the Charming: The Development of the Greek Concept of Magic', in *Ancient Magic and Ritual Power* (eds Marvin Meyer and Paul Mirecki; Leiden: Brill, 2001), 35 [29–42]; Naomi Janowitz, *Magic in the Roman World: Pagans, Jews and Christians* (London: Routledge, 2001), 9–26.

38. See Matthew W. Dickie, *Magic and Magicians in the Greco-Roman World* (London: Routledge, 2003), 49–60, 130–6, 142–61, *passim*; Garrett, *Demise*, 2–5; Janowitz, *Magic*, 13–26; Reimer, *Miracle*, 212–25.

39. Origen, *Philoc.*, 27.8. in *The Philocalia of Origen. A Compilation of Selected Passages from Origen's Works Made by St. Gregory Nazianzus and St. Basil of Caesarea* (trans. G. Lewis; Edinburgh: T&T Clark, 1911), 232.

40. Clement of Alexandria, *Stromata*, 1:23 (ANF 2:336). See also Tertullian, *On Modesty* 21 (ANF 4:99).

are a death sentence, and Ananias's death excommunicates him from the community of goods.'[41] I agree with Robinson and Wall. Furthermore, it will be seen that Ananias' death is tantamount to excommunication.[42] Later, I argue that Peter's words are tantamount to a death sentence with support from Speech-Act Theory.

Speech-Act Theory was introduced into biblical studies by Anthony Thiselton as a response to a scholarly tradition in the discipline which suggested that words were construed as containers of power in ancient Israel.[43] Gerhard von Rad is representative of this tradition:

> At the early mythical level of thought, man's [sic] apperception of the world about him is of it as a unified entity. He makes no distinction between spiritual and material [...] and in consequence he is also unable properly to differentiate between word and object, idea and actuality. Such thought is thus characterized by an inherent absence of differentiation between the ideal and the real, or between word and object.[...] In a way which defies precise rational clarification, every word contains something of the object itself. Thus, in a very realistic sense, what happens in language is that the world is given material expression.[44]

Later, von Rad writes,

> Israel, too, was thus aware that her language possessed possibilities other than those demanded by everyday personal conversation.[...Some words] should simply be brought on the scene as an objective reality endowed with mysterious power. This was, of course, only one possibility among others.[...] Both in her most ordinary and in her sublimest statements, in magic, and in the deepest insights of her theology or prophecy alike, Israel took as her starting point her conviction that the word possessed creative power.[45]

Otto Procksch in his *TDNT* article on λέγω argued for a 'dynamic' conception of language among the ancient Hebrews, where words are imbued with power and work automatically, in contrast to modern speakers who exhibit a 'dianoetic' conception of language where words simply refer to things and convey information.[46] Thiselton responded to this apparent consensus in

---

41. Anthony B. Robinson and Robert W. Wall, *Called to Be Church: The Book of Acts for a New Day* (Grand Rapids: Eerdmans, 2006), 77, 78.

42. See §§4.2.2.2., 5.1.4. and 5.2.1.4. below.

43. Anthony C. Thiselton, 'The Supposed Power of Words in the Biblical Writings', *JTS* 25 (1974): 283–99.

44. Gerhard von Rad, 'The Prophets' Conception of the Word of God', in *The Message of the Prophets* (trans. D. M. G. Stalker; London: SCM Press Ltd, 1968), 60–76, here 61. See his *Old Testament Theology* (2 vols; trans. D. M. G. Stalker; Edinburgh: T&T Clark, 1962, 1965); 2:80–98.

45. Von Rad, 'The Prophets", 65. Closer to the position I am advocating is R. B. Y. Scott (*The Relevance of the Prophets* [New York: The Macmillan Company, 1947], 91–3), although he has more confidence in the 'prophet's inner-psychology' than I attribute.

46. O. Procksh, 'λέγω', *TDNT*, 4:91–100. The position is criticized by James Barr, 'Hypostatization of Linguistic Phenomena in Modern Theological Interpretation', *JSS* 7 (1962): 88–94 [85–94].

Old Testament studies with a challenge from the philosophy of language, specifically from J. L. Austin's writings on 'performative utterances'.[47] In essence, Thiselton argued that what was at stake was not incompatible worldviews (such as dynamic vs. dianoetic), but rather different philosophies of language. He suggested that the power of language derived from culturally appropriate authorities (such as God, kings, or prophets authorized by God) and efficacious procedures (like blessings and curses) undergirded by accepted cultural conventions and institutions. Thus, 'dynamic' and 'dianoetic' 'are not basic alternative accounts of language as a whole, but merely two of many possible ways of accounting for different uses of words'.[48] Thiselton takes blessing and cursing as special cases of the power of performatives which draw their efficacy from social conventions of language use. 'They are effective, in most cases, only when performed by the appropriate person in the appropriate situation.'[49] In countering the widespread idea that blessings and curses have virtually a life of their own, Thiselton explains that a blessing was unable to be retracted, not because the words once spoken were now self-potent, but rather because a 'convention for withdrawing the performative utterance did not exist'.[50]

The ancients, just like people today, had many uses for language, including its performative function. This is plainly visible in Israelite history through prophetic speech, specifically in the oracles that brought the people under judgement in the very act of uttering the accusations and indictments.[51] The power of the prophetic word in the Scriptures of Israel sets a powerful precedent for capturing the imagination of Luke's (model) readers.

With this background it is plausible that the deaths of Ananias and Sapphira are the result of the prophetic indictment by the apostle-prophet Peter. This study is not concerned to discover what Peter *said* as much as to determine what he *did*. Peter's words are performative verdicts that entail and effect divine judgement. Peter indicted the couple for their treachery and condemned them to divine execution. Haenchen claims too much with regard to Peter's motivation when he states that Peter '*wants* to kill – and succeeds'.[52] Luke's material for Peter's character does not display his explicit intentions. What we are given is Peter's action as one speaking on behalf of Israel's exalted Messiah, and sanctioned by the Holy Spirit. It is in fact a divine execution carried out through Peter as representative of the apostles and as one deputized to rule the messianic community.

---

47. Thiselton, 'Supposed Power'. He refers to the works of J. L. Austin, *How to do Things with Words* (2nd edn; eds J. O. Urmson and Marina Sbisa; Oxford: Oxford University Press, 1965), and idem, 'Performative Utterances', in *Philosophical Papers* (3rd edn; eds J. O. Urmson and G. J. Warnock; Oxford: Oxford University Press, 1979), 220–52.
48. Thiselton, 'Supposed Power', 297.
49. Thiselton, 'Supposed Power', 294.
50. Thiselton, 'Supposed Power', 294.
51. See Walter Houston, 'What Did the Prophets Think They Were Doing? Speech Acts and Prophetic Discourse in the Old Testament', *BibInt* 1 (1993): 167–88.
52. Haenchen, *Acts*, 239, emphasis added.

In order to draw this conclusion, it is necessary to demonstrate the presence of three elements in the Lukan narrative. First, there must be accepted conventions for the efficacy of prophetic speech, and specifically the indictment that leads to divine judgement. Second, there must be appropriate authority for the protagonist. Third, there must be evidence of a properly executed procedure, including the corresponding entailments of the social convention. These three elements are derived from Austin's necessary conditions for the successful execution of a speech-act in his famous 1955 William James lectures at Harvard, *How to Do Things with Words* (*HtDTwW* hereafter).[53]

Austin, an 'ordinary language philosopher', embarked on the task of overcoming the positivistic philosophy of language which posited a theory that all meaningful language could be evaluated on the basis of whether it was 'true' or 'false'. In effect, the test is how well the language corresponded to its extra-linguistic referent. *HtDTwW* was Austin's initial attempt to come to grips with the fact that humans sometimes perform deeds in the act of uttering words. Sandy Petrey, who has offered a comprehensive proposal for applying Speech-Act Theory to literary discourse, explains the significance of Austin's theory as follows:

> [S]peech-act theory challenges a foundational principle of other linguistic schools. It shifts attention from what language *is* to what it *does* and sees a *social process* where other linguistic philosophies see a *formal structure*. From a speech-act perspective, all linguistic artifacts, including those that count as literary, must be understood in relation to the sociohistorical context of their production and reception.[...] Speech-act theory addresses rather language's productive force, which depends entirely on where and when it's used. Other linguistic schools address the structure of language in itself; speech-act theory examines the power of language in communities.[54]

Speech-Act Theory is positioned to answer what a person accomplishes with an utterance, and specifically what Peter accomplished through his utterances.

---

53. Austin, *HtDTwW*, 14–15, and the elaboration on 26–38. See idem, 'Performative Utterances', 237–39.

Jonathan Potter ('Wittgenstein and Austin', in *Discourse Theory and Practice: A Reader* [eds M. Wetherell, S. Taylor and S. J. Yates; London: Sage Publications, 2001], 44) states Austin's conditions as such:

(A.i) There must exist an accepted conventional procedure having a certain conventional effect, and further,

(A.ii) the particular persons and circumstances in a given case must be appropriate for the invocation of the particular procedure.

(B) The procedure must be executed by all participants both (i) correctly and (ii) completely.

(C) Often (i) the persons must have certain thoughts, intentions, etc. which are specified in the procedure, (ii) the procedure specifies certain conduct which must be adhered to.

In my use of Austin, I organize the conditions in the following manner: (1) accepted conventions (A.i), (2) appropriate authority (A.ii), and (3) proper execution of procedure, with entailments (B.i.ii and C.i.ii).

In order to demonstrate that Peter's words carry the force of a prophetic indictment that causes two deaths, it will be necessary to do three things. First, this study must describe the conventions that are reflected in Luke-Acts that confirm the divine sanction for oracles that would bring someone under divine judgement. Second, it must show that Peter is authorized to speak on behalf of God with the authority of God's own word. Finally, it must demonstrate that the convention was properly executed – that is, that all the necessary conditions of the prophetic speech were fulfilled.

Therefore, the argument ensues in three successive stages. First, I explore the conventions forming the contextual background to apostolic-prophetic speech in the community-of-goods discourse in Acts 4.32–5.11. This includes both the socio-cultural context of the practice of shared goods and its associated disciplinary actions as well as an exploration of plausible precedents in Luke-Acts and its literary stockpile of efficacious prophetic speech enacting blessing and judgement. This includes a discussion of the roles of the Holy Spirit and of Jesus as Prophet-King announcing salvation and judgement to Israel in the eschatological epoch of Luke's narrative. Second, I elucidate the role and function of the apostolic-prophetic figure in this eschatological framework as he is envisioned in the narrative world of Luke-Acts. In short, Jesus is the Prophet-King like Moses and David; Peter is an apostle-prophet like Jesus. Third, I explore the death of the couple as the execution of divine judgement alongside the tragic demise of the betrayer Judas. Ananias and Sapphira embody the destiny of those who threaten the sanctity of the eschatological, Spirit-filled community of the Messiah and counterfeit its sacred ethos.

All exegetes work with a philosophy of language, explicit or implicit, that fundamentally influences the interpretive decisions they are able to make.[55] Speech-Act Theory is appropriate because it provides a grid to analyse the dynamics of performative utterances and illuminate the performance of the prophetic oracle of judgement in Luke-Acts. The theory is presented more completely below to build the linguistic apparatus for the task ahead.

3.5. Speech-Act Theory as a Socio-Pragmatic Tool for 'Thick' Description

Austin's Speech-Act Theory is a descriptive analytical tool engaging the uses of language in various contexts. It is not an imposition of twentieth

---

54. Sandy Petrey, *Speech Acts and Literary Theory* (New York: Routledge, 1990), 3, his emphasis. See also the exchange between David Gorman ('The Use and Abuse of Speech-Act Theory in Criticism', *PT* 20 [1999]: 93–119) and Sandy Petrey ('Whose Acts? Which Communities? A Reply to David Gorman', *PT* 21 [2000]: 423–33).

55. This point is articulated well by Craig Bartholomew, 'Introduction', in *After Pentecost* (eds C. Bartholomew, C. Greene and K. Möller; SHS 2; Grand Rapids: Zondervan, 2001), xxi–xxxvi.

century philosophy onto the text, but rather a tool for 'thick description'[56] of what is already there. Speech-Act Theory requires that language utterances be understood in their contexts of use, which includes social conventions and expectations. Austin's vision redirected the attention of linguists from the structure of language to its role as a social process within a living community.

Austin dissected a 'speech-act' into three constitutive dimensions: (1) the *utterance* itself ('locutionary act'), (2) the *force* of the utterance ('illocutionary act') and (3) the (intended) *effect* of the utterance ('perlocutionary act'). Austin was insistent that the entire speech-act is the minimal unit for consideration.[57] This has a significant consequence for examining a speech-act in literary discourse, particularly narrative. The narrative boundaries will define the scope of the context for analysing the speech-act. In other words, a speech-act deployed in a narrative will display all its necessary elements, and the narrative drama will reveal whether the speech-act was successful.

It was Austin's student and primary successor in Speech-Act Theory, John R. Searle, who singled out the force of the utterance for evaluation, and thus made analysis of 'speech-acts' into a theory to explain language in general.[58] This way, Peter's statements and questions, the utterances themselves, could have the *force* of informing, predicting, or indicting and condemning. I argue that Peter's statement, 'You have not lied to humans, but to God!' (Acts 5.4d) is in fact an indictment, and not merely an informative assertion. God

---

56. I borrow the term 'thick description' from Clifford Geertz's ('Thick Description: Toward an Interpretive Theory of Culture', in *The Interpretation of Cultures* [New York: Basic Books, 1973], 5–6, 9–10) theory of ethnography, who in turn borrows it from Gilbert Ryle, an 'ordinary language philosopher' of Oxford.

57. Austin, *HtDTwW*, 52, 148. See John Searle, *Speech Acts: An Essay in the Philosophy of Language* (Cambridge: Cambridge University Press, 1969), 16.

The illocutionary act is the crucial aspect that Speech-Act Theory offers, although it has proven difficult to define. Austin, *HtDTwW*, 99–100, defines the illocutionary act as the 'performance of an act *in* saying something as opposed to performance of an act *of* saying something [a locutionary act]'. Further, if the illocutionary act is performing an act *in* saying something, a perlocutionary act is performing an act *by* saying something (see *HtDTwW*, 108, 122, 127–31). Searle nowhere offers a straight definition for the illocutionary act. It is roughly equated with the metaphor of *force*.

The theorists become slippery when referring to perlocutionary effect. A helpful distinction should be made between the *intended* effect and the *actual* effect, where the perlocutionary act corresponds to the former. For example, John Lyons (*Semantics* [2 vols; Cambridge: Cambridge University press, 1977], 2:731) makes this distinction as a helpful rule, but is incorrect to suggest Austin and Searle make the same distinction. Austin seemed to conflate the two, *HtDTwW*, 101–8. Searle recognizes the distinction, but applies both intended and actual effects to perlocutionary acts. Cf. Searle, *Speech Acts*, 25.

Vincent Brümmer, (*Theology and Philosophical Inquiry: An Introduction* [London: MacMillan Press Ltd, 1981], 11–12, 110) labels the effective aspect as per-illocutions to limit the analysis to the intentions of the speaker. 'A speech act fails in its *per-illocutionary* aspect if the speaker does not succeed in bringing about the intended response in the hearer' (12).

sanctioned Peter's indictment with an execution. Likewise, Peter's denunciation of Sapphira, 'How is it that you have conspired to test the Spirit of the Lord? Behold, the feet of those who have buried your husband are at the door, and they shall carry you out (as well)!' (5.9), is not merely a prediction of what was to come, but rather a judicial verdict, a condemnation, that brought her under the divine death sentence. That is the force, or the social action, of the utterance of Peter's words. The actual effect, of course, is the death of the couple. The prophetic speech-act of judgement was successful.

The history of development in Speech-Act Theory has been adequately covered in several places, including many works applying the theory to biblical studies.[59] Some further basic concepts which have been developed in speech-act analysis are necessary to aid in examining various dimensions of a speech-act. This will allow us to address the most important features of the Ananias and Sapphira pericope that have hitherto been neglected.

3.5.1. Necessary Elements of Speech-Act Theory

First, I will pay closer attention to the particular element of contribution from Speech-Act Theory, the elucidation of the force, or the social action, performed by the utterance of a speech-act and various crucial dimensions of the illocutionary act. Next, I adapt the theory for literary discourse with

---

58. Searle invokes Ferdinand de Saussure's categories of *langue* and *parole*, and sets Speech-Act Theory squarely in the *langue* category. See *Speech Acts*, 17. In this way, Searle makes speech-acts parallel to Wittgenstein's theory of 'language games'. See Ludwig Wittgenstein, *Philosophical Investigations* (3rd edn; trans. G. E. M. Anscombe; Oxford: Blackwell Publishing, 2001), §§23–24, 179–80, 288. Searle (*Expression and Meaning: Studies in the Theory of Speech Acts* [Cambridge: Cambridge University Press, 1979], vii–viii) recognizes the connection, but believes he can narrow down human use of language to five basic categories (see below on Searle's taxonomy). See the summary of Searle's collective work on Speech-Act Theory in his *Mind, Language and Society: Philosophy in the Real World* (New York: Basic Books, 1998), 135–61.

59. See esp. Richard Briggs, *Words in Action: Speech Act Theory and Biblical Interpretation* (Edinburgh: T&T Clark, 2001), 3–18, 31–143; idem, 'The Uses of Speech-Act Theory in Biblical Interpretation', *CurBS* 9 (2001): 229–76. See also Hugh C. White, 'Introduction: Speech Act Theory and Literary Criticism', *Semeia* 41 (1988): 1–24; J. Eugene Botha, *Jesus and the Samaritan Woman: A Speech Act Reading of John 4:1–42* (NovTSup 65; Leiden: Brill, 1991), 62–81; idem, 'The Potential of Speech Act Theory for New Testament Exegesis: Some Basic Concepts', *HvTSt* 47 (1991): 277–93; Anthony C. Thiselton, *New Horizons in Hermeneutics: The Theory and Practice of Transforming Biblical Reading* (Grand Rapids: Zondervan Publishing House, 1992), esp. 272–312, 361–7; Derek Tovey, *Narrative Art and Act in the Fourth Gospel* (JSNTSup 151; Sheffield: Sheffield Academic Press, 1997), 70–84; Kevin J. Vanhoozer, *Is There a Meaning in This Text? The Bible, the Reader, and the Morality of Literary Knowledge* (Grand Rapids: Zondervan, 1998), 207–14; Jim W. Adams, *The Performative Nature and Function of Isaiah 40–55* (London: T&T Clark, 2006), 18–63; Bridget Gilfillan Upton, *Hearing Mark's Endings: Listening to Ancient Popular Texts through Speech Act Theory* (BIS 79; Leiden: Brill, 2006), 88–102.

regard to accepted conventions, and the implied collective acceptance of these conventions by a particular community. Finally, I briefly explore the case of deputized agency, offering explanation of how someone can speak on behalf of another, as I suggest Peter does for God.

3.5.1.1. Focusing on the Illocutionary Act

Searle, recognizing the potential in Austin's emphasis on language-as-action, isolated the illocutionary act for evaluation.[60] Petrey explains the social nature of illocutionary actions:

> The same words with the same meaning – the same locutions – have different conventional powers, and one of the most important principles of speech-act theory is that such difference of powers is at least as important in analyzing language as lexical and semantic identity.[...] Locutionary *form* is complete and whole *within* the linguistic utterance; illocutionary *force* is a combination of language and social practice.[61]

It is possible that Peter's locutions ('You have not lied to humans, but to God', 'The feet of those who have buried your husband...shall bury you') could be informative or predictive. However, I argue that the action that Peter achieves, the force, is rather performative prophetic indictment and condemnation. Thus, the effect intended by Peter as a character in this episode was not to get Ananias and Sapphira to believe a certain proposition ('You lied to God'; 'You will soon be [dead and] buried'), but to accuse them formally, placing them under divine judgement.

Searle cautions against two common pitfalls made regarding the illocutionary act. First, there is the confusion between the illocutionary act and the perlocutionary act. He notes that an illocutionary act is successful if it is understood by the audience,[62] even if the actual corresponding perlocutionary act does not take effect. The proper illocutionary effect, in Searle's *Speech Acts*, is understanding. This is important for the current study because, in the words of Walter Houston,

> as long as the prophets' hearers understood that they were warning them, calling for repentance or whatever the particular speech act might be, and understood the content of the warning or whatever it might be, then the prophets had *done* what they set out to do, even if they had not achieved the effect they hoped for.[63]

Second, Searle notes that the single most common mistake in Speech-Act Theory is confusion between features of illocutionary verbs and illocutionary

---

60. Searle, *Speech Acts*, 54–71.
61. Petrey, *Speech Acts*, 12, 13, emphasis his.
62. Searle (*Speech Acts*, 47) calls this the Illocutionary Effect, that is, understanding.
63. Houston, 'What Did', 177. This will have to be modified slightly in light of the definition of 'declarations' below.

acts.⁶⁴ We should not confuse form with function. Peter does not explicitly state, 'I hereby condemn you', and yet God sanctions his indictment of Ananias with an execution.

Searle distinguishes five major types of speech-acts.⁶⁵ The most interesting of these is what he calls a 'declaration', corresponding closest to the original investigation of Austin into 'performatives', which occurs when 'the state of affairs represented in the proposition expressed is realized or brought into existence by the illocutionary force, cases where one brings a state of affairs into existence by declaring it to exist, cases where, so to speak, "saying makes it so"'.⁶⁶ Declarative speech is the act that merges fruitfully the illocutionary force with the perlocutionary effect, keeping them distinct, but inseparable. Searle also proffers various dimensions of illocutionary acts, demonstrating the complexity of interpersonal communication.

3.5.1.2. Dimensions of Illocutionary Acts

Searle advanced Speech-Act Theory further with his recognition of numerous dimensions of variation in which illocutionary acts differ from one another.⁶⁷ Two of these factor into the most important distinctions for the current study and serve as a basis for constructing Searle's classification. These are (1) the illocutionary point or purpose in uttering a statement and (2) the direction of fit.⁶⁸ The point or purpose of the illocutionary act is the essential condition, the identifying marker of the act.⁶⁹ Thus, a command is normally an attempt to get the hearer to do something. The purpose of a description is to represent how something is in the world. The basic point of a promise is to undertake an obligation by a speaker to do something.

The direction of fit, which is always a consequence of the illocutionary point, is concerned with the relationship between an utterance and reality.⁷⁰ The way in which propositional content is related to the world of utterance

---

64. Searle, *Speech Acts*, 70–1; idem, *Expression*, 2, 27–8, demonstrates by showing that some illocutionary verbs mark various features of the illocutionary act, such as the degree of intensity ('suggest' vs 'insist'), or style and manner of performance (e.g., 'bellow', 'hint', 'confide').

65. For Searle's full taxonomy, see his *Expression*, 12–20. Briggs (*Words*, 51) presents a helpful conceptual chart. For Austin's taxonomy, see *HtDTwW*, 148–64.

66. Searle, *Expression*, 16. Thus, Michael Hancher ('Performative Utterance, The Word of God, and the Death of the Author', *Semeia* 41 [1988]: 28 [27–40]) makes the astute observation that divine fiats (like 'Let there be light') cannot be directives (attempts by a speaker to get the hearer to do something, and are vulnerable to failure), but are declarations with the illocutionary effectiveness of altering the extra-linguistic affairs.

67. In *Expression*, 2–8, Searle lists twelve.

68. Searle, *Expression*, 12.

69. For a description of the conditions of the speech-act according to Searle, see *Speech Acts*, 57–71.

70. Searle, *Expression*, 3–4, 12–20; John R. Searle and Daniel Vanderveken, *Foundations of Illocutionary Logic* (Cambridge: Cambridge University Press, 1985), 52–4, 92–6.

is its direction of fit. Essentially, it is the distinction between whether a statement conforms to pre-existing reality (word-to-world), and whether it attempts to bring about a change in reality (world-to-word). Thiselton writes, 'In summary, linguistic *description* reflects or portrays prior states of affairs in word-*to-world* language; whereas world-*to-word* language in priciple [*sic*] can bring about *change to the world to match the uttered word*, of which *promise* is the clearest paradigm.'[71] As declarations, the prophetic indictments in Luke-Acts often carry the weight of both a world-to-word and word-to-world fit. Sandy Petrey writes, 'With the performative [...] the referent is *within* the words and the conventional procedures they enact [...A] successful performative [utterance] is *necessarily* in harmony with a non-verbal [truth] condition.'[72] The Spirit as God's guarantor of the divine βουλή brings to fulfilment the promises and warnings of the prophetic speech. The prophets' accusations and announcements of punishment were themselves the acts that placed Israel under judgement. Peter's words themselves placed Ananias and Sapphira under divine judgement.

3.5.1.3. Accepted Conventions and the Fictive Context of Narrative

Briefly put, the three broad elements necessary for a successful speech-act are as follows: (1) accepted conventions (2) appropriate authority and (3) a properly executed procedure.[73] Petrey points out that the first element is the most fundamental, and the other elements are logical consequences of the requirement for an accepted conventional procedure with conventional effect. He writes,

> [A] convention exists by virtue of trans-individual ratification. Part of what's accepted in any convention is that more than one person is doing the acceptance. Words do things in a social setting.[...T]he things words do are directly endured as well as indirectly ratified by the members of a speech-act community.[...F]rom one end of the performative spectrum to the other, words derive their power to produce what they say from the conventional procedures accepted by a definite collectivity.[74]

Petrey's reading of Austin brings to the fore two crucial aspects necessary to interpret a speech-act: the accepted convention and the community that accepts the convention. 'Social interaction [...] determines just what it is that words do as well as making it possible for them to do anything at all.[...] In order to know to which convention the illocutionary act is conforming, you must know in which community it's being performed.'[75]

This observation creates two corresponding challenges when applying Speech-Act Theory to literary discourse. First, there is the task of identifying

---

71. Thiselton, *New Horizons*, 296, emphasis his.
72. Petrey, *Speech Acts*, 11.
73. Austin, *HtDTwW*, 14–15, 26–38.
74. Petrey, *Speech Acts*, 6, 8.
75. Petrey, *Speech Acts*, 15.

an actual context of use in 'ordinary' linguistic circumstances. Austin sought to exclude certain types of poetic utterances from consideration:

> a performative utterance will, for example, be *in a peculiar way* hollow or void if said by an actor on the stage, or if introduced in a poem, or spoken in soliloquy. This applies in a similar manner to any and every utterance.[...] Language in such circumstances is in special ways – intelligibly – used not seriously, but in ways *parasitic* upon its normal use...[76]

Searle endorses the designation 'parasitic' in applying speech-act analysis to forms of discourse such as fiction and play acting.[77] Austin qualifies his own study to cover only those utterances that take place in 'ordinary circumstances'.[78] However, this could subject all narrative discourse (διήγησις) to the accusation of 'parasitism' because of the fictive elements inherent in all selective emplotment, whether fiction or non-fiction.[79] Mary Louise Pratt observes,

> What is needed is a theory of linguistic representation which acknowledges that representative discourse is always engaged in both fitting words to world and fitting world to words; that language and linguistic institutions in part construct or constitute the world for people in speech communities, rather than merely depicting it. Representative discourses, fictional or nonfictional, must be treated as simultaneously world-creating, world-describing, and world-changing undertakings.[80]

Petrey sums up the problem of literary discourse succinctly with reference to the speech-act of making a bet: 'Like all performative language, that used to make a bet, derives the whole of its force from collective acceptance.

76. Austin, *HtDTwW*, 22, his emphasis; see 104, 122.
77. Searle, *Speech Acts*, 78–9; and see his 'The Logical Status of Fictional Discourse', in *Expression*, 58–75, where he deems fictional discourse as 'pretending' and opposed to 'serious' discourse. See the criticisms in Thomas G. Pavel, 'Ontological Issues in Poetics: Speech Acts and Fictional Worlds', *JAAC* 40 (1981): 167–78.
78. Austin, *HtDTwW*, 22.
79. The topic of 'fictiveness' is raised in Wolfgang Iser, *The Act of Reading: A Theory of Aesthetic Response* (Baltimore: Johns Hopkins University Press, 1978), 180–231; idem, *The Fictive and the Imaginary: Charting Literary Anthropology* (Baltimore: Johns Hopkins University Press, 1993). See also Paul Ricœur, *Time and Narrative* (vol. 3; trans. Kathleen Blamey and David Pellauer; Chicago: University of Chicago Press, 1998), 127–92; Hayden White, *The Content of the Form: Narrative Discourse and Historical Representation* (Baltimore: Johns Hopkins University Press, 1987), 1–57; idem, *Tropics of Discourse: Essays in Cultural Criticism* (Baltimore: Johns Hopkins University Press, 1978), 81–134; idem, 'The Narrativization of Real Events', *CI* 7 (1981): 793–8.
80. Mary Louise Pratt, 'Ideology and Speech-Act Theory', *PT* 7 (1986): 71. Jonathan Culler ('Problems in the Theory of Fiction', *Diacritics* 14 [1984], 10–11) is correct to note that all speech-acts are mimetic in the sense that they are instantiations of established conventions: 'To perform a speech act is to imitate a model, to take on a role of someone performing this particular speech act. The self-consciousness with which introducers perform their introductions, or with which a chairperson says "I hereby call this meeting to order," testifies to the fact that to perform a speech act is to adopt a persona. The more formal the act, the more vivid our sense of this fundamental truth.'

The collectivity can be as small as two people, but performative speech can never be the unilateral act of a single individual.'[81] This statement assumes, along with the analyses of Austin and Searle, the situational context of a spoken utterance in conversation. Yet, how does literary discourse fare in this privileging of spoken utterance? How can one apply Speech-Act Theory to literary discourse, which is in one sense, a 'monologue' where the author or narrator controls the selectivity of discourse? Is it enough to posit a(n implied) community of readers?

This leads to the second task of applying Speech-Act Theory to literary discourse. Luke's 'community' of readers can only be a composite reconstruction. In the best case scenario we simply derive a general reading competency from Luke's text itself, and thus posit a 'model' or 'implied' reader. In the worst case, Luke's text is mirror-read and themes or events in the text are projected onto a hypothetical reconstruction of a 'community', and then this product of the scholar's imagination dictates the possibilities of how the text can mean.[82]

It is at this point – the intersection of Speech-Act Theory's pragmatic concern for context and literary discourse's narrative boundaries – where the theory and the text are mutually enhancing. Speech-Act Theory provides a linguistic apparatus to describe the social and theological dynamics of performative utterances. The text of Luke-Acts provides narrative boundaries for real conversations, which include all of the dimensions of Austin's speech-acts: locutionary, illocutionary and perlocutionary acts. Furthermore, literary theory provides a parallel for the social conventions necessary to examine a particular speech-act – what Iser calls 'literary repertoire'.[83]

> The repertoire consists of all the familiar territory within the text. This may be in the form of references to earlier works, or to social and historical norms, or to the whole culture from which the text has emerged.[...] Thus the repertoire incorporates both the origin and the transformation of its elements, and the individuality of the text will largely depend on the extent to which their identity is changed.[84]

---

81. Petrey, *Speech Acts*, 5.

82. For an example of the latter method, see the statements by Robert J. Karris, 'The Lukan *Sitz im Leben*: Methodology and Prospects', in *SBLSP 1976* (ed. George MacRae; Missoula, MT: Scholars Press, 1976), 219: '[F]or purposes, themes, or tendencies to have complete validity it must be demonstrated that they arise from a concrete situation within Luke's community. Otherwise, it is too easy for them to lose their grounding in reality and to float freely on some high level of abstraction where they can generate other ideas and combine them to form clusters of ideas. These clusters of ideas may have captivating intrinsic beauty, but say little about the reality which they are supposedly designed to explain.' On this topic, see the oft-cited study of Luke Timothy Johnson, 'On Finding the Lukan Community: A Cautious Cautionary Essay', in *SBLSP 1979* (2 vols; ed. Paul J. Achtemeier; Missoula, MT: Scholars Press, 1979), 1:87–100.

83. Iser, *Act*, 53–85.

84. Iser, *Act*, 69. See also the statement on p. 85: '[T]he repertoire organizes his [the reader's] reactions to the text and the problems it contains.[... T]he repertoire forms an organizational structure of meaning which must be optimized through the reading of the text.'

Iser's category of 'repertoire' includes both socio-cultural norms (e.g., community-of-goods discourse) and the literary precedents (e.g., prophetic personae in the Scriptures of Israel), that shape and guide the manner in which the discourse is received by the audience. Iser explains,

> The repertoire of a literary text does not consist solely of social and cultural norms; it also incorporates elements and, indeed, whole traditions of past literature that are mixed together with these norms.[...] The literary repertoire can thus be seen to have a two-fold function: [1] it reshapes familiar schemata to form a background for the process of communication, and [2] it provides a general framework within which the message or meaning of the text can be organized.[85]

There are conventions that frame the reception of Peter's words to the offending couple inscribed within Luke's text, the 'internal repertoire'. The conventions are not disassociated from the discourse, but rather are inscribed in it and they frame its reception. There is also an 'external repertoire' that shapes the reception of the text. The competency of the model reader partly resides in her ability to align her understanding and conception of what is socially acceptable with the perspective of the author or narrator.[86] The community-of-goods discourse would have evoked certain expectations regarding social esteem of the community and its disciplinary practices. The 'accepted conventions' of the efficacy of prophetic speech are part of the shared schemes of Luke and his audience from the many examples found in the Scriptures of Israel. The Scriptures of Israel are a powerful force in governing the 'external repertoire' of the linguistic community.[87] When the narrative drama arrives at Peter's confrontation, already the scene has been set by this literary pretext and the preceding drama of Jesus, from the announcement of the birth of his predecessor (John), to his ascension-exaltation, through to the continuing conflict between the nascent Jerusalem community and the established Jerusalem elite. All of these events, characters and relationships serve as the conventional repertoire for the speech-act. In this sense, Peter's words are more concretely situated than many of the hypothetical utterances

---

85. Iser, *Act*, 79, 81.

86. Lanser (*The Narrative Act: Point of View in Prose Fiction* [Princeton: Princeton University Press, 1981], 16) provides a sophisticated discussion of 'point of view', indicating that this term refers to both the technique of structuring perspective in a text and the ideology that shapes and is projected from a text. The narrative point of view, arising from the 'textual voice', is both the standpoint of observation and the manner of evaluation. More fully, 'point of view subsumes those aspects of narrative structure that concern [1] the mode of presenting and representing speech, perception, and event; [2] the identities of those who speak and perceive; [3] their relationships with one another and with the recipients of their discourses; [4] their attitudes, statuses, personalities, and beliefs' (13–14). '[P]oint of view shapes, even controls, textual meaning and reader response' (18). For Lanser, point of view in a narrative arises out of a dynamic relationship between an author, the speech-act and its reception by an audience.

87. See Steven Davis, 'Anti-Individualism and Speech Act Theory', in *Foundations of Speech Act Theory: Philosophical And Linguistic Perspectives* (ed. Savas L. Tsohatzidis; London: Routledge, 1994), 208–19.

examined by Austin and Searle. The repertoire is both given and needing to be realized. Chapters 4 and 5 examine the expectations associated with the community of shared goods discourse. Chapters 7 and 8 will be concerned to identify the primary elements of the repertoire as it relates to the efficacy of prophetic speech and the authorization of prophetic successors. The only theoretical piece remaining to be covered here is the mechanism of deputized agency.

3.5.1.4. Deputized Agency and Superintendence
Nicholas Wolterstorff offers a helpful elucidation of the possibility of what he calls 'double agency discourse' that helps to fill out the implications for Speech-Act Theory's application to the narrative of Acts.[88] The aspect of Wolterstorff's proposal which is useful for the current study is his cogent argument that one person can be deputized to speak (or write) on behalf of another person. There are cases 'in which one person says something with words which he himself hasn't uttered or inscribed'.[89] In this case there is often interplay between what he calls superintendence and authorization. Superintendence is a direct involvement of the primary discourser (e.g., God) for what is said by the speaker (e.g., prophet). Part of the superintendence in Luke-Acts is indicated by the phrase 'being filled with the Spirit'.[90] Authorization is when

> the discourser *authorizes* the text [or speech] – that is, does one thing or another to the text such that her doing that *counts as* her performing some illocutionary acts, with the consequence that the text becomes the *medium* of those illocutionary acts. To authorize a text is in effect to declare: let this text serve as medium of my discoursing.[91]

This authorization often requires an explicit deputizing of the speaker to serve as the medium of the discourse.[92] However, this does not mean that authority is surrendered to the person deputized. Instead, 'it is to bring it

---

88. Nicholas Wolterstorff, *Divine Discourse: Philosophical Reflections on the Claim that God Speaks* (Cambridge: Cambridge University Press, 1995), esp. 37–57.
89. Wolterstorff, *Divine Discourse*, 38.
90. See Max Turner, 'Spirit Endowment in Luke-Acts: Some Linguistic Considerations', *VoxEv* 12 (1981): 45–63; idem, *Power From on High: The Spirit in Israel's Restoration and Witness in Luke-Acts* (JPTSup 9; Sheffield: Sheffield Academic Press, 1996), 165–9.
91. Wolterstorff, *Divine Discourse*, 41, his emphasis. Searle offers a more complex attempt to explain the assignment of functions and deontic powers to things or persons. See his *Speech Acts*, 33–42; idem, *The Construction of Social Reality* (London: Penguin Books, 1995), 7, 13–43, 99–112, 120–5).
92. Merold Westphal, 'On Reading God the Author', *RS* 37 (2001), 278: 'A God who literally speaks must sometimes speak directly, without the benefit of deputized ambassadors or appropriated secretaries, precisely in order to deputize the ambassadors and to appropriate the writings of the secretaries.' We see this in Luke 3.22, and derivatively in Luke 24.48-49 and Acts 1.8 (Isa. 49.6).

about that one exercises that authority by way of actions performed by that other person acting as one's deputy'.[93] Wolterstorff offers the example of an ambassador (such as an ἀπόστολος).[94] Peter is precisely one who has been commissioned by the risen Christ as an apostle-witness (Acts 1.8, 21-22) and a leader of the messianic community.[95]

By way of summary we can take stock of the basic elements of Speech-Act Theory. The question before us concerns what sort of action(s) did Peter accomplish when he spoke to the couple. The answer given here is that Peter indicted the couple for their deception and in so doing, as God's representative, condemned them to death. The action performed, the force exerted, was indictment and condemnation and the effect was the divinely executed death. Peter's words, particularly those directed at Sapphira, are what Searle calls declarations. Declarations bring about the thing declared. Furthermore, Speech-Act Theory and literary discourse are mutually enhancing. Austin stressed that the total speech-act was the object of analysis. The narrative boundaries of the literary speech-act provide real contexts with each of the three constituent dimensions of a speech-act. Finally, we have a linguistic apparatus to help describe the 'deputized agency' of Peter as one authorized to speak on behalf of God as a vehicle of divine judgement. Before turning to the examination of the inscribed conventions (the literary repertoire) undergirding Peter's speech-acts, it will be necessary to register some qualifying caveats.

3.5.2. The Limits of Speech-Act Theory

Two caveats need to be established before launching into the heart of the argument. First, it will be helpful to interact with the caution of Richard Briggs regarding the usefulness of Speech-Act Theory for biblical interpretation. Second, I note the limitations of Speech-Act Theory in order to make explicit my goals in using this tool of philosophy of language.

In responding to the contributions of the first sustained move to apply the insights of speech theory to biblical studies, *Speech Act Theory and Biblical Criticism* (*Semeia* 41), Martin J. Buss suggested that '[t]he potential contribution of speech act theory can be viewed either [1] in terms of a theoretical reconceptualization of the process of exegesis or [2] in terms of a refinement of exegetical procedures in their application to specific passages'.[96] In other words, Speech-Act Theory can either reconceive the hermeneutical

---

93. Wolterstorff, *Divine Discourse*, 42.
94. Wolterstorff, *Divine Discourse*, 43-5, 50-1, 288-96.
95. It will be the task of §7.1. below to argue the conditions for legitimate authorization of Peter as being authorized to speak on behalf of God for Christ, and of §7.2. below to argue that Peter is indeed characterized as one with such a deputation.
96. Martin J. Buss, 'Potential and Actual Interactions Between Speech Act Theory and Biblical Studies', *Semeia* 41 (1988): 125 [125–34].

task at the macro-level, or it can help to illuminate the dynamics of a particular passage (as in examining inner-narrative conversation). However, the second option has been challenged by Richard Briggs. He deliberates,

> [S]peech-act theory may be utilized as a form of narrative and/or rhetorical criticism, focusing on speech acts within the world of the text.[...] My own view is that this is not an obvious way forward, or rather that in so far as it represents a viable option it is doubtful that speech-act theory is the best suited critical method for developing the narrative-critical tools envisaged.[97]

However, if this study is deemed successful, it will show that prophetic speech within the narrative world of Luke-Acts does necessitate the use of Speech-Act Theory as a philosophy of language to demonstrate how God accomplishes the divine purpose through divinely ordained agents and specifically through their spoken language. Furthermore, as suggested above, the narrative boundaries help to establish an analysis of the entire speech-act, including the actual effects, by framing the socio-pragmatic context of the speech-act with a beginning, middle and end of a particular episode.

Finally, as a conclusion to the introduction of Speech-Act Theory, I state what I do *not* see the theory accomplishing and to contrast it with other approaches. First, it is important to realize that Speech-Act Theory is not rhetorical criticism. Rhetorical criticism focuses on the (intended) effect of poetical composition and expression, whereas the object of this study is the force or point of a speaker's utterances. Rhetorical criticism, in so far as narrative is concerned, is better suited to examine the intended effect of speeches or discourse upon an audience, whether it be an audience in the narrative world (such as Jerusalemites or Athenians) or the audience addressed by the text itself (such as Theophilus). Speech-Act Theory, as I employ it, is specifically designed to describe the dynamics of certain utterances *within* narrative discourse.

Lastly, Speech-Act Theory will not make the story more palatable to the mores of modern ears who find the retribution unjustified, or make the transaction more respectable for those who find the miraculous incredible. Speech-Act Theory does not explain or defend the mechanics of the theological conviction that God speaks or executes judgement through authorized individuals. It is not the aim of this study to defend or deny the represented episode of divine judgement upon Ananias and Sapphira as an actual historical event.

---

97. Briggs, 'The Uses', 264. Similarly, in his conclusion to *Words*, Briggs writes: 'If Austin's particular emphasis on convention-governed performatives such as "I name this ship" is taken as the essence of speech act theory, then theologians are content to leave it to its obvious relevance to liturgical considerations, where it has indeed proved fruitful. Similarly, if it is thought that Austin essentially proposes a "performative use of language" to set alongside more familiar language-related concerns, then "performative utterances" are duly noted, but the purpose of such an exercise is not always clear' (294).

Speech-Act Theory does provide the tools to grasp the performative nature of prophetic language, and can afford a linguistic apparatus to understand the nature of God's mediated interaction with people in Luke-Acts. Particularly, this philosophy of language will give the opportunity to address the long neglected aspect dealing specifically and deliberately with the nature of Peter's verbal actions as he confronted the couple threatening the sacral ethos of the early messianists' community-of-goods.

Chapter 4

SOCIO-HISTORICAL REPERTOIRE I:
THE JERUSALEM CHURCH

4.1. Community-of-Goods and Friendship

In this chapter and the next I examine the socio-cultural discursive conventions surrounding the communities of shared goods in order to compare the literary 'common places' (*topoi*) associated with such practices in the ancient Mediterranean world. The focus will be on three utopian communities that are presented in their literary contexts as actual communities of shared goods associated with disciplinary practices.[1] These communities are 'utopian' (lit. 'no place') not in the sense that they never existed in an actual past, but rather '(e)utopian' (lit. 'good place, paradise') in the sense that they are the embodiments of the highest social and moral values of the communities transmitting the traditions.[2] The goal here is be to establish common discursive conventions as part of the reading competence, the literary repertoire, in the Mediterranean milieu. Particularly, the *topos* of a representation of a community-of-goods would have conditioned a Mediterranean auditor of Acts to expect two primary elements associated with the discourse: (1) laudatory esteem and (2) severe disciplinary actions.

First, it will be necessary to recall some basic features of the ancient economy and how this relates to the establishment of a community-of-

---

1. Therefore, it should be noted that the focus here is on the literary representation of the communities, not the *historical* question of whether or not the communities represented in the literature *actually* existed as described.
2. The term 'Utopia' goes back to Sir Thomas More in his 1515 work by the same name. For recent, pertinent discussion of utopian idealism and communities in the ancient Greek world, see Doyne Dawson, *Cities of the Gods: Communist Utopias in Greek Thought* (New York: Oxford University Press, 1992); and John Ferguson, *Utopias of the Classical World* (Ithica, NY: Cornell University Press, 1975). For biblical-Jewish utopian thoughts, see John J. Collins, 'Models of Utopia in the Biblical Tradition', in *A Wise and Discerning Mind: Essays in Honor of Burke O. Long* (eds Saul M. Olyan and Robert Culley; Providence, RI: Brown Judaic Studies, 2000), 51–67. A popular compendium of scholarship regarding utopian thought and relating it to the 'Kingdom of God' movement is Mary Ann Beavis, *Jesus and Utopia: Looking for the Kingdom of God in the Roman World* (Minneapolis: Fortress, 2006).

goods. Specifically, it will be important to explain the basic principles of reciprocity and the framing values of an embedded economy. In the ancient world economic relationships were structured by fundamental values, and the ideal of friendship directed potential economic transactions between social equals in a manner distinctive to other types of relationships. This will help to establish a basic framework to understand the divine economies of the communities-of-goods discussed below. Justo González would find precedent in each of the communities surveyed below as he states, '[t]he truth is [...] that from the earliest time economics was a theological issue, and still is'.[3]

Next, the focus is on examining the divine economy in Luke-Acts, with special focus on Luke's depiction of the early messianists' community-of-goods. Luke anchors the various perspectives on the use of possessions in his overarching theological agenda of reorienting relationships under the household of God. The God of Israel, for Luke, is a Benefactor who makes particular claims on the characters within Luke's story regarding their use of possessions and specifically their (re)orientation toward trust in God's benevolent generosity.

Finally, in the next chapter, there will be a comparatively brief examination of the communities-of-goods represented by the Pythagorean community as an ideal Greco-Roman type, on the one hand, and the Essenes (as described by Josephus and Philo) and the communities portrayed in *The Community Rule* and *The Damascus Document* of the Dead Sea Scrolls as ideal Jewish types, on the other hand. The focus throughout is on establishing common discursive conventions so the texts are examined as literary artifacts. An auditor recognizing the elements of a representation of a (e)utopian community-of-goods in the ancient world would not have been surprised by the divine execution of a miscreant transgressing the communal ethos of trust and fidelity. The argument is *not* about literary dependence of Acts upon either the sources from the Essene communities or the Pythagorean communities. I am, rather, arguing for *a common social milieu* that gave rise to the literary depictions of ideal friendship communities.

4.1.1. 'Embedded' Economy

4.1.1.1. Symbolic Economic Transactions

A prime example of the discursive conventions surrounding the symbolic nature of possessions in a community-of-agricultural-goods is illustrated in a passage from Diodorus of Sicily concerning the neighbours of the Celtiberians, the Vaccaei. In a brief but revealing passage, Diodorus writes:

> Of the tribes neighbouring upon the Celtiberians, the most advanced is the people of the Vaccaei, as they are called; for this people each year divides among its members

---

3. Justo L. González, *Faith and Wealth: A History of Early Christian Ideas on the Origin, Significance, and Use of Money* (London: Harper & Row, 1990; repr. Eugene, OR: Wipf & Stock, 2002), xiii.

the land which it tills and making the fruits the property of all they measure out his portion to each man, and for any cultivators who have appropriated (νοσφισαμένοις) some part for themselves they have set the penalty as death. (*Hist.* 5.34.3, trans. Oldfather, LCL)

Here, we have both the example of laudatory esteem (they are the most 'advanced' of the Celtiberian's neighbours) and the severe penalty for transgressing the ethos of the communal fruits of labour (death). These features of the community-of-goods discourse were common among the presupposition pools in the ancient Mediterranean world.

Robert Wuthnow, writing about contemporary practice but equally relevant for the ancient Mediterranean world, notes that 'economic commitments are embedded in moral frameworks, and that these frameworks significantly *restrain* our economic behavior'.[4] It is significant to highlight the values undergirding economic practices in the ancient world, particularly those practices of the highly structured relationships in a community-of-goods. Primarily, the structures of reciprocity, honour, and (fictive) kinship and friendship govern the divine economy of shared goods in Luke-Acts. These elements assist in reconstructing the 'moral universe' and social ethos surrounding such practices.

4.1.1.2. Reciprocity and Exchange

Marshall Sahlins offers a generalized discussion of reciprocity in 'primitive' societies in terms of social distance.[5] He examines the social nature of economic transactions in terms of varied degrees of 'vice-versa' exchanges, what one gets for giving something to another. He calls this 'reciprocity' and suggests a continuum of expected exchange relative to the nearness or distance of social relationships.[6] He explains, 'The distance between poles of reciprocity is, among other things, social distance [...T]he spirit of exchange swings from disinterested concern for the other party through mutuality to

---

4. Robert Wuthnow, *Poor Richard's Principle: Recovering the American Dream Through the Moral Dimension of Work, Business, and Money* (Princeton: Princeton University Press, 1996), 3, emphasis his. See also Mark Granovetter, 'Economic Action and Social Structure: The Problem of Embeddedness', *AJS* 91 (1985): 481–510; and the critique in Greta R. Krippner, 'The Elusive Market: Embeddedness and the Paradigm of Economic Sociology', *TSoc* 30 (2001): 775–810.

5. 'Primitive' refers to cultures lacking a political state, and remaining unmodified by the historic penetration of the (modern) state. See Marshall Sahlins, *Stone Age Economics* (New York: Aldine de Gruyter, 1972), 188.

6. Sahlins, 'On the Sociology of Primitive Exchange', in *Stone Age*, 185–275. Sahlins actually offers two broader categories for analytical purposes: 'reciprocity', carried out *between* two parties, and 'pooling/redistribution', the collective action *within* a group (188). Compare the broad, contextualizing essay of Hans van Wees, 'The Law of Gratitude: Reciprocity in Anthropological Theory', in *Reciprocity in Ancient Greece* (eds Christopher Gill, Norman Postlethwaite and Richard Seaford; Oxford: Oxford University Press, 1998), 13–49.

self-interest.'[7] This social distance is gauged by relative distance to kinship relationships,

> a spectrum of sociability, from sacrifice in favor of another to self-interested gain at the expense of another.[...] It follows that close kin tend to share, to enter into generalized exchanges, and distant nonkin to deal in equivalents or in guile. Equivalence becomes compulsory in proportion to kinship distance lest relations break off entirely, for with distance there can be little tolerance of gain and loss even as there is little inclination to extend oneself.[8]

Amenably applied to Acts 4.32–5.11, Sahlins's schema shows how the early Jerusalem community of followers of Jesus, surrounding the nucleus of the apostolic witnesses, formed a close-knit (fictive) kinship group based on their common faith in the risen and exalted Messiah. Engaging the community-of-goods ethos was the embodiment of this unity; rejecting or counterfeiting this ethos was tantamount to degeneration of the communal integrity.

Sahlins explains the continuum of reciprocal exchange-relationships with three basic categories.[9] First there is 'generalized reciprocity' which is the 'gift'. The second type is 'balanced reciprocity', the direct and balanced exchange, which is intolerant of one-way giving. The final type of reciprocal exchange, polar opposite to the first, is 'negative reciprocity', which basically amounts to theft.

Sahlins's schema is a helpful heuristic device that defines reciprocity in relation to social distance. This social matrix helps to prepare for the understanding of how economic transactions, especially ritual transactions like the one where the early messianists proffer money 'at the apostles' feet', can be theologically significant.[10] When Ananias and Sapphira transgressed the ethos of (e)utopian reciprocity, they were also threatening the very fabric of the communal identity as portrayed by Luke. Ananias and Sapphira were pretending to act as insiders; Peter exposed them as dangerous, satanic outsiders.

---

7. Sahlins, *Stone Age*, 191, 193; see 198–200. Sitta von Reden (*Exchange in Ancient Greece* [London: Duckworth, 2003], 3) explains: '[B]oth reciprocity and market exchange are [...] ideologies which appear in many societies in different forms, the transformation of gift exchange based on social relationships and trade based on the anonymous market principle, can be envisioned – at least partly – as an ideological process in which political and social boundaries shift under a shifting perception of in-groups and out-groups.'

8. Sahlins, *Stone Age*, 196.

9. Sahlins, *Stone Age*, 191–6. See also Alvin W. Gouldner, 'The Norm of Reciprocity: A Preliminary Statement', *ASR* 25 (1960): 161–78.

10. Luke Timothy Johnson (*The Literary Function of Possessions in Luke-Acts* [SBLDS 39; Missoula, MT: Scholars Press, 1977], 202) writes, '[T]*he disposition of possessions is a direct symbol of the disposition of the self* [emphasis his]. This is the meaning of having all things in common as an expression of spiritual unity. When believers lay their possessions at the Apostles' feet, therefore, they were symbolically laying themselves there, in a gesture of submission to the authority of the Twelve.'

4.1.2. Primary Social Structures

Two recent studies on the community-of-goods in Acts highlight the social dynamics of honour and shame in the act of giving. In an economic situation where status is the primary currency,[11] honour (both inherited and acquired) is the means of increasing one's wealth.[12] It is imperative to properly nuance the types of reciprocal relationship involved in the ritual transaction of submitting the proceeds of sales at the apostles' feet. It is also necessary to offer a note on the nature of the relationship of the believers as portrayed in Luke's narrative, specifically the bonds of kinship and friendship.

4.1.2.1. Honour/Shame and the Ancient Gift
It has been well established in social-scientific studies of the New Testament that honour and shame were pivotal values in the ancient Mediterranean world.[13] Every public situation became a venue to exchange honour, or a situation of liability to assign shame. Much effort was expended in relationships to sustain an honourable reputation.[14] It is therefore no surprise when Scott Bartchy writes:

> [B]y lying in order to achieve an honor they had not earned, Ananias and Sapphira not only dishonored and shamed themselves as patrons [*sic*] but also revealed themselves to be outsiders, non-kin. By not telling the truth, especially about a matter so central

---

11. See M. I. Finley, *The Ancient Economy* (Sather Classical Lectures 43; rev. edn; Berkeley: University of California Press, 1985), 35–61, 183–8; idem, *Politics in the Ancient World* (Cambridge: Cambridge University Press, 1983), 1–49; Ramsay MacMullen, *Roman Social Relations: 50 B.C. to A.D. 284* (New Haven: Yale University Press, 1974), 88–120.
12. See Julian Pitt-Rivers, 'Honour and Social Status', in *Honour and Shame: The Values of Mediterranean Society* (ed., J. G. Peristiany; London: Weidenfeld and Nicolson, 1965), 19–77.
13. See David A. deSilva, *Honor, Patronage, Kinship & Purity: Unlocking New Testament Culture* (Downers Grove, IL: InterVarsity Press, 2000), 23–93; Bruce J. Malina and Jerome H. Neyrey, 'Honor and Shame in Luke-Acts: Pivotal Values of the Mediterranean World', in *The Social World of Luke-Acts: Models for Interpretation* (ed. Jerome H. Neyrey; Peabody, MA: Hendrickson, 1991), 25–65; Halvor Moxnes, 'Honor and Shame', in *The Social Sciences and the New Testament* (ed. Richard Rohrbaugh; Peabody: Hendrickson, 1996), 19–40; Richard L. Rohrbaugh, 'Legitimating Sonship – A Test of Honour: A Social-scientific Study of Luke 4:1–30', in *Modelling Early Christianity: Social-scientific Studies of the New Testament in its Context* (ed. Philip Esler; London: Routledge, 1995), 183–97.
14. See the survey of various epigraphic texts (confession inscriptions, prayers for justice and [funerary] imprecations for revenge) recovered from Asia Minor by Angelos Chaniotis, 'Under the Watchful Eyes of the Gods: Divine Justice in Hellenistic and Roman Asia Minor', in *The Greco-Roman East: Politics, Culture, Society* (ed. Stephen Colvin; Cambridge: Cambridge University Press, 2004), 1–43. Chaniotis notes how many of the prayers and imprecations were motivated by the need to re-establish honour and / or gain revenge (11–15, 18–21, 39, 43). Relevant to the Ananias and Sapphira episode is the common crime of theft and / or perjury (theft: 1–2, 4, 7, 8, 14–15, 16, 17–19, 23; perjury: 11–13, 33–4), crimes which were expected to be avenged by the gods. I am grateful to Richard Fellows for pointing me to this essay.

to their relationship with their fictive kin group, Sapphira and Ananias seriously violated the honor of the group.[15]

Bartchy is surely correct to state the social devastation positioned against the community and the potential pollution of the group.[16] However, his conflation of benefaction and patronage needs further nuance. While the two forms of reciprocal exchange overlapped, they were not in fact the same thing, as if patronage was the Roman equivalent to the Hellenistic 'euergetism' (benefaction).[17] The situation of exchange in the Jerusalem community-of-goods is closer to Hellenistic benefaction than it is to Roman patronage. This indicates that the honour attributed to those surrendering their wealth on behalf of the needy in the community would not have been exchanged for social superiority (cf. Luke 22.24-27). The aim would have been directed more towards a strengthening of the bonds of communal solidarity and identity formation. Furthermore, the ideological perspective of Luke-Acts militates against the action of bringing goods and proceeds for the apostles to distribute *as patronage* within the community-of-goods.[18] By

---

15. S. Scott Bartchy, 'Community of Goods in Acts: Idealization or Social Reality?', in *The Future of Early Christianity* (ed. Birger A. Pearson; Minneapolis: Fortress Press, 1991), 309-18.
16. See §4.2.2.2. nn. 109-10 below.
17. See Stephan J. Joubert, 'One Form of Social Exchange or Two? "Euergetism", Patronage, and Testament Studies', *BTB* 31 (2001): 17–25; and Peter Garnsey and Greg Woolf, 'Patronage of the Rural Poor in the Roman World', in *Patronage in Ancient Society* (ed. Andrew Wallace-Hadrill; London: Routledge, 1989), 153–70 ('Patronage coexists with charity and euergetism [philanthropy or public benefaction], and support provided by other members of the poor man's family, village or town' [154]); Richard P. Saller, *Personal Patronage Under the Early Empire* (Cambridge: Cambridge University Press, 1982), 3, 7–39; idem, 'Patronage and Friendship in Early Imperial Rome: Drawing the Distinction', in *Patronage* (ed. Wallace-Hadrill), 49–62; Andrew Wallace-Hadrill, 'Patronage in Roman Society: From Republic to Empire', in *Patronage* (ed. Wallace-Hadrill), 63–87 ('Patronage was central to the Roman cultural experience, in a way in which it was foreign to the Greek cultural experience.[...] Rather than offering *the* key to Roman politics, patronage must be seen as one of several methods of generating power, a system actually in competition and conflict with other systems' [65, 71]). See also the criticism of Moxnes, ('Patron-Client Relations and the New Community in Luke-Acts', in *Social World of Luke-Acts* [ed. Neyrey], 241–68) by Alan C. Mitchell, '"Greet the Friends by Name": New Testament Evidence for the Greco-Roman *Topos* on Friendship', in *Greco-Roman Perspectives on Friendship* (ed. John T. Fitzgerald; SBLRBS 34; Atlanta: Scholars Press, 1997), 246 n. 79.

The standard work on euergetism is Paul Veyne, *Bread and Circuses: Historical Sociology and Political Pluralism* (trans. Brian Pearce; London: Allen Lane / The Penguin Press, 1990). See also Frederick Danker, *Benefactor: Epigraphic Study of a Graeco-Roman and New Testament Semantic Field* (St Louis: Clayton Publishing House, Inc., 1982), esp. 26–55.

18. Thus, while Moxnes's ('Patron-Client', 261) assertion of transformation is correct – 'There is, then, a break with the patron-client relationship at its most crucial point: a service performed or a favor done shall *not* be transformed into status and honor' – his construal of the nature of the transaction is not. Mitchell ('New Testament Evidence', 239, 246–57; 'The Social Function of Friendship in Acts 2:44–45 and 4:32–37', *JBL* 111 [1992]: 266–72) is closer with his discussion of the transformation of the friendship convention.

considering Barnabas and the errant couple as the early messianists' 'patrons' Bartchy misreads Luke's radical subversion of the potentially vicious cycle of reciprocal obligation and the nature of the relationships in the early Jerusalem community.[19]

4.1.2.2. Benefaction and Friendship

Richard Ascough does take note of the distinctions in relationships of reciprocity, but does not take enough account of the particular (e)utopian context.[20] Focusing on the precise nature of the couple's 'crime', he suggests that the key to understanding this story is the convention of benefaction in the context of Greco-Roman 'voluntary associations'.[21] Drawing evidence from inscriptions concerned with honouring benefactors, including the honouring of couples, he proposes that the sin of Ananias and Sapphira was that they were attempting to gain more honour than was due them. He proposes:

19. That ancient gift-giving could have an agonistic element, see, T. O. Beidelman, 'Agonistic Exchange: Homeric Reciprocity and the Heritage of Simmel and Mauss', *CulAnth* 4 (1989): 227–59; Terence Turner, '"Agonistic Exchange: Homeric Reciprocity and the Heritage of Simmel and Mauss": A Commentary', *CulAnth* 4 (1989): 260–4; A. R. Hands, *Charities and Social Aid in Greece and Rome* (London: Thames and Hudson, 1968), 26–61; Veyne, *Bread and Circuses*, 77–80, von Reden, *Exchange*, 13–57.

Luke's radical alternative vision is perceived, for example, by Richard Ascough, 'Benefaction Gone Wrong: The "Sin" of Ananias and Sapphira in Context', in *Text and Artifact in the Religions of Mediterranean Antiquity: Essays in Honour of Peter Richardson* (eds Stephen G. Wilson and Michael Desjardins; ESCJ 9; Waterloo, Ontario, Canada: Wilfrid Laurier University Press), 102–5; Brian J. Capper, 'Reciprocity and the Ethic of Acts', in *Witness to the Gospel: The Theology of Acts* (eds I. Howard Marshall and David Peterson; Grand Rapids: Eerdmans, 1998), 516–18; Mitchell, 'New Testament Evidence', 237, 239, 246–57; idem, 'Social Function', 258, 259, 261–2, 264–72.

20. Ascough, 'Benefaction', 97–8.

21. A good collection on Greco-Roman voluntary associations is John S. Kloppenborg and Stephen Wilson, eds, *Voluntary Associations in the Graeco-Roman World* (London: Routledge, 1996). Also relevant are Richard Ascough, 'Translocal Relationships among Voluntary Associations and Early Christianity', *JECS* 5 (1997): 223–41; Philip A. Harland, *Associations, Synagogues, and Congregations: Claiming a Place in Ancient Mediterranean Society* (Minneapolis: Fortress, 2003); Matthias Klinghardt, 'The Manual of Discipline in the Light of Statutes of Hellenistic Associations', in *Methods of Investigation of the Dead Sea Scrolls and the Khirbet Qumran Site: Present Realities and Future Prospects* (ed. Michael O. Wise, et al.; ANYAS 722; New York: The New York Academy of Sciences, 1994), 251–67 (with panel discussion, 267–70); Justin Taylor, *Pythagoreans and Essenes: Structural Parallels* (Paris: Peeters, 2004), 53–69.

Particularly relevant to a critique of Ascough's thesis are Albert Baumgarten, 'Graeco-Roman Voluntary Associations and Ancient Jewish Sects', in *Jews in a Graeco-Roman World* (ed. Martin Goodman; Oxford: Oxford University Press, 1998), 93–111; Sandra Walker-Ramisch, 'Graeco-Roman Voluntary Associations and the Damascus Document', in *Voluntary Associations* (eds John Kloppenborg and Stephen Wilson), 128–45; Moshe Weinfeld, *The Organizational Pattern and the Penal Code of the Qumran Sect: A Comparison with Guilds and Religious Associations of the Hellenistic-Roman Period* (NTOA 2; Fribourg / Göttingen: Univeritatsverlag / Vandenhoeck & Riprecht, 1986), 10–50, 77–80.

The widespread practice of associations setting up honours for their benefactors makes it reasonable for Ananias and Sapphira to expect that in return for their benefaction they would have received the honours due to them. In an attempt to extract more honour than they are due, however, they claim to have given over the entire proceeds of the sale of their land. To have done so would be deemed more generous, and thus deserving of more honour, than to have given only a portion.[22]

In contradistinction to Brian Capper, who argues that benefaction through the selling of property was rare,[23] Ascough rejoins, 'benefaction was commonplace and yet accorded great honour, and it was often accompanied by the suggestion that others should follow suit in supporting the group. It is precisely because dispersing one's wealth was commonplace that we should read this text in the context of benefaction'.[24] Ascough summarizes his understanding of the parenetic force of the passage:

The story serves as a warning to those who would be benefactors in Luke's own Christian community, but who might expect the honours in exchange. The message is not 'give everything or else,' but 'do not seek recognition for more than you have contributed.'[...] Set within the larger context of both Luke-Acts and the world of the voluntary associations, the story of Ananias and Sapphira is a cautionary tale about wanting honours for benefaction, and a warning against those who act according to human conventions rather than divine conventions. While their 'sin' is their lie, their motivation is the desire for greater worldly honour. Their reward for holding back part of the proceeds while claiming to give them all was death. Clearly this is a case of benefaction gone wrong.[25]

Ascough's attempt to locate the (intended) reading context of the Ananias and Sapphira episode is helpful in drawing a wider array of intertextual echoes (i.e., inscriptions). However, Ascough does not fully accomplish his aim; he does not explain the severity of the couple's punishment, nor has he properly contextualized Luke's account.[26] Ascough's explanation of the couple's reward of death due to their corrupt motivation, in the end, is implicated in his critique of his predecessors' attempts: 'it is doubtful whether this is an adequate explanation of this passage'.[27] It is unclear that the early Jerusalem community in Acts so readily assimilates to 'voluntary associations'.[28] There is no indication in Luke's description that the early Jerusalem community's reciprocal honour of their benefactor would have resulted in epigraphic

---

22. Ascough, 'Benefaction', 102.
23. Brian J. Capper 'Community of Goods in the Early Jerusalem Church', *ANRW* II 26.2 (1995), 1742-3 [1730-74]; idem, 'The Palestinian Cultural Context of Earliest Christian Community of Goods', in *The Book of Acts in Its Palestinian Setting* (ed. Richard Bauckham; BAIFCS 4; Grand Rapids: Eerdmans, 1995), 337-41 [323-56].
24. Ascough, 'Benefaction', 102.
25. Ascough, 'Benefaction', 105.
26. See Veyne, *Bread*, 70-200, for a more nuanced discussion of the various types of euergetism (*ob honorem*), and its contrast to the 'gift'.
27. Ascough, 'Benefaction', 92.
28. See Taylor, *Pythagoreans*, 67.

commendation, and therefore increase in public status in the manner of city-wide euergetism. Furthermore, the focus on the act of Ananias and Sapphira as benefaction is too vague to offer any real explanatory power.[29] As Ascough states, 'precisely because dispersing one's wealth was commonplace' the focus should be more on the nature of the relationship within this particular community rather than the putative actions that could be found in any number of contexts. The sphere of 'voluntary associations' is too vague to adequately account for the execution of divine judgement for failing the communal ethos. Alan Mitchell is closer to the mark when he writes,

> [D]ue to their social and ethical implications, friendship traditions became a vehicle Luke used to encourage upper status people in the community to benefit those beneath them.[...] I see Luke challenging the reciprocity ethic in both the Gospel and Acts, especially in Acts 2 and 4, by showing how Christians can become friends regardless of culturally promoted and accepted status divisions and without the need to give with an eye to a return.[30]

Coupled with Luke's subversion of reciprocal obligation, his allusions to the (e)utopian friendship tradition and the eschatological context, the Ananias and Sapphira episode is framed by a highly distinctive literary environment that ultimately defies exact parallel. However, this does not mean that Luke's portrayal would have been foreign or without precedent for his (model) auditors. Luke takes over and adapts common conventions to convey his message.

4.1.2.3. Friendship and (E)utopia

One more caveat is necessary before expounding upon the 'divine economy' of the early Jerusalem messianists as described by Luke. I have thus far found it convenient to fuse the (e)utopian and friendship traditions, a move resisted by Mitchell. He understands the introduction of utopian traditions to obscure the description.[31] Mitchell is rightfully resisting the tendency in previous scholarship to claim that Luke was merely *idealizing* the early Jerusalem community in terms of a mythic Golden Age. Bartchy's primary aim was similar,[32] and both in my view are successful in refuting their interlocutors.[33] Bartchy is able to hold together better than Mitchell the two

---

29. Saller's (*Personal Patronage*, 3) comments regarding patronage are analogous: 'Demonstrating the mere existence of patron-client relationships in imperial Rome is of limited value, since they can be found in one form or another in most societies. It is much more valuable to know how patronage functioned in relation to other political, economic and social institutions. Function is more difficult to prove than existence.'
30. Mitchell, 'New Testament Evidence', 239, 240.
31. Mitchell, 'New Testament Evidence', 240–3, 257; 'Social Function', 257–8.
32. Bartchy, 'Community of Goods'.
33. Chiefly Hans Conzelmann, *Acts of the Apostles* (Hermeneia; trans. J. Limburg, A. T. Kraabel and D. H. Juel; Philadelphia: Fortress, 1987), 24.

traditions, allowing for allusions to the (e)utopian traditions as framing his portrait: 'Luke uses language that echoes Greek utopian hopes to describe the actual meeting of individual needs among the Jewish Christians in the Jerusalem house-churches by means of their pervasive acts of sharing, which Luke believed had indeed happened.'[34] Construing the utopian traditions as *merely* the ideal shadow of a long past or mythic Golden Age, we can agree with Mitchell, that the 'evidence supports the view that Luke had more in mind than alluding to a primitive Christian utopia when he incorporated elements of the Greco-Roman friendship ideal in his summary descriptions of the early Jerusalem community'.[35] However, the two traditions – (e)utopian and friendship – are not *necessarily* in conflict. The (e)utopian traditions, understood as an obtainable 'good place' and transformed by Luke's theological vision, can have the same parenetic effects that Mitchell claims for the transformed friendship *topos*.[36] A better construal is made by Dawson, who argues for two sorts of political utopias in the ancient world. The first is a 'low' (e)utopia, which was a 'comprehensive program for an ideal city-state that *was meant to be put into action,* if possible, and in the meantime to provide a critique of existing institutions and a model for more limited reforms'.[37] The second is a 'high' utopianism, which fits the 'classical utopianism', a 'plan for an ideal city-state that was not meant to be literally enacted'.[38] Luke's portrayal of the early Jerusalem community would have evoked the 'low' (e)utopian traditions, along with those of the Pythagoreans and the Essenes.

4.2. The Divine Economy in Luke-Acts

It is remarkable that only one narrative account of the earliest Jerusalem community has been preserved. Luke is without precedent in his account of the early messianists' community-of-goods in Jerusalem in the days after the risen Christ's exaltation. The lack of precedents has caused many speculations regarding the sources Luke may have used. However, there is a precedent in literary *topoi* contemporaneous with Luke's account. Jacques Dupont was one of the first scholars to clearly demonstrate that

---

34. Bartchy, 'Community of Goods', 318.
35. Mitchell, 'New Testament Evidence', 257.
36. See Wallace-Hadrill's ('Patronage', 66–8, 72) discussion of how Dionysius of Halicarnassus appealed to the 'Golden Age' of Romulus in order to challenge his contemporaries to imitate the ideal. My point is simply that ideal and parenesis are not *necessarily* in conflict.
37. Dawson, *Cities*, 7, emphasis added. Dawson includes in this type those found in Plato's *Laws*, Aristotle's *Politics* 7–8, and Cicero's *On the Republic* and *On the Laws*.
38. Dawson, *Cities*, 7. The prime example is Plato's *Republic*, and Dawson also includes the Cynic / Stoic utopias of the third century BC. Even these, according to Dawson (*Cities*, 4) are meant to inspire reform: '[T]he serious utopia is always meant as a paradigm or goal for social and political reform.'

Luke's account was influenced by the *topoi* of Greco-Roman (e)utopian ideals and friendship traditions.[39] Many others have collected various discursive comparisons with the language in Acts. Luke has provided an idyllic summary of the community life that would have evoked Greco-Roman (e)utopian and friendship ideals[40] and Jewish eschatological hopes.[41] David Mealand helpfully collects various phrases that serve as a point of contact for a common milieu for the Greco-Roman (e)utopian *topoi*.[42] He concludes, 'The writer of Acts seems to have seen the nascent

---

39. Jacques Dupont, 'Community of Goods in the Early Church', in *The Salvation of the Gentiles: Studies in the Acts of the Apostles* (trans. John R. Keating; New York: Paulist Press, 1979), 85–102. This is an abbreviated translation of the French 'La communauté des biens aux premiers jours de l'Eglise', in *Etudes sur les Actes des Apôtres* (LD 45; Paris: Cerf, 1967), 503–19.

40. See Bartchy, 'Community of Goods', 309–18; Lucien Cerfaux, 'La première communauté chrétienne à Jérusalem (Act., II, 41–V, 42)', in *Recueil Lucien Cerfaux: Études d'Exégèse et d'Histoire Religieuse de Monseigneur Cerfaux, réunies a l'occasion de son soixante-dixième anniversaire* (2 vols; BETL 6–7; Gembloux: J. Duculot, 1954), 2:150–2; Henriette Havelaar, 'Hellenistic Parallels to Acts 5.1–11 and the Problem of Conflicting Interpretations', *JSNT* 67 (1997): 63–82; Pieter van der Horst, 'Hellenistic Parallels to the Acts of the Apostles (2.1–47)', *JSNT* (1985): 58–60; Hans Josef Klauck, 'Gütergemeinschaft in der klassischen Antike, in Qumran, und im Neuen Testament', *RevQ* 11 (1982), 47–79; David L. Mealand, 'Community of Goods and Utopian Allusions in Acts II–IV', *JTS* 28 (1977): 96–9; Mitchell, 'New Testament Evidence', 236–57; idem, 'Social Function', 255–72; Gregory E. Sterling, '"Athletes of Virtue": An Analysis of the Summaries in Acts (Acts 2:41–47; 4:32–35; 5:12–16)', *JBL* 113 (1994): 679–96.

41. The majority of studies compare the description of community goods in Acts with the descriptions (by Philo and Josephus) of the Essenes and the Dead Sea Scrolls (particularly 1QS and CD). See the many works by Brian J. Capper, 'The Interpretation of Acts 5.4', *JSNT* 19 (1983), 117–31; idem, '<<In der hand des Ananias...>> Erwagungen zu 1 QS VI, 20 und der Urchristlichen Gütergemeinschaft', *RevQ* 12 (1986), 223–36; idem, 'Community of Goods', 1730–74; idem, 'Palestinian Cultural Context', 323–56; idem, 'Reciprocity', 499–518. See also Leslie J. Hoppe, *There Shall Be No Poor Among You: Poverty in the Bible* (Nashville, Abingdon Press, 2004), 154–5; Klauck, 'Gütergemeinschaft', 52–79; David L. Mealand, 'Community of Goods at Qumran', *TZ* 31 (1975): 129–39; Justin Taylor, 'The Community of Goods among the First Christians and among the Essenes', in *Historical Perspectives: From the Hasmoneans to Bar Kokhba in Light of the Dead Sea Scrolls: Proceedings of the Fourth International Symposium of the Orion Center for the Study of the Dead Sea Scrolls and Associated Literature, 27–31 January, 1999* (eds David Goodblatt, Avital Pinnick, and Daniel Schwartz; Studies on the Texts of the Desert of Judah; Leiden: Brill, 2001), 147–61.

Charles H. Talbert (*Reading Acts: A Literary and Theological Commentary on the Acts of the Apostles* [New York: Crossroad Publishing Company, 1997], 64) also notes Greco-Roman parallels for the elimination of the poor in Seneca, *Epistle* 90.38 and Isocrates, *Aeropagiticus*, 83.

42. Mealand, 'Community of Goods and Utopian Allusions':
(1) μία ψυχή ('one soul'): Arist., *Eth. nic.* 9.8.2 (1168b); D.L. 5.20; Iamb., V.P. 30.167 (see below on [3a])
(2) κοινὰ τὰ φίλων ('friends have their goods in common'): Arist., *Eth. nic.* 9.8.2 (1186b); Plato, *Rep.* 4.424A, 5.449C; *Phaedr.* 279C; D.L. 8.10, 10.11 (attributed to Pythagoras), 6.72 (Diogenes); Photius, *Lexicon* (κοινός); Philo, *Mos.* 1.156f.; Cicero, *Off.* 1.16.51

Christian community as fulfilling the hopes, the promises, and the ideals, not only of Deuteronomy, but also of that same Greek Utopianism.'[43] Klauck agrees, 'Luke himself consciously falls back in his choice of words on the Hellenistic social utopias...Luke wanted to show his Hellenistic readers that all the dreams and ideals of Hellenistic social thinking were exemplarily realized in the early Christian community' (my translation).[44] However, this does not disintegrate the community's distinctives, nor the particular role its representation contributes to Luke's narrative. The intertextual relations add a rich 'texture' to Luke's presentation of the early messianists within his narrative of beginnings. It draws his description of the early messianic community into a wider discourse with dispositions and practices associated with the best of cultural expression. Furthermore, it helps to draw attention to a certain set of associated expectations and practices associated with communal living and discipline. While the maxims would have evoked friendship ideals, the episode of Ananias and Sapphira would have indicated a more extensive practice of sharing goods that was associated with (e)utopian communal 'experiments', as found in traditions about the Pythagoreans and Essenes. What follows will be an examination of the 'moral cosmos' of the early messianists' community of life and goods as it is represented by Luke, as well as a brief look at some details of Luke's idyllic description.

4.2.1. *The Moral Universe of the Early Christian Community-of-Goods*

Wealth and poverty, the use of possessions and the contrast between generosity and greed have occupied no little space within Lukan scholarship,

---

(3a) οὐδὲν (or μηδὲν) ἴδιον ('nothing one's own'): Plato, *Crit* 110D (ἴδιον...οὐδέν); *Rep.* 3.416D (οὐσίαν...μηδεμίαν...ἰδίαν), 5.464D (μηδὲν ἴδιον), 8.543B (ἴδιον...οὐδέν); *Tim.* 18B (μηδὲν...ἴδιον); Euripides, *Andr.* 376, 377 (combined with [4]); Diod. 5.45.5 (Euhemerus); Iamb. V.P. 30.168 combined with [4] with [1] in V.P. 167)

(3b) ἴδιον τε μηδὲν ἡγεῖσθαι ('consider nothing one's own'): D.L. 8.23 (a Pythagorean maxim)

(4) πάντα (or ἅπαντα) κοινά ('everything common'): Plato, *Crit.* 110D (ἅπαντα ... κοινά); *Rep.*5.464D (τὰ δ' ἄλλα κοινά), 8.543B (κοινὰς δὲ πᾶσι); Cicero, *Off.* 1.16.51; Strabo, *Geogr.* 7.3.9; Porph, V.P. 20; Philo, *Hyp.* 11.4 (combined with [3a])

See also Dupont, 'Community of Goods', 89–90, 96–7; van der Horst, 'Parallels (2.1–47)', 58–60; Mitchell, '"Greet the Friends"', 238 n. 54; Sterling, '"Athletes of Virtue"', 692–3.

43. Mealand, 'Community of Goods and Utopian Allusions', 99.

44. Klauck, 'Gütergemeinschaft', 72, 73, 'Lukas selbst greift in seiner Wortwahl bewußt auf die hellenistischen Sozialutopien zurück...Lukas wollte seinen hellenistischen Lesern zeigen, daß all die Träume und Wunschgebilde hellenistischen Sozialdenkens in der christlichen Urgemeinde vorbildlich verwirklicht wurden.' Similarly, Marguerat, 'Ananias and Sapphira', 165: 'The author of Acts wanted to make it known to his readers that the original community, the church of Jerusalem, fulfilled the ideal of sharing which was current in the culture at the time.'

particularly since the post-world war period of the twentieth century.⁴⁵ The fact of the matter is that Luke has no single perspective, no one encompassing proposition, regarding the use of possessions.⁴⁶ Luke's narrative vision cannot be reduced to principles of giving and freedom from greed (e.g., Luke 3.10-14; 12.13-21; Acts 20.35), renunciation (e.g., Luke 18.18-30), (e)utopian sharing (Acts 2.41-47; 4.32–5.11), nor to almsgiving (e.g., Acts 11.27-30). However, general principles can be suggested to undergird the divine economy in the Lukan narrative world. Specifically, the metaphors of the Household of God and God as a generous Benefactor help to encourage and restrain economic commitments for the Lukan characters.⁴⁷ These divine metaphors serve to frame the moral cosmos of economic transactions in the narrative world and theological vision of Luke-Acts.

John Elliott correctly notes the way household becomes an embodied metaphor for the Lukan Jesus to serve 'as the most apposite sphere and symbol of social life for illustrating features of life under the reign of God'.⁴⁸ Joel Green, utilizing the socio-anthropological grid of Clifford Geertz,⁴⁹ argues that the household becomes the new 'culture centre' for the people of God in Lukan perspective.⁵⁰ Green concludes his insightful essay on household baptism in Acts with the following proposal:

45. Several bibliographical surveys of scholarship are helpful. See François Bovon, *Luke the Theologian: Fifty-Three years of research (1950–2005)* (2nd rev. edn; Waco, TX: Baylor University Press, 2006), 442–53, 548–51; John R. Donahue, 'Two Decades of Research on the Rich and Poor in Luke-Acts', in *Justice and the Holy: Essays in Honor of Walter Harrelson* (eds D. A. Knight and P. J. Paris; Atlanta: Scholars Press, 1989), 129–44; Kyoung-Jin Kim, *Stewardship and Almsgiving in Luke's Theology* (JSNTS 155; Sheffield: Sheffield Academic Press, 1998), 13–32; Thomas E. Phillips, *Reading Issues of Wealth and Poverty in Luke-Acts* (Lewiston, NY: Edwin Mellen Press, 2001), 5–43; idem, 'Reading Recent Readings of Issues of Wealth and Poverty in Luke and Acts', *CBR* 1 (2003): 231–69; David P. Seccombe *Possessions and the Poor in Luke-Acts* (SNTU 6; Linz: A. Fuchs, 1982), 11–17.

46. As Luke T. Johnson (*Sharing Possessions: Mandate and Symbol of Faith* [OBT; Philadelphia: Fortress, 1981], 13) quips, 'Although Luke consistently speaks about possessions, he does not speak about possessions consistently.'

47. See, for example, Joel B. Green, *The Theology of the Gospel of Luke* (Cambridge: Cambridge University Press, 1995), 111, 116; Moxnes, 'Patron-Client', 257–8.

48. John Elliott, 'Temple Versus Household in Luke-Acts: A Contrast in Social Institutions', in *Social World of Luke-Acts* (ed. Neyrey), 227. However, there are problems with Elliott's contrast. See the perceptive critiques by Joel B. Green, 'The Demise of the Temple as "Culture Center" in Luke-Acts: An Exploration of the Rending of the Temple Veil (Luke 23.44-49),' *RB* (1994), 510 n. 40.

49. Cf. Clifford Geertz, 'Centers, Kings, and Charisma: Reflections on the Symbolics of Power', in *Local Knowledge: Further Essays in Interpretive Anthropology* (New York: Basic, 1983), 121–46, esp. 122–3.

50. See also the discussion of the household and the *polis* in Dawson, *Cities*, 40–3. Dawson writes, 'The ideal of sharing property was the social cement of a Greek city.[...] It seemed an obvious solution to the perennial conflict between the competitiveness of the households and the city's need for unity: merge the households into one great communal household.[...] The total *koinonia* of the philosophers could seem a merely logical extension of the ordinary *koinonia*' (43).

> The baptism of households entails the unequivocal embrace of the household as the new culture center for the people of God, an active center of social order that embodies and radiates a world-order within which Jesus is Lord of all, hospitality is shared across socio-ethnic lines, and hierarchical lines that define the empire are erased.[51]

The significance of this household metaphor for the early Jerusalem messianists' community-of-goods is that the image of God as benevolent Father, and the relationship between one another as (fictive) kin, motivates and directs economic transactions. This is not an argument for (e)utopian communities generally, but rather a particular theological vision that emerges from the plot of the narrative world of Luke-Acts. Both communal summaries in Acts (2.41-47; 4.32-35) flow from the community's experience of the Holy Spirit (2.1-4, 33, 38-39; 4.31). Both summaries follow the identification of the community in terms of the household, specifically the master-slave relationship (δοῦλοι [καὶ δοῦλαι] μου/σου, 2.18; 4.29).[52] The Spirit is deemed a 'gift' (δωρεά, 2.38) by Peter, a 'promise' (ἐπαγγελία, 2.39) that is for Israel, those near and dispersed, for ὅσους ἂν προσκαλέσηται κύριος ὁ θεὸς ἡμῶν (2.39b). Peter's speech recalls Jesus' own language, who identifies the Spirit as the ἐπαγγελίαν τοῦ πατρός μου (Luke 24.49), made explicit both in Jesus' address before his ascension in Acts (1.4-5) and in Peter's hermeneutical homily (2.33).

The Spirit of Pentecost has motivated the community-of-goods among the Jerusalem community of Jesus' followers as an instantiation of the household of the benevolent God of Israel. As Marguerat reminds us, '[I]t is important to note, the author attributes this communion [of Acts 4.32] to "the whole group of those who believe" *moved by the Spirit of Pentecost*.'[53] As Jesus taught in his Sermon on the Plain (the plain possibly being a socio-symbolic space of levelling in Luke's Gospel, anticipated by Mary [Luke 1.52] and John [Luke 3.5; cf. Isa. 40.4 LXX]), his followers ought to 'love your enemies

---

51. Joel B. Green, '"She and Her Household were baptized" (Acts 16.15): Household Baptism in the Acts of the Apostles', in *Dimensions of Baptism: Biblical and Theological Studies* (eds Stanley E. Porter and Anthony R. Cross; JSNTS 234; London: Sheffield Academic Press, 2002), 90.

52. See Robert L. Brawley, *Text to Text Pours Forth Speech: Voices of Scripture in Luke-Acts* (Indianapolis: Indiana University Press, 1995), 81–2; and his 'Social Identity and the Aim of Accomplished Life in Acts 2', in *Acts and Ethics* (ed. Thomas E. Philips; Sheffield: Sheffield Phoenix Press, 2005), 16–33, esp. 23–4, 26; and Kim, *Stewardship and Almsgiving*, 111–30. H. W. Pleket ('Religious History as the History of Mentality: The "Believer" as Servant of the Deity in the Greek World', in *Faith, Hope and Worship: Aspects of Religious Mentality in the Ancient World* [ed. H. S. Versnel; Leiden: Brill, 1981], 152–92) offers a helpful contextualizing study examining various 'family' terms and their use in religious contexts.

53. Marguerat, 'Ananias', 165 n. 25, emphasis added. Cf. Dupont ('Community of Goods', 95–6) on the communal sharing as a consequence of the unity of heart and soul and (105) on the emphasis of Luke's appellation of 'believers' over 'friends' or 'brothers'; cf. Klauck, 'Gütergemeinschaft', 74.

and do good, and lend not hoping for something in return'⁵⁴ (Luke 6.35). Jesus continues, indicating that the potentially vicious system of reciprocity is not eradicated, but rather redirected and thus transformed. The expected reward comes from God (see Luke 14.14), and this generous practice will demonstrate the character of this new community of givers as 'sons of the Most High, for [God] himself is kind to ungrateful and evil persons' (6.35). Jesus makes the demand explicit: 'Be merciful, just as your Father is merciful' (6.36). Jesus' theological teaching here indicates a complete rearranging of the typical Roman social order of balanced reciprocity.⁵⁵ The motivation is domestically recognizable: the primary identity and social practice is derivative from the household and the *paterfamilias*. Yet, there is a shift to a more prominent head of household – the generous God of Israel.

In Acts, with the community-of-goods flowing from the presence of the Spirit in the midst of the congregation of believers, the redistribution that eradicates need is, as Dupont asserts, 'but the manifestation of a deeper, spiritual communion'.⁵⁶ Thus, Klauck rightly contends, 'Luke understands the community of goods as a visible work of the Spirit, which works in the community' (my translation).⁵⁷ God has bestowed the 'gift' of the Spirit upon the community, and in consequence has motivated a 'divine economy of grace' (Acts 4.33b), a noncompetitive economy built on trust and kinship fidelity. In short, the cycle of obligation now flows from and into the new relationship between God and those who believe.

However, I suggest that this 'economy' (οἰκονομία, 'household management') in Acts is not unlike the double-edged sword of the gospel proclaimed and embodied by Jesus in his Nazareth sermon (Luke 4.16-30; cf. Simeon's prediction in 2.34-35). In both passages there are echoes of Jubilee legislation, transformed by the eschatological context.⁵⁸ The Jubilee

---

54. For this sense of ἀπελπίζω as '(not) expecting return', see BDAG 101 meaning 2. Some commentators see a play on words here between δανείζω and ἀπελπίζω. See Frederick W. Danker, *Jesus and the New Age: A Commentary on St. Luke's Gospel* (rev. edn; Philadelphia: Fortress, 1988), 149.

55. Joel B. Green, *The Gospel of Luke*. (NICNT; Grand Rapids: Eerdmans, 1997), 273–5 is instructive here. He writes, '[T]he ethic Jesus unfolds has its basis in God's own character and is not essentially contractual.[...] If God, and not the emperor, is identified as the Great Benefactor, the Patron, and if people are to act without regard to cycles of obligation, then the politics of the Empire is sabotaged' (274).

56. Dupont, 'Community of Goods', 95; see also O'Toole, '"You Did Not Lie"', 195; Walter E. Pilgrim, *Good News to the Poor: Wealth and Poverty in Luke-Acts* (Minneapolis: Augsburg Publishing House, 1981), 148–9.

57. Klauck, 'Gütergemeinschaft', 74, 'Lukas versteht die Gütergemeinschaft als sichtbares Werk des Geistes, der in der Gemeinde wirkt.' See also Marguerat, 'Ananias', 165 n. 25, '[I]t is important to note, the author attributes this communion to "the whole group of those who believe" *moved by the Spirit of Pentecost*' (emphasis added).

58. On the Jubilee theme in Luke's Gospel, see Sharon H. Ringe, *Jesus, Liberation, and the Biblical Jubilee: Images for Ethics and Christology* (OBT; Philadelphia: Fortress, 1985), 33–90; James A. Sanders, 'Sins, Debts, and Jubilee Release', in *Luke and Scripture: The Function of Sacred Tradition in Luke-Acts* (Craig A. Evans and James A. Sanders;

theme in Luke 4.18-19 is mediated by Isaiah 61.1-2 and 58.6, which has already transformed the ancient theme as Israel's release from the Babylonian captivity.[59] For Luke, this 'release' is 'forgiveness for sins'.[60] Yet, as Jesus continues his sermon (4.23-27), the scriptural fulfilment is not reserved for Jesus' countrymen, or even Israel, alone. At the inauguration of Jesus' public ministry there is already the division of the children of Abraham and the anticipation of inclusion for outsiders (as the examples of the gentile widow and the Syrian Naaman infer). The audience's amazement (ἐθαύμαζον, 4.22) turns to rage (θυμός, v. 28), and the proclaimer of the message of the 'acceptable' (δεκτός, 4.18; Isa. 61.2 LXX) year of the Lord has himself become 'unacceptable' ('no prophet is δεκτός in his own country', 4.24) to those of his hometown.[61]

Just as the Spirit-anointed Messiah divides Israel, so the Spirit-motivated messianic community in Jerusalem finds itself divided by those who cannot submit to the whole-hearted apportioning ethos.[62] It is precisely the eschatologically, Spirit-filled status of the Christian community that brings down the wrath of God upon the couple who attempts deception of the Spirit and the rupture of the sacred bond of trust. It remains to look closer at the specifics of the framing summaries of the community-of-goods.

4.2.2. Messianic (E)utopian Community-of-Goods

In order to demonstrate a reading competency, or extra-textual repertoire, and common milieu of the early Christian discourse on community-of-goods with certain expectations associated with the discourse on communal life and goods in the ancient Mediterranean world it is necessary to look at the specific literary expressions of the discourse. We pay attention to their generic form and examine the similarities and distinctives. Among the various perspectives

---

Minneapolis: Fortress, 1993), 84–92; and Robert B. Sloan, *The Favorable Year of the Lord: A Study of Jubilary Theology in the Gospel of Luke* (Austin: Schola Press, 1977), who concludes with suggestions for the socio-political, eschatological, and cultic ramifications for Luke's theology.

59. See the discussion in James A. Sanders, 'From Isaiah 61 to Luke 4', in *Luke and Scripture*, 46–69.

60. Luke 1.77; 3.3; 5.20; 7.48; 11.4; 23.34; 24.47; Acts 2.38; 5.31; 10.43; 13.38; 26.18.

61. James A. Sanders ('Isaiah in Luke', in *Luke and Scripture*, 23, 24–5) writes, 'Here is a word tally in the Lukan passage: the Jubilee will come at a time *acceptable to God*; and the prophet who wrests a prophetic challenge to his own people out of their identifying traditions, precisely by the hermeneutic of the freedom of God as Creator of all peoples, is himself *not acceptable to them*.[...] The passage stresses what is acceptable to God, not what is acceptable to the faithful: it disengages any thought that God's agenda must follow Israel's.'

62. So John O. York, *The Last Shall Be First: The Rhetoric of Reversal in Luke* (JSNTS 46; Sheffield: JSOT Press, 1991), 172.

of the proper use of possessions in Luke-Acts the Jerusalem community-of-goods arises as one instantiation. The picture of the community-of-goods in Acts 2.42-47 and 4.32–5.11 is actually more complex than this: there is a melding of at least two known variations of practicing a community of life and goods, and, in the second summary, an example of disciplinary action via divine execution.

4.2.2.1. The Character of the Christian Community-of-Goods
Justin Taylor draws attention to the variations in community-of-goods practices represented in Acts 2.44-45 and 4.32-35.[63] Taylor compares the practices of these kinds of communities among the early Jerusalem messianists with the practice among the Essenes[64] and the Pythagoreans. He concludes that there are references to at least three types of practices: (1) an absolute community-of-goods with formal sharing,[65] (2) sharing private goods made accessible to one's 'friends',[66] and finally, (3) a community welfare fund maintained by voluntary donations.[67]

Taylor begins by examining the description of 2.44-45, and suggests that the phrase 'they had all things in common' should be taken literally. For Taylor, like Brian Capper, both the community at Qumran and Jesus' followers formed *actual* communities of common life and goods. He sees a similar version in Acts 4.34-35, but juxtaposed with the 'friendship' maxim in 4.32, connected by Luke's redactional link in 4.33, a third type of communal practice is created. Following Capper, Taylor suggests that the stories of Barnabas and Ananias and Sapphira require a:

> situation where property initially belongs to an individual, who has full rights over it, including the price obtained for its sale, but which then becomes in full the property of the community, in such a way that the previous owner has no right to retain it.[...]

---

63. Taylor, 'Community of Goods', 147–61. Capper ('Community of Goods', 1773; 'Palestinian Cultural Context', 352–3, 55) recognizes the different descriptions among the Essenes, but does not develop this theme.

64. Taylor utilizes data from Josephus, Philo, and the Dead Sea Scrolls, thus indicating his assumption that the Qumran documents represent Essene communities.

65. Acts 2.44-45; 4.34-35; 1QS 6.13-25.

66. Acts 4.32; Essenes in Josephus, *J.W.* 2.127; the Pythagoreans in Iamb. *V.P.* 30.167–69; Plato's Guardians *Rep.* 3.416d, 5.462c. The community-of-goods is not entirely consistent in Plato's *Republic*. See the entire discussion in 414d–20b; Cf. also 464d, 543b; *Crit.* 110d; *Tim.* 18b; and the criticism in Aristotle *Pol.* 2.1261a–1263b. See Darrell Dobbs, 'Aristotle's Anticommunism', *AJPS* 29 (1985): 29–46; Capper, 'Reciprocity', 507–8, n. 36; Dawson, *Cities*, 42–3, 93–9; Ferguson, *Utopias*, 64–7; Johnson, *Sharing Possessions*, 124–5; Mitchell, 'New Testament Evidence', 241 nn. 63, 70.

67. The result of the Lukan redaction of the material in Acts 4.32-35; CD 14.11b-16; Philo's Essenes in *Hypoth.* 11.4–11. Philo's treatise *Hypothetica* is preserved only in Eusebius' *Praep. evang.* 8.11.1–19. See §5.2.1. below. Capper ('Palestinian Context', 352) makes a comparison of the daily meal-fellowship of the Essenes described by Philo in this text with the Christian distribution in Acts 6.1-6.

So a candidate who presented part of his property, while declaring that it was the whole, would be embezzling the community that had acquired provisional rights to the whole property, as well as making false declaration.⁶⁸

Applying this logic to the Ananias and Sapphira episode, Taylor writes,

> It seems reasonable to think that Ananias, with the consent of his wife, made such a transfer of their assets upon entering the community described in Acts 2:44–45 but kept back part, although they were obliged to hand over all and declared that they were doing so.⁶⁹

Capper, who offers a more extensive argument for the thesis represented in the summary of Taylor above, utilizes *The Community Rule* (1QS) from Khirbet Qumrân to 'fill in the gaps' of Luke's narrative summary and illustrations.⁷⁰ Capper's primary agenda is to offer evidence for the historicity of Luke's presentation of the formal property-sharing in the earliest Jerusalem community. While working from the premise that the early Christian community designated itself in a fashion similar to the community portrayed in *The Community Rule*,⁷¹ he looks at the episode with Ananias and suggests that this situation is best explained as the failure of a novitiate in the initiation ritual of becoming integrated as a full member into the community, which included the formal sharing of goods. Drawing a parallel between the description found in 1QS 6.13-23,⁷² where after a fifth stage in the initiation process the candidate surrenders his property to be accounted for and kept distinct (for the safety of the community *and* the novitiate),

---

68. Taylor, 'Community of Goods', 158. See Capper, 'Acts 5.4', 117–31; 'Community of Goods', 1741–52; 'In der Hand des Ananias', 230–5; 'Palestinian Cultural Context', 337–40.
69. Taylor, 'Community of Goods', 158.
70. See the incisive challenge from Richard Bauckham, ('The Early Jerusalem Church, Qumran, and the Essenes', in *The Dead Sea Scrolls as Background to Postbiblical Judaism and Early Christianity: Papers from an International Conference at St. Andrews in 2001* [ed. James R. Davila; STDJ 46; Leiden: Brill, 2003], 65, 71, 78, 84, 87–9) following Gabriele Boccaccini (*Beyond the Essene Hypothesis: The Parting of the Ways between Qumran and Enochic Judaism* [Grand Rapids: Eerdmans, 1998]) who argues that the Qumran sect broke off from mainline Essenism, and therefore its sectarian documents would have had little influence outside the sect. Also, relevant but dated is Leander E. Keck, 'The Poor Among the Saints in Jewish Christianity and Qumran', ZNW 57 (1966): 54–78.
71. Capper follows Max Wilcox (*The Semitisms of Acts* [Oxford: Clarendon Press, 1965], 93–100) with the observation that ἦσαν ἐπὶ τὸ αὐτό at Acts 2.44 reflects the semitic idiom להיות ליחד ('to be together') found in 1QS. The 'together' was for the Essenes a technical term designating the Essene community. It is possible that the phrase εἶχον παντα κοινά was an epexegetical expression to explain the more semitic phrase not able to carry in Greek the technical significance which it had in its semitic source. Wilcox also argued that the Greek προσετίθει...ἐπὶ τὸ αὐτό ('to add together') in Acts 2.47 reflects the semitic Qumran idiom להוסיף ליחד.
72. For the assessment of 1QS and the various stages of initiation, see below §5.3.2.2.

the candidate can experience the common life with the prerogative to reject it before the process is complete. A sixth stage includes the merging of the goods into the community treasury, and only then the candidate becomes a full member of the community. Thus,

> Peter's point [in his rhetorical questions of Acts 5.4] is that Ananias had abused the very procedure which was designed to protect him. To keep some insurance expressed mistrust of the Church and a selfishness which opposed the whole ethic of the group. Yet more seriously, it meant premeditated dishonesty and deception in the course of a ceremony central to the community's life.[73]

Thus, Ananias being in the stages between initial conversion and full surrender has sinned a crime falling 'awkwardly between embezzlement and deception'.[74] Capper is correct to point out that the actions of Barnabas and Ananias and Sapphira were not supererogatory, but rather in line with what is presented as common practice of the entire community.[75] Capper is surely also correct to point to the fact that the actions of laying the proceeds at the apostles' feet was more than an *ad hoc* gesture.[76] The repetition of the action[77] points to a ritual gesture, adding a sacred significance to the submission of the possessions and profits.

Both Capper and Taylor relegate Luke's compositional strategy and narrative logic to an enigma in the placement of the story of Ananias and Sapphira, proposing that it fits better with and originally accompanied the first summary in 2.44-45.[78] Perhaps Capper and Taylor too quickly configure

---

73. Capper, 'Community of Goods', 1747. Cf. idem, 'Community of Goods', 337–8: 'If Acts 5:4 indicates that the donation of property by Ananias and Sapphira was seen by Peter as voluntary, this may not actually contradict the existence of formal community of property with the earliest church in Jerusalem. Community of property can be both voluntary and formally organized [...] Ananias and Sapphira were under no compulsion to enter this inner group, but if they wanted to, they had to obey its rules, which they signally failed to do by withholding some of their property.'

74. Capper 'Acts 5.4', 128. Capper ('In der Hand des Ananias') draws further evidence of this initiation process in the phrase ἐν τῇ σῇ ἐξουσίᾳ, which he mounts evidence is a technical accounting term equal to בידך, literally 'in the hand'. 'Hand' in Biblical Hebrew, argues Capper, carries the connotation of 'power' or 'authority' in the economic sense. See Capper, 'Community of Goods', 1747–50.

75. See Capper, 'Acts 5.4', 118; idem, 'Community of Goods', 1742–3; idem, 'Palestinian Cultural Context', 340 (where he concedes that surrender of major lands may have been rare). See Richter Reimer, *Women*, 13; and Pilgrim, *Good News*, 152, who holds together Barnabas as a model to imitate and as a norm for the entire community.

76. Capper, 'Acts 5.4', 120–1; idem, 'Community of Goods', 1744–52; idem, 'Palestinian Cultural Context', 337–40; see Havelaar, 'Hellenistic Parallels', 77; Strelan, *Strange Acts*, 204.

77. Acts 4.35, 37; 5.2.

78. Capper ('Community of Goods', 1740) writes, 'I would make so bold as to suggest that the original Semitic statement concerning the יחד and, therefore, the property-sharing which that pattern of social organization entailed, was the original introduction to the story of Ananias and Sapphira, for which it would have provided the necessary preamble. The story as a whole, probably passed from Hebrew or Aramaic into Greek before it reached

Luke's presentation of the early Jerusalem community-of-goods to the description of *The Community Rule*.[79] This is a common tendency since the discovery of the scrolls at Khirbet Qumrân, and particularly to summarily relate the death of Ananias and Sapphira with the disciplinary measures in 1QS 6.24-25.[80] Certainly Luke views the messianic community as open to outsiders (in contrast to the Qumran sectarians), in fact, appealing for them to join.[81] Furthermore, the community did not harbour protected secrets or mysteries. What is also certain is that Luke was not emphasizing a progressive initiation ritual in Acts 4.32–5.11. While contemporary discourse surrounding communities-of-goods included descriptions of similar initiation rituals (as with the Pythagoreans and the Essenes presented below), and therefore such may have contributed to the presupposition pool and expectancy for the literary *topos*, Luke's emphasis is on the authority of Peter and the divine sanction of his indictment for transgressing the ethos, and finally on the twice repeated 'fear' (Acts 5.5, 11) that resulted from the incident among those that heard. Finally, as noted by Taylor above, the text itself proffers Ananias and Sapphira as an example of the third type of practice of shared goods. Thus an absolute community-of-goods is not indispensible to Luke's depiction. The ethos is defined by a disposition of generosity and unity,

---

Luke's hands. The author of Acts, however, is responsible for detaching the introduction and using it as a building-block in his summaries, first at 2.44-45, and then, in a rather more stylized version, at 4.32 and 34.'

Taylor ('Community of Goods', 158) writes, 'The story [of Ananias and Sapphira] should therefore be associated, like that of Barnabas, with the first summary, 2:44–45, which describes a strict community of goods. Why Luke placed it after the second summary, where he seems to intend to describe a less strict practice, one can only guess. Perhaps he merely wanted to fill out his description with two exemplary narratives, one positive, the other negative.'

79. See the criticisms from Ascough, 'Benefaction', 94–5; Marguerat, 'Ananias and Sapphira', 163. Havelaar, 'Hellenistic Parallels', 76–7, defends Capper's position.

80. See as general parallels, Sherman E. Johnson, 'The Dead Sea Manual of Discipline and the Jerusalem Church of Acts', *ZAW* 66 (1954): 106–20; reprinted in *The Scrolls and the New Testament* (ed. Krister Stendahl; New York: Crossroad, 1992), esp. 130–6, 141–2 (subsequent page numbers from reprint); Richter Reimer, *Women*, 18–19; and for analogy of disciplinary actions, Göran Forkman, *The Limits of the Religious Community: Expulsion from the Religious Community within the Qumran Sect, within Rabbinic Judaism, and within Primitive Christianity* (Lund: CWK Gleerup, 1972), 173; and J. Gwyn Griffiths, *The Divine Verdict: A Study of Divine Judgment in the Ancient Religions* (SHR 52; Leiden: Brill, 1991), 122.

81. See the summary statement of Martin Hengel apropos to Acts regarding early Christian attitudes toward proselytizing mission, 'Die Ursprünge der christlichen Mission', *NTS* 18 (1971), 38: 'History and theology of the early Christians is "missions-history" and "missions-theology". A church and theology that forgets or denies the missionary message, as a messenger of salvation in a world threatened by evil, abandons itself and its reason for being.' ('Geschichte und Theologie des Urchristentums sind "Missionsgeschichte" und "Missionstheologie". Eine Kirche und Theologie, die die missionarische Sendung als Boten des Heils in eine vom Unheil bedrohte Welt vergißt oder verleugnet, gibt ihren Grund und damit sich selber auf.')

aiming to eradicate need.⁸² This does not denigrate the symbolic nature of the giving nor delegitimize the ritual represented.

With the amount of space dedicated to the Ananias and Sapphira episode, Luke signals the importance of the couple's demise, God's solemn protection of the messianic community, and the result of reverent fear among all those who heard. In the case of (e)utopian communities-of-goods it becomes a matter of life and death, a thesis that is strengthened below with the examples of the discourse as it appears among the Pythagorean and Essene traditions. Before this, it is beneficial to inquire into the severity of the couple's punishment and how this contributes to Luke's engagement with the community-of-goods discourse.

4.2.2.2. Discipline and Extirpation

What precisely is the couple's sin? And why does it merit such severe divine retribution? Peter's direct accusations include lying to the Holy Spirit and keeping back some of the profit of the sale of the land (5.3), lying to God (5.4), and putting the Spirit of the Lord to the test (5.9). The combination of three factors contributed to the severe execution of divine judgement upon the deceitful couple: (1) the context of the community-of-goods with its associated disciplinary practices of excommunication, (2) the sanctity and guarantee on the community with the presence of the Holy Spirit, and (3) the fact that transgressing both of these – the (e)utopian ethos and holy communion with the divine – often resulted in death, either social or physical.

The first factor will be demonstrated more fully as other instantiations of the community-of-goods discourse are explored below. It can be suggested here that the Ananias and Sapphira episode is an example of the consequences of failing the trust of the (e)utopian communal ethos, in fact counterfeiting the unity of the messianists' ethos by their conspiratorial deception.⁸³ In the Pythagorean tradition, failing the rigorous initiation process resulted in a social death.⁸⁴ Josephus portrays expulsion from the Essene community in dire and near fatal terms.⁸⁵ The regulations for discipline in *The Community Rule* (1QS 6.24-25) are less severe, but indicate the association of exclusion and punitive retribution.⁸⁶

Henriette Havelaar, in a search for Hellenistic parallels to the Ananias and Sapphira episode, offers the most imaginative proposal yet regarding the generic form of the text.⁸⁷ Havelaar's innovative conclusion is this: '[W]e encounter here in the Ananias and Sapphira story a highly stylized form of excommunication given shape with the help of the literary form of the rule

---

82. This is also stressed by Pilgrim, *Good News*, 149–50, 151.
83. See below on §8.1.2., comment on Acts 5.1 discussing how Ananias and Sapphira form a subversive challenge by counterfeiting the unity of the Jerusalem messianists.
84. See §5.1.4. below.
85. See §5.2.1.4. below.
86. See §5.3.2.2. below.
87. Havelaar, 'Hellenistic Parallels', 63–82.

miracle of punishment.'[88] Havelaar draws from Gerd Theissen and Rudolf Pesch for the form-critical designation of a rule miracle of punishment.

Theissen designates the Ananias and Sapphira episode as the only rule miracle of punishment in the New Testament.[89] He defines rule miracles as those which 'seek to reinforce sacred prescriptions. They may be classified according as they justify rules, reward behaviour in accordance with the rules or punish behaviour contrary to the rules'.[90] After briefly surveying some examples of rule miracles in Hellenistic and Jewish sources, he concludes:

> [I]n the Jewish rule miracles the issue is almost always one of life or death. Breaches of the law lead to death; observance of the law preserves from death. The law does not chastise; it kills.[...I]t is a sign of great seriousness about the observance of the divine will: *in the presence of God the issue is one of life or death* [emphasis added]. The Greek punishment miracles are more humane, more educative, and this is certainly no accident.[91]

As a result of this construal, Havelaar identifies the sin of Ananias and Sapphira as blasphemy: 'If we read the crime of Ananias and Sapphira as a far more severe offense than the lying about the value of their property, their sudden cruel death seems more proportionate to the crime.'[92]

Havelaar also follows Pesch in his exposition of the elements of the 'punishing norms miracle' (*Normenwunder*) or 'penal miracle' (*Strafwunder*). Pesch lays out the characteristics, with their corresponding verses in Acts, as such:

> *Intro*: (*1*) description of the setting and introduction of the main characters (5:1); (*2*) the violation of the norm, the action punishable, the appearance of the first transgressor (5:2); *Center*: (*3*) the 'penal word' from the authority figure representing the norm (5:3–4) (in detail: [a] the speech introduction, [b] an address, [c] the reproach with responsible statement, [d] and argument to the grounds of the reproach, [e] another reproach with renewed responsibility statement); (*4*) the stating of the punishment (5:5a); *the End*: (*5*) an admiration motif ('fear') (5:5b); (*6*) the demonstration of the penal miracle (5:6).

The second half of the pattern is varied in Acts:

---

88. Havelaar, 'Hellenistic Parallels', 82, from the abstract. Gerd Lüdemann, (*Early Christianity According to the Traditions in Acts: A Commentary* [trans. John Bowden; London: SCM, 1989], 66; *The Acts of the Apostles: What Really Happened in the Earliest Days of the Church* [Amherst, NY: Prometheus Books, 2005], 80–1) proposes the historical nucleus of the story was about a member who offended against sacred law and was therefore expelled by the head of the community.

89. Gerd Theissen, *The Miracle Stories of the Early Christian Tradition* (ed. John Riches; trans. Francis McDonagh; Philadelphia: Fortress, 1983), 109.

90. Theissen, *Miracle Stories*, 106.

91. Theissen, *Miracle Stories*, 110.

92. Havelaar, 'Hellenistic Parallels', 79. Havelaar goes on to suggest that the crime was more of an intentional violation of the eighth and ninth commandments of the Decalogue.

Intro: (*1*) situation info, and appearance of the confident (5:7); (*2*) questioning the confident by the authority representing the norm (5:8a–b) (in detail: [a] speech intro, [b] question concerning the true circumstances); (*3*) answer of the confident (5:8:c–d) (in detail: [a] speech intro, [b] answer: lie); *Center*: (*4*) 'Penal word' from authority representing norm (v.9) (in detail: [a] speech intro, [b] reproach with responsibility statement (in question form), [c] announcement of punishment with demonstration); (*5*) stating the punishment (5:10a); *The End*: (*6*) demonstration (5:10b); (*7*) admiration motif (5:11).[93]

Pesch interprets the summary theologically, seeing the community practice as the concretizing of the resurrection of Jesus (4.33) and the fulfilment of eschatological promises rather than realizing some utopian ideal.[94] He does not explicitly detail the normative practice of a formal sharing of goods, but rather stresses the voluntary nature of the giving.[95] 'The narrative wants to maintain rather that the Christian community is the place of freedom where no one is forced to lie or shall be so. The distinction between "life" and "death" serves to encourage the freedom: Choose life!'(my translation).[96]

Havelaar continues with a hardly parallel anthology of examples illustrating divinely instigated death and lying to, cheating, or offending a deity. The examples offered include a man who is driven mad for disbelieving in the healing power of a statue,[97] a man who is denied offspring for not returning money entrusted to him by foreigners,[98] a man who is bitten by a fish because he does not keep his vow to give 10 per cent of his earnings to Asclepius,[99] a banker who is punished by death for withholding money entrusted to him,[100]

---

93. Rudolf Pesch, *Die Apostelgeschichte (Apg 1-12)* (EKKNT V/1; Zürich: Benziger Verlag, 1986), 195. See Theissen, *Miracle Stories*, 72–4; Williams, *Miracle Stories*, 28–30.

94. Pesch, *Apostelgeschichte*, 186–8, compares the Qumran writings and Acts, pointing out the reference to Deut. 15.4 in Acts 4.34, and citing 1QS 1.11-13 as pointing to the biblical tradition as the primary intertext.

95. This leaves his form-critical analysis susceptible to the critique of Witherington (*Acts*, 218–19) that if they were under no obligation to give, this could not have been a rule miracle, violating a sacred rule, law, or taboo. Witherington affirms the possibility of a punitive miracle (218), but mitigates this claim in siding with Derrett ('Right of Property') in his psychologizing explanation of death by shock (216).

96. Pesch, *Apostelgeschichte*, 203, 'Die Erzählung will vielmehr behaupten, daß die christliche Gemeinde der Ort von Freiheit ist, an dem niemand zur Lüge genötigt wird bzw. werden darf. Die Unterscheidung von »Leben« und »Tod« in der Gemeinde dient der Ermutigung der Freiheit: Wähle das Leben!'.

97. Havelaar, 'Hellenistic Parallels', 67–8, citing Lucian, *Philops* 20.1–26. Of the various comparisons Havelaar makes between this and the Ananias and Sapphira story, the most convincing is the miraculous punishment.

98. Havelaar, 'Hellenistic Parallels', 68–9, citing Herodotus, *Hist*. 6.86. In both there is lying about money, but the punishments being compared by the fact that they are 'extreme' seems to be a stretch.

99. Havelaar, 'Hellenistic Parallels', 69–70. See literature cited there.

100. Havelaar, 'Hellenistic Parallels', 70–1. See literature cited there. Helpful parallels are the immediate death by divine judgement and the crime of perjury with regard to an economic situation.

and various mentions of perjurious lying to a god.¹⁰¹ Havelaar rejects any Old Testament parallels outright, stating that they simply do not convince.¹⁰² Combining the strengths of previous interpretations, each stressing either the rule miracle of punishment or the social act of excommunication, Havelaar suggests that Luke has presented the *content* of an excommunication story in the *form* of a rule miracle of punishment. For Havelaar, the most pertinent Hellenistic parallel to the episode in Acts is the Pythagorean excommunication of failed novitiates. Both are consequences of failing the community-of-goods ethos, both are fatal (literally or socially), and both are permanent, without recourse to appeal. Havelaar's thesis furthers the discussion a great deal, but the limited scope of the essay to Greco-Roman parallels precludes examination of the Jewish stream of tradition, which is indispensable for Luke's story.¹⁰³

There is, in fact, precedent for the severity of the couple's punishment, not only in the death of Judas,¹⁰⁴ but also in Peter's warning to those who 'do not heed' the Prophet like Moses (Acts 3.22-23). Peter warns with language alluding to Lev. 23.29 LXX, 'And it shall be that every person that does not heed the prophet shall be utterly destroyed from among the people' (Acts 3.23). Johnson construes the deaths of Ananias and Sapphira as 'fulfillment' of Peter's threat, as 'an immediate fulfillment in the narrative [...] where the failure to heed the prophetic authority of the Apostles leads to ultimate extermination from the people, death'.¹⁰⁵ While Johnson's proposal makes sense out of the wider co-text of the story, taking into account the conflict

---

101. Havelaar, 'Hellenistic Parallels', 71–3. Citations are from Plato, Ovid, Sextus, Appian, and Virgil.

102. Havelaar, 'Hellenistic Parallels', 73, n. 31. Havelaar does find possibility in the excommunication of a rabbi eventually leading to the death of his brother-in-law in *Baba Metzi'a* 59b. Recognized are the various criteria that could be established to consider a parallel: 'An ideal parallel [...] would be a text in which exactly the same events are described, with other main characters. Such a parallel has not been found' (64). Yet, with the criteria and examples Havelaar presents, it is unclear why the parallel with Achan in Josh. 7 is rejected, who is guilty of misusing wealth, transgresses a communal norm (the 'ban'), and is punished by death. In the Achan episode we have (1) the description of the setting and introduction of the main figures (Achan, Joshua and Israel attacking Ai, Josh. 7.1, 2-5); (2) the actual trespass of a certain rule (withholding possessions under the 'ban', 7.1, 11); (3) the 'Strafwort' from an authority holding the rather precisely formulated assumptions by which the offender is judged as guilty (YHWH's rebuke to the interceding Joshua, 7.13-15, 20-21); (4) the punishment (Achan and everything associated with him is stoned, 7.24-25); (5) the admiration motif (missing in Josh.); and (6) the demonstration (a heap of stones raised as a memorial, 7.26). Compare Havelaar's application of Pesch's model to the Ananias segment (66). Granted, Achan does not die via direct miraculous divine punishment, nor is there the admiration motif ('great fear'), but this episode offers a closer parallel *in form* to the Ananias and Sapphira narrative than any of the Hellenistic narratives Havelaar offers.

103. With Williams' (*Miracle Stories*, 62 n. 15) critique of Havelaar. Compare Williams' (*Miracle Stories*, 29–30) description of *semitic* punitive miracle.

104. See §8.1.1. below.

105. Johnson, *Literary Function*, 192; see 205; idem, *Acts*, 92–3.

motif, it is not nuanced enough for the actual indictment laid down by Peter, lying to and testing the (Holy) Spirit.

William Horbury has expounded the tradition of 'excommunication and extirpation ("cutting off from community")' in the Scriptures of Israel and later Jewish traditions.[106] Arguing for evidence of an actual practice of excommunication in Second Temple Judaism, Horbury suggests that the practice of exclusion was associated with two overlapping Pentateuchal contexts: admission to the temple congregation and loyalty to the covenant.[107] He argues that 'in the case of the covenant [...] exclusion was a surrogate for, or preliminary to, the death penalty'.[108] As with the biblical tradition, according to Horbury, in later pre-rabbinic and rabbinic tradition, '[f]ailure to uphold certain observances and belief has throughout incurred [...] a penalty which in theory and sometimes in practice is capital, but which is represented or prepared for by excommunication'.[109] With evidence of this practice, and the precedent from the scriptural texts, it is probable that excommunication as a means of preparing for or resulting in death would have been included in the cultural repertoire of Luke's account of the death of Ananias and Sapphira. In other words, Havelaar is correct in the inventive fusion of the *content* of excommunication and the *form* of a rule miracle of punishment.

However, it is not enough to identify the sin as *blasphemy* and assume that this then explains the severity of the retribution.[110] It is necessary to give attention to the peculiar context of the community-of-goods discourse *and* the eschatological context of the Spirit's presence. It is the combination of the Spirit's guarantee upon the messianic community and the context of communal life and goods which bears upon the execution of divine judgement in this instance. If the mass of evidence surveyed by Chaniotis for Asia Minor is analogous to the sentiments of the wider Mediterranean milieu, it was

---

106. William Horbury, 'Extirpation and Excommunication', in *Jews and Christians in Contact and Controversy* (Edinburgh: T&T Clark, 1998), 43–66.

107. Horbury, 'Extirpation', 46–9.

108. Horbury, 'Extirpation', 46; cf. 47, 48, 55–9, 62, 63, 66. See Forkman (*Limits*, 33) in his study of expulsion and the Old Testament, 'expulsion and death as a rule coincide – either in that one put the deviator to death, or that the execution of the punishment is transferred to a higher power'.

109. Horbury, 'Extirpation', 66. Horbury ('Extirpation', 59–62) notes how 'extirpation' (Heb. כרת) was used as (1) a penalty guard for covenantal signs and festival observance, (2) divinely or humanly inflicted death penalty, and (3) as dispossession. He concludes, 'Extirpation, as the covenantal death penalty for which exclusion could prepare or substitute, was thus distinct from, yet linked with, excommunication' (62).

110. While there may be some echoes of Luke 12.10 with the unforgivable sin of blaspheming the Holy Spirit, the different contexts militate against equating the admonition of Jesus with the judgement against the couple. Jesus speaks of a context of confessional testimony and synagogal trial (Luke 12.8-12), whereas the Ananias and Sapphira episode is concerned with inner-communal discipline. Correctly noted by Acough, 'Benefaction', 92 n. 2.

expected for the deity to punish wrongdoers in everyday life.[111] Furthermore, in the ancient world the pollution of disobedience was understood as contagious, threatening to contaminate the entire community. Therefore, in this sense, Strelan is surely correct: 'It is the holiness of God and the holiness of the Spirit of the Lord against which Ananias and Sapphira sin. That, in turn, means that the holiness of the community is affected. [...S]o Peter must root out Ananias and Sapphira and purify the new Israel.'[112]

What is the significance of the eschatological context? On this issue, Forkman is instructive. Forkman's study of expulsion from ancient Jewish communities is guided by three crucial questions: (1) Which deviations brought about expulsion?, (2) How was the expelling carried out? and (3) Which theological motifs were connected with expulsion?[113] In his treatment of the Scriptures of Israel, he notes that two motifs dominate the texts: holiness and covenant. Thus, as in Horbury's study, covenant is a common stream in the various discourses. However, in Luke-Acts the theme of (Mosaic) covenant is pushed to the background,[114] overshadowed by the proclamation of the in-breaking kingdom of God and the mediation of Israel's relationship with the God of Israel through the Prophet-Messiah, Jesus.[115] Forkman's comments are relevant to the Ananias and Sapphira episode when he writes:

> That the kingdom of God was near, also meant a need for decision.[...] This need for a decision at the prospect of the coming kingdom explains the 'intolerant' feature in

---

111. See Chaniotis, 'Watchful Eyes', 7, 9, 11, 18, 19, 21, 22, 24, 33, 39, 43. See also Hendrik S. Versnel, 'Beyond Cursing: The Appeal to Judice in Judicial Prayers', in *Magika Hiera: Ancient Greek Magic and Religion* (eds Christopher A. Faraone and Dirk Obbink; Oxford: Oxford University Press, 1991), 60–106. Versnel concludes, 'It appears that in these [Greek and Latin] regions people had a choice of options when it came to interacting with the supernatural; the fact that in the case of a justified complaint they so often opted for the deferential judicial prayer instead of the traditional *defixio* [binding spell] speaks volumes about their belief in divine power and its direct involvement in human affairs' (93).

112. Strelan, *Strange Acts*, 200; see 208. The extermination of Achan's family in Joshua 7 illustrates this point. On the potentially contagious nature of pollution, see also, for example, Chaniotis, 'Watchful Eyes', 2–3; E. R. Dodds, *The Greeks and the Irrational* (Sather Classical Lectures 25; Berkeley: University of California Press, 1951), 35–8, 43–8; Forkman, *Limits*, 28–9, 32; Griffiths, *Divine Verdict*, 78–85, 90, 93; Gary G. Miles and Garry Trompf, 'Luke and Antiphon: The Theology of Acts 27–28 in Light of Pagan Beliefs about Divine Retribution, Pollution, and Shipwreck', *HTR* 69 (1976): 260–1, 262, 263.

113. Forkman, *Limits*, 12–14, *passim*.

114. This feature of Luke's narrative has caused Robert F. O'Toole ('Acts 2:30 and the Davidic Covenant of Pentecost', *JBL* 102 [1983]: 246, 250, 256) to erroneously exclude the role of the Sinai covenant in Luke's portrayal of Pentecost, and Luke's wider theology: 'Although the Sinai covenant appears in his Institution Narrative [Luke 22.20] and in Acts 7.38, Luke has not worked this covenant into his theology' (257). I suggest that it is worked into Luke's theology through the recurrent motif of the blessing and cursing, now enacted through relationship to the risen Christ. The Mosaic covenant is not neglected, it is transformed.

115. See Forkman, *Limits*, 188–90.

the Jesus fellowship. Only he who puts aside everything else is 'fit for the kingdom of God' and can enter into the Jesus fellowship (Luke 9:62). Because of this there is no trace of partial expulsion in the synoptics either. In the same way as one cannot partially join the kingdom of God, one cannot be expelled partially from the Christian community either.[116]

Luke's propensity to portray allegiance to the kingdom as exclusive is demonstrated not only with the injunctions against sharing allegiances in Jesus' teachings,[117] but also the polarizing proclamation of Peter.[118] The kingdom of God, with its exclusive claims, has been established in a preliminary way with the resurrection-ascension-exaltation of Jesus to the right hand of the Father (Acts 2.32-36).[119] The community-of-goods, as a concrete expression of the apostolic witness to the resurrection (Acts 4.33) is a prolepsis of the eschatological blessing of the reign of God,[120] and with it, the eschatological judgement of that which is opposed to the kingdom. Ananias (and by inference, Sapphira) having a heart filled by Satan, has aligned himself with all that will be eradicated in the age to come. The cosmic struggle between the Holy Spirit and Satan, waging in the exchange between Peter and the deviant couple, results in a final victory and an ultimate defeat. As the corpses of Ananias and Sapphira are carried across the threshold of the door (Acts 5.9b) they are removed from the locus of God's presence. In this incident, unique within Luke-Acts, failure of the divine harmony results not in mere expulsion from the community household or relational space, but ultimately in extermination.[121]

4.3. Summary and Looking Ahead

In summary, the moral universe of the early Jerusalem messianists' community-of-goods was framed by a sense of a new relationship of the Household of God, who is Benevolent Father, established by the way of Jesus. The gift of the Spirit was both the model and the enablement for the proper use of possessions for the benefit of the community. In the case of the nascent community of the followers of Jesus established in Jerusalem, Luke

---

116. Forkman, *Limits*, 189.
117. Luke 9.57-61; 11.33-36; 14.26-35; 16.13; 18.24-25.
118. Acts 2.38-40; 4.19-20; 5.29-32.
119. On the resurrection-ascension-exaltation complex, see below §7.1.3.
120. See Marguerat's ('Ananias', 163) interpretation of the significance of the term ἐκκλησία used for the first time in Acts 5.11: 'ἐκκλησία here designates the community of Jerusalem as a prototype of the eschatological community of salvation'.
121. Similarly Havelaar ('Hellenistic Parallels', 80) concludes, 'Ananias and Sapphira died miraculously from no observable causes, they fell suddenly, they were carried out by the young men and were buried immediately. This procedure neither matches the officially ordained "death penalty" as mentioned by Josephus, nor the pseudo-burial as depicted by Iamblichus. At the same time, *the effect of the couple's death is clear: they were definitely expelled from the community* [emphasis added], which, as noted at the end of the story, reacted with great fear.'

presents them as actualizing a (e)utopian-friendship ethos. With this ethos came expectations of laudatory praise for the embodied ideal, as well as a severe discipline for those who broke the rules.

The question regarding the sin of the couple and the proportionate sanction is clarified by due attention to the discursive context, both socio-culturally and theologically. Both the (e)utopian-friendship ethos and the presence of the Holy Spirit bear down on the consequences of the couple's lie. Luke is not presenting a pattern here for imitation, and therefore it is not proposed here that Luke was suggesting that every transgression in a Christian community-of-goods would have resulted in death. Luke does not present a pattern or principle. His narrative is not reducible to such, but as a dramatic unfolding of a plot it engages the community-of-goods discourse in its cultural milieu and offers a distinctive illustration of the swift execution of divine judgement and protection of the community.[122] In light of Theissen's study, the Ananias and Sapphira episode is an encapsulation of the intersection of Jewish and Hellenistic culture: the (e)utopian-friendship *topos* is melded with the life-or-death solemnity of transgressing divine law.

What has also come to light is the association of certain linguistic conventions surrounding the community-of-goods discourse, especially the positive (and parenetic) appeal of the practice and the expectation for severe and potentially irreversible disciplinary measures. This points to the fact that Peter's words are uttered in a quasi-judicial setting, and would have carried the force of more than just an informative rebuke. The supposition of linguistic conventions can only be tentative at this stage, but will be strengthened with the survey of the Hellenistic and Jewish examples below.

---

122. Strelan (*Strange Acts*, 205–6) aptly summarizes: 'We can safely conclude that in both Jewish and non-Jewish communities deceit, duplicity, and infidelity in matters of financial trust were seen as very serious crimes and were punished severely.'

Chapter 5

SOCIO-HISTORICAL REPERTOIRE II:
PAGAN AND JEWISH EXAMPLES

This chapter discusses the discursive conventions associated with the community-of-goods *topoi* in traditions surrounding the Pythagorean and Essene groups, as well as the literary instantiations of the practice in the Dead Sea Scrolls. This chapter further argues that Luke's negative illustration in the episode of Ananias and Sapphira is not as 'strange' in the ancient world as it may appear in modern contemporary context. The examples surveyed below show a widespread literary repertoire which prepared ancient readers to expect both laudatory esteem and severe discipline associated with the (e)utopian ethos of community-of-goods discourse.

5.1. The Divine Economy of the Pythagoreans

For many in the Mediterranean region the epitome of the Hellenistic ideal community was embodied in the traditions regarding Pythagoras of Samos (c. 570–480 BCE) and his secretive religio-mathematical community.[1] Traditions surrounding this charismatic saint-philosopher and his followers included a (e)utopian community-of-goods with intensive communal solidarity and fidelity. Issues regarding the 'historical Pythagoras' are far beyond the scope of this study; we are more concerned with the discursive conventions and literary *topoi* arising from and feeding into the traditions.[2] More specifically, I

---

1. Johan Thom ('"Don't Walk on the Highways": The Pythagorean *Akousmata* and early Christian Literature', *JBL* 113 [1994]: 93 [93–112]) notes how 'the revival of Pythagorean ideas that gained momentum in the first century BC should be of great interest to NT scholars'. Thom's article covers only the transmission and interpretation of the 'oral sayings' (ἀκούσματα).

2. See W. K. C. Guthrie (*A History of Greek Philosophy. Vol. 1: The Earlier Presocratics and the Pythagoreans* [Cambridge: Cambridge University Press, 1962], 146 and n. 1) who deems the history of Pythagoreanism as 'perhaps the most controversial subject in all Greek philosophy': 'No one can claim to have plumbed [...] "the bottomless pit" of research on the Pythagoreans.'

See the brief history of research in Walter Burkert, *Lore and Science in Ancient Pythagoreanism* (trans. E. L. Minar, Jr; Cambridge, MA: Harvard University Press, 1972),

examine the discourse regarding the community-of-goods and the communal discipline for transgressing the community ethos.³ It is important to discuss the moral universe framing the practice of shared goods among the Pythagoreans, but first we must note the problems and limitations of sources.

5.1.1. The Problems and Limitations of the Sources

When comparing Lukan discourse on the early messianists' community-of-goods with the similar discourse of Pythagorean community-of-goods one is confronted with divergence of the nature and date of the sources for the latter.⁴ The primary extant sources for the traditions of Pythagoras and his community are the *Lives* of Diogenes Laertius (c. 225–50 CE),⁵ Porphyry (c. 233–305 CE),⁶

1–14; David L. Balch, 'Neopythagorean Moralists and the New Testament Household Codes', *ANRW* II. 26.1 (1996): 381–9; and Holger Thesleff, 'The Pythagoreans in the Light and Shadows of Recent Research', in *Mysticism: Based on Papers read at the Symposium on Mysticism held at Åbo on the 7th–9th September, 1968* (eds Sven S. Hartman and Carl-Martin Edsman; Stockholm: Almqvist & Wiksell, 1970), 77–90.

3. This indicates the narrow scope with which this study will be concerned with the traditions of Pythagoras and his followers, for it virtually neglects those aspects that preoccupy most scholarly inquiry such as astronomy, mathematics, musical theory and even the Pythagorean sayings (ἀκούσματα, σύμβολα). Compare the amount of space devoted to these other topics in Burkert, *Lore*, 166–92 (sayings), 299–368 (astronomy), 369–400 (musical theory), 401–84 (number theory). While this reflects both ancient and modern concerns with the Pythagorean tradition, it provides what is here deemed 'moral cosmos', that is, background to the Pythagorean practice of community-of-goods.

Compare the relative brevity given to questions regarding Pythagorean communal practice. See Burkert, 'Craft Versus Sect: The Problem of Orphics and Pythagoreans', in *Jewish and Christian Self-Definition. Vol. 3: Self-Definition in the Greco-Roman World* (ed. Ben F. Meyer and E. P. Sanders; Philadelphia: Fortress, 1982), 1–22, 183–9, where discussion of Pythagorean community is shared with Orphism.

4. A comprehensive discussion of the problems involved is provided by Burkert, *Lore*, 97–120. The primary work on sources of the Pythagorean tradition was accomplished by Armand Delatte, *Études sur la littérature pythagoricienne* (Paris: Champion, 1915); Isidore Lévy, *Recherches sur les sources de la légende de Pythagore* (Paris: Leroux, 1926); and Ernst Rhode, 'Die Quellen des Iamblichus in seiner Biographie des Pythagoras', *RM* 26 (1871): 554–76, and 27 (1872): 23–61.

See also Walter Burkert, 'Hellenistiche Pseudopythagorica', *Phil* 105 (1961), 226–46; Guthrie, *History*, 166–71; J. A. Philip, 'The Biographical Tradition – Pythagoras', *TAPA* 90 (1959): 185–94; Christoph Riedweg, *Pythagoras: His Life, Teaching, and Influence* (trans. Steven Rendall; London: Cornell University Press, 2005), 42–97; Justin Taylor, *Pythagoreans and Essenes: Structural Parallels* (Paris: Peeters, 2004), 3–11.

5. All citations of Diogenes Laertius, Greek and English, come from LCL, edited by R. D. Hicks (2 vols; Cambridge: Harvard University Press, 1925–1972).

6. Greek citation for Porphyry *De Vita Pythagorica* (V.P.) come from Édouard des Places, ed., *Porphyroi Vie de Pythagore / Lettre à Marcella* (Collection Budé; Paris: Les Belles Lettres, 1982). English translations follow David R. Fideler, ed., *The Pythagorean Sourcebook and Library: An Anthology of Ancient Writings Which Relate to Pythagoras and Pythagorean Philosophy* (comp. and trans. K. S. Guthrie; Grand Rapids: Phanes Press, 1988), 123–35.

and Iamblichus (c. 250–325 CE).⁷ This means that the extant source-texts are more than a century later than Luke's writings, and more than six centuries after Pythagoras and his followers. However, these biographers often use and appeal to previous sources, many dating to the time of, and before, Aristotle (384–322 BCE).⁸ In addition to being late, the biographers do not seem to be critical sifters of the traditions they received.⁹ For the purposes of the present study, it is sufficient to demonstrate that Pythagorean discourse was 'in the air' around the time that Luke would have written his works. This would indicate a common milieu, even if merely a literary *topos*, for the hermeneutical shaping of traditions depicting community-of-goods and the disciplinary practices associated with them. With Aristotle, the present study is more interested in the Pythagoreans and their beliefs and practices rather than with Pythagoras the man.¹⁰

The most persuasive element to demonstrate the presence and influence of Pythagorean discourse in the Judaean region during the period in question is the adoption of Pythagorean customs in the practices of the Essenes, or at least the facilitation of a direct comparison between the two communities, as with Josephus' description (*Ant.* 15.371).¹¹ Josephus *assumes* that his readers will be familiar with the Pythagoreans *and* their communal practices. Furthermore, Pythagoras and his way of life were proliferated by the fusion with the Platonic tradition, which virtually absorbed and propagated Pythagorean doctrine.¹² In

---

7. All citations, Greek and English, of Iamblichus, *De Vita Pythagorica* (*V.P.*) come from John Dillon and Jackson Hershbell, eds, *Iamblichus: On the Pythagorean Way of Life: Text, Translation, and Notes* (Atlanta: Scholars Press, 1991). Besides Dillon and Hershbell's introduction (*Iamblichus*, 17–29), see Dominic J. O'Meara, *Pythagoras Revived: Mathematics and Philosophy in Late Antiquity* (Oxford: Clarendon, 1989), 30–105, and 109–215 (for Iamblichus' influence).

8. It is standard to divide the tradition with Aristotle. See Burkert, *Lore*, 15–16, 28–83 (esp. 79, 82), 109; Lévy, *Les Sources*, 1–19, and J. A. Philip, *Pythagoras and Early Pythagoreanism* (Toronto: University of Toronto Press, 1966), 5–6, 8–19. Burkert (*Lore*, 109) writes, 'It is only in post-Aristotelian sources that biographical and historical details regarding Pythagoras and the Pythagoreans are to be found.'

9. Burkert (*Lore*, 105) summarizes, 'On the whole, the "later" tradition seems not so much the result of unscrupulous falsification as of simpleminded, naive compilation and transmission of whatever could be found, contradictions and all.'

10. See Burkert, *Lore*, 2, 13, 15–16, 28–30 and n. 8, 46, 66, 216. Unlike Aristotle, we will not be preoccupied with distinguishing between Pythagorean and Platonic innovations.

11. Sterling ('"Athletes of Virtue"', 688–93) deems the descriptions as literary *topoi*.

12. See Burkert (*Lore*, 8, 13, 15–16, 53–96): 'In fact, Plato remained the principal source for all later Pythagoreans – Plato's myths, and in particular the *Timaeus*.[...] Later, neo-Pythagoreanism converges, in the philosophical realm, with Neoplatonism' (96). See also Charles H. Kahn, *Pythagoras and the Pythagoreans: A Brief History* (Cambridge: Hackett Publishing, 2001), 3, 4, 49, 57, 63, 65, 71, 78–9, 95 n. 3, 96–7, 105, 133, 134, 137–8, 157–8, 162; J. A. Philip, 'Aristotle's Monograph *On the Pythagoreans*', *TAPA* 94 (1963): 197–8; Riedweg, *Pythagoras*, 23, 118–19, 124–8; Taylor, *Pythagoreans*, 104–5; C. J. de Vogel, *Pythagoras and Early Pythagoreanism: An Interpretation of Neglected Evidence on the Philosopher Pythagoras* (Assen: Van Gorcum, 1966), 192–217.

the Hellenistic period, Pythagoras and his followers were associated in various texts with friendship economy and possibly influencing utopian politics.[13]

Pythagorean traditions were transmitted in a vast number of writings and locations from the fourth century BCE to the third century CE.[14] Aristotle (384–322 BC) wrote about Pythagorean teachings, some of which are preserved in the works of Plutarch, Alexander of Aphrodisias, Aelian, and Iamblichus.[15] Diogenes Laertius (5.25), in his biography of Aristotle, mentions two books concerning the Pythagoreans, Πρὸς τοὺς Πυθαγορείους and Περί τῶν Πυθαγορείων.[16] The primary sources of the *Lives* come from students of Aristotle, Aristoxenus (native of Tarentum,[17] southern Italy; fourth century BCE),[18] Dicaearchus (native of Messine, Sicily; c. 350 BCE–285),[19] and the historian Timaeus of Tauromenium, Sicily (c. 345 BCE–250).[20] Some of the important intermediaries include Neanthes of Cyzicus (in Asia Minor; c. third century BCE),[21] Hermippus of Smyrna, student of Callimachus (third century BCE),[22] and Alexander Polyhistor (first century BCE).[23] Further, we are indebted

---

13. See the discussions in Ferguson, *Utopias*, 46–8, 62–4, 72 (on the influence of the Pythagoreans on Plato and his *Republic*); Dawson, *Cities*, 14–18, 20 (Dawson doubts actual Pythagorean influence on Plato's politics in *Republic* [16–17, 18], but recognizes the perception of such by Timaeus and Aristoxenus [18]).

14. See the accounts of Burkert, *Lore*, 15–120; Guthrie, *History*, 146–71; Kahn, *Pythagoras*, 23–138; Philip, *Pythagoras*, 8–23; Riedweg, *Pythagoras*, 114–28.

15. See Lévy, *Les Sources*, 10–19; and Burkert, *Lore*, 29 and n. 5. On Aristotle's sources, see Burkert, *Lore*, 47, and more comprehensively, Philip, 'Aristotle's Monograph'.

16. Philip ('Aristotle's Monograph', 197) concludes 'that Aristotle wrote two monographs on the Pythagoreans, later re-edited as one.' Cf. Burkert, *Lore*, 29 n. 5. See D.L. 8.34.

17. Tarentum became the centre of Pythagoreanism after the group was expelled from Croton. See D.L. 8.39. Consult Burkert, *Lore*, 116; Riedweg, *Pythagoras*, 19–20, 104–6. See Aristotle, *Pol.* 1320b9–11, mentioned by Riedweg, *Pythagoras*, 112, 157 n. 75.

18. Fragments from Aristoxenos are collected in Fritz Wehrli, ed., *Die Schule des Aristotles. Heft II Aristoxenos* (Basel: Benno Schwabe & Co, 1954).

See Burkert, *Lore*, 106–8; Kahn, *Pythagoras*, 69–71; Lévy, *Les Sources*, 43–9; Rhode, 'Quellen', 555–62; Riedweg, *Pythagoras*, 40–1, 104–6, 123–4. Kahn (*Pythagoras*, 69) writes, 'He [Aristoxenus] was apparently the first to write a *Life* of Pythagoras, and many of the more marvelous or moralistic features of the later biography (as preserved by Diogenes Laertius, Porphyry, and Iamblichus) must go back to this lost work of Aristoxenus.'

19. Fragments from Dicaearchus are collected in Fritz Wehrli, ed., *Die Schule des Aristotles. Heft I Dikaiarchos* (Basel: Benno Schwabe & Co, 1944).

See, Kahn, *Pythagoras*, 68–9; Lévy, *Les Sources*, 49–52.

20. Fragments from Timaeus are collected in Felix Jacoby, ed., *Die Fragmente der griechischen Historiker* (Berlin: Weidmann / Leiden: Brill, 1923–), 3B:581–658. This collection will hereafter be referred to as *FGrHist*.

See, Lévy, *Les Sources*, 53–9; Riedweg, *Pythagoras*, 13, 16–17, 102.

21. Fragments from Neanthes are collected in *FGrHist* 2A:191–202.

See Burkert, *Lore*, 102; Lévy, *Les Sources*, 60–4.

22. See Burkert, *Lore*, 102–3; Lévy, *Les Sources*, 65–6.

23. Fragments from Alexander are collected in *FGrHist* 3A:96–126.

See Burkert, *Lore*, 53–4; with a comprehensive treatment in A.-J. Festugière, 'Les mémoires pythagoriques cites par Alexandre Polyhistor', *REG* 58 (1945): 1–65.

to many more for transmitting these traditions throughout the Mediterranean environment in later times,[24] including Apollonius of Tyana (Asia Minor; c. 1–97 CE),[25] Nicomachus of Gerasa (Roman Syria; c. 60–120 CE),[26] Numenius of Apamea (Syria; late second century CE).[27] Cicero attests Pythagorean influence in Rome in the first century BCE.[28]

Therefore, it can be safely stated that heterogeneous Pythagorean traditions circulated throughout the Hellenistic period, in a wide range of geographical locations along the Mediterranean, with contact in Roman Palestine during the era which Luke narrates *and* in which he writes. From this it can be assumed that Luke's implied audience could have had a basic knowledge of the Pythagorean traditions and thus would have made the necessary connections to frame the discourse with a certain association of expectations for the community-of-goods ethos and discipline, partly informed by Pythagorean discourse. This should be sufficient to establish a discursive context for community-of-goods and associated disciplinary practices.

5.1.2. The Moral Cosmos of the Pythagorean Community

In order to situate the discourse on the (traditions concerning) practices of the Pythagorean community-of-goods, it is beneficial to survey the Pythagorean 'moral universe' which included a cosmic harmony, universal kinship, and divine origins of the central teachings reserved for those initiated into the community. Throughout the tradition, to varying degrees, 'religious' and 'scientific' elements are intermingled producing a rich heritage of 'mathematical piety'.[29] As Guthrie maintains, 'Philosophy for Pythagoras and his followers had to be first and foremost the basis for a way of life: more than that, for a way of eternal salvation.'[30]

---

24. For an account of the varieties of Neo-Pythagoreanism in the first centuries CE, see John Dillon, *The Middle Platonists: A Study of Platonism 80 B.C. to A.D. 220* (London: Duckworth, 1977), 341–83; O'Meara, *Pythagoras Revived*, 9–29. O'Meara is concerned to contextualize Iamblichus' work and influence.

25. Fragments from Apollonius are collected in *FGrHist* 4A:132–47.
See Burkert, *Lore*, 100–1; Kahn, *Pythagoras*, 141–6; Lévy, *Les Sources*, 104–10. Lévy (*Les Sources*, 130–7) also offers a section on Philostratus' *Life of Apollonios*, which depicts Apollonius as a Pythagorean saint. See Taylor, *Pythagoreans*, 5–6, 16, 19–20, 21, 27, 30, 31.

26. Fragments from Nicomachus are collected in *FGrHist* 4A:112–23.
See Burkert, *Lore*, 98–9; Dillon, *Middle Platonists*, 352–61; Kahn, *Pythagoras*, 110–18; Lévy, *Les Sources*, 95–102, 103–4. Kahn (*Pythagoras*, 116) writes: 'Nicomachus thus serves as the major authority for the most irrational [e.g., magic and theosophical numerology] tendency in later Neopythagorean and Neoplatonic traditions.'

27. See Burkert, *Lore*, 95; Dillon, *Middle Platonist*, 361–79; Kahn, *Pythagoras*, 118–33.

28. See Kahn, *Pythagoras*, 73, 89–93; Riedweg, *Pythagoras*, 123–4.

29. On identifying the divisions of Pythagorean followers by emphasizing one stream or the other, see below n. 58.

30. Guthrie, *History*, 182. See also Kahn, *Pythagoras*, 51–2.

Persistent throughout the transmission of the Pythagorean traditions is the primacy of numerical and musical theories. According to Aristotle, for the Pythagoreans things 'are' numbers, or 'consist of' numbers.[31] The whole of reality is numerical in nature. This idea mutates through various formulations, with postulates on first principles (ἀρχαί), and a sacralizing of numbers as the key to understanding the mysteries of the universe. The cosmos was balanced in a harmonic equilibrium.[32] This notion is manifested throughout Pythagorean musical theory,[33] astronomy,[34] politics[35] and ethics.[36] The primary moral significance of this harmonic moral philosophy is the *quasi*-egalitarian nature of the relationships within the community as is manifest through the communal property.[37]

One significant feature of the community was its protective secrecy of the Master's divine teachings. Among the many secret teachings guarded by the community were the sacred doctrines on numbers,[38] the publishing of which resulted in excommunication (Empedocles and Plato) and even fatal divine retribution (Hippasus).[39] Concerning Pythagorean secrecy, Burkert explains:

> Pythagorean silence and secrecy should also be seen in the context of cult and ritual. [...] All mysteries have secrets; the ritual is interpreted in a ἱερὸς λόγος which may not be disclosed to the uninitiated, and the initiate also learns secret passwords, σύμβολα, συνθήματα. All kinds of societies that are bound together by cult have their esoteric aspect – even political clubs, trade guilds, and those of physicians.[40]

---

31. See Burkert, *Lore*, 31 and n. 15, citing Aristotle, *Met.* 987b28; 1083b17; 1090a22, et al. Cf. Guthrie, *History*, 212-13, 220, 229, 234-6 (quoting many relevant passages from Aristotle); Kahn, *Pythagoras*, 27-9; Riedweg, *Pythagoras*, 23, 80-7.

32. See Kahn, *Pythagoras*, 24-6, 63-5.

33. See Burkert, *Lore*, 369-400; Guthrie, *History*, 220-6; Riedweg, *Pythagoras*, 13-14, 27-30.

34. Burkert, *Lore*, 299-368; Riedweg, *Pythagoras*, 83-4.

35. See the studies by Edwin L. Minar, *Early Pythagorean Politics in Practice and Theory* (Baltimore: Waverly Press, 1942); and Kurt von Fritz, *Pythagorean Politics in Southern Italy: An Analysis of the Sources* (New York: Columbia University Press, 1940). Fritz is more suspicious of the sources than Minar, and is correct in distinguishing the Pythagorean politics inside and outside their ἑταίρια.

36. See Guthrie, *History*, 182-212; Robert Navon, 'An Introduction to the Pythagorean Teachings', in *The Pythagorean Writings: Hellenistic Texts from the 1st Cent. B.C.-3rd Cent. A.D.* (ed. Robert Navon; trans. from Greek and Latin by Kenneth Guthrie and Thomas Taylor; Kew Gardens, NY: Selene Books, 1986), 22-7; Philip, *Pythagoras*, 134-50.

37. Peter Kingsley (*Ancient Philosophy, Mystery, and Magic: Empedocles and Pythagorean Tradition* [Oxford: Clarendon, 1995], 292-8, 317-34) offers insightful criticisms of a propensity in modern scholarship to try and rid the Pythagorean tradition of images embarrassing to modern philosophy.

38. So Guthrie, *History*, 153. See Burkert, *Lore*, 178-81, 447-65; idem, 'Craft', 18.

39. See the passages quoted in §5.1.4. below.

40. Burkert, *Lore*, 178. Edwin L. Minar ('Pythagorean Communism', *TAPA* 75 [1944], 39) writes, 'The phrasing of Iamblichus and Diogenes makes it clear that this silence is purely a ritual matter connected with the mystery-like instruction and religious ceremonies of the order.'

Burkert also explains the dialectic between philosophy and politics, 'In fact, cult society and political club are in origin virtually identical. Every organized group expresses itself in terms of a common worship, and every cult society is active politically as a ἑταιρία.'[41]

Another salient feature of the community was their communal solidarity and fidelity in friendship.[42] This 'friendship is identified with the harmonious relationships underlying reality. [...It] becomes synonymous with harmonious relations the Pythagoreans discovered in nature and in which they required their members to participate'.[43] The community exhibited relations of fictive kinship manifest in communal goods (and life), common meals, various perpetual ritual taboos and dietary restrictions.[44] 'The Pythagoreans, too, formed a "brotherhood," in accordance with the ancient custom of colleagues bound together in a cult.'[45] The Pythagoreans were not quick to make friends, but many sayings and anecdotes indicate they were careful on not deliberately making enemies either.[46] Thom avers, 'The theoretical universality of Pythagorean friendship was counterbalanced by an exclusiveness based on initiation, a common way of life, and shared doctrines.'[47] For the Pythagoreans this meant exclusivism where 'outsiders' are regarded as impure.[48] This feature caused no little strife with blood relations who were not invited into the pledge of good faith (Iamblichus, V.P. 35.257). Like the Essenes (and inhabitants of Qumran) the community lived in a constant state of strictly regulated purity, usually reserved for priests during their time of service. This also meant a gruelling initiation ritual to enter the community (with varying grades of members), which, if failed, resulted in a social death of excommunication.

41. Burkert, *Lore*, 119.
42. Minar (*Pythagorean Politics*, 15–94; and 'Communism', 42–6) distinguishes between the earliest Pythagorean (aristocratic) community-of-goods and the later, broader traditions of friendship.
See also the instructive essay of Johan C. Thom, '"Harmonious Equality": The *Topos* of Friendship in Neopythagorean Writings', in *Greco-Roman Perspectives on Friendship* (ed. John T. Fitzgerald; SBLRBS 34; Atlanta: Scholars Press, 1997), 77–103; and de Vogel, *Pythagoras*, 150–9.
43. Thom, '"Harmonious Equality"', 93, 102. See also de Vogel, *Pythagoras*, 81–2. Minar, ('Communism', 45) writes, 'The central point of Pythagorean thought throughout its history was harmony, the fitting together of the parts in any whole – the cosmos, society, or the individual.'
44. See Porphyry, V.P. 34–36; Iamblichus, V.P. 21.98–99. On the dietary restrictions, see Burkert, *Lore*, 180–5; Robert M. Grant, 'Dietary Laws Among Pythagoreans, Jews, and Christians', *HTR* 73 (1980), 299–302; Riedweg, *Pythagoras*, 31–3, 67–71.
45. Burkert, *Lore*, 179–80. Taylor (*Pythagoreans*, 71–91) offers a helpful survey of 'oriental priesthoods and religious brotherhoods'.
46. See Thom, '"Harmonious Equality"', 87, 90, 97, 100.
47. Thom, '"Harmonious Equality"', 97 (and see n. 58). In fact, this is the only caveat Thom offers, and one gets the sense that not enough attention has been paid in his article to the sectarian aversion to 'outsiders'. Perhaps this is due to Thom's focus on the *neo-*pythagorean discourse on friendship, particularly Iamblichus.
48. See Taylor, *Pythagoreans*, 19–20, 41–3, 46–8.

We now turn to the relevant passages illustrating the rich and fantastic communal life of the Pythagoreans and their associated disciplinary practices. The examples demonstrate that the community-of-goods was a matter of life and death, and the communal solidarity was protected by divine guarantee.

5.1.3. The Pythagorean Community-of-Goods

Beginning with Diogenes Laertius (citing Timaeus), we note what became common maxims during the Hellenistic period:[49]

> According to Timaeus, he [sc. Pythagoras] was the first to say, 'Friends have all things in common' and 'Friendship is equality'; indeed, his disciples did put all their possessions into one common stock. (8.10b, Hicks, LCL)[50]

Porphyry, citing Nicomachus as his source, relays the grand initial reception Pythagoras received in the city of Croton.[51] More than two thousand people welcomed him with such enthusiasm that they built a massive auditorium (ὁμακοεῖος παμμέγεθες), in which both boys and women were admitted. He continues:

> His ordinances and laws were received by them as divine precepts, and they would do nothing to transgress even one. Indeed, they held all property in common and counted him among the gods. (*V.P.* 20, trans. Guthrie, emended)[52]

Here we see the connection between the veneration of Pythagoras and his teachings, and the resulting community-of-goods.

Iamblichus also recounts the community established in Croton, the first city to have been graced by the great teacher. He writes:

> After receiving from him [sc. Pythagoras] laws and ordinances, as if they were divine precepts, without which they did nothing, they remained of like mind with the entire gathering of disciples. Praised and deemed blessed by those around them, they held their possessions in common, as stated before,[53] and reckoned Pythagoras henceforth

---

49. Cf. Delatte, *Diogène Laërce*, 111, 168; Mealand, 'Community of Goods and Utopian Allusions'.

50. Cf. Timaeus *FGrHist* 566 F 13.

Diogenes Laertius (8.23) records another instance of this doctrine of commonality of possessions in a section on Pythagoras' teaching on just conduct: '[Pythagoras taught] to deem nothing one's own' (ἴδιόν τε μηδὲν ἡγεῖσθαι).

51. On Pythagorean politics and influence in Croton, including the revolt and dispersion, see especially Minar, *Pythagorean Politics*, 7–94; also Burkert, *Lore*, 113–20, 141–5, Riedweg, *Pythagoras*, 11–18, 61, 103–6.

52. *FGrHist* 1063 F 1. Parallel to Iamblichus *V.P.* 30, 166.

53. Dillon and Hershbell (*Iamblichus*, 55 n. 7) place a note here suggesting that this reference to a previous note does not correspond to Iamblichus' text, and therefore indicates this may be a passage from Nicomachus.

among the gods, as a beneficent guardian spirit (*daimon*) and most benevolent to humanity. (*V.P.* 6.30, Dillon and Hershbell)

The parallels with Acts on the description with the community are noteworthy. The school of Pythagoras received his teachings as binding divine precepts.[54] 'They remained of like mind.'[55] They were 'praised and deemed blessed by those around them'[56] and 'they held their possessions in common'.[57]

Continuing with Iamblichus' work, he elaborates on the high estimation of Pythagoras. Pythagoras is considered to be a distinctive type, alongside the divine and the human. He proposed correct doctrines regarding the divine and the cosmos, about motion, and the movements of heavenly bodies, mathematics, metaphysics, and all 'scientific matters' (τὰ ἐπιστημονικὰ πάντα). Iamblichus says,

> Again, the best civil polity, living with others, '*friends have things in common*' [emphasis added] worship of the gods, reverence for the dead, legislation and education, silence and forbearance for other living beings, self-control and sound-mindedness, sagacity and piety, and other good things. (*V.P.* 6.32, Dillon and Hershbell)

This passage indicates the way in which the Pythagorean community was understood as an alternative society with its own 'constitution' (πολιτεία) and schematizing frames of reference.

Iamblichus (*V.P.* 18.80–81) also notes how Pythagoras separated his school into two groups, the 'Pythagoreans' (true followers) and 'Pythagorists' (the emulators of the true followers). Of these two groups Iamblichus writes,

> Then he [Pythagoras] ordered that the property of the Pythagoreans be held in common, and that their common life should be permanent. The others he ordered to retain their own possessions, but to meet together to study with one another. (*V.P.* 18.81, Dillon and Hershbell)

This section goes on to divulge the distinction between the μαθηματικοί (advanced students) and the ἀκουσματικοί (probationers).[58] It demonstrates

---

54. Cf. Acts 2:42; ἦσαν δὲ προσκαρτεροῦντες τῇ διδαχῇ τῶν ἀποστόλων.
55. παρέμειναν ὁμονοοῦντες; cf. Acts 2:46, προσκαρτεροῦντες ὁμοθυμαδόν.
56. εὐφημούμενοι καὶ παρὰ τῶν πέριξ μακαριζόμενοι; cf. Acts 2:47, ἔχοντες χάριν πρὸς ὅλον τὸν λαόν; 4:33, χάρις τε μεγάλη ἦν ἐπὶ πάντας αὐτούς.
57. τὰς τε οὐσίας κοινὰς ἔθεντο; cf. Acts 2:44, εἶχον ἅπαντα κοινά; 4:32, ἦν αὐτοῖς ἅπαντα κοινά.
58. It would appear that Iamblichus did not represent this distinction well. See Burkert, *Lore*, 192–208; Guthrie, *History*, 192–3; Riedweg, *Pythagoras*, 106–8.
  It would appear more so that the division derived from an intra-sectarian dispute among those who followed the secret 'oral sayings' primarily concerning ritual and worship (ἀκουσματικοί) and those who wanted to further develop the 'scientific' insights of the tradition (μαθηματικοί). Burkert (*Lore*, 197) writes: 'In fact, the modern controversies over Pythagoras and Pythagoreanism are basically nothing more than the continuation of the ancient quarrel between *acusmatici* and *mathematici*. Is there nothing more in the doctrine of Pythagoras than what is indicated by the *acusmata*, with which the Pythagoras legend

that there are at least two different ways the Pythagorean community could practice shared goods: (1) a pure commonality of possessions (cf. Acts 2.44a; 4.32) and (2) a retaining of private property made available to other members of the community (cf. Acts 2.45; 4.34-35).[59]

A lengthy passage regarding the contribution of Pythagoras and his community to humanity is worth quoting in length, for it reveals the discursive links between cosmology and economic ethics – the Pythagorean divine economy. In chapter 30 of his *Life*, a chapter on the virtue of Justice, Iamblichus writes:

> We can best understand how he practiced justice and taught it to human beings if we consider it from its first principle and from which first causes it originates, and if we discern the first cause of injustice.[...] The first principle of justice, then, is the concept of the common and equal, and the idea that all should approximate nearly as possible in their attitudes to having one body and one soul in which all have the same experience, and should call that which is mine and that which belongs to another by the same name, just as Plato, who learned from the Pythagoreans, also maintains [cf. Plato, *Rep*. 462-64]. This, then, he of mortals best established, by having banished everything private in customs, and by having increased what is common as far as the lowliest possessions, which are causes of discord and tumult. For all things were common and the same for all, and no one possessed anything privately. And if someone were satisfied with the community, he used the things in common most justly; but if not, he got back his own property, and indeed more than he had contributed to the common stock, and so left. Thus from its first source, Pythagoras established justice in the best manner. (*V.P.* 30.167–68, Dillon and Hershbell)[60]

Here we see Iamblichus rooting Pythagoras' communal ethos in the unifying cosmological first principle of justice (δικαιοσύνη), which affects the well-being of humankind. This ethos is a common experience of the community having 'one body and one soul'[61] and not taking private property. While this picture is later mitigated in this same chapter (*V.P.* 30.170) where Pythagoras is said to have inherited property and managed it well, it demonstrates both the embodied ethic of shared goods and roots it in the cosmological principle of unity.

Finally, we take note of two passages regarding the Pythagorean discourse on the bond of friendship. Porphyry writes:

---

and the theory of metempsychosis are of course closely connected? Or was there from the beginning, behind these religious and mythical features, whose existence cannot be denied by the modern scholar any more than it could by the *mathematici*, a new, scientific approach to philosophy, mathematics, and the study of the world's nature?'
Kahn (*Pythagoras*, 72), following Burkert, suggests that the ἀκουσματικοί are replaced by the Cynics and the μαθηματικοί are absorbed into the Platonic-scientific tradition. Cf. Dawson, *Cities*, 129-30, 245.
59. On the various modes of shared possessions, see Taylor, 'The Community of Goods', 152-6, 158-9. See §4.2.2.1. above.
60. Cf. Aristoxenus fr. 33 Wehrli, 17-18.
61. ἑνὸς σώματος καὶ μιᾶς ψυχῆς; cf. Acts 4:32, καρδία καὶ ψυχὴ μία.

> His friends he loved exceedingly, being the first to declare that 'The goods of friends are common,' and that 'A friend is another self'. (*V.P.* 33, Guthrie)

Furthermore, Iamblichus notes how this sense of (fictive) kinship in the Pythagorean community incensed blood relatives who were excluded from the sharing of goods. He writes:

> But their relatives were especially indignant because the Pythagoreans gave the right hand as a pledge of good faith only to Pythagoreans, and to no other relatives except parents; also because they offered their possessions in common to one another, but excluded their relatives. (*V.P.* 35.257, Dillon and Hershbell)[62]

This particularism and exclusivism is a distinctive shared by the Essene sectarians, but not with the Christians (as represented by Luke). However, all shared in the practices of close friendship or (fictive) kinship bonds.

However, these bonds of friendship were not entered into lightly. The process of initiation was difficult and fraught with ascetic demands and dire consequences for failure.

5.1.4. Initiation and Excommunication

In a section source-credited to Timaeus,[63] Iamblichus divulges the initiation ritual by which Pythagoras tested potential students (*V.P.* 17.71–79). Apparently, Pythagoras scrutinized behaviour, relationships, desires, reactions, and such. Whomever he examined in such a manner was subjected to a three year supervisory period. If they passed the previous test they were initiated into a five year period of silence to test 'how they were disposed to self-control' (πῶς ἐγκρατείας ἔχουσιν). That the Pythagorean community was an alternative political realm is evidenced by the structuring of the community and management of its 'household':

> At this time, then, the things belonging to each, that is, their possessions, were held in common, given to those disciples appointed for this purpose who were called 'politicians,' and experienced in household management and skilled in legislation. The candidates themselves, then, if they appeared worthy of sharing in his teaching, having been judged by their way of life and other virtuousness, after the five year silence, became 'esoterics' and heard Pythagoras within a curtain, and also saw him. Before this, they shared his discourses through mere hearing, being outside the curtain

---

62. Cf. Apollonius *FGrHist* 1064 F 2, lines 117–20. Cf. lines 138–9 (Iamblichus *V.P.* 259): 'His friends he considered equal to the blessed gods, the others were hardly worth mentioning, and counted nothing at all' (τοὺς μὲν ἑταίρους ἦγεν ἴσον μακάρεσσι θεοῖσι, τοὺς δ' ἄλλους ἡγεῖτ' οὔτ' ἐν λόγῳ οὔτ' ἐν ἀριθμῷ).

63. *FGrHist* 556 F 13. See Burkert, *Lore*, 104 n. 37,192 n. 1; followed by Dillon and Hershbell, *Iamblichus*, 97 n. 1. Rhode, ('Quellen', 32) suggests §§68–73 come from Apollonius.

and never seeing him, while submitting over a long period to a test of their characters. (V.P. 17.72, Dillon and Hershbell)[64]

Iamblichus continues with a fascinating account of the failure of initiation:

> If they were rejected, they received double their property, and a tomb was raised by their 'fellow-hearers' [...] *as if they were dead* [emphasis added]. And on meeting them, they met them as if they were somebody else; for they said those who themselves had been moulding were dead, since they expected them to be good and noble as a result of their lessons. (V.P. 17.73, Dillon and Hershbell)

Iamblichus expounds upon this social death with what appears to be an account of the same social process from a different source[65] with mention of specific 'fatalities'. If after the period of testing the novice

> were found still clumsy and hard of understanding, after raising for such a one a stele and memorial in the school (just as it is said to have been done for Perillus the Thurian, and Cylon, leader of the Sybarites, who were rejected by them) they would expel him from the school of the Pythagoreans. They would load him with much gold and silver (for these things were stored in common for them, and were administered in common by those suitable for this purpose, whom they called 'managers' because of their post). And if they ever met him by chance, they considered him someone wholly other than he who, according to them, had died. (V.P. 17.74, Dillon and Hershbell)

This poignant account of the radical stakes involved in the communal fellowship or excommunication provides a germane parallel to the high stakes in the Ananias and Sapphira episode, where failure to conform to the communal ethos meant life or death.[66]

Closely linked with the rigorous communal initiation, and its cause, is the sacredness with which they held the Master's teachings. Exposing the teachings to the uninitiated resulted in expulsion, and even death by divine retribution in at least one case. Diogenes Laertius records the testimony of Timaeus, recalling the story of Empedocles, who was apparently expelled for publishing the secrets of the group.

> Timaeus in the ninth book of his *Histories* says he [*sc*. Empedocles] was a pupil of Pythagoras, adding that, having been convicted at that time of stealing his discoveries, he was, like Plato, excluded from taking part in the discussions of the school. (8.54, Hicks, LCL)

Diogenes Laertius continues his account from another source:

---

64. Cf. Diogenes Laertius, 8.10.
65. Rhode ('Quellen', 32) suggests this comes from Nicomachus, along with the quote of the Letter of Lysis that follows (see below).
66. We are reminded of Havelaar ('Hellenistic Parallels', 77–80) who, in combining the *Gattungen* of miracle of punishment *and* excommunication stories, suggests this ritual of social death as the most informative parallel to the Ananias and Sapphira episode in light of its literary context.

> Neanthes states that down to the time of Philolaus and Empedocles all Pythagoreans were admitted to the discussion. But when Empedocles himself made them public property by his poem, they made a law that they should not be imparted to any poet. He says the same thing also happened to Plato, for he too was excommunicated. (8.55, Hicks, LCL)[67]

Recalling that for the Pythagoreans philosophy and community was the means to salvation, the implication of this sanction is a shameful 'death'. Furthermore, this breach of ethos meant a permanent division, shattering the 'harmony' of the school.

Iamblichus confirms the 'fatal' consequences of publicizing the secret teachings when he refers to the tragedy of Hipparchus who carelessly revealed the divine mysteries of Pythagoras' teaching to those who were uninitiated. After describing the rigorous testing process and the consequences of failing these tests (*V.P.* 17.71–74), he cites a (pseudonymous) letter from Lysis to Hipparchus:[68]

> Hence also Lysis, in rebuking Hipparchus for having shared doctrines with uninitiated persons who had attached themselves to him without training in the sciences and theory, says: 'They say you philosophize in public with ordinary people, the very thing Pythagoras deemed unworthy, as you learned, Hipparchus, with zeal, but you did not maintain, having tasted, good fellow, Sicilian extravagance, which ought not to happen to you a second time. If you repent of your decision, I will be pleased, but if not, *you are dead* [emphasis added]. 'For,' he says, 'it is pious to remember the divine and human precepts of the famous one, not to share the good things of wisdom with those who have their souls in no way purified. For it is not lawful to give any random person things acquired with diligence after so many struggles, or to divulge to the profane the mysteries of the Eleusinian goddesses [Demeter and Persephone]. For those who have done these things are equally unjust and impious. (*V.P.* 17.75, Dillon and Hershbell)

Notice here how the transgressing of the ethos of the community is impious and equal to social death. In the moral universe of the Pythagoreans it was unacceptable to expose the secrets that were so hardly earned through the initiation. By contrast to the early followers of Jesus, the Pythagoreans thought the sacred status of their teaching rendered it for the 'esoterics' and not available for the wider, profane public.

Another (truly) fatal tragedy of one who foolishly revealed the secrets of the divine teaching is a certain Hippasus.[69] Regarding Hippasus, Iamblichus writes in a manner reminding us of Luke's account of the premature death of Judas (Acts 1.18-19):

---

67. See Neanth. *FGrHist* 84 F 26.
68. On this letter, see Burkert, 'Hellenistiche Pseudopythagoricas', 17–28. He dates it to around the second half of the third century BC (pp. 24–5). The full Greek text of the letter can be found in Thesleff, *Pythagorean Texts*, 111–14.
69. See Burkert, *Lore*, 206–8, 455–61, Riedweg, *Pythagoras*, 26, 107. Philip, *Pythagoras*, 26–30, discusses Hippasus without mention of traditions concerning his death.

> On the matter of Hippasus in particular: he was a Pythagorean, but because of having disclosed and given a diagram for the first time of the sphere from the twelve pentagons, *he perished in the sea since he committed impiety*. (V.P. 18.88, Dillon and Hershbell, emphasis added)

In another place, Iamblichus recalls both traditions of excommunication and the death of one (Hippasus?) punished by divine power as a result of publishing the secret teachings of Pythagoras:

> And Pythagoras is said to have taught first this very thing to those associating with him: that, free from all incontinence of will, they should guard in silence whatever discourse they heard. At any rate, he who first revealed the nature of commensurability and incommensurability to those unworthy to share in these doctrines was hated so violently, they say, that he was not only banished from their common association and way of life, but a tomb was even constructed for him. As one who had once been their companion, he had truly departed from life with human beings.
> Others say that even the divine [δαιμόνιον] power was indignant with those who published Pythagoras' doctrines. For that man perished at sea as an offender against the gods who revealed the construction of a figure having twenty angles: this involved inscribing the dodecahedron, one of the five figures called 'solid', within a sphere. Some, however, maintained that the one who broke the news about the irrationals and incommensurability suffered this fate. (V.P. 34.246–47, Dillon and Hershbell)

Here, in this miscellaneous section of Iamblichus' *Life*, we see the polemical traditions against those who would transgress the ethos of retaining the secret mathematical mysteries for the initiated alone. While the 'crime' of the miscreant is not directly an economic transgression of the community-of-goods, it is an infraction of the communal fidelity to which this exclusive community shared, and resulted in either social or physical death.

5.1.5. Summary and Connection with Acts

The very nature of the Pythagorean moral universe makes it impossible to have a direct parallel to the messianists' community-of-goods and the episode with Ananias and Sapphira in Acts 4.32–5.11. Their secrecy prohibited the transmission of their specific linguistic conventions surrounding their community of life and goods and the associated disciplinary practices.[70] However, even with the shroud of secrecy come echoes of discursive framing, which included kinship solidarity, veneration of the divine teachings, and the communal pledge leading to either life or death. From the widespread Pythagorean discourse, an ancient auditor would have in his cultural competency the expectations that such practice was associated with life or death recompense. It was similar with the Essenes, a Jewish community moulded into the (e)utopian repertoire of Pythagorean community of life and goods.

70. So Thesleff, 'Recent Research', 88.

5.2. The Divine Economy of the Essenes

The practices of the Essenes and the communities envisioned by the Dead Sea Scrolls provide Jewish examples of the common milieu in which Luke wrote and represented.[71] The traditions regarding community-of-goods among the Essenes, similar to the Pythagoreans, have source problems. However, these are not as varied as with the latter, primarily because we have three primary sources contemporaneous with the communities.[72] The scholarly issues surrounding the sources on the Essenes focus more on how well they reflect the realities of actual practice, and scholarly proposals attempting to

---

71. The task of demonstrating any actual direct dependence or borrowing from one community to another lies beyond the scope of the present work. For arguments that the Essenes were *directly* influenced by Pythagorean teachings (through the Therapeutae), see Justin Taylor, *Pythagoreans and Essenes: Structural Parallels* (Paris: Peeters, 2004), esp. 93–107. Taylor compares the Pythagorean and Essene ways of life (15–35, 41–51), and examines the parallels with Greco-Roman voluntary associations (53–69), oriental priesthoods and religious brotherhoods (71–91), before concluding that direct influence is the most probable solution to the highly distinctive elements shared by the Pythagoreans and Essenes. See also John Dillon, 'The Essenes in Greek Sources: Some Reflections', in *Jews in the Hellenistic and Roman Cities* (ed. John R. Bartlett; London: Routledge, 2002), 126–7; André Dupont-Sommer, 'Le probleme des influences étrengères sur la sect juive de Qoumrân', *RHPR* 35 (1955): 86–91; Thomas F. Glasson, *Greek Influence in Jewish Eschatology* (London: SPCK, 1961), 48–56; Moses Hadas, *Hellenistic Culture: Fusion and Diffusion* (New York: Columbia University Press, 1959), 194–6, 218; Isidore Lévy, *La légende de Pythagore de Grèce en Palestine* (Paris: Champion, 1927), 231–4, 264–93; idem, *Recherches esséniennes et pythagoriciennes* (Geneva: Droz / Paris: Minard, 1965), 57–63; Doron Mendels, 'Hellenistic Utopias and the Essenes', *HTR* 72 (1979): 207–22 (arguing for utopian influence on the first Essenes, especially from Iambulus' Heliopolitans); Schürer, *History*, 2:589–90. Peter Gorman ('Pythagoras Palestinus', *Phil* 127 [1983]: 30–42) argues that there was already a 'Jewish Pythagoras' borrowing from the Pentateuch in Alexandrian Jewish tradition, deriving mostly from Neanthes, that supported the absorbing of Pythagorean tradition.

Martin Hengel (*Judaism and Hellenism* [2 vols; trans. John Bowden; London: SCM Press, 1974], 1:243–7) stresses the importance not of direct dependence, but that the Essenes could be presented as 'Jewish Pythagoreans'. He writes, 'Thus it is possible in theory that the founder of the Essene community knew Pythagorean doctrines. Nevertheless, direct dependence is improbable. The Essene community wanted only to represent the genuine intention of the Torah and the prophetic writings and to defend its own Jewish heritage against all alien influences. Thus the alien influences were accepted only unconsciously or in a polemic apologetic situation' (245). See now his 'Qumran and Hellenism', in *Religion in the Dead Sea Scrolls* (eds John J. Collins and Robert A. Kugler; Grand Rapids: Eerdmans, 2000), 46–56.

For arguments that the early Christians were directly influenced by Essene practice and teaching, see especially Capper, 'Community of Goods'; and 'Palestinian Cultural Context'; and see the criticism by Bauckham, 'Early Jerusalem Church', 65, 71, 78, 84, 87–9.

72. The classical sources on the Essenes are collected in Alfred Adam and Christoph Burchard, eds, *Antike Berichte über die Essener* (Berlin: de Gruyter, 1972), with (German) commentary; and with fewer texts (perhaps because the later writers are largely dependent upon Philo, Josephus, and Pliny [cf. Schürer, *History*, 560 n. 15]), but with more introduction, in Geza Vermes and Martin D. Goodman, eds, *The Essenes According to the Classical Sources* (Sheffield: JSOT, 1989).

harmonize the descriptions (primarily between Josephus and the documents from Qumran).[73] This study makes no assumptions regarding the contentious identification of the inhabitants of Khirbet Qumrân as one of the many communities of Essenes,[74] and it is not crucial for the argument. The two composite descriptions, of the Essenes (via Josephus and Philo)[75] on one hand, and the community/ies represented by the scrolls of the Judaean Desert (in *The Community Rule* [1QS] and the *Damascus Document* [CD]), on the other, will be treated in separate sections primarily as independent attestation of examples of extra- and intra-community discourse, respectively. The goal of this survey is to garner discursive conventions surrounding communities of goods and life and the disciplinary practices associated with them.

5.2.1. Josephus[76] and Philo[77] on Essene Communities-of-Goods

Josephus, writing to a Roman audience, divides the Jewish people into four groups: the Sadducees, the Pharisees, the Essenes, and what he deems 'the fourth philosophy' – the zealots. For Josephus, the Essenes serve as the

---

73. See the monograph by Todd S. Beall, *Josephus' Description of the Essenes Illustrated by the Dead Sea Scrolls* (SNTSMS 58; Cambridge: Cambridge University Press, 1988).
See also Roland Bergmeier, *Die Essener-Berichte des Flavius Josephus: Quellenstudien zu den Essenertexten im Werk des jüdischen Historigraphen* (Kampen: Kok Pharos, 1993). Bergmeier focuses more on identifying the sources in Josephus and Philo.
74. See the studies, with their documentation, of Per Bilde, 'The Essenes in Philo and Josephus', in *Qumran Between the Old and New Testaments* (eds F. H. Cryer and T. L. Thompson; Sheffield: Sheffield Academic Press, 1998), 32–4; Boccaccini, *Beyond the Essene Hypothesis*, *passim*; Martin Goodman, 'A Note on the Qumran Sectarians, the Essenes and Josephus', *JJS* 46 (1995): 161–6; Murphy, *Wealth*, 401–46; Schürer, *History*, 2:583–90; Hartmut Stegemann, 'The Qumran Essenes – Local Members of the Main Jewish Union in the Late Second Temple Times', in *The Madrid Qumran Congress: Proceedings of the International Congress on the Dead Sea Scrolls, Madrid 18–21 March, 1991* (2 vols; ed. Julio Trebolle Barrera and Luis Vegas Montaner; Leiden: Brill, 1992), 1:83–166 (who concludes the Qumran settlement was an outpost for all Essenes, a quiet research retreat, p. 161); James C. VanderKam, *The Dead Sea Scrolls Today* (Grand Rapids: Eerdmans, 1994), 71–98; Geza Vermes, 'The Qumran Community, the Essenes, and Nascent Christianity', in *The Dead Sea Scrolls: Fifty Years After their Discovery: Proceedings of the Jerusalem Congress, July 20–25, 1997* (eds Lawrence Schiffman, Emanuel Tov and James C. VanderKam; Jerusalem: Israel Exploration Society, 2000), 581–6; Vermes and Goodman, *Essenes*, 12–14.
75. Valuable information also comes from Pliny the Elder (*N.H.* 5.17.4 [73]), but does not add anything extra to what Josephus and Philo attest. He does notice their reputation as 'admirable beyond all others in the whole world' and those who live without money, among other things. The Latin text is in Adam and Burchard, *Antike Berichte*, 38; and with English translation in Vermes and Goodman, *The Essenes*, 32–3.
76. All citations of Josephus come from *Josephus*, trans. H. St J. Thackeray, et al. 13 vols. LCL (Cambridge: Harvard University Press, 1926–1965).
77. All citations of Philo come from *Philo*, trans. F. H. Colson and G. H. Whitaker. 10 vols. LCL (Cambridge: Harvard University Press, 1929–1962).

supreme example of virtuous and honourable Judaism.[78] In fact, as Mason (who has provided the best commentary on Josephus' discourse on the Essenes thus far) notes, the Essenes serve Josephus' apologetic rhetoric in his *Jewish War* to present the supreme example of Judaean piety and philanthropy, and to serve as a foil to 'the reckless rebel tyrants, whose hot-headed behavior precipitated the revolt'.[79] Josephus mentions the Essenes more than a dozen times, with three highly significant references (*Life* 10–12; *J.W.* 2.119–61; *Ant.* 18.18–22), one with the suggestion that he actually submitted himself to the Essene way of life for a time (*Life*, 11).[80] For all the groups Josephus mentions, he Hellenizes his descriptions to make them more intelligible for his intended audience.[81] In his *Antiquities* he casts the Essenes in light of the Pythagoreans – 'This is a group [the Essenes] which follows a way of life taught to the Greeks by Pythagoras'[82] – followed by the story of Manaēmus, an Essene, who foretold the reign of Herod, in order to declare that 'many of these men have indeed been vouchsafed a knowledge of divine things *because of their virtue*'.[83]

Philo also discusses the Essenes as the supreme example of Jewish piety and civic virtue (*Prob.* 75–91; *Hypoth.* 11.1–18).[84] In Philo's treatise *Every*

---

78. See Steve Mason, *Josephus and the New Testament* (Peabody: Hendrickson, 1992), 132–5, 215, 222, 224; Tessa Rajak, 'Ciò che Flavio Giuseppe vide: Josephus and the Essenes', in *Josephus and the History of the Greco-Roman Period: Essays in Memory of Morton Smith* (eds Fausto Parente and Joseph Sievers; Leiden: Brill, 1994), 141–60.

79. Steve Mason, 'What Josephus Says about the Essenes in his *Judean War*', in *Text and Artifact in the Religions of Mediterranean Antiquity: Essays in Honour of Peter Richardson* (eds Stephen G. Wilson and Michael Desjardins; Ontario: Wilfrid Laurier University Press, 2000), 439.

80. Josephus actually claims to have submitted himself to all three groups (αἱρέσαι), the Sadducees, the Pharisees, and the Essenes. Certainly he exaggerates when with his claims of 'hard labor' and participation. So Tessa Rajak, *Josephus: The Historian and His Society* (2nd edn; London: Duckworth, 2002), 34–5.

81. See Per Bilde, *Flavius Josephus between Jerusalem and Rome: His Life, his Works, and their Importance* (JSPSup 2; Sheffield: Sheffield Academic Press, 1988), 165–7; idem, 'Essenes', 64, 66–8; Dillon, 'Essenes', 127–8; Mason, *Josephus*, 68, 132. Mason ('What Josephus Says', 426–7) also suggests that part of the reason for Josephus oscillating between forms of the name, Ἐσσαῖοι and Ἐσσηνοί, was because the latter was more familiar to his Greco-Roman readers.

82. Josephus, *Ant.* 15.371. Bergmeier (*Essener-Berichte*, 81–93, 104–5) argues for a 'Pythagorized-Essene' source that largely undergirds Josephus' description of the Essenes in *J.W.* 2.119–61 and *Ant.* 18.18–22. However, Bergmeier does not sufficiently address the redactional qualities in both Philo's and Josephus' texts, nor the possibility of the pervasiveness of a common discourse.

83. Josephus, *Ant.* 15.379, emphasis added. We recall that Josephus introduced the Essenes through two individuals associated with the group who proffer accurate prophecies (Judas in *Ant.* 13.311–13 [// *J.W.* 1.78]; and Simon in *Ant.* 17.346–48 [// *J.W.* 2.113]).

84. Philo also refers to a Jewish community in Egypt called the Therapeutai, for which he dedicates an entire treatise, *On the Contemplative Life*. This treatise begins with an allusion to a work on the Essenes, which may refer to the *Hypothetica*, the treatise *That Every Good Person is Free*, or some other lost work. On this, see Kenneth Schenck, *A Brief Guide to Philo* (Louisville: Westminster / John Knox Press, 2005), 21.

Good Man is Free, he presents the Essenes as the Jewish examples of moral excellence, alongside those surveyed from the Greeks, Persians, and Indians.[85] In Philo's *Hypothetica*, preserved only by Eusebius' *Praeparatio Evangelica* (8.11.1–19),[86] the Essenes are presented 'as a popular voluntary association of pious, mature Jews, living in cities and villages in Judaea, organized in "communistic" societies with common property, meals and clothes'.[87] Philo's account of the Essene community of life and goods focuses only on the 'positive' aspects, without mention of disciplinary practices associated with the group.

What follows is a brief survey of the primary statements about the Essene community of life and goods from Philo and Josephus. Bilde summarizes well the portrayal of the Essenes in Philo and Josephus:

> Both writers describe Judaism as a sort of ideal 'philosophy', able to compete with Greek philosophical schools and with Hellenistic-Roman religions. In this general context they present the Essenes as the Jewish elite. They describe the Essenes as representing the highest quality of Judaism and Jewish values and, therefore, as the best bid of the Jewish people in the international, Hellenistic-Roman, religio-philosophical debate on social ethics, legislation and the ideal and utopian society.[88]

Both Philo's and Josephus' descriptions of the Essenes are valuable precisely because they stand as intermediaries between the Jewish and Greco-Roman cultures. Precisely as outsiders to the Essene way of life (even if Josephus did 'taste' it for a short while) their depictions are intriguing as the use of a literary discourse to represent the Jewish virtuous elite in terms of Greco-Roman (e)utopian *topoi*.

5.2.1.1. Virtuous (Common) Life and Honourable Reputation
To begin, we note the laudatory language used to represent the good reputation of the Essenes. In the conclusion of Josephus' brief discourse on the Essenes in his *Antiquities* he notes the honourable repute of the Essenes along with their practice of sharing property.

For recent discussions, see Mary Ann Beavis, 'Philo's Therapeutai: Philosopher's Dream or Utopian Construction?', *JSP* 14 (2004): 30–42 (in response to Troels Enberg-Pedersen, 'Philo's *De Vita Contemplativa* as a Philosopher's Dream', *JSJ* 30 [1999]: 40–61); Beavis, *Jesus and Utopia*, 58–68; and Joan E. Taylor and Philip R. Davies, 'The So-Called Therapeutai of *De Vita Contemplativa*: Identity and Character', *HTR* 91 (1998): 3–24.

85. Significantly, Philo begins this treatise with reference to the 'saintly Pythagoreans' and interpretations of some of their ἀκούσματα (*Prob.* 2) as the paradigm for a new 'way' for life. For further discussion about Pythagorean, among other Hellenistic (Stoic and Platonic), influence on Philo's thought, see Dillon, *Middle Platonists*, 139–83.

86. Eusebius preserves Philo's larger work entitled *Pro Iudaeis Apologia*, in his *Praep. Evang.* 8.11.1–19, of which *Hypothetica* is postulated as part.

87. Bilde, 'Essenes', 39.

88. Bilde, 'Essenes', 62.

They deserve admiration in contrast to all others who claim their share of virtue because such qualities as theirs were never found before among any Greek or barbarian people, nay, not even briefly, but have been among them in constant practice and never interrupted since they adopted them from of old. Moreover, they hold their possessions in common, and the wealthy man receives no more enjoyment from his property than the man who possesses nothing. The men who practise this way of life number more than four thousand.[89] (*Ant.* 18.20, Feldman, LCL)

A similar commemoration concludes another discussion of the Essenes in Philo's *Hypothetica*:

Such then is the life of the Essenes, a life so highly to be prized that not only commoners but also great kings look upon them with admiration and amazement, and the approbation and honours which they give add further veneration to their venerable name. (*Hypoth.* 11.18, Colson, LCL)

In this apologetic text, the Essenes are offered as examples of virtue and communal life, exemplary even to kings. They are like a voluntary association that works for the common good, shares food and clothing, and cares for one another's needs.

In Josephus' history of the *Jewish War* he offers a fuller account of the way of life of the Essenes (2.119–61). On their community-of-goods, he writes:

Riches they despise, and their community of goods is truly admirable; you will not find one among them distinguished by greater opulence than another. They have a law that new members on admission to the sect shall confiscate their property to the order, with the result that you will nowhere see either abject poverty or inordinate wealth; the individual's possessions join the common stock and all, like brothers, enjoy a single patrimony. (*J.W.* 2.122, Thackeray, LCL)

Indicative here is the focus on proper communal balance expressed through economic use of resources. Also seen here is indication of a probationary period and ritual initiation. Finally, the designation of members as 'brothers' (ἀδελφοῖς) demonstrates the close relational distance of (fictive) kinship. The Essene's manner of life, commendable as ideal to Josephus' Roman audience, is expressed supremely through their handling of wealth, which frames this community's ethos as a family of like-minded souls.

Philo notes how the Essenes, a name which he traces to ὁσιότης ('holiness', *Prob.* 75; *Hypoth.* 11.1),[90] direct their efforts of labour for the benefit of one another and care for the needs of each in the community:

Some of them labour on the land and others pursue such crafts as co-operate with peace and so benefit themselves and their neighbors. They do not hoard gold and silver or acquire great slices of land because they desire revenues therefrom, but provide

---

89. Philo (*Prob.* 75) gives the same number of 4,000. Schürer (*History*, 562 n. 1) notes the debate about Josephus being dependent on Philo.
90. This suggestion is generally rejected today. See Vermes and Goodman, *The Essenes*, 1–2, for a summary of scholarly suggestions.

what is needed for the necessary requirements of life. For while they stand almost alone in the whole of mankind in that they have become moneyless and landless by deliberate action rather than by lack of good fortune, they are esteemed exceedingly rich, because they judge frugality with contentment to be, as indeed it is, an abundance of wealth. (*Prob.* 76b–77, Colson, LCL)

We notice here the stock philosophical reversal of rich-poor status through virtuous living and the shunning of excess.[91] The divine economy of the Essenes, according to Philo, here focuses on a harmonious existence emphasizing cooperation and contentment. Indeed, according to Philo, the Essenes take as their defining standards the love of God, the love of virtue and the love of humanity (*Prob.* 83). He expands the manner in which they do this as such:

Indeed, a multitude of proofs are presented concerning their love of God, by a continued purity throughout the whole of life, by avoiding oaths and avoiding falsehood, and by their belief that the Deity is the cause of all good things and nothing bad; concerning their love of virtue by abstaining from love of either money or reputation or pleasure, by self-control, endurance, again by frugality, simple living, contentment, humility, respect for the law, steadiness, and all such qualities; concerning their love of humanity, benevolence, equality and fellowship beyond all description concerning which is it not unreasonable to say a few words. (*Prob.* 84, Colson, LCL, translation emended)

Philo expands the love of humanity and their remarkable benevolence, equality and fellowship with the following illustrations:

First of all then no one's house is his own in the sense that it is not shared by all, for besides the fact that they dwell together in communities, the door is open to visitors from elsewhere who share their convictions. Again they all have a single treasury and common disbursements; their clothes are held in common and also their food through their institution of public meals. In no other community can we find the custom of sharing roof, life and board more firmly established in actual practice. And that is no more than one would expect. For all wages which they earn in the day's work they do not keep as their own private property, but throw them into the common stock and allow the benefit thus accruing to be shared by those who wish to use it. The sick are not neglected because they cannot provide anything, but have the cost of their treatment lying ready in the common stock, so they can meet expenses out of the greater wealth in full security. To the elder men too is given the respect and care which real children give to their parents, and they receive from countless hands and minds a full and generous maintenance for their latter years. (*Prob.* 86–87, Colson, LCL)

Here Philo exhibits the communal living, the common stock of earned wages, and the care for the sick and elderly (which again is framed in terms of kinship categories). Philo continues by describing the patient endurance of persecution of the Essenes, the Jewish 'athletes of virtue' (§88), who exhibit 'the clearest evidence of a complete and supremely happy life' (§91b). Philo's

---

91. See David L. Mealand, 'Philo of Alexandria's Attitude to Riches', *ZNW* 69 (1978): 256–64; and the exchange between T. Ewald Schmidt ('Hostility to Wealth in Philo of Alexandria', *JSNT* 19 [1983]: 85–97) and Mealand ('The Paradox of Philo's Views on Wealth', *JSNT* 24 [1985]: 111–15).

description helps to orient an informed reading of Luke's presentation of the early Jerusalem messianists and their idyllic common life. These believers, even in the midst of persecution, are put on display as the embodiment of the highest ideals.

5.2.1.2. Communal Solidarity and Hospitality

In Josephus' description, the Essenes occupy every city throughout Judaea. Mason proposes that Josephus 'evidently means to stress that Essenes truly are representative of the best Judeans: they are *not* some isolated group, but their healthful presence is felt throughout Judean society'.[92] Furthermore, Josephus comments on the group's collective solidarity and hospitality to others identified in the group as though they were 'intimate friends':

> They occupy no one city, but settle in large numbers in every town. On the arrival of any of the sect from elsewhere, all the resources of the community are put at their disposal, just as if they were their own; and they enter the houses of men whom they have never seen before as though they were their most intimate friends.[...] In every city there is one of the order expressly appointed to attend to strangers, who provides them with raiment and other necessities. (*J.W.* 2.124, 125, Thackeray, LCL)

This description further illustrates the close (fictive) kinship dynamics of 'generalized reciprocity'. Also noteworthy is the quasi-nomadic description of this community, which presents an ethos of generous xenophilia that would have been important for the early Christian communities with their hospitality toward itinerant evangelists and travelling prophets.

5.2.1.3. Moneyless Economy and General Reciprocity

Analogous to the subversion of the vicious cycle of reciprocity in the Lukan theological vision, Josephus notes the '(e)utopian economy' among the Essenes:

> There is no buying or selling among themselves, but each gives what he has to any in need and receives from him in exchange something useful to himself; they are, moreover, freely permitted to take anything from any of their brothers without making any return. (*J.W.* 2.127, Thackeray, LCL)

Like Josephus, Philo describes the 'purity' of their (e)utopian economy, not corrupted by production of weapons or any commercial goods,

> for they don't even know the dream of commerce, either traffic or retail trade or seafaring; they set aside the inducements that lead one into covetousness. (*Prob.* 78, Colson, LCL, translation emended)

---

92. Mason, 'Essenes', 436–7; see 430.

These descriptions illustrate the alternative society practised among the Essenes. They indicate that the community is built on trust as among those of a single household. We are reminded here of Sahlins's crucial distinctions regarding reciprocity arranged according to social distance.[93] The (e)utopian economy of the Essenes described by Josephus and Philo indicates the closest nature of relationships.

5.2.1.4. Initiation Ritual and Discipline
Like the Pythagoreans, the communal solidarity of the Essenes is marked by a rigorous testing period. This probationary period progresses through stages, each apparently binding for life. Josephus describes the initiation period of testing as such:

> A candidate anxious to join their sect is not immediately admitted. For one year, during which he remains outside the fraternity, they prescribe for him their own rule of life.[...] Having given proof of his temperance during this probationary period, he is brought into closer touch with the rule and is allowed to share the purer kind of holy water, but is not yet received into the meetings of the community. For after this exhibition of endurance, his character is tested for two years more, and only then, if found worthy, is he enrolled in the society. (*J. W.* 2.137–38, Thackeray, LCL)

Community membership is not taken lightly. The intimate nature of communal fellowship is mirrored by the severe standard of disciplinary measures. Josephus describes the consequences of being expelled from the community as dreadful, and potentially fatal. He writes,

> Those who are convicted of serious crimes they expel from the order; and the ejected individual often comes to a most miserable end. For, being bound by their oaths and usages, he is not at liberty to partake of other men's food, and so falls to eating grass and wastes away and dies of starvation. This has led them in compassion to receive many back in the last stage of exhaustion, deeming the torments which have brought them to the verge of death are a sufficient penalty for their misdoings. (*J. W.* 2.143–44, Thackeray, LCL)

This is the closest we come to communal discipline in the presentations of Philo and Josephus. Philo has no parallel.[94] What is noteworthy here is that exclusion from the community is a life or death matter. One gets the sense that Josephus may be (over)emphasizing the severity of the situation of being ejected from the community, as if he must conform his description to some prescribed conventions. Referring to their practices of jurisprudence, Josephus notes how Essenes are scrupulously careful with their rulings, which are irrevocable. He follows by noting how they revere only God above Moses,

---

93. See §4.1.1.2. above.
94. The situation is similar with the Pythagorean traditions. Iamblichus transmits traditions regarding the 'fatal' consequences of failing the initiation ritual, whereas Diogenes Laertius and Porphyry do not.

and blasphemy against him is punished with death (*J.W.* 2.145b). Mason offers insightful commentary of Josephus' depiction of the Essenes' efficiently stern jurisprudence:

> Josephus credits the Essenes with peerless precision and justice (ἀκριβέστατοι καὶ δίκαιοι) in the administration of laws ([*War*] 2.145). They practise a severe discipline, with capital punishment legislated for anyone who reviles God or the lawgiver Moses. [...] Whereas the Pharisees are only *reputed to be* [emphasis his] the most precise in the laws (*War* 1.110; 2.162; *Life* 191), his celebration of the Essenes here has no such quality.[...] Josephus considers it a powerful attraction of the Judean law code that it leaves no loopholes (*Apion* 2.276–77), that its justice is sure and swift (2.178) and that numerous crimes merit the death penalty (2.214–17).[95]

Mason's comments indicate that severe judgement without delay is in fact a virtue alongside a community that embodies the ideal of Jewish life and practice presented for a Greco-Roman audience. Set within this wider socio-cultural repertoire, the Ananias and Sapphira episode is not so strange or offensive, but is rather further evidence of the early messianists' communal virtue and divine favour for those with similar cultural sensibilities. With Luke's description of the community in such ideal terms, one would expect to find severe disciplinary measures for those who transgress the communal ethos. Narrating relentless judgement which results in death would have added to the assurance that the community being depicted was in fact the pure exemplar of the cultural ideals.

5.2.1.5. Summary and Connection with Acts

For both Philo and Josephus, the community of life and goods is the primary evidence of the supreme example of the Jewish virtuous elite. The Essenes are presented as the pinnacle of virtue and worthy of honourable esteem, as the early messianic community is among the people in Acts. They are the model of generous hospitality, friendship, and generalized reciprocity. Josephus, who was geographically (and perhaps socially) closer than Philo to the Essene communities in Palestine, notes their rigorous initiation ritual, and the dreadful consequences of transgressing the communal ethos. In short, Philo and Josephus present venerable examples of a Jewish community, supremely illustrated by their community of life and goods, with many common *topoi* comparable to the many traditions of the Pythagorean and messianist community of life and goods. Regardless of whether Philo's and Josephus' description correspond to the actual practices of the community, they demonstrate that there were certain elements forming a broad Mediterranean reading competency, a presupposition pool, with regard to community-of-goods and associated practices. The one glimpse of disciplinary practices, in Josephus' account, seems as if it is shaped to conform to the severity associated with failing the (e)utopian communal ethos: exclusion is equated with death.

---

95. Mason, 'Essenes', 443, 444.

A similar communal practice is evinced by two documents recovered at Khirbet Qumrân, *The Community Rule* (1QS) and *The Damascus Document* (CD). The Qumran Covenanters are the final example to be surveyed of conventions surrounding communities-of-goods and the associated disciplinary practices.

5.3. *The Communities of Khirbet Qumrân*

The practices of community life and goods as portrayed in the Qumran documents (*The Community Rule* and *The Damascus Document*) are valuable precisely because they are intra-communal texts composed for the regulation of life within the community. It is most likely that Luke-Acts was also composed for those who adhered to the faith it expounded, who would have been able to recognize Luke's echoes and allusions to the Scriptures of Israel. However, unlike Luke-Acts, it is crucial to recognize the distinctive genre of the Qumran texts as communal regulations. The parallels with the summaries of communal life in the narrative of Acts have a limited value. A regulation text is designed for the generalization of life, and therefore we are not surprised at the lack of the spectacular episodes of disciplinary action as we have in Acts' account. Each of the two texts will be examined separately as literary instantiations of the *topos* of community-of-goods without any attempt to harmonize them or speculate on how they may have been received in actual, historical communities that may have inhabited Khirbet Qumrân or elsewhere in Judaea.[96] The use of the term 'community' in this section refers to those groups which are projected from the texts as literary (re)constructions.[97]

Fortunately for the current study, the fundamental work on the use of possessions and economic matters has been comprehensively discussed by the

---

96. Klauck ('Gütergemeinschaft', 65–6) suggests that 1QS and CD represent two stages of the Qumran communal movement. The former is an earlier stage, while the latter represents the community scattered with the Jewish War, Khirbet Qumrân serving as a centre for the dispersed. Mealand ('Qumran', 138) seems to suppose the reverse situation, CD first, followed by a formation of communal living as in 1QS. Capper ('Palestinian Cultural Context', 334 n. 32) suggests perhaps a relationship in the opposite direction of Klauck, where males from CD communities passed over to the celibate lifestyle of 1QS after raising their families. Each of these theories seems too simplistic for the actual use of these texts in historical communities.

97. See the discussion in Philip R. Davies, 'Communities in the Qumran Scrolls', *PIBA* 17 (1994): 55–68; idem, 'The Judaism(s) of the Damascus Document', and Sarianna Metso, 'The Relationship Between the Damascus Document and the Community Rule', in *The Damascus Document: A Centennial of Discovery. Proceedings of the Third International Symposium of the Orion Center, 4–8 February 1998* (eds Joseph M. Baumgarten, Esther G. Chazon and Avital Pinnick; Leiden: Brill, 2000), 27–43 and 85–93, respectively; and Catherine M. Murphy, *Wealth in the Dead Sea Scrolls and in the Qumran Community* (STDJ 40; Leiden: Brill, 2002), 3.

thorough work of Catherine Murphy[98] and the valuable summary offered by Gordon Zerbe.[99] Therefore the discussion can be expedited in lieu of space constraints. The following discussion is heavily indebted to these two works. I proceed by examining the passages concerning communal goods in *The Community Rule* (1QS)[100] and then *The Damascus Document* (CD).[101] I begin by setting the stage with a brief overview of the 'moral cosmos' of the Dead Sea Scrolls in general focusing primarily on the 'divine economy' of the renewed covenant and regulations of purity and holiness.

5.3.1. The Moral Universe of the Renewed Covenant

The documents recovered at Khirbet Qumrân share a common life-world defined by covenant renewal and a heightened sense of holiness structured by intense purity regulations.[102] These elements will be illustrated from the two texts under consideration. 1QS opens with a covenant renewal ceremony that defines the identity of the community associated with the *Rule*. Joining the

---

98. See previous note.
99. Gordon M. Zerbe, 'Economic Justice and Nonretaliation in the Dead Sea Scrolls: Implications for New Testament Interpretation', in *The Bible and the Dead Sea Scrolls: The Princeton Symposium on the Dead Sea Scrolls. Vol 3: The Scrolls and Christian Origins* (ed. James H. Charlesworth; Waco, TX: Baylor University Press, 2006), 319–55.
100. All Hebrew for 1QS comes from Florentino García Martínez and Eibert J. C. Tigchelaar, eds, *The Dead Sea Scrolls: Study Edition* (2 vols; Leiden: Brill / Grand Rapids: Eerdmans, 1997–98), 1:68–98 (1QS), 1:510–44 (4Q255–64), 2:1132, 1134–36 (5Q11, 13). Also consulted are the photographic images in James H. Charlesworth, ed., *The Dead Sea Scrolls: The Rule of the Community: Photographic Multi-language Edition* (Philadelphia: American Interfaith / World Alliance, 1996). See Murphy, *Wealth*, 104–5 nn. 1–3 for more resources.

All English translations come from Geza Vermes, *The Complete Dead Sea Scrolls in English* (5th edn; New York / London: Penguin Books, 1997), 98–124, unless otherwise noted.

101. All Hebrew for CD comes from García Martínez and Tigchelaar, *Study Edition*, 1:550–626 (CD-A–B, including 4Q266–73), 2:1134 (5Q12), 2:1152–54 (6Q15). Also consulted are the photographic images in Magen Broshi, ed., *The Damascus Document Reconsidered* (Jerusalem: The Israel Exploration Society, 1992). For more resources, see Maxine Grossman, *Reading for History in the Damascus Document: A Methodological Method* (STDJ 45; Leiden: Brill, 2002), 1 nn. 1–2; Charlotte Hempel, *The Damascus Texts* (Sheffield: Sheffield Academic Press, 2000), 10–14; Murphy, *Wealth*, 26–7 nn. 4, 6.

All English translations come from Vermes, *Complete*, 125–53, unless otherwise noted.

102. See Forkman, *Limits*, 70–4; Murphy, *Wealth*, 97–9, 117–37; Helmer Ringgren, *The Faith of Qumran: Theology of the Dead Sea Scrolls* (exp. edn; ed. James H. Charlesworth; trans. Emilie T. Sander; New York: Crossroad, 1963), 201–2; Moshe Weinfeld, 'The Covenant in Qumran', and Sarianna Metso, 'Qumran Community Structure and Terminology as Theological Statement', in *The Bible and the Dead Sea Scrolls: The Princeton Symposium on the Dead Sea Scrolls. Vol 2: The Dead Sea Scrolls and the Qumran Community* (ed. James H. Charlesworth; Waco, TX: Baylor University Press, 2006), 59–69 and 289–90, respectively.

community (היחד) is deemed as 'entering the covenant' (1QS 1.18), and for those who join this voluntary commitment entails offering

> all their knowledge, powers and possessions into the Community of God, that they may purify their knowledge in the truth of God's precepts and order their powers according to His ways of perfection and all their possessions according to his righteous counsel. (1QS 1.11b-13a, trans. Vermes)

In this invitation we see already the intersection of the community's relationship before the God of Israel and a distinctive observance defined by the precepts of the divine Law subjecting economic practice. Likewise in CD, the community is designated as the 'new covenant' (הברית החדשה, CD-A 6.19; 8.21; CD-B 19.33-34; 20.12). In CD-A 13.11-12 there is a comparable statement to the passage quoted above from 1QS. Included in rules for the Guardian (המבקר) – who is to instruct the congregation in the works of God, love the community as a father loves his children, care for them in distress as a shepherd cares for his sheep, and assure that none are oppressed or broken (CD-A 13.7-10) – is the following:

> [11] He shall examine every man entering his Congregation with regard to his deeds, understanding, strength, ability and possessions, [12]and shall inscribe him in his place according to his rank in the lot of L[ight]. (CD-A 13.11-12, trans. Vermes)[103]

Weinfeld sees here an interpretation of the Deuteronomic exhortation to love God in total with all one's being (Deut. 6.5). For Weinfeld, the aspect of the person mentioned as מאד ('strength / might') becomes a concrete expression through the giving of one's property to the community.[104] Weinfeld concludes:

> Worship of God by דעת, כח, and הון is expressed by the members of the Qumran sect in a practical manner; i.e., the member is obliged to contribute to the sect from his knowledge, his strength, and his property.[...] Loyalty to the company, which is אל יחד, is like loyalty to God himself, that should be, בכל מאדך, בכל לבבך, בכל נפשך (Deut 6:5). Knowledge, strength, and wealth are the practical interpretation of ל ב and of מאד of Deuteronomy, in the Qumran sect.[105]

Whether or not one follows Weinfeld in this precise equation, it is certain that for the communities projected in both 1QS and CD worship of God was expressed through various means, one of which was with proper use of possessions as determined by the 'divine economy' of the regulations.[106] In this, there is a common fusion of piety towards the divinity and harmonious

---

103. See the comments from Murphy, *Wealth*, 59–60, particularly those regarding the 'alternative *oikonomia*' (60).
104. Weinfeld, 'Covenant', 68–9.
105. Weinfeld, 'Covenant', 69.
106. Murphy (*Wealth*, 48–9, 60, 90, 97–8, 120–30 [esp. 122], 133, 136) argues in a similar direction to Weinfeld for CD and 1QS.

relationships with fellow members of the group, as it was seen among the messianist, Pythagorean, and Essene communities examined above.

The community collectively portrayed in the Dead Sea Scrolls is a fiercely eschatological sectarian group, viewing itself as the true Israel, the eschatological remnant of God's holy people awaiting the 'time of God's glory'. Their daily lives were regulated by a strict holiness code and the corresponding desire to ward off pollution and root out moral wickedness from their midst.[107] The complex theories regarding the groups' developmental histories need not detain us here from examining *The Community Rule* and *The Damascus Document* as literary instantiations of communal living. Gordon Zerbe summarizes the theological framework of the documents found at Qumran comparing them with the Jesus movement:

> Admittedly, neither the covenanters of the Dead Sea Scrolls nor Jesus' followers would have thought of social morality as a separate ethical category. They would have agreed that these topics [economic justice and nonretaliation] fall under the heading of obligation to neighbor and belong more generally to keeping God's commands and to maintaining holiness.[108]

Particularly, as Zerbe argues, 'social morality is integral to the issue of "purity"...'[109] For both 1QS and CD, economic justice is a matter of uncleanness and defilement, and transgression of the ethos risks polluting the holiness of the entire community. Forkman argues, referring to 1QS 3.5 as an allusion to Lev. 13.45, 'He who was totally expelled from the sect was considered as unclean as a leper.'[110] As we shall see in *The Community Rule* (1QS 7.25) and *The Damascus Document* (4QD^a 11.14-16), members were forbidden to associate with the expelled, or else they would suffer the same social contamination of death.

---

107. See Forkman, *Limits*, 44, 46, 55-7, 74-7; Klauck, 'Gütergemeinschaft', 67; Lawrence H. Schiffman, *Sectarian Law in the Dead Sea Scrolls: Courts, Testimony, and the Penal Code* (BJS 33; Chico, CA: Scholars Press, 1983), 161-8, 215-16; Taylor, *Pythagoreans*, 20, 46-7, 65, 105-6. See also Bertil Gärtner, *The Temple and The Community in Qumran and the New Testament: A Comparative Study in the Temple Symbolism of the Qumran Texts and the New Testament* (Cambridge: Cambridge University Press, 1965), 16-46, for an examination of temple symbolism at Qumran. Cf. Murphy, *Wealth*, 143-52.

108. Zerbe, 'Economic Justice', 319. The present study is concerned with what Zerbe calls 'economic justice', which he defines as 'expectations for maintaining just relationships with one's neighbour, particularly in matters pertaining to wealth, money, commerce, or possessions, usually marked on the one hand by prohibitions against wrong patterns (e.g., 'unjust wealth'), and on the other hand by expectations to attend to the welfare of one's neighbour or to engender certain attitudes in relation to possessions and money' (319).

109. Zerbe, 'Economic Justice', 324. However, we agree with the criticisms of Corrado Martone ('The Nature of Impurity at Qumran', in *Fifty Years After* [eds Schiffman, Tov and VanderKam], 610-16) that all cultic impurities should not be identified with moral 'sin'.

110. Forkman, *Limits*, 44. It should be noted, however, that this section of the *Rule* deals not with one expelled, but with one who refuses to enter the Covenant. See also Klauck, 'Gütergemeinschaft', 67; Murphy, *Wealth*, 146. Cf. above §4.2.2.2. nn. 108-9, on pollution and contamination.

This introduction is best concluded with two quotes from Murphy, who summarizes the communal ethos and moral cosmos as a theological vision. The quotes come from her introduction and her conclusion, appropriately framing a discussion in the way that covenant fidelity and radical holiness framed the 'divine economy' of the Qumran Covenanters:

[T]his symbolic world [of the Qumran communities] was governed by commitment to radical covenant fidelity. Economic transactions will provide community members with so many occasions to apply the Torah command to love God with their whole strength and to love their neighbors. This symbolic system of covenant fidelity allows several other frameworks of meaning to be integrated with a radical Torah ethic, including the wilderness experience of Israel's past, the cultic context of sacrificial acts, and the eschatological ideals of a restored Temple and an economy turned on its head.[111]

[T]he Qumran community not only idealized its economy or projected its ideal form into the eschatological future, but actually attempted to realize the promised redemption and past covenant in the society they created. Their ideal, and thus their provisional economy, was motivated by radical covenant fidelity and was modeled on the system of sanctification that the Temple was supposed to provide. Their economic system was thus profoundly grounded in Torah and was radically conservative in relation to other social groups.[112]

Covenant faithfulness and cultic purity regulate all interactions, especially economic transactions, within the communities represented by the Dead Sea Scrolls, particularly *The Community Rule* and *The Damascus Document*.

5.3.2. The Community Rule

5.3.2.1. Introduction
The Community Rule (סרך היחד), also sometimes called *The Manual of Discipline*, is positioned as one of the primary legal texts governing life and behaviour among those living in the community. Apparently having a long development, the current text of 1QS is composite with at least three or four recensions.[113] For heuristic purposes, the focus here will be on the final text of 1QS, with notations of other manuscripts in the footnotes.

---

111. Murphy, *Wealth*, 24.
112. Murphy, *Wealth*, 455.
113. Sarianna Metso, *The Textual Development of the Qumran Community Rule* (STDJ 21; Leiden: Brill, 1997), 69–149 (esp. the stemma on 147); idem, 'The Redaction of the Community Rule', *Fifty Years After* (eds Schiffman, Tov and VanderKam), 377–84; idem, 'The Textual Traditions of the Qumran *Community Rule*', in *Legal Texts and Legal Issues: Proceedings of the Second Meeting of the International Organization for Qumran Studies Cambridge 1995* (eds Moshe Bernstein, Florentino García Martínez, John Kampen; Leiden: Brill, 1997), 141–7 (stemma on 145); and (mentioned by Murphy, *Wealth*, 105–10) Philip S Alexander and Geza Vermes, *Qumran Cave 4.XIX: Serekh ha-YaHad and Two Related Texts* (DJD 26; Oxford: Clarendon, 1998). In light of these nuanced studies, Forkman's (*Limits*, 61–2) theory of linear addition would have to be modified, and, derivatively, perhaps also

Based on the scribal markings, Murphy divides the structure of 1QS into four major sections: (1) 1QS 1.1–4.26, (2) 5.1–7.25, (3) 8.1–9.2, and (4) 9.3–11.22.[114] She proffers five basic generic categories for the material: (1) introductions, (2) liturgical norms of covenant initiation and renewal, (3) principals of communal organization, (4) rules of communal discipline, and (5) guidelines or instructional standards for the wise leader.[115] It is in categories (2) and (4) that one would expect to find the discursive conventions surrounding the community-of-goods and its associated disciplinary practices.

Finally, by means of introduction, Murphy suggests three primary rationales for voluntary offering of wealth in 1QS: (1) covenant fidelity, (2) sacrificial offering, and (3) unity in the holy spirit.[116] Zerbe's conclusions are in line with Murphy as he writes, 'it is doubtful that the motivation for their community-of-goods can primarily be attributed to [ascetic] eschatological renunciation. [...] Rather, emphasis is on communal life in anticipation of God's future restoration, not on poverty or ascetic renunciation as such.'[117]

5.3.2.2. Initiation and Discipline

In the first section of covenant initiation and renewal (1QS 2.25b–3.12), both primary themes of covenant and purity come through clearly.[118] If one does not join the covenant, he is unfit to be counted among the upright and unfit for the righteous counsel. He is 'unclean / defiled' (טמא)! The same is the case with the next section of covenant initiation and renewal (5.7b–6.1b). Entering the council of the community (עצת היחד) is entering into the covenant of God (ברית אל), requiring an oath to be guided completely by the Law of Moses as revealed primarily to 'the sons of Zadok, the Priests, Keepers of the Covenant and seekers of His will' (1QS 5.9) and then to the multitude. Further, the one entering the covenant 'shall undertake by the Covenant to separate from all the men of injustice who walk in the way of wickedness' (1QS 5.10-11). Here we see the strong sectarian tendency that assimilation into the communal ethos conversely means separation from outsiders (cf. 1QS

---

his thesis that 'the development within the sect is one which goes towards greater emphasis of the holiness motif' (78).

These traditions of the text are verified by other fragments discovered in Caves 4 (4Q256–64, 280, 286–87, 502) and 5 (5Q11, 13) at Qumran. See the helpful parallel charts in Murphy, 'Appendix B: Parallel Passages on Wealth in all Rule Manuscripts', in *Wealth*, 495–512.

114. Murphy, *Wealth*, 110–15, esp. Tables 7 ('Repetition of generic categories in the four major sections of 1QS') and 8 ('Texts mentioning wealth in the Qumran Rule manuscripts arranged by section and generic categories') (112, 115). See also her 'Appendix C: Outline of the Rule of the Community (1QS) Based on Paragraph Markings' (513–17).

115. Murphy, *Wealth*, 112–14.

116. Murphy, *Wealth*, 117–55.

117. Zerbe, 'Economic Justice', 333.

118. Schiffman, *Sectarian Law*, 156: 'A major theme, if not *the* major theme, of the *Manual of Discipline* is entry in the sect [...] characterized as an obligation, taken freely, to comply with the complex set of rules and regulations by which the sect lived.'

1.10-11; 9.16-17, 21-23; 10.18-20; 11.1-2).[119] Wealth (הון)[120] was a symbol of communal membership, occurring

> alongside various other terms in 1QS: knowledge, strength, Torah, judgment, counsel, purity/pure food, service. In each case, the terms appear in passages concerned to establish or maintain communal boundaries, whether by assimilation of the initiate, by alienation of the errant member or outsider, or by the assertion of executive authority.[121]

It is the third section on covenant initiation (1QS 6.13b-23) that has served New Testament scholars (like Capper and Taylor) with the parallel to the practice of community-of-goods in Acts 2 and 4. Murphy has demonstrated that the community viewed this action of voluntary offering as a sacrificial offering to God in a manner parallel to the sacred offerings of the Exodus wilderness sanctuary.[122]

Below is the prescription for the ritual-initiation period. I have interpolated with ordinal numbers in the English translation where I understand the seven stages to take place.

> [13b]Every man, born of Israel, who freely pledges himself [14]to join the Council of the community (עצה היחד) shall [1st] be examined by the Guardian at the head of the Congregation (הרבים) concerning his understanding and his deeds. If he is fitted to the discipline, [2nd] he shall admit him [15]into the Covenant that he may be converted to the truth and depart from all injustice; and he shall instruct him in all the rules of the Community. And later, [3rd] when he comes to stand before the Congregation, they shall all deliberate his case, [16]and according to the decision of the Council of the Congregation he shall either enter or depart. [4th] After he has entered the Council of the Community he shall not touch the pure Meal of [17]the Congregation until one {full}[123] year is completed, and until he has been examined concerning his spirit and deeds; nor shall he have any share in the property of the Congregation. [18]Then [5th] when he has completed one year within the Community, the Congregation shall deliberate his case with regard to his understanding and observance of the Law. And if it be his destiny, [19]according to the judgment of the Priests and the multitude of the men of their Covenant, to enter the company of the Community, his property and earnings shall be handed over to the [20]Bursar [המבקר] of the Congregation who shall register it to his account and shall not spend it for the Congregation. He shall not touch the Drink of the Congregation until [21]he has completed a second year among the men of the Community. [6th] But when the second year has passed, he shall be examined, according to the judgment of the Congregation, and if [22]it be his destiny, to enter the Community, then [7th] he shall be inscribed among his brethren in the order of his rank for the Law, and for justice, and for the pure Meal; his property shall be merged and he shall offer his counsel and judgment to the Community. (1QS 6.13b-24, trans. Vermes, slightly emended)

119. See Zerbe, 'Economic Justice', 331 and n. 45.
120. For other terms used of wealth in 1QS, including the term ממון relevant to Luke (16.9, 11, 13), see Murphy, *Wealth*, 155–8.
121. Murphy, *Wealth*, 136.
122. Murphy, *Wealth*, 137–53.
123. From 4Q256 according to Vermes, *Complete*, 106. Cf. García Martínez and Tigchelaar, *Study Edition*, 1:514.

Presented here is the most detailed prescription for the integration of a new member into the community. It is imperative to realize that the deepest stage, the highest ideal, of communal membership includes the 'mixing' of one's property into the communal stockpile.[124] Furthermore, the gradual integration of the novice's resources stresses the voluntary nature of the action.[125] This freedom existed within a system of ritually structured norms and value constraints (e.g., honour / shame dynamics). The legal discourse presents in unambiguous terms the symbolic power of possessions to represent oneself and his commitment and assimilation into the community life.

The rules of communal discipline (1QS 6.24–7.25) begin with penalties for those who lie about property.[126]

> [24] *These are the Rules by which they shall judge at a Community (Court of) Inquiry according to the cases.* [25]*If one of them has lied deliberately in matters of property, he shall be excluded from the pure Meal of the Congregation for one year and shall do penance with respect to one quarter of his food.* (1QS 6.24-25, trans. Vermes)

Murphy suggests two possible reasons for fronting this regulation for lying, either because it was the most commonly contested point of law or because it was the most concrete symbol of faithfulness to the communal ethos. She opts for the latter because the sectarian penal code relied on sapiential-apocalyptic texts which likewise favour economic matters in the criteria of eschatological judgement.[127] Furthermore, the conclusion of the penal code indicates that it is framed by reference to improper use of wealth. It is concluded with strictures against mixing one's pure food or property with an apostate, which will result in expulsion along with the original offender.[128]

> [22]{...} If, after being in the Council of the Community {...} for ten full years, [23] {...} the spirit of any man has failed, so that he has betrayed the Community and departed from [24]the Congregation to walk in the stubbornness of his heart, he shall return no more to the Council of the Community. Moreover, if any member of the Commu[nity h]as[129] shared [25]with him his food or property wh[ich...] of the Congregation, his sentence shall be the same; [he] shall be ex[pelled]. (1QS 7.22-25, trans. Vermes)

124. Forkman, *Limits*, 58, 63; Schiffman, *Sectarian Law*, 162.
125. Capper, 'Community of Goods', 1745, 1746–7; idem, 'Palestinian Cultural Context', 329, 337–40; Murphy, *Wealth*, 141.
126. See Murphy, 'Appendix D: Arrangement of the Rules of Communal Discipline in 1QS VI 24–VII 25', in *Wealth*, 519–22.
127. Murphy, *Wealth*, 53, suggests the following texts: *Sibilline Oracle* 2.56–148, *1 Enoch* 91–104, and *2 Enoch* 39–66. Murphy offers an interesting suggestion for the significance of the judgement: 'If this judgment is an example of *lex talionis*, then the nature of lying about money or wealth becomes clear: it is lying about what one brings into the community on a regular basis, the produce of one's daily work' (54).
128. Murphy, *Wealth*, 155; cf. 81 and n. 140. See Zerbe, 'Economic Justice', 331 and n. 43. Contrast this with the simplistic referential interpretation of this text by Forkman (*Limits*, 63): 'The one expelled, to put it simply, had to walk the path of the novice, but in the opposite direction.'
129. Vermes does not indicate the lacuna in the text here or in the next line; I added the brackets to indicate this. See Charlesworth, *Rule*, 44.

Schiffman also reads the hierarchy of seriousness as determined by the stringency of punishment, '[t]he most serious offenses come at the beginning and at the end'.[130]

Similar regulations are directed toward those who transgress the Law of Moses generally in 1QS 8.20-27.[131] For those who sin inadvertently, they are to be excluded from the pure meal and the Council. The penance for such a one should last two years. However, if one sins with deliberation, he is to be *permanently* expelled with no recourse for restitution.[132] Further, 'no man of holiness shall be associated in his property or counsel in any matter at all' (1QS 8.23). The community and the expelled are socially barred from one another.

5.3.2.3. Summary

The Community Rule firmly dictates strict guidelines regarding the use of property. The currency of this 'divine economy' is covenant fidelity.[133] Honour and privilege in this Community are concretely embodied by the gradual surrender of one's possessions and their fusion into the common life. Punishments are meted for transgressing this ethos. The economic aspect frames the first regulations of communal discipline (1QS 6.24–7.25). The punishment is not as harsh for transgressing the communal ethos by lying as it is in Acts. However, the ultimate penalty for betrayal of the community is expulsion, the social death. This is meted out for deliberate transgression (7.22-24; 8.22-23; 9.1) as well as for sharing food or possessions with the expelled member (7.25). The parallel to the laudatory esteem is the progressive depth of covenant fidelity expressed through the amassing privileges experienced at the various levels of the novitiate. Discipline for lying begins with a reduction in rations, but the range extends to complete, irreversible expulsion. A model reader of 1QS may have found the deaths of Ananias and Sapphira severe compared to their own legislation, but they would not have found it foreign to the expectations of a community living in the eschatological presence of the Holy Spirit. The incident, rather, would most likely have been evidence of the divine guarantee upon a holy, elect community living in accord with divine stipulations.

It is divulged below that 1QS is distinctive in envisioning an *actual* community of shared goods. By contrast, *The Damascus Document* presupposes private property of which some is to be made public within the limits of the communal

---

130. Schiffman, *Sectarian Law*, 157.

131. This section is included in that which Metso (*Textual Development*, 144, 146; 'Textual Traditions', 143, 144) considers to have been absent from the original due to its lack in 4QS^e (4Q259). See García Martínez and Tigchelaar, *Study Edition*, 1:530–3.

132. See the comments by Schiffman, *Sectarian Law*, 158, 168–73.

133. See Murphy, *Wealth*, 161: 'Shared goods do not render members equal, but neither are goods any longer as a basis of distinction between members. Rather, rank is based on one's covenant fidelity, symbolized in part by the commitment to share goods, and rank is assessed by the entire community that participates in that commitment.'

identity. However, *The Damascus Document* is included in this discussion because of the highly symbolic form of 'wealth' as a principal means of covenant fidelity and proper kinship relations. Its fundamental importance is attested by its place in the Dead Sea Scrolls collection, by its ideological overlap with 1QS, and by the severity with which it deals with economic matters as constitutive of community identity. In many ways it broadens the scope of the 'divine economy' among the Qumran covenanters (when compared to 1QS) while still representing elements of (e)utopian and friendship discourses.

5.3.3. The Damascus Document

5.3.3.1. Introduction

The Damascus Document, sometimes referred to as the *Zadokite Document* or the *Damascus Covenant*, is distinctive among the documents found in Khirbet Qumrân, for it was known before the discovery of the Dead Sea Scrolls. VanderKam recounts how Solomon Schechter, a Jewish scholar working in Old Cairo at the turn of the twentieth century, found two copies in the *geniza* of the Ezra Synagogue in 1896 and published them in 1910. These texts were called A (with sixteen columns) and B (with two columns, labelled 19–20, and overlap considerably with A, columns 7–8[134]). The numbers come from the medieval copyists in the tenth and twelfth centuries CE.[135] Versions of the document were recovered in several of the caves at Qumran (4Q266–73, 5Q12, 6Q15).[136] These versions have added considerably to the textual witness of *The Damascus Document*, including additional opening lines and an opening admonition not attested in CD, as well as an appended expulsion ritual.[137] It is generally acknowledged that *The Damascus Document* can be divided into two broad categories: admonition and laws.[138] Murphy affirms that 'despite the variables of generic category and therefore possibly of public function, an interest in the disposition of wealth remains constant'.[139]

Murphy offers three major categories on wealth in *The Damascus Document*: (1) those illustrating the community's history, (2) those illustrative of communal relations, and (3) those related to communal ideals. The second

---

134. CD-B 19 corresponds to CD-A 7.5-10, 8.2-21. CD-B 20 has no parallel. See Hempel, *Damascus Texts*, 31–3.
135. VanderKam, *Dead Sea Scrolls*, 55–6; Hempel, *Damascus Texts*, 15–17; Murphy, *Wealth*, 4–6. A fuller discussion is provided by Stefan C. Ref, 'The Damascus Document from the Cairo Genizah: Its Discovery, Early Study and Historical Significance', in *Centennial of Discovery* (eds Baumgarten, Chazon and Pinnick), 113–27.
136. See the helpful parallel charts in Murphy, 'Appendix A: Parallel Passages on Wealth in all Damascus Document Manuscripts', in *Wealth*, 457–93.
137. See Hempel, *Damascus Texts*, 26–7, 41–2; García Martínez and Tigchelaar, *Study Edition*, 1:580–3, 598–9, 604–5.
138. Charlotte Hempel, *The Laws of the Damascus Document: Sources, Tradition and Redaction* (STDJ 29; Leiden: Brill, 1998), 8–14; idem, *Damascus Texts*, 26–53; Murphy, *Wealth*, 32–4.
139. Murphy, *Wealth*, 33.

category is most relevant to the present study. The third category helps to define the various elements of the ideological background framing the discourse.[140]

Murphy's first category is also suggestive of the ideological texture of the document and its stance concerning the proper use of wealth.[141] There are general denunciations of unjust wealth (CD-A 8.2b-12a // CD-B 19.15-24a) and damning rhetoric against the improper handling of sacrifices or defilement of the temple (CD-A 6.15b-17a).[142] Furthermore, in a revealing passage, 'the princes of Judah' are indicted for a long list of things, including wallowing 'in the ways of fornication and wicked wealth (ובהון רשעה)', and striving intensely for wealth and vicious gain (CD-A 8.5, 7 // CD-B 19.17, 19). There is resonance with earlier indictments anticipated in CD-A 4.13–5.15. There, wealth (הון) is presented as one of the 'nets of Belial' along with lust and defilement of the temple (CD-A 4.17) that snares Israel in the last days.

'Corresponding to this sharp condemnation of unjust wealth in CD is the theme of communal solidarity and support for the needy.'[143] Murphy hears an echo of Isaiah 58.6 in CD-A 13.9-10, the passage immediately preceding the passage quoted above in the introduction of the 'The Moral Universe of the Renewed Covenant' as an example of submission of property as symbolic of entering the covenant. Below I set the CD passage alongside the Isaiah passage with the parallels underlined:

> ⁹He shall love them as a father loves his children, and shall carry them in all their distress like a shepherd his sheep. ¹⁰He shall <u>loosen</u> all the <u>chains</u> which bind them that in his Congregation there may be none that are <u>oppressed</u> or broken. (CD-A 13.9-10, trans. Vermes, emended)

> ⁶Is not this the fast that I choose: to <u>loose</u> the <u>bonds</u> of injustice, to undo the thongs of the yoke, to let the <u>oppressed</u> go free, and to break every yoke? ⁷Is it not to share your bread with the hungry, and bring the homeless poor into your house; when you see the naked, to cover them, and not to hide yourself from your own kin? (Isa. 58.6-7, NRSV)

Murphy understands the significance of this allusion as a means whereby 'the Damascus covenanters create the community envisioned by Third Isaiah when they relieve their neighbors' economic distress by freeing the oppressed, feeding the hungry, housing the homeless, and caring for community members'.[144] As she goes on to note, the community has a mandatory collection to care for a group precisely of this description, 'the fatherless', 'the poor and the needy, the aged sick and the man who is stricken (with disease), the captive taken by foreign people, the virgin with no near kin, and the ma[id for] whom no man

---

140. Murphy, *Wealth*, 93–101. The 'communal ideals' are primarily biblical themes and imageries shaping the discourse, like the Ideal wilderness community, the Deuteronomic exhortation to covenant fidelity, sabbatical and Jubiliary legislation, prophetic critiques against unjust wealth, etc.'
141. Grossman, *Reading for History*, is helpful with this.
142. See Zerbe, 'Economic Justice', 322–4, who offers more examples.
143. Zerbe, 'Economic Justice', 324.
144. Murphy, *Wealth*, 43–4.

cares' (CD-A 14.14-16, trans. Vermes). The allusion is strengthened by the suggestion of Zerbe that the denunciation of CD-A 8.6 – 'and each man hated his fellow, and they hid themselves, each man from him who is flesh of his flesh'[145] – echoes Isaiah 58.7. Further, Zerbe claims that 'all of the occurrences of the hithpa'el of עלם ("to hide oneself") in the Hebrew Bible refer to the refusal to help someone in need (Deut 22:1, 3–4; Isa 58:7; Ps 55:2 [55:1 ET]; Job 6:16)'.[146]

This reference to Isa. 58.6, precisely as a programmatic mission to free the oppressed, is familiar to students of Luke-Acts (Luke 4.18-19). The Jubilee motif is one particular frame which undergirds the 'divine economy' of *The Damascus Document* as it does in the theological vision of Luke-Acts (see §4.2.1. above).[147] Wealth is imbued with theological symbolism in *The Damascus Document*, and as such approaches (e)utopian economic language and themes.

5.3.3.2. *Economic Transactions as Community Boundary Markers*

The Damascus Document assumes the retention of private property and marriage (e.g., CD-A 7.6-9; 9.10b-16a; 12.6b-11a; 13.15-18; 16.10-12; 19.3-5; 4Q271 3.4-15). In this sense, *The Damascus Document* does not represent the absolute (e)utopian community-of-goods and life.[148] However, possessions are highly significant as symbolic boundary markers for communal identity. There is a difference between how economic transactions are conducted with fellow members of the community and with those outside the community. The continuation of the section of CD-A 13 quoted above indicates the role of the Guardian / Examiner (המבקר) in supervising economic matters. It reads:

> ...[12b]No member [13]of the camp shall have authority to admit a man to the Congregation against the decision of the Guardian of the camp. [14] No member of the Covenant of God shall give or receive anything from the sons of Dawn[149] [15]except hand to hand.[150] No man shall form any association for buying or selling without informing [16]the Guardian of the camp and shall act on (his) advice and they shall not go {astray... (CD-A 13.12b-16a, trans. Vermes, emended)[151]

145. The translation comes from Zerbe, 'Economic Justice', 325.
146. Zerbe, 'Economic Justice', 326.
147. See Murphy, *Wealth*, 66–71, 79–83, 99–100; Zerbe, 'Economic Justice', 325–8.
148. Klauck, 'Gütergemeinschaft', 64–5.
149. Vermes has a possible alternate reading here of 'sons of the Pit' (this phrase exists in CD-A 6.15). The final *reš* could be rendered as a *taw*, thus changing השחר to השחת. Chaim Rabin, *The Zadokite Documents* (Oxford: Clarendon, 1954), 67. See the following two footnotes.
150. I have translated כף לכף more literally here where Vermes has 'for a price'. However, the phrase would indicate not exchange of money but rather a bartering, which seems more likely. See Joseph M. Baumgarten, 'The "Sons of Dawn" in CDC 13:14–15 and the Ban on Commerce among the Essenes', *IEJ* 33 (1983): 81–5.
151. Cf. CD-A 12.6-11, where the members of the community are admonished against defrauding a Gentile *in order that* he may not blaspheme. See Forkman, *Limits*, 43, 45; Murphy, *Wealth*, 88–90.

The translation here is influenced by the thesis of Baumgarten correcting the early (mis)transcription of Rabin.[152] The issue, in particular, is the nature of the transaction mentioned in vv. 14–15a, whether dealings with the 'sons of Dawn' are intra-communal transactions or business with outsiders. Hempel, following Baumgarten, opts for the former, indicating a distinction between the manner of economic transaction between insiders and outsiders.[153] Economic transactions with outsiders were conducted with money as a distancing medium. Murphy states, 'The price, or cash transacted, was a necessary buffer that shielded the sectarian from defilement in a more sinful economy.'[154] Intra-communal economic transactions were carried through via generalized reciprocity, a bartering of sorts. Baumgarten explains,

> This rule [of lines 14–15...] concerns not avoidance of contacts with outsiders, but the internal economic relations among members of the community. These relations are to be predicated not on the commercial basis of buying and selling (שא...יתן), but the fraternal concept of mutual help and exchange of services (כף לכף).[155]

The legislation resembles closer relations also with the injunction for a monthly contribution of at least two days' wages as a charity to support the needy in the community (CD-A 14.12-19).[156] In this text it is the Examiner and the judges (המבקר והשופטים) of the community that distribute the charity. Murphy offers some suggestive interpretive possibilities for this practice. From the reconstruction aided by 4QD^a 10.1.11, with the phrase '[...th]ese are the foundation walls of the assembly',[157] she sees a possible echo of Ezek. 22.29-31 indicating that the monthly contribution is a means of building the foundation walls for the future messianic city.[158] Alternatively, she suggests that the monthly charity may be understood in terms of an alternative religious or economic institution. Finally, and not mutually exclusive, she suggests an interpretation where this feature is an extension of the kinship support

---

152. Rabin, *Zadokite Documents*, 67. It would seem Baumgarten ('CDC 13:14–15') has swayed the scholarly opinion. He is followed by, e.g., James H. Charlesworth, ed., *The Dead Sea Scrolls: Hebrew, Aramaic, and Greek Texts with English Translations. Vol. 2: Damascus Document, War Scroll and Related Documents* (Tübingen: Mohr / Louisville: Westminster / John Knox Press, 1995), 55 n. 203; Hempel, *Laws*, 123–5; Murphy, *Wealth*, 58.
153. Hempel, *Laws*, 125. Contra, e.g., Zerbe, 'Economic Justice', 327 n. 27.
154. Murphy, *Wealth*, 58.
155. Baumgarten, 'CDC 13:14–15', 83. Baumgarten immediately appeals to what I have labelled the '(e)utopian economy' in Philo's (*Prob.* 78) and Josephus' (*J.W.* 2.127) descriptions of the Essenes (see §5.2.1.3. above). Compare the discussion of Sahlins's construal of reciprocity above, §4.1.1.2.
156. Hempel (*Damascus Texts*, 41; *Laws*, 138) notes that in 4QD^a 10.1.6 there is not room for the words 'every month', and so this text may indicate a one time collection.
157. 4Q266 10.1.11: הקהל [יסוד]ות אוש[י] ואן[ה יסודות See García Martínez and Tigchelaar, *Study Edition*, 1:594.
158. Murphy, *Wealth*, 86. She sees further warrant for this suggestion in the possible echo of Ezek. 22.26- 27 in CD-A 10.14-21 (69). See also Zerbe, 'Economic Justice', 325.

system. 'The association has replaced the family.'[159] In any case, the economic relations within the group have an idealist quality leaning towards the (e) utopian-friendship ethos. For the community projected from *The Damascus Document* the motivation is linked with messianic redemption and 'envisioned as a temporary correlative to the atoning sacrifice anticipated in the coming messianic age [CD-A 14.19]'.[160]

5.3.3.3. Initiation and Discipline

The process of initiation is less complex in *The Damascus Document* than it is in 1QS. In CD-A 15.5b–16.6a (supplemented by 4QD^a 8.1) the novice is to swear with 'the oath of the Covenant' (CD-A 15.6) and be examined by the Guardian / Examiner (המבקר).[161] Already noted above is the role of the Guardian / Examiner in scrutinizing those who join in regard to deeds, insight, strength, might and wealth (CD-A 13.11-12) and supervising economic associations and transactions (CD-A 13.12b-16a). It is often mentioned that the initiation process is light when compared to that in 1QS 6.13-23.[162] Even if less stringent, there are remarkable similarities with the *Rule*. These include primary regulations concerning one who lies about wealth in the penal code (CD-A 14.20-21) and restrictions concerning associations with expelled or apostate members (CD-B 20.6-10). Distinctive to *The Damascus Document* is the (possibly) capital nature of crimes concerning wealth (CD-A 9.16–10.3)[163] and an expulsion ritual at the end attested by Qumran fragments (4QD^a 11.14b-16) which also condemns one who would associate with the apostate.

The penal code in CD, as in 1QS 6.24-25, begins with legislation on punishing those who lie about money (ממון). The manuscript is heavily damaged, but fortunately able to be supplemented by 4QD^a 10.1.14 and 4QD^d 11.1.4-5.[164] It reads,

---

159. Murphy, *Wealth*, 86. This would not be too far from the interpretation of the household nature of the 'divine economy' of the early Jerusalem messianists or the Pythagoreans suggested in §4.2.1. and §5.1.3. above, respectively.

160. Murphy, *Wealth*, 87.

161. Further comment on the procedure can be found in Forkman, *Limits*, 63–4; Hempel, *Laws*, 73–90.

162. Forkman, *Limits*, 64; Hempel, *Laws*, 76; Zerbe, 'Economic Justice', 327. Hempel (*Damascus Texts*, 36) also notes the comparable procedure in 1QS 5.7c-9a.

163. Murphy (*Wealth*, 55–6) gives four arguments in favour of viewing the regulations of CD-A 9.22–10.3 as capital: (1) the preceding co-text refers to capital cases, and the present passage is a subsidiary case of the same phenomenon, (2) the passage is followed by restrictions for witnesses, indicating the capital nature of the crime, (3) the contribution of wealth in CD and 1QS is framed as a matter of fidelity to Torah, and (4) violations regarding wealth are treated elsewhere in the document as worthy of complete judgement or expulsion. Murphy correctly identifies 'capital' punishment with expulsion. Compare Forkman, *Limits*, 48–50, 64–5, 133–4; Horbury, 'Extirpation', 57–8.

164. See Murphy, *Wealth*, 52–3.

> ²⁰[...And the ma]n who <lies> knowingly with regard to riches, they shall ex[clude from the pure food] ²¹[...and he shall be] punished for six days. (CD-A 14.20-21, trans. García Martínez and Tigchelaar)

Damage to the manuscript makes it impossible to ascertain the exact punishment prescribed. However, from what is extant it can be seen that the punishment is perhaps less severe than in 1QS 6.25. Here it is a punishment for six days, versus the one year exclusion from the pure meal of the congregation.[165] Here we recall Murphy's suggestion for the significance of fronting the regulations on lying because it is the most concrete symbol of behavioural fidelity to the covenant and community.[166]

Expulsion from *The Damascus Document* community is a consequence of lack of diligence in the ways of the community. CD-B 19.33–20.27a presents various threats for permanent and temporary expulsion. Those who defected from the new covenant in the land of Damascus 'shall not be counted in the assembly of the people, they shall not be inscribed in their lists, from the day of the gathering in {of the teacher}' (CD-B 19.35, trans. García Martínez and Tigchelaar).[167] The ultimate threat is extirpation at the end of the age, coming at the end of the passage:

> ²⁵And all, among those who entered the covenant, transgressing the limits of the law, when ²⁶the glory of God is manifested to Israel, shall be cut off from amongst the camp, and with them all who acted wickedly against ²⁷ᵃJudah in the days of its chastenings. (CD-B 20.25-27a, trans. García Martínez and Tigchelaar)

Following this threat is a promise for those who would remain faithful. In between the opening and closing threats lies a passage concerning expulsion and the dangers of associating with the expelled. The passage discusses the defector and warns against associating with him.

> ³ᵇ ... When his works become apparent, he shall be expelled from the congregation, ⁴as one whose lot did not fall among those taught by God. According to his trespass, the men of knowledge shall reprove him, ⁵until the day when he returns to stand along with the men of perfect holiness. {for} ⁶{his lot is not in the midst of m} But when his works become apparent according to the interpretation of the Torah in which walk ⁷the men of perfect holiness, let no man share with him in wealth or labor, ⁸for all the holy ones of the Most High have cursed him. And thus (is) the judgment of their neighbors concerning anyone who rejects, the first ⁹and the last, who put abominations upon their heart {and have placed} and walk in the wantonness

---

165. Murphy (*Wealth*, 53) notes that 1QDᵈ has sixty days (ששים יום). See also Zerbe, 'Economic Justice', 328 n. 30.
166. See nn. 127-8 above.
167. Heb: לא יחשבו בסוד עם בכתבם לא יכתבו מיום האסף {יור מורה}. See García Martínez and Tigchelaar, *Study Edition*, 1:578. The final words in the manuscript are corrupt. See Broshi, *Damascus Document*, 44. Charlesworth (*Damascus Document*, 32) has transcribed them with a line drawn through them indicating deletion by a scribe.

of ¹⁰ᵃtheir heart. They have no portion in the house of Torah. (CD-B 20.3-10a, trans. Charlesworth, emended)¹⁶⁸

A similar admonition occurs in the expulsion ceremony recovered in 4QDᵃ 11.1-20. With no parallel in CD, the threat here is more explicit than in the passage cited above. It reads:

> ¹⁴ᵇAnd the one who has been expelled will leave, and the man ¹⁵who eats from his riches, and the one who inquires about his welfare [ושלומו], {the one who has been expelled}¹⁶⁹ and the one who agrees with him. ¹⁶And his sentence will be written down by the Inspector's [המבקר] hand, as an engraving, and his judgment will be complete. (4Q266 11.14b-16, trans. García Martínez and Tigchelaar, emended)

The Hebrew here is ambiguous, in that the punishment of those who associate with the man is construed either as (1) expulsion along with the apostate (if the verb ויצא governs the following relative clauses beginning with אשר) or (2) simply the inscription of their crime in the Examiner's registry. Murphy argues for the latter, appealing to other mentions of inscription in the *Damascus Document*, including the initial inscription of wealth upon initiation (CD-A 13.11-12) and the only other mention of inscription of a crime, that of lying in regard to wealth (CD-A 9.16-23).¹⁷⁰ We may demur however, for it seems that the latter option does not preclude the former. Yes, the transgression is recorded. However, this does not necessarily exclude the associate from experiencing the penalty of expulsion. In light of the example of CD-A 9.16-23 offered as an example by Murphy, on her own account of the consequences of these 'capital' offences, the 'complete' judgement is in fact expulsion.¹⁷¹ I suggest, therefore, that in 4QDᵃ 11.14-16 the penalty for associating with an expelled member is itself expulsion.

Therefore, in the community where wealth and possessions are symbolic of the community identity, there is the danger of the social death, which, without repentance, will result in final extermination when the glory of the Lord is revealed. The rest of the community is warned not to 'share with him in wealth or labor' (CD-B 20.7). Those familiar with the severity of the (e)utopian community-of-goods disciplinary measures would have heard resonances with the *topos*, albeit with the particular thrust of the eschatological permutations advanced by *The Damascus Document*.

---

168. I have interpolated the marks of scribal deletion from the Hebrew text. See Broshi, *Damascus Document*, 46; Charlesworth, *Damascus Document*, 34.
169. The text here has been emended by the scribe. Consult Murphy, *Wealth*, 90.
170. Murphy, *Wealth*, 91: 'The penalty for the one who associates with the apostate is that his action will be inscribed by the Examiner permanently, and his judgement will be complete. This is not as severe as in 1QS VII 22-25, where the violator is himself expelled from the community.' Contrast Hempel, *Laws*, 182–3. She suggests an interpretation similar to Murphy. However, she is not content with the interpretation and speculates that parts of the passage have been lost.
171. See Murphy, *Wealth*, 54–6.

5.3.3.4. Summary

By way of summary, the community of the *Damascus Document* can be said to represent traces of the (e)utopian communal traditions of sharing possessions among community members as among close (fictive) kinship relations. As with the *Rule*, regulations concerning lying about possessions crown the penal code. Possessions among this community would serve as communal boundary markers, with differing means of economic transactions among community members and between community members and outsiders. The prophetic denunciations against unjust wealth and the corresponding theme of communal solidarity and support for the needy serve as identity markers. The initiation process is less rigorous than in 1QS, but there is more discussion of the dangerous consequences of transgressing the communal ethos with the threats of expulsion and, ultimately, eschatological extermination.

5.4. Summary and Conclusions for Socio-Historical Context

In summary, the divine economy as manifest in the community-of-goods discourse demonstrably has two major features. First, there is the laudatory esteem of such communities as (e)utopian ideals embodying the most commendable practices and relationships among its members. Each of the communities discussed were presented as an ideal community encouraging a (e)utopian alternative society. Possessions were weighted with symbolic importance to indicate the nature of harmonious relationships among members of the communities. Second, the discourse is associated with severe disciplinary practices. In the one instance of transgressing the ethos among the early Jerusalem messianists, the couple is struck dead by divine judgement. With the Pythagoreans, failure of the initiation process results in a social death. Josephus includes in his account of expelled members a stress on the dismal condition of apostates. Examples in the Qumran legislation are less severe, but are consistent by portraying transgressions concerning property as the most severe breach of communal solidarity. It should therefore be taken into consideration that the deaths of Ananias and Sapphira are severe in this milieu, but not out of place or incommensurate with the expectations of the socio-cultural *topos*. The story of Ananias and Sapphira is not unbefitting in the ancient Mediterranean world which told stories about the restoration of society back to a harmonious, paradisiacal state of origin. The episode is not a liability staining the tapestry of Luke-Acts with embarrassingly unjustifiable divine violence. The story could rather function as a comfort and assurance of divine favour upon the early history of the nascent messianic ἐκκλησία for those who are a part of this community.

Chapter 6

Inscribed Conventions: Divine Deputation and the Pattern of Salvation and Judgement

The action Peter performed in his confrontation with Ananias and Sapphira was an indictment that caused death. Wrapped up in his formal accusations (that the couple has lied to the Holy Spirit and tested the Spirit of the Lord) was the divinely sanctioned judicial sentence and execution. In order to understand how this can be, one must identify the social conditions that would make it possible to construe Peter's words as condemnatory actions. Drawing from the insights of Speech-Act Theory, we should expect to find both an 'external' and an 'internal' linguistic repertoire for the conventions inscribed into Luke-Acts.

The 'external' repertoire includes the social discourse of community-of-goods and its associated disciplinary practices as well as the numerous examples in the Scriptures of Israel where the prophetic word was efficacious in bringing about either blessing or judgement. As it was argued in the previous two chapters, the community-of-goods discourse was associated with laudatory esteem and severe disciplinary practices. The Ananias and Sapphira episode, as the negative illustration of the early messianists' community-of-goods, would have evoked expectations for severe disciplinary action as a result of transgressing that ethos. Furthermore, the peculiar context, where the eschatological presence of the Holy Spirit clashed with a satanic threat to the community, only heightened the stakes. Opposing the divine in these circumstances led to the couple's death.

The 'external' repertoire would also include the stories in the Scriptures of Israel where a divinely authorized person, such as a prophet, spoke powerfully sanctioned words to effect blessing or judgement. A few examples should suffice to establish such episodes as fertile precedents for the performative potential of the prophetic declaration.

There is also the 'internal' repertoire of the profound potency of a divinely endorsed utterance. The inscribed conventions undergirding effective prophetic speech in Luke-Acts include the fundamental empowerment of the Holy Spirit, and the drama of Jesus as the Prophet-King addressing Israel with 'the sword of his mouth' that brings both blessing and judgement. Because the persona of Peter in Acts is inseparably linked to the established persona of Jesus in Luke's Gospel, it is necessary to explore the plotline of Jesus as the Prophet-King pronouncing both judgement and salvation to Israel. The framing patterns of character types from Moses (Israel's principal prophet) and David (Israel's divinely appointed ruler) merge into a unique portrait of Jesus as one both bringing divine rule and divine deliverance through his life, death and resurrection. The plot emerges from the earliest scenes of Luke's Gospel, such as the infancy and baptism episodes, and continues through to the end of the narrative. In this unfolding story traditional stereotypes from Israel's sacred history imbue the story of Jesus with particular significance. Stock images of Israel rejecting prophetic messengers who in turn confront the rebellious generation form a conflict that drives Luke's gospel plotline. Jesus journeys his way up to Jerusalem, approaching the city as both the rightful heir to the Davidic throne and as the lamenting prophet bearing the news of impending judgement. It is precisely this storyline that establishes the 'internal' repertoire for the performance of divine speech leading up to Peter's encounter with Ananias and Sapphira. After exploring these dynamic elements around and within Luke-Acts, this chapter rounds out with the examination of certain passages illustrating further dimensions of speech-acts within the narrative of Acts.

6.1. External Literary Repertoire: Effective Prophetic Speech in the Scriptures of Israel

The actions and utterances of the prophets in the Scriptures of Israel are a rich field of suggestive inquiry. Prophetic warnings and indictments in Luke-Acts are performed against the backdrop of prophetic customs and expectations created by the world projected in the (Greek) Scriptures of Israel.[1] Even the forms of prophetic speech, such as accusing questions and assertions, seem to have influenced Luke's portrayal of prophetic protagonists. Luke transforms these traditions by combining the customary prophetic paradigm with the royal messianic fulfilment to create a fusion that transforms both traditions.

6.1.1. Accusing Questions and Assertions

A common feature of prophetic condemnations of individuals in the Scriptures of Israel is an accusation that comes in the form of a question. When Samuel confronts Saul for his disobedience in not putting all Amalek under the ban, Samuel asks: 'What is the sound of this flock in my ears, and

---

1. There were, of course, Hellenistic prophetic conventions as well. However, for Luke-Acts, the prophetic conventions in the Scriptures of Israel were the primary background. See David E. Aune, *Prophecy in Early Christianity and the Ancient Mediterranean World* (Grand Rapids: Eerdmans, 1983), 23–79; Christopher Forbes, *Prophecy and Inspired Speech in Early Christianity and its Hellenistic Environment* (Peabody, MA: Hendrickson, 1995), 103–81, 188–217.

the noise of these oxen I hear?' (1 Kgdms 15.14). Again, Samuel brings the word of the Lord, 'Are you not small before him [the Lord], leading a tribe of Israel? And yet, the Lord anointed you to be king over Israel.[...] So why did you not give heed to the voice of the Lord, but rather you rushed to store up the spoils and do evil in the sight of the Lord?' (2 Kgdms 15.17, 19). The continuation of Samuel's pronouncement fuses accusing questions with impending condemnation.

> Is there as much pleasure for the Lord in whole burnt offerings and sacrifices as in hearing the voice of the Lord? Behold, giving heed is above a good sacrifice, and obedience above the fat of rams.
> For sin is as divination; an idol is pain and suffering. Because you have rejected the word of the Lord, the Lord shall also reject you so that you will not be king over Israel. (1 Kgdms 15.22-23)

This whole episode of Samuel's confrontation with Saul is framed by the regret of the Lord for making Saul ruler over Israel (1 Kgdms 15.11, 35). The Lord expresses his will through Samuel, indicating the powerful use of the prophetic word to convey the divine intention.

In Nathan's rebuke to David, after telling his seductively indicting parable, Nathan uses both question and assertion: 'Why have you disparaged the word of the Lord to do evil in his eyes? Urias the Chettite you have slain with a sword, and his wife you have taken to be your own wife, and [furthermore] you have killed him with the sword of the sons of Ammon' (2 Kgdms 12.9). Nathan continues to pronounce upon David a punishment that corresponds to his crime: the sword shall never depart from his house, and David's wives will be given to his neighbour (2 Kgdms 12:10-13). Nathan also conveys forgiveness to the penitent David, but announces that the child of David and Bathsheba will not live.

The narratives of Elijah prove especially fruitful here. From the beginning of 4 Kingdoms, Elijah is a troubler of the wayward kings of the northern kingdom. The word of the Lord comes through Elijah to accuse king Ahaziah with a damning question, repeated three times in the episode (4 Kgdms 1.3, 6, 16): 'Is it because there is no God in Israel, that you go to enquire from Baal fly, the God of Akkaron? This should not be! This bed to which you have gone up, from there you shall not come down, for you will surely die' (4 Kgdms 1.6). Here, the present accusation of idolatry indicts Ahaziah's pretension that the God of Israel has been absent. Ahaziah's sickness is interpreted to be God's punishment for idolatry. Death will come 'according to the word of the Lord which Elijah spoke' (4 Kgdms 1.17). Moreover, the soldiers sent to collect Elijah are struck down by divine fire that comes at the word of Elijah (4 Kgdms 1.10, 12, 13-14).

Two more examples from Isaiah illustrate an interrogative form of indictment against individuals by the prophets. In Isa. 37, the Lord answers king Hezekiah's prayers with a word from Isaiah against Sennacherib. Isaiah speaks of Zion's resistance to the Assyrian assault, itself an insult to Israel's God: 'Whom have you insulted and provoked? Against whom have you lifted up your voice? Have you not raised your eyes toward heaven against the Holy One of Israel?' (Isa. 37.23 LXX).

When confronting Hezekiah later on for the foolish act of showing all his treasures to Babylonian emissaries, Isaiah drills him with questions: 'What did these men say? And from where did they come to you?' (Isa. 39.3 LXX // 4 Kgdms 20.14). The prophet warns Hezekiah that everything will be carried off to Babylon (Isa. 39.4-8 // 4 Kgdms 20.15-19). Again, questions precede the pronouncement of a dire future for Hezekiah's descendents. The prophet extracted the information from the king before declaring God's judgement.

These examples show a large precedent for the form of Peter's speech in Acts 5.1-11. In other words, the external repertoire would allow Luke's hearers to understand Peter's questions and statements as prophetic accusations and condemnations against Ananias and Sapphira.[2] The form of Peter's speech as questions and accusations is another element that invites the hearer to frame his confrontation with the couple as prophetic indictment.

6.2. Internal Repertoire: Effective Prophetic Speech in Luke-Acts

Examples of performative language are a prominent feature of Luke-Acts. Throughout his narrative, Luke exhibits a penchant for performative language. The Ananias and Sapphira pericope is only one example of the way in which Luke employs divine judgement as a consequence of transgressing the rule of the Messiah and resisting the divine economy. While this consequence is severe in the Lukan narrative world, it is not unique (e.g., Judas, Luke 22.21-22; Acts 1.18-20; cf. the performance of angelic speech in Luke 1.19-20, 22, 62-64). The creative power of the prophetic utterance is a dynamic force serving as the vehicle for God's promise, judgement, and revelation. For example, Jesus' prophetic commission predicts, but also directs the movement of the mission from Jerusalem to Judaea, Samaria, and to the 'uttermost part of the earth' (Acts 1.8). This is just the direction in which the narrative plot of Acts unfolds. Peter's speech at Pentecost evokes the response of repentance, as the audience is 'cut to the heart' (Acts 2.37), and three thousand are converted to become followers of Jesus. Peter speaks in the Name of Jesus to the lame beggar outside the Beautiful Gate, commanding him to walk, and he is restored. The prophetic word performs the healing (Acts 3.1-10). Paul challenges the magician Elymas, 'a Jewish false prophet' (Acts 13.6), and curses him with blindness, in a symbolic and ironic judgement (Acts 13.4-12). It seems that for Luke the prophetic word was a powerful force that could cause change in the world.

---

2. These and other examples are discussed by Claus Westermann, *Basic Forms of Prophetic Speech* (trans. Hugh C. White; Cambridge: Lutterworth Press / Louisville: Westminster / John Knox Press, 1991), 129–68. His insight into the literary forms of the prophetic speech continues to exert influence, but his account of the provenance and development of these forms has not been widely accepted.

Ultimately for Luke there is divine support for these conventional frameworks. The Spirit is the principal power cradling the nascent community and its leaders. God acts through the Holy Spirit, the Spirit of prophecy, to fulfil the divine promises and to guide God's agents of salvation. The Spirit is integral to the climactic ministry of Jesus, who brings salvation and judgement to Israel. Also, the Spirit, as the 'promise of the Father', is intimately linked to the continuing mission of God's people under the resurrected and enthroned Messiah. For Luke, God's prophets are baptized and filled with the Spirit in order to continue God's mission of liberating and restoring Israel, leading to the Gentiles also being saved and added to the community of believers.

6.2.1. *The Holy Spirit: The Divine Performance*

'The Holy Spirit plays a preeminent role in Luke's writings.'[3] As a result, the persona of the Holy Spirit in Luke-Acts has captured the imagination of many Lukan scholars.[4] There has been much effort invested into understanding the importance of the Holy Spirit as the Jewish theological background and context of much of Luke's narrative,[5] as a character within the narrative,[6] and the ethical-theological and missiological function of the Spirit as a driving force in the socio-rhetorical narrative logic of the text.[7]

---

3. François Bovon, *Luke the Theologian: Fifty-Three years of research (1950–2005)* (2nd rev. edn; Waco, TX: Baylor University Press, 2006), 228.

4. See the surveys and bibliographies in Bovon, *Theologian*, 225–72, 536–40, 643; Max Turner, *Power from on High: The Spirit in Israel's Restoration and Witness in Luke-Acts* (JPTSup 9; Sheffield: Sheffield Academic Press, 1996), 20–79. I am indebted to Turner's survey of scholarship, and the stamp of his thought is evident in what follows.

5. Here background refers to portrayals in the Scriptures of Israel and other earlier Jewish writings. Context refers to Jewish writings of the period roughly contemporaneous with Luke's writings, like the writings of Qumran, for instance. These two categories overlap. See Robert P. Menzies, *The Development of Early Christian Pneumatology with special reference to Luke-Acts* (JSNTSup 54; Sheffield: Sheffield Academic Press, 1991), 52–112; Turner, *Power*, 82–138; idem, *The Holy Spirit and Spiritual Gifts in the New Testament Church and Today* (rev. edn; Peabody: Hendrickson, 1996), esp. 1–18, 57–135; Matthias Wenk, *Community-Forming Power: The Socio-Ethical Role of the Spirit in Luke-Acts* (JPTSup 19; Sheffield: Sheffield Academic Press, 2000), 54–118; Ju Hur, *A Dynamic Reading of the Holy Spirit in Luke-Acts* (London: T&T Clark, 2001), 37–86. See also John R. Levison, *The Spirit in First-Century Judaism* (Leiden: Brill Academic Publishers, Inc., 2002).

6. See Hur, *Dynamic Reading*; William H. Shepherd, Jr, *The Narrative Function of the Holy Spirit as a Character in Luke-Acts* (SBLDS 147; Atlanta: Scholars Press, 1994).

7. Joseph A. Fitzmyer, 'The Role of the Spirit in Luke-Acts', in *The Unity of Luke-Acts* (ed. J. Verheyden; BETL 142; Leuven: Leuven University Press, 1999), 65–83; Jacob Jervell, 'Sons of the Prophets: The Holy Spirit in the Acts of the Apostles', in *The Unknown Paul: Essays on Luke-Acts and Early Christian History* (Minneapolis: Augsburg, 1984), 96–121; Max Turner, 'The Spirit of Prophecy and the Ethical/Religious Life of the Christian Community', in *Spirit and Renewal: Essays in Honor of J. Rodman Williams* (ed. Mark W. Wilson; JPTSup 5; Sheffield: Sheffield Academic Press, 1994), 166–90; Turner, *Power*, *passim*; Wenk, *Power*, *passim*.

This seems to be clearly the case in Acts 5.3, 4, where Peter's indictment to Ananias indicates a direct offence against the Holy Spirit. After a brief elucidation of the insights of previous scholars for the importance of the Spirit as a pervading presence in the narrative world of Luke-Acts, I discuss how the Spirit operates dynamically in the divine economy in Luke-Acts, and in particular as part of the repertoire of prophetic speech. The aim of the present section is to understand the socio-cultural and spiritual setting and tone of the interaction between Peter and the couple, and more importantly that Peter interprets the engagement as a confrontation between the Spirit-filled community and the Satan-filled heart of the counterfeits. It is a confrontation between eschatologically renewed life and ultimate judgement unto death.

There is a consensus that the Spirit is 'the Spirit-of-prophecy' in Luke-Acts. However, there is divergence of opinion about what this actually means.[8] Some scholars see the Spirit as the gift of salvation, the impetus for a new covenant life.[9] For others, the consensus designation excludes

---

8. There has been a productive debate among Pentecostal-Charismatic scholars. The question of the Spirit's role in Luke-Acts was the impetus in a debate between Menzies and Turner. The most relevant texts from M. M. B. Turner and R. P. Menzies in the debate concerning Luke-Acts are these (arranged chronologically): Turner, 'Jesus and the Spirit in Lucan Perspective', *TynB* 32 (1981): 3–42; Menzies, (his Aberdeen PhD dissertation); Menzies, 'The Distinctive Character of Luke's Pneumatology', *Paraclete* 25 (1991): 17–30; Menzies, 'Spirit and Power in Luke-Acts: A Response to Max Turner', *JSNT* 49 (1993): 11–20; Turner, 'The Spirit of Christ and "Divine" Christology', in *Jesus of Nazareth: Lord and Christ. Essays on the Historical Jesus and New Testament Christology* (eds Joel B. Green and Max Turner; Carlisle: Paternoster / Grand Rapids: Eerdmans, 1994), 413–36; Turner, 'Ethical/Religious Life'; Turner, *Power* (a much revised version of his 1980 dissertation); Turner, 'The "Spirit of Prophecy" as the Power of Israel's Restoration and Witness', in *Witness to the Gospel: The Theology of Acts* (eds I. Howard Marshall and David Peterson; Grand Rapids: Eerdmans, 1998), 327–48; Menzies, 'The Spirit of Prophecy in Luke-Acts and Pentecostal Theology: A Response to Max Turner', *JPT* 15 (1999): 49–74; Turner, 'The Spirit and Salvation in Luke-Acts', in *The Holy Spirit and Christian Origins: Essays in Honor of James D. G. Dunn* (ed. Graham N. Stanton, Bruce W. Longenecker and Stephen C. Barton; Grand Rapids: Eerdmans, 2004), 103–16; Turner, 'Luke and the Spirit: Renewing Theological Interpretation of Biblical Pneumatology', in *Reading Luke: Interpretation, Reflection, Formation* (eds Craig G. Bartholomew, Joel B. Green and Anthony C. Thiselton; SHS 6; Grand Rapids: Zondervan, 2005), 267–93.

9. James D. G. Dunn, *Baptism in the Holy Spirit: A Re-examination of the New Testament Teaching on the Gift of the Spirit in Relation to Pentecostalism Today* (London: SCM Press, 1970), following Hans von Baer, *Der Heilege Geist in den Lukasschriften* (Stuttgart: Kohlhammer, 1926) in the significance of the transition in dispensational ages (compare the influential and well known development of this thesis in Hans Conzelmann, *The Theology of Saint Luke* [trans. Geoffrey Buswell; London: Faber and Faber, 1961]); see also Dunn, *Jesus and the Spirit: A Study of the Religious and Charismatic Experience of Jesus and the First Christians Reflected in the New Testament* (Grand Rapids: Eerdmans, 1975), 135–96.

the work of miracles and ethical cleansing associated with the Spirit.[10] Still others understand Luke to have fused the Spirit of prophecy with the Spirit of salvation.[11]

Max Turner provides one of the most comprehensive accounts of the role of the Spirit in Luke-Acts. He offers five points of consensus in the ways scholars understand the role of the Spirit in Luke-Acts:

(1) The essential background for Luke's pneumatological material is Jewish and deeply rooted in the Scriptures of Israel.
(2) The Spirit is the uniting motif and the driving force within the Lukan salvation history, and establishes the legitimacy of the mission to which this leads.
(3) For Luke the Spirit is largely the Spirit-of-prophecy; in Acts especially as an 'empowering for witness'.
(4) Luke shows relatively little interest in the Spirit as the power of spiritual, ethical and religious renewal of the individual.
(5) Luke's ideas develop beyond Judaism by giving the Spirit functions that centre on God's Messiah.[12]

The scholarly understanding of Luke's narrative characterization of the Spirit presents a solid foundation for the following discussion which examines the narrative construction of social reality in Luke-Acts. The Spirit of prophecy is the pervading presence driving the Lukan narrative forward. The Spirit

---

10. E. Schweizer, 'πνεῦμα, κτλ', *TDNT* 6:389–455; followed by Youngmo Cho, *Spirit and Kingdom in the Writings of Luke and Paul: An Attempt to Reconcile these Concepts* (Milton Keynes: Paternoster, 2005), esp. 110–97; Menzies, *Development*; and *Empowered*; Roger Stronstad, *The Charismatic Theology of St Luke* (Peabody: Hendrickson, 1984); idem, *The Prophethood of All Believers: A Study in Luke's Charismatic Theology* (JPTSup 16; Sheffield: Sheffield Academic Press, 1999). A variation on this theme is the position of Gonzalo Haya-Prats, *L'Esprit force de l'église* (trans. José J. Romero and Hubert Faes; Paris: Cerf, 1975), where charismata (vivifying bestowals of the eschatological plenitude) and kerygmatic (the preaching mission of the apostles) endowments are two aspects of the one Spirit of prophecy, not a fusion of two different conceptions. For him, any salvific effects of the Spirit are secondary to the primary prophetic witness. See also John M. Penney, *The Missionary Emphasis of Lukan Pneumatology* (JPTSup 12; Sheffield: Sheffield Academic Press, 1997).

11. Amongst this position there are various representations and emphases. Included here are Jacob Kremer, *Pfingstbericht und Pfingstgeshehen: Eine exegetische Untersuchung zu Apg 2,1-13* (Stuttgart: KBW, 1973); James B. Shelton *Mighty in Word and Deed: The Role of the Holy Spirit in Luke-Acts* (Peabody: Hendrickson, 1991); Hee-Seong Kim, *Die Geistaufe des Messias: Eine kompositionsgeschichtliche Untersuchung zu einem Leitmotiv des lukanischen Doppelwerks* (Berlin: Lang, 1993); and the developing position of James D. G. Dunn, 'Baptism in the Spirit: A Response to Pentecostal Scholarship on Luke-Acts', *JPT* 3 (1993): 3–27 (repr. in *The Christ and the Spirit: Volume 2. Pneumatology* [Grand Rapids: Eerdmans, 1998], 222–42).

12. Max Turner, *Holy Spirit*, 36–41.

compels the action along the βουλὴ τοῦ θεοῦ, which is informed by the Scriptures of Israel. The Spirit and the Scriptures guide the fulfilment of the promises of Israel's God.

The Spirit emerges immediately in the narrative of Acts as the means (διά) of Jesus giving instructions (ἐντειλάμενος) to his disciples, whom he had chosen (1.2).[13] Therefore, Jesus is highlighted as the charismatic teacher of Israel in the beginning of the narrative of God's continuing mission. The Holy Spirit is linked to Jesus' authority over his followers, and to the forty-day period of Jesus' presenting himself alive with 'many convincing proofs' and speaking about the kingdom of God (1.3). The Spirit gives a 'face' to the promise of the Father, also mentioned in Luke 24.49.[14]

Acts is clear about the connection, describing the reception of the promise as receiving 'power when the Holy Spirit has come upon you' (1.8). This power is explicitly linked to the apostles' role as 'witnesses', a term which again links this prologue of Acts to the concluding scenes of Luke's Gospel. There Jesus appears to his disciples in order to offer proof of his risen bodily existence, to reveal the plan concerning himself in 'the law of Moses and the Prophets and the Psalms' (Luke 24.44), and 'to open their minds to understand the Scriptures' (24.45). A summary of the kerygmatic proclamation is provided by Jesus: 'Thus it is written that the Christ is to suffer and to rise from the dead on the third day, and repentance for[15] the forgiveness of sins will be preached in his name to all nations, beginning from Jerusalem' (24.46-47). In announcing this mission, Jesus transforms the identity of the disciples: 'You are witnesses of these things' (24.48). Jesus issues the command to stay in Jerusalem to receive the promise of his Father.

To sum up, the Holy Spirit undergirds the actions and speech of the divinely authorized agents in Luke-Acts. The Spirit effects Israel's salvation and empowers the messianic community for mission. The ministries of Jesus (Luke 3.22) and the Church (Acts 2.1-4) are each inaugurated by the descent of the Spirit. Through these agents the people of God will hear God's message of salvation and judgement.

---

13. I take the prepositional phrase διὰ πνεύματος ἁγίου to modify only ἐντειλάμενος, and not to include ἐξελέξατο. With J. M. Creed, 'The Text and Interpretation of Acts i,1-2', *JTS* 35 (1934): 176-82; Turner, *Power*, 335 n. 47; Mikeal C. Parsons and Martin M. Culy, *Acts. A Handbook on the Greek Text* (Waco: Baylor University Press, 2003), 3. But, Johnson (*Acts*, 24) sees the prepositional phrase modifying both verbs. Haenchen (*Acts*, 139) sees it modifying ἐξελέξατο.

14. That is, Acts 1.4 is repeating the same promise as in Luke 24.49, rather than referring back to it. The referent of the promise in Luke 24.49 is not immediately clear. The clearest referent would be not a promise from Jesus, but the prophecy of John the Baptist in Luke 3.16.

15. εἰς is represented by P[75] ℵ B, et al; καί is represented by A C D W, et al.

6.2.2. Jesus as Prophet-King Pronouncing Salvation and Judgement

Three main stock images dominate the persona of Jesus in Luke-Acts: the Davidic royal Messiah, the Isaianic anointed Servant, and the Mosaic eschatological Prophet. The royal Messiah and the eschatological Prophet are the most vital for the pericope under consideration (Acts 4.32–5.11).[16] The images of the messianic king executing righteous judgement[17] and the divinely authorized prophetic word[18] are commanding precedents for the execution of divine judgement through the deputized agency of Peter as an apostle-prophet. Both images impinge on the construction of Peter's character in Acts, and are perhaps nowhere more explicitly manifest in Peter's (apostolic) authority than in his encounter with Ananias and Sapphira.

Jesus himself is the paradigm for Luke's protagonists in Acts. Therefore it is important to understand the persona of Jesus and how that shapes the subsequent personae of his followers. For this reason, a brief survey of Luke's characterization of Jesus as the Prophet-King is in order.

Luke Johnson persuasively demonstrates that in both Luke and Acts the author uses prophecy as a literary source for portraying his characters and for the overall structuring of his work.[19] Prophecy is a force that drives the Lukan plot, rooting the story of Jesus in the continuation of redemptive history preserved in the Scriptures of Israel.[20] It creates expectations from the beginning of Luke's story in the infancy narratives (Luke 1–2), continuing through to the end as Paul interprets the division among Jews

---

16. Isaiah is of course fundamental to the Lukan narrative, but as far as Peter's encounter with the deceiving couple is concerned, it is the Davidic-messianic and Mosaic-prophetic images that dominate Peter's persona. The influence of Isaiah on Luke's text is documented in Bart J. Koet, 'Isaiah in Luke-Acts', in *Isaiah in the New Testament* (eds Steve Moyise and Maarten J. J. Menken; London: T&T Clark, 2005), 79–100; David W. Pao, *Acts and the Isaianic New Exodus* (Grand Rapids: Baker Academic, 2000). Mark L. Strauss (*The Davidic Messiah in Luke-Acts: The Promise and its Fulfillment in Lukan Christology* [JSNTSup 110; Sheffield: Sheffield Academic Press, 1995], 198–336) suggests that the Lukan Jesus of the Gospel is a fusion of the Isaianic imagery with royal Davidic messianism.

17. Isa. 11.1-10, esp. v. 4c-d; *Pss. Sol.* 17.21-46, esp. vv. 24-25, 35, 43.

18. Deut. 1.6–4:40; 32.1-47; 2 Kgdms 12.10-12; 3 Kgdms 14.1-18; 17.1, 7; 22.16-36; 4 Kgdms 5.24-27.

19. Johnson, *The Gospel of Luke* (SP 3; Collegeville, MN: The Liturgical Press, 1991), esp. 17–21; idem, *Acts*, esp. 12–14.

20. See Joel B. Green, 'The Problem of a Beginning: Israel's Scriptures in Luke 1–2', *BBR* 4 (1994): 61–86. Green carefully distinguishes between a 'promise-fulfillment' scheme and a self-conscious continuation of the redemptive story. See also Green, *Luke*, 51–8. Compare Brian S. Rosner, 'Acts and Biblical History', in *The Book of Acts in Its Ancient Literary Setting* (eds Bruce W. Winter and Andrew D. Clarke; vol. 1 of *The Book of Acts in Its First Century Setting*, ed. B. W. Winter; Grand Rapids: Eerdmans, 1993), 65–82, although his category of 'biblical history' is ambiguous.

in Rome through the words of the prophet Isaiah (Acts 28.25-28[21]). The stock image of the Mosaic eschatological prophet provides a rhetorically powerful link to the religious and cultural patterns and literary types for organizing a narrative of the continuing story of God's promises stretching from Abraham to the gospel's arrival in Rome.

However, Jesus explodes the prophetic boundary as Israel's messianic King of the line of David. Jesus is the Prophet-King, his character fusing both the typologies of Moses and David into one powerful unique persona advocating and initiating the reign of God.[22] Luke equates the kingship of Jesus functionally with the kingdom of God.[23] This has implications both for Luke's characterization of Jesus and Jesus' followers. Jesus occupies the throne of David, exalted to God's right hand. The church occupies the space of God's kingdom, awaiting the time of its consummation.[24] For Luke, the Prophet-King is marked by rejection, which paradoxically is the source of salvation and judgement for Israel. The Prophet-King's divine vindication also results in the extension of the blessing of Abraham to the nations. Thus, to understand what it means to call Peter an apostle-prophet it is necessary to understand what it means to call Jesus a Prophet-King.

---

21. Some 'Western' versions (36, 307, 383, 614; lacuna in D) contain verse 29, καὶ ταῦτα αὐτοῦ εἰπόντος ἀπῆλθον οἱ Ἰουδαῖοι, πολλὴν ἔχοντες ἐν ἑαυτοῖς συζήτησιν. W. A. Strange (*The Problem of the Text of Acts* [SNTSMS 71; Cambridge: Cambridge University Press, 1992], 44) considers this as an 'addition' that is consonant with the tendency in the Western readings to make the entry and exit of characters more pronounced. See Eldon Jay Epp, *The Theological Tendency of Codex Bezae Cantabrigiensis in Acts* (SNTSMS 3; Cambridge: Cambridge University Press, 1966; repr. Eugene, OR: Wipf & Stock, 2001), 114; Bruce M. Metzger, *A Textual Commentary on the Greek New Testament* (3rd edn; Stuttgart: United Bible Society, 1971), 502.

22. Jack D. Kingsbury ('Jesus as the "Prophetic Messiah" in Luke's Gospel', in *The Future of Christology: Festschrift L.E. Keck* [eds A. J. Malherbe and W. A. Meeks; Minneapolis: Fortress, 1993], 29–42) presents a mediating position denying that Luke uses the title 'prophet' for Jesus, but does use the adjective 'prophetic' for Jesus' ministry. This distinction between adjective and noun cannot be sustained; note Luke 4.24, 13.33; Acts 3.22; 7.37. Kingsbury attempts to make 'prophet' a designation in opposition to 'Messiah' in Luke 9.7-9, 18-20 in comparison with Luke 3.15-17, where John exclusively claims the former title and Jesus exclusively claims the latter. More likely, Luke 9.7-9, 18-27 evokes continuity between John's mortal fate as a prophet and Jesus' impending suffering in Jerusalem (9.22) rather than contrasting their 'prophetic' and 'messianic' vocations. Kingsbury's sharp contrast is undercut by his own assertions that Jesus fulfils Moses' prediction that God would raise up a prophet like himself (Acts 3.22; 7.37; Deut. 18.15-16, 18) as Messiah, showing that the two are not in polar opposition.

23. Robert F. O'Toole, 'The Kingdom of God in Luke-Acts', in *The Kingdom of God in 20th-Century Interpretation* (ed. Wendell Willis; Peabody: Hendrickson, 1987), 147–62; Turner, *Power*, 290–7.

24. Green, *Luke*, 760–1.

6.2.2.1. The Preparation and Anointing of the Messiah

In the Gospel of Luke, Jesus publicly addresses Israel with the voice of both king[25] and prophet.[26] Luke references Jesus' royal lineage and status strategically throughout his two volumes. There are clusters at the beginning of Jesus' ministry (birth narratives and baptism), the transfiguration, the arrival at Jerusalem, and the passion and resurrection, and in the speeches in Acts (Peter: Acts 2.14-41; Paul: Acts 13.16-41; James: Acts 15.13-21). Jesus is identified as a prophet early in his ministry; later Peter proclaims that 'God anointed him with the Holy Spirit and with power, and he went about doing good and healing all who were being oppressed by the devil, for God was with him' (Acts 10.38). Both patterns, messianic and prophetic, converge in the character of Jesus leading to his rejection by the Jewish people and the divine vindication which exalts him to the throne of God.

6.2.2.1.1. The Birth of the Messiah

The highest expectations for Jesus' status and destiny are raised by Gabriel's address to Mary.[27] 'He will be great, and will be called the Son of the Most

---

25. Strauss (*Davidic Messiah*) sees a pervasive influence of a Davidic-messianic type in Lukan Christology. Strauss has overstated the case in trying to avoid the error of overestimating the prophetic dimension of Luke's characterization of Jesus. See also Cristoph Burger, *Jesus als Davidssohn. Eine traditionsgeschichtliche Untersuchung* (FRLANT, 98; Göttingen: Vandenhoeck & Ruprecht, 1970), 107–52 (who wrongly argues that Jesus' status as Davidic Messiah plays no role in his earthly ministry); Augustin George, *Études sur l'œuvre de Luc* (SB; Paris: Gabalda, 1978), 257–82; Scott W. Hahn, 'Kingdom and Church in Luke-Acts: From Davidic Christology to Kingdom Ecclesiology', in *Reading Luke* (eds Bartholomew, Green and Thiselton), 294–326; Kingsbury, '"Prophetic Messiah"'; O'Toole, 'Kingdom'; idem, *Luke's Presentation of Jesus: A Christology* (SubBi 25; Rome: Editrice Pontificio Instituto Biblico, 2004), 113–40. O'Toole (*Luke's Presentation*, 155–79), too sharply distinguishes between Jesus as 'Christ' and Jesus as 'Son of God', the latter for O'Toole being the demarcation of Jesus' divinity.

26. The literature on Luke's prophetic pattern for Jesus is extensive. See T. R. Carruth, 'The Jesus-as-Prophet Motif in Luke-Acts' (PhD diss.; Baylor University, 1973); J. Severino Croatto, 'Jesus, Prophet like Elijah, and Prophet-Teacher like Moses in Luke-Acts', *JBL* 124 (2005): 451–65; Paul F. Feiler, 'Jesus the Prophet: The Lucan Portrayal of Jesus as the Prophet like Moses' (PhD diss.; Princeton Theological Seminary, 1986); G. R. Greene, 'The Portrayal of Jesus as Prophet in Luke-Acts' (PhD diss.; Southern Baptist Theological Seminary, 1975); Adrian Hastings, *Prophet and Witness in Jerusalem: A Study of the Teaching of Saint Luke* (New York: Helicon, 1958); Johnson, *Literary Function*, 60–9; idem, *Living Jesus: Learning the Heart of the Gospel* (New York: HarperSanFrancisco, 1999), 159–75; Menzies, *Development*, 146–204; Robert J. Miller, 'Elijah, John, and Jesus in the Gospel of Luke', *NTS* 34 (1988): 611–22; Paul Minear, *To Heal and Reveal: The Prophetic Vocation According to Luke* (New York: The Seabury Press, 1976), 102–21; David P. Moessner, *Lord of the Banquet: The Literary and Theological Significance of the Lukan Travel Narrative* (Harrisburg, PA: Trinity Press International, 1989), *passim*; O'Toole, *Luke's Presentation*, 29–54; Roger Stronstad, *Prophethood*, 35–53; David L. Tiede, *Prophecy and History in Luke-Acts* (Philadelphia: Fortress Press, 1980), *passim*; Wenk, *Power*, 191–231.

27. See Robert C. Tannehill, 'What Kind of King? What Kind of Kingdom?', and 'Israel in Luke-Acts: A Tragic Story', in *The Shape of Luke's Story: Essays on Luke-Acts*

High, and the Lord God will give him the throne of his father David, and he will reign over the house of Jacob forever, and his kingdom will have no end' (Luke 1.32-33). Luke already established that Jesus' legal father, Joseph, was a descendant of David (1.27). Gabriel tells Mary that she will conceive through the power of the Spirit. 'Jesus is Son of God in consequence of his extraordinary conception.'[28]

When Mary expresses her adoration of God, she integrates her account of her experience into the continuing story of God's powerful acts on behalf of Israel. Mary calls God 'her Saviour' (1.47) and 'the Mighty One who has done great things for me' (1.49), evoking the corporate memory of God's power and deliverance in the Exodus.[29] Mary interprets Gabriel's announcement in terms of God's reversing of fortunes, and she traces the story back to the promise God gave to Abraham and his offspring (1.55).[30]

At the moment of Jesus' birth, he is heralded by angels, yet accompanied by shepherds (Luke 2.1-20). The angels approach the shepherds and announce that 'today in the city of David there has been born for you a Saviour, who is Christ the Lord' (2.11). A dissonance is created between the high claims of salvation and royalty and the humble place where the coming king is born.[31]

At the birth of John, Jesus' cousin, John's father Zacharias bursts out with Spirit inspired praise, blessing God for having 'raised up a horn of salvation for us in the house of David his servant' (Luke 1.69). He links this with God's fulfilment of the promise made to Abraham (1.72-73). John is the 'prophet of the Most High' (1.76), commissioned to prepare the way of the Lord and to be a preacher of salvation and forgiveness of sins (1.76b-77).

Jesus expresses self-conscious recognition of his identity as the Son of God when he is left behind in Jerusalem after Passover. When his parents find him and ask why he has stayed behind, Jesus replies, 'Why is it that you were searching for me? Did you not know that I must be about my Father's business (ἐν τοῖς τοῦ πατρός μου)?' (Luke 2.49).

6.2.2.1.2. The Baptism and Testing of the Messiah
God himself confirms Jesus' status of sonship at Jesus' baptism,[32] uniting Spirit and sonship, in calling out, 'You are my beloved son, in you I am

---

(Eugene, OR: Cascade Books, 2005), 48–55 and 105–24, respectively, for a discussion of the expectations raised in the infancy narratives and an argument that the expectations are overturned and transformed. In 'What Kind of King?', Tannehill argues for a transformed version of kingdom expectations as the church acts as an interim community realizing partially a social policy of Jesus' kingdom-restoration for Israel (esp. 52–5).

28. Green, *Luke*, 184; See also Hahn, 'Kingdom', 303; Strauss, *Davidic Messiah*, 93–4.
29. Acts 2.11; cf. Deut. 11.2-7; LXX Ps. 70.19; Sir. 17.8, 10; 36.7; 42.21.
30. See Green, *Luke*, 82–105; idem, 'The Social Status of Mary in Luke 1,5–2,52: A Plea for Methodological Integration', *Bib* 73 (1992): 457–72; idem, *The Theology of the Gospel of Luke* (Cambridge: Cambridge University Press, 1995), 94.
31. See Mark Coleridge, *The Birth of the Lukan Narrative: Narrative as Christology in Luke 1–2* (JSNTSup 88; Sheffield: Sheffield Academic Press, 1993), 219–23.
32. Strauss, *Davidic Messiah*, 200–8; Turner, *Power*, 188–201.

well-pleased' (Luke 3.22).³³ The audience already knows that Jesus is God's Son by virtue of his extraordinary conception, but he will have to embrace his identity through his loyalty to God's purpose. By participating in John's baptism, Jesus demonstrates his solidarity with the people of Israel and his fundamental orientation around God's purpose.³⁴ With regard to Jesus' status as the royal Messiah, his position is revealed gradually from his conception to his resurrection, ascension, and exaltation.³⁵ Jesus' baptism in the Jordan indicates that he is anointed for service, clearly evoking the patterns of the Davidic Messiah and the Isaianic Servant.³⁶

Following Jesus' anointing, the Spirit leads him into the wilderness, where he recapitulates Israel's testing. The temptation is in effect a battle raging over who is allowed to control the perspective of Israel's story and the reading of the sacred Scriptures. Jesus' answers are all quotations from Deuteronomy, and as such they evoke the authoritative Mosaic voice, indicating Jesus' unequivocal obedience to his Father and his readiness to embark on his public mission. Turner says that Jesus as 'the Davidic messianic Son [...] represents *Israel* in an eschatological replay of the wilderness testing of Moses and Israel'.³⁷ Strauss aptly summarizes the episode,

> The scene is antitypical of the experience of Israel in the wilderness. While God's son Israel (Exod. 4.22-23) failed when tested in the wilderness, Jesus the true Son remains obedient and emerges victorious. Jesus' forty days of temptation in the wilderness are analogous to Israel's forty years, and the three Old Testament passages Jesus cites (Deut. 8.3; 6.13, 16) are all related to Israel's failures in the wilderness. The interpretive key to the account lies in Deut. 8.2-3, where Moses recalls how 'the Lord your God led you in the wilderness these forty years, that he might humble you, testing you to know what was in your heart...' (1) Israel was tested with hunger so that she would learn dependence on God (Deut. 8.3) but failed to do so; Jesus depends wholly on God for his sustenance, quoting Deut. 8.3 (Lk. 4.4; Mt. 4.3, 4). (2) Israel was commanded to worship God alone (Deut. 6.13-15) but turned to idolatry (Deut. 9.12; Judg. 3.5-7); Jesus rejects the devil's offer of the kingdoms of the world in exchange for worship, quoting Deut. 6.13 (Lk. 4.5-7; Mt. 4.8-9). (3) Israel doubted God's power and put him to the test at Massah/Meribah (Deut. 6.16; Exod. 17.1-7); Jesus refuses to throw himself from the temple and so test the Lord God, citing Deut. 6.16 (Lk. 4.9-12). As the messianic king and Son of

---

33. Greek: 'σὺ εἶ ὁ υἱός μου ὁ ἀγαπητός, ἐν σοὶ εὐδόκησα.' The Western tradition (D) reads 'Υἱός μου εἶ σύ, ἐγὼ σήμερον γεγέννηκά σε' which draws out more explicitly the connection to Davidic messianism with its allusion to a royal psalm (Ps. 2.7 LXX).

34. See Green, *Luke*, 184-5.

35. See George, *Études*, 281-2; Strauss, *Davidic Messiah*, 144-5; Robert C. Tannehill, *The Narrative Unity of Luke-Acts: A Literary Interpretation* (2 vols; Minneapolis: Fortress, 1994), 1:238-9.

36. See Green, *Luke*, 184-7; John Nolland (*Luke* [3 vols; WBC 35; Nashville: Thomas Nelson Publishers, 1989-1993], 1:157-65) stresses the echoes of Isa. 42.1-7 (163). See Darrell L. Bock, *Luke* (2 vols; BECNT; Grand Rapids: Baker Books, 1994, 1996), 1:341-5, for other suggestions of intertextual allusions.

37. Turner, *Power*, 207, emphasis his.

God [...] Jesus represents the nation and fulfills the task of eschatological Israel in the wilderness.[38]

As Brawley and Green have pointed out, the temptation narrative has a polarizing function for the rest of Luke-Acts.[39] From this point on in the narrative, all opposition to Jesus is polarized between God and Satan.

The testing shows that Jesus has proved himself ready for the task ahead. He begins his ministry in Nazareth, where his message of 'the Favorable (δεκτός) year of the Lord' (Luke 4.19. cf. Isa. 61.2) is rejected by his countryfolk because 'no prophet is welcome (δεκτός) in his hometown' (4.24).[40] The rejection of Jesus is salvation for humanity, as Jesus is vindicated by God through his resurrection and exaltation, and at the same time, a fatal mistake for those who persist in rejecting God's Prophet-King (cf. Acts 3.23).

6.2.2.2. The Story of Lukan Messianic Prophecy: The Lineage of Rejected Prophets

Jesus claims prophetic status in his inaugural address to the synagogue in Nazareth, where he claims to be the fulfilment of Isaiah's prophecy of the servant anointed by the Spirit of the Lord (Luke 4.16-30). With the announcement of this status comes the introduction to the story of a prophet rejected by his own people. Anticipating the response of his townsfolk to his calling and ability, Jesus declares, 'Truly I say to you, no prophet is welcome in his hometown' (4.24). He uses as examples the ministries of Elijah and Elisha, prophets who performed their miracles outside Israel as a result of their rejection by Israelite royalty.[41]

Another story recalling the ministries of the great prophets is told in Luke 7.1-17. Jesus heals the servant of a Roman centurion and then raises a widow's son from the dead. The crowd's response is a doxological acclamation, 'A great prophet has risen among us', and 'God has visited (ἐπεσκέψατο) his people' (7.16).[42] The miracles of the prophet are recognized as an action of God on behalf of God's people. The crowd, in effect, scripts Jesus into the role of the eschatological prophet.

At this point, Jesus' reputation reaches the current Jewish royalty, Herod the tetrarch (Luke 9.7-9, 19).[43] Herod was 'perplexed with anxiety'

---

38. Strauss, *Davidic Messiah*, 215–16; Turner (*Power*, 205) quotes the same passage suggesting the pervasive influence of Birger Gerhardsson, *The Testing of God's Son* (Lund: Gleerp, 1966).
39. See above §2.3.4.
40. See §4.2.1. n. 59 above.
41. 3 Kgdms 17.17-24 for Elijah and the widow Sarepta; 4 Kgdms 5 1-14 for Elisha and Naaman.
42. Compare the use of ἐπισκοπή in Luke 19.44, where Jesus indicts Jerusalem for not recognizing the visitation of God, and prophesies the impending destruction of the city as a result.
43. See David Ravens, 'Luke 9.7–62 and the Prophetic Role of Jesus', *NTS* 36 (1990): 119–29.

(διηπόρει)⁴⁴ upon hearing that John, whom Herod had executed, had been raised from the dead. Some took Jesus to be an appearance of Elijah, or 'one of the prophets of old who had risen' (9.8). In other words, Jesus evoked a sacred pattern of the persona of those who acted on behalf of God in the sacred traditions of Israel.

Another indication that Jesus' reputation evoked the script of a prophet is how he was treated after his arrest. In the house of the high priest, Jesus was blindfolded, beaten, and ridiculed with calls to, 'Prophesy! Who is the one who hit you?' (Luke 22.64). Jesus is abused in the role of a prophet.⁴⁵ Further, Jesus is accused of claiming to be the 'Son of God' (22.67-71). Having reached Jerusalem, the city does not disappoint, but plays out its role in the drama of the rejected prophet (13.33-35).

Jesus is heralded as a prophet by the weary disciples travelling to Emmaus (Luke 24.13-35). Coming alongside Cleopas and his travelling companion, the risen Jesus hears his own story relayed back to him, muddled and confused. The disciples claim that Jesus was 'a prophet mighty in deed and word in the sight of God and all the people' (24.19), but determine that the accompanying stranger is the only one in Jerusalem unaware of the things that transpired in the previous days. In fact, the unrecognized Jesus is the only one who does know what transpired and interprets the events through the Scriptures of Israel and opens their eyes.⁴⁶

The Lukan Jesus himself understands his role as a prophet and links it with his fate in Jerusalem, the city 'that kills the prophets and stones those sent to her' (Luke 13.34). Jesus mentions the series of prophets from Abel to Zacharias⁴⁷ in a long story of rejection and execution (11.46-52). He finally lays the blame for this failure to receive God's messengers at the feet of 'this generation'. David Moessner points out that the phrase 'this generation'⁴⁸ in Luke's Gospel is an allusion to the wilderness generation of the Exodus narrative.⁴⁹ Moessner's work on the central section of Luke (9.51–19.44) took

---

44. Compare Acts 10.17, where Peter experiences this 'anxious perplexity' over the vision of the animals.

45. *Pace* David Hill, *New Testament Prophecy*, London: Marshall, Morgan and Scott, 1979, (52) who suggests that Jesus was accused before the court as a *false* prophet. The violence, as presented in Luke (and Mark 14.65) is gratuitous, not related to judging the veracity of Jesus' prophetic vocation.

46. See Robert L. Brawley, *Centering on God: Method and Message in Luke-Acts* (Louisville: Westminster / John Knox Press, 1990), 130–1.

47. Sometimes it is suggested that the Lukan Jesus extends the lineage of the prophets from Abel to Zacharias to include the first and last prophet in the Hebrew Bible. However, this can not be certain because, as Green (*Luke*, 475 n. 82) notes, (1) there are various possibilities for the reference to Zacharias (consult J. M. Ross, 'Which Zechariah?', *IBS* 9 [1987]: 70–3) and (2) the question of the canonical order of the Hebrew (and Greek) Scriptures remains unsettled.

48. ἡ γενεὰ αὕτη [ταύτη], Luke 7.31; 11.29-32, 50-51; 17.25; 21.32; cf. Luke 9.41; 16.8.

49. Num. 32.13; Deut. 2.14; 29.21; 32.5, 20. Moessner, *Lord*, 63–6, 92–114; idem, 'Jesus and the Wilderness Generation: The Death of the Prophet like Moses according to

its lead from O. H. Steck, who concerned himself with the rejected prophet motif in early Christian writings.[50] Steck identified a four-fold Deuteronomic conception of Israel's history. Moessner describes it as follows:

A) The history of Israel is one long, persistent story of a 'stiff-necked,' rebellious, and disobedient people.
B) God sent his messengers, the prophets, to mediate his will (i.e., the Law), to instruct and admonish (parenesis) them in his will, and to exhort them to repentance lest they bring upon themselves judgment and destruction.
C) Nevertheless, Israel en masse rejected all these prophets, even persecuting and killing them out of their stubborn 'stiff-neckedness.'
D) Therefore, Israel's God had 'rained' destruction upon them in 722 and 587 B.C.E. and would destroy them in a similar way if they did not heed his word.[51]

This historical outline helps clarify the rejection of Jesus as a prophet in Luke-Acts, and Luke's presentation of a continued 'rebellion' of many within Israel in an unrelenting rejection of Jesus. The storyline ties together the polarity of opposition in the Gospel and Acts. When Peter urges the people at Pentecost to 'be saved from this wicked generation' (Acts 2.40), he casts his audience into a continuing narrative of Israel's persisting rebellion. Peter's accusing question to Sapphira also carries forward this characterizing motif of rebellion: 'Why is it that you have conspired to put the Spirit of the Lord to the test?' (5.9). Testing the Spirit of God is a theme that also pervades the description of

---

Luke', in *SBL 1982 Seminar Papers* (ed. Kent H. Richards; Atlanta: Society of Biblical Literature, 1982), 319–40; idem, 'The "Leaven of the Pharisees" and "This Generation": Israel's Rejection of Jesus According to Luke', in *Reimaging the Death of the Lukan Jesus* (ed. Dennis D. Sylva; Frankfurt: Hain, 1990), 79–107, 190–3 (revised in *JSNT* 34 (1988): 21–46 = *The Synoptic Gospels: A Sheffield Reader* [ed. Craig A. Evans and Stanley E. Porter; Sheffield: Sheffield Academic Press, 1995], 268–93).

Contra R. Maddox, The *Purpose of Luke-Acts* (Edinburgh: T&T Clark, 1982), 111–15, who offers five possibilities for this phrase ([1] The Jewish people as a whole, [2] the human race, [3] Luke's generation, [4] Jesus' generation extending to Luke's generation by a few individuals, and [5] the last phase of history), showing a lack of nuance for Luke's literary-theological language. Indeed, the discussion of this phrase is more appropriate to Maddox's discussion of Luke's orientation towards Judaism (ch. 2) rather than his discussion of Lukan eschatology (ch. 5) where it is located.

Jon A. Weatherly (*Jewish Responsibility for the Death of Jesus in Luke-Acts* [JSNTSup 106; Sheffield: Sheffield Academic Press, 1994], 100–7) rightly criticizes Moessner for making Jesus' denunciation of 'this generation' as a blanket condemnation of Jews generally.

50. Odil Hannes Steck, *Israel und das gewaltsame Geschick der Propheten: Untersuchungen zur Überlieferung des deuteronomistischen Geschichtsbildes im Alten Testament, Spätjudentum und Urchristentum* (WMANT, 23; Neukirchen-Vluyn: Neukirchener Verlag, 1967). See also Michael Knowles, *Jeremiah in Matthew's Gospel: The Rejected-Prophet Motif in Matthean Redaction* (JSNTSup 68; Sheffield: Sheffield Academic Press, 1993), esp. 96–161, for the extension of Steck's work into the Gospel of Matthew.

51. Moessner, *Lord*, 84. Consult Steck, *Israel*, 60–4.

Israel wandering in the desert after the Exodus.[52] Those of Peter's audience in Jerusalem who refuse to repent and Ananias and Sapphira in Acts 5.1-11 are associated with the theme of diabolical opposition to the purposes of God and the Prophet-King. In this way, they continue the polarizing interpretation that Luke has established in his narrative.

6.2.2.3. The Shape of Lukan Messianic Prophecy: Jesus as a Prophet-King like Moses and David

6.2.2.3.1. The Prophet-King's Exodus to Jerusalem

Moses is the paradigm of all prophetic voices in the traditions of Israel.[53] As such, he is a formative model for the Lukan prophets. The pattern of a new Exodus shapes the role of God's prophet starting with Jesus, who initiates the restoration of Israel and continuing with the emergent messianic community which journeys along the way of the divine plan.[54] Jesus embodies the vocation of the eschatological Mosaic Prophet and transfers this prophetic vocation to his witnesses so they can continue the work of Israel's restoration and proclaim the gospel to the nations.

Jesus is the prophet *par excellence* in the Luke's 'narrative world'. While the title of 'prophet' does not exhaust the Lukan persona of Jesus,[55] it is an essential aspect to his character. Jesus is the Prophet like Moses, and the story of Moses' life can be seen as a structuring paradigm for the Gospel and Acts.[56] There is a reciprocal relationship between the two stories; Luke retells the story of Moses through Stephen (Acts 7.20-44), in a manner that highlights

---

52. Exod. 17.2, 7; Num. 14.22; Deut. 33.8.

53. Dale C. Allison, *The New Moses: A Matthean Typology* (Edinburgh: T&T Clark, 1993), 11–112; Michael Fishbane, *Biblical Interpretation in Ancient Israel* (Oxford: Clarendon Press, 1985), 257–61, 374; Wayne Meeks, *The Prophet-King: Moses Traditions and the Johannine Christology* (Leiden: Brill, 1967), esp. 125–9, 137–8, 154–6, 177–81, 198–204, 220–27; R. B. Y. Scott, *The Relevance of the Prophets* (New York: The Macmillan Company, 1947), 59, 62–71; Howard M. Teeple, *The Mosaic Eschatological Prophet* (SBLMS 10; Philadelphia: Society of Biblical Literature, 1957), esp. 29–94, 100–22.

54. The usage of 'New Exodus' refers to the tradition that emerged in the Scriptures of Israel and later Jewish writings applying the paradigm of Yahweh's deliverance of Israel from Egypt to later times, such as the return from exile. The theme is presented by Jindřich Mánek, 'The New Exodus in the Books of Luke', *NovT* 2 (1957): 8–23. The formative influence and transmission of this tradition through the Isaianic writings is discussed by Pao, *Acts*; Rikki E. Watts, *Isaiah's New Exodus in Mark* (Grand Rapids: Baker Academic, 1997); and Strauss, *Davidic Messiah*, 263–305 (who argues against the Deuteronomic New Exodus suggested by Moessner [*Lord*, 56–79, 260–88] in favour of the Isaianic New Exodus [esp. 275–305]).

55. *Pace* Croatto, 'Jesus', who allows his own theo-political horizons to eclipse the voice of the Lukan text.

56. See Moessner, *Lord*, 46–79, 114–31, 260–88; Morna D. Hooker, '"Beginning with Moses and From All the Prophets"', in *From Jesus to John: Essays on Jesus and New Testament Christology in Honour of Marinus de Jonge* (ed. Martinus C. De Boer; JSNTSup 84; Sheffield: JSOT Press, 1993), 228–30.

the elements of Jesus' story. Twice Luke evokes the promise of Deut. 18.15-19 by God to raise up a prophet like Moses (Acts 3.22-23; 7.37), interpreting the promise in a teleological manner that is fulfilled in Jesus.

Luke Johnson has argued for a close connection between the story of Moses in Stephen's sermon and the structure of the story about Jesus and his followers.[57] Stephen's speech can be read as a summary of Luke's Gospel and demonstrates how Luke read the Scriptures. In the speech the story of Moses unfolds in two stages, both defined by rejection by his people. The first rejection comes when he was born into the time of Egyptian oppression and attempts to help alleviate Israelite suffering (Acts 7.17-29), and the second comes when he had led the Israelites out of Egypt and they wanted to turn back (Acts 7.35-43). Johnson correlates the dual rejection of Moses to the story of Jesus in Luke-Acts. Jesus' death was akin to Moses first rejection, and Jesus' resurrection is like Moses' second sending. Johnson writes, 'The second sending of Moses, then, is structurally the same as the resurrection of Jesus; it is an establishment in power, and a second chance for the people to accept him as the agent of God's salvation.'[58] Israel's second rejection of Moses was definitive, and final. Those who rejected Moses the second time were themselves rejected by God. Stephen's speech indicates a structural paradigm used by Luke for the relationship of Israel to Jesus and his presence through his (apostles-)witnesses and their testimony. Stephen casts his callous audience in the role of the wicked generation on the verge of being rejected and judged by God for rejecting God's Prophet. Stephen embodies the rejected Prophet like Moses as he is executed in a manner reminiscent of the death of Jesus (Acts 7.59-60; Luke 23.34, 46).[59]

An explicit convergence of the messianic and prophetic vocations comes to the forefront in Luke's Gospel in the events surrounding Jesus' transfiguration. The news that arrives to the perplexed Herod is a result of Jesus' sending of the Twelve with authority over demons and diseases (Luke 9.1) to proclaim the kingdom of God and to perform healings (9.2, 6). The ministry of the Twelve results in a multitude pursuing Jesus for more teaching and healing (9.11). Jesus performs a miracle of multiplying bread and fish, which evokes the memory of God's provision for Israel (Exod. 16.4-36), and the miraculous provision through Elisha (4 Kgdms 4.42-44).[60] This miracle leads to the question of Jesus' identity, which Jesus' pursues with his disciples. Located here in Luke's Gospel is Peter's bold confession ('[You are] the Christ of God', 9.20), followed by Jesus' enigmatic passion-resurrection prediction coupled with the directives of the high cost of discipleship (9.22-27).

---

57. Johnson, *Literary Function*, 70–8.
58. Johnson, *Literary Function*, 74. See also H. Alan Brehm, 'Vindicating the Rejected One: Stephen's Speech as a Critique of the Jewish Leaders', in *Early Christian Interpretation of the Scriptures of Israel: Investigations and Proposals* (eds Craig A. Evans and James A. Sanders; JSNTSup 148; Sheffield: Sheffield Academic Press, 1997), 266–97.
59. On this, see §2.3.3. n. 58 above.
60. Green, *Luke*, 365.

The scene moves to the Transfiguration encounter with Moses and Elijah (9.28-36), followed by a rebuke of 'this unbelieving and perverted generation', evoking the drama of Sinai with Moses' ascent and descent up the mountain to receive the covenant stipulations and the ensuing rebellion with the golden calf (9.7-21; Deut. 4.10-24).[61] Moessner summarizes the comparison:

> What was true of the miraculous signs and feeding in the wilderness for the *laos* of God has become true again for the *laos* of God in Luke: 'You have been rebellious against the Lord from the day that I knew you' (Deut. 9:24; cf. 8:3, 15–20).[...] The *whole generation*, the disciples and all, are like their Horeb counterparts – one disobedient, rebellious mass.[62]

The disciples display their inability to 'hear' (8.4-15) and exhibit the disposition of 'this generation', vying for status (9.46-48), attempting to control the prerogative of Jesus by hindering an unassociated exorcist (9.49-50). When Jesus commences his journey, the disciples demonstrate misplaced zeal as a response to Jesus' prophetic rejection in a village of the Samaritans (9.51-56;[63] see 4 Kgdms 1.9-16). After reiterating the demands of following Jesus on his journey (9.57-62), Jesus appoints and sends seventy(-two)[64] others to prepare the way for his arrival. He sends them as 'harvesters' in the eschatological gathering of God's people.[65] Moessner elucidates,

> To Journey with Jesus means to participate in the self-unveiling of his authority as the Son as he advances to Jerusalem [emphasis his]! And this revelation is the effecting of salvation for those who receive him and his ambassadors which is most sublimely mirrored in the eschatological joy of the home-meal fellowship.[...T]o reject these ambassadors is simultaneously the rejection of Jesus who commissioned them (v.1) and of God who sent Jesus.[...] The time of eschatological decision has arrived. Those who reject this pleading call down upon themselves the final judgment of the reign of God.[66]

Hence, the drama unfolding in Luke here indicates a dense reservoir of messianic and prophetic images. Jesus is like Moses in his ascending and descending the mountain of Sinai, his exodus (cf. Luke 9.31), and his appointing seventy elders (Num. 11.16-18). Yet, Jesus is also like David because he is again identified by

---

61. Moessner, *Lord*, 56–70, 92–114.
62. Moessner, *Lord*, 66, 64, emphasis his.
63. Longer readings of verses 54-56 include αὐτοὺς ὡς Ἠλίας ἐποίσεν (9.54), αὐτοῖς καὶ εἶπεν, Οὐκ οἴδατε οἵου πνεύματός ἐστε ὑμεῖς (9.55), and ὁ γὰρ υἱὸς τοῦ ἀνθρώπου οὐκ ἦλθεν ψυχὰς ἀνθρώπων ἀπολέσαι ἀλλὰ σῶσαι (9.56), all of which are omitted in P[45, 75], ℵ, B, L, et al. Metzgar (*Textual Commentary*, 148–9) suggests that they are glosses derived from some extraneous source.
64. Consult the comprehensive treatment of this textual problem addressed by J. Verheyden, 'How Many Were Sent according to Lk 10,1?', in *Luke and His Readers* (eds Bieringer, Van Belle and Verheyden), 193–238.
65. Moessner, *Lord*, 136–43.
66. Moessner, *Lord*, 142, 138, 143.

God as 'My Son' (Luke 9.35), he sends royal ambassadors (ἀπόστολος, 9.10) and he conducts a mission to reunify Israel under his own rule.[67]

Jesus' divine sonship confirmed at his baptism is echoed at his transfiguration (Luke 9.28-36). When on the mountain, as when in the Jordan, God speaks from heaven: 'This is my Son, the Chosen One, listen to him!' (9.35).[68] At this moment the royal Davidic and prophetic Mosaic imageries fuse in a glorious summit of that which is anticipated in eschatological fulfilment. Jesus' address and claim to God as Father for himself[69] and Israel[70] bespeaks of the covenant language which established the Davidic 'house'[71] and Israel as a people.[72] Jesus, having been affirmed by the voice of God and the companionship of Elijah and Moses on the mountain, sets out for Jerusalem proleptically sharing in the eschatological banquet of redemption through his practice of meal fellowship along the way. Like both Moses and David, Jesus advocated sharing the blessings of God through meal fellowship.[73]

Two passages in Luke's Gospel explicitly link the kingdom of God with Jesus' presence and ministry.[74] In response to an accusation that Jesus 'casts out demons by Beelzebul, the ruler of demons' (Luke 11.15), Jesus argues that a kingdom divided against itself would not stand, and offers the alternative with its implication: 'But if I cast out demons by the finger of God, then the kingdom of God has come upon you' (11.20).[75] Jesus' exorcisms are manifestations of God's liberating power over Satan. The kingdom has arrived in power through Jesus' action of casting out demons. Furthermore, these exorcisms provide a sign requested of Jesus by his opponents (11.16); the kingdom is right under their noses, but stiff-necks prevent them from seeing.

When the Pharisees confront Jesus about the time of the kingdom (Luke 17.20), Jesus responds with a rebuke for those seeking signs (17.22-37): 'The Kingdom of God is not coming with empirical observation (παρατηρήσεως) [...] for behold, the Kingdom of God is in your midst (ἡ βασιλεία τοῦ θεοῦ

---

67. See Jacob Jervell, 'The Lost Sheep of the House of Israel: The Understanding of the Samaritans in Luke-Acts', in *Luke and the People of God: A New Look at Luke-Acts* (Minneapolis: Augsburg Publishing House, 1972), 113–32; David Ravens, *Luke and the Restoration of Israel* (JSNTSup 119; Sheffield: Sheffield Academic Press, 1995), 47, 72–106; Hahn, 'Kingdom', 305.

68. See commentary by Strauss, *Davidic Messiah*, 263–72.

69. Luke 2.49; 9.26; 10.21, 22; 11.2; 22.29, 42; 23.34, 46; 24.49; Acts 1.4, 7; 2.33.

70. Luke 6.36; 11.13; 12.32; 15.11-32.

71. 2 Kgdms 7.13-16; Ps. 2.7.

72. Exod. 4.22-23; 19.5-6. See Strauss, *Davidic Messiah*, 35; Hahn, 'Kingdom', 298; Brawley, *Centering*, 116–17.

73. For Moses, see Moessner, *Lord*, 266–77, mentioning provisions for various feasts (Deut. 12.15-16, 20; 14.22-29; 15.22; 26.12). For David, see Hahn, 'Kingdom', 308, citing 2 Sam. 9.7, 10, 13; 1 Kgs 2.7.

74. O'Toole, 'Kingdom', 150.

75. See Carroll, *Response*, 85 n. 188; Green, *Luke*, 456–7; Edward J. Woods, *The 'Finger of God' and Pneumatology in Luke-Acts* (JSNTSup 205; Sheffield: Sheffield Academic Press, 2001), 101–214.

ἐντὸς ὑμῶν ἐστιν)'[76] (17.20-21). Jesus follows up with teaching to his disciples concerning the coming of the Son of Man, and so Jesus' response to the Pharisees would indicate that he was implying an intimate connection between God's reign and his own ministry.

6.2.2.3.2. Jesus' Prophetic Indictment of Jerusalem

Perhaps the most poignant demonstration of the performative prophetic word is Jesus' indictment of Jerusalem as 'the city that kills the prophets and stones those sent to her' (Luke 13.34) and which does not know 'the things which make for peace' (19.42). Jesus correlates the attack by Jerusalem on those of the household of God with the retribution against Jerusalem of having its own house(hold)[77] 'abandoned' (ἀφίεται, 13.35). Here, we see the conflict of desires between Jesus and Jerusalem.[78] Jesus desires to shelter the holy city with maternal nurture, while Jerusalem will have none of it. This conflict 'must' (δεῖ) increase until Jesus and Jerusalem are mutually 'rejected', leading to death. Jesus' mission resolutely thrusts him into confrontation with the 'abandoned' house (9.51, αὐτὸς τὸ πρόσωπον ἐστήρισεν; 13.22). Here the accusation is the murdering of the prophets, and this indictment brings Israel under judgement.[79] Like many other prophetic declarations in the Scriptures of Israel, there is conditionality to this pronouncement. However, as the narrative progresses it becomes clear that Jerusalem is aligned opposite the purposes of God, thus sealing its fate to destruction.

As Jesus approaches Jerusalem, concluding his journey, he weeps over the city (Luke 19.41). He mourns with a 'searing oracle of doom [...] with an elaborate statement of judgments and sentences.'[80] Jesus here predicts the levelling of Jerusalem as a result of the city's failure 'to recognize the time of [their] visitation (ἐπισκοπῆς)' (19.44). Tiede masterfully illustrates the dynamic pattern of the polarizing of Israel between blessing and judgement in this passage: '[T]he "visitation" of the prophet-king who comes in the name of the Lord has already been a proving of Israel. The visitation now spells judgment and destruction for the city instead of the redemption of Jerusalem, or peace, or the immediate appearance of the kingdom (19:11).'[81] Jesus brings Israel under judgement through his prophetic indictment. The referent of the performative utterance is *within* the speech-act of prophetic pronouncement.

---

76. ἐντός could indicate 'within', but this internalizing ('spiritualizing') of the kingdom is resisted by the wider presentation of the kingdom in Luke-Acts.

77. On οἶκος here as referring to more than the temple-as-building, see Green, *Luke*, 539; Johnson, *Luke*, 219; Nolland, *Luke*, 2:742, 743. Pace Bock, *Luke*, 2:1250.

78. See the use of θέλω in 13.31, 34 (x2). Consult Green, *Luke*, 534; Nolland, *Luke*, 2:742.

79. Notice the *present* passive of ἀφίημι.

80. David L. Tiede, *Prophecy and History in Luke-Acts* (Philadelphia: Fortress, 1980), 80.

81. Tiede, *Prophecy*, 81. Tellingly, Tiede juxtaposes the passage with Stephen's speech in Acts 7.

This is not mere prediction of the future, but a prophetic condemnation[82] of the city now destined for siege and the Temple now destined for ruin. C. H. Dodd has already demonstrated the possibility that this prophecy is not necessarily an *ex eventu* 'prediction' created after the event of 70 CE and projected back on to the Jesus-tradition.[83]

Closer to a simple prediction is Jesus' statement responding to some who marvel at the glory of the Temple's adornment. In contrast to this admiration is Jesus' alternative vision – 'there will not be one stone left upon another' (Luke 21.6). Jesus uses this opportunity to warn his audience regarding the violence of the days ahead, the 'days of vengeance, in order that all things which are written may be fulfilled' (21.22). Furthermore, Borg is correct to note that Jesus' 'threat pointedly reversed the ideology of resistance rooted in the Temple.[…] These [echoes of the Scriptures, particularly day-of-Yahweh passages] make it clear that the fall of Jerusalem was understood as the judgment of God: these are days of retribution, of great distress, and wrath upon his people.'[84]

Finally, as Jesus completes his 'necessary' 'death march', he utters a damning oracle against Jerusalem to the women who mourn him (Luke 23.28-31).[85] Here, Jesus makes explicit the causal connection of his own suffering and death and the ominous fate of Jerusalem: 'For if they do these things in the green tree, what will happen in the dry?' (23.31). Green comments, 'Jesus' proverb, together with the expression "the days are surely coming" [v. 29], intimates the certainty and imminence of judgment.'[86] Jesus' prophetic indictment, both verbally and through his own self-sacrifice in the divine plan, achieves a successful outcome, even if not felicitous in the eyes of this weeping prophet.

6.2.2.3.3. The 'Raising-Up' of the Prophet-King in Jerusalem

The constellation of royal Davidic appellations increases dramatically with Jesus' arrival in the vicinity of Jerusalem. Approaching Jericho, he is seen

---

82. See Marcus Borg, 'Luke 19:42-44 and Jesus as Prophet?', *Forum* 8 (1992), 104-5.

83. C. H. Dodd, 'The Fall of Jerusalem and the "Abomination of Desolation"', *JRS* 37 (1947): 47-54. See Marcus J. Borg, *Conflict, Holiness and Politics in the Teachings of Jesus* (Harrisburg, PA: Trinity Press International, 1998), 197-203; idem, 'Luke 19:42-44'. Green (*Luke*, 691) explains the hermeneutical significance of the connection with the first destruction of the Jerusalem Temple: 'Those connections urge an analogous interpretation of the Jerusalem that failed to recognize the entry of Jesus as "the time of your visitation from God."[…] Luke has it that Jerusalem's rejection of Jesus is reminiscent of its historic betrayal of the covenant that led to the first destruction of Jerusalem and the exile. As Israel of old fell to its enemies on account of divine judgment for its unfaithfulness, so Jerusalem will be judged for its inconstancy.'

84. Borg, *Conflict*, 202-3.

85. See Jerome Neyrey, 'Jesus' Address to the Women of Jerusalem (Lk 23:27b-31): A Prophetic Judgment Oracle', *NTS* 29 (1983): 74-86.

86. Green, *Luke*, 816.

as 'Jesus, Son of David' by a desperate blind man (Luke 18.35-43). The anonymous healed blind man[87] is a transition figure between the rich ruler (18.18-34) and Zacchaeus (19.1-27), indicating the chasm between those who 'do not want this man [Jesus] to rule over us' (19.14b) and the disciples who laud Jesus as he enters Jerusalem: 'Blessed is the king who comes in the name of the Lord!' (19.38). It is the latter group who inadvertently anticipate the events of Jesus' exaltation, as he passes through death and moves on to the right hand of God. Jesus' entry into Jerusalem echoes the performance of the king in Zechariah's prophecy (Zech. 9.9-10), which seems to draw on the tradition of Solomon's coronation ceremony (1 Kgdms 1.32-35). In addition, in his climactic messianic banquet with his disciples (Luke 22.14-38), Jesus makes a covenant (διατίθημι) with the Twelve and confers upon them *his* kingdom (Luke 22.29), of which he is the legitimate heir.

The designations of king and saviour are ironically applied to Jesus during his passion.[88] Jesus is tried as the Christ, the Son of God before the Council (Luke 22.67-71) and as the Christ, the King of the Jews before Pilate (23.2-3, 11). Jesus is crucified as the King of the Jews (23.38) and with irony,

> Even the rulers were sneering, 'He *saved* others, let him *save* himself if he is the *Christ* of God, the Chosen One'. And the soldiers ridiculed him, coming and bringing to him sour wine, and saying, 'If you are the *King* of the Jews, *save* yourself!' (23.35b-37, emphasis added)

Even the criminals crucified with Jesus indicate his royal status, both with varying elements of irony. One insults him saying, 'Are you not the Christ? Save yourself, and us!' (23.39). The other displays radical trust, defending Jesus and placing his faith in this shamed victim. He entreats, 'Jesus, remember me when you come into your kingdom' (23.42). Having passed through death to divine vindication,[89] Jesus is raised and exalted to the throne of God.

6.2.2.3.4. Proclaiming the Risen Prophet-King

Finally, in three strategic junctures in the speeches in Acts, Jesus' Davidic rule is proclaimed as a means of salvation and blessing for Israel and the nations. Peter, in his speech at Pentecost, interprets the outpouring of the Spirit as evidence of Jesus' exaltation because exaltation is a precondition for the outpouring of the Spirit (2.32-33).[90] Furthermore, Peter employs David as an authoritative prophetic voice bearing witness to Jesus as exalted Messiah and

---

87. The name 'Bartimaeus' in Mark 10.46(-52) is dropped. Matt. 20.29-34 has two anonymous blind men.

88. Brawley, *Centering*, 51; O'Toole, 'Kingdom of God', 156-7.

89. See the comments of Agustín del Agua, 'The Lucan Narrative of the "Evangelization of the Kingdom of God": A Contribution to the Unity of Luke-Acts', in *The Unity of Luke Acts* (ed. J. Verheyden, BETL 142. Leuven, Leuven University Press, 1999), 654.

90. Strauss, *Davidic Messiah*, 131-47; Darrell L. Bock, *Proclamation from Prophecy and Pattern: Lucan Old Testament Christology* (JSNTSup 12; Sheffield: JSOT, 1987), 156-87.

Lord quoting from Ps. 15.8-11 LXX as proof that David looked for one to sit on his throne who would be resurrected because God would not abandon him to Hades or allow his 'holy one' to decay (2.27, 31). In a manner similar to Jesus (Luke 20.41-44), Peter quotes David, from Ps. 109.1 LXX, to assert that Jesus is Lord, exalted not merely in Jerusalem, but to the very throne of God. Jesus, not David, is the one who ascended. Peter's conclusion is that all Israel can know with certainty (ἀσφαλῶς; cf. ἀσφάλεια in Luke 1.4) that God has made Jesus both Lord and Christ (2.36). Green remarks, 'In these two ways – the witness of the Spirit and the witness of Scripture – the divine performance and the divine voice are also brought to bear in the resurrection apologetic of Acts.'[91]

Paul makes a similar argument in his inaugural missionary address at the synagogue in Psidian-Antioch (Acts 13.16-41).[92] Paul emphasizes Jesus' divine sonship (appealing to Ps. 2.7) and his eternal kingdom through his incorruptible life (with reference to Ps. 15.10 LXX). Paul scripts Jesus into the sacred historical drama running from the Exodus, through the judges, to David (13.17-23). Jesus is the climax of this history, fulfilling the covenant promises made to David (2 Kgdms 7.6-16),[93] and securing blessings for all Israel (quoting Isa. 55.3 LXX). The ancient promises of God have been executed through Jesus' life, death and resurrection. The ensuing pattern of Jewish rejection and turning to the Gentiles commences the following week when Paul and Barnabas return. Israel is divided, and many embody the role of scoffers from Hab. 1.5, a passage which Paul used to warn those who did not respond appropriately with faith to be forgiven and liberated (Acts 13.38-39, 40-41). Jesus encounters the nations through Paul and Barnabas as witnesses (13.46-48, with reference to Isa. 49.6; cf. Luke 2.32; Acts 1.8).

Finally, in James' speech to the Jerusalem Council, he appeals to the rebuilding of the 'tent of David' to affirm the divine necessity of the Gentile inclusion into the people of God (Acts 15.13-21).[94] James' use of Scripture is

---

91. Joel. B. Green, '"Witnesses of His Resurrection": Resurrection, Salvation, Discipleship, and Mission in the Acts of the Apostles', in *Life in the Face of Death: The Resurrection Message in the New Testament* (ed. Richard N. Longenecker; Grand Rapids: Eerdmans, 1998), 230.
92. Strauss, *Davidic Messiah*, 148–80; Bock, *Proclamation*, 240–57.
93. See the comparative chart in Strauss, *Davidic Messiah*, 154–5.
94. Strauss, *Davidic Messiah*, 180–93. Jervell (*Luke*, 92–3) goes too far to state that the restoration of Israel is an established fact. So does Craig A. Evans ('The Twelve Thrones of Israel: Scripture and Politics in Luke 22:24–30', in *Luke and Scripture*, 170) who states, 'In *no sense* is this reign [of the apostles as bestowed in Luke 22.28-30] achieved in Acts' (emphasis added) If the 'reign' is defined primarily by service and characterized according to Jesus' service (Luke 22.26-27), then it does occur proleptically through the apostles' preaching, teaching, performance of liberating miracles, bestowal of the Spirit by the laying on of their hands, by their brokering the communal goods and table fellowship. See Carroll (*Response*, 84): 'While this process of Israel's "restoration" has already begun in Acts, the final establishment of the kingdom remains an eschatological hope.' Similarly Brawley (*Centering*, 93) writes, 'The allusions to the leadership of the apostles in Acts 2:41-47; 4:32-37; 6:2 indicate that the apostles lead as just such servants.'

usually interpreted as more directly relevant to the church than to the person of Christ.[95] Even if this is accurate, the Christology is implied: salvation comes through the grace of the Lord Jesus (cf. Peter's testimony, Acts 15.11) and with this the prophets agree (so James' sermon, Acts 15.15-18).[96] Whether the 'tent of David' refers to the Davidic dynasty restored through Jesus' enthronement or the Davidic kingdom now manifest in the messianic people of God, the reciprocity is clear: Jesus is the Davidic king ruling over the Davidic kingdom, which is the manifest kingdom of God moving towards consummation at Jesus' return. The important point here is to stress that God has initiated a move to include the Gentiles into the people of God, which was part of the divine plan from the beginning.[97]

6.2.3. Further Examples Clarifying Performative Prophetic Speech

Having argued for a precedent for Peter's persona and his performative utterances in the person of Jesus and his prophetic speech-acts, this chapter concludes by extending the discussion beyond the Jerusalem section of Acts (1–5) in order to demonstrate further instances of the performative potency of the prophetic word, either by negative example (an unsuccessful speech-act) or positive parallel example (a prophetic curse). First, we examine Peter's confrontation with Simon Magus, arguing that Peter's rebuke should be construed as a warning, not a curse, due to the narrative co-textual constraints, but exhibiting the efficacy of the prophetic word nonetheless. Next, we follow Paul to Cyprus, where he encounters the false prophet, Bar-Jesus. Paul condemns Bar-Jesus to (temporary) blindness as a consequence of a divinely sanctioned imprecation. Finally, the Sons of Sceva provide an advantageous perspective on the composition of speech-acts as social actions through their failure to exorcize the spirits. This will allow a discussion of the aspects leading to the non-success of a speech-act before continuing on with an examination of Luke's strategy for guiding his auditors in understanding the nature of apostolic-prophetic authority.

6.2.3.1. The Apostle-Prophet and the Magician (Acts 8.9-25)
The encounter between Simon Magus and Simon Peter illustrates further elements of performative-prophetic language in Luke-Acts.[98] The pericope

---

95. Thus, Bock (*Proclamation*), whose primary interest resides in Lukan Christology, has no discussion of this pericope.
96. Strauss (*Davidic Messiah*, 187–92) surveys four prominent views, opting for a modified understanding that the 'booth of David' refers to the restored Davidic dynasty through Jesus' ministry, death and resurrection.
97. So Strauss, *Davidic Messiah*, 180, 185.
98. See the statement by Garrett (*Demise*, 77) noting Luke's masterful contrast between Christian signs and the magician's tricks: 'Luke actually *capitalizes on the outward similarity of Christian signs and of magic* [italics hers], constructing his narrative so as to suggest

concerning Simon Magus is set within the larger discourse about Philip's spreading the gospel into Samaria and beyond.[99] In a dramatic way the encounter contrasts the 'magical' use of language with what is here deemed the prophetic-performative use of language.[100] Magical practice uses manipulative formulae to perform μαγείαι (Acts 8.11), whereas 'performative' speech is an empowerment by the Holy Spirit to perform σημεῖα καὶ δυνάμεις μεγάλας (Acts 8.6, 13).[101] Attention is continually focused on to the message of the word of God and its authority, as opposed to the person who is performing.[102] It would appear that, for Luke, magic was a real threat of being confused with genuine divine power, and therefore it needed to be distinguished from true miracles performed by the authority and power of God.

Compared with the remarkable embellishments of the tradition arising from the encounter between Peter and Simon,[103] Acts here proves to be

that Simon mistook the former for the latter.[...This] creates a pretext for the protagonists to dispel the notion that there is *any* similarity of importance between Christians and magicians. Christian authority is in no way like magical-satanic authority, for the latter can be bought but the former is solely a gift of God. The Holy Spirit can be and is used by God to confirm the word proclaimed by God's servants, but it cannot be used to bring glory to an individual.' See also Klauck (*Magic*, 18–19): 'These "mirrorings" [between the acts of Philip and of Simon] show that the experiential world in which the author and his readers lived was aware that most religious phenomena were ambiguous and required interpretation. Without interpretation, the phenomena have no value; this is what makes it so difficult to distinguish the working of miracles from magical activity.' See further idem, 97–102.

99. See F. Scott Spencer, *The Portrait of Philip in Acts: A Study of Roles and Relations* (JSNTSup 67; Sheffield: JSOT Press, 1992).

100. See C. K. Barrett, 'Light on the Holy Spirit from Simon Magus (Acts 8, 4–25)', in *Les Actes des Apôtres: Traditions, rédaction, théologie* (ed. J. Kremer; BETL 48; Leuven: Leuven University Press, 1979), 294 [281-95].

101. See Garrett's (*Demise*, 63) contrast of Simon and Philip in their motives and the relationship between their performance and their message: 'Philip's "signs" (*sēmeia*) were not regarded by Luke as random displays of power (as were, presumably, Simon's unspecified magic tricks, *mageiai*), but, rather, as virtual reenactments of the word that Philip preached. Sign and proclamation were coherent, and therefore mutually reinforcing.'

102. Acts 8.4 (εὐαγγελιζόμενοι τὸν λόγον), 5 (ἐκήρυσσεν), 6 (ἐν τῷ ἀκούειν αὐτοὺς καὶ βλέπειν τὰ σημεῖα ἃ ἐποίει), 12 (ἐπίστευσαν...εὐαγγελιζομένῳ...), 21 (οὐκ ἔστιν σοι μερὶς οὐδὲ κλῆρος ἐν τῷ λόγῳ τούτῳ). Contrast the focus of attention on the person of Simon: Simon was a man 'λέγων εἶναί τινα ἑαυτὸν μέγαν' (8.9c), 'ᾧ προσεῖχον πάντες' (8.10a) who were calling him 'ἡ δύναμις τοῦ θεοῦ ἡ καλουμένη μεγάλη' (8.10b), and 'προσεῖχον δὲ αὐτῷ...as ταῖς μαγείαις ἐξεστακέναι αὐτούς' (8.11). See Spencer, *Portrait*, who provides a superior literary study of the role of Philip in Acts.

103. For the development of the traditions about Simon Magus, including his purported role as the founder of Gnosticism, see *Acts of Peter* 4–32; *Clementine Recognitions* 10; *Pseudo Clementine Homilies* 2.22–24 [20.21]; Justin, *Apology* 1.26.1–3; 1.56.2; idem, *Dialogue with Trypho* 120.6; Irenaeus, *Against Heresies* 1.23; Hippolytus, *Refutation* 6.9–20; and Epiphanius, *Panarion* 21.1–4. Cf. Karlmann Beyschlag, *Simon Magus und die christliche Gnosis* (WUNT 16; Tübingen: Mohr Siebeck, 1974); idem, 'Zur Simon-Magus-Frage', ZTK 68 (1971): 395–415; L. Cerfaux, 'Simon le magicien à Samarie', in *Recueil Lucien Cerfaux* (BETL 6–7; Gembloux: J. Duculot, 1954), 1:259–62; K. Rudolph, 'Simon – Magus oder Gnosticus? Zur Stand der Debatte', TRu 42 (1977): 279–359; H. Waitz, 'Simon Magus in der altchristlichen Literatur', ZNW 5 (1904): 121–43.

momentous but reserved. Simon the magician is an ambivalent character, demonstrating both the marks of conversion (belief and baptism, 8.13), but also exhibiting the disposition of avarice and the desire to manipulate divine authority (8.18-19; cf. 8.9-11).[104] Simon was one who had practised magic in Samaria saying he was someone great and one who commanded attention from the inhabitants of Samaria. Simon is lauded as 'the Power of God which is called[105] Great' (8.10). This designation aligns Simon with the counterfeit power of Satan and, later, with the misplaced worship given to Peter (10.25-26), Herod (12.22-23) and Paul and Barnabas (14.11-18), which is either rejected or accepted with dire consequences. Being dazzled by the association between the apostles' laying on of hands and the bestowal of the (Holy) Spirit,[106] Simon offers money (χρήματα, 8.18; cf. 4.37[!]) in order to purchase the authority of the apostles for himself. In this request, he betrays a disposition toward exploitation and perfidious dealing and one who denigrates divine power with avarice.[107]

Peter's response is most pertinent to the present study. Peter rebukes Simon and corrects his misapprehensions of the Spirit of God. Wolfgang Dietrich correctly remarks, 'Peter with threatening speech addresses the strange request, the basic idea in v. 20 is explained: The Spirit and its gift are not manipulatable (in this case through money), because it belongs to the giver not to the receiver' (my translation).[108]

The pattern of performative speech among Lukan prophetic protagonists adds real suspense to the encounter between Peter and Simon Magus. Jesus' declarative direction of the expansion of the witness in Acts 1.8 has begun to move precisely as he said it would (Acts 8.1c). The prophetic-regal word is coming to fruition. The Ananias and Sapphira pericope adds further suspense by illustrating the severity of the apostle-prophet's condemnation against those who would prove to oppose the communal ethos. Therefore, up through verse 23, there is the real prospect that Peter's scowling rebuke of the magician could lead to his immediate death. As a result, it is remarkable that Simon is given the space to plead for mercy asking the apostles to intercede on his behalf.

The fact that Simon the magician offers to pay Peter and John to obtain the authority to bestow the Spirit confirms his recognition of the undergirding divine authorization of Peter and his forceful verbal rebuke. In some ways,

---

104. I am inclined to consider Simon's attempt at extortion as a lapse from a shallow faith commitment rather than to construe his confession and baptism as insincere. So Klauck, *Magic*, 20–1; Spencer, *Portrait*, 122–6.

105. The participle καλουμένη is read by ℵ, A, B, C, D, E, 33, 1739, but is omitted in Ψ, 36, 307, 453.

106. ℵ, B, et al. read πνεῦμα; P[45, 74], A, D, et al. read πνεῦμα ἅγιον.

107. Negative associations often accompany those accused of magic. See Barrett, 'Light', 286–8; Garrett, *Demise*, 70.

108. Wolfgang Dietrich, *Das Petrusbild der lukanischen Schriften* (BWANT 94; Stuttgart: Kohlhammer, 1972), 254, 'Seinem Ansinnen tritt Petrus mit einer Drohrede entgegen, deren Leitgedanke in V. 20 entfaltet wird: Der Geist bzw. dessen Verleihung ist nicht manipulierbar (in diesem Fall durch Geld), weil er in die Verfügung des Gebers und nicht des Empfängers gehört.'

Peter's indictment of Simon is less severe than his indictment of Ananias and Sapphira.[109] Peter does not *explicitly* align Simon with Satan, as he does with Ananias (Acts 5.3; 8.21b). Yet, as Garrett argues, the association is implicit in the accusing appellation of 'magic'. Peter utters a threatening rebuke to Simon,

> May your silver be with you in destruction because you thought you could acquire the gift of God with money![110] You have no part or portion in this word, for your heart is not right before God. (8.20-21)

Peter assigns Simon to destruction (ἀπώλειαν) and denies him a part or portion (οὐκ...μερὶς οὐδὲ κλῆρος) in the word (τῷ λόγῳ τούτῳ) because of his treacherous proposition. Peter has effectively positioned Simon in the damning space of excommunication.[111] Peter's statement, while appearing to be a performative curse, carries rather the force of a stern warning.[112] This can be seen in (1) Peter's lending opportunity for repentance and (2) the corresponding perlocutionary effect in the narrative co-text: Simon is jolted to beg for intercession on his behalf.

Peter offers the opportunity for repentance (Acts 8.22) because he perceives the desperate state of Simon, being in (or, headed towards) 'the gall of bitterness and in the bondage of unrighteousness' (8.23). This final allegation could be taken as either a clarification for Simon's need to 'repent' or a harsh condemnation of the path Simon is on – either as warning or curse.[113] Grammatically both explanations are possible. The inference is predicated on Peter's perception (ὁρῶ),[114] and the first part could indicate a destination in a sense, as Barrett translates, 'You are destined for bitter anger, that is, to experience the wrath of God (on the assumption you do not repent).'[115] Finding it difficult to correspond σύνδεσμον ἀδικίας with this

---

109. So Johnson, *Literary Function*, 216.

110. Colourful is the translation of J. B. Philips: 'To hell with you and your money!'; quoted in Fitzmyer, *Acts*, 406. See Haenchen, *Acts*, 304.

111. Schuyler Brown, *Apostasy and Perseverance in the Theology of Luke* (Rome: Pontifical Biblical Institute, 1969), 111.

112. Barrett, *Acts*, 1:414; Beyer, 'The Challenge', 114. However, Beyer's attempt to make only the money the object of 'the curse' remains unpersuasive.

113. Depending on the force of γάρ, being either explanatory or causal.

114. D, E, 614, *pc* have θεωρεῶ.

115. Barrett, *Acts*, 1:416, taking εἰς as metaphorically spatial ('leading to'), χολή, as metaphorically referring to anger, with πικρία intensifying that anger, 'bitter anger, wrath'. Codex Bezae reads ἐν πικρίας χολῇ καὶ συνδέσμῳ ἀδικίας θεωπῶ σε ὄντα, thus replacing εἰς with ἐν clarifying the reference to Simon's present state (See C. F. D. Moule, *An Idiom Book of New Testament Greek* [2nd edn; Cambridge: Cambridge University Press, 1959], 69; Jenny Read Heimerdinger, *The Bezan Text of Acts: A Contribution of Discourse Analysis to Textual Criticism* [JSNTSup 236; Sheffield: Sheffield Academic Press, 2002], 192–5) and making Peter's inner perception more apparent. See Josep Rius-Camps, and Jenny Read-Heimerdinger, *The Message of Acts in Codex Bezae: A Comparison with the Alexandrian Tradition. Volume 2: Acts 6.1 – 12.25: From Judea and Samaria to the Church in Antioch* (JSNTSup 302; London: T&T Clark, 2006), 2:138, 145.

translation, Barrett opts instead for a description of Simon's present state, 'You are full of bitter poison, bound by unrighteousness.'[116] He suggests an allusion to Deut. 29.17 (LXX, MT; 29.18, English), where Moses pronounces a curse on one who turns away to idolatry, lest there grow among Israel a root with gall and bitterness.[117] The phrase σύνδεσμον ἀδικίας occurs in Isa. 58.6,[118] where the Lord declares that it is not a fast that will please God, but rather feeding the hungry, sheltering the poor, clothing the naked, and remembering one's kin (Isa. 58.7), in other words participating in the jubilary divine economy of generosity and liberation. That the Lukan Jesus joined this verse to his citation of Isa. 61.1 in his Nazareth sermon indicates a connection for Luke-Acts between this passage and the divine economy of salvation and judgement. Simon has displayed a disposition aligning himself with Judas and Ananias and Sapphira, attempting to engage a proposition with money for self-gain. Simon's request could recall the blasphemous transaction required by Satan to supposedly transfer authority to Jesus in exchange for worship (Luke 4.6).[119] Furthermore, his offer of money (χρῆμα) to the apostles recalls the transaction of Barnabas' submission to the apostles (4.37), but in fact evidences the opposite of friendship (φιλία) and common fellowship (κοινωνία). Simon reveals a corrupt attitude toward τὴν δωρεὰν τοῦ θεοῦ (8.20b), which is power to bestow the Spirit.[120]

Simon's response indicates the gravity with which he received Peter's chastisement. He clearly understood the potential deadly effects of Peter's words. He was dangling in the thin, dangerous space between the prophetic threat and the prophetic imprecation.[121] He begs for the apostles to intercede on his behalf to the Lord 'so that nothing of what you said may come upon me' (8.24). Barrett recognizes that Simon may have taken χολὴν πικρίας and σύνδεσμον ἀδικίας as punishments, but that he may also be referring to Peter's

---

116. Barrett, *Acts*, 1:417.
117. Greek: μή τίς ἐστιν ἐν ὑμῖν ῥίζα ἄνω φύουσα ἐν χολῇ καὶ πικρίᾳ.
118. So Johnson, *Acts*, 149. See Barrett, *Acts*, 1:416; Fitzmyer, *Acts*, 407; Haenchen, *Acts*, 305.
119. See Garrett, *Demise*, 72, 146–7 nn. 50–1.
120. So Johnson, *Literary Function*, 215. See Barrett, 'Light'; Tannehill, *Narrative Unity*, 2:107.
121. The musings of George Steiner (*After Babel: Aspects of Language and Translation* [3rd edn; Oxford: Oxford University Press, 1998], 153–4) on the difference between the false and the true prophet are appropriate here: 'The relation of the genuine prophet (*nabi*) to the future is, in the classic period of Hebrew feeling, unique and complex. It is one of "evitable" certitude. In as much as he merely transmits the word of God, the prophet cannot err. His uses of the future of the verb are tautological. The future is entirely present to him in the literal presentness of his speech-act. But at the same moment, and this is decisive, his enunciation of the future make that future alterable. If man [*sic*] repents and changes his conduct, God can bend the arc of time out of foreseen shape.[...] The force, the axiomatic certainty of the prophet's prediction lies precisely in the possibility that the prediction will go unfulfilled.[...] Thus "behind every prediction of disaster there stands a concealed alternative."' (The final statement quotes Martin Buber, *The Prophetic Faith* [New York: Harper and Row, 1949], 103).

'curse' in verse 20 (ἀπώλεια).¹²² In either case, Simon's fear is evidence that there was recognition of the powerful efficacy in the words of God's apostle-prophets according to the narrative world of Luke-Acts. The threat was immediate and, in light of Ananias and Sapphira, not just something to be feared as taking effect only in the future at the last judgement.¹²³ Peter's rebuke was more than a potential reservation for eschatological condemnation – it was *potentially* the ticket to take him there.

Simon is associated with the self-seeking transactions of Judas and the deviant couple.¹²⁴ All of these are exposed by the prophetic figure, and indicted for their misgivings. In this way, Simon serves as another foil to demonstrate Peter's apostolic-prophetic authority. The Western text brings out further associations between Peter and the Magus with an additional clause in verse 24. In place of ἐπ' ἐμὲ ὧν εἰρήκατε Codex Bezae has μοι τούτων τῶν κακῶν ὧν εἰρήκατε μοι, and is followed by ὃς πολλὰ κλαίων οὐ διελίμπανεν, 'and he did not cease much weeping'. Rius-Camps and Read-Heimerdinger note how the latter clause seems to be an intended allusion to Peter's distress after his denial of Jesus (Luke 22.62, ἔκλαυσεν πικρῶς).¹²⁵ This association could be taken as either a confirmation of the Magus's contrition, or a parody of Peter's genuine repentance. Conversely, Garrett cites examples of weeping by an opponent as a sign of defeat of Satan or of a magician, as when the devil weeps in shame after an unsuccessful attack on Job in *Testament of Job* 27.¹²⁶ The fact that Simon disappears from the narrative leaves the audience with unresolved ambivalence¹²⁷ warning against the dangerous seduction of magic.¹²⁸

---

122. Barrett, *Acts*, 1:417–18. *Pace* Haenchen (*Acts*, 305): 'in fact, there has been no such warning of multiple disasters as would justify the wording μηδὲν ὧν (=τούτων ἃ) εἰρήκατε; this is not, however, intended to illustrate the confusion in Simon's mind, but is a harmless Lucan formulation [...] which underlines the dangerous power of the apostolic words'. It is possible that Simon understood himself to be being cursed with 'perishing' (8.20) and the prospect of entering into 'the gall of bitterness and chains of iniquity' (8.23).

123. With Klauck, *Magic*, 21; Spencer, *Portrait*, 125. *Pace* Garrett, *Demise*, 71, 72, 146, n. 46.

124. See Reimer (*Miracle*, 115–40, esp. 134 [on Simon]) discussing the avoidance of avarice and the danger of wealth for miracle workers.

125. Rius-Camps, and Jenny Read-Heimerdinger, *Message*, 2:139.

126. Garrett, *Demise*, 73. She also cites *Hermas Mandate* 11:14. See also idem pp. 41–2.

127. So Klauck, *Magic*, 23.

128. As Garrett (*Demise*, 69) writes, 'Simon's submission to the cleansing ritual demonstrates the superiority of Christianity to magic: even a competitor recognizes something better when he sees it.' Garrett remains convinced of a negative portrayal of Simon's character and motives throughout, interpreting even his plea for intercession (Acts 8.24) as insincere (72).

6.2.3.2. The Missionary-Prophet and the False Prophet (Acts 13.1-12)

Whereas the confrontation between Peter and Simon may have implicitly echoed the *topos* of God's true prophet confronting the false prophet,[129] this theme becomes explicit in Paul's cursing of Elymas. This is the first significant event of Barnabas' and Saul's ('Paul's') first missionary journey after being selected by the Holy Spirit and confirmed by the community for a special work (Acts 13.2-3; cf. 14.26-27, where the work is said to have been 'fulfilled'). At the beginning of the gentile mission, just as at the beginning of the Gospel's spread to Samaria (8.4-25), God's prophetic agents encounter an opposing servant of Satan. Having been sent by the Holy Spirit to Cyprus,[130] they reach the city of Paphos and find a certain μάγος, a Jewish ψευδοπροφήτης whose name was Bar-Jesus. He was most likely a court advisor[131] of Sergius Paulus, the proconsul, himself 'a man of intelligence' (13.7), who summoned Barnabas and Saul to hear the word of God. However, Elymas[132] ὁ μάγος was opposing them, and seeking to turn the proconsul away from the faith.[133] It is this circumstance that causes Paul to indict Elymas with a harsh list of accusations and to curse him blind. In this case, as with Ananias and Sapphira, but unlike the story of Simon the magician, the curse takes effect immediately. The servant of darkness is consigned to a world without light, and Paul triumphs over this 'son of the devil' causing the proconsul to believe and respond in the way common to acts of the Lord through a commissioned servant, with 'amazement' (13.12; see Luke 2.38; 4.32; 9.43).

In the confrontation between Paul and Elymas, the narrator offers highest commendation for Paul, saying he was 'filled with the Holy Spirit'. In this state Paul glares (ἀτενίσας)[134] at Elymas and offers four indictments: 'Oh! [1] Full of all deceit and all fraud, [2] son of the devil, [3] enemy of all righteousness, [4] will you stop twisting the straight paths of the Lord?' (13.10). After his indictment – in the form of a rhetorical question (cf. §6.1.1. above)! – Paul

---

129. Garrett, Demise, 67–8.

130. One should be reminded that Barnabas is originally from Cyprus (Acts 4.36) and there is already a Christian presence in Cyprus (11.19-20). Kee (*Every Nation*, 160) notes that there is evidence of a Jewish presence as early as the third century BCE, citing 1 Macc. 15.23; 2 Macc. 12.2. Note Alanna Nobbs, 'Cyprus', in *The Book of Acts in its Graeco-Roman Setting* (ed. David W. J. Gill and Conrad Gempf; vol. 2 of *The Book of Acts in its First Century Setting*, ed. Bruce W. Winter; Grand Rapids: Eerdmans, 1994), 279–89.

131. See Klauck (*Magic*, 51) for a discussion about the presence of court astrologers employed by Roman officials. Rick Strelan ('Who Was Bar Jesus [Acts 13.6-12]?', *Bib* 85 [2004]: 66 [65–81]) claims μάγος meant simply a court advisor citing Josephus, *Ant*. 20.7.2. Garrett (*Demise*, 81) calls him a 'court magician' implying a negative connotation.

132. D05 reads Ἐτοιμᾶς. As a result of this, some have drawn a parallel to a certain magician, Ἄτομος, in Josephus, *Ant*. 20.7.2. See Metzger, *Commentary*, 402–3.

133. Codex Bezae, with E syr[hmg] cop[G67], includes ἐπ(ε)ιδὴ ἥδιστα ἤκουεν αὐτῶν, 'because he was listening to them with the greatest pleasure'. According to Metzger (*Commentary*, 404) this addition heightens the threat of replacement to Elymas posed by the ministers of the word.

134. See the comprehensive study of Rick Strelan, 'Strange Stares: ATENIZEIN in Acts', *NovT* 41 (1999): 235–55.

speaks the divine curse upon Elymas: 'And now, behold, the hand of the Lord is upon you, and you will be blind and not see the sun for a time' (13.11).[135] The narrator explains that immediately (παραχρῆμα; see 5.10) a mist and darkness fell upon Elymas, and he sought for someone who could lead him by the hand. The response of the proconsul serves to authenticate the miracle as did the response of the crowds for the miracles of Jesus and Peter.[136]

Garrett is certainly right to note the association of Elymas as a servant of Satan at the level of Luke's narrative.[137] She notes the human representation of superhuman figures, indicating that in this pericope there is actually a confrontation between the Holy Spirit and Satan, with the result that Satan is humbled and Paul, called to be a light to the Gentiles, turns darkness upon itself. Paul's first accusation characterizes the magician as a charlatan.[138] The final predication confirms the designation of 'false prophet' and sets Elymas in contrast to a true prophet, John the Baptist, who 'made straight' the paths of the Lord (Luke 3.4).[139] Bar-Jesus is one who sets himself against the 'Way' of the Lord.[140] He is aligned with Satan in his attempt to pervert the divine economy and by his opposition to God's anointed servants. At the literary level, there is yet a starker contrast: this magician calls himself 'Bar-('son of') Jesus', but in fact he proves to be the 'son of the devil'.[141] Strelan has argued that the threat of Elymas was not his magical practices, but rather his teaching the righteousness of God in a false way.[142] However, Strelan too sharply divides what cannot be divided in the text. Strelan correctly perceives the primary danger not as syncretism,[143] but rather as a Jewish prophet

---

135. Beyer ('The Challenge', 141–55) stretches the credibility of his thesis by labelling this episode a mere 'foretelling' or 'predicting' on the part of Paul. He notes the absence of explicit curse formula and so neglects the dynamics of performative language in Luke-Acts as well as the fundamental divine undergirding. Beyer denies that Elymas could be cursed blind by appealing to Paul's own experience of blindness. This demonstrates lack of attention to the different circumstances surrounding each episode. This episode fits Beyer's own criteria perfectly for a punitive imprecation (23, 27).

136. Luke 7.16-17; 9.43; Acts 3.10; 4.21. So Garrett, *Demise*, 85.

137. Garrett, *Demise*, 79–87; followed by Gaventa, *Acts*, 191–5.

138. Barrett ('Light', 289), argues that ῥαδιουργία tends to have the sense of falsification or forgery in money matters. Note *BDAG*, 902–3.

139. So Garrett, *Demise*, 81.

140. Pao (*New Exodus*, 68) sees here a reference to Isa. 40.3 which is 'used to distinguish those who belong to the people of God from those who do not'. See Pao's discussion of the passage on pp. 201–2.

141. See Barrett, *Acts*, 1:617; Klauck, *Magic*, 49. However, *pace* Klauck, I think it goes beyond the evidence to suggest that Bar-Jesus thought himself to be a disciple of Jesus, and therefore an 'insider' in the Christian community in Paphos. It remains to be established that Luke envisaged a *Christian* community in Paphos by the time Barnabas and Saul arrived (although with Acts 11.19 this is a possibility). Strelan ('Bar Jesus', 74–6, 77) notes that Luke stresses ὄνομα (Acts 13.6, 8) and reserves the nominative case exclusively of Jesus, except with Bar-Jesus.

142. Strelan, 'Bar Jesus'.

143. Argued by Pesch, *Apostelgeschichte*, 2:21, 26; Klauck, *Magic*, 54.

claiming to represent the God of Israel to the gentile proconsul without proper authorization or insight.[144] In doing so, Bar-Jesus is misrepresenting God, and is marked by his appeal to magical authority (μάγος mentioned twice, verses 6, 8). Strelan is correct to state that, for Luke, '[v]alid authority only comes from those who have been given it by Jesus through the legitimate apostles, teachers, and prophets who through prayer and fasting and the laying on of hands, have been set apart by the Holy Spirit for such work (13.1-3)'.[145] However, Strelan unhelpfully divorces the magician's perverse teaching from his magical powers in a way unwarranted by the Lukan text. Because the Lukan narrator twice stresses Bar-Jesus' role of μάγος, it is better to understand his 'corruption of the straight paths of the Lord' as occurring, at least partly, through his magical practice.[146]

In lucid manner Luke portrays Bar-Jesus as becoming the dark photographic negative of Paul's heroic image before Paul's conversion.[147] Both characters oppose Christian witness; both are confronted by the power of God; both are struck blind for a time; both are 'led about by the hand'. There are important differences as well.[148] Is it that, as Klauck states, 'we see Paul fighting against his own shadow, the dark parts of his own personality'?[149] Or, is there a

---

144. Strelan, 'Bar Jesus', 68–71, 74, 81. Strelan writes, 'Bar Jesus has been proclaiming the word and will of God in Paphos, but from Luke's perspective, he has interpreted the ways of God falsely. That is the point of this whole episode' (70).

145. Strelan, 'Bar Jesus', 71.

146. Strelan ('Bar Jesus', 73) writes, 'It is his teaching about the way of the Lord that is delusional, not his magical power or pagan syncretism.' I challenge Strelan's 'either / or' (either magic or corrupt teaching) and replacing it with a 'both / and' (corruption partly through illicit magic).

Strelan also assumes, rather than argues, that Bar-Jesus is a threat to the *Christian* community in Paphos, and *therefore* exists the necessity for Paul to curse him. He offers no evidence for such a distinctive community, and the evidence he does cite for false prophets and false teachers arising from the community ('Bar Jesus', 70–1) is already an element of intra-communal discourse (cf. Matt. 7.15 [arguably], 2 Cor. 11.13; Gal. 1.9; 2 Thess. 2.11; 2 Pet. 2.1; 1 John 4.1; Rev. 19.20 [sic]). Günter Klein ('Der Synkretismus als theologisches Problem in der ältesten christliche Apologetik', *ZTK* 64 [1967]: 61–7) also suggests Bar-Jesus may have claimed to be a disciple of Jesus.

147. Garrett, *Demise*, 84–5; Johnson, *Acts*, 227; Klauck, *Magic*, 54–5; Strelan, 'Bar Jesus', 65 n. 4; Tannehill, *Narrative Unity*, 2:163 n. 15.

For the appropriateness of the language of 'conversion' here, see the nuanced perspective of Michael J. Gorman, *Apostle of the Crucified Lord: A Theological Introduction to Paul and His Letters* (Grand Rapids: Eerdmans, 2004), 59–60.

148. Garrett (*Demise*, 84) suggests three differences: (1) Bar-Jesus is one who 'makes straight paths crooked' (13.10), but Paul is led to 'a street called straight' (9.11); (2) Bar-Jesus is blinded by 'a mist and darkness' (13.11), but Paul is blinded by radiant light (9.3; 22.11; 26.13); and (3) Paul made a transition from darkness to light, but Bar-Jesus is not relieved within the narrative. She concludes, 'The differences in experience signify the diverging paths or "ways" of their lives.' Note also Johnson, *Acts*, 227.

149. Klauck, *Magic*, 55. Klauck refers to Johnson, *Acts*, 227 and Tannehill, *Narrative Unity*, 2:163 n. 15, but fails to notice how both authors downplay this psychological association.

looser literary comparison meant to contrast two opposing Jewish-prophetic representations of fulfilling the vocation of 'light to the Gentiles'?[150] Sergius Paulus represents the nations, poised at the outset of Paul's' missionary journeys, confronted by two portrayals of Israel's God, one mediated by false prophecy and another represented by the agent of God's exalted Messiah. Primarily to be noticed is the contrast between darkness and light, blindness and sight.[151] Elymas is blinded by a 'mist and darkness', whereas Paul is blinded by a light 'brighter than the sun' (Acts 26.13). Throughout the narrative concerned with Paul's ministry, it becomes clear that light carries symbolic significance illuminating the scriptural theme of salvation to the Gentiles with allusions to Isa. 42.6; 49.6. Stretching from Simeon's proclamation in Luke 2.30-32 through to Paul's defence before Agrippa in Acts 26.15-18, and on to Paul's arrival in Rome (28.25-28), the symbolism of light and darkness, seeing and blindness, becomes a cohesive image.[152] In the immediate co-text of Acts 13, there is contrast between Elymas and Paul, who is fulfilling the vocation of Israel to be a light for the ἐθνῶν (Acts 13.47; cf. Isa. 42.6; 49.6). Therefore, Paul is the heroic foil to the 'false prophet' Elymas who is misrepresenting the God of Israel and 'perverting the straight paths of the Lord'. It can be stated that Elymas embodies his dark deception (from Luke's perspective) as he was leading astray the proconsul Sergius Paulus and attempting to hinder the true 'word of God' (13.7). Elymas is another character who tries to derail 'the way of the Lord' which was prepared by John the Baptist (Luke 3.4) and continues through Paul and his companions.

With regard to Paul's imprecation, there are two aspects to be noted. First, the formula of the curse echoes with a 'biblical ring' to it.[153] Plümacher notes, 'Even the curses of the apostle are held in biblical tone.'[154] Johnson

---

150 With Johnson, *Acts*, 227: '[I]t is Paul as "Light of the Gentiles" (as we shall soon be told he is, 13:47) who blinds the master of the dark arts; and it is the Holy Spirit that fills the prophet Paul who casts into confusion the "false prophet" Bar-Jesus [who is "full of deception and fraud"].'

151. Dennis Hamm studies this theme in Luke's Gospel ('Sight to the Blind: Vision as Metaphor in Luke', *Bib* 67 [1986]: 457–77) and in Acts ('Paul's Blindness and its Healing: Clues to Symbolic Intent [Acts 9; 22 and 26]', *Bib* 71 [1990]: 63–72). See also the voyeuristic musings of Stephen D. Moore, 'The Gospel of the Look', *Semeia* 54 (1991): 159–96.

152. See Tannehill, *Narrative Unity*, 2:121–22: 'Thus the one who is called to be a light to the nations and to open the eyes of the Jews and Gentiles has encountered the Messiah in light and is himself a healed blind man, forced by the Messiah's light to recognize his own blindness and to receive his sight through him. The story of Paul is necessary to complete the story begun in Luke 1–2, for it is with Paul that the crucial prophecy of light to the Gentiles, as well as for Israel, begins to be fulfilled as the gospel moves through the Mediterranean world.' Also Gaventa, *Acts*, 193–4.

153. Witherington (*Acts*, 402) says that verse 11 'seems to involve a form of oath curse' but he does not define this term nor does he offer examples of antecedents or conventions of what this 'form' may be.

154. Eckhard Plümacher, *Lukas als hellenistischer Schriftsteller: Studien zur Apostelgeschichte* (SUNT 9; Göttingen, 1972), 47 n. 58 ('Auch die Flüche der Apostel sind in biblischem Ton gehalten'), who is quoted by Barrett, *Acts*, 1:617; and Klauck, *Magic*, 53.

notes how the phrase 'the hand of the Lord is upon you' echoes passages in the Septuagint such as Judg. 2.15 and 1 Kgdms 12.15, where the 'hand of the Lord' is an active force against the rebellious people of God.[155] Garrett suggests a possible echo of Deut. 28.28-29, and adduces *The Community Rule* (1QS 2.11-19) of the Qumran sectarians as evidence for employment of Deuteronomy's curses in their condemnation of idolatry.[156] Emphasized is the missionary-prophet's ability to speak on behalf of God and curse the magician false-prophet with efficacious divine authority. The curse comes about from Paul's effective imprecatory speech-act undergirded by divine authorization. It is as if through speech Paul is able to move the 'hand of God'.

The second noteworthy aspect was noted above: the punishment fits the crime. The magician who is 'twisting (διαστρέφων) the straight paths of the Lord' and attempting 'to turn (διαστρέψαι) the proconsul away from the faith' is sent down the twisted road of darkness. The picture is one of the blind leading the blind and now Elymas bodily exhibits the scene. The Spirit-filled missionary-prophet has exposed the false prophet filled with 'deceit and fraud' and cursed him with powerful imprecatory speech.

In summary, Elymas, as a 'false prophet', is not properly authorized by the God who raised Jesus from the dead. The point of the episode is not syncretism, but rather the misrepresentation of the truth of God. It is a narrative about the truly authorized prophet confronting the false prophet and demonstrating the validity of the 'word of God' (13.7) through efficacious, if terrible, wonders and amazing teaching (13.12). Elymas had no recourse to superior power; he was condemned by the authorized agent specifically chosen by the Holy Spirit (13.2, 4).

6.2.3.3. *An Unsuccessful Speech-Act: The Sons of Sceva (Acts 19.8-20)*

An enlightening case of lack of authorization is the unsuccessful exorcism by the Sons of Sceva,[157] who were apparently trying to imitate Paul in employing the Name of Jesus to expel demons. In this case there is a contrast between

---

155. Johnson, *Acts*, 224.
156. Garrett, *Demise*, 82-3.
157. This passage is riddled with textual problems. There is wide divergence between the AT and the WT. At the crux of the matter is verse 14. Codex Vaticanus (B03) reads: ἦσαν δέ τινος Σκευᾶ Ἰουδαίου ἀρχιερέως ἑπτὰ υἱοὶ τοῦτο ποιοῦντες. Codex Bezae (D05) has a considerably longer version: ἐν οἷς καὶ υἱοὶ Σκευᾶ τινος ἱερέως ἠθέλησαν τὸ αὐτὸ ποιῆσαι. ἔθος εἶχαν τοὺς τοιούτους ἐξορκίζειν, καὶ εἰσελθόντες πρὸς τὸν δαιμονιζόμενον ἤρξαντο ἐπικαλεῖσθαι τὸ ὄνομα λέγοντες· παραγγέλλομέν σοι ἐν Ἰησοῦ ὃν Παῦλος ἐξελθεῖν κηρύσσει ('Among whom also the sons of a certain priest Sceva wished to do the same thing. They had a custom to exorcize such persons, and they went in to the one who was demonized and began to invoke the Name, saying, "We command you to come out by Jesus, whom Paul preaches."'). The differences include: (1) the priestly status of Sceva (B03 = *Jewish high* priest; D05 = priest [P38 agrees with B03]); (2) the difference between current action (B03 = 'doing this'; D05 = 'desiring to do this') (3) the number of sons (B03 = seven; D05 = no number given [syr^hmg has ἑπτά] [the number 'seven' potentially creates problems with ἀμφότεροι ('both') in v. 16]). Strange (*Problem*, 187) suggests that ἐν οἷς be taken as 'At

Paul as an authorized exorcist (19.12; cf. 16.16-18) and the 'sons'[158] of a (Jewish high)[159] priest who were not authorized to use the Name of Jesus, and so were themselves expelled from the house (19.13-16). The failed exorcism is a prime example of what Austin would have called a 'misinvocation', and more precisely a 'misappropriation' due to the lack of proper authority.[160]

The episode is couched between Paul's bestowal of the baptism of the Holy Spirit on disciples of John the Baptist in Ephesus (Acts 19.1-7) and the riots of the Ephesian silversmiths who are threatened by the waning interest in their product (19.23-41).[161] In this way the themes of Spirit-filling and the seductive power of wealth frame the episode contrasting the victorious ministry of Paul and the failed attempt of the priestly exorcists. Of particular interest is the immediate co-text where Paul withdraws from the Ephesian synagogue, due to some who 'were becoming hardened and disobedient, speaking evil of the Way before the multitude' (19.9), going to go to the school of Tyrannus.

The next scene is a dramatic vista of the power of God that resembles magical power.[162] It is therefore important to note that ὁ θεός is the subject, and Paul is the instrument. This mitigates the view that Paul's σουδάρια and σιμικίνθια[163] are conduits of power controllable through magical formulae or technique. The insult to the failed exorcists is heightened by the inversion of prophetic action and magical-exorcistic word: the missionary-prophet performs through extraneous articles, whereas the Sons of Sceva prove to utter ineffectual words. The ineptitude of the exorcists is further accentuated by the reversal of knowledge. Garrett notes that this episode of a botched exorcism presents characters who attempt to emulate the successful exorcist, Paul, apparently using their knowledge of the source of his power (19.10), the Name of Jesus, but demonstrating that they do not in fact know Jesus nor are they authorized by him.[164] Garrett states, 'what is important is

---

that time', thus making the new group of exorcists in v. 14 different from the ones in v. 13, and also Gentile, not Jewish.

Metzger (*Commentary*, 470-1) focuses mainly on the numbers. For an argument that the WT is an attempt to solve apparent exegetical difficulties, see Ernst Haenchen, 'Zum Text der Apostelgeschichte', *ZTK* 54 (1957): 28-9. For an argument that the AT appears to be an attempt to simplify an obscure, more original WT, see W. A. Strange, 'The Sons of Sceva and the Text of Acts 19:14', *JTS* 38 (1987): 97-106.

158. Strelan ('Bar Jesus', 75) argues that 'sons' here could mean disciples. Klauck (*Magic*, 100) deems the designation a 'stage name'. Cf. the options listed in Barrett, *Acts*, 2:909.

159. For the textual variants, see n. 157 above.

160. Austin, *HtDTwW*, 17-18, 34-5. Garrett (*Demise*, 98-9) states that what was crucial for Luke was 'the question of *agency* [emphasis hers] in assessing miraculous deeds. In Luke's view the difference between Christian "signs and wonders" on the one hand and non-Christian "magic" on the other lay in the source of the instrumental power'.

161. See Lynn Allan Kauppi, *Foreign But Familiar Gods. Greco Romans Read Religion in Acts* (LNTS 277; London: T&T Clark, 2006), 94-106.

162. See Klauck, *Magic*, 97-8.

163. See T. J. Leary, 'The "Aprons" of St Paul – Acts 19:12', *JTS* 41 (1990): 527-9.

164. Garrett, *Demise*, 92, 157 n. 35; also Klauck, *Magic*, 99.

not whether the exorcist "knows" the name of Jesus, but whether the demons "know" the exorcist as one who has truly been invested with authority to call upon that holy name'.[165]

These exorcists are described as part of a group of Jewish exorcists who go around attempting to wield (ὀνομάζειν) the Name of the Lord Jesus over those having evil spirits, saying, 'I adjure (ὁρκίζω) you by Jesus whom Paul preaches.'[166] The Sons of Sceva were doing this very thing, and proved laughable. After scoffing at the illegitimate charmers, the demonized man leaps on them, subdues (both / all of [ἀμφότεροι])[167] them and defeats (ἴσχυσεν) them, so that they flee out of the house naked and wounded (19.16). The result recalls the Ananias and Sapphira episode: fear came over those that heard of it. This episode further results in massive conversion and voluntary burning of magical books in an act of repentance and rejection of magical practice. The consequence is uproar among the silversmiths who are losing business for lack of interest in their product (19.23-41).

The episode with the Sons of Sceva serves as a foil to emphasize Paul's authority and the effectiveness of his ministry. Three times there is mention of the name of Jesus (Acts 19.5, 13, 17) embedded in a plot that culminates in the growth of the 'word of the Lord' (19.20). It is after the defeat of the failed exorcists and the mass conversion to follow 'the Way' by turning from magical practice that Paul determines to go to Jerusalem (19.21; cf. Luke 9.51). Johnson aptly concludes,

> The present passage [Acts 19.1-20] therefore compresses into three vivid scenes [the Spirit-baptism of disciples of John, the preaching of Paul in the synagogues and the school of Tyrannus and the failed exorcism leading to mass conversion and repentance] the essence of Paul's prophetic ministry as an apostle and serves to 'legitimate' him firmly in the reader's eyes as having fulfilled precisely what was predicted of him, before his own series of calamities and defenses begin.[168]

In summary, this story demonstrates the negative aspect of the performative power of speech in Acts. Without the proper authorization, there cannot be a successful speech-act of exorcism in the world of Luke-Acts. The Name of Jesus cannot be domesticated or controlled through invocation. The power associated with that Name cannot be manipulated by contenders who stake arbitrary claims on divine authority. The implication is that if it were Paul demanding the unclean spirits to come out of the man that they would have been impelled to do so, just as evil spirits were going out of those who came into contact with Paul's sweaty clothes.

This passage facilitates a discussion of unsuccessful speech-acts, which clarifies the socio-pragmatic dynamics that make up the social process of

---

165. Garrett, *Demise*, 93.
166. On the use of ὀνομάζειν and ὁρκίζειν, see Garrett, *Demise*, 92, 155 nn. 21-2, and the literature cited there.
167. See Metzger, *Commentary*, 471-2.
168. Johnson, *Acts*, 344.

prophetic speech in the ancient world. In discussing the possibility of performing actions through speech, Austin describes various forms of speech-act failures ('infelicities'), which offer great insight into how he was analysing the various conditions for a speech-act to be successful.[169] The two main categories of infelicities are what Austin calls 'misfires' and 'abuses'. A 'misfire' occurs when an act is 'purported but void', for example, if a wedding is presided over by an unordained minister. An 'abuse' occurs when the act is 'professed but hollow', as when a groom speaks his wedding vow but does not intend to honour it. Austin mentions various types of misfires such as a 'misinvocation' (there exists no such procedure), 'misapplications' (the procedure in question is not applicable to the circumstances), and 'misexecutions' (the purported act is vitiated by a flaw or incompletion in the conduct of the ceremony).[170] By indicating the possible non-success of a speech-act, Austin grounds his theory of performatives in the extra-linguistic conventions of social action. In the case of the Sons of Sceva there is a clear 'misfire', for they are not authorized by God in the manner of Paul.

6.3. Summary and Conclusions

This chapter has been occupied with the fundamental question of the socio-literary conventions inscribed into Luke-Acts which undergird Peter's speech-acts. It has surveyed both the 'external' and 'internal' literary repertoires, which establish a convention for efficacious prophetic speech to achieve the accusation and condemnation of those indicted by the prophetic word. Furthermore, it has reviewed the specific prophetic conventions inscribed into the narrative of Luke-Acts, specifically the fundamental role of the Holy Spirit in sanctioning prophetic speech, as well as the dramatic pattern of Jesus as the Prophet-King addressing Israel in salvation and judgement. Finally, this chapter examined three passages in Acts that clarify further various dimensions of speech-acts. The episode of Peter confronting Simon Magus (Acts 8.9-25) helps to distinguish different social actions (e.g., warning versus imprecation) as depicted in narrative portrayal. The confrontation between Paul and Elymas (Acts 13.1-2) offers a direct parallel with Peter's indictment of Ananias and Sapphira (5.1-11), where the utterance of the prophetic figure accomplishes its purpose in condemning the offender. Finally, the failure of the Sons of Sceva (Acts 19.8-20) illustrates when performative speech fails to accomplish its goals because the speakers are not authorized according to the proper extra-linguistic conventions.

The next chapter turns to examine the strategy of the Lukan text to guide the reader in understanding the nature of the encounter between Peter and

---

169. Austin, *HtDTwW*, 15–24.

170. Ronald Grimes ('Infelicitous Performances and Ritual Criticism', *Semeia* 41 [1988], 103–22) offers an elaboration of the possible 'infelicities' of speech-acts with attention to ritual acts.

the couple. The current chapter has established the necessary conventions for the performance of efficacious prophetic oracles of judgement in Luke-Acts. The next chapter will be concerned with the demonstration of Peter as being in fact represented as an effective prophetic speaker according to these conventions.

Chapter 7

LEGITIMATE AUTHORITY: APOSTOLIC-PROPHETIC SUCCESSION AND THE CHARACTERIZATION OF PETER

Having established a theoretical grid for understanding the necessary conditions for performative language (§3), and having explored the socio-cultural repertoire of the embedded discourse of community-of-goods (§§4–5) and socio-literary conventions undergirding the authorized prophetic speech (§6), it is now pertinent to establish that Peter is in fact characterized as an apostle-prophet, that is, that he is authorized to speak the divine judgement upon the deceiving couple. In order to argue that the illocutionary force of Peter's statements and rhetorical questions are in fact prophetic indictment and condemnation, it is necessary to establish that Peter is in fact characterized as one having appropriate prophetic authority.[1] This chapter progresses in two stages. First, I build a case for the literary strategy which leads one to understand the characterization of one authorized as an apostle-prophet.[2] Second, I argue that Peter is a character aligned with the theological and ideological perspective of the narrator and is characterized in a manner indicating that he is deputized with apostolic-prophetic authority.

7.1. Apostolic Commission and Prophetic Transference

Having argued for the manifestation of the royal-messianic and eschatological-prophetic repertoire that converges in the character of Jesus, now I examine the way in which this convergence (trans)forms the character of the messianic-prophetic community. The messianic-prophetic community derives its identity from the Prophet-King.[3] All three primary stock images – Davidic Messiah,

---

1. See Austin, *HtDTwW*, 14–15, 34–5; Searle, *Construction*, 104–12.
2. On 'strategy', see Iser, *Act*, 86–103.
3. See Agustín del Agua, 'The Lucan Narrative of the "Evangelization of the Kingdom of God". A Contribution to the Unity of Luke-Acts', in *The Unity of Luke Acts* (ed. J. Verheyden; BETL 142; Leuven: Leuven University Press, 1999), 639–61; Hahn, 'Kingdom', 294–326; Jervell, 'The Twelve on Israel's Thrones: Luke's Understanding of the Apostolate', in *Luke and the People of God*, 75–112; and Gerhard Lohfink, *Die Sammlung Israels: Eine Untersuchung zur lukanischen Ekklesiologie* (SANT 39; Munich: Kösel, 1975).

Isaianic Servant, and Mosaic Prophet – impinge upon the character of the community as it derives its identity from the risen Jesus. After a brief survey of Luke's prophetic-messianic community in his Gospel, we then move on to Acts in order to complete the necessary background to understand the inscribed conventional framework undergirding Peter's apostolic-prophetic authority.

7.1.1. Covenanting Jesus' Kingdom: The Twelve and Their Thrones to Judge Israel

In Luke's Gospel, the community surrounding Jesus bears the marks of both prophetic-eschatological and royal-messianic features. The main role of the disciples in the Gospel is to be *with* Jesus.[4] Early on Jesus separates twelve disciples to be his apostles (Luke 6.12-16; 9.1-6, 10), but their distinctive function remains undefined until the climactic Passover banquet-meal in Jerusalem (22.14-38). These apostles participate in Jesus' ministry, are allocated authority to preach the kingdom, and perform the liberating miracles, like healings and exorcisms. However, they often prove to be aligned with 'the leaven of the Pharisees' (12.1b; cf. 9.46-48; 22.24-27) as imitating the disposition of a counterfeit household mismanaging Israel (12.41-48; 14.7-11; 16.1-31). Yet, Jesus confers upon the Twelve a regal status of leadership over the eschatological people of God (22.28-30). The nascent messianic community is the bearer of the 'promise of the Father' and the commission to take the message of repentance for the forgiveness of sins to the nations (24.45-49).

During the course of the Last Supper, Jesus identifies the Twelve disciples as those who will sit on thrones to judge the twelve tribes of Israel (22.28-30). Here, Jesus claims the kingdom as '*my* kingdom' (22.30), confirming the exuberant praise given to Jesus upon his entrance into Jerusalem (19.38). After pledging his disciples this status, Jesus specifically addresses Peter to confer upon him the responsibility of strengthening his brothers (22.31-32). Peter begins to fulfil this commission when he interprets the situation in light of Scripture in the replacement of Judas (Acts 1.12-26; Pss. 68.26; 108.8 LXX), which was a necessary precondition for the advancement of the restoration of Israel by restoring the symbolic Twelve.[5] The story of the early Jerusalem church in Acts is largely the story of the new apostolic leadership coming into

---

4. Green, *Theology*, 102–5.
5. See Arie W. Zwiep, *Judas and the Choice of Matthias* (WUNT 2. Reihe 187; Tübingen: Mohr Siebeck, 2004), esp. 127–74. Cf. Nelson P. Estrada, *From Followers to Leaders: The Apostles in the Ritual of Status Transformation in Acts 1–2* (JSNTSup 255; London: T&T Clark International, 2004), who argues that the main thrust of this passage is the ritual of status transformation following Mark McVann ('Rituals of Status Transformation in Luke-Acts: The Case of Jesus the Prophet' in *The Social World of Luke-Acts: Models for Interpretation* [ed. Jerome H. Neyrey; Peabody: Hendrickson, 1991], 333–60).

conflict with the presently established high priestly and Herodian dynasties.[6] Peter is transformed from being one who denies his association with Jesus (Luke 22.33-34, 54-62) to one who preached the resurrected Christ with confidence (παρρησία, Acts 4.13) even under threat (4.18, 21; 5.18, 33) and physical harm (5.40-41).

Another amazing transformation occurs from the content of Jesus' message where the object is the kingdom of God to the content of the apostolic preaching where the object is the life, death and resurrection of Jesus as the means of inaugurating the kingdom of God. This is a natural progression, not disjunctive, for Luke. Both Luke's Gospel and Acts are *themselves* witnesses of the gospel of the kingdom of God. The gospel is the narrative of the in-breaking of the kingdom through the person and actions of Jesus; Acts is the retrospective and prospective glances to this fulfilment and its kerygmatic proclamation to the nations. Just as the kerygma of the kingdom of God characterized Jesus' preaching, so his prophets-witnesses are identified by the same message. The 'kingdom of God' is often used as a summary of the missionary preaching.[7]

The church, for Luke, is not equated with the kingdom of God. The church celebrates, announces and anticipates the kingdom, but it is not synonymous with it.[8] The thrones awaiting Jesus' apostles (22.29-30) await a future

---

6. Jervell (*Luke*, 94) writes, 'The leaders of the people have relinquished any right to rule over the people, and the Twelve have now become the new leaders of Israel, as Luke 22:30 makes clear.[...] They rule not over a special synagogue or a sect, a new organization or congregation, but simply over Israel. The history of the people continues in the church. As Jesus addressed the people as a whole and made demands on them, so do the Twelve.' However, their rule is rejected by many, as was Jesus', and causes division in Israel. Jervell neglects mention here of the necessary eschatological consummation required by Luke's text.

7. Acts 8.12, 19.8; 20.25; 28.23, 31. See Luke 10.9, 11; Acts 1.3; 14.22.

8. *Contra* Hahn, 'Kingdom'. Hahn makes some mistaken inferences resulting in a premature fusion of kingdom and church. (1) He argues that the 'breaking of bread' is the *fulfilment* of the promise 'to eat and drink at my table in my kingdom' (Luke 22.30) so that eucharistic celebration (the post-resurrection communal meals) is itself the kingdom (319; also 307-8). Green's proposal (*Luke*, 760-1) is better. He argues that the meals in Acts 'do not constitute the "fulfillment of Passover," but should nevertheless draw into the presence and continued experience of God's people the significance of meal sharing as this has been developed in the ministry of Jesus: times of celebration and eschatological anticipation, characterized by a reversal of normal status-oriented concerns and conventions.' The meals are an *anticipation* of the eschatological kingdom banquet, not a *fulfilment* of it. (2) Like the first point, Hahn argues that the kingdom has indeed come when Jesus eats with the disciples on the way to Emmaus (Luke 24.30-35). In line with Hahn's sacramental theology ('Kingdom', 319; and his *The Lamb's Supper: The Mass as Heaven on Earth* [London: Darton, Longman and Todd Ltd, 1999]), he stresses the imminence of the kingdom *in the meal* by Luke's fronting (vis-à-vis Matthew and Mark) Jesus' statement 'I will not eat it [the Passover meal] until it is fulfilled in the kingdom of God' (Luke 22.16; cf. Matt. 26.29; Mark 14.25). But, again, Hahn fails to recognize the unfulfilled eschatological consummation, as well as the fact that the meal Jesus refers to is a *Passover meal*, whereas the meal in Luke 24 is not. With Green, *Luke*, 759 n. 51, 760.

occupancy. Luke explicitly links the prophetic authority of the apostles with the kingship of Jesus in Acts through titular appellation. The designation of ἀπόστολος carries with it both the force of a royal ambassador and, for Luke, a prophetic successor commissioned to continue the Spirit-anointed vocation.[9] Furthermore, they are referred to as servants (δοῦλοι) of God (Acts 2.18), a designation harking back to the honourable status of those in the genuine household of God. The two main characters that carry the plot forward, Peter and Paul, are characterized through their actions and speeches as prophetic successors. The role of Peter as a regal leader is carried forward through the narrative from the Last Supper pericope where Jesus confers a kingdom upon his apostles.[10] It is the apostles who realize the transformation of the kingdom-proclamation of Jesus: from the objective to the subjective genitive.[11] The apostles display their proleptic regal authority through the overseeing of the spread of the gospel message and authorizing the message through their bestowing the Spirit by the laying on of hands.

The apostles-witnesses demonstrate their role as regal leaders through their position of preeminently witnessing to the resurrection (Luke 24.48;

---

(3) Finally, Hahn ('Kingdom', 308, 310–11) prematurely fuses the references to the Mosaic and Davidic covenants in his reading of the 'new covenant in my blood' as shifting the immediate reference from Exod. 24.6-8 to Jer. 31.31 (an either / or?), and so the emphasis from the Mosaic covenant to the renewal of the Davidic covenant. Hahn rightly reads the surrounding co-text of Jeremiah's prophecy to include the restoration of the Davidic kingdom, but he neglects the primary aspects of the Mosaic covenant. He is correct to assert that '[t]he only kingdom established on the basis of a covenant in Scripture is the kingdom of David' (312), but does not recognize that Jer. 31.31-34 is about the renewal of the *Mosaic* covenant, and the discontinuity is not disparity between the shape of the two covenants (Mosaic and 'Jermeian'), but the manner in which they will be enacted (i.e., written on their hearts). Further Hahn does not seem to recognize that for the Davidic kingdom to encompass all Israel, it must be understood against the backdrop of the Mosaic covenant. As Jon Levenson (*Sinai and Zion: An Entry into the Jewish Bible* [New York: HarperSanFrancisco, 1985], 210) writes, '[T]he Sinaitic and Davidic covenants, at least as the latter appears in 2 Samuel 7 and Psalm 89, are of radically different types. The former is a *treaty*; the latter is a *grant*.[...] The Davidic covenant chooses as vassal an Israelite, therefore, someone bound by Sinaitic norms, but the relationship does not have to be seen as directly involving Israel. It takes the form of a special alliance of YHWH and David.' See also Johnson, *Luke*, 339; Carroll, *Response*, 83–4.

9. See K. Rengstorff, 'ἀπόστολος', *TDNT*, 1:424–37; Klaus Haacker ('Verwendung und Vermeidung des Apostelbegriffs im lukanischen Werk', *NovT* 30 [1988]: 9–38) stresses Luke's cautious use of the term.

10. Jervell, *Luke*, 89–96; Evans, 'Twelve Thrones', 154–70 (he argues for the background of Dan. 7.9-27 and Ps. 122.3-5 and their interpretation in contemporary Judaism); Andrew Clark, 'The Role of the Apostles', in *Witness to the Gospel: The Theology of Acts* (eds. I. Howard Marshall and David Peterson; Grand Rapids: Eerdmans, 1998), 169–81; Hahn, 'Kingdom', 306–20.

11. Furthermore, for Luke, the apostles serve as the guarantee of the veracity of the Gospel tradition. See Haacker, 'Apostelbegriffs', 38; Clark, 'Role', 170–1. For a historical argument along these lines, see Richard Bauckham, *Jesus and the Eyewitnesses: The Gospels as Eyewitness Testimony* (Grand Rapids: Eerdmans, 2006), 93–7, 108, 114–32, 271–89.

Acts 1.22; 2.32; 4.33; 5.32; 10.39, 41-42) and their overseeing of the mission extending to Samaria (Acts 8.14-24) and Peter's (initially reluctant) role in the mission to the Gentiles (10.9-16, 28). The apostles-witnesses act as an authorizing bridge of continuity from Jesus to the spreading messianic community. Philip brings the 'good news about the Kingdom of God and the name of Jesus Christ' (8.12) to Samaria. Philip's mission is legitimated not only by the divinely wrought signs (τὰ σημεῖα), but also by the reception of his ministry by the apostolic leaders from Jerusalem. Peter and John are sent to Samaria, and the Holy Spirit is bestowed through the laying on of their hands (8.15-17). This serves Luke's interests in demonstrating the continuity of the Jesus-tradition.[12]

The gentile mission is superintended by the apostles-witnesses. While Peter was speaking to Cornelius and his household, the Spirit fell upon them (Acts 10.44). Yet, while the apostles-witnesses are important for the continuity from Jesus to the emerging and growing community, they do not control the Spirit or dictate the terms by which the Spirit is given to those whom God chooses.[13] Furthermore, Paul, the great missionary to the Gentiles, shows his own submission to the Jerusalem church and the leadership of the apostles.[14]

Giving witness to Jesus' resurrection (Acts 4.33) is presented as testimony to Jesus' exaltation. Peter, in preaching to Cornelius, indicates that the apostolic witness has been commissioned by God (10.39, 41-42).[15] Therefore, as Peter speaks, he does so as one who witnesses to the exaltation of Jesus in his divinely vindicated resurrection, and as one chosen by God for this task. When Peter confronts the Jerusalem hierocracy, they are scripted into the narrative of those who would be found as enemies of God (θεομάχοι, 5.39), along with the 'raging nations' and 'kings and rulers aligned against God in battle' (4.25-28; Ps. 2.1-2). In like manner, when Peter confronts the inner threat of Ananias and Sapphira as those who oppose the Messiah by attempting to counterfeit the communal ethos, he does so in the context of the eschatological community, which is marked by the kingdom-establishing resurrection of the Lord Jesus (4.33). It is in the context of the manifest kingdom that the eschatological judgement proves fatal (Luke 19.27). The kingdom motif is immanent in the pericope of the communal goods (Acts

---

12. Clare S. Rothschild, *Luke-Acts and the Rhetoric of History: An Investigation of Early Christian Historiography* (Tübingen, Mohr Siebeck, 2004), 213-89.

13. See Beverly Roberts Gaventa, 'Initiatives Divine and Human in the Lukan Story World', in *The Holy Spirit and Christian Origins: Essays in Honor of James D.G. Dunn* (eds Graham N. Stanton, Bruce W. Longenecker and Stephen C. Barton; Grand Rapids: Eerdmans, 2004), 79-89.

14. Acts 9.26-30; 11.27-30; 12.25. See Johnson, *Literary Function*, 217-20.

15. Jervell (*Luke*, 89) writes, 'Luke takes great pains to show, prove, and demonstrate Jesus' messiahship and resurrection. It is precisely of that that the apostles are witnesses. Consequently, it must be shown that their authority goes back further than Jesus, namely to God himself.' Jervell (*Luke*, 83-9) argues cogently for the divine sanction of the apostolate throughout Luke-Acts. Also Green, *Luke*, 258-9, 759.

4.32–5.11), and it forms a crucial conventional framework for Peter's persona as an apostle-prophet like Jesus. This is particularly so in the recurrent motif of conflict between the nascent messianic community and rebellious Israel, represented by the established temple elite and the deceiving couple.

It remains to demonstrate more specifically how Luke portrays Jesus' deputizing of the apostles-witnesses with his messianic-prophetic authority in the Acts of the Apostles. The moment of the outpouring of the Spirit is precisely the moment of actual transference of the ministry of liberation from Jesus to his apostles-witnesses. This is the moment when the promise of the Father is given to Jesus' disciples (Luke 24.49; Acts 1.4-5, 8). It is Jesus, as the risen Lord, who pours out the Spirit upon his followers (Acts 2.33). There are three lines of evidence that demonstrate the convention of prophetic succession: (1) Jesus' prophetic commission to the disciples, which results in the transformation of their identity; (2) the paradigmatic framing of Jesus' ascension like the ascension of Elijah (and so, like the transference of the spirit to Elisha, the prophetic successor); and (3) the prophetic character pronounced as characteristic of the new community, interpreted via the emblematic citation from the prophet Joel.

7.1.2. *Apostolic Commission: Witness as Identity*

The choice of the apostles-witnesses is enacted through a speech-act.[16] Jesus declares his apostles to be witnesses of the unfolding of the plan of God interpreted reciprocally against the background of the hermeneutical 'script' of the Scriptures of Israel. Jesus, in his final farewell address (Luke 24.36-49) rehearses the divine plan for messianic suffering and vindication which enables the proclamation of repentance and forgiveness of sins. Jesus' statement, 'ὑμεῖς μάρτυρες τούτων' (24.48) gains new significance with the unfolding narrative of Acts; this seemingly simple referential statement becomes a commission. With the underlying authority of 'the promise of the Father' (Acts 1.4) the disciples will be authorized to proclaim in Jesus' name the message of repentance and forgiveness of sins to all nations beginning from Jerusalem (Luke 24.47).

---

16. Terence Y. Mullins ('New Testament Commission Forms, Especially in Luke-Acts', *JBL* 95 (1976): 603–14) offers some general form-critical observations concerning commission forms in Luke-Acts. See also, Benjamin J. Hubbard, 'Commissioning Stories in Luke-Acts: A Study of their Antecedents, Form and Content', *Semeia* 8 (1977): 103–26 (although he does not include Acts 1.1-14 as a commission form here); idem, 'The Role of Commissioning Accounts in Acts', in *Perspectives on Luke-Acts* (ed. Charles H. Talbert; Danville, VA: Association of Baptist Professors of Religion / Edinburgh: T&T Clark, 1978), 187–98 ('So the commission is the charter of the apostles for their entire missionary activity to follow' [196]). See also D. W. Palmer, 'The Literary Background of Acts 1.1-14', *NTS* 33 (1987): 427–38, for a critique of these earlier studies, and an examination specific to the passage at hand.

Luke fuses the voice of his narrator with the voice of Jesus in Acts 1.4b-5, sliding from third person to first person address. This reciprocally draws from and adds to Jesus' prophetic authority. Literally translated, it reads, 'He [Jesus] commanded them not to leave Jerusalem, but to "wait for the promise of the Father, which you heard from me..."' This fusion roots the authority of Luke in the perspective of God's risen Prophet-King, while at the same time making Jesus the director of the events in Acts.[17] Luke's history does not attempt to create an authoritative persona of objectivity and detachment, as perhaps other Greco-Romans historians ventured to do.[18]

When Jesus again reiterates the promise to receive the Holy Spirit (Acts 1.5-8), so the disciples will receive power for their mission beginning in Jerusalem and moving centrifugally outward to the end of the earth, the promise is succeeded again, as in the Gospel (Luke 24.50-53),[19] by the narration of Jesus' ascension (Acts 1.9-11). Therefore, Jesus has commissioned his disciples as 'witnesses' to the predetermined plan of God fulfilled through God's Messiah. The Messiah has transferred the mission and promises Spirit-enabled ability to carry it out.[20] The apostles, among whom Peter emerges as a leading spokesman, preside precisely as prophetic successors to Jesus in the continuing drama of God's completion of the divine promise given to Abraham (Gen. 12.1-3; 15.1-21; 17.7; 22.16-18) and claimed by both Mary (Luke 1.55) and Zechariah (1.72-73) in their doxologies, and by Peter in

---

17. See Palmer, 'Literary Background', 428. D. P. Moessner ('"Managing" the Audience: Diodorus Siculus and Luke the Evangelist on Designing Authorial Intent', in *Luke and His Readers: Festschrift A. Denaux* [ed. R. Bieringer, G. van Belle, J. Verheyden; Leuven: Leuven University Press, 2005], 77 [61–80]) writes, 'The risen Jesus who opens the Scriptures and gives the charge in Luke 24,44–49 breaks into and takes over the voice of the narrator in Acts 1,1–4a→1,4b–5. [...T]he *prooemial* voice of this linking passage has shifted from the narrator to the main actor and speaker of the previous volume (cf. Acts 1,1b). It would appear that Luke is vouchsafing a narrative continuity (cf. τὸ συνεχές) for his two 'books' and thus providing a hermeneutic barometer for his readers.' For other examples of this unannounced change from indirect to direct speech, see Pieter W. van der Horst, 'Hellenistic Parallels to the Acts of the Apostles: 1 1–26', *ZNW* 74 (1983): 18–19.

18. Loveday Alexander, 'Fact, Fiction and the Genre of Acts', *NTS* 44 (1998): 383–9, 393, suggests that this attempt to create an 'objective and detached' persona frames the authoritative perspective of Herodotus, for example. 'Luke's prefaces effectively collapse the distinction between outsider (observer) and insider (believer) which was so important in the construction of the [ancient Hellenistic] historian's critical *persona*' (399).

19. This reading assumes the longer reading of Luke 24.51 including καὶ ἀνεφέρετο εἰς τὸν οὐρανόν, represented by P[75] ℵ[2] A B C, et al.; omitted in ℵ* D, et al. See Mikeal C. Parsons, *The Departure of Jesus in Luke-Acts. The Ascension Narratives in Context* (JSNTSup 21; Sheffield: JSOT, 1987), 37–51, for a rejection of the longer reading. See A. W. Zwiep, 'The Text of the Ascension Narratives (Luke 24, 50–3; Acts 1, 1–2, 9–11)', *NTS* 42 (1996): 219–44 for a compelling refutation.

20. Palmer ('Literary Background', 429) writes that Acts 1.8 'is only a commission by anticipation, awaiting its fulfillment at Pentecost.[...] Thus one can speak of a commission in Acts 1 only with some hesitation'.

his speech in Solomon's Portico (Acts 3.25).[21] Jesus' address directed to the apostles (Acts 1.2; Luke 24.33) indicates the continuing role they are to play in God's redemptive history, continuing the work Jesus had accomplished.[22] The substance of their witness is disclosed in Peter's speech initiating the replacement of Judas: the apostolic witness testifies to Jesus' resurrection (Acts 1.22). This is exactly the performance of the apostles in the summary passage describing the community illustrated by Barnabas and Ananias and Sapphira: 'With great power the apostles were giving witness to the resurrection of the Lord Jesus' (4.33). Peter acts and speaks to the couple as one commissioned by the Lord Jesus to testify to the resurrection. This witness is linked to the unity of the early community and the community-of-goods, which the offending couple counterfeits. Therefore, it is crucial to understand Luke's regal and soteriological significance to Jesus' resurrection.[23] It is the substance of the apostolic witness, which is itself characterized by the Spirit-filled apostolic-prophetic succession. Jesus, the anointed messianic prophet, has commissioned his ἀπόστολοι and transferred the Spirit-aided power to them in order to make them his witnesses to Israel and the nations (cf. Isa. 49.6).

The crucial passage dramatizing the significance of the resurrection is the Pentecost episode with Peter's hermeneutical homily (Acts 2.1-41). It is in this sermon that we are invited to reflect retrospectively on what has been accomplished in the plot of Luke's narrative so far. This sermon also frames the expectations of what is to come. The sermon casts a retrospective shadow across the preceding events. In Acts 2.32-36, Peter interprets Jesus' ascension as an aspect of the resurrection-ascension-exaltation complex. Jesus pours out the Spirit as the risen and exalted Lord. The ascension, it seems, is a crucial aspect in the prophetic succession patterned after the ascension of the prophet Elijah, and the transference of his prophetic ministry. However, it is also unlike the ascension of Elijah in that Luke fuses the prophetic (Moses-Elijah) typologies with the royal (David) typologies in his characterization of Jesus.

7.1.3. Ascension-Exaltation as Prerequisite for Prophetic Transference

The ascension is the bridge from the Gospel to Acts and the bridge from Jesus' earthly ministry to his heavenly reign, his enthronement at the right

---

21. Nils A. Dahl, 'The Story of Abraham in Luke-Acts', in *Studies in Luke-Acts* (eds L. E. Keck and J. L. Martyn; Philadelphia: Fortress Press, 1968), 139–58; Robert L. Brawley, 'Abrahamic Covenant Traditions and the Characterization of God in Luke-Acts' and Sabine van den Eynde, 'Children of the Promise: On the Διαθήκη-Promise to Abraham in Lk 1,72 and Acts 3,25', in *Unity* (ed. Verheyden), 110–32 and 469–82, respectively.

22. Turner, *Power*, 290–303; Wenk, *Power*, 242–6.

23. See the excellent study by Kevin L. Anderson, *'But God Raised Him from the Dead': The Theology of Jesus' Resurrection in Luke-Acts* (Milton Keynes: Paternoster, 2006).

hand of God. The ascension, while closing the Gospel of Luke and opening Acts,[24] functions in the theological unity of Luke and Acts to draw a line of continuity between the work of Jesus and the ministry of the apostles-witnesses.[25] The ascension is a crucial juncture intersecting Jesus' pledge of bestowing the promise of the Father, the commission of witness, and, reaching through the prediction of the angelic messengers, to the return of Jesus 'in the same way [they] watched him go to heaven' (Acts 1.11). The ascension links the eschatological mission of Jesus' followers with Jesus' future return.[26]

What is the function of the ascension narrative in the Lukan writings?[27] What expectations does it create in the ensuing plot of the continuation of 'all Jesus began to do and teach'? For many scholars, Jesus' exaltation is polarized, being aligned either with his resurrection or his ascension.[28] For

24. Parsons, *Departure*, 65–113, 151–86, 199.
25. This position reads the ascension narrative in Luke 24.50-53 and Acts 1.2, 9-11 as the same event. So Gerhard Lohfink, *Die Himmelfahrt Jesu: Untersuchungen zu den Himmelfahrts- und Erhöhungstexten bei Lukas* (Munich: Kösel, 1971), 160–1. This rejects the position of P. A. Van Stempvoort ('The Interpretation of the Ascension in Luke and Acts', *NTS* 5 [1958–59]: 32–4) that ανελήμφθη refers to Jesus' death rather than his ascension. Luke's use of the verbs αναφέρω (Luke 24.51), αναλαμβάνω (Acts 1.2, 11, 22); cf. ανάλημψις in Luke 9.51), επαίρω (Acts 1.9) and αναβαίνω (Acts 2.34) all refer to Jesus' ascension.
26. Carroll (*Response*, 127–8) rightly criticizes Haenchen (*Acts*, 150–2) and Scott G. Wilson ('The Ascension: A Critique and an Interpretation', *ZNW* 59 [1968]: 269–81) for not distinguishing between the setting of Luke and his audience on the one hand, and the setting presupposed *within* the narrative, on the other.
27. Stempvoort ('Interpretation', 30) sums up the difficulty of interpreting this episode: 'The Ascension texts of Luke in his Gospel and in the Acts belong to those parts of the New Testament about which discussion never ends.'
28. Eric Franklin ('The Ascension and the Eschatology of Luke-Acts', *SJT* 23 [1970]: 191–200) is correct to see the ascension as related to the exaltation of Christ, but exceeds the evidence that 'Luke found *the full eschatological act of God* in relation to the person of Jesus to be expressed, not in the Parousia, but in the Ascension' (192, emphasis added). Here, Franklin virtually ignores the import of the resurrection(!). In his fuller treatment (*Christ the Lord: A Study in the Purpose and Theology of Luke-Acts* [Philadelphia: The Westminster Press, 1975], 29–41), Franklin solidifies his error: 'This [Luke's scheme] is controlled by his thought of the ascension as an event which, separate from the resurrection, is understood as the actual moment of the glorification of Jesus.[...] Without it [the ascension], even with the resurrection – at least as Luke describes it – he would not have been other than the prophets' (30, 35). Franklin recognizes the evidence of the resurrection as glorification (Luke 22.69; 23.42-43; 24.26; Acts 3.15-16; 4.10; 5.30-31; 10.40-43; 13.33) but dismisses it as inconsistency on Luke's part. 'All this points to the conclusion that Luke's scheme is an artificial one and is most likely to have been of his own making. It is the vehicle which he uses, when he spells out his beliefs, when he is developing his argument, to emphasize and to justify his contention that Jesus is the present Lord' (33). Finally, Franklin ('Review of A.W. Zwiep, *The Ascension of the Messiah in Lukan Christology*', *JTS* 50 [1999]: 230–6) has criticized Zwiep (see below, n. 30) indicating that he remains firm in his initial position: '[T]he ascension, when seen through the eyes of faith, demonstrates the status of Jesus. Essential and pivotal though the resurrection is, it is the ascension which actually effects the full reality of Jesus. It glorifies and universalizes him in a way which the resurrection does

others, the ascension has been understood integrally as part of the resurrection-ascension-exaltation complex.[29] This has been challenged by Arie Zwiep, who offers the most comprehensive analysis of the Lukan Ascension texts to date.[30] Zwiep suggests, rather, that Luke never fuses the resurrection-exaltation with the ascension-departure. They are separate narrative elements in the Lukan story. Zwiep offers a robust challenge to the integrated view, but in the end proves unpersuasive. His form-critical method restricts his ability to follow Luke's narrative logic.[31] Two main problems exist in Zwiep's assessment: (1) he sharply distinguishes the ascension-departure, narrated in Luke 24.50-51 and Acts 1.1-14 from the resurrection-exaltation,[32] and (2) he interprets the ascension-departure as primarily the end of Jesus' ministry (dissecting Lukan salvation history into a three-part scheme like Conzelmann), thus relegating Jesus to virtual inactivity in the interim period between the ascension and the Parousia.[33] More likely, Jesus' ascension belongs with resurrection as the divinely vindicated exaltation of Jesus. They may be temporally separated (forty days, Acts 1.3), but these events are soteriologically and theologically

not.[...] The ascension does not merely make Jesus available for the parousia, it actually anticipates it, releases its first-fruits and even inaugurates what the parousia will complete, the overthrow of Satan and all that hinders God's rule' (234, 235). Rightly, Franklin ('Review', 235) admits, 'Only in Peter's sermon at Pentecost is the ascension pin-pointed as the moment of exaltation' (cf. *Christ the Lord*, 33). Both readings, I argue, of Acts 2.32-35 by Franklin and Zwiep are inadequate.

29. See the helpful survey of positions in R. F. O'Toole, 'Luke's Understanding of Jesus' Resurrection-Ascension-Exaltation', *BTB* 9 (1979): 106–14. O'Toole correctly identifies the ascension as part of the wider complex including resurrection and exaltation, but with little argued support. See also Anderson, *Resurrection*, 46–7, 213–18; John F. Maile, 'The Ascension in Luke-Acts,' *TynB* 37 (1986): 29–59.

30. Arie W. Zwiep, *The Ascension of the Messiah in Lukan Christology* (NovTSup 87; Leiden: Brill, 1997). See his comprehensive review of scholarship, pp. 1–35.

31. Zwiep follows Lohfink (*Himmelfahrt*) in identifying the 'form' of Luke's Ascension as *Entrückung* – 'rapture'. For a critique of Lohfink's rigid application of the 'form' to Luke, see Maile, 'Ascension', 40–4. Maile's criticisms similarly apply to Zwiep.

32. Zwiep, *Ascension*, 'Luke sharply distinguishes the resurrection-exaltation from the ascension and never presents Jesus' ἀνάλημψις (*Entrückung*) [rapture] as the occasion of his *exaltio ad dexteram*.[...] For Luke, the exaltation of Jesus, traditionally articulated with the help of the symbol of the session at the right hand of God, took place on the day of the resurrection, not forty days later on the day of the ascension' (197, 163).

33. Zwiep, *Ascension*, 167–85. He writes, 'Luke advocates an "absentee Christology", i.e., a christology that is dominated by the (physical) absence *and present inactivity* [emphasis his] of the exalted Lord.[...] The ascension opens up an interim period in which Jesus is absent. Since the ascension of Christ does make his presence known but he does so in spiritual ways. Christ is not actively involved in the course of history, or at least it is not Luke's main concern to develop this theme...' (182). Zwiep follows his *Doktorvater* in interpreting Luke in this manner. See James D. G. Dunn, *Unity and Diversity in the New Testament: An Inquiry in the Character of Earliest Christianity* (2nd edn; London: SCM Press, 1990), 224–5: 'In Earliest Christianity, in the Synoptic tradition and in Acts hardly any role is attributed to the exalted Christ.'

Zwiep indicates direct (though not uncritical) influence of Conzelmann's tri-partite salvation-historical schema on p. 171, n. 1; also 12–13.

connected, even inseparable.[34] In this complex, perhaps, Jesus' resurrection is his coronation, and his ascension is his enthronement. Together, they demonstrate the divine exaltation of this Prophet-King.[35]

Where Zwiep and I do concur is that Luke's narrative links Jesus' ascension with the outpouring of the Spirit in a manner where Jesus transfers his prophetic authority and vocation to his apostles-witnesses.[36] Two primary traditions of Moses and Elijah lay in the background of Luke's composition of the ascension narratives. Jesus' ascent with the result of sending the Spirit is reminiscent of Moses' departure and designation of Joshua as his successor[37] and Elijah's ascent and bestowal of his spirit to Elisha.[38] The Moses- and Elijah-allusions elsewhere in Luke-Acts heighten the plausibility of availability and volume.[39]

---

34. For support of this claim from ascension discourse in the second century, see David R. McCabe, 'Acts of Ascension: History, Exaltation and Ideological Legitimation', in *Reading Acts in the Second Century* (eds Todd Penner and Rubén Dupertuis; London: Equinox, *forthcoming*).

35. J. F. Maile ('Ascension', 55-8) provides an apt summary of the significance of the ascension narratives for Luke-Acts:

(1) The Ascension is the confirmation of the exaltation of Christ and his present Lordship.

(2) The Ascension is the explanation of the continuity between the ministry of Jesus and that of the church.

(3) The Ascension is the culmination of the resurrection appearances.

(4) The Ascension is the prelude to the sending of the Spirit.

(5) The Ascension is the foundation of Christian Mission (per #4 above).

(6) The Ascension is the pledge of the return of Christ in his glory.

36. Zwiep (*Ascension*, 185) writes: 'As the public ministry of Jesus was inaugurated by the descent of the Spirit in visible form upon him (Lk 3:21–22), so the period of the Church is initiated by the outpouring of the Spirit "upon all flesh" (Acts 2:17) on the day of Pentecost.[...] Luke exploits the rapture-preservation [sic] paradigm for *christological* reasons, the rapture-transmission of the Spirit connection of Elijah-Elisha cycle for *salvation-historical* (soteriological/ecclesiological) reasons.' The dissection of the *Gattung* is unjustified, but the other connections are surely there.

37. Num. 27.15-23; Deut. 31.14-23; 34.9–Josh 1.9; *As. Mos.* 1:6–9.

38. 4 Kgdms 2.1-18.

39. Moses: Luke 9.30-31, 33; 20.37; Acts 3.22-23; 7.20-44. Elijah: Luke 4.24-27; 7.11-17, 36-50; 9.30-31, 33, 51. Compare the proposal of Kenneth D. Litwak (*Echoes of Scripture in Luke-Acts: Telling the History of God's People Intertextually* [JSNTSup; Edinburgh: T&T Clark, 2005], 148, 150–1, 154): 'This transfer of prophetic role via giving of the Spirit to one's successor is an important element for both Moses and Elijah. [...] Through the echoing of this scene from the Scriptures of Israel [4 Kingdoms 2.1-10], but not primarily of the vocabulary, Luke frames his discourse so that his audience expects a transfer from Jesus to his disciples of Jesus' mission of proclaiming the kingdom of God, though the precise content of the message of the kingdom changes.[...] Just as the story in 4 Kingdoms 2 may be seen as a prophetic commissioning narrative, so the accounts in Luke 24 and Acts 1 may be seen as prophetic commissionings, identifying valid, legitimate successors.' Also Roger Stronstad, *The Prophethood of All Believers: A Study in Luke's Charismatic Theology* (JPTSup 16; Sheffield: Sheffield Academic Press, 1999), 48, 53, 64, 71.

As stated above, Moses, as the model prophet, is an apt exemplar framing Luke's christology.[40] The tradition concerning Moses' death / departure seems to have developed from the ambiguities surrounding his burial in the ancient tradition: 'And Moses, the servant of the Lord, died (ἐτελεύτησεν) in the land of Moab [...] and no one has seen his place of burial to this day' (Deut. 34.5-6). In Philo's account (*Vit. Mos.* 2.291), Moses' death is paradoxically presented as a 'passing away' and a 'taking up' (ἀναλαμβανόμενος). The unknown location of his grave becomes a 'special tomb' (ἐξαίρετος μνῆμα).[41] Although the 'rapture' terminology is present, it seems that Philo is preserving traditions of the assumption of Moses' immortal soul into heaven.[42] Josephus describes Moses' departure in terms of an assumption with a cloud, but written as death lest they say, 'he had gone back to the Deity' (*Ant.* 4.326).[43] Zwiep is certainly correct to assert that Moses' final ascent was patterned after his ascent on Sinai to receive the Law, rather than *vice versa*.[44]

More important here, for Luke's depiction of the ascension, is the tradition of Moses appointing Joshua as his successor. In Numbers 27.15-23 Moses beseeches the Lord to appoint a successor to lead the congregation. The Lord responds to Moses by electing Joshua, 'a man who has the spirit in him' (Num. 27.18, ἄνθρωπον ὃς ἔχει πνεῦμα ἐν ἑαυτῷ). Moses is to put some of his glory (δόξα; Heb. הוד) upon Joshua. Moses lays his hands upon Joshua (27.23; cf. Luke 24.50) before Eleazar the priest and the congregation. Then, in Deuteronomy 31.14-23, the Lord commissions Joshua as God manifests in a cloud. The Lord recites a song (31.22) of the ensuing rebellion of Israel, and commissions Joshua with the reassurance of his presence (31.23; Josh. 1.5). Deuteronomy 34.9 (LXX) states, 'And Joshua, the son of Naue, was filled with the spirit of understanding (πνεύματος συνέσεως), for Moses laid his hands upon him.' Granted, the connotations of 'spirit' are quite different between the commissioning of Joshua and the commissioning of the apostles-witnesses, but the parallels are correlative.

Elijah's ascension is the most established paradigm for rapture-ascent in the Jewish tradition, and Elijah-echoes elsewhere in Luke-Acts heighten the plausibility of these allusions.[45] Indeed the Elijah-type is not 'pure' for the narration of Elijah's ascent to heaven (4 Kgdms 2.1-18) contains no cloud, but rather occurs in a whirlwind (συσσεισμός), and Elijah is lifted by a flaming

---

40. See §6.2.2.3.1. above. See also Zwiep, *Ascension*, 64–71.
41. Palmer, 'Literary Background', 432. Further, Moses' end is compared with the ascensions of Enoch and Elijah (*Quaest in Gen.* 1.86), noted by Zwiep, *Ascension*, 66, n. 2.
42. So Zwiep, *Ascension*, 66–7.
43. Palmer, 'Literary Background', 432. The phrase 'he had gone back to the Deity' (πρὸς τὸ θεῖον αὐτὸν ἀναχωρῆσαι) is used of Enoch (*Ant.* 1.85: ἀνεχώρησε πρὸς τὸ θεῖον). Also *Ant.* 3.96, again of Moses (πρὸς τὸ θεῖον ἀνακεχωρηκέναι).
44. Zwiep, *Ascension*, 66 n. 2, 71 n. 6.
45. Luke 4.24-27; 7.11-17, 36-50; 9.30-31, 33, 51. See Zwiep, *Ascension*, 58–63, 104–6, 110, 114–15, 181, 185, 194.

chariot with flaming horses. However, the cloud is roughly equivalent to the chariot as the vehicle of conveyance.[46] Just as the focus of Elijah's ascension is on the transfer of his ministry to Elisha,[47] so it is in Acts that the focus is on the legitimate transfer of Jesus' ministry to his apostles-witnesses as we follow the plot from commission to Spirit-outpouring.[48] This factors into the criteria for replacing Judas (Acts 1.22). Just as Elisha performs prophetic actions in the manner of Elijah, so the apostles are characterized like the prophet Jesus.

However, the Elijah ascension-preservation tradition is inadequate to explain the full significance of the Lukan Jesus' ascension. This Jesus is not merely absent and inactive![49] Robert O'Toole demonstrated that Jesus is present in Acts through his activity as Lord of his church in guidance and protection, through the preaching of his witnesses, through the Holy Spirit, through his Name, by saving those who call upon him and performs miracles (Acts 9.34).[50] Jesus actively reigns from his exalted position on the divine

---

46. Zwiep (*Ascension*, 105 and n. 2) is correct to see a double function for the cloud, both as concealment (as in the transfiguration, Luke 9.34) and the vehicle of conveyance.

47. The prophets of Jericho recognizing him as Elijah's successor, 4 Kgdms 2.15. Zwiep (*Ascension*, 59) writes: 'Elijah's ascension marks the conclusion of his earthly career and is *conditio sine qua non* for the transfer of his spirit to Elisha, the fulfillment of which is closely related to Elisha's seeing Elijah go to heaven.'

48. This story is equally about the climax of the career of Elijah as it is about the transfer of the spirit to Elisha. So Palmer, 'Literary Background', 435. *Pace* Zwiep, *Ascension*, 59.

Further, I concur with Zwiep that it is the exaltation proper which is the *conditio sine qua non* for the outpouring of the Spirit. However, I find his divorce of the ascension-preservation (*sic*) from the resurrection-exaltation unjustified for Luke-Acts. See above, n. 36.

49. *Contra* Zwiep. See above, n. 33.

50. Robert F. O'Toole, 'Activity of the Risen Jesus in Luke-Acts', *Bib* 62 (1981): 471-98. He concludes, 'Luke's christology shapes his ecclesiology. The risen Lord acts and is present to the whole life of his church. He leads the Christians. Their mission is Christ' mission. He gives his followers their mission and directs them. When they are persecuted, he encourages, supports, and protects them. His power enables them to perform miracles. When they preach, he preaches; when they are heard, he is heard. Their salvation, a present experience and reality, comes only from him. They are baptized in his name and realize his presence in the Eucharist. Certainly, the Father and the Spirit are active, but a church without considerable activity on the part of the risen Christ is not Lukan' (498).

See also Strauss, *Davidic Messiah*, 177, arguing that the missionaries proclaiming the gospel are representatives of Jesus himself. Through these envoys, Jesus himself is being a light to the nations.

Cf. G. W. MacRae, '"Whom Heaven Must Receive Until the Time": Reflections on the Christology of Acts', *Interp* 27 (1973): 151-65. MacRae focuses on the absence of Jesus, but recognizes, similar to O'Toole, the active presence of Jesus through the Spirit, his name, recalled history and in the lives of his followers.

This balance between Jesus' absence and his presence, what Parsons (*Departure*, 160-4) calls the 'empty center', creates a narrative tension between the comforting activity of Jesus in his church in the present and a longing anticipation for his return in the future.

throne. Jesus suffers in the persecution of his disciples (9.4). Jesus, while having departed bodily from his apostles-witnesses, is by no means inactive, merely waiting for his eschatological return. Jesus is decisively involved in the continued restoration of Israel and the mission to the Gentiles.

The two heavenly messengers further verify the nature of the commission, linking Jesus' pledge with the coming of the Spirit at Pentecost (Acts 1.10b-11). They direct the disciples' attention away from gazing into the sky toward their correct response to Jesus' commission.[51] With the assurance of Jesus' return, the men go up to Jerusalem to await the Promise of the Father in prayer. As Parsons comments, 'In Acts, Luke expanded the ascension narrative by means of "apocalyptic stage props" so that the departure of Jesus in his sequel volume provides the impetus for the gift of the Spirit and the mission of the church.'[52]

Peter interprets the resurrection-ascension-exaltation as the inducement for the outpouring of the Spirit in Acts 2.33-34. In the immediate co-text, Peter has appealed to Ps. 15.8-11 LXX to interpret the events of Jesus' passion and resurrection.[53] Peter infers (οὖν) from Jesus' resurrection-as-exaltation that the Spirit, which is evidenced before the crowd, has been poured out. The Spirit is evidence that Jesus has been exalted to God's right hand. Hence, Peter recites 109.1 LXX as evidence that Jesus, not David, has ascended to God's right hand, and so (οὖν) Peter declares that God has made Jesus both Lord and Christ.[54] Zwiep denies that Acts 2.33-34 refers to Jesus' ascension in the present context. He does this by dissecting the passage into Luke's redaction and his likely source, consigning the reference to ascension (2.34, ἀνέβη εἰς τοὺς οὐρανούς) to tradition coming from a Jewish-Palestinian milieu.[55] This

---

See the theological-historical study by Douglas Farrow, *Ascension and Ecclesia: On the Significance of the Doctrine of the Ascension for Ecclesiology and Christian Cosmology* (Edinburgh: T&T Clark, 1999); and a more popular treatment by Gerrit Scott Dawson, *Jesus Ascended: The Meaning of Christ's Continuing Incarnation* (London: T&T Clark, 2004). Dawson takes less account of biblical scholarship than Farrow.

51. Mullins, 'Commission Forms', 609; Palmer, 'Literary Background', 429–30, 435.

52. Parsons, *Departure*, 150.

53. Litwak (*Echoes of Scripture*, 175–9) offers a persuasive rebuttal and nuance to Bock's (*Proclamation*, 180) assertion that '[a] clearer presentation of a direct prophecy [Ps. 15.8-11] fulfilled [in Acts 2.25-32] could not exist'. Litwak (*Echoes of Scripture*, 177) writes, 'Peter reads Psalm 15 in a new way in the light of Jesus' resurrection, thus revising its apparent, non-messianic meaning.' Also Donald Juel, 'Social Dimensions of Exegesis: The Use of Psalm 16 in Acts 2', *CBQ* 43 (1981): 543–56; David P. Moessner, '*Two* Lords "at the Right Hand"? The Psalms and an Intertextual Reading of Peter's Pentecost Speech (Acts 2:14–36)', in *Literary Studies in Luke-Acts: Essays in Honor of Joseph B. Tyson* (eds Richard P. Thompson and Thomas E. Phillips; Macon, GA: Mercer University Press, 1998), 215–29.

54. See Moessner, 'The Psalms', 229–32; and H. Douglas Buckwalter, *The Character and Purpose of Luke's Christology* (SNTSMS 89; Cambridge: Cambridge University Press, 1996), 194–6; Turner, *Power*, 273–9; idem, '"Trinitarian" Pneumatology in the New Testament? – Towards an Explanation of the Worship of Jesus', *AsTJ* 57 (2002), 177–80.

breakdown is unwarranted. While Zwiep's attempt to defend Luke as one who used sources, rather than merely composing *ex nihilo*, is to be applauded,[56] this treats Luke as an incompetent writer unable to manage his sources or integrate them into a coherent narrative.[57] Within the narrative, Acts 2.34 in context cannot but recall Acts 1.9-11 as an event, and following Acts 2.33 the 'ascending into heaven' done here must be part of the resurrection-ascension-exaltation complex resulting in the outpouring of the Spirit.

In summary, for Luke the ascension is part of a wider soteriological and theological complex that includes Jesus' resurrection and exaltation to the right hand of God. Jesus' ascension from Mt Olivet recalls the paradigmatic ascension of Jewish tradition – the departure of Elijah and the transference of his 'spirit' to Elisha. Yet, this intertextual echo is not sufficient to explain the significance for Jesus' ascension. The element of the cloud as a vehicle of conveyance and concealment recalls Jesus' transfiguration (Luke 9.28-36) with the presence of Moses and Elijah. Jesus is exalted not merely as a prophet awaiting some eschatological vocation (like Elijah); he is rather the Prophet-King who occupies the throne of David – not merely in Jerusalem, but at the right hand of God. Jesus' ascension, as the climax of his resurrection appearances, is a prelude to the outpouring of the Spirit. Both Elijah(/ Moses)- and David-typologies are necessary to understand the significance of the ascension-exaltation of Jesus in the narrative logic of Acts. David is not one who transfers his spirit to successors. Moses and Elijah do this, and Jesus accomplishes this in a way unparalleled in Jewish tradition before or since. Jesus sends the very Spirit of God, and transforms the community of those who follow him into a community of messianic prophets. When Peter speaks as a witness to Jesus, he speaks as an apostolic-prophetic successor to Jesus the exalted Prophet-King, Lord of the Spirit.

7.1.4. *Pentecost: Prophetic Transference and Vocation*

Luke's Pentecost, with its explanatory sermon citing the prophetic text of Joel, is paradigmatic for the text of Acts in the way that the Nazareth sermon of Luke 4.18-30 is paradigmatic for Luke's Gospel.[58] Thus, it is important

---

55. Zwiep, *Ascension*, 154–6. Zwiep rightly sees the logical flow pointing to resurrection in Acts 2.25-32, which is interpreted as exaltation in verse 33. But his relegating ἀνέβη εἰς τοὺς οὐρανούς to 'traditional material' does not interpret Peter's speech – it merely speculates about possible source-influence.

56. Zwiep, *Ascension*, 163.

57. The same criticisms apply to Franklin's attempt to explain the Lukan correlation of resurrection with exaltation as inconsistent redaction. See his *Christ the Lord*, 32–3.

58. Wenk, *Power*, 232 (and the literature cited there). To Wenk's list, add the important studies: Huub van de Sandt, 'The Fate of the Gentiles in Joel and Acts 2: An Intertextual Study', *ETL* 66 (1990): 56–77, Marion L. Soards, *The Speeches in Acts: Their Content, Context, and Concerns* (Louisville: Westminster / John Knox Press, 1994), 33. Turner (*Power*, 267) goes further suggesting that Peter's Pentecost sermon is possibly the hermeneutical key to the whole of Luke-Acts!

to understand the significance of Pentecost, the event of the outpouring of the Spirit and the beginning of the empowerment for the apostolic mission in the narrative logic of Luke's work to understand the rest of Acts. Pentecost casts a retrospective vision over the πρῶτος λόγος (Acts 1.1), giving shape to the prophecy of John (Luke 3.16-17), and through Peter's proclamation, interprets the event of Jesus' resurrection, which is Luke's primary soteriological event. Pentecost further anticipates the fulfilment of Jesus' prophetic commission in Acts 1.8, where reconstituted Israel has been restored to its vocational position as witnesses to God's salvific work (Isa. 32.15; 43.10-12; 49.6-7). The outpouring of the Spirit onto the community of Jesus' disciples has crucial importance for the conventional framework of the Lukan social order. Therefore, it is essential to follow Luke's narrative into the intersection between the continuation of 'all Jesus began to do and teach' (Acts 1.2) and the transference of plot development to the actions of Jesus' apostles-witnesses.

Pentecost marks a watershed moment for the apostles-witnesses with regard to the activity of the Spirit. The Spirit-enabled manifestations (Acts 2.1-4) cause a diverse crowd to gather at the sound (2.6) and they hear 'invasive charismatic praise'[59] miraculously in their own native languages.[60] Divergent and potentially shameful interpretations ('drunkenness') cause Peter to hermeneutically guide explanation of the event through kerygmatic speech resulting in an appeal for repentance and conversion.

How does the Pentecost episode contribute to the narrative logic that prepares the audience for interpreting the Ananias and Sapphira episode? What does Peter's interpretive speech indicate about the conventional framework that the narrator presents as the undergirding divine social order in the narrative world?[61] It comprises the explicit manifestation of the Holy Spirit's impetus for all prophetic actions throughout the narrative of Acts. Pentecost is the very moment of prophetic commissional transference. Pentecost is a vital part of Israel's restoration and renewal. Most clearly in Peter's discourse, we see that the coming of the Spirit is the result of the enthronement of Jesus at the very right hand of God, and so those who give witness to his resurrection are ambassadors of the highest king, Christ the Lord. Two points are worth noting. First, the result of the outpouring of the Spirit-of-Prophecy upon the messianic community is a universal vocation to

---

59. The phrase is Turner's (*Power*, 271); *contra* Menzies (*Development*, 211), who sees the speech as missiological proclamation because the audience says that they hear in their own languages 'uttering the mighty works (μεγαλεῖα) of God' (2.11). Turner's strongest rebuttal is to demonstrate that extolling God's mighty acts was the expected and regular feature of Jewish praise from the song of Moses (Exod. 15) to the *Magnificat* and *Benedictus* (Luke 1).

60. On the phenomena of *glossolalia* and Christian prophecy in general, see Forbes, *Prophecy*, 44–74, 218–50.

61. On Peter's speeches in Acts 2 and 3, see Richard F. Zehnle, *Peter's Pentecost Discourse: Tradition and Lukan Reinterpretation in Peter's Speeches of Acts 2 and 3* (SBLDS 15; Nashville: Abingdon Press, 1971).

every member of the community to participate in eschatological prophecy. Second, Peter as one of the apostles-witnesses, separated out for the task of leadership, illustrates the efficacy of Spirit-inspired prophetic speech. Peter as an apostle-prophet calls Israel to repentance, making the people liable in their ignorance, and persuades a multitude to convert to the way of the messianic community.

Paul Minear provocatively suggested that for Luke there was a 'prophethood of all believers'.[62] He was followed by the Pentecostal scholar Roger Stronstad in expounding Luke's 'charismatic theology'.[63] Peter clearly sets the eschatological stage through his programmatic citation of the prophet Joel.[64] Setting his interpretation of the Pentecost events eschatologically (Acts 2.17, ἐν ταῖς ἐσχάταις ἡμέραις),[65] Peter indicates that the community will be characterized by prophecy. Twice, Luke indicates that 'they shall prophesy' (προφητεύσουσιν; Acts 2.17, 18).[66] In arguing that the prophetic vocation has been transferred from Jesus to his disciples, the Joel passage is shown to be programmatic for the characterization of the community, and, Peter specifically. Some questions help to frame the discussion: what is the relationship between the outpouring of the Spirit as an event, and Peter's charismatic interpretation? As Peter identifies the Spirit explicitly as the Spirit of Prophecy, what is the shape of prophetic manifestations? That is, how does this prophetic vocation manifest itself through the community, and Peter in particular? How does the Joel citation create anticipations for the characterization of Peter as a prophet?

Peter's speech can be structured in four fluid parts, following the 'script' of three prophetic Scriptures. First, based on Joel 3.1-5 LXX, Peter proclaims the

---

62. Paul S. Minear, *To Heal and to Reveal: The Prophetic Vocation According to Luke* (New York: The Seabury Press, 1976), 87.

63. Roger Stronstad, *The Charismatic Theology of St. Luke* (Peabody: Hendrickson, 1984); idem, *Prophethood*.

64. See Craig A. Evans, 'The Prophetic Setting of the Pentecost Sermon', ZNW 74 (1983): 148–50; idem, (expanded in) 'The Prophetic Setting of the Pentecost Sermon', in *Luke and Scripture*, 212–24; F. O. Francis, 'Eschatology and History in Luke-Acts', *JAAR* 37 (1969): 49–63; van de Sandt, 'Fate', 56–77; Hubbard, 'Commissioning Accounts', 195; Bock, *Proclamation*, 156–69; Carroll, *Response*, 128–37; Brawley, *Text to Text*, 79–83; Litwak, *Echoes of Scripture*, 155–68.

65. The phrase 'ἐν ταῖς ἐσχάταις ἡμέραις' seems to be a textual alteration from the texts of Joel that have come down to us. LXX Joel 3.1 has 'μετὰ ταῦτα'. Most commentators reject Haenchen's view (*Acts*, 179) that 'μετὰ ταῦτα' is original to Luke. Some have suggested the influence of Isa. 2.2 here. See Franz Mussner, '"In den letzten Tagen" (Apg 2, 17a)', *BZ* 5 (1961): 263–5; Robert B. Sloan, '"Signs and Wonders": A Rhetorical Clue to the Pentecost Discourse', in *With Steadfast Purpose: Essays on Acts in Honor of Henry Jackson Flanders, Jr.* (ed. Naymond H. Keathley; Waco: Baylor University, 1990), 145–62; Carroll, *Response*, 135 n. 69; Litwak, *Echoes of Scripture*, 156.

66. The second of these, in v. 18, is an addition to the Joel text as we have it. See Gerhard Schneider, *Die Apostelgeschichte* (2 vols; HTKNT 5; Freiberg: Herder, 1980, 1982), 1:268–9.

Spirit as evidence of the inaugurated 'last days' which will mean a resurgence of prophecy in the vocation of all participants in the messianic age (Acts 2.14-21). Next, Peter interprets the events of the recent Passover season, to which the apostles are witnesses (2.32) as being in accordance with the βουλῇ καὶ προγνώσει of God (2.23). Appealing to David's prophecy in Ps. 15.8-11 LXX, Peter declares the fulfilment of the psalmist's hope occurring in the resurrection of Jesus (Acts 2.22-28). In a dramatic climax, Peter draws together the outpouring of the Spirit and Jesus' resurrection with an appeal to Ps. 109.1 LXX. Jesus' resurrection was exaltation by God to heavenly enthronement, where Jesus mediates the promise of the Father and pours out the Holy Spirit. The conclusion of this tightly structured proclamation is that the Jesus 'whom you crucified' has been made by God both Lord and Christ (2.36). The perlocutionary effect of Peter's rhetorical performance is precisely in line with Peter's invitation: The audience asks, 'What shall we do?' (2.37).

Assuming that the text of Joel used by Luke is the same as that of the Septuagint, scholars have often noted theologically significant changes made to the Joel text in Peter's citation.[67] The fact that Peter emphasizes prophecy as the result of this theophanic event is key. However, what is not always noted is that while Peter is explicating the charismatic speech, he is also embodying it.[68] Crucial here is Luke's use of the verb ἀποφθέγγομαι to describe both the charismatic speech of those filled with the Spirit (Acts 2.4) and Peter as he addresses the crowd (2.14). Peter's interpretation is as much Spirit-inspired speech as the doxological languages spoken in 2.4. Peter relays God's action[69] to locate the prophetic encounter between Israel and its God at the intersection of the apostolic testimony concerning the risen Christ.[70] With Joel's prophecy as the hermeneutical pattern to characterize the community, Peter perceives the eschatological community as those who prophesy, see visions, and have (revelatory) dreams (2.17). They are honoured with the appellation 'slaves (δοῦλοι and δοῦλαι) of God' (2.18). As it turns out, the 'wonders and signs' of the Joel text (Acts 2.19) become characteristic of the Spirit-empowered witnesses (Acts 2.43; 4.16, 22, 30; 5.12; 6.8; 8.6, 13; 14.3; 15.12).

Peter's citation of Joel frames the activity of preaching and miracles as eschatological events with apocalyptic tenor. Many have attempted to correlate the τέρατα ἄνω and the σημεῖα κάτω with events previously narrated,

---

67. See Bock, *Proclamation*, 158–64; Turner, *Power*, 269–70; Zehnle, *Pentecost Discourse*, 28–34.

68. See C. H. Giblin, 'Complementarity of Symbolic Event and Discourse in Acts 2, 1–40', in *Studia Evangelica* (vol. 6; ed. Elizabeth A. Livingstone; Berlin: Akademie Verlag, 1969), 189–96.

69. λέγει ὁ θεός, Acts 2.17; not in Joel 3.1 LXX.

70. See Richard J. Dillon, 'The Prophecy of Christ and His Witnesses According to the Discourses of Acts,' *NTS* 32 (1986): 544–56.

contemporaneous with the Pentecost-event, or with future events.[71] Most significant is the performative apocalyptic language that weighs the whole event, and the ensuing community, with cosmological significance. Rather than try to correlate each reference of 'wonders and signs' with heavenly or earthly portents, it is better to view the citation as a whole as performative prophetic discourse framing the current events (through Peter's speech) and the subsequent narrative developing from the events.[72] Rather than trying to figure out which events and actions are 'wonders', and which are 'signs', and whether or not 'blackened sun' and the 'bloody moon' have already passed or are still to come, the entire speech frames the prophetic discourse as *apocalyptic*, indicating an epochal in-breaking of God's presence on to Mount Zion through this messianic community.

Therefore, it can be shown that the community brought to birth through the outpouring of the Spirit is a community characterized by prophecy. This community receives the renewed prophetic vocation transferred from the risen and exalted Christ. Peter emerges as a leader of this community, speaking on behalf of the (apostles-)witnesses who lead the messianic people of God into the burgeoning period of world mission. Jesus has commissioned his apostles-witnesses, spanning the period of mission between his ascension and his return. The Spirit as the Spirit-of-prophecy is available to all in this community to accomplish the mission of the exalted Prophet King. When Peter speaks, both in his public proclamation of the gospel and in his private inner-communal regulation, he speaks as a Spirit-filled, Messiah-commissioned apostle-prophet.

The apostles-prophets are shaped by the character of Jesus in how they perform their witness and in what they do. The character parallels have often been noticed.[73] The apostles-prophets both preach to Israel proclaiming the

---

71. Bock (*Proclamation*, 167) notes four possible correlations of reference: (1) to the ministry of Jesus, (2) to the future ministry of the Apostles in the power of the Spirit, (3) to the cosmic signs accompanying the crucifixion, and (4) to future cosmic signs associated with the Day of the Lord. He opts for the fourth reference. Turner (*Power*, 273–4) suggests that these should not be exclusive of one another, as does Sloan ('Signs and Wonders', 155–8, 161). Stronstad (*Prophethood*, 55–6) correlates the 'wonders above' with the heavenly noise, the 'signs below' with the fiery tongues atop the disciples. Stronstad demonstrates his correlation *ad absurdum* with a suggestion that Peter's Pentecost sermon took place on the Temple mount, and thus the 'blackened sun' and the 'bloody moon' would result from a rising sun.

72. See the instructive comments from Litwak, *Echoes of Scripture*, 157–68. Discourses perform to shape identities and societies in the most profound ways. The discourses in Acts, including, but not limited to, the speeches, are meant to initiate the reader into a 'world' encapsulating Luke's theological vision and social order.

73. Andrew C. Clark, *Parallel Lives: The Relation of Paul to the Apostles in the Lucan Perspective* (Carlisle: Paternoster Press, 2001); David P. Moessner, 'Paul in Acts: Preacher of Eschatological Repentance to Israel', *NTS* 34 (1988), 96–104; idem, 'Paul and the Pattern of the Prophet like Moses in Acts,' in *SBL 1983 Seminar Papers* (ed. Kent H. Richards; Missoula: Scholars Press, 1983), 203–12; idem, '"The Christ Must Suffer": New Light on The Jesus-Peter, Stephen, Paul Parallels in Luke-Acts', *NovT* 28 (1986), 220–

good news of the kingdom and calling Israel to repentance, as did Jesus, and they also perform liberating miracles demonstrating the messianic power in the eschatological era of the exalted 'Christ and Lord'.

Both Peter's Pentecost speech (Acts 2.14-40) and his Temple speech (3.12-26) focus on the rhetorical effect of persuading the audience to repentance. In the very speech-act of proclamation, Peter brings his audience under divine obligation.[74] On Pentecost, those who listened were convicted (2.37) under the weight of Peter's message and pleaded for a remedy to their plight. Luke often distinguishes between the people (λαός) and their leaders, but the 'ignorance motif'[75] (Acts 3.17)[76] indicates that all Jerusalem is complicit in the rejection and 'put[ting] to death the Leader of life' (3.15). On the day of Pentecost, Peter informs his audience of what God has accomplished among them (2.14, 'Let it be known to you'; 2.22, 'performed in your midst, just as you yourselves know') leading to a directive to repent (2.38). In Solomon's Portico, Peter commands his audience to repent so that (οὖν…εἰς + infinitive) their sins may be wiped out and the times of refreshing may come.[77] Tannehill emphasizes the divine initiative to confront Israel through the apostolic-prophetic deputation: 'Thus repentance is not only a requirement, as in [Acts] 3:19, but is the intended result of the active intervention of God and God's servant through the mission. God does not simply wait for repentance

---

56; Robert F. O'Toole, *The Unity of Lukan Theology: An Analysis of Luke-Acts* (GNS 9; Wilmington: Michael Glazier, 1984), 62–94; idem 'Parallels between Jesus and His Disciples in Luke-Acts: A Further Study', *BZ* 27 (1983): 195–212; Susan Marie Praeder, 'Jesus-Paul, Peter-Paul, and Jesus-Peter Parallelisms in Luke-Acts: A History of Reader Response', in *SBL 1984 Seminar Papers* (ed. Kent H. Richards; Missoula: Scholars Press, 1984), 23–39; Charles H. Talbert, *Literary Patterns, Theological Themes, and the Genre of Luke-Acts* (SBLMS; Missoula: Scholars Press, 1974), 15–33.

74. Robert C. Tannehill, 'The Function of Peter's Mission Speeches in the Narrative of Acts', in *The Shape of Luke's Story: Essays on Luke-Acts* (Eugene, OR: Cascade Books, 2005), 169–84; idem, *Narrative Unity*, 2:26–42, 48–58.

75. Also Luke 9.45; 18.34; 24.16, 31; Acts 4.10; 13.38; 28.22, 28.

76. For the intensity of the Western tradition, see Epp, *Theological Tendency*, 42–51; Josep Rius-Camps and Jenny Read-Heimerdinger, *The Message of Acts in Codex Bezae: A Comparison with the Alexandrian Tradition. Volume 1: Acts 1.1 – 5.42: Jerusalem* (JSNTSup 257; London: T&T Clark, 2004), 231–3.

77. The eschatological perspective of this speech is highly complex and the idiosyncratic language has produced a number of interpretations. See C. K. Barrett, 'Faith and Eschatology in Acts 3', in *Glaube und Eschatologie* (eds E. Grasser and O. Merk; Tübingen: Mohr Siebeck, 1985), 1–17; Hans F. Bayer, 'Christ-Centered Eschatology in Acts 3:17–26,' in *Jesus of Nazareth: Lord and Christ. Essays on the Historical Jesus and New Testament Christology* (eds Joel B. Green and Max Turner; Grand Rapids: Eerdmans, 1994), 236–50; Bock, *Proclamation*, 187–98; Carroll, *Response*, 137–54; Dennis Hamm, 'Acts 3:12–26: Peter's Speech and the Healing of the Man Born Lame', *PRSt* 11 (1984): 199–217; Donald Juel, 'Hearing Peter's Speech in Acts 3: Meaning and Truth in Interpretation', *WW* 12 (1992): 43–50; William Kurz, 'Acts 3:19–26 as a Test of the Role of Eschatology in Lukan Christology', in *SBL 1977 Seminar Papers* (ed. Paul J. Achtemeier; Missoula: Scholars, 1977), 309–23.

but seeks to create it.'[78] Hence, it is the apostolic-prophetic speech-act that brings Jerusalem under obligation for the death of the Prophet-King, and also creates the opportunity for Israel to respond appropriately.

Furthermore, it is in his Temple speech that Peter identifies Jesus as the Prophet like Moses, predicted in Deut. 18.15, 18 (Acts 3.22). Here Peter combines this quote with the threat of Lev. 23.29, 'And it shall be that every person that does not heed that prophet shall be utterly destroyed from among the people' (Acts 3.23).[79] The fate of all Israel is now decided based on their response to the Prophet like Moses. Rejection of the 'raised prophet'[80] by rejecting his messengers results in divine retribution.

7.1.5. Summary: Commission and Transference Strategy

In summary, concerning the strategy by which Luke-Acts guides the reader in forming the process of apostolic commission and prophetic transference, we can state the points covered so far. First, we see that Jesus confers a kingdom on his apostolic nucleus (Luke 22.28-30). Second, as witnesses to Jesus' resurrection, the apostles' identity is transformed by the commission to proclaim what they have seen (Luke 24.46-49; Acts 1.4-5, 8). Third, by means of a highly allusive ascension-exaltation scene, Luke signals the anticipation of prophetic transference (Luke 24.50-53; Acts 1.9-11). Fourth, the transference is effected with the outpouring of the Holy Spirit onto the messianic community by the exalted 'Lord and Christ' signalling the beginning of the eschaton (Acts 2.1-41). Peter, as the apostolic spokesman, interprets and embodies the eschatological prophetic persona. It remains to fill out the details on Peter's characterization to confirm his identity as the apostolic-prophet successor *extraordinaire*.

7.2. Peter: The Character of the Apostolic-Prophetic Successor Par Excellence

Much of any plot is advanced through the lives of and interactions between characters. This is true of Acts 4.32–5.11. It begins with a description, setting the scene, of the early messianic community sharing in common goods and being directed by the witness of the apostles, who broker the goods. Barnabas is introduced here,[81] with origins as a diasporic Jew from Cyprus,

---

78   Tannehill, *Narrative Unity*, 2:56.
79.   See Johnson, *Acts*, 74.
80.   In 3.22, ἀνίστημι is a *double entendre* for the commissioning of the prophet and the raising of the dead Jesus.
81.   In the Western tradition (D), Barnabas is introduced in Acts 1.23, set as the alternative to Matthias. See Rius-Camps and Read-Heimerdinger, *Message*, 1:109, 113, 129–31, 133–6; Jenny Read-Heimerdinger, 'Barnabas in Acts: A Study of His Role in the Text of Codex Bezae', *JSNT* 72 (1998), 34–5, 41–63.

one Joseph who has his name changed by the apostles. More crucially, the encounter between the prophet Peter and the deceiving couple indicates cosmic dimensions to the early community's existence. Involved in this drama is not merely human encounters, but the empyrean struggle between God and Satan. Contrasted here are opposing 'fillings', one with the Spirit (Acts 4.31) and one with a heart filled with Satan (Acts 5.3), and opposing agendas, one guided by the Spirit and one counterfeit, which is exposed. This section looks at characterization to interpret the dynamics of relational involvement, and further underscore the gravity with which the confrontation between the apostle-prophet and the wayward couple enhances the dynamic performance of this pericope. The primary aim of this chapter is to demonstrate that Peter is in fact characterized as an apostle-prophet in Acts 1–5, and particularly that he is authorized to speak the prophetic indictment / condemnation upon Ananias and Sapphira resulting in their death.[82] While examining the dynamics of Peter's character, it is necessary to process some categories from literary theory to help answer the question, how is the character reconstructed from the text?[83]

7.2.1. Peter: Characterization and Relational Interaction

It is becoming an axiom in modern literary studies that characters are constructed by readers.[84] John Darr has written persuasively on the

---

82. While the information contained in Acts 8.14-24; 9.32–11.18; 12.1-19; and 15.7-11 add significantly to a full characterization of Peter, a full examination of these passages is beyond the scope of this work, and will only be referenced for brief illustration. For a fuller treatment of the character of Peter in Luke-Acts, see Raymond E. Brown, Karl P. Donfried, John Reumann (eds), *Peter in the New Testament: A Collaborative Assessment by Protestant and Roman Catholic Scholars* (London: Geoffrey Chapman Publishers, 1973), 39–56, 109–28; Wolfgang Dietrich, *Das Petrusbild der lukanischen Schriften* (BWANT 94; Stuttgart: Kohlhammer, 1972); Terence V. Smith, *Petrine Controversies in Early Christianity* (WUNT 2.15; Tübingen: Mohr Siebeck, 1985), 160-2; Christoph Zettner, *Amt, Gemeinde und kirchliche Einheit in der Apostelgeschichte des Lukas* (EHS.T 423; Frankfurt: Lang, 1991), 132–45; Timothy Wiarda, *Peter in the Gospels: Patterns, Personality and Relationship* (WUNT 2.127; Tübingen: Mohr Siebeck, 2000), 99–106, 133–6, 167–70.

83. The question is posed this way by Shlomith Rimmon-Kenan (*Narrative Fiction: Contemporary Poetics* [2nd edn; London: Routledge, 2002], 36–40, 59), who has aided the more efficient construals of characterization in Lukan studies (Gowler, Hur). She notes that there are two preliminary debates concerning the ontology of characters summarized in two questions: (1) People or words? (2) Being or doing? (31–6). These debates need not detain us here. It is inadequate to polarize characters to one side or the other along these continua; characters are both persons-in-words and agents-in-plots.

84. See the technical discussion by John A. Darr, *On Character Building: the Reader and the Rhetoric of Characterization in Luke-Acts* (Louisville: Westminster / John Knox Press, 1992), 37–59 and idem, *Herod the Fox: Audience Criticism and Lukan Characterization* (JSNTSup 163; Sheffield: Sheffield Academic Press, 1998), 64–91. Also Robert Alter, *The Art of Biblical Narrative* (New York, Basic Books, 1981), 114–30; Robert L. Brawley, *Centering on God: Method and Message in Luke-Acts* (Louisville: Westminster / John

compositional rhetoric of building characters from the data contained in the text coupled with extratextual factors (like conventional character-types, cultural scripts, and contemporary social norms).[85] He suggests four overarching criteria for constructing characters: (1) frame of reference, (2) character indicators, (3) narrative sequence and (4) socio-cultural literacy. A reader / auditor pieces together a portrayal of a particular character in her encounter with the character throughout the narrative journey. This is no less so for specific characterizing traits that script characters into particular roles and vocations, with the accompanying status-functions, like that of apostle-prophet.

7.2.1.1. Frame of Reference
The first criterion is the rhetorical approach that identifies how the character is presented, the frame of reference whereby the character is scripted into a narrative-world. Darr suggests that there are two primary frames of reference for Luke-Acts: the narrator's perspective and the divine perspective.[86] The narrator's perspective regulates the audience's evaluation of a character with reliable commentary and 'narrative asides' providing privileged information, and governs the construction of social reality as it emerges from the narrative world.[87] The divine frame of reference, God's own perspective, manifests in the Lukan narrative through the Holy Spirit (Spirit-inspired speech), the oracles of Scripture, angelic announcements, heavenly voices, and visions. Ju Hur has developed what Darr calls the 'divine frame of reference', which establishes narrative authority, drawing

Knox Press, 1990), 107–10; Fred W. Burnett, 'Characterization and Reader Construction of Characters in the Gospels' and David McCracken, 'Character in the Boundary: Bakhtin's Interdividuality in Biblical Narratives', in *Semeia* 63 (1993), 1–28 and 29–42, respectively; David B. Gowler, *Host, Guest, Enemy, and Friend: Portraits of the Pharisees in Luke and Acts* (New York: Peter Lang, 1991), 29–75, 321–32; Ju Hur, *A Dynamic Reading of the Holy Spirit in Luke-Acts* (London: T&T Clark, 2001), 115–28; David Rhoads and Kari Syreeni, eds, *Characterization in the Gospels: Reconceiving Narrative Criticism* (JSNTSup 184; Sheffield: Sheffield Academic Press, 1999); William H. Shepherd, Jr, *The Narrative Function of the Holy Spirit as a Character in Luke-Acts* (SBLDS 147; Atlanta: Scholars Press, 1994), 43–90; Elizabeth Struthers Malbon and Adele Berlin, eds, *Characterization in Biblical Literature* (*Semeia* 63; Atlanta: Scholars Press, 1993).
    85.   Darr, *Character Building*, 38–47; idem, *Herod*, 68–78. Darr follows Wolfgang Iser (*The Implied Reader: Patterns of Communication in Prose Fiction from Bunyan to Beckett* [Baltimore: Johns Hopkins University Press, 1974] and *The Act of Reading: A Theory of Aesthetic Response* [Baltimore: Johns Hopkins University Press, 1978]) in distinguishing between a *text*, described as a framework or pattern to guide reading, filled with gaps, and a *literary work*, defined as that which is generated when a text is read, filling the gaps. For both, the *literary work* is the proper object of interpretation.
    86.   Darr, *Character Building*, 50–3; idem, *Herod*, 80–2. See also idem, 'Narrator as Character: Mapping a Reader Oriented Approach to Narration in Luke-Acts', *Semeia* 63 (1993), 43–60.
    87.   See Steven M. Sheeley, *Narrative Asides in Luke-Acts* (JSNTSup 72; Sheffield: JSOT Press, 1992), 149–59, *passim*.

attention to the various ways that God, who is an 'offstage character',[88] guides and regulates evaluative decisions.[89] Together the narrator's perspective with the divine frame of reference offers the most authoritative and reliable vantage point to evaluate a character, event, setting, or object within the story.[90] Darr writes, 'Much like the narrator's perspective, the divine frame of reference provides the audience with a consistent and highly authoritative guide for constructing and/or evaluating characters and their roles in the action.'[91]

---

88. Darr, *Character Building*, 51; idem, *Herod*, 81; Daniel Marguerat, *The First Christian Historian: Writing the 'Acts of the Apostles'* (SNTSMS 121; Cambridge, Cambridge University Press, 2002), 85–108, esp. 89–90. Contrast the formalist-semiotic stance of Brawley, *Centering*, 110–24.

89. Hur, *Dynamic Reading*, 87–114, 284–6. Hur (*Dynamic Reading*, 101 n. 38 [following Mark. A. Powell, *What Are They Saying About Acts?* (New York: Paulist Press, 1991), 57]) refers to the triune theological frame of reference for the narrator including a theocentric, christocentric and pneumatocentric point of view.

90. Darr (*Character Building*, 53–9; *Herod*, 83–9) extended Luke's rhetorical poetics to include, alongside the frames of reference, (1) a model of proper perception (through the eyewitness' accounts) and (2) models of proper response to the protagonists.

Therefore, the narrative of Luke-Acts is itself construed by the model author as reliable and authoritative Spirit-inspired narrative giving witness to the kingdom of God and the story of Jesus through the Lukan prologue (Luke 1.1-4). See Hur, *Dynamic Reading*, 284; Robert G. Hall, *Revealed Histories: Techniques for Ancient Jewish and Christian Historiography* (JSPSup 6; Sheffield: JSOT Press, 1991), 172, 205–8; and the various works from David P. Moessner 'The Appeal and Power of Poetics (Luke 1:1-4): Luke's Superior Credentials (παρηκολουθηκότι), Narrative Sequence (καθεξῆς), and Firmness of Understanding (ἡ ἀσφάλεια) for the Reader', in *Jesus and the Heritage of Israel: Luke's Narrative Claim Upon Israel's Legacy* (ed. D. P. Moessner; Harrisburg, PA: Trinity Press International, 1999), 84–123; idem, 'The Meaning of καθεξῆς in the Lukan Prologue as a Key to the Distinctive Contribution of Luke's Narrative among the "Many"', in *The Four Gospels 1992: Festschrift Frans Neirynck* (eds F. Van Segbroeck, C. M. Tuckett, G. van Belle, et al.; 2 vols; Leuven: Leuven University Press, 1992), 2:1513–28; idem, 'The Lukan Prologues in the Light of Ancient Narrative Hermeneutics: Παρηκολουθηκότι and the Credentialed Author', in *The Unity of Luke-Acts* (ed. J. Verheyden; BETL 142; Leuven: Leuven University Press, 1999), 399–417; idem, 'Dionysius' Narrative "Arrangement" (οἰκονομία) as the Hermeneutical Key to Luke's Re-Vision of the "Many"', in *Paul, Luke, and the Graeco-Roman World: Essays in Honour of Alexander J.M. Wedderburn* (eds, A. Christophersen, C. Claussen, J. Frey and B. Longenecker; JSNTSup 217; Sheffield: Sheffield Academic Press, 2002), 149–64; idem, 'Ministers of Divine Providence: Diodorus Siculus and Luke the Evangelist on the Rhetorical Significance of the Audience in Narrative "Arrangement"', in *Literary Encounters with the Reign of God: Studies in Honor of R.C. Tannehill* (eds S. H. Ringe and H. C. P. Kim; London: T&T Clark, 2004), 304–23; idem, '"Managing" the Audience: Diodorus Siculus and Luke the Evangelist on Designing Authorial Intent', in *Luke and His Readers: Festschrift A. Denaux* (eds R. Bieringer, G. van Belle and J. Verheyden; BETL 182; Leuven: Leuven University Press, 2005), 61–80; and a helpful condensation of his arguments in 'How Luke Writes', in *The Written Gospel* (eds M. Bockmuehl and D. Hagner; Cambridge: Cambridge University Press, 2005), 149–70.

The narrator of Luke-Acts displays an overall positive disposition towards Peter when compared to the narratives of Matthew and Mark.[92] Peter becomes aligned with the narrator's authoritative perspective and disseminates it through his Spirit-inspired speeches (Acts 2.14-40; 3.12-26; and 4.8). Peter becomes the protagonist in the beginning of Acts set in Jerusalem (1.12–5.42).[93] In these ways, Peter is legitimated as a reliable character and aligned with the narrator's theological and ideological perspective.

7.2.1.2. Character Indicators
Recognizing now how a model author guides the evaluation of characters, it is important to ask, what data is available to build characters? Character indicators are the raw data that an audience uses to construe the characters they encounter. Gowler, who applied the methodology of Rimmon-Kenan to apprehend the Lukan presentation of the Pharisees[94] suggests that characters can be apprehended upon (descending) scales of reliability and explicitness. The scale of reliability helps to calibrate the significance of character indicators.[95] Gowler suggests the scale of explicitness occurs through (1) direct definition and (2) indirect presentation. Characterization arises from both telling and showing. I suggest that (3) *inter-character relationships and associations* should be added to this scale.

---

91. Darr, *Character Building*, 53.
92. See Terence V. Smith, *Controversies*, 160–2. Smith notes that compared to Mark and Matthew, Luke omits various aspects, like the stinging rebuke by Jesus where the apostles are identified with Satan (Mark 8.33; Matt. 16.23; cf. Luke 9.20-27), Peter's swearing and cursing (Mark 14.71; Matt. 26.74; cf. Luke 22.54-62), etc. Further, Luke's account of Peter's call is more developed, Jesus' prediction of Peter's denial is preceded by a directive to 'strengthen his brothers', and Luke 24.34 gives full expression to Jesus' resurrection appearance to Peter. See Brown, Donfried and Reumann (eds), *Peter*, 110–14, 127–8.
93. To designate Peter a protagonist is not to make the corresponding claim that his initiative or action drives the narrative. Correctly, Roberts Gaventa, 'Initiatives Divine', *Holy Spirit* (eds Stanton, Longenecker, Barton) 79–89. Robert Banks' essay in the same volume ('The Role of Charismatic and Noncharismatic Factors in Determining Paul's Movements in Acts', 117–30) inadvertently offers helpful nuances to Gaventa's position.
94. Gowler, *Host*, 55–75; Rimmon-Kenan, *Narrative Fiction*, 59–67.
95. Compare Alter's (*Biblical Narrative*, 116–17) ascending 'hierarchy of reliability' ('a scale of means, in ascending order of explicitness and certainty, for conveying information about the motives, the attitudes, the moral nature of characters', [116]) conflating the scales of reliability and explicitness. At the lowest level of the continuum is the revelation of the character through actions or appearance, which causes the reader to rely on inference. In the middle is direct speech, by the character himself or by other characters about him. Here the claims must be weighed. Inner speech offers comparatively more certainly, although the reader may still question the motive behind the intention. Finally, at the top level of certainty, Alter places 'the reliable narrator's explicit statement of what the characters feel, intend, desire' (117). Also Brawley, *Centering*, 110; Darr, *Character Building*, 43–7; idem, *Herod*, 73–8.

7.2.1.2.1. Direct Description

Gowler writes, 'Direct definition plays a critical part in characterization, because it creates in the mind of the reader an explicit, authoritative, and static impression of a character.'[96] The most obvious examples are the descriptive terms linking Peter with the 'disciples' and the 'apostles'.[97] Take, for example, the narrator's description of Peter and his companions in Luke 9. Jesus has invited Peter, James and John to come up a mountain to pray. Jesus is accompanied by Moses and Elijah. 'But Peter and those with him were burdened with sleep' (Luke 9.32). It is likely that this portrayal figures the disciples with 'spiritual dullness'.[98] Other examples include the narrator's description of Peter being 'filled with the Holy Spirit' (Acts 4.8). This is the highest recommendation of Peter's character, and authorizes whatever it is that Peter speaks in the immediate co-text. When the narrator states that 'Peter, standing with the Eleven, raised his voice and declared (ἀπεφθέγξατο) to them [the Jewish crown in Jerusalem]...' (Acts 2.14), we not only get a picture of Peter distinguished among the apostles, but as one whose speech is associated with the Spirit-enabled speech of those who experienced the outpouring of the Holy Spirit (Acts 2.4).[99]

Besides the narrator, other characters can offer direct descriptions, although these are subject to the fluctuating scale of reliability. As Jesus is exalted by angelic messengers (Luke 1.32-33), Spirit-filled prophecy (1.69-72; 2.29-32), and the heavenly voice (3.22b), his perspective is aligned with that of the narrator and the divine frame of reference. Therefore, when Jesus tells Simon (Peter) that 'from now on you will be catching people' (5.8) in the context of a miraculous catch of fish, Peter's vocational identity is transformed into what is later revealed as the eschatological gathering of Israel (9.1-6; 10.1-24).[100] Another example is the ironic designation of Peter as a man who was 'with' Jesus from the παιδίσκη in the courtyard of the house of the high priest (22.56; cf. Acts 4.13b). It is ironic because this character, associated with the household of one of Jesus' prime enemies, speaks the truth concerning Peter, which he denies. Being with Jesus is the primary identification of the

---

96. Gowler, *Host*, 57. Rimmon-Kenan (*Narrative Fiction*, 60) writes, 'Definition is akin to generalization and conceptualization. It is also both explicit and supra-temporal. Consequently, its dominance in a given text is liable to produce a rational, authoritative and static impression.'

97. Indeed, to get a full characterization of Peter, we would have to explore not just his character as an individual, but also the collective characterizations of the 'disciples' and 'apostles'. See McCracken, 'Interdividuality'.

98. The phrase is Green's (*Luke*, 383); cf. Nolland, *Luke*, 2:500 ('human frailty').

99. It is the same verb used of both utterances, ἀποφθέγγομαι. Cf. Acts 26.25.

100. Brawley, *Centering*, 140–1. Also Moessner, *Lord*, 134–43. Dietrich (*Petrusbild*, 80) suggests, 'Hence, one could suppose that our history shows, in view of the post-Easter primacy of the first apostle, attempts to project backward, and glorifying the picture of Peter' ('Man könnte daher vermuten, daß unsere Geschichte Ansätze zu einem im Blick auf die nachösterliche Vorrangstellung des Erstapostels zurückprojizierten, glorifizierenden Petrusbild zeige.').

disciples in Luke's Gospel,[101] and is the primary identification mentioned by Peter in Acts 1.21-22. Therefore, Peter's denial is set in sharp contrast to this identification by the slave-girl and to Peter's subsequent boldness with which he will proclaim the apostles' identity as 'witnesses' (Acts 1.22; 2.32; 3.15; 4.20; 5.32).

An interesting hybrid perspective exists in the narrator's description of one character's direct description of another character.[102] We learn from the narrator in Luke 6.13-14 that Jesus separated twelve of his disciples and named them 'ἀπόστολοι' and that it was Jesus who gave Simon the name 'Πέτρος'. Like the renaming of Joseph as 'Βαρναβᾶς' by the apostles (Acts 4.36), this change of name indicates the new relationship between the leader and the follower. Further, it may indicate an association with a 'rock', which is a term that itself becomes associated with the proper 'hearing' of Jesus' words (Luke 6.48).[103]

Another example of this hybrid perspective is the narrator's description of Peter and John through the eyes of the Jerusalem hierocracy (Acts 4.13). They (the rulers and elders and scribes and Annas, the high priest, and Caiaphas and John and Alexander, and all who were of high priestly descent, 4.5-6) are the subject of four verbs of cognition in the description of the narrator:

> Not only did they *observe* (θεωροῦντες) the confidence of Peter and John, and *realize* (καταλαβόμενοι) that they were uneducated and untrained men, they *were marveling* (ἐθαύμαζον), and they also *began to recognize* (ἐπεγίνωσκον) them as having been with Jesus. (Acts 4.13)

Peter and John are described as ἄνθρωποι ἀγράμματοί ... καὶ ἰδιῶται and as 'having been with Jesus'. However, this description is given by the narrator *from the perspective of* the rulers and elders of the people. An interesting tension is created from two factors. First, there is a potentially negative description of Peter and John, that they are 'uneducated and untrained', but this comes from the enemies of Jesus and his apostles-witnesses mediated through the narrator. Second, this potentially negative status marker, made all the more acute by the contrasting presence of the scribes (γραμματεῖς, 4.5; contrast the term for 'uneducated', ἀγράμματος), actually highlights the emphasis on the Spirit-enabled ability of Peter (and John) to speak with boldness (παρρησία) before the leaders of the people, who *are* educated and trained, but lack the Holy Spirit. It is from this depiction of Peter and John

---

101. Green, *Theology*, 102–3.
102. Tannehill (*Narrative Unity*, 2:106–7) recognizes this phenomenon in the narrator's describing the perception of Simon Magus that the Spirit is bestowed through the laying on of hands, and so offers to purchase this authority, rather than recognizing it as a gift (Acts 8.18).
103. See Brawley, *Centering*, 142–3; Dietrich, *Das Petrusbild*, 94; Green, *Luke*, 259; Nolland, *Luke*, 1:270. Compare also the tradition preserved in Matt. 16.18, where Πέτρος is directly juxtaposed to πέτρα.

in the public sphere that the narrative moves into the private space of the Christian community (Acts 4.23–5.11).[104]

7.2.1.2.2. Indirect Presentation

Direct description is basically a straightforward means of providing data for character-building. Indirect presentation, by contrast, is more ambiguous and open to a wider range of interpretive possibilities. Rimmon-Kenan proposes four main categories of indirect presentation of characters: (1) character speech (both inward and spoken), (2) actions, (3) external appearance, and (4) environment (physical and social [e.g., familial]).[105]

The most important indicator for the indirect presentation of the Lukan Peter's character is his *speech*. Toward the beginning of Luke's Gospel we hear Peter reluctantly obey Jesus' order to cast out into the deep to let down the nets for a catch. Peter responds, 'Master (ἐπιστάτα), we worked hard all night and caught nothing, but at your word I will let down the nets' (Luke 5.5). After a miraculous catch of fish, Peter reveals his penitent disposition by responding to Jesus with the words, as he falls at Jesus' knees, 'Depart from me, for I am a sinful man, O Lord (κύριε)!' (5.8). The narrator explains Peter's motivation: 'for amazement (θάμβος) seized him and all those with him as a result of the great catch of fish which they had taken' (5.9). We see Peter as one who is outspoken, and yet willing to repent when he is confronted with his faults. Peter is shown to be one who submits to Jesus' authority, having addressed him in a manner indicating Jesus' right over Peter's own boat. Peter's response to Jesus leads to his participation into Jesus' own ministry.

Peter often speaks on behalf of the other disciples, indicating his role of prominence, even among the Twelve. It is Peter who correctly designates Jesus' identity as the 'Christ of God' (Luke 9.20),[106] although it is unclear from the text how Peter came to this conclusion. However, Peter demonstrates that he has not fully grasped the Messiah's identity when he offers to pay homage to Moses and Elijah alongside the transfigured Jesus (9.33).[107] Here the narrator assists in understanding the folly of Peter's request offering an explanatory aside: 'not knowing what he was saying' (9.33c).

---

104. Note the division of the text by Johnson, *Acts*, 82–93; Scott F. Spencer, *Journeying Through Acts: A Literary-Cultural Reading* (Peabody, MA: Hendrickson, 2004), 62–8.

105. Rimmon-Kenan, *Narrative Fiction*, 61–7; See Gowler, *Host*, 61–70; Hur, *Dynamic Reading*, 147–62; Shepherd, *Narrative Function*, 88.

106. See Dietrich, *Petrusbild*, 94–104. This is all the more interesting in light of Jack Kingsbury's ('"Prophetic Messiah"', 34–5) argument that Peter's confession is parallel to Jesus' self-designation as God's Anointed (Luke 4.18), set in the inclusio marked by God's own evaluation of Jesus as 'God's Son'. Also Jack Dean Kingsbury, *Conflict in Luke: Jesus, Authorities, Disciples* (Minneapolis: Fortress Press, 1991), 50–3.

107. Cf. Dietrich, *Petrusbild*, 112–16. Again Peter addresses Jesus as ἐπιστάτης, indicating a recognition of authority, but not grasping the fullness of Jesus' identity. P[45] reads διδάσκαλε, a designation reserved for outsiders elsewhere in Luke (cf. 7.40; 9.38; 10.25; 11.45; 12.13; 18.18; 19.39; 20.21, 28, 39; 21.7).

In another episode, in the context of Jesus' teaching in parables, Peter interrupts Jesus to query about Jesus' intended audience. Peter asks, 'Lord (κύριε), are you telling this parable to us, or to everyone else as well?' (Luke 12.41). Peter's question is telling about his concern to differentiate 'us' (the disciples; 12.1, 22) from the larger crowd that has gathered around Jesus (12.1, 13, 16). The possibilities are initially open as to whether Peter's concern is to *include* the wider crowd in the blessing pronounced upon those who remain alert for the coming κύριος, or whether his concern is to differentiate the disciples and *exclude* the wider crowd.[108] It is more likely that it is to be understood as a concern for differentiation and exclusion, due to the fact that Jesus' indirect response includes not just commendation and blessing (12.43, the tri-fold promise of blessing in the previous parable in 12.37 [μακάριοι, and ἀμήν], 12.38 [μακάριοι]), but also grave threat and warning (12.45-48). Du Plessis indicates that the change in Jesus' conversational goals is a reaction to Peter's 'deficient discipleship'.[109] Furthermore, this parable is couched in a didactic discourse that began with a warning: 'Beware of the leaven of the Pharisees, which is hypocrisy' (12.1b). The Pharisees were rebuked by Jesus for seeking status and preeminence (11.43) as a sign of their inward corruption (11.39-44). Later they are cast into the role of stewarding a counterfeit household with values of status-seeking that were incommensurate with the household and kingdom of God (14.7-24). Peter, in his question, is exhibiting the very anxiety that Jesus warns against in Luke 12.22-34, of which the narrator has told the audience is directed to the disciples (12.22). Jesus' response to Peter (12.42-48) is both a confirmation of the disciples' privileged position with its accompanying responsibility and a corresponding threat.[110] Peter, once again, displays a complex disposition as one who understands Jesus' position as κύριος (12.41; cf. 12.36, 37, 42, 43, 45, 46, 47), but who is also at odds with the cultural revaluation of the servant Lord (12.37b).

Peter is found again grasping for recognition of the disciples' privileged status when he responds to Jesus' denunciation of the wealthy ruler's clinging to his riches (Luke 18.23-28). Peter says, 'Behold, we have left our own [possessions] to follow you' (18.28), precisely what Jesus required of the wealthy ruler (18.22). Jesus affirms the disciples' sacrifice, but removes their privileged status by offering the blessing of the kingdom of God to whomever will do the same (18.29-30). This desire to assert privileged status through distinction is a flaw in Peter's character, as a representative of the disciples, which carries through into Acts (Luke 9.46-48; 22.24-30; Acts 6.2-4; 10.13-17a).

---

108. J. G. du Plessis, 'Why Did Peter Ask His Question and How did Jesus Answer Him? Or: Implicature in Luke 12:35–48', *Neot* 22 (1988): 318; Green, *Luke*, 503. This indicates that Peter's question functions to do more than just prepare for the following parable, distinguish the applicability of the parables, or focus the attention of the reader, *pace* Marshall, *Luke*, 540; Nolland, *Luke*, 2:705.

109. Du Plessis, 'Implicature', 320.

110. Du Plessis, 'Implicature', 319–20.

Peter's boisterous personality is also apparent in the complex episode of his denial (Luke 22.31-34, 54-62).[111] Peter's role is as a supportive character confirming the prophetic reliability of Jesus as one who predicts both Peter's denial and his restoration. The focus of the narrative is on Jesus, his farewell discourse over the Passover meal, and his arrest leading up to his suffering. After Jesus corrects the disciples for their quarreling over status positions (22.25-27) and confers upon them an exalted status in the future kingdom (22.28-30), he singles out Peter for address. Jesus explains that Satan has demanded to sift Peter, but that Jesus has interceded so that his faith may not fail, and once Peter has returned, Jesus commissions him to strengthen his brothers (22.31-32). Peter responds brazenly with an assurance of his devotion: 'Lord (κύριε), with you I am ready to go both to prison and to death!' (22.33), to which Jesus predicts Peter's tri-fold denial. Peter's boldness is ironic, both because he completely fulfils Jesus' prediction of his weakness and because he will later experience both prison (Acts 4.3; 5.18; 12.3) and the real threat of death (12.1-19).

Peter's speech in Acts reveals further his role as a leader of the Christian community. Peter exhibits charismatic exegesis to interpret the present situation of the community (Acts 1.15-22) in a manner similar to Jesus' interpreting the situation by opening the Scriptures to the travellers on their way to Emmaus (Luke 24.25-27) and the collection of his disciples (24.44-49). Tannehill remarks,

> Peter is now an interpreter of Scripture and of God's purpose for the Church. His insight into Scripture and God's purpose will also be demonstrated in his missionary speeches, but even before the mission begins he is presented as one who knows what 'was necessary' to fulfill Scripture (v. 16) and what Scripture indicates to be 'necessary' now (1:20–22). *Peter is taking over a major function of the departed Jesus.*[112]

Peter is also the privileged protagonist who interprets the events of Jesus' ascension to heaven as exaltation (2.33-36), the outpouring of the Holy Spirit on Pentecost as eschatological fulfilment (2.14-40) and the healing of the temple beggar as a result of God's glorifying and raising Jesus (3.12-26).[113] It is Peter who emerges as the spokesman of the apostles-witnesses (and therefore of the Christian community) (1.12; 2.14, 38; 3.6, 12; 4.8; 5.3, 8, 29[114]).

Therefore, in Acts, what was already evident in the Gospel, becomes expressed most positively that Peter speaks on behalf of the community

---

111. Dietrich, *Petrusbild*, 116–57.
112. Tannehill, *Narrative Unity*, 2:20, emphasis added.
113. See Dietrich, *Petrusbild*, 195–216 for the Pentecost speech, and 216–30 for the Temple speech.
114. In Codex Bezae (D) it is Peter alone who answers the Sanhedrin. See Joseph Crehan, 'Peter According to the D-Text of Acts', *TS* 18 (1957), 599–600; Rius-Camps and Read-Heimerdinger, *Message*, 1:342–3.

which gives witness to the resurrected-exalted Jesus and through whom Jesus continues his work (Acts 1.1). Peter's speech presents a complex character who often speaks correctly, although presumptuously. In Acts, Peter's speeches focalize the perspective of the narrator, framing the events as christologically, pneumatologically and theologically significant affairs.[115] Therefore, it is most appropriate that Peter's prophetic indictment of Ananias and Sapphira (Acts 5.1-11) comes as an expression of divinely authorized *speech* governing and guaranteeing the sacral nature of the community's ethos and witness.

Another character indicator is a character's *action*. Peter's actions, especially in Acts, serve to promote the construal of his character as apostolic-prophetic. In the Gospel, the actions that are specifically set apart are Peter's speech. In the Jerusalem section in Acts (1.12–8.3, esp. 1.12–5.42), Peter is promoted as the character through which the narrative action flows. Peter proves to be a prophet like John the Baptizer, in his preaching of repentance (2.38; 3.19 cf. Luke 3.3), and more significantly a prophetic successor to the Prophet-Messiah, Jesus. Already mentioned is Peter's charismatic interpretation of Scripture (1.20; 2.17-21, 25-28; 3.22-23, 24-25). Peter also displays the prophetic endowment of performing miracles; he, like Jesus, is marked by 'signs and wonders' (3.7-10; 4.30; 5.1-11, 12, 15[116]; cf. 2.22; 10.38).[117] Peter's acts of preaching have already been addressed above under the consideration of his speech.

Two other character indicators are *external appearance* and environment. The former is not an instrument used by the model author of Luke-Acts to advance the characterization of Peter. There is nothing akin to the physiognomic associations of Jesus' physical and social development in Luke 2.52, or the (dazzling) white clothing of the heavenly messengers accompanying Jesus' empty tomb (Luke 24.4) and Jesus' ascension into heaven (Acts 1.10). There is no correlation between Peter's physical appearance and his character implicit as it is with the lame beggar in Acts 3–4.[118]

---

115. The classic study of speeches in Acts is Martin Dibelius, 'The Speeches in Acts and Ancient Historiography', in *The Book of Acts: Form, Style, and Theology* (trans. Mary Ling; ed. K. C. Hanson; London: SCM Press, 1956; repr. Minneapolis: Fortress, 2004), 49–86. The most comprehensive study to date is Soards, *Speeches*. See also, Tannehill, 'Function', 169–84.

116. Codex Bezae (D) makes the role of Peter (and his shadow) unequivocal as the instrument of the people's healing by adding ἀπηλλάσσοντο γὰρ ἀπὸ πάσης ἀσθενείας ὡς εἶχεν ἕκαστος αὐτῶν. See Metzger, *Commentary*, 330; Rius-Camps and Read-Heimerdinger, *Message*, 1:318, 323. Epp (*Theological Tendency*, 156-7), notes the addition, and suggests that the D-reading is an attempt to bring out the parallel with Paul's handkerchiefs (Acts 19.12, ...καὶ ἀπαλλάσσεσθαι ἀπ' αὐτῶν τὰς ὅσους...). On the power of Peter's shadow, see Dietrich, *Petrusbild*, 238-9.

117. See the parallels noted by Clark, *Parallel Lives*, 209–29; Johnson, *Literary Parallels*, 60–9; O'Toole, 'Parallels', *passim*; Praeder, 'Parallelisms', 34–6; Talbert, *Literary Patterns*, 16, 18–20.

118. Consult Mikeal C. Parsons, 'The Character of the Lame Man in Acts 3–4', *JBL* 124/2 (2005): 295–312, and now his full study, *Body and Character in Luke and Acts: The Subversion of Physiognomy in Early Christianity* (Grand Rapids: Baker Academic, 2006).

The model author does employ *environment* as a crucial factor informing Peter's characterization. Peter's household serves as a base of operations for Jesus' early ministry in Capernaum, in Galilee (Luke 4.38-41). Perhaps more significant is Peter's place in the social space of family and kinship associations. The audience learns that Peter is married (by inference from his having a mother-in-law, Luke 4.38). As a fisherman, he would have most likely had a lower status as a manual labourer, but he is also one who owns his own boat, having business partners (the sons of Zebedee, 5.10).[119] However, his status in the divine economy is substantially raised by his election as one of Jesus' twelve apostles (Luke 6.12-16; Acts 1.13), upon whom Jesus confers *his* kingdom (Luke 22.28-30). Having this chosen position, Peter emerges as the apparent leader of the apostles, being particularly commissioned to strengthen his fellow apostles after the time of trial (22.32b). Also significant is Peter's presence in the courtyard of the house of the high priest, the locale for his infamous denial (22.54-62). It is important to give Peter the credit for following Jesus, even if at a distance (22.54b).

More importantly in the beginning of Acts, Peter emerges as the leader of the *Jerusalem* community (Acts 1.12; cf. Luke 24.52-53).[120] The apostles are the core cluster of the nascent Christian community (Luke 24.33, 48-49; Acts 1.12-13; 2.42; 4.33-35), the fictive kin-group. It can be inferred that Peter and John are pious Jews as they head to the Jerusalem Temple at the hour of prayer (Acts 3.1). The apostles' position as 'outsiders' in the Sanhedrin throughout Acts 4–5 serves to indict the Sanhedrin for their stiff-necked refusal to accept Israel's divinely vindicated Messiah. Thus, social location presses into the aspect of relationships and associations, which are crucial to any character construal.

7.2.1.2.3. Inter-Character Relationships

Darr insists character analysis must take account of the interdependence of plot and character (e.g., how one responds to the plan of God), the geographical and cultural settings evoking specific expectations (e.g., the Jerusalem Temple or a meal set in a symposium type-scene), and how characters interact with one another. In fact, the last of these is the most revealing. Darr writes, 'The fundamental matrix within which we construct a character is the web of interrelationships that develops among all of the figures in the story world.

---

119. Green, *Luke*, 231.
120. Richard Bauckham, 'James and the Jerusalem Church', in *The Book of Acts in its Palestinian Setting* (ed. Richard Bauckham; vol. 4, *The Book of Acts in its First Century Setting*, ed. B. W. Winter; Grand Rapids: Eerdmans, 1995), 415–50; Milton Moreland, 'The Jerusalem Community in Acts: Mythmaking and the Sociorhetorical Functions of a Lukan Setting', in *Contextualizing Acts: Lukan Narrative and Greco-Roman Discourse* (eds Todd Penner and Caroline Vander Stichele; SBLSymS 20; Atlanta: Society of Biblical Literature, 2003), 285–310.

In other words, characters are delineated largely in terms of each other, just as we are defined by our relationships in real life.'[121]

It has already been noted above that the disciples' primary role in Luke's Gospel is to be *with* Jesus, from the beginning of his ministry through to his ascension-exaltation (συνελθόντων, Acts 1.21; cf. Luke 8.38; 9.18; 22.14, 28 [ὑμεῖς δέ ἐστε οἱ διαμεμενηκότες μετ' ἐμοῦ], 49, 56).[122] Therefore, the apostles-witnesses derive their primary identity from the identity of the crucified and risen Prophet-King. Peter's relationship to Jesus is his primary identifying characteristic.[123] On the other hand, Peter is also set in stark contrast to Judas and the Jerusalem elite.

Throughout the Gospel, Peter remains a device to enhance the Lukan characterization of Jesus.[124] Often Peter is a voice that opens the stage to clarify or enhance Jesus' words (Luke 5.8; 8.45; 9.20; 12.41; 18.28). Peter's denial functions to verify Jesus' prophetic prediction (22.34, 54-62). On the first day of the week, following Jesus' execution, Peter serves to verify the empty tomb, responding with the common response to divine visitation of awe (24.12).[125]

Peter is also associated with James and John as a distinct inner group within the Twelve. At least twice these three are separated out and given a privileged participation in remarkable events. Jesus allows these three into the room where he raised a deceased girl (Luke 8.51). Further, these three are the only ones Jesus allows to come up the mountain with him for the event of his transfiguration (9.28). Later, it is Peter and John that Jesus sends to prepare Jesus' last Passover meal (22.8). One is also reminded that Peter and John are singled out for their journey to pray in the Temple in Acts 3.1-5.

There are two important negative foils that enhance the characterization of Peter in Luke-Acts. First, Peter is juxtaposed with Judas as followers of

---

121. Darr, *Character Building*, 41; cf. idem, *Herod*, 72–3.

122. See Schuyler Brown, *Apostasy and Perseverance in the Theology of Luke* (AnBib 36; Rome: Pontifical Biblical Institute, 1969), 53–81.

123. It is also important to realize, with Timothy Wiarda ('Peter as Peter in the Gospel of Mark', *NTS* 45 [1999]: 20–1, 26–34, 35–6), commentating on Mark's Gospel, but here relevant to Luke-Acts, that Peter's character is not to be absorbed into the collectivity of the disciples or as 'representative' of some typology. See also Burnett, 'Characterization', 7, 11–19; Petri Merenlahti, 'Characters in the Making: Individuality and Ideology in the Gospels', in *Characterization* (eds Rhoads and Syreeni), 49–72; Meir Sternberg, *The Poetics of Biblical Narrative: Ideological Literature and the Drama of Reading* (Bloomington: Indiana University Press, 1985), 253–5, 325–8, 346–8.

124. R. Alan Culpepper's (*Anatomy of the Fourth Gospel: A Study in Literary Design* [Philadelphia: Fortress Press, 1983], 104) statements concerning the Fourth Gospel are appropriate for Luke's Gospel: 'In John's narrative world the individuality of all the characters except Jesus is determined by their encounter with Jesus. The characters represent a continuum of responses to Jesus which exemplify misunderstandings the reader may share and responses one might make to the depiction of Jesus in the gospel. The characters are, therefore, particular kinds of choosers.'

125. Verse 12 is omitted in D, but present in P⁷⁵, ℵ, A, B, et al. Metzger (*Commentary*, 184) notes that the verse is often viewed as an interpolation derived from John 20.3, but that the UBS Committee was inclined to explain the similarity as a result of shared tradition.

Jesus. In Luke 22.1-13, the apostate Judas is contrasted with the obedient Peter and John. Green observes,

> All belong to the circle of the twelve, but whereas the former [Judas] becomes an agent of Satan to betray Jesus in exchange for money, the latter [Peter and John] are presented as exemplary disciples. Their portrayal as table servants (cf. 12:37, 17:7–10; 22:24–27) anticipates their roles as leaders in the book of Acts (3:1, 3, 11; 4:13, 19; 8:14).[126]

Also, there is a stark contrast between Jesus' determination for Judas and for Peter. Judas has no future in the continuing divine economy: '...but woe to that man by whom he [the Son of Man] is betrayed' (Luke 22.22b). In contrast, Jesus commissions Peter to strengthen his brothers after he has turned again (ἐπιστρέφω).[127] In this way, Peter is to Judas what Barnabas is to Ananias and Sapphira. Peter and Barnabas have a future in the ongoing narrative journey of Luke-Acts. Judas and the condemned couple merely remain in infamy for their heinous crimes against God and the community; they have no future in the continuing journey. Furthermore, there is an austere contrast between Peter and Judas in Peter's portrayal of Judas in Acts 1.16-20.[128] Peter is presented as the ideal apostle in distinction to Judas, the ultimate apostate. Peter is one who passes divine judgement (also Acts 5.1-11); Judas is one who is under divine retribution.

Second, Peter as an apostle is contrasted with the Jerusalem Temple elite as a divinely appointed leader over restored Israel.[129] Peter displays competence and ability in ruling the burgeoning Christian community (Acts 5.1-11), whereas the rulers and elders of the people show themselves incompetent to rule over their constituents and are held captive by the will of the people (4.21-22; 5.26, 28). Peter is one who is filled with the Spirit (4.8), whereas the Jerusalem rulers and elders are those who are filled with jealousy (5.17), and who have crucified Jesus and continually reject God's vindicated Messiah

---

126. Green, *Luke*, 756.
127. The term ἐπιστρέφω is a term Luke favours to be synonymous with repentance. See Luke 1.16, 17 (cf. Mal. 4.6), John will *turn* back the sons of Israel to the Lord their God; 17.4, 'And if he sins against you seven times a day, and *returns* to you seven times, saying, "I repent," forgive him'; 22.32, 'once you have *turned* again, strengthen your brothers'; Acts 3.19, 'Repent, and *turn* to God'; 9.35, 'And those who lived at Lydda and Sharon saw Aeneas healed, and they *turned* to the Lord'; 11.21, 'And the hand of the Lord was with them, and a large number who believed *turned* to the Lord'; 14.15, 'you should *turn* from these vain things to a living God'; 15.19 'Therefore it is my judgment that we do not trouble those who are *turning* to God from among the Gentiles...'; 26.18,' to open their eyes so that they may *turn* from darkness to light and from the dominion of Satan to God'; 26.20, 'that they should repent and *turn* to God'; 28.27 (cf. Isa. 6.10), 'Lest they should see with their eyes, And hear with their ears, And understand with their heart and *return*, And I should heal them.'
128. Dietrich, *Petrusbild*, 166–94. This passage will be explored further below when considering the characterization of Judas, §8.1.1.
129. See Jervell, 'The Twelve'. See §2.3.3. above.

(4.10-11, 21, 25-29; 5.28, 30-33; 7.51-53). The people hold the apostles in high esteem (5.13b), but the rulers and elders fear the people (4.21; 5.26). Even the people are presented as responding appropriately to the miraculous healing (4.21b), which is recognized as undeniable by the Sanhedrin (4.16). Yet, the rulers and elders refuse to recognize their complicity in the unjust execution of Jesus, and therefore the authority of Jesus' Name or of his representatives – the apostles-witnesses. Gamaliel's advice to the Council brings out the deep irony of the confrontation: throughout Acts 3–5, when dealing with Jesus' apostles-witnesses, one is not dealing with mere men and human devices, but with God and the divine purpose. Peter's encounter with Ananias and Sapphira only heightens the warning Gamaliel gives to the Council: to oppose the apostles is to be found fighting against God (5.39, θεομάχοι), which the condemned couple find leads to death. The confrontation between Peter and the apostles and the Jerusalem elite merely serves to solidify the solidarity between Jesus and his followers.[130] Jerusalem continues its role as the persecutor of God's prophets (Luke 13.33-35; Acts 7.52-53).

7.2.1.3. Narrative Sequence
The third main criterion Darr suggests for character-building is paying attention to the narrative sequence, the unfolding of the narrative plot – reading from left to right, as it were. Darr notes that *characters are cumulative.* That is, characters are successively constructed and assessed throughout the reading of a text.[131] This requires the recognition that characters are unfolded with the sequence of the narrative (from beginning to middle to end), and attempting to construct a character based on a reversed reading (from back to front) will result in distortion.[132] Therefore, it would be too simplistic and inadequate to simply state that Peter is a wholly positive character in light of his role in the Jerusalem section of Acts (1–5). On the one hand, Peter is a complex character evolving, with a shift in disposition between Luke and Acts.[133] The Gospel itself prepares the reader for this shift with Peter's role in witnessing the empty tomb (Luke 24.12) and the mention of the appearance of the risen Lord to Simon (Peter) (24.34). On the other hand, there is a

---

130. Tannehill, *Narrative Unity*, 2:68–71; idem, 'Composition'.
131. We recall that Luke and Acts would have most likely been performed orally in the ancient world. See William D. Shiell, *Reading Acts: The Lector and the Early Christian Audience* (BIS 70; Leiden: Brill, 2004); Bridget G. Upton, *Hearing Mark's Endings: Listening to Ancient Popular Texts Through Speech Act Theory* (BIS 79; Leiden: Brill, 2006); Harry Y. Gamble, *Books and Readers in the Early Church: A History of Early Christian Texts* (New Haven: Yale University Press, 1995), esp. 203–41, 321–34.
132. Darr (*Character Building*, 74) warns, 'If one ignores the constraints of narrative order, one can (re)make a character almost at will.'
133. See the comments about character development in classical literature, with reference to Plutarch's *Lives*, by Christopher Gill, 'The Question of Character-Development: Plutarch and Tacitus', *CQ* n.s. 33 (1983), 472–80.

consistency to Peter's character, in his strong will and vocal manner. From the beginning Peter is outspoken in his reluctance to alter his habits (5.5), and this same disposition exerts itself when Peter is given the vision of the unclean animals (Acts 10.9-16). The heavenly voice commands Peter, 'Arise, Peter, sacrifice and eat' (10.13). Peter responds with an ironic contradiction, 'By no means, Lord (κύριε)[!]. For, I have never eaten anything profane or unclean' (10.14). There is also a transformation that takes place. When Peter experiences trials in the Gospel, he denies Jesus. In Acts, he denies himself (cf. Luke 9.22-24) as he experiences trials with determined resolve and persecution with celebration that he can be counted worthy to suffer for Jesus' Name (Acts 5.41).

7.2.1.4. Socio-Cultural Literacy

The final criterion for character building involves the role of the extra-textual repertoire necessary to make sense out of the narrative.[134] Darr writes, 'Suffice it to say that an awareness of both Hellenistic literary conventions (character types and typical situations) and intertextual connections between Luke-Acts and the LXX is necessary for a complete interpretation of characters in Luke-Acts.'[135] As this was the focus of §§4–6 above, it is not necessary to repeat that investigation here. It is sufficient to recall that the characterization of Jesus and Peter includes primarily the fusion between the prophetic and messianic types and that the authority of the Prophet-King, Jesus, is transferred to the apostles through the type-scenes of prophetic succession and commission (Luke 24.48-51; Acts 1.4-8). The disciples themselves are anointed with the Holy Spirit, sent by the risen-exalted Lord (Acts 2.1-4, 33-36). The apostles operate with the Spirit-enabled ability to perform 'signs and wonders' (Acts 2.43; 5.12). Peter confronts the miscreant couple for transgressing the (e)utopian ethos of the eschatological community-of-goods. Such socio-cultural norms are scripted into the fabric of the narrative world of Luke-Acts.[136]

It is also important to remember that the primary intertext for Luke-Acts is the (Greek) Scriptures of Israel. Luke makes a concerted effort to root his

---

134. Darr, *Character Building*, 48–9; idem, *Herod*, 89–91, 92–136 (where he argues that literary pattern of the Philosopher and Tyrant governs the portrayal of the encounters between Jesus and Herod).

135. Darr, *Herod*, 89.

136. James Garvey ('Characterization in Narrative', *Poetics* 7 [1978]: 75) argues for four implicational norms that appear at the textual level: (1) *logical*: deductions made in accordance with reasonable inference (Peter has a mother-in-law; therefore Peter is married), (2) *cultural*: norms specific to certain cultural contexts (in Jewish culture, eating pork makes one unclean), (3) *generic*: norms explained by reference to certain forms or genres (supra-sensual knowledge indicates prophetic endowment in Jewish culture, Luke 22.7-13, 34, 61; Acts 5.3, 9), and (4) *co-textual*: conclusions drawn from the inner-logic of a text ('woe to the one who betrays the Son of Man, and Judas betrays Jesus' implies woe to Judas). See Gowler, *Host*, 61–2; Shepherd, *Narrative Function*, 79.

narrative in the continuing story of Israel and Israel's God.[137] Therefore, it is crucial to recognize that the model reader of Luke-Acts will be one with a carefully attuned ear to the scripts and norms projected from the narrative world of the Scriptures of Israel.

7.2.1.5. Summary for Peter's Characterization
In this section I offered a grid for understanding the process of character-building with a concrete illustration of the characterizing data giving rise to the representation of Peter. Through direct description, the narrator portrays Peter in Acts as one 'filled with the Spirit'. More significantly, through indirect presentation, Peter's complex character emerges as one who speaks with divine authorization and acts with Spirit-enabled 'signs and wonders'. Peter's perspective throughout the Jerusalem section in Acts (1–5) is identical with the narrator's perspective and the divine perspective. The narrator even uses Peter's speeches to interpret key events. From the beginning of Luke's Gospel, through the Jerusalem section in Acts, the reader encounters a character who is both developing into a faithful apostle-witness, and who is transformed by his commission from the risen Christ. By the time Peter encounters Ananias and Sapphira, who threaten the community under his charge (as the representative of the apostles), he is authorized to speak on behalf of God with divine legitimation and authority. The model reader will recognize that the messianic and prophetic types have derivatively shaped the characters of the apostles, so that when Peter speaks and acts publicly, before the people of Jerusalem and their leaders, or in the privacy of the Christian communal fellowship, he does so as an apostle-prophet, 'with great power [...] giving witness to the resurrection of the Lord Jesus' (Acts 4.33). To get a fuller picture of the dynamics in the encounter between Peter and Ananias and Sapphira, it is necessary to examine the ways in which they are characterized in this brief episode. The final chapter of the body of this study will continue the examination of characterization with Judas, and subsequently with the aberrant couple. This allows the conclusion of the application of Speech-Act Theory to the passage, examining the successful execution of the oracle of divine judgement.

137. See Green, 'Problem of a Beginning'; idem, *Luke*, 51–8; Litwak, *Echoes*, 66–115.

Chapter 8

SUCCESSFUL EXECUTION: ANANIAS AND SAPPHIRA UNDER THE SPEECH-ACT OF DIVINE JUDGEMENT

This final chapter brings together all the strands of the various contexts that set the discursive framing for the Ananias and Sapphira episode. Here, I argue that the apostolic-prophetic speech-act of indictment and condemnation was successfully executed by Peter, and divinely sanctioned to bring about the intended effect. In §§4–5, the case was made that the Ananias and Sapphira episode is located in community-of-goods discourse, and therefore the expectations of severe disciplinary practices frame the account. In §6 there was an argument for a socio-literary repertoire that would have undergirded performative prophetic speech in Luke-Acts. In §7 there was a description of the Lukan strategy designed to guide the auditor in recognizing the conventions of legitimation and authorization. It has been argued that Luke-Acts consistently offers cues for the model audience to build the persona of Peter as one who emerges with apostolic-prophetic authority able to speak on behalf of God, which includes, in at least one instance, the authority to condemn a nefarious couple to their death. This final chapter continues with an exploration of the characterization of those apostates condemned to die as a consequence of divine displeasure. Part of the characterization of Ananias and Sapphira comes from the couple's indirect association with the characterization of Judas (cf. §7.2.1.2.3. above), a polarizing instrument of Satan. Therefore, it is essential to understand the characterization of Judas in order to understand the full impact of the encounter between the apostle-prophet Peter and the iniquitous duo.

8.1. *The Characterization of those Condemned to Die*

8.1.1. *Judas the Betrayer*

The Lukan characterization of Judas presents a despicable character who experiences a gruesome death as a 'fitting end' for his treacherous betrayal of the Son of Man. Judas' character emerges from the shadows of the collective identity of the disciples, and the Twelve, to reveal an enemy within the ranks of Jesus' elect apostles. His hideous death exposes his apostasy as deserving divine punishment, as presented from the point of view of the narrator.

The narrator of Luke's Gospel offers the first crucial piece of data through direct description of the character of Judas in the list of the Twelve apostles: 'Judas Iscariot, who became a traitor (προδότης)' (Luke 6.16b).[1] Therefore, from this introduction of Judas he is labelled a traitor, one who defected from the community of Jesus' closest followers. The next mention of Judas is found in Luke 22.3, where it is said of him that 'Satan entered into Judas, who was called Iscariot, being of the number of the Twelve.' Here Judas is completely aligned with the diabolical opposition to Jesus and his ministry of the kingdom of God which began during Jesus' time of πειρασμός in the wilderness (Luke 4.1-13). Judas' betrayal begins with agreement with the chief priests and officers how he might 'hand over' (πῶς... παραδῷ) Jesus to them. Judas, having given them reason to be glad (ἐχάρησαν), agrees to accept money and consents to their plan, and begins to seek an opportune time (ἐζήτει εὐκαιρίαν) so that he might hand Jesus over apart from the crowds (22.6).

Further developments in Judas' character are made primarily through two reliable characters who provide crucial clues to Judas' characterization in Luke-Acts: Jesus and Peter. Twice, Jesus confirms the narrator's direct description of Judas. First, Jesus indirectly refers to Judas as the one who will betray him: 'Behold, the hand of the one betraying me is with me on the table' (Luke 22.21; cf. 6.16b).[2] The narrator has already identified Judas as the betrayer, so there is no question who is intended at this point in the narrative.[3] Furthermore, Jesus indicates the condemnation of this betrayer with a prophetic cry of 'woe' (22.22) indicating only sorrow and divine judgement lay ahead for such a one who does not alter his course.[4] Second, Jesus identifies Judas through an accusing question when he confronts Judas at the time of his arrest. The narrator makes it explicit that Judas was one of the Twelve and that he was leading the multitude coming to arrest Jesus (22.47). Judas approaches Jesus to kiss him, and Jesus responds, 'Judas, are you betraying (παραδίδως) the Son of Man with a kiss?' (22.48). Jesus' rhetorical question condemns Judas as one who is most despicable, betraying with a gesture of intimacy.[5]

---

1. On προδότης see Arie W. Zwiep, *Judas and the Choice of Matthias* (WUNT 2.187; Tübingen: Mohr Siebeck, 2004), 48, n. 58 (and literature cited there), 68–72, 139. The parallel with Menelaus in 2 Macc. 4–5 is particularly interesting because he is said to have stolen (νοσφισάμενος) some of the sacred vessels of the Temple at an opportune time (καιρὸν εὐφυῆ) (2 Macc. 4.32), and he is labelled a traitor (προδότην γεγονότα), becoming allied with Antiochus Epiphanes (2 Macc. 5.15-16)!
2. Johnson (*Luke*, 340) asserts that the biblical sense of 'hand' as 'power' indicates that Luke's statement does not require Judas' physical presence at the table, but may 'simply indicate how the fact of the betrayal overshadows the meal'. Compare the similar reference to Ananias's 'authority' (ἐξουσία) over the profit from selling his property before he submitted it to the apostles (Acts 5.4b) and the argument made by Brian Capper ('«In der hand des Ananias...» Erwagungen zu 1 QS VI, 20 und der Urchristlichen Gutergemeinschaft', *RevQ* 12 [1986], 223–36) to the effect that ἐν τῇ σῇ ἐξουσίᾳ is a technical accounting term equal to בידך in the *Community Rule*.
3. *Contra* Nolland, *Luke*, 3:1060.
4. See Bock, *Luke*, 1:583, 2:1734; Johnson, *Luke*, 108; Nolland, *Luke*, 1:287.
5. Note 2 Kgdms 15.5-6; 20.9-10; Prov. 27.6. See Zwiep, *Judas*, 69–70.

The description of Judas in Acts 1.15-26 comes through the voices of both the narrator and Peter. In fact, when Scripture is employed to frame Judas' treachery, it is unclear whether it is the narrator or Peter who speaks.[6] Ideologically, this is inconsequential, for Peter speaks here to represent the perspective of the narrator. After Jesus had ascended, the eyewitnesses return to Jerusalem and enter the upper room, joining a remnant of the Jesus-movement numbered at about (ὡσεί) one hundred and twenty.[7] With the community displaying a continual disposition of prayer (1.14), Peter stands up in the midst of them and speaks about the defection of Judas and the need for a replacement in terms of the divine necessity (ἔδει, 1.16; δεῖ, 1.22). Peter basically reiterates what is already known about Judas. Peter says that he became a leader / guide (γενομένου ὁδηγοῦ) to those who arrested Jesus. This comports with what the narrator said about Judas in Luke 22.47, where Judas is preceding (προήρχετο) the crowd. Peter also reiterates that Judas was 'counted among us (κατηριθμημένος ἦν ἐν ἡμῖν) and received his portion (ἔλαχεν τὸν κλῆρον) in this ministry' (Acts 1.17; 1.25). This corresponds with the narrator's emphasis upon Judas' place among the Twelve (Luke 22.3, 47). His place among the Twelve is further stressed through the prayer of the community for the Lord to reveal which one of the men God had chosen to occupy 'this ministry and apostleship from which Judas turned aside to go to his own place' (1.25). Thus, having firmly established Judas' place among the Twelve, his turning aside (παρέβη, 1.25; cf. ἀπελθὼν in Luke 22.4) indicates that he has defected in following the way of the Messiah and potentially threatened the integrity of the kingdom conferred upon the apostles by Jesus (Luke 22.28-30).

The narrator describes the horrific end of Judas in vivid terms (Acts 1.18-19). First, the narrator exposes the depth of Judas' crime: with the reward for his wickedness (μισθοῦ τῆς ἀδικίας) he purchased a field (ἐκτήσατο χωρίον). Then, the narrator describes how, 'falling headlong, he burst open in the middle and all his entrails gushed out' (1.18b). Next, there is an etiological explanation for the name of the field, Hakeldama, being translated from the Aramaic as 'Field of Blood' (1.19). It is these two verses that sum up the character of Judas and his significance in Luke-Acts: Judas is an apostate whose life is terminated by divine retribution.

Luke's symbolic use of possessions betrays the heinous disposition of Judas. Johnson summarizes this perspective in his published dissertation,

---

6. Peter begins his speech in verse 16, but he is interrupted by the narrator in verse 18 with a narrative aside to bring the audience up to speed on the events to which Peter refers. The narrative aside covers at least through verse 19. Thus, it is difficult to say whether or not Peter's speech picks up at verse 20 or verse 21. For the language of narrative aside, see Sheeley, *Narrative Asides*. See Zwiep, *Judas*, 150–1.

7. Many scholars suggest a symbolic value for the number 120. For those who see symbolic significance, see, for example, Johnson, *Acts*, 34; Kee, *Every Nation*, 40; Talbert, *Reading Acts*, 30; Zwiep, *Judas*, 133. For an opposing view, see Bruce, *Acts*, 44 n. 66; Fitzmyer, *Acts*, 222.

> There is no mention of suicide here [cf. Matt 27.3-10]; rather his [Judas'] death appears as a divine punishment, executed, ironically, on the property he had bought for himself.[...] Judas' apostasy from the Twelve is expressed by the buying of a field, his perdition is expressed by the emptiness of that field, and that empty property in turn expresses the vacancy of the apostolic office which can now be assumed by another.[8]

Judas' action of purchasing a field, as an act of acquisition, is in direct contradiction to the way of discipleship (Luke 18.28-30) and the ethos of the Spirit-filled community in Acts (2.44-45; 4.32, 34-37). In Luke-Acts, in contrast to Matthew (27.3-10), Judas displays no remorse for his crime. He simply indulges in the reward for his wickedness by purchasing land.

The auditors of Acts would have immediately recognized Judas' death as divine retribution informed by the cultural repertoire of divine retribution.[9] As with Ananias and Sapphira, the 'mysterious' death of Judas as divine punishment is inferred from the fact that there is no direct agency attributed as the cause of the death, and from a widely current literary *topos* on the 'fitting end', or the death of the wicked as punishment.[10]

The Scripture citations employed to frame the events of Judas' betrayal and death come from the Psalms (of David). Peter declares that 'the Scripture (τὴν γραφήν) had to be fulfilled...' (1.16). In fact, the Scripture cited comes from two psalms, 68.26 LXX and 108.8b LXX.[11] The first part of the quotation states, 'Let his (αὐτοῦ) homestead be made desolate (ἔρημος),[12] and let no

---

8. Johnson, *Literary Function*, 180, 181. Cf. Brawley, *Text to Text*, 62, 63 (with the order of the text revised slightly): 'Voices of scripture interpret the death of Judas – implicitly his construct of world – as a bleak absurdity. Judas buys a field for a homestead, but inside and outside invert, habitation becomes uninhabitable, livable becomes unlivable. Judas bursts open and his bowels gush out.[...] With the demise of Judas, the homestead becomes an oxymoron.[...] The grotesque evisceration diminishes Judas to a bloody pile of the organs that produce feces – absurd.'

For a comparison of the tradition(s) of the death of Judas in Matthew and Acts, see Pierre Benoit, 'The Death of Judas', in *Jesus and the Gospel* (2 vols; trans. Benet Weatherhead; London: Darton, Longman & Todd, 1973-74), 2:189-207; William Klassen, *Judas: Betrayer or Friend of Jesus?* (London: SCM Press, 1996), 160-76; Zwiep, *Judas*, 104-8.

9. See Zwiep, *Judas*, 76, 'For Luke, the death of Judas is not an accident or a tragic mishap – although strictly speaking this is not excluded by the words of the text – but an act of divine punishment.'

10. See §5.1.4 above. For examples of death as divine punishment see Zwiep, *Judas*, 63-72, 147-9; van der Horst, 'Hellenistic Parallels 1 1-26', 24-5. Note the extensive discussion in G. W. Trompf, *Early Christian Historiography: Narratives of Retributive Justice* (London: Continuum, 2000), 10-106, and Rick van de Water, 'The Punishment of the Wicked Priest and the Death of Judas', *DSD* 10 (2003): 395-419.

11. See Gert J. Steyn, *Septuagint Quotations in the Context of the Petrine and Pauline Speeches of the Acta Apostolorum* (CBET 12; Kampen: Kok Pharos, 1995), 43-62; Zwiep, *Judas*, 91-4, 150-4.

12. Ps. 68.26 LXX reads, 'Let *their* (αυτῶν) habitation be made desolate (ἠρημωμένη, perfect participle).

man dwell in it',[13] indicating that the divine retribution is in fact framed by the Scriptures. Moessner, looking to the broader context of the psalm, writes,

> Peter [...] appears to be looking back and describing the 'things that have happened' (Lk. 24.18) in terms of a plot found in Scripture. Judas is identified in the 'script' as a persecutor of a (God's) righteous, suffering servant (cf. the offering of 'vinegar' [ὄξος] as part of the *suffering* [emphasis his], Ps. 68.21 and Lk. 23.36).[14]

Brawley considers the alterations to the text by Peter as justified, both because of the post-resurrection vantage point of reading (cf. Luke 24),[15] and because of the representative nature of both Jesus and Judas with regard to the psalm. He writes,

> The psalm has two facets, suffering and oppression, and the two facets reflect Jesus as well as Judas.[...] As Judas is a singular case of the opposition reflected in the plural in the psalm, so also Jesus, like the psalmist, is a particular servant (*pais*) [Ps. 68.17] among God's servants (*douloi*) also reflected in the plural (Ps 68:37).[16]

Just as Jesus represents a corporate identity of God's servants, so Judas is one who represents a larger group, those who persecuted and opposed God's servant(s). Therefore, with Moessner and Brawley, one can affirm that the broader context of the psalm is invoked, indicating that, for Luke, the Scriptures offered a paradigm for understanding the recent events. This both justifies Jesus' choice of Judas as an apostle and offers assurance to the reader that Judas' defection was not something that derailed the plan of God.

The other part of Peter's (the narrator's?) appeal to Scripture comes from Psalm 108.8 LXX, 'his office of overseer (ἐπισκοπή), let[17] another take'. In the recontextualization of the psalm, this is an imprecatory request, indicating that the quotation refers primarily to Judas' death, and secondarily to the replacement by Matthias.[18] Judas' action appeared to have threatened the assurance of God's salvific action through the Messiah, and the integrity of the kingdom conferred upon the apostles by Jesus (Luke 22.28-30). However, Peter explains that this very thing – Judas' defection – was not only anticipated, but necessitated as a crucial aspect of the divine drama as projected by the 'script' of the Scriptures.[19]

---

13. The phrase from Ps. 68.26 LXX, ἐν τοῖς σκηνώμασιν αὐτῶν, appears to have been shortened to ἐν αὐτῇ in Acts 1.20, effecting a change in focus from the house of Judah to the land, making it more applicable to the situation of Judas.
14. Moessner, 'The "Script"', 223.
15. Brawley, *Text to Text*, 65.
16. Brawley, *Text to Text*, 67.
17. The LXX has the optative, λάβοι, whereas Acts has the imperative, λαβέτω. This comports with the recasting in light of the divine δεῖ.
18. So Brawley, *Text to Text*, 70.
19. See the complex logic of Moessner, 'The "Script"', 224, encompassing the identity of the apostles as 'witnesses to his resurrection'.

The final note on Judas is a comparison of his defection with the other apostles' perseverance (Acts 1.22-25). Therefore, Judas' portion (κλῆρος, 1.17) becomes the lot (κλῆρος, 1.26) that falls on Matthias. Whereas Judas had been counted among (κατηριθμημένος) the apostles, now Matthias becomes numbered (συγκατεψηφίσθη) with the Eleven (1.26). The discourse of Judas' punishment is absorbed into a discourse on the replacement of Judas and the reconstitution of the Twelve as a prerequisite for the outpouring of the Spirit at Pentecost.

Judas' character is primarily built from the raw data of direct description. There is no ambiguity to the evaluation concerning Judas in the Lukan narrative. Judas never speaks in direct language. Yet, there are significant insights to be gleaned from the inferences from other character indicators. Judas' actions are indicated by a number of verbs. Luke uses spatial images symbolically. Most effective are Judas' relationships and associations. I will draw out more explicitly these elements from the summary of Judas' description above.

Judas' primary action is his betrayal (παραδίδωμι) of Jesus (Luke 22.4, 6, 21, 48; cf. 6.16b). He does this for money (ἀργύριον), which the narrator refers to as his μισθός τῆς ἀδικίας (Acts 1.18) which he uses to buy a field (χωρίον). Thus his primary identifying action is derived from his primary identifying relationship: Judas betrays the Son of Man. As a result of this action, in anticipation of it, Jesus pronounces upon him the surety of the divine retribution he subsequently experiences. Jesus declares the inevitability of the betrayal of the Son of Man (Luke 22.21-22), 'but woe to that man by whom he is betrayed!' (22.22b).

Furthermore, Judas' action of entering into agreement with the enemies of Jesus causes him to form an alliance which makes him an enemy of God. When the narrator says of Judas that he consented (ἐξωμολόγησεν) and acts in accordance with the scheming of the chief priests and scribes by seeking an opportune time to hand Jesus over to them apart from the people, this stands in stark contrast to Luke's use of this term and its cognates elsewhere.[20] In Luke 10.21, the term is on Jesus' lips as an adulation to God as he rejoices in the Holy Spirit at the results of the returning of the seventy-(two): 'I praise you (ἐξομολογοῦμαί σοι), O Father...'[21] The verb ὁμολογέω is used in Luke 12.8 where Jesus declares, 'Whoever confesses (ὁμολογήσῃ) me before others, the Son of Man will confess (ὁμολογήσει) him also before the angels of God.' Particularly in light of this last usage-association, Judas' action of agreeing (ἐξομολογέω) to participate in the scheme of the enemies of Jesus demonstrates the heinousness of his character.[22] Judas enters into (verbal)

20. Note Klassen, *Judas*, 121.
21. See also how Mary 'was giving thanks (ἀνθωμολογεῖτο) to God' in Luke 2.38.
22. Brown (*Apostasy*, 85) labels Judas' agreement as 'blasphemous'. In terms of a speech-act, we see that Judas has aligned himself through verbal commitment with the enemy. Elsewhere in Luke-Acts (ἐξ)ὁμολογέω indicates verbal action. See Acts 7.17 (God's promise spoken to Abraham); 19.18 (referring to the confession of the converted Ephesians); 23.8 (concerning the Pharisees' confession of resurrection, angels and spirits); and 24.14 (Paul confesses to Felix his association with the Way).

agreement with the opposition to God's Messiah, and therefore God.[23] Judas takes the enemies of Jesus beyond their impasse to have him executed. *Judas actually becomes the key to fulfilling the diabolical schemes.*[24]

Another crucial character indicator for building Judas' character is Luke's metaphorical use of Judas' environments and spatial movements. Two verbs indicate Judas' defection, one at the beginning of the scheme to execute Jesus (ἀπελθών, Luke 22.4) and the other being at the end of the pericope explaining the death of Judas and his replacement by Matthias (παρέβη...πορευθῆναι, Acts 1.25). Brown focuses on Luke's theological journey motif as a metaphor for discipleship to contrast Judas's 'crooked' departure from the fold of Jesus' followers. Brown writes,

> In view of the theological pregnancy in Luke's use of the spatial image [of discipleship as journey] it is fair to assume that Judas' 'departure' (Lk 22,4: ἀπελθών) from Jesus has a significance that is scarcely possessed in Mark (14,10)...*Judas' unauthorized departure from Jesus has as its consequences his passing over to the side of Jesus' enemies*, the chief priests and officers; it represents a definitive rupture of the bond of discipleship. Judas' downfall occurs at this point. His death is divine punishment for his apostasy (Acts 1, 18) and not a despairing rejection of divine mercy (cf. Mt 27, 3-5).[25]

Judas' separation from the followers of Jesus happens in his movement toward the chief priests and the officers.

When the community prays for God to reveal the chosen replacement for Judas, the ministry of apostleship is defined as that 'from which Judas turned aside to go to his own place' (Acts 1.25). This second verb, παραβαίνω, further indicates the separation of Judas from Jesus and the community of discipleship. Judas turned away from his privileged election as one of the Twelve, those to whom Jesus conferred (διατίθεμαι, Luke 22.29) his own kingdom, with an eschatological place to rule Israel.

One of the most important character indicators is a character's relationships and associations. Most importantly regarding Judas' relationships, he is aligned with Satan and with the enemies of Jesus who plot to have him killed. Judas' action of betrayal is so diabolical that the narrator says that Satan and Judas become one in action and intent: Satan entered *into* Judas (Luke 22.3, Εἰσῆλθεν δὲ σατανᾶς εἰς Ἰούδαν).[26] This means that Judas' seeking for an opportune time (εὐκαιρίας) should remind the reader of the devil's departure after the temptation until an appropriate time (χαιρός).[27] Furthermore, Judas

---

23. Klassen (*Judas*, 120-2) suggests that the term indicates Judas was filing a formal complaint against Jesus.
24. Note Brown, *Apostasy*, 92-3. 'Judas is the "brain" whose cool planning frees Jesus' enemies from their embarrassment and impotence' (93).
25. Brown, *Apostasy*, 82, emphasis added.
26. Green (*Luke*, 753-4) notes that this phrase refers more to evil dominion over disposition rather than spatial corruption with illustration from 1QS 3.20-24.
27. Green, *Luke*, 753. See the description of the criminal Menelaus in 2 Macc. 4-5, above n. 1.

is depicted as taking on the disposition of the chief priests and scribes in plotting for an opportune time *away from the crowds*, who might intervene on Jesus' behalf (Luke 22.2, 6).[28] Here, Judas makes a full swing in opposition to the narrator's theological and ideological perspective on how to relate Jesus to the crowds. Judas joins the chief priests and scribes in their seeking (ζητέω, 22.2, 6) for an opportune time to separate Jesus in order to put him to death. This means also that when Jesus speaks to the crowd that has come to arrest him saying, 'This is yours, the hour and the power of darkness' (22.53b), he includes Judas. Therefore, Judas is separated from Jesus both spatially (Luke 22.4, ἀπελθών; cf. Acts 1.25, παρέβη Ἰούδας πορευθῆναι εἰς τὸν τόπον τὸν ἴδιον) and temporally (Luke 22.6, εὐκαιρίας; 22.53b, αὕτη ἐστὶν ὑμῶν ἡ ὥρα).[29]

More pertinently, Judas was the 'leader' or 'guide' (ὁδηγός) of those who arrested Jesus (Acts 1.16; cf. Luke 22.47, ἰδοὺ ὄχλος...προήρχετο αὐτούς). Brawley insightfully notes how Judas, as the leader of those who arrested Jesus, *renews the polarizing opposition to Jesus and his Way*. Judas 'becomes the paradigm for Jews who separate from the community judged by the reconstituted twelve and who go their own way'.[30] With Brown, viewing Judas through the theological metaphor of 'the Way', we can say that Judas is a sort of antithesis to John the Baptist, paving the way that runs in opposition to 'the Way of the Lord' (Luke 1.76; 3.4; Isa. 40.3) at the beginning of Luke's second book.

Finally, Judas is contrasted with the faithful disciples. It was already mentioned in the discussion of Peter how Judas is contrasted with Peter, the former being one who has no future (Luke 22.22b) except to remain in infamous memory, whereas Peter is commissioned to strengthen his brothers after he has returned (22.32) and his faith did not fail on account of Jesus' intercession. Furthermore, Judas goes 'to his own place' (Acts 1.25). While this action stands in contrast to the consistency of the other apostles who accompanied Jesus, as 'he went in and out among them' (1.21), there are various interpretations of the phrase 'his own place'. Zwiep suggests five interpretations, including the going to his own field, which symbolizes his apostasy, and prefers the option that the phrase ἴδιος τόπος 'is a euphemism for his postmortem state, in Luke's view γέεννα'.[31] The direction of Judas' separation from his apostleship due to his betrayal and financial indulgence further contrasts him with the faithful disciples. While the others have left τὰ ἴδια (Luke 18.28), Judas has purchased a field with blood money. While Peter and John return to their own (Acts 4.23, ἦλθον πρὸς τοὺς ἰδίους) after being released from the inquisition of the Sanhedrin, Judas can only 'go to his own

28. Johnson, *Luke*, 332.
29. Klassen (*Judas*, 119, 123, 124) stresses that Luke does not actually depict the kiss.
30. Brawley, *Centering*, 92. Cf. idem, *Text to Text*, 67, with reference to the fuller context to Psalm 68 LXX. See §2.3.4. above.
31. Zwiep, *Judas*, 166-8, quote from 167. Luke's use of γέεννα in Luke 12.5 makes this a viable option in Luke's cosmology.

place' (τὸν τόπον τὸν ἴδιον), his solitary and shameful death, fitting for one who makes war with God.

This concludes the characterization of Judas, which is deemed important for the present study due to Judas' role in Acts as a paradigm for opposition to God and God's Messiah, as well as one who exemplifies the fate of those who make war with God (Acts 5.39) and die as a result of divine punishment. Moreover, Judas is an example of defective discipleship, having purchased a field (χωρίον) with the reward for his wickedness. In this way, Luke signals to his audience a rhetorically powerful illustration by which to understand both the obedient submission of the early Christian community-living with shared goods, so that 'all who were owners of lands (χωρίων) or houses would sell them and bring the proceeds of the sale and lay them at the apostles' feet' (Acts 4.34-35), for which Barnabas is a positive example (4.37), and the deviant couple is the negative example (5.3, 8, χωρίον). Also in this way, Luke signals that Ananias and Sapphira have an oscillating disposition, partly fulfilling the community ethos of shared goods, but also holding back some of the price of their transaction for selfish gains. It is necessary to fill out the details of the characterization of Ananias and Sapphira in what follows.

8.1.2. Ananias and Sapphira and Divine Displeasure

All of the conditions of the apostolic-prophetic speech-act of divine judgement were satisfied, and therefore Peter's utterances successfully executed the divine condemnation upon Ananias and Sapphira. Luke offers the boundaries for the entire speech-act in his narrative, showing that Peter's action in confronting the couple was accomplished from the position of an apostolic-prophetic successor to the Prophet-King, Jesus. This confrontation takes place in the context of an eschatological community of shared goods, and as a dynamic encounter between a leader of this messianic community and a couple who threaten the Spirit-empowered practice of (e)utopian sharing, which is a response to the presence of the Holy Spirit in their midst and a manifestation of the nascent community's witness to the saving implications of the resurrection of Jesus Christ (Act 4.33). What follows will be a verse-by-verse exploration of Acts 4.32–5.11 to demonstrate the contribution Speech-Act Theory has made to the illumination of the Ananias and Sapphira episode. It will be helpful to recall that this summary of the early messianic community-of-goods (as with the initial summary in Acts 2.41-47) follows the action of the Holy Spirit filling the place where the community is located (4.31), and therefore, the social ethos is presented as a direct consequence of the Holy Spirit's presence.

4.32 – The summary begins by identifying the group as those who were 'believers' (τοῦ...πλήθους τῶν πιστευσάντων; cf. 2.44), and the most remarkable characteristic of this group is their unity 'in heart and mind' (ἦν καρδία καὶ ψυχὴ μία). It was argued above (§§4–5) that this language (along with what immediately follows) would have recalled the social-utopian ideals of the Hellenistic mind.

The 'Western text' (D) adds a negative clause, 'and there was no distinction among them',[32] to stress the harmonious kinship-type relations within the messianic community. This clause emphasizes the unity, but it does not add anything significant to the picture of the community's action of sharing common goods. This poetical composition stresses the balance of a common unity coupled with the absence of division.

This unity, illustrated by the communal sharing, would have tapped into a socio-literary convention of representing communities whose relationships would have been symbolically defined by a general reciprocity. In the current instance of the messianic community, 'no one claimed private ownership of any possessions, but rather all things were common among them' (οὐδὲ εἷς τι τῶν ὑπαρχόντων αὐτῷ ἔλεγεν ἴδιον εἶναι ἀλλ' ἦν αὐτοῖς ἅπαντα κοινά). This language would have evoked 'friendship' ideals among Greco-Roman auditors,[33] and it is all the more striking that Luke stresses the unity based in the common faith as 'believers'.[34]

4.33 – Bridging the gap between the initial description of the community-of-goods and the one in the following verse, Luke describes the central role of the apostolic witness, defined by 'great power' (δύναμις μεγάλη). Located here in the summary, the apostolic witness (1.8, 22) again roots the communal ethos and its practice of shared goods in the Spirit-empowered mission.

The Ananias and Sapphira episode is surrounded by two summaries, one concerning the community of shared goods (4.32-35), and the other concerned with the 'signs and wonders' performed by the apostles (5.12-16). Both incidents of the episode, that with the husband and that with the wife, conclude with the reaction among the populace (5.5, 11). Marguerat was correct to note how both summaries frame the episode to indicate how it functioned in Luke's focus on the mission of the ἐκκλησία.[35] The mention of the apostolic witness precisely to the resurrection of Jesus Christ serves to emphasize the role of this community and its ethos within the divine economy[36] and how this has been initiated by the raising of God's Messiah.[37]

This missiological focus is internally rooted in the central role of the apostolic witness, which is coupled with 'great (divine) favour' (χάρις μεγάλη). The divine χάρις mentioned here is probably to be distinguished from the high esteem with which the populace considered the messianic community in the first communal summary (2.47).[38] The community enjoys the favour of God, who approves of both the community's practice of the 'divine economy' and the apostolic leadership who superintend the caring of needs by distributing

32. καὶ οὐκ ἦν διάκρισις ἐν αὐτοῖς οὐδεμία.
33. See §4.2 above.
34. Dupont, 'Community of Goods', 95-6.
35. Marguerat, 'Ananias and Sapphira', 163; idem, 'La mort', 216.
36. See §4 above.
37. See §§7.1.2.–7.1.3. above.
38. With Barrett, *Acts*, 1:254; *pace* Rius-Camps and Read-Heimderdinger, *Message*, 1:286.

the proceeds as each has need (4.35). The way of life of this community would have appealed to divine favour and popular human esteem alike.

4.34-35 – 'For there was not a needy person among them.' The γάρ here indicates a correlating explanation. It could be explicative of the χάρις μεγάλη, or of the previous statements about the unity, practice of sharing and divine favour generally. This clause indicates the composition of the messianic community, and this characterization is described as a result of (γάρ) the manner in which many of the community who owned property (κτήτορες),[39] both 'lands' (χωρία) or 'houses' (οἰκίαι), were selling them (πωλοῦντες) and were bringing (ἔφερον) the value (τιμή) of the things being sold (πιπρασκομένων) and they were placing it (ἐτίθουν) at the apostles' feet. The imperfect tenses indicate that these actions were not a spontaneous, one-time event, but rather a regular practice in the early Jerusalem community. Furthermore, with the allusion to the language of the jubilary legislation in Deuteronomy 15.4,[40] it was noted above that here Luke's portrait would have appeared as fulfilment of Jewish eschatological hopes.

Several aspects of this verse are noteworthy. First, this verse seems to mitigate a representation of an 'absolute' community of shared goods indicated by verse 32 (cf. 2.44-45). It was noted with the discussion of Taylor above that there were three types of communal sharing in the ancient world: (1) an absolute community-of-goods with formal sharing, (2) sharing private goods made accessible to one's 'friends', and finally, (3) a community welfare fund maintained by voluntary donations.[41] The community did not have even one needy person among them because when need arose, the proceeds of the sale of lands or houses was distributed by the overseeing of the apostolic leadership. Another imperfect verb leads the next clause clarifying how the funds were distributed, 'it was given to each as any had need'.

Second, it is worth pausing to consider what should be included in the 'lands' and 'homes' here. Logically, it would seem that these properties were excess properties, and not the fundamental locations of living, thus causing a vicious cycle of eradicating need in the short term while creating a disastrous need in the long term. In fact, the positive example of Barnabas is presented with aorist verbs indicating the sale of 'a field' (singular, 4.37). However, Luke foregrounds the continuing practice of generosity without clarifying the details in every case of who sold what and how much extra they could have retained.

Third, it is important to notice that the proceeds are brought to the feet of the apostles, a location that links the actions of Barnabas (4.37) and of the miscreant couple (5.2 [10]) together making the boundaries of the pericope a coherent unit. With this attention given to the role of the apostles in the 'divine economy' (this role being absent from the initial summary of communal life in 2.44-45), Luke prepares his audience for the fundamental role that the

---

39. Bruce (*Greek Text*, 160)
40. Deut. 15.4 LXX: οὐκ ἔσται ἐν σοὶ ἐνδεής.
41. See §4.2.2.1. above.

representative of the apostles – Peter – will play in the execution of divine judgement upon Ananias and Sapphira. The constant reference to the apostles indicates that Luke is not focusing on 'a community of equals' without distinction of role or hierarchy. This community is not a democracy. It is, rather, a following of the 'way of the Lord', a people coming together under the representative leadership of the apostolic successors to Jesus, representing his rule and proclaiming the message of his resurrection-exaltation to divine power.

Together, this summary of the community-of-life-and-goods manifest through a community welfare fund maintained by voluntary donations, with the focus on the role of the apostolic nucleus, creates an atmosphere of eschatological fulfilment and holiness of social order. The presence of the Holy Spirit within this messianic community (4.31) is necessarily resulting in a sacred social order of economic harmony and dynamic witness to the acts of God in raising Jesus Christ and restoring Israel.

4.36-37 – Again the authority of the apostles is foregrounded with the introduction of Joseph, 'called Barnabas by the apostles', which is translated as 'son of encouragement' (a role he will fill in the narrative of Acts; see 9.27; 11.23-24). Barnabas is the positive illustration of communal generosity as he is depicted as one who sold a field (ἀγρός),[42] and then as one who brought the money (χρῆμα) and laid it at the apostles' feet. Barnabas models the ethos of the 'divine economy'.

5.1 – The illustration of Ananias and Sapphira is the negative corollary to the generosity of Barnabas. We are introduced to a man, named Ananias, and his wife Sapphira. Like Barnabas, they sell (ἐπώλησεν) a piece of property (κτῆμα; see 2.45, and the cognate κτήωρ in 4.34).

The information supplied to construct the characters of Ananias and Sapphira is sparse, but decisive. Most of the character data comes from the narrator and Peter, with only one quick self-condemning affirmation from the lips of Sapphira. Ananias has no time to speak. The dire perspective of the narrator on these characters is tightly controlled through direct description. The narrative begins with a description of the couple's actions of selling a piece of property or land (κτῆμα, 5.1; χωρίον, 5.3, 8; cf. 1.18), withholding some of the price, and then bringing only part of the proceeds to lay at the feet of the apostles (5.2). This is set in stark contrast to Barnabas (Acts 4.36-37) who sells land and brings the (full) proceeds to lay at the apostles' feet. Peter, having what appears to be charismatic insight into the truth of the transaction,[43] interprets the action of Ananias and Sapphira as lying to the Holy Spirit, and to God (5.3, 4) and as testing the Spirit of the Lord (5.9).

The primary indirect presentation of the couple comes through their approach to the community, Ananias with less than the full proceeds, and

---

42. Codex Bezae has χωρίον here, making the connections with Judas, on the one hand, and with Ananias, on the other hand, more obvious. See Rius-Camps and Read-Heimerdinger, *Message*, 1:293.

43. Johnson (*Acts*, 88) notes that 'the ability to see into the hearts of others is the mark of a prophet (Luke 5:22; 7:39; 9:47; 24:38; *Joseph and Aseneth* 23:8)'.

Sapphira without knowledge of her husband's demise, both with hearts filled by Satan (note the συν- compounds in 5.1, 2, 9). The wife speaks (5.8b), but her words only confirm her complicity in the conspiracy to deceive and test the Spirit of the Lord. Ananias remains in silent infamy. The couple exists primarily as a conspiratorial unity counterfeiting the Spirit-enabled community and its (e)utopian ethos. Part of what constitutes the severity of their crime is their subversive action to create a counter-community through their unified actions of withholding and deceiving. They offer a shadow-mirror image of the communal ethos in the way that Bar-Jesus reflected the opposite of Paul (Acts 13.4-12). Through this couple, Satan had infiltrated the messianists and attempted to set a root of discord. Exposing the potential rupture in the community's unified ethos means protecting and guaranteeing divine favour for Peter and those under his leadership.

5.2 – With his wife's knowledge, Ananias is the subject of three actions, withholding some of the price, and what amounts to mimicking Barnabas' generous action by bringing only part of the proceeds and laying it at the apostles' feet.

The use of the rare verb νοσφίζομαι to designate the couple's crime (Acts 5.2, 3) is telling.[44] Richter Reimer has efficiently collected references to νοσφίζεσθαι in relevant Greco-Roman literature to compare with the use of the word in Acts. Beside the biblical passages, she notes the following uses. Josephus (*Ant.* 4.8.29 [274]) uses the term to interpret Deut. 22.1 (on not being guilty of 'appropriating' the goods of others). Polybius (10.16.6) discusses vows of soldiers not to retain spoils of war for themselves, because the property is common to all. Xenophon (*Cyr.* 4.2.42) discusses a situation similar to Polybius. Diodorus Siculus mentions a particularly stimulating parallel with our passage in Acts. In his ethnography discussing the Celtiberians, Diodorus mentions the neighbouring Vaccaei who have a community-of-goods: 'for any cultivators who have appropriated (νοσφισαμένοις) some part for themselves they have set the penalty as death' (*Hist.* 5.34.3, trans. Oldfather, LCL).[45] Richter Reimer mentions a few other examples and concludes:

> [T]he concept of νοσφίζεσθαι is not used synonymously with κλέπτω, 'steal,' [...] or with ἁρπάζω, 'rob' [...] The actions of 'stealing' and 'robbing' are committed by outsiders who break in, usually with violence. 'Keeping back' or 'pilfering' is something different: it is done by 'insiders,' secretly and without violence.[...] The keeping back occurs only when the property does not belong, or no longer belongs, to oneself. [...T]he action of keeping back is directed against the common property that exists also for my sake, or that belongs to a community of which I am a member. The keeping back injures the community.[46]

---

44. This verb only appears elsewhere in the Greek scriptures at Joshua 7.1 (of Achar), 2 Macc. 4.32 (of Menelaus), and Titus 2.10 ('pilfer').
45. All citations of Diodorus come from *Diodorus of Sicily*, trans. C. H. Oldfather, et al., 12 vols. LCL (Cambridge: Harvard University Press, 1933–1967).
46. Richter Reimer, *Women*, 8–9.

Richter Reimer insists that the offender will have already been aware of the consequences for violating the community he or she participates in from the vows to submit to the community's rules. The verb common to these episodes used in Acts indicates a crime committed against the community, and worse, against the God of that community.

Environmentally, it is crucial to note that this whole scene takes place inside the bounds of the early Christian communal space. Compositionally, the spatial movement in Acts exposes the inner workings of the community beginning with Acts 4.23, which does not pan outside the inner-community space again until 5.11-12. The couple's movement is toward the community, even though they hold back part of their proceeds, and therefore themselves. As with Judas, there is an inner penetration of Satan into their 'hearts' (cf. Luke 22.3). With Ananias and Sapphira, as with Judas, there is an enemy *within* the camp.[47]

With regard to relationships and associations, it has already been noted that the couple is the negative contrast to the positive foil of Barnabas, each episode being an illustration of the community-of-goods. Brown writes, 'Barnabas' donation was in reality what the offering of Ananias and Sapphira pretended to be: an act of total and spontaneous generosity.'[48] The couple goes through the same motions as Barnabas, but their transaction with their land (χωρίον, 5.3, 8; cf. 4.34) is done as a double dealing, one hand reaching out toward the community with a gift while the other hand was pulling back, concealing a portion of the proceeds. In this way, the couple is lexically and dispositionally associated with the transaction of Judas, who purchased a field (χωρίον) with the reward for his wickedness (Acts 1.18). Finally, the couple is a foil to Peter, who executes prophetic judgement upon the community under his apostolic leadership. Peter displays his loyalty to the Messiah and his community by 'giving witness to the resurrection' (4.33) and judging the people of God. The couple displays disloyalty by exhibiting a duality in their engagement of the communal ethos.

5.3 – More can be said of the couple's character based on Peter's accusations. Peter indicts Ananias because Satan has filled his heart 'to lie to the Holy Spirit (ψεύσασθαι [...] τὸ πνεῦμα τὸ ἅγιον; cf. ἐψεύσω ... τῷ θεῷ [5.4]). The verbal construction, infinitive plus accusative, could mean, according to Johnson, 'to falsify'.[49] In this sense, the couple were counterfeiting the Spirit's work, fraudulently mimicking the ethos of the community. More commonly, the infinitive (+ person-thing) is understood in the sense of an attempt to deceive the Holy Spirit, which would make it an exact parallel to the second verbal construction in verse 4, aorist plus dative, indicating that lying to the Holy Spirit is the same as lying to God. Furthermore, this deceit occurs through the 'holding back' (νοσφίσασθαι) some of the price of the land.[50]

47. See Brown, *Apostasy*, 98–114, with comparisons on 106–7.
48. Brown, *Apostasy*, 99.
49. Johnson, *Acts*, 88, 92.
50. Barrett, *Acts*, 1:266.

Next, Peter begins his inquisition, rattling off a series of indicting questions exposing Ananias' fraud and deceit. The first question is a veiled accusation, in a manner of indictment familiar to the prophetic genre. Peter indicts Ananias, but does not overtly speak the form of an explicit condemnation (i.e., 'you will therefore die'). Peter does not voice the impending consequences, and yet, the divine sanction causes his indictment to *count as* a condemnation unto death. The accusing questions remind us of the similar forms encountered in the Scriptures of Israel when the prophetic figure confronted individuals.[51] The fact that Peter does not explicitly articulate the punishment to Ananias makes this episode distinctive, but it does not reduce the performative nature of Peter's language. It certainly does not require that the auditor posit natural consequences for Ananias' death (e.g., shock, overwhelming guilt).

'*Why has Satan filled your heart to lie to the Holy Spirit and to keep back for yourself part of the price of the land?*' This is the question / indictment Peter hurls at Ananias. The question indicates further the role of the Holy Spirit in directing and guiding the ethos of shared goods among the community, for this offence was an attempt to deceive not just the community, but also the God of this community (5.4). Peter's question here is loaded with accusations, including association with the diabolical opposition to the messianic 'way' (as with Judas, Luke 22.3) and violation of the inner-sanctity of the community. The use of the verb νοσφίζεσθαι again indicates that Ananias had pledged his proceeds for the benefit of the wider community fund, and that the personal ownership was therefore relinquished. To hold back was to violate the unity of generosity and corporate benefit. To hold back was to dissociate oneself from the unity 'in heart and mind'.

Furthermore, it was argued above that reference to Satan indicated another level of interaction not immediately apparent to all characters in the story.[52] The temptation narrative in Luke 4.1-13 polarizes all allegiances for either God or Satan. The role of Satan in Luke 4 is similar to that in Acts 5. Satan functions as 'the devil', an adversary who lures God's agents with temptations, as with Peter in Luke 22.31. However, the role of Satan in the narrative world of Luke-Acts is not restricted to temptation of God's elect. Satan is one who 'falls like lightening' as a result of the mission of the seventy(-two) who were casting out demons (Luke 10.18). Satan is the chief of a kingdom, which would be threatened if it was the source of Jesus' own exorcisms (Luke 11.18). Satan is also the one who 'binds' a crippled woman (Luke 13.16) and 'oppresses' some (Acts 10.38). The devil is associated with the Jewish false prophet and magician, Elymas who is 'full of deceit and fraud' and does not cease to make crooked the straight paths of the Lord (Acts 13.10). Finally, Satan is associated with darkness and with a power that is in opposition to God (Acts 26.18).

However, to polarize opposition to Jesus is not to 'demonize' the Jewish people as a whole, who, in large, tend to be opposed to the work of God's

---

51. See §6.1.1. above.
52. See §2.3.4. above.

Messiah and his witnesses.[53] The very fact that Judas and Ananias are 'entered into' by or 'filled' with Satan should serve as a warning to the messianic community that opposition to God's plan or agents does not always arise from without the community. Ananias serves precisely as an indication that, for Luke, the dangerous conflict is not 'Jews versus Christians' but rather 'hearing the word of God and obeying (Luke 11.28) versus disobeying'.

5.4 – Following Peter's initial interrogative accusation is a series of questions indicating the nature of Ananias' crime in the community. These questions imply that Ananias gave his wealth voluntarily (cf. those who came under the obligation of Qumran's *Community Rule*), and when initially pledged the decision could be reversed. However, once given, and what seems to be implied but not explicitly stated, represented as a certain amount of funds, must be completely handed over to the authority and distribution of the community as overseen by the apostolic leadership. Peter's scathing questions here seem to indicate that Ananias misrepresented the amount of the funds, and by so doing he had counterfeited the ethos and unity of corporate generosity.

'*While it remained, did it not remain yours? And after it was sold, was it not still in your authority?*' It seems inescapable that these questions indicate the voluntary nature of the giving. We may recall the insightful 'middle ground' of Capper's reading of this passage, where he sees Ananias, being in the stages between initial conversion and full surrender, has sinned a crime falling 'awkwardly between embezzlement and deception'.[54] With concern to establish the historical veracity of the narrative's representation, Capper helps to make sense out of much of the dynamics of this encounter, and to recreate a plausible context in which this encounter may have taken place (or would have been perceived to have taken place). However, with focus on what is literarily foregrounded, the correlations between the scene in Acts and initiation descriptions and prescription in *The Community Rule* (1QS 6.24-25) must remain tentative, and the distinctives should not be overlooked.

It seems plausible from Peter's questions that there was a stage of probation in the act of pledging and giving with a possibility of withdrawal. However, once the amount is registered and the gift presented, the full amount is required as a means of keeping fidelity and solidarity with the communal obligation.

'*Why did you set this deed in your heart? You did not lie to humans, but to God!*' Peter comes back with one more damning question, and leads into a direct accusation – Ananias has offended God. Here, Peter indicates that even if Satan had filled his heart (5.3), Ananias was not beyond personal guilt, as it was with Judas.

5.5 – '*Hearing these words, Ananias fell down and died.*' Luke establishes three actions in direct relationship. With a present participle (ἀκούων) Luke established a cotemporaneous relationship between the response of Ananias 'breathing his last' (ἐξέψυξεν) and the speaking of Peter ('as he [Ananias] heard these words'). It would seem that from this construction Luke is indicating a

---

53. See §2, n. 1 above on the motif of division within Israel.
54. Capper 'Acts 5.4', 128. See also §4.2.2.1. above for the fuller discussion.

direct relationship between Peter's utterances ('these words') and Ananias' death. This study has been concerned to describe the conditions for which such a performative speech could occur.

Conventions were in place that indicated that prophetic indictment came through accusing questions. Furthermore, within the narrative world of Luke-Acts, the Prophet-King, empowered by the Spirit at his baptism, embarked on a mission to liberate God's covenant people in a manner that divided Israel between those who accepted his mission and manner of service and those who did not. In like manner, Peter, as a representative of the apostolic leadership commissioned by the risen Christ, blessed those who were submissive (like Barnabas) and excluded those who were rebellious (like Judas and Ananias).[55] Peter was authorized to speak on behalf of God, and his verbal confrontation with the deceptive Ananias resulted in the death of this wicked detractor.[56]

'*And great fear came upon all those who heard.*' The corresponding result among the populace was a 'great fear' that mirrors the 'great grace' (4.33) of the divine favour. God had defended and guaranteed the sanctity of the communal ethos of generosity and unity, and the *topos* of community-of-goods discourse indicates that severe disciplinary practices were expected to accompany the practice of (e)utopian sharing of goods.[57] This 'great fear', or 'reverential awe' reflects both a positive endorsement of the community's divine sanction and a (negative) warning to those who would scorn or oppose the call to exclusive obedience to God through messianic association (cf. Acts 5.13-14).

<u>5.6</u> – The final verse of the Ananias scene depicts the young men (νεώτεροι) as wrapping Ananias' corpse and taking it out to bury it. Perhaps Richter Reimer is correct to note that the burial of the deceitful couple by the community should be considered as a final work of love.[58] The community remained faithful to its obligation to care for the remains of one of its members, even when that member had broken solidarity with the wider community.[59]

Furthermore, the possibility that the burial of Ananias was an act of love should not be excluded from the action of removing the body of the deceiver as an act of removing the pollution from the sacred group.[60] We may

---

55. See §6 above.
56. See §7 above.
57. See §§4.2.2.2., 5.1.4., 5.2.1.4., 5.3.2.2., and 5.3.3.3. above.
58. Richter Reimer, *Women*, 22.
59. See the comments by Robert L. Wilken, 'Christianity as a Burial Society', in *The Christians as the Romans Saw Them* (New Haven: Yale University Press, 1984), 31–47, esp. 34.
60. See §§4.2.2.2., nn. 108–9 above. See the remarks concerning corpse pollution among Jewish / Christian communities in Byron R. McCane, *Roll Back the Stone: Death and Burial in the World of Jesus* (Harrisburg: Trinity Press International, 2003), 50–1, 55–6, 70–2, 112–15. Furthermore, while few details regarding the burial rituals (or lack thereof) are given for Ananias and Sapphira, there is conspicuous lack of mention about mourning, which, when compared to the burial of Stephen (Acts 8.2), suggests duty apart from sorrow. See the comments about dishonourable burial and the associated prevention of mourning in McCane, *Roll Back*, 95–6, 99, 102–4.

recall the suggestion of Havelaar that this episode is 'a highly stylized form of excommunication given shape with the help of the literary form of the rule miracle of punishment'.[61] Ananias has effectively been excluded from the community. The threat of discord and its potential for pollution have been removed.

5.7-8 – Sapphira comes in 'after an interval of about three hours' ignorant of what had transpired with her husband. Peter responds (ἀπεκρίθη) to her entry with an imperative: 'Tell me whether you sold the field for such and such.' She replies, 'Yes, indeed; for such and such.' Here is the only place one of the couple is allowed to speak, and only enough to demonstrate complicity in the conspiracy to deceive. The focus here is on the continuation of the exposing of the lie of the couple. Luke does not seem concerned with the questions that preoccupy many contemporary commentators (such as why Peter does not show compassion to Sapphira by kindly informing her of her husband's death or why he does not allocate time for repentance).

O'Toole labels the structure of Acts 5.1-11 as 'diptych', indicating a strategy of repetition and gradation of severity.[62] Both panels begin by introducing the characters (5.1a, 7a). Next there is the mention of the crime (5.1b-2a, 8) followed by, or within, Peter's speech, and containing Peter's reaction (5.3-4, 8, 9). Both panels contain action at the apostles' feet (5.2c, 10a). Both parties fall dead as an immediate consequence of the confrontation with Peter (5.5a, 10a), and both are removed and buried by the young men (5.6, 10b). Finally, for both parts this results in 'great fear' among those who heard of it (5.5b, 11). O'Toole is correct to recognize the intensification,[63] both in the identification of the couple's crime (from lying to 'testing / tempting') and in Peter's indictments (from a statement of the crime, 'You have lied…', to an accusation plus pronouncement, 'You have conspired…you will be carr[ied] out [and buried].'). Peter plays the central role throughout the episode, and the scene is carried along through his speech-acts. The crucial thing to remember is that these two panels cannot be separated from each other, with one interpreted independently from the other. The significance of this diptych structure, coupled with the narrative boundaries, indicate that Peter's words, regardless of their surface form, act in a similar manner. In other words, Peter's encounter with each of the couple results in actions of indictment and execution *as a result of divine judgement relayed through the venue of Peter's condemnatory accusations*. The evidence is their immediate death.

5.9 – More suggestive is the accusation Peter lays on Sapphira: the couple conspired 'to test the Spirit of the Lord' (συνεφωνήθη ὑμῖν πειράσαι τὸ πνεῦμα κυρίου). There are possible echoes here with the indictments of the wilderness generation who are said to have 'tested' (ἐπείρασαν) the Lord ten times and are therefore refused entry into the land.[64] If Peter's invitation to the Jerusalem audience of his Pentecost speech evokes similar imagery – 'Be saved from this

---

61. Havelaar, 'Hellenistic Parallels', 82.
62. O'Toole, '"You Did Not Lie"', 185-97; Also Marguerat, 'Ananias', 158-62.
63. O'Toole, '"You Did Not Lie"', 192.

perverse generation!' (Acts 2.40) – then the echo is more plausible.[65]

With regard to Sapphira, the ancient prophetic form of prophetic indictment is more closely resembled than with her husband. Peter indicts her with an accusing question (*'Why have you conspired to test the Spirit of the Lord?'*), and then articulates her demise, beginning with the indicator, 'Behold!' He explicitly names her punishment of death, 'The feet of those who buried your husband are at the door and they shall carry you out as well!'

<u>5.10</u> – Again, Luke coordinates Peter's speech with the demise of Sapphira using the term παραχρῆμα, 'immediately'. Here, there is an irony of submission, for Sapphira falls at Peter's feet, the location of the proceeds that represent her duplicitous self. The same verb used of her husband's death – ἐξέψυχεν – is used here, a verb reserved to describe only the death of the wicked in Acts.[66]

Then the νεώτεροι return finding Sapphira dead and do just what Peter had said. The comments regarding burial under verse 6 equally apply here.

<u>5.11</u> – Peter's apostolic-prophetic authority is here manifest in a terrible manner, evoking fear upon all who heard of the incident. God sanctioned Peter's words with fatal consequences in order to protect the sanctity of the community and remove the polluting disharmony. In fact, it is here that Luke uses the political designation ἐκκλησία of the messianic community for the first time. The exercise of discipline by the apostolic-prophetic successors seems to indicate a fulfilment of status for the nascent messianic community as a new, alternative social order. As it was argued in §2.3.3., in the immediate co-text, this serves to contrast the legitimate claims of authority by the apostolic leaders over against the incompetent Jerusalem hierocracy. From here, Luke cascades into another summary of apostolic 'signs and wonders' which leads into an intensification of conflict with the Jerusalem elite.

8.2. Summary and Conclusion

In summary, Ananias and Sapphira are aligned with Judas, who is condemned to death as a result of divine judgement. With this association, the death of the couple following immediately with the utterances of Peter tips the scale in favour of construing the couple's death as a result of divine judgement. The inscribed conventions for prophetic speech in Luke-Acts, and the characterization of Peter as an apostle-prophet deputized to speak on behalf of God to the messianic community all point to Peter's words as performative apostolic-prophetic speech-acts that *themselves* function as the vehicle to bring the couple under divine judgement. Satan's tactic to infiltrate the community has failed. The effect of the Spirit-empowered apostolic-prophetic speech has been successful. God has guaranteed the sanctity of the messianic ethos in the divine economy.

64. Num. 14.22; cf. Exod. 17.1-7; LXX Pss. 77.41, 56; 94.9; 106.14
65. See also §6.2.2.2. above for the discussion of the phrase 'ἡ γενεὰ ταύτη'.
66. Also in the death of the wicked Herod, Acts 12.23.

Chapter 9

CONCLUSION

9.1. Summary of Argument

It is now time to summarize and reiterate the claims made in this study. The main argument has been directed towards demonstrating that in Acts 5.1-11 Peter's words are instrumental in the execution of divine judgement upon Ananias and Sapphira. The primary conceptual tools utilized for this task came from Speech-Act Theory, a philosophy of language which understands communicative utterance as a socially conditioned and socially constructive action. From the socio-linguistic grid of Speech-Act analysis we described the hermeneutical components of this narrative text which guide a reader to understand the force of Peter's verbal confrontation with Ananias and Sapphira as a condemnation-unto-death. Peter's prophetic indictment performed the execution of divine judgement upon the couple.

We began with an exploration of the literary co-text surrounding the Ananias and Sapphira episode in Acts in order to elucidate both the compositional logic of the plot of Acts 1–5 and the specific contribution of Acts 4.32–5.11 in this narrative flow. Acts 5.1-11 is embedded in a narrative summary of community-of-goods discourse (4.32-35). The couple's deceit is the negative corollary to Barnabas's embodiment of the unifying ethos of the early Jerusalem messianists (4.36-37). Acts 4.32–5.11 is itself embedded in a wider narrative plot of the community life of a messianic group, which is largely composed of a subplot of conflict between this community and the established Jerusalem hierocracy. The pericope about Ananias and Sapphira contributes greatly to the plot and subplot. It was argued that the episode demonstrates the divine guarantee upon the messianic community, where the attempt to lie to the Holy Spirit, and, as a result, to disrupt the internal unity of the group, was met with the gravest consequences. It was also argued that in this ensuing plot of inner-community growth and inter-community conflict, the successful speech-act of judgement offered a picture of divine legitimation upon the apostolic leadership over against the incompetent Jerusalem hierocracy. As a matter of fact, the direct reference to Satan as the agent who filled Ananias' heart exposes the continued motif of polarizing allegiances. Those who oppose the messianic community are found to be the enemies of God. On the other side of the pericope, with the escalation of the threat against the apostolic leadership, the severe judgement on Ananias and Sapphira serves to raise the stakes and build suspense with the evidently real peril meted out for opposing God's servants. All of this helped to establish the boundaries with which the linguistic exchange between Peter and the couple should be understood.

The largest portion of the exploration here is dedicated to the socio-literary elements of the deadly verbal encounter where fatally accurate apostolic-prophetic speech served as a divine death sentence. In digest, Peter's words create and reinforce the powerful social reality in which the apostolic-prophetic word performs the will of God. This reality itself is sustained by pre-established conventions of how words can perform in certain contexts by particularly authorized agents. Speech-Act Theory is a pragmatic philosophy of language which demands that analysis of actions performed by language be described in their context of use. That is, the entire speech-act is the basic unit of analysis, and this includes (1) the accepted conventions that create the utterance to count as a certain type of speech-act, (2) the legitimately represented authority, and (3) a successfully executed procedure in line with the accepted convention and the expected outcomes. Narrative discourse offers the full framework for each of these elements to be explored. In the case of Acts 5.1-11, Peter's utterances to Ananias and Sapphira performed a divine death sentence successfully as a result of Peter's speaking with divinely deputized authority in a tradition where the performance of a prophetic indictment brings about the condemnation of the accused. Peter's words occurred in an eschatologically charged context where the messianic community lived in idyllic unity and shared their goods and the proceeds from sales of their lands as a result of the Holy Spirit's presence in their midst. This community-of-goods *topos* set up a particular literary competence among audiences of the ancient Mediterranean world which would have added to the tone of reception for this episode of divine judgement. Furthermore, with mention of offence against the Holy Spirit, and with the influence of Satan, there is a cosmic element revealed to the entire episode.

As a negative illustration of the community-of-goods ethos represented by the messianists in Acts, it was necessary to describe this ancient *topos* that captured the imagination of so many creative social engineers in the ancient world. This socio-historical discourse of shared life and goods shaped Luke's portrayal of the early Church as the fulfilment of both Greco-Roman (e) utopian ideals and Jewish eschatological hopes. The Pythagoreans served as the archetypal Greco-Roman exemplars of the discourse, while the Essenes, as described by Josephus and Philo, served as the quintessential exemplars for the Jewish world. These varied, yet highly consistent depictions of model communities in the ancient world expressed through a common life of shared goods, indicate a common ideal of the proper relationships among communities living according to the divine economy, which was the manifestation of cosmic harmony in the world. In each broad tradition about these communities, we saw that the descriptions of these communities were associated with (1) laudatory esteem of the group and (2) severe disciplinary actions against those who transgressed the communal ethos. Each of these communities attached a symbolic significance to the proper use of possessions and wealth, indicating that the use of possessions revealed one's status in, and solidarity with, the wider community. The *Community Rule* and the *Damascus Document* from Khirbet Qumrân, each in their own ways, revealed a similar finding about the ideals concerning the use of possessions among members of the community and discipline for those who broke the rules. These Jewish examples are particularly relevant because of their common eschatological underpinnings shared with the Jerusalem church as presented by Luke. All of these examples serve as independent attestations of a common discourse in the ancient Mediterranean world which would have framed the way ancient auditors would have received the summaries of the early messianists' community-of-goods and the types of expectations they would have had when presented with a breach of the communal ethos. The fear experienced by those who heard of the incident in the narrative of Acts (5.5, 11) would likely have been the same reaction the narrative was meant to evoke from its model audience: a reverent fear of the God who protected the sanctity of this messianic community. The ancient world provides a rich paradigm for understanding the narrative as something other than 'repulsive' or 'offensive'. In this context, a plausible reading, according to 'the grain' of the text, would have provided comfort and encouragement for those who self-identified with the messianic community spawned from this Jerusalem core. Even those who refrained from association with the community (cf. Acts 5.13) could have found appreciation for the description in light of the discursive *topos* instantiated in the traditions of the Pythagoreans and the Essenes.

The community-of-goods discourse made up a prime aspect of the socio-cultural reading competence, the external repertoire, that would have hermeneutically framed the reception of the Ananias and Sapphira episode in the ancient world. As far as the literary repertoire goes, prophetic speech provides a generic category to frame Peter's words. This includes both the paradigms gathered in the Scriptures of Israel, and, because this study self-consciously read Luke-Acts as a coherent story, the paradigm of Jesus as the Prophet-King in the Gospel of Luke. The prophets of the Scriptures serve as a pattern both in their divinely enabled words and deeds, and also in the details of the form of their verbal interaction. They often accused their opponents through questions and damning assertions, as did Peter to Ananias and Sapphira.

Both the prophetic pattern and the authority by which Peter condemned the couple were derived primarily from the character of Jesus in Luke-Acts. In Luke's characterization of Jesus there is a transformation of the prophetic personae, and so, the authority with which prophetic speech is deployed. In Luke-Acts, there is a fusion of the royal-messianic and prophetic figures in a manner that creates a distinctive precedent for the character of Peter. Empowered by the Holy Spirit for a ministry that both comforts and challenges Israel, Jesus defines the boundaries of legitimate authority in Luke-Acts. Jesus is a prophet for Luke, but he is much more than that; he is the one declared by God to be both 'Lord and Christ' (Acts 2.36). The character of Peter is patterned after the example of Jesus, and his authority derives directly from the royal-prophetic persona of Jesus as the Prophet-King. As a legitimate apostolic-prophetic successor to Jesus, Peter and the apostles continue Jesus' ministry of bringing salvation and judgement to Israel and the nations.

The execution of the divine death sentence on Ananias and Sapphira is one way Peter is portrayed as stewarding the rule over the restored people of God on behalf of the Messiah (cf. Luke 22.32). The characterization of Peter throughout Acts is increasingly one of a Spirit-enabled, divinely deputized leader who acts on behalf of God and his Christ. Peter does this through mighty signs and wonders and bold speech. Peter counts as an apostle-prophet under the conditions that he has been granted a position (i.e., throne) in the leadership of restored Israel (Luke 22.28-30), has been ordained a prophet by Jesus (prophetic succession, Acts 1.4-11), speaks under the inspiration of the Spirit of Prophecy sent by the Lord of the Spirit (Acts 2.14-40; 4.8; cf. 6.8; 7.55; 13.9), and, finally, Peter exhibits the character traits of a prophet like Moses-and-Jesus (Acts 2.17-18; 4.29-30; 5.12). Peter as an apostle-prophet utters questions and statements, which count as an apostolic-prophetic judicial indictment and condemnation in the context of the eschatological, Spirit-filled community, embodying and giving witness to the divine economy. These conventional realities are ultimately undergirded by raw divine power: God acts through the Spirit to accomplish liberation and the salvific reversal of fortunes. God has ordained the Prophet-King, Jesus, to rule over the restored people. God sends the Spirit to empower the disciples to continue the work Jesus began. God protects the integrity of the messianic community. God kills Ananias and Sapphira through the voice of his servant Peter.

All of these elements point to the performative function of Peter's language. Ananias and Sapphira are aligned with Satan, and therefore Judas, as those condemned to die under divine displeasure. Ananias and Sapphira transgress the community-of-goods ethos, forming a counterfeit unity characterized by deception and self-aggrandizement, and are therefore placed under severe punitive retribution. In the eschatological context where the community is filled with the Spirit of God, this transgression results in death. Peter confronts the couple as a divinely empowered leader, authorized to speak divine condemnation on these offenders, and does so with success.

9.2. Prospects for Further Research

The application of Speech-Act Theory to New Testament and early Christian utterance opens a world of possibilities yet to be explored. Many other New Testament passages remain to be illuminated by the exploration of speech as a social action in various contexts. Additionally, as a theological tool, the application of Speech-Act Theory here to prophetic speech has brought awareness of the fundamental role of the Holy Spirit in more than simply a missiological function in Luke-Acts. The present study opens many possibilities for Speech-Act Theory to refine exegetical procedures in their application to specific passages.[1]

Among the many passages that remain to be explored with Speech-Act Theory are other examples of divine judgement, like the punishment of Zechariah by the angel Gabriel for not believing his message (Luke 1.20, 64). Another obvious passage is the narrative of Jesus cursing the fig tree in Mark (11.12-14, 20-25; cf. Matt. 21.18-22; no par. in Luke). In this tradition, speech plays a fundamental role in both Jesus' prophetic sign-act and in the expression of basic faith offered to Jesus' disciples, a faith that can 'move mountains'.

Speech-Act Theory also holds promise in exploring passages concerning the opposite side of divine judgement, divine favour. For example, in Luke 5.17-26 Jesus brings restoration to a paralysed man by offering him forgiveness of sins and wholeness in body. All of this is accomplished by the power of his authoritative word.

A more complex example of a passage that could be illuminated by Speech-Act Theory is Paul's 'insult' to the high priest in Acts 23. The complexities include the role of the Jerusalem Temple in Luke-Acts[2] and the particulars of the force of Paul's invective. Paul is struck at the command of Ananias, the high priest, and snaps back with an insult and accusation of violating the Law (23.3). It may be that Paul reacts in anger without regard to the high priest's

---

1. In respectful disagreement with Briggs, 'The Uses of Speech-Act Theory in Biblical Interpretation', *CurBS* 9 (2001), 264; idem, *Words in Action: Speech Act Theory and Biblical Interpretation* (Edinburgh: T&T Clark, 2001), 294.

2. The role of the Jerusalem Temple poses a complex problem for the interpretation of Luke-Acts. Scholarship has been divided over whether the Temple is a wholly positive institution or a subverted institution in the Lukan text. Those that argue that the Temple is wholly positive include Michael Bachmann, *Jerusalem und der Tempel: Die geographisch-theologischen Elemente in der lukanischen Sicht des jüdischen Kultentrums* (Stuttgart: Kohlhammer, 1980); K. Baltzer, 'The Meaning of the Temple in the Lukan Writings', *HTR* 58 (1965): 263–77; C. K. Barrett, 'Attitudes to the Temple in the Acts of the Apostles', in *Temple Amicitiae: Essays on the Second Temple presented to Ernst Bammel* (ed. William Horbury; JSNTSup 48; Sheffield: Sheffield Academic Press, 1991), 345–97; J. Bradley Chance, *Jerusalem, the Temple, and the New Age in Luke-Acts* (Macon, GA: Mercer University Press, 1988); J. M. Dawsey, 'Confrontation in the Temple: Luke 19:45–20:47', *PRSt* 11 (1984): 153–65; idem, 'The Origin of Luke's Positive Perception of the Temple', *PRSt* 18 (1991): 5–22; Francis D. Weinert, 'The Meaning of the Temple in the Gospel of Luke', PhD diss., Fordham University, 1979; idem, 'The Meaning of the Temple in Luke-Acts', *BTB* 11 (1981): 85–9; idem, 'Luke, the Temple and Jesus' Saying about Jerusalem's Abandoned House (Luke 13:34-35)', *CBQ* 44 (1982): 68–76, idem, 'Luke, Stephen and the Temple in Luke-Acts', *BTB* 17 (1987): 88–91.

Those who argue that Luke subverts the Temple, or replaces it with either Jesus or the church, are G. K. Beale, *The Temple and the Church's Mission: A Biblical Theology of the Dwelling Place of God* (Downers Grove: InterVarsity Press, 2004), 169–92 (not differentiating between the Synoptics), and 201–44 (for Acts); John Elliott, 'Temple Versus Household in Luke-Acts: A Contrast in Social Institutions', in *The Social World of Luke-Acts: Models of Interpretation* (ed. Jerome H. Neyrey; Peabody, MA: Hendrickson, 1991), 211–40; Joel B. Green, 'The Demise of the Temple as "Culture Center" in Luke-Acts: An

position,³ but it may also be that there is a stronger thrust behind Paul's words, especially in light of the impending doom expected for the city of Jerusalem and its Temple (Luke 19.43-44; 21.6; 23.29-31). If the knowledge of the fall of Jerusalem under the Roman general Titus lies in the extra-textual repertoire of the audience's competence, then Paul's words would carry a foreboding condemnation of the high priest for the events to come.

In final conclusion, each of these examples demonstrates a rich field of inquiry for further research. Just as Speech-Act Theory helped to offer a fuller, 'thicker', description of the episode concerning Ananias and Sapphira, so examination of the social and pragmatic contexts of early Christian utterance can elucidate further areas of how words functioned to perform actions in the ancient world.

Exploration of the Rending of the Temple Veil (Luke 23.44–49)', *RB* (1994), 495–515; Bruce W. Longenecker, 'Rome's Victory and God's Honour: The Jerusalem Temple and the Spirit of God in Lukan Theodicy', in *The Holy Spirit and Christian Origins: Essays in Honor of James D.G. Dunn* (eds Graham N. Stanton, Bruce W. Longenecker and Stephen C. Barton; Grand Rapids: Eerdmans, 2004), 90–102; Michael McKeever, 'Sacred Space and Discursive Field: The Narrative Function of the Temple in Luke-Acts', PhD diss., Graduate Theological Union, 1999; Nicholas H. Taylor, 'Luke-Acts and the Temple', in *The Unity of Luke-Acts* (ed., J. Verheyden; BETL 142; Leuven: Leuven University Press, 1999), 709–21; Steve Walton, 'A Tale of Two Perspectives?: The Place of the Temple in Acts', in *Heaven on Earth: The Temple in Biblical Theology* (eds T. Desmond Alexander and Simon Gathercole; Carlisle: Paternoster, 2004), 135–49; Peter W. L. Walker, *Jesus and the Holy City: New Testament Perspectives on Jerusalem* (Grand Rapids: Eerdmans, 1996), 57–112.

Philip F. Esler (*Community and Gospel in Luke-Acts: The Social and Political Motivations of Lucan Theology* [SNTSMS 57; Cambridge: Cambridge University Press, 1987], 131–63) holds that Luke's view of the Temple is ambivalent. Peter Head ('The Temple in Luke's Gospel', in *Heaven on Earth* (eds Alexander and Gathercole), 101–19) offers a survey of scholarship on the Temple in Luke without drawing any conclusions.

3. So e.g., William J. Larkin, *Acts* (IVPNTCS 5; Downers Grove: InterVarsity Press, 1995), 328.

BIBLIOGRAPHY

Primary Sources

The Ante-Nicene Fathers. Edited by Alexander Roberts and James Donaldson. 1885–87. 10 vols. Repr. Peabody, MA: Hendrickson, 1994.
Aristoxenos, Fritz Wehrli, ed. *Die Schule des Aristotles. Heft II Aristoxenos.* Basel: Benno Schwabe & Co., 1954.
Broshi, Magen, ed. *The Damascus Document Reconsidered.* Jerusalem: The Israel Exploration Society, 1992.
Charlesworth, James H., ed. *The Dead Sea Scrolls:* The Rule of the Community: *Photographic Multi-language Edition.* Philadelphia: American Interfaith / World Alliance, 1996.
Dicaearchus, Fritz Wehrli, ed. *Die Schule des Aristotles, Heft I Dikaiarchos.* Basel: Benno Schwabe & Co., 1944.
Diodorus of Sicily. Translated by C. H. Oldfather, et al. 12 vols. Loeb Classical Library. Cambridge: Harvard University Press, 1933–67.
Diogenes Laertius. Translated by R. D. Hicks. 2 vols. Loeb Classical Library. Cambridge: Harvard University Press, 1925–72.
Fideler, David R., ed. *The Pythagorean Sourcebook and Library: An Anthology of Ancient Writings Which Relate to Pythagoras and Pythagorean Philosophy.* Compiled and translated by Kenneth Sylvan Guthrie; Grand Rapids: Phanes Press, 1988.
García Martínez, Florentino, and Eibert J. C. Tigchelaar, eds. *The Dead Sea Scrolls: Study Edition.* 2 vols. Leiden: Brill / Grand Rapids: Eerdmans, 1997–98.
Hesiod. Translated by Hugh G. Evelyn White. Loeb Classical Library. Cambridge: Harvard University Press, 1954.
Iamblichus, On the Pythagorean Way of Life: Text, Translation, and Notes. Translated with notes by John Dillon and Jackson Hershbell. SBL Texts and Translations 29 Greco-Roman Religion Series 11. Atlanta: Scholars Press, 1991.
Josephus. Translated by H. St J. Thackeray, et al. 13 vols. Loeb Classical Library. Cambridge: Harvard University Press, 1926–65.
The Nicene and Post-Nicene Fathers. Series 1. Edited by Philip Schaff. 1886–89. 14 vols. Repr. Peabody, MA: Hendrickson, 1994.
Origen. *The Philocalia of Origen: A Compilation of Selected Passages from Origen's Works Made by St. Gregory Nazianzus and St. Basil of Caesarea.* Translated by George Lewis. Edinburgh: T&T Clark, 1911.
Philo. Translated by F. H. Colson and G. H. Whitaker. 10 vols. Loeb Classical Library. Cambridge: Harvard University Press, 1929–62.
Places, Édouard des, ed. *Porphyre: Vie de Pythagore / Lettre a Marcella.* Collection Budé; Paris: Les Belles Lettres, 1982.
Plato. *Complete Works.* Edited by John M. Cooper. Indianapolis / Cambridge: Hackett Publishing Company, 1997.
Vermes, Geza. *The Complete Dead Sea Scrolls in English.* 5th edn; New York / London: Penguin Books, 1997.

Secondary Sources

Adam, Alfred, and Christoph Burchard, eds. *Antike Berichte über die Essener*. Berlin: de Gruyter, 1972.
Adams, Jim W. *The Performative Nature and Function of Isaiah 40–55*. London: T&T Clark, 2006.
Agua, Agustín del. 'The Lucan Narrative of the "Evangelization of the Kingdom of God": A Contribution to the Unity of Luke-Acts'. Pages 639–61 in *The Unity of Luke Acts*. Edited by J. Verheyden. Bibliotheca Ephemeridum Theologicarum Lovaniensium 142. Leuven: Leuven University Press, 1999.
Alexander, Loveday. 'Fact, Fiction and the Genre of Acts'. *New Testament Studies* 44 (1998): 383–99. Repr. pages 133–63 in *Acts in its Ancient Literary Context*. Library of New Testament Studies 298. London: T&T Clark, 2005.
Alexander, Philip S., and Geza Vermes. *Qumran Cave 4.XIX: Serekh ha-YaHad and Two Related Texts*. Discoveries of the Judean Desert 26. Oxford: Clarendon, 1998.
Allen, Jr, Oscar Wesley. *The Death of Herod: The Narrative and Theological Function of Retribution in Luke-Acts*. Society of Biblical Literature Dissertation Series 158. Atlanta: Scholars Press, 1997.
Allison, Dale C. *Jesus of Nazareth: Millenarian Prophet*. Minneapolis: Fortress, 1999.
———, *The New Moses: A Matthean Typology*. Edinburgh: T&T Clark, 1993.
Alston, William P. 'Illocutionary Acts and Linguistic Meaning'. Pages 29–49 in *Foundations of Speech Act Theory: Philosophical and Linguistic Perspectives*. Edited by Savas L. Tsohatzidis. London: Routledge, 1994.
———, *Illocutionary Acts and Sentence Meaning*. London: Cornell University Press, 2000.
Alter, Robert. *The Art of Biblical Narrative*. New York: Basic Books, 1981.
Anderson, Kevin L. *'But God Raised Him from the Dead': The Theology of Jesus' Resurrection in Luke-Acts*. Paternoster Biblical Monographs. Milton Keynes: Paternoster, 2006.
Anne-Etienne, Sr, and C. Combet-Galland. 'Actes 4/32–5/11'. *Etudes théologiques et religieuses* 52 (1977): 548–53.
Anscombe, G. E. M. 'On Brute Facts'. *Analysis* 18 (1958): 69–72.
Ascough, Richard. 'Benefaction Gone Wrong: The "Sin" of Ananias and Sapphira in Context'. Pages 91–110 in *Text and Artifact in the Religions of Mediterranean Antiquity: Essays in Honour of Peter Richardson*. Studies in Christianity and Judaism / Études sur le Christianisme et le Judaïsme Number 9. Edited by Stephen G. Wilson and Michael Desjardins. Waterloo, Ontario, Canada: Wilfrid Laurier University Press, 2000.
———, 'Translocal Relationships among Voluntary Associations and Early Christianity', *Journal of Early Christian Studies* 5 (1997): 223–41.
Aune, David E. *Prophecy in Early Christianity and the Ancient Mediterranean World*. Grand Rapids: Eerdmans, 1983.
Austin, J. L. *How to do Things with Words*. 2nd edn. Edited by J. O. Urmson and Marina Sbisa. Oxford: Oxford University Press, 1965.
———, 'Performative Utterances'. Pages 220–52 in *Philosophical Papers*. 3rd edn. Edited by J. O. Urmson and G. J. Warnock. Oxford: Oxford University Press, 1979.
Baban, Octavian D. *On the Road Encounters in Luke-Acts: Hellenistic Mimesis and Luke's Theology of the Way*. Milton Keynes: Paternoster, 2006.
Bachmann, Michael. *Jerusalem und der Tempel: Die geographisch-theologischen Elemente in der lukanischen Sicht des jüdischen Kultentrums*. Stuttgart: Kohlhammer, 1980.
Baer, Hans von. *Der Heilege Geist in den Lukasschriften*. Stuttgart: Kohlhammer, 1926.
Balch, David L. 'Neopythagorean Moralists and the New Testament Household Codes'. *Aufstieg und Niedergang der römischen Welt* 26.1: 380–411. Part 2, *Principat* 26.1. New York: de Gruyter, 1996.
———, 'Rich and Poor, Proud and Humble in Luke-Acts'. Pages 214–33 in *The Social World of the First Christians: Essays in Honor of Wayne Meeks*. Edited by L. Michael White

and O. Larry Yarbrough. Minneapolis: Fortress Press, 1995.

Baltzer, K. 'The Meaning of the Temple in the Lukan Writings'. *Harvard Theological Review* 58 (1965): 263–77.

Banks, Robert. 'The Role of Charismatic and Noncharismatic Factors in Determining Paul's Movements in Acts'. Pages 117–30 in *The Holy Spirit and Christian Origins: Essays in Honor of James D.G. Dunn*. Edited by Graham N. Stanton, Bruce W. Longenecker and Stephen C. Barton. Grand Rapids: Eerdmans, 2004.

Barr, James. 'Hypostatization of Linguistic Phenomena in Modern Theological Interpretation'. *Journal of Semitic Studies* 7 (1962): 85–94.

Barrett, C. K. 'Attitudes to the Temple in the Acts of the Apostles'. Pages 345–97 in *Temple Amicitiae: Essays on the Second Temple presented to Ernst Bammel*. Edited by William Horbury. Journal for the Study of the New Testament: Supplement Series 48. Sheffield: Sheffield Academic Press, 1991.

———, *A Critical and Exegetical Commentary on The Acts of the Apostles*. 2 vols. Edinburgh: T&T Clark, 1994, 1998.

———, 'Faith and Eschatology in Acts 3'. Page 1–17 in *Glaube und Eschatologie*. Edited by E. Grasser and O. Merk. Tübingen: Mohr Siebeck, 1985.

———, 'Light on the Holy Spirit from Simon Magus'. Pages 281–95 in *Les Acts des Apôtres: Traditions, rédaction, théologie*. Edited by J. Kremer. Bibliotheca Ephemeridum Theologicarum Lovaniensium 48. Leuven: Leuven University Press, 1979.

Barstad, Hans. 'The Understanding of the Prophets in Deuteronomy'. *Scandinavian Journal of the Old Testament* 8 (1994), 236–51.

Bartchy, S. Scott. 'Community of Goods in Acts: Idealization or Social Reality?' Pages 309–18 in *The Future of Early Christianity: Essays in Honor of Helmut Koester*. Edited by Birger A. Pearson. Minneapolis: Fortress Press, 1991.

Bartholomew, Craig. 'Before Babel and After Pentecost: Language, Literature and Biblical Interpretation'. Pages 131–70 in *After Pentecost: Language and Biblical Interpretation*. Edited by C. Bartholomew, C. Greene, K. Möller. Scripture and Hermeneutics Series 2. Grand Rapids: Zondervan, 2001.

———, 'Introduction'. Pages xxi–xxxvi in *After Pentecost: Language and Biblical Interpretation*. Edited by C. Bartholomew, C. Greene, K. Möller. Scripture and Hermeneutics Series 2. Grand Rapids: Zondervan, 2001.

Bartholomew, Craig, Colin Green and Karl Möller, eds. *After Pentecost: Language and Biblical Interpretation*. Scripture and Hermeneutics Series 2. Grand Rapids: Zondervan, 2001.

Bartholomew, Craig, C. Stephen Evans, Mary Healy and Murray Rae, eds. *'Behind' the Text: History and Biblical Interpretation*. Scripture and Hermeneutics Series 4. Grand Rapids: Zondervan / Carlisle: Paternoster, 2003.

Bauckham, Richard. 'The Early Jerusalem Church, Qumran, and the Essenes'. Pages 63–89 in *The Dead Sea Scrolls as Background to Postbiblical Judaism and Early Christianity: Papers from an International Conference at St. Andrews in 2001*. Edited by James R. Davila. Studies on the Texts of the Desert of Judah 46. Leiden: Brill, 2003.

———, 'James and the Jerusalem Church'. Pages 415–80 in *The Book of Acts in its Palestinian Setting*. Edited by Richard Bauckham. Vol. 4 of *The Book of Acts in Its First Century Setting*. Edited by Bruce W. Winter. Grand Rapids: Eerdmans / Carlisle: Paternoster, 1995.

———, *Jesus and the Eyewitnesses: The Gospels as Eyewitness Testimony*. Grand Rapids: Eerdmans, 2006.

Bauckham, Richard, ed. *The Book of Acts in its Palestinian Setting*. Vol. 4 of *The Book of Acts in Its First Century Setting*. Edited by Bruce W. Winter. Grand Rapids: Eerdmans / Carlisle: Paternoster, 1995.

———, *The Gospels for All Christians: Rethinking the Gospel Audiences*. Grand Rapids / Cambridge: Eerdmans, 1998.

Baumgarten, Albert. 'Graeco-Roman Voluntary Associations and Ancient Jewish Sects'. Pages 93–111 in *Jews in a Graeco-Roman World*. Edited by Martin Goodman. Oxford: Oxford University Press, 1998.

Baumgarten, Joseph M. 'The "Sons of Dawn" in CDC 13:14–15 and the Ban on Commerce among the Essenes'. *Israel Exploration Journal* 33 (1983): 81–5.

Bayer, Hans F. 'Christ-Centered Eschatology in Acts 3:17–26'. Pages 236–50 in *Jesus of Nazareth: Lord and Christ. Essays on the Historical Jesus and New Testament Christology*. Edited by Joel B. Green and Max Turner. Grand Rapids: Eerdmans, 1994.

Beale, Gregory K. *The Temple and the Church's Missions: A Biblical Theology of the Dwelling Place of God*. Downers Grove: InterVarsity Press, 2004.

Beall, Todd S. *Josephus' Description of the Essenes Illustrated by the Dead Sea Scrolls*. Society for New Testament Studies Monograph Series 58. Cambridge: Cambridge University Press, 1988.

Beavis, Mary Ann. *Jesus and Utopia: Looking for the Kingdom of God in the Roman World*. Minneapolis: Fortress, 2006.

———, 'Philo's Therapeutai: Philosopher's Dream or Utopian Construction?' *Journal for the Study of the Pseudepigrapha* 14 (2004): 30–42.

Begg, Christopher T. 'The Function of Josh 7,1–8,29 in the Deuteronomistic History'. *Biblica* 67 (1986): 320–33.

Benoit, Pierre. 'The Death of Judas'. Pages 189–207 in vol. 2 of *Jesus and the Gospel*. 2 vols. Translated by Benet Weatherhead. London: Darton, Longman & Todd, 1973–74.

———, *Jesus and the Gospel*. 2 vols. Translated by Benet Weatherhead. London: Darton, Longman & Todd, 1973–74.

Berger, Klaus. *Identity and Experience in the New Testament*. Translated by Charles Muenchow. Minneapolis: Fortress Press, 2003.

Bergmeier, Roland. *Die Essener-Berichte des Flavius Josephus: Quellenstudien zu den Essenertexten im Werk des jüdischen Historigraphen*. Kampen: Kok Pharos, 1993.

Berlin, Isaiah, et al. *Essays on J.L. Austin*. Oxford: Clarendon Press, 1973.

Bertolet, Rod. 'Are There Indirect Speech Acts?' Pages 335–49 in *Foundations of Speech Act Theory: Philosophical and Linguistic Perspectives*. Edited by Savas L. Tsohatzidis. London: Routledge, 1994.

Betori, Giuseppe. *Perseguitati a causa del Nome: Strutture dei racconti di persecuzione in Atti 1,12–8,4*. Analecta biblica 97. Rome: Pontifical Biblical Institute, 1981.

Beyer, Robert. 'The Challenge: Restoring the Seven So-Called "Punitive Miracles" in Acts to the Prophetic Genre'. ThD diss., Lutheran School of Theology, 1984.

Beyschlag, Karlmann. *Simon Magus und die christliche Gnosis*. Wissenschafliche Untersuchungen zum Neuen Testament 16; Tübingen: Mohr Siebeck, 1974.

———, 'Zur Simon-Magus-Frage'. *Zeitschrift für Theologie und Kirche* 68 (1971): 395–415.

Bilde, Per. 'The Essenes in Philo and Josephus'. Pages 32–68 in *Qumran Between the Old and New Testaments*. Edited by Frederick H. Cryer and Thomas L. Thompson. Sheffield: Sheffield Academic Press, 1998.

———, *Flavius Josephus between Jerusalem and Rome: His Life, his Works, and their Importance*. Journal for the Study of the Pseudepigrapha: Supplement Series 2. Sheffield: Sheffield Academic Press, 1988.

Bingham Kolenkow, Anitra. 'Persons of Power and their Communities'. Pages 133–44 in *Magic and Divination in the Ancient World*. Edited by Leda Ciraolo and Jonathan Seidel. Ancient Magic and Divination II. Leiden: Brill, 2002.

Black, David Allen, with Katharine Barnwell and Stephen Levinsohn, eds. *Linguistics and New Testament Interpretation: Essays in Discourse Analysis*. Nashville: Broadman Press, 1992.

Blaiklock, E. M. 'The Acts of the Apostles as a Document of First Century History'. Pages 41–54 in *Apostolic History and the Gospel: Biblical and Historical Essays presented to F.F. Bruce on his 60th Birthday*. Edited by W. Ward Gasque and Ralph P. Martin.

London: Paternoster Press, 1970.

Block, Fred. 'Karl Polanyi and the Writing of *The Great Transformation*'. *Theory and Society* 32 (2003): 275–306.

Bock, Darrell L. *Acts*. Baker Exegetical Commentary on the New Testament. Grand Rapids: Baker Books, 2007.

———, *Luke*. 2 vols. Baker Exegetical Commentary on the New Testament. Grand Rapids: Baker Books, 1994, 1996.

———, *Proclamation from Prophecy and Pattern: Lucan Old Testament Christology*. Journal for the Study of the New Testament: Supplement Series 12. Sheffield: JSOT, 1987.

———, 'Proclamation from Prophecy and Pattern: Luke's Use of the Old Testament for Christology and Mission'. Pages 280–307 in *The Gospels and the Scriptures of Israel*. Edited by Craig A. Evans and W. Richard Stegner. Journal for the Study of the New Testament: Supplement Series 104. Sheffield: Sheffield Academic Press, 1994.

Bond, Helen K. *Caiaphas: Friend of Rome and Judge of Jesus?* Louisville: Westminster / John Knox Press, 2004.

Borg, Marcus. *Conflict, Holiness and Politics in the Teachings of Jesus*. Harrisburg, PA: Trinity Press International, 1998.

———, 'Luke 19:42–44 and Jesus as Prophet?' *Forum* 8 (1992), 99–112.

Botha, J. Eugene. *Jesus and the Samaritan Woman: A Speech Act Reading of John 4:1–42*. Supplements to Novum Testamentum 65. Leiden: Brill, 1991.

———, 'The Potential of Speech Act Theory for New Testament Exegesis: Some Basic Concepts'. *Hervormde teologiese studies* 47 (1991): 277–93.

Bovon, François. *Luke the Theologian: Fifty-five Years of Research (1950–2005)*. 2nd rev. edn. Waco, TX: Baylor University Press, 2006.

Braun, Herbert. 'Qumran und das Neue Testament: Ein Bericht über 10 Jahre Forschung (1950–59)'. *Theologische Rundschau* 29 (1963): 142–76.

Brawley, Robert. 'Abrahamic Covenant Traditions and the Characterization of God in Luke-Acts'. Pages 110–32 in *The Unity of Luke Acts*. Edited by J. Verheyden. Bibliotheca Ephemeridum Theologicarum Lovaniensium 142. Leuven: Leuven University Press, 1999.

———, 'The Blessing of All the Families of the Earth: Jesus and Covenant Traditions in Luke-Acts'. Pages 252–268 in *SBL 1994 Seminar Papers*. Edited by Eugene H. Lovering, Jr.

———, *Centering on God: Method and Message in Luke-Acts*. Louisville: Westminster / John Knox Press, 1990.

———, *Luke-Acts and the Jews: Conflict, Apology, and Conciliation*. SBLMS 33. Atlanta: Scholars Press, 1987.

———, 'Social Identity and the Aim of Accomplished Life in Acts 2'. Pages 16–33 in *Acts and Ethics*. Edited by Thomas E. Philips. Sheffield: Sheffield Phoenix Press, 2005.

———, *Text to Text Pours Forth Speech: Voices of Scripture in Luke-Acts*. Indianapolis: Indiana University Press, 1995.

Brehm, H. Alan. 'Vindicating the Rejected One: Stephen's Speech as a Critique of the Jewish Leaders'. Pages 266–97 in *Early Christian Interpretation of the Scriptures of Israel: Investigations and Proposals*. Edited Craig A. Evans and James A. Sanders. Journal for the Study of the New Testament: Supplement Series 148. Sheffield: Sheffield Academic Press, 1997.

Bremer, Jan-Maarten. 'The Reciprocity of Giving and Thanksgiving in Greek Worship'. Pages 127–37 in *Reciprocity in Ancient Greece*. Edited by Christopher Gill, Norman Postlethwaite and Richard Seaford. Oxford: Oxford University Press, 1998.

Bremmer, Jan N. 'The Birth of the Term "Magic"'. Pages 1–11 in *The Metamorphosis of Magic from Late Antiquity to the Early Modern Period*. Edited by Jan N. Bremmer and Jan R. Veenstra. Groningen Studies in Cultural Change 1. Leuven: Peeters, 2002.

Briggs, Richard S. 'The Uses of Speech-Act Theory in Biblical Interpretation'. *Currents in Research: Biblical Studies* 9 (2001): 229–76.

——, *Words in Action: Speech Act Theory and Biblical Interpretation*. Edinburgh: T&T Clark, 2001.
Brodie, Thomas L. 'The Accusing and Stoning of Naboth (1 Kgs 21:8–13) as one component of the Stephen Text (Acts 6:9–14, Acts 7:58a)'. *Catholic Bible Quarterly* 45 (1983): 417–32.
——, *The Crucial Bridge: The Elijah-Elisha Narrative as an Interpretive Synthesis of Genesis-Kings and a Literary Model for the Gospels*. Collegeville, MN: The Liturgical Press, 2000.
——, 'Greco-Roman Imitation of Texts as a Partial Guide to Luke's Use of Sources'. Pages 17–46 in *Luke-Acts: New Perspectives from the Society of Biblical Literature Seminar*. Edited by Charles H. Talbert. New York: Crossroad, 1984.
——, 'Jesus as the New Elisha: Cracking the Code'. *Expository Times* 93 (1981–82): 39–42.
——, 'Luke-Acts as an Imitation and Emulation of the Elijah-Elisha Narrative'. Pages 78–85, 172–4 in *New Views on Luke and Acts*. Edited by Earl Richard. Collegeville, MN: The Liturgical Press, 1990.
——, 'Luke 7,36–50 as an Internalization of 2 Kings 4,1–37: A Study in Luke's Use of Rhetorical Imitation'. *Biblica* 64 (1983): 457–85.
——, 'Luke 9:57–62: A Systematic Adaptation of the Divine Challenge to Elijah (1 Kings 19)'. Pages 237–45 in *SBL 1989 Seminar Papers*. Edited by David J. Lull. Atlanta: Scholars Press, 1989.
——, 'Towards Unraveling Luke's Use of the Old Testament: Luke 7. 11–17 as an *Imitatio* of 1 Kings 17. 17–24'. *New Testament Studies* 32 (1986): 247–67.
——, 'Towards Unraveling the Rhetorical Imitation of Sources in Acts: 2 Kgs 5 as One Component of Acts 8,9–40'. *Biblica* 67 (1986): 41–67.
Brooke, George. 'Luke-Acts and the Qumran Scrolls: The Case of MMT'. Pages 72–90 in *Luke's Literary Achievement: Collected Essays*. Edited by C. M. Tuckett. Journal for the Study of the New Testament: Supplement Series 116. Sheffield: Sheffield Academic Press, 1995.
——, 'The Qumran Scrolls and the Study of the New Testament'. Pages 3–18 in *The Dead Sea Scrolls and the New Testament*. Minneapolis: Fortress, 1995.
Broshi, Magen, ed. *The Damascus Document Reconsidered*. Jerusalem: The Israel Exploration Society, 1992.
Brown, Gillian and George Yule. *Discourse Analysis*. Cambridge Textbooks in Linguistics. Cambridge: Cambridge University Press, 1983.
Brown, Paul B. 'The Meaning and Function of Acts 5:1–11 in the Purpose of Luke-Acts'. ThD diss., Boston University School of Theology, 1969.
Brown, Raymond. *The Birth of the Messiah: A Commentary on the Infancy Narratives in the Gospels of Matthew and Luke*. Rev. edn. New York: Doubleday, 1993.
Brown, Raymond E., Karl P. Donfried and John Reumann, eds. *Peter in the New Testament: A Collaborative Assessment by Protestant and Roman Catholic Scholars*. London: Geoffrey Chapman Publishers, 1973.
Brown, Schuyler. *Apostasy and Perseverance in the Theology of Luke*. Rome: Pontifical Biblical Institute, 1969.
Bruce, F. F. *The Acts of the Apostles: The Greek Text with Introduction and Commentary*. Rev. edn. Grand Rapids: Eerdmans / Leicester Apollo, 1990.
——, *The Book of Acts*. Rev. edn. Grand Rapids: Eerdmans, 1988.
Brümmer, Vincent. *Theology and Philosophical Inquiry: An Introduction*. London: MacMillan Press Ltd, 1981.
Büchsel, Friedrich. 'Noch einmal: Zur Blutgerichtsbarkeit des Synedrions'. *Zeitschrift für die neuetestamentliche Wissenschaft und die Kunde der älteren Kirche* 33 (1934): 84–7.
Buckwalter, H. Douglas. *The Character and Purpose of Luke's Christology*. Society for New Testament Studies Monograph Series 89. Cambridge: Cambridge University Press, 1996.

Burger Cristoph. *Jesus als Davidssohn. Eine traditionsgeschichtliche Untersuchung*. Forschungen zur Religion und Literatur des Alten und Neuen Testaments, 98. Göttingen: Vandenhoeck & Ruprecht, 1970.

Burkert, Walter. 'Craft Versus Sect: The Problem of Orphics and Pythagoreans'. Pages 1–22, 183–9 in *Jewish and Christian Self-Definition. Volume Three: Self-Definition in the Greco-Roman World*. Edited by Ben F. Meyer and E. P. Sanders. Philadelphia: Fortress, 1982.

——, 'Hellenistiche Pseudopythagoricas'. *Philologus* 105 (1961), 16–43, 226–46.

——, *Lore and Science in Ancient Pythagoreanism*. Translated by Edwin L. Minar, Jr. Cambridge, MA: Harvard University Press, 1972.

Burnett, Fred W. 'Characterization and Reader Construction of Characters in the Gospels'. *Semeia* 63 (1993): 1–28.

Burridge, Richard A. 'Who Writes, Why, and for Whom?' Pages 99–115 in *The Written Gospel*. Edited by Markus Bockmuehl and Donald A. Hagner. Cambridge: Cambridge University Press, 2005.

Buss, Martin J. 'Potential and Actual Interactions Between Speech Act Theory and Biblical Studies'. Pages 125–34 in *Speech Act Theory and Biblical Criticism*. Semeia 41. Edited by H. C. White. Decatur, GA: Scholars Press, 1988.

Cadbury, Henry J. *The Book of Acts in History*. Eugene, OR: Wipf & Stock, 1955.

——, *The Making of Luke-Acts*. Peabody, MA: Hendrickson, 1958.

——, 'The Speeches in Acts'. Pages 402–27 in *The Beginnings of Christianity. Part 1: The Acts of the Apostles. Volume V: Additional Notes to the Commentary*. Edited by F. J. Foakes-Jackson and Kirsopp Lake. London: MacMillan and Co., 1933.

——, 'The Summaries in Acts'. Pages 392–402 in *The Beginnings of Christianity. Part 1: The Acts of the Apostles. Volume V: Additional Notes to the Commentary*. Edited by F. J. Foakes-Jackson and Kirsopp Lake. London: MacMillan and Co., 1933.

Capper, Brian J. 'Community of Goods in the Early Jerusalem Church'. *Aufstieg und Niedergang der römischen Welt* II 26.2 (1995): 1730–74.

——, '<<In der hand des Ananias...>> Erwagungen zu 1 QS VI, 20 und der Urchristlichen Gütergemeinschaft'. *Revue de Qumran* 12 (1986), 223–36.

——, 'The Interpretation of Acts 5.4'. *Journal for the Study of the New Testament* 19 (1983): 117–31.

——, 'The Palestinian Cultural Context of Earliest Christian Community of Goods'. Pages 323–56 in *The Book of Acts in its First Century Setting. Volume 4: The Book of Acts in Its Palestinian Setting*. Edited by Richard Bauckham. Grand Rapids: Eerdmans / Carlisle: Paternoster Press, 1995.

——, 'PANTA KOINA: A Study of Earliest Christian Community of Goods in Its Hellenistic and Jewish Context'. PhD diss., Cambridge University, 1985.

——, 'Reciprocity and the Ethic of Acts'. Pages 499–518 in *Witness to the Gospel: The Theology of Acts*. Edited by I. Howard Marshall and David Peterson. Grand Rapids / Cambridge: Eerdmans, 1998.

Carroll, John T. *Response to the End of History: Eschatology and Situation in Luke-Acts*. Society of Biblical Literature Dissertation Series 92. Atlanta: Scholars Press, 1988.

Carruth, T. R. 'The Jesus-as-Prophet Motif in Luke-Acts'. PhD diss., Baylor University, 1973.

Casey, Robert P. 'Simon Magus'. Pages 151–63 in *The Beginnings of Christianity. Part 1: The Acts of the Apostles. Volume V; Additional Notes to the Commentary*. Edited by F. J. Foakes-Jackson and Kirsopp Lake. London: MacMillan and Co., 1933.

Cassidy, Richard J. *Society and Politics in the Acts of the Apostles*. Maryknoll: Orbis Books, 1987.

Cerfaux, Lucien. 'La première communauté chrétienne à Jérusalem (Act., II, 41–V, 42)'. Pages 125–56 in vol. 2 of *Recueil Lucien Cerfaux: Études d'Exégèse et d'Histoire Religieuse de Monseigneur Cerfaux, réunies a l'occasion de son soixante-dixième anniversaire*. 2 vols.

Bibliotheca Ephemeridum Theologicarum Lovaniensium 6–7. Gembloux: J. Duculot, 1954.

———, 'Simon le magician à Samarie'. Pages 259–62 in vol. 1 of *Recueil Lucien Cerfaux: Études d'Exégèse et d'Histoire Religieuse de Monseigneur Cerfaux, réunies a l'occasion de son soixante-dixième anniversaire*. 2 vols. Bibliotheca Ephemeridum Theologicarum Lovaniensium 6–7. Gembloux: J. Duculot, 1954.

Chance, J. Bradley. *Jerusalem, the Temple, and the New Age in Luke-Acts*. Mercer, GA: Mercer University Press, 1988.

Chaniotis, Angelos. 'Under the Watchful Eyes of the Gods: Divine Justice in Hellenistic and Roman Asia Minor'. Pages 1–43 in *The Greco-Roman East: Politics, Culture, Society*. Edited by Stephen Colvin. Cambridge: Cambridge University Press, 2004.

Charlesworth, James H. *The Old Testament Pseudepigrapha*. 2 vols. New York: Doubleday, 1983, 1985.

Charlesworth, James H., ed. *The Dead Sea Scrolls: Hebrew, Aramaic, and Greek Texts with English Translations. Vol. 2: Damascus Document, War Scroll and Related Documents*. Tübingen: Mohr / Louisville: Westminster / John Knox Press, 1995.

———, *The Dead Sea Scrolls:* The Rule of the Community: *Photographic Multi-language Edition*. Philadelphia: American Interfaith / World Alliance, 1996.

Childs, Brevard. 'Speech-act Theory and Biblical Interpretation'. *Scottish Journal of Theology* 58 (2005): 375–92.

Cho, Youngmo. *Spirit and Kingdom in the Writings of Luke and Paul: An Attempt to Reconcile these Concepts*. Milton Keynes: Paternoster, 2005.

Clark, Andrew C. *Parallel Lives: The Relation of Paul to the Apostles in the Lucan Perspective*. Paternoster Biblical and Theological Monographs. Carlisle: Paternoster Press, 2001.

———, 'The Role of the Apostles'. Pages 169–90 in *Witness to the Gospel: The Theology of Acts*. Edited by I. Howard Marshall and David Peterson. Grand Rapids: Eerdmans, 1998.

Co, Maria Anicia. 'The Major Summaries in Acts (Acts 2,42–47; 4,32–35; 5,12–16): Linguistic and Literary Relationship'. *Ephemerides theologicae lovanienses* 68 (1992): 49–85.

Coleridge, Mark. *The Birth of the Lukan Narrative: Narrative as Christology in Luke 1–2*. Journal for the Study of the New Testament: Supplement Series 88. Sheffield: JSOT Press, 1993.

Collins, John J. 'Models of Utopia in the Biblical Tradition'. Pages 51–67 in *A Wise and Discerning Mind: Essays in Honor of Burke O. Long*. Edited by Saul M. Olyan and Robert Culley. Providence, RI: Brown Judaic Studies, 2000.

Cook, John G. *The Interpretation of the New Testament in Greco-Roman Paganism*. Studien und Texte zu Antike und Christentum 3. Tübingen: Mohr Siebeck, 2000.

Conzelmann, Hans. *Acts of the Apostles*. Hermeneia. Translated by J. Limburg, A. T. Kraabel and D. H. Juel. Philadelphia: Fortress Press, 1987.

———, *The Theology of Saint Luke*. Translated by Geoffrey Buswell. London: Faber and Faber, 1961.

Cotterell, Peter and Max Turner. *Linguistics and Biblical Interpretation*. Downers Grove: InterVarsity Press, 1989.

Crawford, Timothy G. 'Taking the Promised Land, Leaving the Promised Land: Luke's Use of Joshua for a Christian Foundation Story'. *Review and Expositor* 95 (1998): 251–61.

Creed, J. M. 'The Text and Interpretation of Acts i,1–2'. *Journal of Theological Studies* 35 (1934): 176–82.

Crehan, Joseph. 'Peter According to the D-Text of Acts.' *Theological Studies* 18 (1957): 596–603.

Croatto, J. Severino. 'Jesus, Prophet like Elijah, and Prophet-Teacher like Moses in Luke-Acts'. *Journal of Biblical Literature* 124 (2005): 451–65.

Cryer, Frederick H. 'Magic in Ancient Syria – Palestine – and in the Old Testament'. Pages 97–149 in *Witchcraft and Magic in Europe: Biblical and Pagan Societies*. Edited by Bengt Ankarloo and Stuart Clark. Philadelphia: University of Pennsylvania Press, 2001.

Culler, Jonathon. 'Problems in the Theory of Fiction'. *Diacritics* 14 (1984): 2–11.

Culpepper, R. Alan. *Anatomy of the Fourth Gospel: A Study in Literary Design*. Philadelphia: Fortress Press, 1983.

Cunliffe-Jones, Hubert. 'Ananias and Sapphira (Acts 4:31–5:11)'. *Congregational Quarterly* 27 (1949): 116–21.

Dahl, Nils A. 'The Story of Abraham in Luke-Acts'. Pages 139–58 in *Studies in Luke-Acts*. Edited by L. E. Keck and J. L. Martyn. Philadelphia: Fortress Press, 1968.

Danker, Frederick W. *Benefactor: Epigraphic Study of a Graeco-Roman and New Testament Semantic Field*. St Louis: Clayton Publishing House, Inc., 1982.

———, *Jesus and the New Age: A Commentary on St. Luke's Gospel*. Rev. edn. Philadelphia: Fortress, 1988.

Darr, John A. *Herod the Fox: Audience Criticism and Lukan Characterization*. Journal for the Study of the New Testament: Supplement Series 163. Sheffield: Sheffield Academic Press, 1998.

———, 'Irenic or Ironic? Another Look at Gamiliel before the Sanhedrin (Acts 5:33–42)'. Pages 121–39 in *Literary Studies in Luke-Acts: Essays in Honor of Joseph B. Tyson*. Edited by Richard P. Thompson and Thomas E. Philips. Macon, GA: Mercer University Press, 1998.

———, 'Narrator as Character: Mapping a Reader-Oriented Approach to Narration in Luke Acts'. *Semeia* 63 (1993): 43–60.

———, *On Character Building: the Reader and the Rhetoric of Characterization in Luke-Acts*. Louisville: Westminster / John Knox Press, 1992.

Dascal, Marcelo. 'Speech Act Theory and Gricean Pragmatics: Some Differences that Make a Difference'. Pages 323–34 in *Foundations of Speech Act Theory: Philosophical and Linguistic Perspectives*. Edited by Savas L. Tsohatzidis. London: Routledge, 1994.

Davies, Philip R. 'Communities in the Qumran Scrolls'. *Proceedings of the Irish Biblical Association* 17 (1994): 55–68.

———, 'The Judaism(s) of the Damascus Document'. Pages 27–43 in *The Damascus Document: A Centennial of Discovery, Proceedings of the Third International Symposium of the Orion Center, 4–8 February 1998*. Edited by Joseph M. Baumgarten, Esther G. Chazon and Avital Pinnick. Leiden: Brill, 2000.

———, 'Review of Todd S. Beall, *Josephus' Description of the Essenes Illustrated by the Dead Sea Scrolls*'. *Journal of Theological Studies* 41 (1990): 64–9.

Davis, Steven. 'Anti-Individualism and Speech Act Theory'. Pages 208–19 in *Foundations of Speech Act Theory: Philosophical and Linguistic Perspectives*. Edited by Savas L. Tsohatzidis. London: Routledge, 1994.

Dawsey, James M. 'Confrontation in the Temple: Luke 19:45–20:47'. *Perspectives in Religious Studies* 11 (1984): 153–65.

———, 'The Origin of Luke's Positive Perception of the Temple'. *Perspectives in Religious Studies* 18 (1991): 5–22.

Dawson, Doyne. *Cities of the Gods: Communist Utopias in Greek Thought*. New York: Oxford University Press, 1992.

Deissmann, Adolf. *Light from the Ancient East: The New Testament Illustrated by Recently Discovered Texts of the Graeco-Roman World*. Rev. edn. London: Houghton & Stoughton, 1927.

Delatte, Armand. *Études sur la littérature pythagoricienne*. Paris: Champion, 1915.

Delatte, Armand, ed. and comm. *La vie de Pythagore de Diogène Laërce*. Brussels: Lamertin, 1922.

Derrett, J. Duncan M. 'Ananias, Sapphira, and the Right of Property'. *Downside Review* 89 (1971), 225–32.

deSilva, David A. *Honor, Patronage, Kinship & Purity: Unlocking New Testament Culture.* Downers Grove, IL: InterVarsity Press, 2000.

Dibelius, Martin. 'The Speeches in Acts and Ancient Historiography'. Pages 49–86 in *The Book of Acts: Form, Style, and Theology*. Translated by Mary Ling. Edited by K. C. Hanson. London: SCM Press, 1956. Repr. Minneapolis: Fortress, 2004.

——, *Studies in the Acts of the Apostles*. Edited by Heinrich Greeven. London: SCM Press, 1973.

Dickie, Matthew W. *Magic and Magicians in the Greco-Roman World*. London: Routledge, 2003.

Dietrich, Wolfgang. *Das Petrusbild der lukanischen Schriften*. Beiträge zur Wissenschaft vom Alten und Neuen Testament 94. Stuttgart: Kohlhammer, 1972.

Dillon, John. 'The Essenes in Greek Sources: Some Reflections'. Pages 117–28 in *Jews in the Hellenistic and Roman Cities*. Edited by John R. Bartlett. London: Routledge, 2002.

——, *The Middle Platonists: A Study of Platonism 80 B.C. to A.D. 220*. London: Duckworth, 1977.

Dillon, John and Jackson Hershbell, eds. *Iamblichus: On the Pythagorean Way of Life: Text, Translation, and Notes*. Texts and Translations 29. Greco-Roman Religion Series 11. Atlanta: Scholars Press, 1991.

Dillon, Richard J. 'The Prophecy of Christ and His Witnesses According to the Discourses of Acts'. *New Testament Studies* 32 (1986): 544–56.

Dobbeler, Axel von. *Der Evangelist Philippus in der Geschichte des Urchristentums: Eines prosopographische Skizze*. Texte und Arbeiten zum neutesamentlichen Zeitalter 30. Tübingen: Francke, 2000.

Dobbs, Darrell. 'Aristotle's Anticommunism'. *American Journal of Political Science* 29 (1985): 29–46.

Dodd, C. H. 'The Fall of Jerusalem and the "Abomination of Desolation"'. *Journal of Roman Studies* 37 (1947): 47–54.

Donahue, John R. 'Two Decades of Research on the Rich and Poor in Luke-Acts'. Pages 129–44 in *Justice and the Holy: Essays in Honor of Walter Harrelson*. Edited by Douglas A. Knight and Peter J. Paris. Atlanta: Scholars Press, 1989.

Du Plessis, J. G. '*Speech Act Theory*: Speech Act Theory and New Testament Interpretation with Special Reference to G.N. Leech's Pragmatic Principles'. Pages 129–42 in *Text and Interpretation: New Approaches in the Criticism of the New Testament*. Edited by P. J. Hartin and J. H. Petzer. New Testament Tools and Studies 15; Leiden: Brill, 1991.

——, 'Why Did Peter Ask His Question and How Did Jesus Answer Him? Or: Implicature in Luke 12:35–48'. *Neotestamentica* 22 (1988): 311–24.

Dunn, James D. G. *Baptism in the Holy Spirit: A Re-examination of the New Testament Teaching on the Gift of the Spirit in Relation to Pentecostalism Today*. London: SCM Press, 1970.

——, 'Baptism in the Spirit: A Response to Pentecostal Scholarship on Luke-Acts'. *Journal for Pentecostal Theology* 3 (1993): 3–27. Repr. pages 222–42 in *The Christ and the Spirit: Volume 2. Pneumatology*. Grand Rapids: Eerdmans, 1998.

——, *Jesus and the Spirit: A Study of the Religious and Charismatic Experience of Jesus and the First Christians Reflected in the New Testament*. Grand Rapids: Eerdmans, 1975.

——, *Unity and Diversity in the New Testament: An Inquiry in the Character of Earliest Christianity*. 2nd edn; London: SCM Press, 1990.

Dupont-Sommer, André. 'Le probleme des influences étrengères sur la sect juive de Qoumrân'. *Revue d'histoire et de philosophie religieuses* 35 (1955): 75–92.

Eco, Umberto. 'Between Author and Text'. Pages 67–88 in *Interpretation and Overinterpretation*. Edited by Stefan Collini. Cambridge: Cambridge University Press, 1992.

——, 'Interpretation and History'. Pages 23–43 in *Interpretation and Overinterpretation*. Edited by Stefan Collini. Cambridge: Cambridge University Press, 1992.

——, *The Limits of Interpretation*. Advances in Semiotics. Bloomington: Indiana University Press, 1990.
——, 'Overinterpreting Texts'. Pages 45–66 in *Interpretation and Overinterpretation*. Edited by Stefan Collini. Cambridge: Cambridge University Press, 1992.
——, *The Role of the Reader: Explorations in the Semiotics of Texts*. Bloomington: Indiana University Press, 1979.
——, *Semiotics and the Philosophy of Language*. Indianapolis: Indiana University Press, 1986.
Ehrman, Bart D. *Jesus: Apocalyptic Prophet of the New Millennium*. Oxford: Oxford University Press, 1999.
Elliott, John. *A Home for the Homeless: A Sociological Exegesis of 1 Peter, Its Situation and Strategy*. London: SCM Press, 1981.
——, 'Household/Family in the Gospel of Mark as a Core Symbol of Community.' Pages 36–63 in *Fabrics of Discourse: Essays in Honor of Vernon K. Robbins*. Edited by David B. Gowler, L. Gregory Bloomquist and Duane F. Watson. Harrisburg, PA: Trinity Press International, 2003.
——, 'Household Meals versus Temple Purity. Replication Patterns in Luke-Acts'. *Biblical Theology Bulletin* 21 (1991): 102–8.
——, 'The Jesus Movement was Not Egalitarian but Family-Oriented'. *Biblical Interpretation* 11 (2003): 173–210.
——, 'Jesus was Not an Egalitarian. A Critique of an Anachronistic and Idealist Theory'. *Biblical Theology Bulletin* 32 (2002): 75–91.
——, 'Temple Versus Household in Luke-Acts: A Contrast in Social Institutions'. Pages 211–40 in *The Social World of Luke-Acts: Models of Interpretation*. Edited by Jerome H. Neyrey. Peabody, MA: Hendrickson, 1991.
Enberg-Pedersen, Troels. 'Philo's *De Vita Contemplativa* as a Philosopher's Dream'. *Journal for the Study of Judaism* 30 (1999): 40–61.
Epp, Eldon J. *The Theological Tendency of Codex Bezae Cantabriensis in Acts*. Society for New Testament Studies Monograph Series 3. Cambridge: Cambridge University Press, 1966. Repr. Eugene, OR: Wipf & Stock, 2001.
Ervin, H. *Conversion-Initiation and the Baptism of the Holy Spirit: An Engaging Critique of James D.G. Dunn's Baptism in the Holy Spirit*. Peabody: Hendrickson, 1984.
Esler, Philip F. *Community and Gospel in Luke-Acts: The Social and Political Motivations of Lucan Theology*. Society for New Testament Studies: Monograph Series 57. Cambridge: Cambridge University Press, 1987.
Estrada, Nelson P. *From Followers to Leaders: The Apostles in the Ritual of Status Transformation in Acts 1–2*. Journal for the Study of the New Testament: Supplement Series 255. London: T&T Clark International, 2004.
Evans, Craig A. 'Jesus and the Continuing Exile of Israel'. Pages 77–100 in *Jesus and the Restoration of Israel: A Critical Assessment of N.T. Wright's Jesus and the Victory of God*. Edited by Carey C. Newman. Downers Grove: InterVarsity, 1999.
——, 'The Prophetic Setting of the Pentecost Sermon'. *Zeitschrift für die neuetestamentliche Wissenschaft und die Kunde der älteren Kirche* 74 (1983): 148–50. ('The Prophetic Setting of the Pentecost Sermon'. Pages 212–24 in *Luke and Scripture: The Function of Sacred Tradition in Luke-Acts*. Edited by Craig A. Evans and James A. Sanders. Minneapolis: Fortress Press, 1993.)
——, 'The Twelve Thrones of Israel: Scripture and Politics in Luke 22:24–30'. Pages 154–70 in *Luke and Scripture: The Function of Sacred Tradition in Luke-Acts*. Edited by Craig A. Evans and James A. Sanders. Minneapolis: Fortress Press, 1993.
Evans, Craig A., and James A. Sanders, eds. *Luke and Scripture: The Function of Sacred Tradition in Luke-Acts*. Minneapolis: Fortress Press, 1993.
——, *Paul and the Scriptures of Israel*. Journal for the Study of the New Testament: Supplement Series 83. Sheffield: JSOT Press, 1993.

Evans, Craig A., and William Richard Stegner, eds. *The Gospels and the Scriptures of Israel*. Sheffield: Sheffield Academic Press, 1994.
Evans, Donald D. *The Logic of Self-Involvement: A Philosophical Study of Everyday Language with Special Reference to the Christian Use of Language about God as Creator*. London: SCM Press, 1963.
Eynde, Sabine van den. 'Children of the Promise: On the Διαθήκη-Promise to Abraham in Lk 1,72 and Acts 3,25'. Pages 469–82 in *The Unity of Luke Acts*. Edited by J. Verheyden. Bibliotheca Ephemeridum Theologicarum Lovaniensium 142. Leuven: Leuven University Press, 1999.
Fann, K. T., ed. *Symposium on Austin*. London: Routledge and Keagan Paul, 1969.
Farris, Stephen. *The Hymns of Luke's Infancy Narratives: Their Origin, Meaning and Significance*. Journal for the Study of the New Testament: Supplement Series 9. Sheffield: JSOT Press, 1985.
Feiler, Paul F. 'Jesus the Prophet: The Lucan Portrayal of Jesus as the Prophet like Moses'. PhD diss., Princeton Theological Seminary, 1986.
Ferguson, John. *Utopias of the Classical World*. London: Thames and Hudson, 1975.
Festugière, A.-J. 'Les mémoires pythagoriques cites par Alexandre Polyhistor'. *Revue des études grecques* 58 (1945): 1–65.
———, 'Sur une nouvelle édition du "De Vita Pythagorica" de Jamblique'. *Revue des études grecques* 50 (1937): 470–94.
Finkel, Asher. 'Jesus' Preaching in the Synagogue on the Sabbath (Luke 4.16–28)'. Pages 325–41 in *The Gospels and the Scriptures of Israel*. Edited by Craig A. Evans and W. Richard Stegner. Journal for the Study of the New Testament: Supplement Series 104. Sheffield: Sheffield Academic Press, 1994.
Finley, M. I. *The Ancient Economy*. Sather Classical Lectures 43 Updated Edition. Berkeley: University of California Press, 1985.
———, *Politics in the Ancient World*. Cambridge: Cambridge University Press, 1983.
Fish, Stanley. 'How to Do Things with Austin and Searle: Speech Act Theory and Literary Criticism'. *Modern Language Notes* 91 (1976): 983–1025.
———, 'With Compliments of the Author: Reflections on Austin and Derrida'. *Critical Inquiry* 8 (1982): 693–721.
Fishbane, Michael. *Biblical Interpretation in Ancient Israel*. Oxford: Clarendon Press, 1985.
———, *Biblical Text and Texture: A Literary Reading of Selected Texts*. Oxford: Oneworld Publications, 1998.
Fitzmyer, Joseph A. *The Acts of the Apostles: A New Translation with Introduction and Commentary*. Anchor Bible 31. New York: Doubleday, 1998.
———, 'Jewish Christianity in Acts in Light of the Qumran Scrolls'. Pages 233–57 in *Studies in Luke-Acts*. Edited by Leander Keck and J. Louis Martyn. Nashville: Abingdon, 1966.
———, *Luke the Theologian: Aspects of his Teaching*. New York: Paulist Press, 1989.
———, 'The Role of the Spirit in Luke-Acts'. Pages 65–83 in *The Unity of Luke Acts*. Edited by J. Verheyden. Bibliotheca Ephemeridum Theologicarum Lovaniensium 142. Leuven: Leuven University Press, 1999.
———, 'Satan and Demons in Luke-Acts'. Pages 146–74 in *Luke the Theologian: Aspects of his Teaching*. New York: Paulist Press, 1989.
Foakes-Jackson, F. J. *The Acts of the Apostles*. Moffat New Testament Commentary. London: Hodder and Stoughton, 1931.
Foakes-Jackson, F. J., and Kirsopp Lake, eds. *The Beginnings of Christianity*. Part one: *The Acts of the Apostles*. 5 vols. London: Macmillan, 1922–33.
Forbes, Christopher. *Prophecy and Inspired Speech in Early Christianity and its Hellenistic Environment*. Peabody, MA: Hendrickson, 1995.
Ferguson, L. W. 'Locutionary and Illocutionary Acts'. Pages 160–85 in *Essays on J.L. Austin*. I. Berlin, et al. Oxford: Clarendon Press, 1973.

Forkman, Göran. *The Limits of the Religious Community: Expulsion from the Religious Community within the Qumran Sect, within Rabbinic Judaism, and within Primitive Christianity*. Lund: CWK Gleerup, 1972.

Francis, F. O. 'Eschatology and History in Luke-Acts'. *Journal of the American Academy of Religion* 37 (1969): 49–63.

Franklin, Eric. 'The Ascension and the Eschatology of Luke-Acts'. *Scottish Journal of Theology* 23 (1970): 191–200.

———, *Christ the Lord: A Study in the Purpose and Theology of Luke-Acts*. Philadelphia: The Westminster Press, 1975.

———, 'Review of A.W. Zwiep, *The Ascension of the Messiah in Lukan Christology*'. *Journal of Theological Studies* 50 (1999): 230–6.

Freedman, David N., ed. *The Anchor Bible Dictionary*. 6 vols. New York: Doubleday, 1992.

Fritz, Kurt von. *Pythagorean Politics in Southern Italy: An Analysis of the Sources*. New York: Columbia University Press, 1940.

Furneaux, William M. *The Acts of the Apostles: A Commentary for English Readers* Oxford: Clarendon Press, 1912.

Gallagher, Robert L., and Paul Hertig, eds. *Mission in Acts: Ancient Narratives in Contemporary Context*. Maryknoll, NY: Orbis Books, 2004.

Gamble, Harry Y. *Books and Readers in the Early Church: A History of Early Christian Texts*. New Haven: Yale University Press, 1995.

García Martínez, Florentino, 'Magic in the Dead Sea Scrolls'. Pages 13–33 in *The Metamorphosis of Magic from Late Antiquity to the Early Modern Period*. Edited by Jan N. Bremmer and Jan R. Veenstra. Leuven: Peeters, 2002.

Garnsey, Peter, and Greg Woolf. 'Patronage of the Rural Poor in the Roman World'. Pages 153–70 in *Patronage in Ancient Society*. Edited by Andrew Wallace-Hadrill. London: Routledge, 1989.

Garrett, Susan. *The Demise of the Devil: Magic and the Demonic in Luke's Writings*. Minneapolis: Fortress Press, 1989.

Garrison, Roman. *Redemptive Almsgiving in Early Christianity*. Journal for the Study of the New Testament: Supplement Series 77. Sheffield: JSOT Press, 1993.

Gärtner, Bertil. *The Temple and The Community in Qumran and the New Testament: A Comparative Study in the Temple Symbolism of the Qumran Texts and the New Testament*. Cambridge: Cambridge University Press, 1965.

Garvey, James. 'Characterization in Narrative'. *Poetics* 7 (1978): 63–78.

Gasque, W. Ward. *A History of the Criticism of the Acts of the Apostles*. Grand Rapids: Eerdmans, 1975.

Geertz, Clifford. 'Centers, Kings, and Charisma: Reflections on the Symbolics of Power'. Pages 121–46 in *Local Knowledge: Further Essays in Interpretive Anthropology*. New York: Basic, 1983.

———, 'Thick Description: Toward an Interpretive Theory of Culture'. Pages 3–30 in *The Interpretation of Cultures*. New York: Basic Books, 1973.

Gehring, Roger W. *House Church and Mission: The Importance of Household Structures in Early Christianity*. Peabody, MA: Hendrickson, 2004.

Gen, Raymond M. 'The Phenomena of Miracles and Divine Infliction in Luke-Acts: Their Theological Significance'. *Pneuma* 11 (1989): 3–19.

George, Augustin. *Études sur l'œuvre de Luc*. Sources bibliques. Paris: Gabalda, 1978.

Gerhardsson, Birger. *The Testing of God's Son*. Lund: Gleerp, 1966.

Giblin, C. H. 'Complementarity of Symbolic Event and Discourse in Acts 2, 1–40'. Pages 189–96 in *Studia Evangelica*. Vol. 6. Edited by Elizabeth A. Livingstone. Berlin: Akademie Verlag, 1969.

Gill, Christopher. 'The Question of Character-Development: Plutarch and Tacitus'. *Classical Quarterly* n.s. 33 (1983), 469–87.

Gill, Christopher, Norman Postlethwaite and Richard Seaford, eds. *Reciprocity in Ancient Greece*. Oxford: Oxford University Press, 1998.

Gill, David W. J., and Conrad Gempf, eds. *The Book of Acts in Its First Century Setting: Volume 2: Graeco-Roman Setting*. Grand Rapids: Eerdmans / Carlisle: Paternoster, 1993.

Glasson, Thomas F. *Greek Influence in Jewish Eschatology*. London: SPCK, 1961.

González, Justo L. *Faith and Wealth: A History of Early Christian Ideas on the Origin, Significance, and Use of Money*. London: Harper & Row, 1990. Repr. Eugene, OR: Wipf & Stock, 2002.

Goodman, Martin. 'A Note on the Qumran Sectarians, the Essenes and Josephus'. *Journal of Jewish Studies* 46 (1995): 161–6.

Gorman, David, 'The Use and Abuse of Speech-Act Theory in Criticism'. *Poetics Today* 20 (1999): 93–119.

Gorman, Michael J. *Apostle of the Crucified Lord: A Theological Introduction to Paul and His Letters*. Grand Rapids: Eerdmans, 2004.

Gorman, Peter. 'Pythagoras Palestinus'. *Philologus* 127 (1983): 30–42.

Gouldner, Alvin W. 'The Norm of Reciprocity: A Preliminary Statement'. *American Sociological Review* 25 (1960): 161–78.

Gowler, David B. *Host, Guest, Enemy and Friend: Portraits of the Pharisees in Luke and Acts*. Emory Studies in Early Christianity 2. New York: Peter Lang, 1991.

Graf, Fritz. 'Excluding the Charming: The Development of the Greek Concept of Magic'. Pages 29–42 in *Ancient Magic and Ritual Power*. Edited by Marvin Meyer and Paul Mirecki. Leiden: Brill, 2001.

———, *Magic in the Ancient World*. Translated by Franklin Philip. Cambridge, MA: Harvard University Press, 1997.

Granovetter, Mark. 'Economic Action and Social Structure: The Problem of Embeddedness'. *American Journal of Sociology* 91 (1985): 481–510.

Grant, Robert M. 'Dietary Laws Among Pythagoreans, Jews, and Christians', *Harvard Theological Review* 73 (1980): 299–310.

Green, Joel B. 'The Demise of the Temple as "Culture Center" in Luke-Acts: An Exploration of the Rending of the Temple Veil (Luke 23.44–49)', *Revue biblique* (1994): 495–515.

———, 'Good News to Whom? Jesus and the "Poor" in the Gospel of Luke'. Pages 59–74 in *Jesus of Nazareth: Lord and Christ: Essays on the Historical Jesus and New Testament Christology*. Edited by Joel B. Green and Max Turner. Grand Rapids: Eerdmans / Carlisle: Paternoster, 1994.

———, *The Gospel of Luke*. New International Commentary on the New Testament. Grand Rapids: Eerdmans, 1997.

———, 'Internal Repetition in Luke-Acts: Contemporary Narratology and Lucan Historiography'. Pages 283–99 in *History, Literature and Society in the Book of Acts*. Edited by Ben Witherington III. Cambridge: Cambridge University Press, 1996.

———, 'The Problem of a Beginning: Israel's Scriptures in Luke 1–2'. *Bulletin for Biblical Research* 4 (1994): 61–86.

———, '"She and her household were baptized" (Acts 16.15): Household Baptism in the Acts of the Apostles'. Pages 72–90 in *Dimensions of Baptism: Biblical and Theological Studies*. Edited by Stanley Porter and Anthony R. Cross. JSNTS 234. London: Sheffield Academic Press, 2002.

———, 'The Social Status of Mary in Luke 1,5–2,52: A Plea for Methodological Integration'. *Biblica* 73 (1992): 457–72.

———, *The Theology of the Gospel of Luke*. New Testament Theology. Cambridge: Cambridge University Press, 1995.

———, '"Witnesses of His Resurrection": Resurrection, Salvation, Discipleship, and Mission in the Acts of the Apostles'. Pages 227–46 in *Life in the Face of Death: The Resurrection*

Message in the New Testament. Edited by Richard N. Longenecker. Grand Rapids: Eerdmans, 1998.

Greene, G. R. 'The Portrayal of Jesus as Prophet in Luke-Acts'. PhD diss., Southern Baptist Theological Seminary, 1975.

Greenspahn, F. E. 'Why Prophecy Ceased'. *Journal of Biblical Literature* 108 (1989): 37–49.

Gregory, Andrew. 'The Reception of Luke and Acts and the Unity of Luke-Acts'. *Journal for the Study of the New Testament* 29 (2007): 459–72.

Grice, H. Paul. *Studies in the Way of Words*. Cambridge, MA: Harvard University Press, 1989.

Griffiths, J. Gwyn. *The Divine Verdict: A Study of Divine Judgment in the Ancient Religions*. Studies in the History of Religions (Supplements to *Numen*) 52. Leiden: Brill, 1991.

Grimes, Ronald. 'Infelicitous Performances and Ritual Criticism'. Pages 103–22 *Speech Act Theory and Biblical Criticism*. *Semeia* 41. Edited by H. C. White. Decatur, GA: Scholars Press, 1988.

Grossman, Maxine. *Reading for History in the Damascus Document: A Methodological Method*. Studies on the Texts of the Desert of Judah 45. Leiden: Brill, 2002.

Haacker, Klaus. 'Verwendung und Vermeidung des Apostelbegriffs im lukanischen Werk'. *Novum Testamentum* 30 (1988): 9–38.

Hadas, Moses. *Hellenistic Culture: Fusion and Diffusion*. New York: Columbia University Press, 1959.

Haenchen, Ernst. *The Acts of the Apostles: A Commentary*. 14th edn. Translated by R. McL. Wilson. Oxford: Basil Blackwell, 1971.

———, 'Zum Text der Apostelgeschichte'. *Zeitschrift für Theologie und Kirche* 54 (1957): 22–55.

Hahn, Scott W. 'Kingdom and Church in Luke-Acts: From Davidic Christology to Kingdom Ecclesiology'. Pages 294–326 in *Reading Luke: Interpretation, Reflection, Formation*. Edited by Craig Bartholomew, Joel B. Green and Anthony C. Thiselton. Scripture and Hermeneutics Series 6. Grand Rapids: Zondervan, 2005.

———, *The Lamb's Supper: The Mass as Heaven on Earth*. London: Darton, Longman & Todd, 1999.

Hall, Robert G. *Revealed Histories: Techniques for Ancient Jewish and Christian Historiography*. Journal for the Study of the Pseudepigrapha: Supplement Series 6. Sheffield: JSOT Press, 1991.

Halliday, M. A. K. *Language as Social Semiotic: The Social Interpretation of Language and Meaning*. London: Edward Arnold, 1978.

Hamm, Dennis. 'Acts 3,1–10: The Healing of the Temple Beggar as Lucan Theology'. *Biblica* 67 (1986): 305–19.

———, 'Acts 3:12–26: Peter's Speech and the Healing of the Man Born Lame'. *Perspectives in Religious Studies* 11 (1984): 199–217.

———, 'Paul's Blindness and its Healing: Clues to Symbolic Intent (Acts 9; 22 and 26)'. *Biblica* 71 (1990): 63–72.

———, 'Sight to the Blind: Vision as Metaphor in Luke'. *Biblica* 67 (1986): 457–77.

Hancher, Michael. 'Beyond a Speech-Act Theory of Literary Discourse: Review of Mary Louise Pratt's *Toward a Speech Act Theory of Literary Discourse*'. *Modern Language Notes* 92 (1977): 1081–98.

———, '"Grice's "Implicature" and Literary Interpretation: Background and Preface'. Conference Paper for the Twentieth Annual Meeting Midwest Modern Language Association, Minneapolis, MN, 2–4 November 1978, accessed on the internet at http://mh.cla.umn.edu/grice.html on June 07, 2006.

———, 'Performative Utterance, The Word of God, and the Death of the Author'. Pages 27–40 in *Speech Act Theory and Biblical Criticism*. *Semeia* 41. Edited by H. C. White. Decatur, GA: Scholars Press, 1988.

Hanson, K. C., and Douglas E. Oakman. *Palestine in the Time of Jesus: Social Structures and Social Conflicts*. Minneapolis: Fortress Press, 1998.

Harari, Yuval. 'What is a Magical Text? Methodological Reflections Aimed at Redefining Early Jewish Magic'. Pages 91–124 in *Officina Magica: Essays on the Practice of Magic in Antiquity*. Edited by Shaul Shaked. Institute of Jewish Studies in Judaica 4. Leiden: Brill, 2005.

Harland, Philip A. *Associations, Synagogues and Congregations: Claiming a Place in the Ancient Mediterranean Society*. Minneapolis: Fortress, 2003.

Harris, William V. 'Between Archaic and Modern: Some Current Problems in the History of the Roman Economy'. Pages 11–29 in *The Inscribed Economy: Production and Distribution in the Roman Empire in the Light of Instrumentum Domesticum; The Proceedings of a Conference Held at the American Academy in Rome on 10-11 January, 1992*. Ann Arbor: University of Michigan Press, 1993.

Hastings, Adrian. *Prophet and Witness in Jerusalem: A Study of the Teaching of Saint Luke*. New York: Helicon, 1958.

Havelaar, Henriette. 'Hellenistic Parallels to Acts 5.1–11 and the Problem of Conflicting Interpretations'. *Journal for the Study of the New Testament* 67 (1997): 63–82.

Hay, David M. 'Moses Through New Testament Spectacles'. *Interpretation* 44 (1990): 240–52.

Haya-Prats, Gonzalo. *L'Esprit force de l'église*. Translated by José J. Romero and Hubert Faes. Paris: Cerf, 1975.

Hays, Richard B., and Green, Joel B. 'The Use of the Old Testament by New Testament Writers'. Pages 222–38 in *Hearing the New Testament: Strategies for Interpretation*. Edited by Joel B. Green. Grand Rapids: Eerdmans, 1995.

Head, Peter. 'The Temple in Luke's Gospel'. Pages 101–19 in *Heaven on Earth: The Temple in Biblical Theology*. Edited by T. Desmond Alexander and Simon Gathercole. Carlisle: Paternoster, 2004.

Hellerman, Joseph H. *The Ancient Church as Family*. Minneapolis: Fortress, 2001.

Helm, Paul. 'Speaking and Revealing'. *Religious Studies* 37 (2001): 249–58.

Hempel, Charlotte. *The Damascus Texts*. Companion to the Qumran Scrolls 1. Sheffield: Sheffield Academic Press, 2000.

——, *The Laws of the Damascus Document: Sources, Tradition and Redaction*. Studies on the Texts of the Desert of Judah 29. Leiden: Brill, 1998.

Hendricks, William O. 'Review of Mary Louise Pratt's *Toward a Speech Act Theory of Literary Discourse*'. *Language* 55 (1979): 475–6.

Hengel, Martin. *Acts and the History of Earliest Christianity*. Translated by John Bowden. London: SCM Press, 1979.

——, *Between Jesus and Paul: Studies in the Earliest History of Christianity*. Translated by John Bowden London: SCM Press, 1983.

——, 'Die Ursprünge der christlichen Mission'. *New Testament Studies* 18 (1971): 15–38.

——, 'Eye-Witness Memory and the Writing of the Gospels'. Pages 70–96 in *The Written Gospel*. Edited by Markus Bockmuehl and Donald A. Hagner. Cambridge: Cambridge University Press, 2005.

——, *Judaism and Hellenism*. 2 vols. Translated by John Bowden. London: SCM Press, 1974.

——, 'Qumran and Hellenism'. Pages 46–56 in *Religion in the Dead Sea Scrolls*. Edited by John J. Collins and Robert A. Kugler. Studies in the Dead Sea Scrolls and Related Literature. Grand Rapids: Eerdmans, 2000.

Hill, Craig C. 'Acts 6.1–8.4: Division or Diversity?' Pages 129–53 in *History, Literature and Society in the Book of Acts*. Edited by Ben Witherington III. Cambridge: Cambridge University Press, 1996.

——, *Hellenists and Hebrews: Reappraising Division within the Early Church*. Minneapolis: Fortress, 1992.

Hill, David. *New Testament Prophecy*. London: Marshall, Morgan and Scott, 1979.
Holdcroft, David. 'Indirect Speech Acts and Propositional Content'. Pages 350–64 in *Foundations of Speech Act Theory: Philosophical and Linguistic Perspectives*. Edited by Savas L. Tsohatzidis. London: Routledge, 1994.
Hooker, Morna D. '"Beginning with Moses and From All the Prophets"'. Pages 216–30 in *From Jesus to John: Essays on Jesus and New Testament Christology in Honour of Marinus de Jonge*. Edited by Martinus C. De Boer. Journal for the Study of the New Testament: Supplement Series 84. Sheffield: JSOT Press, 1993.
——, *The Signs of a Prophet: The Prophetic Actions of Jesus*. Harrisburg, PA: Trinity Press International, 1997.
Horbury, William. 'Extirpation and Excommunication'. *Vetus Testamentum* 35 (1985): 13–38. Reprinted in idem, *Jews and Christians in Contact and Controversy*. Edinburgh: T&T Clark, 1998, 43–66.
Hornsby, Jennifer. 'Illocutions and its Significance'. Pages 187–207 in *Foundations of Speech Act Theory: Philosophical and Linguistic Perspectives*. Edited by Savas L. Tsohatzidis. London: Routledge, 1994.
Horst, Pieter W. van der. 'Hellenistic Parallels to Acts (Chapter 3 and 4)'. *Journal for the Study of the New Testament* 35 (1989): 37–46.
——, 'Hellenistic Parallels to the Acts of the Apostles: 1 1–26'. *Zeitschrift für die Neutestamentliche Wissenschaft* 74 (1983): 17–26.
——, 'Hellenistic Parallels to the Acts of the Apostles (2.1–47)'. *Journal for the Study of the New Testament* 25 (1985): 49–60.
Houston, Walter. 'What Did the Prophets Think They Were Doing? Speech Acts and Prophetic Discourse in the Old Testament'. *Biblical Interpretation* 1 (1993): 167–88.
Hubbard, Benjamin J. 'Commissioning Stories in Luke-Acts: A Study of their Antecedents, Form and Content'. *Semeia* 8 (1977): 103–26.
——, 'The Role of Commissioning Accounts in Acts'. Pages 187–98 in *Perspectives on Luke-Acts*. Edited by Charles H. Talbert. Danville, VA: Association of Baptist Professors of Religion / Edinburgh: T&T Clark, 1978.
Hull, John M. *Hellenistic Magic and the Synoptic Tradition*. SBT, 2.28; London: SCM Press, 1974.
Hur, Ju. *A Dynamic Reading of the Holy Spirit in Luke-Acts*. London: T&T Clark, 2001.
Iser, Wolfgang. *The Act of Reading: A Theory of Aesthetic Response*. Baltimore, MD: Johns Hopkins University Press, 1978.
——, *The Fictive and the Imaginary: Charting Literary Anthropology*. Baltimore, MD: Johns Hopkins University Press, 1993.
——, *The Implied Reader: Patterns of Communication in Prose Fiction from Bunyan to Beckett*. Balitmore, MD: Johns Hopkins University Press, 1978.
Jakobson, R. 'Closing Statement: Linguistics and Poetics'. Pages 350–7 in *Style in Language*. Edited by Thomas A. Sebeok. Cambridge, MA: M.I.T. Press, 1960.
Janowitz, Naomi. *Magic in the Roman World: Pagans, Jews and Christians*. Religion in the First Christian Centuries. London: Routledge, 2001.
Jeremias, Joachim. *Jerusalem in the Time of Jesus: An Investigation into the Economic and Social Conditions during the New Testament Period*. Translated by F. H. and C. H. Cave. Philadelphia: Fortress Press, 1969.
——, 'Zur Geschichtlichkeit des Verhörs Jesu vor dem hohen Rat'. *Zeitschrift für die neutestamentliche Wissenschaft* 43 (1950–51): 145–50.
Jervell, Jacob. *Die Apostelgeschichte*. Göttingen: Vandenhoeck & Ruprecht, 1998.
——, 'The Lost Sheep of the House of Israel: The Understanding of the Samaritans in Luke-Acts'. Pages 113–32 in *Luke and the People of God: A New Look at Luke-Acts*. Minneapolis: Augsburg Publishing House, 1972.
——, *Luke and the People of God: A New Look at Luke-Acts*. Minneapolis: Augsburg Publishing House, 1972.

———, 'Sons of the Prophets: The Holy Spirit in the Acts of the Apostles'. Pages 96–121 in *The Unknown Paul: Essays on Luke-Acts and Early Christian History*. Minneapolis: Augsburg, 1984.

———, 'The Twelve on Israel's Thrones: Luke's Understanding of the Apostolate'. Pages 75–112 in *Luke and the People of God: A New Look at Luke-Acts*. Minneapolis: Augsburg Publishing House, 1972.

———, *The Unknown Paul: Essays on Luke-Acts and Early Christian Historiography*. Minneapolis: Augsburg, 1984.

Johnson, Luke Timothy. *The Acts of the Apostles*. Sacra Pagina 5. Collegeville, MN: The Liturgical Press, 1992.

———, *The Gospel of Luke*. Sacra Pagina 3. Collegeville, MN: The Liturgical Press, 1992.

———, *The Literary Function of Possessions in Luke-Acts*. Society of Biblical Literature Dissertation Series 39. Missoula, MT: Scholars Press, 1977.

———, *Living Jesus: Learning the Heart of the Gospel*. New York: HarperSanFrancisco, 1999.

———, 'On Finding the Lukan Community: A Cautious Cautionary Essay'. Pages 87–100 in vol. 1 of *SBL 1979 Seminar Papers*. 2 vols. Edited by Paul J. Achtemeier. Missoula, MT: Scholars Press, 1979.

———, *Sharing Possessions: Mandate and Symbol of Faith*. OBT. Philadelphia: Fortress, 1981.

Johnson, Sherman E. 'The Dead Sea Manual of Discipline and the Jerusalem Church of Acts'. *Zeitschrift für alttestamentliche Wissenschaft* 66 (1954): 106–20. Reprinted in *The Scrolls and the New Testament*. Edited by Krister Stendahl, with James H. Charlesworth New York: Crossroad, 1992, 129–42.

Joubert, Stephan J. 'One Form of Social Exchange or Two? "Euergetism", Patronage, and Testament Studies'. *Biblical Theology Bulletin* 31 (2001): 17–25.

Juel, Donald. 'Hearing Peter's Speech in Acts 3: Meaning and Truth in Interpretation'. *Word and World* 12 (1992): 43–50.

———, 'Social Dimensions of Exegesis: The Use of Psalm 16 in Acts 2'. *Catholic Biblical Quarterly* 43 (1981): 543–56.

Juster, Jean. *Les Juifs dans l'empire romain: Leur condition juridique, économique et sociale*. 2 vols. Paris: Paul Guethner, 1914.

Kahn, Charles H. *Pythagoras and the Pythagoreans: A Brief History*. Indianapolis / Cambridge: Hackett Publishing, 2001.

Karris, Robert J. 'The Lukan *Sitz im Leben*: Methodology and Prospects'. Pages 219–33 in *SBL Seminar Papers 1976*. Edited by George MacRae. Missoula, MT: Scholars Press, 1976.

Kauppi, Lynn Allan. *Foreign But Familiar Gods: Greco-Romans Read Religion in Acts*. Library of New Testament Studies 277. London: T&T Clark, 2006.

Keck, Leander E. 'The Poor Among the Saints in Jewish Christianity and Qumran'. *Zeitschrift für die neutestamentliche Wissenschaft und die Kunde der älteren Kirche* 57 (1966): 54–78.

Kee, Howard C. *Good News to the Ends of the Earth: The Theology of Acts*. London: SCM Press / Philadelphia: Trinity Press International, 1990.

———, *Medicine, Miracle and Magic in New Testament Times*. Cambridge: Cambridge University Press, 1986.

———, *To Every Nation Under Heaven: The Acts of the Apostles*. Harrisburg, PA: Trinity Press International, 1997.

Kenyon, Frederic G. *The Chester Beatty Biblical Papyri, Fasciculus II, The Gospels and Acts*. London: Emery Walker Ltd, 1933.

Kilgallen, John J. 'Persecution in the Acts of the Apostles'. Pages 143–60 in *Luke and Acts*. Edited by Gerald O'Collins and Gilberto Marconi. New York: Paulist Press, 1991.

———, 'What the Apostles Proclaimed at Acts 4,2'. Pages 233–48 in *Resurrection in the New Testament: Festschrift J Lambrecht*. Edited by R. Bieringer, V. Koperski and B. Lataire. Leuven: Leuven University Press, 2002.

Kim, Hee-Seong. *Die Geistaufe des Messias: Eine kompositionsgeschichtliche Untersuchung zu einem Leitmotiv des lukanischen Doppelwerks*. Berlin: Lang, 1993.

Kim, Kyoung-Jin. *Stewardship and Almsgiving in Luke's Theology*. Journal for the Study of the New Testament: Supplement Series 155. Sheffield: Sheffield Academic Press, 1998.

Kimball, Charles A. *Jesus' Exposition of the Old Testament in Luke's Gospel*. Journal for the Study of the New Testament: Supplement Series 94. Sheffield: Sheffield Academic Press, 1994.

Kingsbury, Jack D. *Conflict in Luke: Jesus, Authorities, Disciples*. Minneapolis: Fortress Press, 1991.

———, 'Jesus as the "Prophetic Messiah" in Luke's Gospel'. Pages 29–42 in *The Future of Christology: Festschrift L.E. Keck*. Edited by A. J. Malherbe and W. A. Meeks. Minneapolis: Fortress, 1993.

Kingsley, Peter. *Ancient Philosophy, Mystery, and Magic: Empedocles and Pythagorean Tradition*. Oxford: Clarendon, 1995.

Kittel, G., and G. Friedrich, eds. *Theological Dictionary of the New Testament*. Translated by G. W. Bromiley. 10 vols. Grand Rapids: Eerdmans, 1964–76.

Klassen, William. *Judas: Betrayer or Friend of Jesus?* London: SCM Press, 1996.

Klauck, Hans-Josef. 'Gütergemeinschaft in der klassischen Antike, in Qumran, und im Neuen Testament'. *Revue de Qumran* 11 (1982): 47–79.

———, *Magic and Paganism in Early Christianity: The World of the Acts of the Apostles*. Translated by Brian McNeil. Minneapolis: Fortress Press, 2000.

Klein, Günter. 'Der Synkretismus als theologisches Problem in der ältesten christliche Apologetik'. *Zeitschrift für Theologie und Kirche* 4 (1967): 40–82.

Klinghardt, Matthias. 'The Manual of Discipline in the Light of Statutes of Hellenistic Associations'. Pages 251–67 in *Methods of Investigation of the Dead Sea Scrolls and the Khirbet Qumran Site: Present Realities and Future Prospects*. Edited by Michael O. Wise, Norman Golb, John J. Collins and Dennis G. Pardee. Annals of the New York Academy of the Sciences 722. New York: The New York Academy of Sciences, 1994.

Kloppenborg, John S., and Stephen Wilson, eds. *Voluntary Associations in the Graeco-Roman World*. London: Routledge, 1996.

Koenig, John. *The Feast of the World's Redemption: Eucharistic Origins and Christian Mission*. Harrisburg, PA: Trinity Press International, 2000.

Koet, Bart J. 'Isaiah in Luke-Acts'. Pages 79–100 in *Isaiah in the New Testament*. Edited by Steve Moyise and Maarten J. J. Menken. London: T&T Clark, 2005.

Knowles, Michael. *Jeremiah in Matthew's Gospel: The Rejected-Prophet Motif in Matthean Redaction*. Journal for the Study of the New Testament: Supplement Series 68. Sheffield: Sheffield Academic Press, 1993.

Kremer, Jacob. *Pfingstbericht und Pfingstgeshehen: Eine exegetische Untersuchung zu Apg 2,1–13*. Stuttgart: KBW, 1973.

Krippner, Greta R. 'The Elusive Market: Embeddedness and the Paradigm of Economic Sociology'. *Theory and Society* 30 (2001): 775–810.

Kuecker Aaron J. 'The Spirit and the "Other," Satan and the "Self": Economic Ethics as a Consequence of Identity Transformation in Luke-Acts'. Pages 81–103 in *Engaging Economics: New Testament Scenarios and Early Christian Reception*. Edited by Bruce W. Longenecker and Kelly D. Liebengood. Grand Rapids: Eerdmans, 2009.

Kurz, William. 'Acts 3:19–26 as a Test of the Role of Eschatology in Lukan Christology'. Pages 309–23 in *SBL 1977 Seminar Papers*. Edited by Paul J. Achtemeier. Missoula: Scholars, 1977.

Labov, William. *Language in the Inner City*. University Park: University of Pennsylvania Press, 1972.

Lake, Kirsopp. 'The Communism of Acts II and IV–VI and the Appointment of the Seven'. Pages 140–51 in *The Beginnings of Christianity. Part 1: The Acts of the Apostles. Volume V: Additional Notes to the Commentary*. Edited by F. J. Foakes-Jackson and Kirsopp Lake. London: MacMillan and Co., 1933.

———, 'The Death of Judas'. Pages 22–30 in *The Beginnings of Christianity. Part 1: The Acts of the Apostles. Volume V: Additional Notes to the Commentary*. Edited by F. J. Foakes-Jackson and Kirsopp Lake. London: MacMillan and Co., 1933.

Lake, Kirsopp, and Cadbury, Henry J. 'Acts of the Apostles: English Translation and Commentary'. Pages 1–352 in *The Beginnings of Christianity. Part 1: The Acts of the Apostles. Vol. IV: English Translation and Commentary*. Edited by F. J. Foakes-Jackson and Kirsopp Lake. London: MacMillan and Co., 1933.

Lange, Armin. 'The Essene Position on Magic and Divination'. Pages 377–435 in *Legal Texts and Legal Issues: Proceedings of the Second Meeting of the International Organization for Qumran Studies, Cambridge 1995*. Edited by Moshe Bernstein, Florentino García Martínez, and John Kampen. Leiden: Brill, 1997.

Lanser, Susan Sniader. *The Narrative Act: Point of View in Prose Fiction*. Princeton: Princeton University Press, 1981.

Larkin, William J. *Acts*. IVP New Testament Commentary Series. Downers Grove: InterVarsity Press, 1995.

Leary, T. J. 'The "Aprons" of St Paul – Acts 19:12'. *Journal of Theological Studies* 41 (1990): 527–9.

Lepore, Ernest, and Robert Van Gulick, eds. *John Searle and His Critics*. Oxford: Blackwell, 1993.

Levenson, Jon D. *Sinai and Zion: An Entry into the Jewish Bible*. New York: HarperSanFrancisco, 1985.

Levison, John R. *The Spirit in First-Century Judaism*. Leiden: Brill Academic Publishers, Inc., 2002.

Lévy, Isidore. *La légende de Pythagore de Grèce en Palestine*. Paris: Champion, 1927.

———, *Recherches esséniennes et pythagoriciennes*. III Hautes Études de Monde Gréco-Romain 1. Geneva: Droz / Paris: Minard, 1965.

———, *Recherches sur les sources de la légende de Pythagore*. Paris: Leroux, 1926.

Litwak, Kenneth D. *Echoes of Scripture in Luke-Acts: Telling the History of God's People Intertextually*. Journal for the Study of the New Testament: Supplement Series. Edinburgh: T&T Clark, 2005.

Lohfink, Gerhard. *Die Himmelfahrt Jesu: Untersuchungen zu den Himmelfahrts- und Erhöhungstexten bei Lukas*. Munich: Kösel, 1971.

———, *Die Sammelung Israels: Eine Untersuchung zur lukanischen Ekklesiologie*. Studien zum Alten und Neuen Testaments 39. Munich: Kösel, 1975.

Longenecker, Bruce W. 'Rome's Victory and God's Honour: The Jerusalem Temple and the Spirit of God in Lukan Theodicy'. Pages 90–102 in *The Holy Spirit and Christian Origins: Essays in Honor of James D.G. Dunn*. Edited by Graham N. Stanton, Bruce W. Longenecker and Stephen C. Barton. Grand Rapids: Eerdmans, 2004.

Lüdemann, Gerd. *The Acts of the Apostles: What Really Happened in the Earliest Days of the Church*. Amherst, NY: Promethius Books, 2005.

———, *Early Christianity According to the Traditions in Acts: A Commentary* Translated by John Bowden; London: SCM, 1989.

Lyons, John. *Language and Linguistics: An Introduction*. Cambridge: Cambridge University Press, 1981.

———, *Semantics*. Vol. 2. Cambridge: Cambridge University Press, 1977.

Mack, Burton L. *Rhetoric and the New Testament*. Guides to Biblical Scholarship: New Testament Series. Minneapolis: Fortress, 1990.

MacMullen, Ramsay. *Roman Social Relations: 50 B.C to A.D. 284*. New Haven: Yale University Press, 1974.

Maddox, Robert J. *The Purpose of Luke-Acts*. Göttingen: Vandenhoeck und Ruprecht, 1982.
Maile, John F. 'The Ascension in Luke-Acts'. *Tyndale Bulletin* 37 (1986): 29–59.
Malina, Bruce J., and Jerome H. Neyrey. 'Honor and Shame in Luke-Acts: Pivotal Values of the Mediterranean World'. Pages 25–65 in *The Social World of Luke-Acts: Models for Interpretation*. Edited by Jerome H. Neyrey. Peabody, MA: Hendrickson, 1991.
Mánek, Jindřich. 'The New Exodus in the Books of Luke'. *Novum Testamentum* 2 (1957): 8–23.
Margolis, Joseph. 'Literature and Speech Acts'. *Philosophy and Literature* 3 (1979): 39–52.
——, 'Review of Mary Louise Pratt's *Toward a Speech Act Theory of Literary Discourse*'. *The Journal of Aesthetics and Art Criticism* 36 (1977): 225–8.
Marguerat, Daniel. 'Ananias and Sapphira (Acts 5. 1–11): The Original Sin'. Pages 155–78 in *The First Christian Historian: Writing the 'Acts of the Apostles'*. Translated by Ken McKinney, Gregory J. Laughery and Richard Bauckham. Society for New Testament Studies Monograph Series 121. Cambridge: Cambridge University Press, 2002.
——, 'Ananias et Saphira (Actes 5, 1–11): Le viol du sacré'. *Lumière et vie* 42 (1993): 51–63.
——, *The First Christian Historian: Writing the 'Acts of the Apostles'*. Translated by Ken McKinney, Gregory J. Laughery and Richard Bauckham. Society for New Testament Studies Monograph Series 121. Cambridge: Cambridge University Press, 2002.
——, 'La mort d'Ananias et Saphira (AC 5.1–11) dans la stratégie narrative de Luc'. *New Testament Studies* 39 (1993): 209–26.
——, 'Magic and Miracle in the Acts of the Apostles' Pages 100–24 in *Magic in the Biblical World: From the Rod of Aaron to the Ring of Solomon*. Edited by Todd Klutz. Journal for the Study of the New Testament: Supplement Series 245. London: T&T Clark, 2003.
——, 'Terreur dans l'Église: le drame d'Ananias et Saphira (Actes 5:1–11)'. *Foi et vie* 91 (1992): 77–88.
Marshall, I. Howard. *Acts*. Tyndale New Testament Commentaries. Leicester: Intervarsity Press / Grand Rapids: Eerdmans, 1980.
——, *Luke: Historian and Theologian*. 3rd edn. London: Paternoster Press, 1970.
——, 'The Significance of Pentecost'. *Scottish Journal of Theology* 30 (1977): 347–69.
Marshall, I. Howard, and David Peterson, eds. *Witness to the Gospel: The Theology of Acts*. Grand Rapids / Cambridge: Eerdmans, 1998.
Martone, Corrado. 'The Nature of Impurity at Qumran'. Pages 610–16 in *The Dead Sea Scrolls: Fifty Years After their Discovery: Proceedings of the Jerusalem Congress, July 20–25, 1997*. Edited by Lawrence Schiffman, Emanuel Tov and James C. VanderKam. Jerusalem: Israel Exploration Society, 2000.
Mason, Steve. 'Chief Priests, Sadducees, Pharisees and Sanhedrin in Acts'. Pages 115–77 in *The Book of Acts in its Palestinian Setting*. Edited by Richard Bauckham. Vol. 4 of *The Book of Acts in its First Century Setting*. Edited by Bruce W. Winter. Grand Rapids: Eerdmans, 1995.
——, *Josephus and the New Testament*. Peabody, MA: Hendrickson, 1992.
——, 'What Josephus Says about the Essenes in his *Judean War*'. Pages 434–67 in *Text and Artifact in the Religions of Mediterranean Antiquity: Essays in Honour of Peter Richardson*. Edited by Stephen G. Wilson and Michael Desjardins. Ontario: Wilfrid Laurier University Press, 2000.
McCabe, David R. 'Acts of Ascension: History, Exaltation and Ideological Legitimation'. In *Reading Acts in the Second Century*. Edited by Todd Penner and Rubén Dupertuis. London: Equinox, *forthcoming*.
McCane, Byron R. *Roll Back the Stone: Death and Burial in the World of Jesus*. Harrisburg, PA: Trinity Press International, 2003.
McComiskey Douglas S. *Lukan Theology in the Light of the Gospel's Literary Structure*. Carlisle: Paternoster, 2004.

McCoy, W. J. 'In the Shadow of Thucydides'. Pages 3–32 in *History, Literature and Society in the Book of Acts*. Edited by Ben Witherington III. Cambridge: Cambridge University Press, 1996.

McCracken, David. 'Character in the Boundary: Bakhtin's Interdividuality in Biblical Narratives'. *Semeia* 63 (1993): 29–42.

McKeever, Michael. 'Sacred Space and Discursive Field: The Narrative Function of the Temple in Luke-Acts'. PhD diss., Graduate Theological Union, 1999.

McVann Mark. 'Rituals of Status Transformation in Luke-Acts: The Case of Jesus the Prophet'. Pages 333–60 in *The Social World of Luke-Acts: Models for Interpretation*. Edited by Jerome H. Neyrey. Peabody: Hendrickson, 1991.

Mealand, David L. 'Community Goods and Utopian Allusions in Acts II–IV'. *Journal of Theological Studies* 28 (1977): 96–9.

——, 'Community of Goods at Qumran'. *Theologische Zeitschrift* 31 (1975): 129–39.

——, 'The Paradox of Philo's Views on Wealth'. *Journal for the Study of the New Testament* 24 (1985): 111–15.

——, 'Philo of Alexandria's Attitude to Riches'. *Zeitschrift für die neutestamentliche Wissenschaft und die Kunde der älteren Kirche* 69 (1978): 256–64.

Meeks, Wayne A. *The Prophet-King: Moses Traditions and the Johannine Christology*. Novum Testamentum Supplements 14. Leiden: Brill, 1967.

——, 'Simon Magus in Recent Research'. *Recherches de science religieuse* 3 (1977): 137–42.

Mendels, Doron. 'Hellenistic Utopias and the Essenes'. *Harvard Theological Review* 72 (1979): 207–22.

Menoud, Philippe-H. 'La mort d'Ananias et de Saphira (Actes 5. 1–11)'. Pages 146–54 in *Aux de sources la tradition chrétienne Mélanges offerts à M. Maurice Goguel à l'occasion de son soixante-dixiime anniversaire*. Edited by O. Cullman and P.-H. Menoud. Biblothéque Theologique. Neuchâtel: Delachaux et Niestlé, 1950.

Menzies, Robert P. *The Development of Early Christian Pneumatology with special reference to Luke-Acts*. Journal for the Study of the New Testament: Supplement Series 54. Sheffield: Sheffield Academic Press, 1991.

——, 'The Distinctive Character of Luke's Pneumatology'. *Paraclete* 25 (1991): 17–30.

——, *Empowered for Witness: The Spirit in Luke-Acts*. Sheffield: JSOT Press, 1994.

——, 'Luke and the Spirit: A Reply to James Dunn'. *Journal for Pentecostal Theology* 4 (1994): 115–38.

——, 'Spirit and Power in Luke-Acts: A Response to Max Turner'. *Journal for the Study of the New Testament* 49 (1993): 11–20.

——, 'The Spirit of Prophecy in Luke-Acts and Pentecostal Theology: A Response to Max Turner'. *Journal for Pentecostal Theology* 15 (1999): 49–74.

Merenlahti, Petri. 'Characters in the Making: Individuality and Ideology in the Gospels'. Pages 49–72 in *Characterization in the Gospels: Reconceiving Narrative Criticism*. Edited by David Rhoads and Kari Syreeni. Journal for the Study of the New Testament: Supplement Series 184. Sheffield: Sheffield Academic Press, 1999.

Metso, Sarianna. 'Qumran Community Structure and Terminology as Theological Statement'. Pages 283–300 in *The Bible and the Dead Sea Scrolls: The Princeton Symposium on the Dead Sea Scrolls. Vol 2: The Dead Sea Scrolls and the Qumran Community*. Edited by James H. Charlesworth. Waco, TX: Baylor University Press, 2006.

——, 'The Redaction of the Community Rule'. Pages 377–84 in *The Dead Sea Scrolls: Fifty Years After their Discovery: Proceedings of the Jerusalem Congress, July 20–25, 1997*. Edited by Lawrence Schiffman, Emanuel Tov and James C. VanderKam. Jerusalem: Israel Exploration Society, 2000.

——, 'The Relationship Between the Danascus Document and the Communty Rule'. Pages in 85–93 *The Damascus Document: A Centennial of Discovery. Proceedings of the Third International Symposium of the Orion Center, 4–8 February 1998*. Edited by Joseph M. Baumgarten, Esther G. Chazon and Avital Pinnick; Leiden: Brill, 2000.

——, *The Textual Development of the Qumran Community Rule*. Studies on the Texts of the Desert of Judah 21. Leiden: Brill, 1997.

——, 'The Textual Traditions of the Qumran *Community Rule*'. Pages 141–7 in *Legal Texts and Legal Issues: Proceedings of the Second Meeting of the International Organization for Qumran Studies Cambridge 1995*. Edited by Moshe Bernstein, Florentino García Martínez and John Kampen. Leiden: Brill, 1997.

Metzger, Bruce M. *A Textual Commentary on the Greek New Testament*. 3rd edn. Stuttgart: United Bible Societies, 1971.

Miles, Gary G., and Garry Trompf. 'Luke and Antiphon: The Theology of Acts 27–28 in Light of Pagan Beliefs about Divine Retribution, Pollution, and Shipwreck'. *Harvard Theological Review* 69 (1976): 259–67.

Miller, Robert J. 'Elijah, John, and Jesus in the Gospel of Luke'. *New Testament Studies* 34 (1988): 611–22.

Minar, Edwin L. *Early Pythagorean Politics in Practice and Theory*. Baltimore: Waverly Press, 1942.

——, 'Pythagorean Communism'. *Transactions and Proceedings of the American Philological Association* 75 (1944): 34–46.

Minear, Paul S. *To Heal and to Reveal: The Prophetic Vocation According to Luke*. New York: The Seabury Press, 1976.

Mitchell, Alan C. '"Greet the Friends by Name": New Testament Evidence for the Greco-Roman *Topos* on Friendship'. Pages 225–62 in *Greco-Roman Perspectives on Friendship*. Edited by John T. Fitzgerald. Society of Biblical Literature Resources for Biblical Study 34. Atlanta: Scholars Press, 1997.

——, 'The Social Function of Friendship in Acts 2:44–45 and 4:32–37'. *Journal of Biblical Literature* 111 (1992): 255–72.

Mitford, T. B. 'Roman Cyprus'. *Aufstieg und Niedergang der römischen Welt: Geschichte und Kultur Roms im Spiegel der neueren Forschung*. Edited by H. Temporini and W. Haase. II.7.2 (1980): 1286–1384.

Moessner, David P. 'The Appeal and Power of Poetics (Luke 1:1–4): Luke's Superior Credentials (παρηκολουθηκότι), Narrative Sequence (καθεξῆς), and Firmness of Understanding (ἡ ἀσφάλεια) for the Reader'. Pages 84–123 in *Jesus and the Heritage of Israel: Luke's Narrative Claim Upon Israel's Legacy*. Edited by D. P. Moessner. Harrisburg, PA: Trinity Press International, 1999.

——, '"The Christ Must Suffer": New Light on the Jesus-Peter, Stephen, Paul Parallels in Luke-Acts'. *Novum Testamentum* 28 (1986): 220–56.

——, 'Dionysius' Narrative "Arrangement" (οἰκονομία) as the Hermeneutical Key to Luke's Re-Vision of the "Many"'. Pages 149–64 in *Paul, Luke, and the Graeco-Roman World: Essays in Honour of Alexander J.M. Wedderburn*. Edited by A. Christophersen, C. Claussen, J. Frey and B. Longenecker. Journal for the Study of the New Testament: Supplement Series 217. Sheffield: Sheffield Academic Press, 2002.

——, 'How Luke Writes'. Pages 149–70 in *The Written Gospel*. Edited by M. Bockmuehl and D. Hagner. Cambridge: Cambridge University Press, 2005.

——, 'Jesus and the Wilderness Generation: The Death of the Prophet Like Moses according to Luke'. Pages 319–40 in *SBL 1982 Seminar Papers*. Edited by Kent H. Richards. Atlanta: Scholars Press, 1982.

——, 'The "Leaven of the Pharisees" and "This Generation": Israel's Rejection of Jesus According to Luke'. Pages 79–107, 190–93 in *Reimaging the Death of the Lukan Jesus*. Edited by Dennis D. Sylva. Frankfurt: Hain, 1990. Rev. in *Journal for the Study of the New Testament* 34 (1988): 21–46. Repr. pages 268–93 in *The Synoptic Gospels: A Sheffield Reader*. Edited by Craig A. Evans and Stanley E. Porter. Sheffield: Sheffield Academic Press, 1995.

——, *Lord of the Banquet: The Literary and Theological Significance of the Lukan Travel Narrative*. Harrisburg, PA: Trinity Press International, 1989.

———, 'The Lukan Prologues in the Light of Ancient Narrative Hermeneutics: Παρηκολουθηκότι and the Credentialed Author'. Pages 399–417 in *The Unity of Luke-Acts*. Edited by J. Verheyden. Bibliotheca Ephemeridum Theologicarum Lovaniensium 142. Leuven: Leuven University Press, 1999.

———, 'Luke 9:1–50: Luke's Preview of the Journey of the Prophet Like Moses of Deuteronomy'. *Journal of Biblical Literature* 102 (1983): 575–605.

———, '"Managing" the Audience: Diodorus Siculus and Luke the Evangelist on Designing Authorial Intent'. Pages 61–80 in *Luke and His Readers: Festschrift A. Denaux*. Edited by R. Bieringer, G. van Belle and J. Verheyden. Bibliotheca Ephemeridum Theologicarum Lovaniensium 182. Leuven: Leuven University Press, 2005.

———, 'The Meaning of καθεξῆς in the Lukan Prologue as a Key to the Distinctive Contribution of Luke's Narrative among the "Many"'. Pages 1513–28 in *The Four Gospels 1992: Festschrift Frans Neirynck*. Vol. 2. Edited by F. Van Segbroeck, C. M. Tuckett, G. van Belle and J. Verheyden. Leuven: Leuven University Press, 1992.

———, 'Ministers of Divine Providence: Diodorus Siculus and Luke the Evangelist on the Rhetorical Significance of the Audience in Narrative "Arrangement"'. Pages 304–23 in *Literary Encounters with the Reign of God: Studies in Honor of R.C. Tannehill*. Edited by S. H. Ringe and H. C. P. Kim. London: T&T Clark, 2004.

———, 'Paul and the Pattern of the Prophet Like Moses in Acts'. Pages 203–12 in *SBL 1983 Seminar Papers*. Edited by Kent H. Richards. Atlanta: Scholars Press, 1983.

———, 'Paul in Acts: Preacher of Eschatological Repentance to Israel'. *New Testament Studies* 34 (1988): 96–104.

———, 'The "script" of the Scriptures in Acts: suffering as God's "plan" (βουλή) for the world for the "release of sins"'. Pages 218–50 in *History, Literature and Society in the Book of Acts*. Edited by Ben Witherington III. Cambridge: Cambridge University Press, 1996.

———, 'Two Lords "at the Right Hand"? The Psalms and an Intertextual Reading of Peter's Pentecost Speech (Acts 2:14–36)'. Pages 215–32 in *Literary Studies in Luke-Acts: Essays in Honor of Joseph B. Tyson*. Edited by Richard P. Thompson and Thomas E. Phillips. Macon, GA: Mercer University Press, 1998.

Moessner, David P., ed. *Jesus and the Heritage of Israel: Luke's Narrative Claim upon Israel's Legacy*. Harrisburg, PA: Trinity Press, 1999.

Möller, Karl 'Words of (In-)evitable Certitude? Reflections on the Interpretation of Prophetic Oracles of Judgment'. Pages 352–86 in *After Pentecost: Language and Biblical Interpretation*. Edited by Craig Bartholomew, Colin Greene, Karl Möller. Scripture and Hermeneutics Series 2. Grand Rapids: Zondervan, 2001.

Moore, Stephen D. 'The Gospel of the Look'. *Semeia* 54 (1991): 159–96.

———, *Literary Criticism and the Gospels: The Theoretical Challenge*. New Haven: Yale University Press, 1989.

Moreland, Milton. 'The Jerusalem Community in Acts: Mythmaking and the Sociorhetorical Functions of a Lukan Setting'. Pages 285–310 in *Contextualizing Acts: Lukan Narrative and Greco-Roman Discourse*. Edited by Todd Penner and Caroline Vander Stichele. Society of Biblical Literature Symposium Series 20. Atlanta: Society of Biblical Literature, 2003.

Morris, Ian. Foreword to *The Ancient Economy*, by M. I. Finley. Sather Classical Lectures 43. Revised and updated edition. Berkeley: University of California Press, 1999.

———, 'Review Article: The Athenian Economy Twenty Years after *The Ancient Economy*'. *Classical Philology* 89 (1994): 351–66.

Morton, A. Q., and G. H. C. MacGregor. *The Structure of Luke and Acts*. London: Hodder and Stoughton, 1964.

Moule, C. F. D. *An Idiom Book of New Testament Greek*. 2nd edn. Cambridge: Cambridge University Press, 1959.

Moxnes, Halvor. *The Economy of the Kingdom: Social Conflict and Economic Relations in Luke's Gospel*. Overtures in Biblical Theology. Philadelphia: Fortress, 1988.

——, 'Honor and Shame'. Pages 19–40 in *The Social Sciences and the New Testament*. Edited by Richard Rohrbaugh. Peabody: Hendrickson, 1996.
——, 'Patron-Client Relations and the New Community in Luke-Acts'. Pages 241–68 in *The Social World of Luke-Acts: Models for Interpretation*. Edited by Jerome H. Neyrey. Peabody, MA: Hendrickson, 1991.
——, 'Social Relations and Economic Interaction in Luke's Gospel: A Research Report'. Pages 58–75 in *Luke-Acts: Scandinavian Perspectives*. Edited by Petri Luomanen. Göttingen: Vandenhoeck & Ruprecht, 1991.
Moxnes, Halvor, ed. *Constructing Early Christian Families: Family as Social Reality and Metaphor*. London: Routledge, 1997.
——, 'Early Christian Families'. *Biblical Interpretation* 11 (2003): 115–246.
Moyise, Steve. 'Intertextuality and the Study of the Old Testament in the New Testament'. Pages 14–41 in *The Old Testament in the New Testament: Essays in Honour of J.L. North*. Edited by Steve Moyise. Journal for the Study of the New Testament: Supplement Series 189. Sheffield: Sheffield Academic Press, 2000.
Moyise, Steve, ed. *Old Testament in the New Testament: Essays in Honour of J. L. North*. Journal for the Study of the New Testament: Supplement Series 189 Sheffield: Sheffield Academic Press, 2000.
Mullins, Terence Y. 'New Testament Commission Forms, Especially in Luke-Acts'. *Journal of Biblical Literature* 95 (1976): 603–14.
Murphy, Catherine M. *Wealth in the Dead Sea Scrolls and in the Qumran Community*. Studies on the Texts of the Desert of Judah 40. Leiden: Brill, 2002.
Murphy, Nancey. *Anglo-American Postmodernity: Philosophical Perspectives on Science, Religion, and Ethics*. Colorado: Westview Press, 1997.
Mussner, Franz. '"In den letzten Tagen" (Apg 2, 17a)'. *Biblische Zeitschrift* 5 (1961): 263–5.
Najman, Hindy. *Seconding Sinai: The Development of Mosaic Discourse in Second Temple Judaism*. Leiden: Brill, 2003.
Navon, Robert, ed. *The Pythagorean Writings: Hellenistic Texts from the 1st Cent. B.C.–3rd Cent. A.D*. Translated from Greek and Latin by Kenneth Guthrie and Thomas Taylor. Kew Gardens, NY: Selene Books, 1986.
Neireck, F. 'The Miracle Stories in the Acts of the Apostles. In Introduction'. Pages 169–213 in *Les Actes des Apôtres: Traditions, rédaction, théologie*. Edited by J. Kremer. Leuven: Leuven University Press, 1999.
Neusner, Jacob. *Judaism When Christianity Began: A Survey of Belief and Practice*. Louisville / London: Westminster John Knox Press, 2002.
Neyrey, Jerome H. 'Jesus' Address to the Women of Jerusalem (Lk 23:27b–31): A Prophetic Judgment Oracle'. *New Testament Studies* 29 (1983): 74–86.
——, 'The Symbolic Universe of Like-Acts: "They Turn the World Upside Down"'. Pages 271–304 in *The Social World of Luke-Acts: Models for Interpretation*. Edited by Jerome H. Neyrey. Peabody, MA: Hendrickson, 1991.
Neyrey, Jerome H., ed. *The Social World of Luke-Acts: Models for Interpretation*. Peabody, MA: Hendrickson, 1991.
Nobbs, Alanna. 'Cyprus'. Pages 279–89 in *The Book of Acts in its Graeco-Roman Setting*. Edited by David W. J. Gill and Conrad Gempf. *The Book of Acts in its First Century Setting*. Edited by Bruce W. Winter. Grand Rapids: Eerdmans, 1994.
Noorda, S. J. 'Scene and Summary. A Proposal for Reading Acts 4, 32–5, 16'. Pages 475–83 in *Les Actes des Apôtres: Traditions, rédaction, théologie*. Edited by J. Kremer. Leuven: Leuven University Press, 1979.
Norwood, Jr, M. Thomas. 'Serious Stewardship: A Second Look at the Ananias and Sapphira Narrative'. *Journal for Preachers* 3 (1979): 4–8.
O'Day, Gail R. 'Acts'. Pages 394–403 in *The Women's Bible Commentary*. Edited by Carol A. Newsom and Sharon H. Ringe. London: SPCK, 1992.

O'Meara, Dominic J. *Pythagoras Revived: Mathematics and Philosophy in Late Antiquity.* Oxford: Clarendon, 1989.
O'Rourke, John J. 'Possible Uses of the Old Testament in the Gospels: An Overview'. Pages 15–25 in *The Gospels and the Scriptures of Israel.* Edited by Craig A. Evans and W. Richard Stegner. Journal for the Study of the New Testament: Supplement Series 104. Sheffield: Sheffield Academic Press, 1994.
O'Toole, Robert F. 'Activity of the Risen Jesus in Luke-Acts'. *Biblica* 62 (1981): 471–98.
——, 'Acts 2:30 and the Davidic Covenant of Pentecost'. *Journal of Biblical Literature* 102 (1983): 245–58.
——, 'The Kingdom of God in Luke-Acts'. Pages 147–62 in *The Kingdom of God in 20th-Century Interpretation.* Edited by Wendell Willis. Peabody: Hendrickson, 1987.
——, *Luke's Presentation of Jesus: A Christology.* Subsidia biblica 25. Rome: Editrice Pontificio Instituto Biblico, 2004.
——, 'Luke's Understanding of Jesus' Resurrection-Ascension-Exaltation'. *Biblical Theology Bulletin* 9 (1979): 106–14.
——, 'Parallels between Jesus and His Disciples in Luke-Acts: A Further Study'. *Biblische Zeitschrift* 27 (1983): 195–212.
——, *The Unity of Lukan Theology: An Analysis of Luke-Acts.* Good News Studies 9. Wilmington: Michael Glazier, 1984.
——, '"You Did Not Lie to Us (Human Beings) but to God" (Acts 5,4c)'. *Biblica* 76 (1995): 182–209.
Ohmann, Richard. 'Literature as Act'. Pages 81–107 in *Approaches to Poetics: Selected Papers from the English Institute.* Edited by Seymour Chatman. New York: Columbia University Press, 1973.
——, 'Speech Acts and the Definition of Literature'. *Philosophy and Rhetoric* 4 (1971): 1–19.
——, 'Speech, Literature and the Space Between'. *New Literary History* 4 (1974): 47–63.
Osiek, Carolyn, and David L. Balch. *Families in the New Testament World: Households and House Churches.* Louisville: Westminster / John Knox Press, 1997.
Overholt, Thomas W. *Channels of Prophecy: The Social Dynamics of Prophetic Activity.* Minneapolis: Fortress Press, 1989.
Palmer, D. W. 'The Literary Background of Acts 1.1–14'. *New Testament Studies* 33 (1987): 427–38.
Pao, David W. *Acts and the Isaianic New Exodus.* Grand Rapids: Baker Academic, 2000.
Parker, Robert. 'Pleasing Thighs: Reciprocity in Greek Religion'. Pages 105–25 in *Reciprocity in Ancient Greece.* Edited by Christopher Gill, Norman Postlethwaite and Richard Seaford. Oxford: Oxford University Press, 1998.
Parsons, Mikeal C. *Body and Character in Luke and Acts: The Subversion of Physiognomy in Early Christianity.* Grand Rapids: Baker Academic, 2006.
——, 'The Character of the Lame Man in Acts 3–4'. *Journal of Biblical Literature* 124 (2005): 295–312.
——, *The Departure of Jesus in Luke-Acts: The Ascension Narratives in Context.* Journal for the Study of the New Testament: Supplement Series 21. Sheffield: JSOT Press, 1987.
Parsons, Mikeal C., and Martin M. Culy. *Acts: A Handbook on the Greek Text.* Waco: Baylor University Press, 2003.
Parsons, Mikeal C., and Richard Pervo. *Rethinking the Unity of Luke and Acts.* Minneapolis: Fortress, 1993.
Patrick, Dale *The Rhetoric of Revelation in the Hebrew Bible.* Overtures in Biblical Theology. Minneapolis: Fortress Press, 1999.
Pavel, Thomas G. 'Ontological Issues in Poetics: Speech Acts and Fictional Worlds'. *The Journal of Aesthetics and Art Criticism* 40 (1981): 167–78.
Penney, John M. *The Missionary Emphasis of Lukan Pneumatology.* Journal for Pentecostal Theology: Supplement Series 12. Sheffield: Sheffield Academic Press, 1997.

Perrot, C. 'Ananie et Saphire: Le jugement ecclésial et la justice divine'. *L'année canonique* 25 (1981): 109–24.
Pervo, Richard I. 'Must Luke and Acts Belong to the Same Genre?' Pages 309–16 in *SBL 1989 Seminar Papers*. Edited by David J. Lull. Atlanta: Scholars Press, 1989.
Pesch, Rudolf. *Die Apostelgeschichte (Apg 1–12)*. Evangelisch-katholischer Kommentar zum Neuentestament V/1. Zürich: Benziger Verlag, 1986.
Petrey, Sandy. *Speech Acts and Literary Theory*. London: Routledge, 1990.
——, 'Whose Acts? Which Communities? A Reply to David Gorman'. *Poetics Today* 21 (2000): 423–33.
Pezzoli-Olgiati, Daria. 'From μαγεία to Magic: Envisaging a Problematic Concept in the Study of Religion'. Pages 3–19 in *A Kind of Magic: Understanding Magic in the New Testament and its Religious Environment*. Edited by Michale Labahn and Bert Jan Lietaert Peerbilte. London: T&T Clark, 2007.
Philip, J. A. 'Aristotle's Monograph *On the Pythagoreans*'. *Transactions of the American Philological Association* 94 (1963): 185–98.
——, 'The Biographical Tradition – Pythagoras'. *Transactions of the American Philological Association* 90 (1959): 185–94.
——, *Pythagoras and Early Pythagoreanism*. Toronto: University of Toronto Press, 1966.
Phillips, Thomas E. *Reading Issues of Wealth and Poverty in Luke-Acts*. Lewiston, NY: Edwin Mellen Press, 2001.
——, 'Reading Recent Readings of Issues of Wealth and Poverty in Luke and Acts'. *Currents in Biblical Research* 1 (2003). 231–69.
Pilgrim, Walter. *Good News to the Poor: Wealth and Poverty in Luke-Acts*. Minneapolis: Augsburg Publishing House, 1981.
Pitt-Rivers, Julian. 'Honour and Social Status'. Pages 19–77 in *Honour and Shame: The Values of Mediterranean Society*. Edited by J. G. Peristiany. London: Weidenfeld and Nicolson, 1965.
Pleket, H. W. 'Religious History as the History of Mentality: The "Believer" as Servant of the Deity in the Greek World'. Pages 152–92 in *Faith, Hope and Worship: Aspects of Religious Mentality in the Ancient World*. Edited by H. S. Versnel. Leiden: Brill, 1981.
Plümacher, Eckhard. *Lukas als hellenistischer Schriftsteller: Studien zur Apostelgeschichte*. Studien zur Umwelt des Neuen Testaments 9. Göttingen, 1972.
Polanyi, Karl, 'The Economy as Instituted Process'. Pages 243–70 in *Trade and Market in the Early Empires*. Polanyi, Karl, Conrad M. Arensberg and Harry W. Pearson. New York: Free Press, 1957.
——, *The Great Transformation: The Political and Economic Origins of Our Time*. Boston: Beacon, 1944. Reprinted 2001.
Porter, Stanley E. 'Literary Approaches to the New Testament: From Formalism to Deconstruction and Back'. Pages 77–128 in *Approaches to New Testament Study*. Edited by Stanley E. Porter, Journal for the Study of the New Testament: Supplement Series 120. Sheffield: Sheffield, 1995.
——, 'Magic in the Book of Acts'. Pages 107–21 in *A Kind of Magic: Understanding Magic in the New Testament and its Religious Environment*. Edited by Michale Labahn and Bert Jan Lietaert Peerbilte; London: T&T Clark, 2007.
Potter, Jonathan. 'Wittgenstein and Austin'. Pages 39–46 in *Discourse Theory and Practice: A Reader*. Edited by M. Wetherell, S. Taylor and S. J. Yates. London: Sage Publications, 2001.
Praeder, Susan M. 'Jesus-Paul, Peter-Paul, and Jesus-Peter Parallelisms in Luke-Acts: A History of Reader Response'. Pages 23–39 in *SBL 1984 Seminar Papers*. Edited by Kent H. Richards. Atlanta: Scholars Press, 1984.
Pratt, Mary Louise. 'Ideology and Speech-Act Theory'. *Poetics Today* 7 (1986): 59–72.
——, *Toward a Speech Act Theory of Literary Discourse*. Bloomington: Indiana University Press, 1977.

Prete, Benedetto. 'Anania e Saffira (At 5:1–11): Componenti letterarie e dottrinali'. *Rivista Biblica* 36 (1988): 463–86.
Quinn, Philip L. 'Can God Speak? Does God Speak?' *Religious Studies* 37 (2001): 259–69.
Rabin, Chaim. *The Zadokite Documents*. Oxford: Clarendon, 1954.
Rad, Gerhard von. *Old Testament Theology*. 2 vols. Translated by D. M. G. Stalker. Edinburgh: T&T Clark, 1962, 1965.
——, 'The Prophets' Conception of the Word of God.' Pages 60–76 in *The Message of the Prophets*. Translated by D. M. G. Stalker. London: SCM Press Ltd, 1968.
Rajak, Tessa. 'Ciò che Flavio Giuseppe vide: Josephus and the Essenes'. Pages 141–60 in *Josephus and the History of the Greco-Roman Period: Essays in Memory of Morton Smith*. Edited by Fausto Parente and Joseph Sievers. Leiden: Brill, 1994.
——, *Josephus: The Historian and his Society*. 2nd edn. London: Duckworth, 2002.
Ravens, David. 'Luke 9.7–62 and the Prophetic Role of Jesus'. *New Testament Studies* 36 (1990): 119–29.
——, *Luke and the Restoration of Israel*. Journal for the Study of the New Testament: Supplement Series 119. Sheffield: Sheffield Academic Press, 1995.
Read-Heimerdinger, Jenny. 'Barnabas in Acts: A Study of His Role in the Text of Codex Bezae'. *Journal for the Study of the New Testament* 72 (1998): 23–66.
——, *The Bezan Text of Acts: A Contribution of Discourse Analysis to Textual Criticism*. Journal for the Study of the New Testament: Supplement Series 236. Sheffield: Sheffield Academic Press, 2002.
Reden, Sitta von. *Exchange in Ancient Greece*. London: Duckworth, 2003.
Ref, Stefan C. 'The Damascus Document from the Cairo Genizah: Its Discovery, Early Study and Historical Significance'. Pages 109–31 *The Damascus Document: A Centennial of Discovery. Proceedings of the Third International Symposium of the Orion Center, 4–8 February 1998*. Edited by Joseph M. Baumgarten, Esther G. Chazon and Avital Pinnick; Leiden: Brill, 2000.
Reicke, Bo. *Glaube und Leben der Urgemeinde. Bemerkungen zu Apg. 1–7*. Zürich: Zwingle-Verlag, 1957.
Reimer, Andy M. *Miracle and Magic: A Study in the Acts of the Apostles and the Life of Apollonius of Tyana*. Journal for the Study of the New Testament: Supplement Series 235. Sheffield: Sheffield Academic Press, 2002.
——, 'Virtual Prison Breaks: Non-Escape Narratives and the Definition of "Magic"'. Pages 125–39 in *Magic in the Biblical World: From the Rod of Aaron to the Ring of Solomon*. Edited by Todd Klutz. Journal for the Study of the New Testament: Supplement Series 245. London: T&T Clark, 2003.
Reimer, Ivoni Richter. *Women in the Acts of the Apostles: A Feminist Liberation Perspective*. Translated by Linda M. Maloney. Minneapolis: Fortress, 1995.
Rhoads, David, and Kari Syreeni, eds. *Characterization in the Gospels: Reconceiving Narrative Criticism*. Journal for the Study of the New Testament: Supplement Series 184. Sheffield: Sheffield Academic Press, 1999.
Rhode, Ernst. 'Die Quellen des Iamblichus in seiner Biographie des Pythagoras'. *Rheinisches Museum* 26 (1871): 554–76; 27 (1872): 23–61.
Richard, Earl. 'Pentecost as a Recurrent Theme in Luke-Acts'. Pages 133–49 in *New Views on Luke Acts*. Edited by Earl Richard. Collegeville, MN: The Liturgical Press, 1990.
Ricœur, Paul. *From Text to Action: Essays in Hermeneutics, II*. Translated by Kathleen Blamey and John B. Thompson. Evanston, IL: Northwestern University Press, 1991.
——, 'Philosophical Hermeneutics and Biblical Hermeneutics'. Pages 89–101 in *From Text to Action: Essays in Hermeneutics, II*. Translated by Kathleen Blamey and John B. Thompson. Evanston, IL: Northwestern University Press, 1991.
Riedweg, Christoph. *Pythagoras: His Life, Teaching, and Influence*. Translated by Steven Rendall. London: Cornell University Press, 2005.

Rimmon-Kenan, Shlomith. *Narrative Fiction: Contemporary Poetics*. 2nd edn. London: Routledge, 2002.
Ringe, Sharon H. *Jesus, Liberation, and the Biblical Jubilee: Images for Ethics and Christology*. Overtures in Biblical Theology. Philadelphia: Fortress, 1985.
Ringgren, Helmer. *The Faith of Qumran: Theology of the Dead Sea Scrolls*. Expanded edn. Edited by James H. Charlesworth. Translated by Emilie T. Sander. New York: Crossroad, 1963.
Rius-Camps, Josep and Jenny Read-Heimerdinger. *The Message of Acts in Codex Bezae: A Comparison with the Alexandrian Tradition. Volume 1: Acts 1.1 – 5.42: Jerusalem*. Journal for the Study of the New Testament: Supplement Series 257. London: T&T Clark, 2004.
——, *The Message of Acts in Codex Bezae: A Comparison with the Alexandrian Tradition. Volume 2: Acts 6.1 – 12.25: From Judea and Samaria to the Church in Antioch*. Journal for the Study of the New Testament: Supplement Series 302. London: T&T Clark, 2006.
Robbins, Vernon K. 'Interpreting the Gospel of Mark as a Jewish Document in a Graeco-Roman World'. Pages 47–72 in *New Perspectives on Ancient Judaism*. Edited by Paul V. M. Flesher. Lanham, Maryland: University Press of America, 1990.
Roberts Gaventa, Beverly. 'Initiatives Divine and Human in the Lukan Story World'. Pages 79–89 in *The Holy Spirit and Christian Origins: Essays in Honor of James D.G. Dunn*. Edited by Graham N. Stanton, Bruce W. Longenecker and Stephen C. Barton. Grand Rapids: Eerdmans, 2004.
——, 'Toward a Theology of Acts: Reading and Rereading'. *Interpretation* 42 (1998): 146–57.
——, 'What Ever Happened to Those Prophesying Daughters?' Pages 49–60 in *A Feminist Companion to the Acts of the Apostles*. Edited by Amy-Jill Levine. London: T&T Clark International, 2004.
Robinson, Anthony B., and Robert W. Wall. *Called to Be Church: The Book of Acts for a New Day*. Grand Rapids: Eerdmans, 2006.
Rohrbaugh, Richard L. 'Legitimating Sonship – A Test of Honour: A Social-scientific Study of Luke 4:1–30.' Pages 183–97 in *Modelling Early Christianity: Social-scientific Studies of the New Testament in its Context*. Edited by Philip Esler. London: Routledge, 1995.
Römer, Thomas, and Jean-Daniel Machi. 'Luke, Disciple of the Deuteronomistic School'. Translated by Ms A. Champendal. Pages 178–87 in *Luke's Literary Achievement: Collected Essays*. Edited by C. M. Tuckett. Journal for the Study of the New Testament: Supplement Series 116. Sheffield: Sheffield Academic Press, 1995.
Rosner, Brian S. 'Acts and Biblical History'. Pages 65–82 in *The Book of Acts in Its Ancient Literary Setting*. Edited by Bruce W. Winter and Andrew D. Clarke. Vol. 1 of *The Book of Acts in Its First Century Setting*. Edited by B. W. Winter. Grand Rapids: Eerdmans, 1993.
Ross, J. M. 'Which Zechariah?' *Irish Biblical Studies* 9 (1987): 70–3.
Rothschild, Clare S. *Luke-Acts and the Rhetoric of History: An Investigation of Early Christian Historiography*. Tübingen, Mohr Siebeck, 2004.
Rudolph, K. 'Simon – Magus oder Gnosticus? Zur Stand der Debatte'. *Theologische Rundschau* 42 (1977): 279–359.
Ruef, S. J. 'Hananias und Sapphira. A Study of Community-Disciplinary Practices Underlying Acts 5,1–11'. PhD diss., Harvard University, 1960.
Saddock, Jerrold M. 'Toward a Grammatically Realistic Typology of Speech Acts'. Pages 393–406 in *Foundations of Speech Act Theory: Philosophical and Linguistic Perspectives*. Edited by Savas L. Tsohatzidis. London: Routledge, 1994.
Saller, Richard P. 'Patronage and Friendship in Early Imperial Rome: Drawing the Distinction'. Pages 49–62 in *Patronage in Ancient Society*. Edited by Andrew Wallace-Hadrill. London: Routledge, 1989.

———, *Personal Patronage Under the Early Empire.* Cambridge: Cambridge University Press, 1982.
Sanders, Jack T. 'The Prophetic Use of the Scriptures in Luke-Acts'. Pages 191–8 in *Early Jewish and Christian Exegesis: Studies in Memory of William Hugh Brownlee.* Edited by Craig A. Evans and William F. Stinespring. Atlanta: Scholars Press, 1987.
Sanders, James A. 'From Isaiah 61 to Luke 4'. Pages 46–69 in *Luke and Scripture: The Function of Sacred Tradition in Luke-Acts.* By Craig A. Evans and James A. Sanders. Minneapolis: Fortress, 1993.
———, 'Isaiah in Luke'. Pages 14–25 in *Luke and Scripture: The Function of Sacred Tradition in Luke-Acts.* By Craig A. Evans and James A. Sanders. Minneapolis: Fortress, 1993.
———, 'Sins, Debts, and Jubilee Release'. Pages 84–92 in *Luke and Scripture: The Function of Sacred Tradition in Luke-Acts.* By Craig A. Evans and James A. Sanders. Minneapolis: Fortress, 1993.
Sandt, Huub van de. 'An Explanation of Acts 15.6-21 in the Light of Deuteronomy 4.29–35 (LXX)'. *Journal for the Study of the New Testament* 46 (1992): 73–97.
———, 'The Fate of the Gentiles in Joel and Acts 2: An Intertextual Study'. *Ephemerides theologicae lovanienses* 66 (1990): 56–77.
Scheidel, Walter, and Sitta von Reden, eds. *The Ancient Economy.* New York: Routledge, 2002.
Scheidweiler, Felix. 'Zu Act 5 4'. *Zeitschrift für die Neutestamentliche Wissenschaft* 49 (1958): 136–7.
Schenck, Kenneth. *A Brief Guide to Philo.* Louisville: Westminster / John Knox Press, 2005.
Schiffman, Lawrence H. *Sectarian Law in the Dead Sea Scrolls: Courts, Testimony, and the Penal Code.* Brown Judaic Studies 33. Chico, CA: Scholars Press, 1983.
Schmidt, T. Ewald, 'Hostility to Wealth in Philo of Alexandria'. *Journal for the Study of the New Testament* 19 (1983): 85–97.
Schmitt, J. 'L'église de Jerusalem, ou la "restauration" d'Israel'. *Revue de Sciences Religieuses* 27 (1953) 209–18.
Schneider, Gerhard. *Die Apostelgeschichte.* 2 vols. Herders theologischer Kommentar zum Neuen Testament 5. Freiberg: Herder, 1980, 1982.
Schottroff, Luise. *Befreiungserfahrungen: Studien zur Sozialgeschichte des Neuen Testaments.* Munich: Kaiser Verlag, 1989.
Schubert, Judith M. 'The Image of Jesus as the Prophet like Moses in Luke-Acts as Advanced by Luke's Reinterpretation of Deuteronomy 18:15, 18 in Acts 3:22 and 7:37'. PhD diss., Fordham University, 1992.
Schürer, Emil. *The History of the Jewish People in the Age of Jesus Christ (175 B. C. – A. D. 135).* Revised and edited by M. Black, G. Vermès, F. Millar and M. Goodman. 3 vols. Edinburgh: T&T Clark, 1973–87.
Schwartz, Daniel R. 'Non-joining Sympathizers (Acts 5:13–14)'. *Biblica* 64 (1983): 550–5.
Scobie, Charles H. H. 'A Canonical Approach to Interpreting Luke: The Journey Motif as a Hermeneutical Key'. Pages in 327–49 *Reading Luke: Interpretation, Reflection, Formation.* Edited by Craig G. Bartholomew, Joel B. Green and Anthony C. Thiselton. Scripture and Hermeneutics Series 6. Grand Rapids: Zondervan, 2005.
Scott, J. M. 'Paul's Use of the Deuteronomistic Tradition'. *Journal of Biblical Literature* 112 (1993): 645–65.
Scott, R. B. Y. *The Relevance of the Prophets.* New York: The Macmillan Company, 1947.
Searle, John R. 'Austin on Locutionary and Illocutionary Acts'. Pages 141–59 in *Essays on J.L. Austin.* I. Berlin, et al. Oxford: Clarendon Press, 1973.
———, *The Construction of Social Reality.* London: Penguin Books, 1995.
———, *Expression and Meaning: Studies in the Theory of Speech Acts.* Cambridge: Cambridge University Press, 1979.
———, *Intentionality: An Essay in the Philosophy of Mind.* Cambridge: Cambridge University Press, 1983.

———, 'Literary Theory and Its Discontents'. *New Literary History* 25 (1994): 637–67.
———, 'The Logical Status of Fictional Discourse'. Pages 58–75 in *Expression and Meaning: Studies in the Theory of Speech Acts*. Cambridge: Cambridge University Press, 1979.
———, *Mind, Language and Society: Philosophy in the Real World*. New York: Basic Books, 1998.
———, 'Reiterating the Differences: A Reply to Derrida'. *Glyph* 1 (1977): 198–208.
———, *Speech Acts: An Essay in the Philosophy of Language*. Cambridge: Cambridge University Press, 1969.
———, 'What is an Institution?' Unpublished paper accessed at http://ist-socrates.berkeley.edu/~jsearle/EconomistsJOIE,10Jan05.doc on April 25, 2006.
Searle, John R., and Daniel Vanderveken. *Foundations of Illocutionary Logic*. Cambridge: Cambridge University Press, 1985.
Seccombe, D. P. *Possessions and the Poor in Luke-Acts*. Linz: SNTU, 1982.
Sheeley, Steven M. *Narrative Asides in Luke-Acts*. Journal for the Study of the New Testament: Supplement Series 72. Sheffield: JSOT Press, 1992.
Seim, Turid K. *The Double Message: Patterns of Gender in Luke-Acts*. Studies of the New Testament and its World. Edinburgh: T&T Clark, 1994.
Shelton, James B. 'A Reply to James D.G. Dunn's "Baptism in the Spirit: A Response to Pentecostal Scholarship on Luke-Acts"'. *Journal for Pentecostal Theology* 4 (1994): 139–43.
———, *Mighty in Word and Deed: The Role of the Holy Spirit in Luke-Acts*. Peabody, MA: Hendrickson, 1991.
Shepherd, Jr, William H. *The Narrative Function of the Holy Spirit as a Character in Luke-Acts*. Society of Biblical Literature Dissertation Series 147. Atlanta: Scholars Press, 1994.
Sherwin-White, A. N. *Roman Society and Roman Law in the New Testament*. Oxford: Clarendon Press, 1963.
Shiell, William D. *Reading Acts: The Lector and the Early Christian Audience*. Biblical Interpretation Series 70. Leiden: Brill Academic Publishers, Inc., 2004.
Skeat, T. C. 'A Codicological Analysis of the Chester Beatty papyrus Codex of Gospels and Acts (P[45])'. Pages 141–57 in *The Collected Biblical Writings of T. C. Skeat*. Edited by J. K. Elliott. Novum Testamentum Supplement 113. Leiden: Brill, 2004.
Sloan, Robert B. *The Favorable Year of the Lord: A Study of Jubilary Theology in the Gospel of Luke*. Austin: Schola Press, 1977.
———, '"Signs and Wonders": A Rhetorical Clue to the Pentecost Discourse'. Pages 145–62 in *With Steadfast Purpose: Essays on Acts in Honor of Henry Jackson Flanders, Jr*. Edited by Naymond H. Keathley. Waco: Baylor University, 1990.
Smith, David E. *The Canonical Function of Acts: A Comparative Analysis*. Collegeville, MN: The Liturgical Press, 2002.
Smith, Dennis E. *From Symposium to Eucharist: The Banquet in the Early Christian World*. Minneapolis: Fortress, 2003.
Smith, Jonathan Z. 'Trading Places'. Pages 13–27 in *Ancient Magic and Ritual Power*. Edited by Marvin Meyer and Paul Mirecki. Leiden: Brill, 2001.
Smith, Terence V. *Petrine Controversies in Early Christianity*. Wissenschaftliche Untersuchungen zum Neuen Testament 2.15. Tübingen: Mohr Siebeck, 1985.
Soards, Marion L. *The Speeches in Acts: Their Content, Context, and Concerns*. Louisville: Westminster / John Knox Press, 1994.
Spencer, F. Scott. *Journeying Through Acts: A Literary-Cultural Reading*. Peabody, MA: Hendrickson, 2004.
———, 'Out of Mind, Out of Voice: Slave-girls and Prophetic Daughters in Luke-Acts'. *Biblical Interpretation* 7 (1999): 133–55.
———, *The Portrait of Philip in Acts: A Study of Roles and Relations*. Journal for the Study of the New Testament: Supplement Series 67. Sheffield: JSOT Press, 1992.

Spivak, Gayatru Chakravorty. 'Revolutions That as Yet Have No Model: Derrida's *Limited Inc*'. *Diacritics* 10 (1980): 29–49.

Squires, John T. 'Acts'. Pages 1213–67 in *Eerdmans Commentary on the Bible*. Edited by James D. G. Dunn and John W. Rogerson. Grand Rapids: Eerdmans, 2003.

———, *The Plan of God in Luke-Acts*. Society for New Testament Studies Monograph Series 76. Cambridge: Cambridge University Press, 1993.

Stacey, W. D. *Prophetic Drama in the Old Testament*. London: Epworth Press, 1990.

Steck, Odil Hannes. *Israel und das gewaltsame Geschick der Propheten. Untersuchungen zur Überlieferung des deuteronomistischen Geschichtsbildes im Alten Testament, Spätjudentum und Urchristentum*. Wissenschaftliche Monographien zum Alten und Neuen Testament, Bd.23. Neukirchen-Vluyn: Neukirchener Verlag, 1967.

Stegemann, Hartmut. 'The Qumran Essenes – Local Members of the Main Jewish Union in the Late Second Temple Times'. Pages 83–166 in *The Madrid Qumran Congress: Proceedings of the International Congress on the Dead Sea Scrolls, Madrid 18–21 March, 1991*. 2 vols. Edited by Julio Trebolle Barrera and Luis Vegas Montaner; Leiden: Brill, 1992.

Steiner, George. *After Babel: Aspects of Language and Translation*. 3rd edn. Oxford: Oxford University Press, 1998.

Stempvoort, P. A. Van. 'The Interpretation of the Ascension in Luke and Acts'. *New Testament Studies* 5 (1958–59): 30–42.

Sterling, Gregory E. '"Athletes of Virtue": An Analysis of the Summaries in Acts (2:41–47; 4:32–35; 5:12–16)'. *Journal of Biblical Literature* 113/4 (1994): 679–96.

———, *Historiography and Self-Definition: Josephos, Luke-Acts and Apologetic Historiography*. Supplements to Novum Testamentum 64. Leiden: Brill, 1992.

Sternberg, Meir. *The Poetics of Biblical Narrative: Ideological Literature and the Drama of Reading*. Bloomington: Indiana University Press, 1985.

Steyn, Gert J. *Septuagint Quotations in the Context of the Petrine and Pauline Speeches of the Acta Apostolorum*. Contributions to Biblical Exegesis and Theology 12. Kampen: Kok Pharos, 1995.

Strange, W. A. *The Problem of the Text of Acts*. Society for New Testament Studies Monograph Series 71. Cambridge: Cambridge University Press, 1992.

———, 'The Sons of Sceva and the Text of Acts 19:14'. *Journal of Theological Studies* 38 (1987): 97–106.

Strauss, Mark L. *The Davidic Messiah in Luke-Acts: The Promise and its Fulfillment in Lukan Christology*. Journal for the Study of the New Testament: Supplement Series 110. Sheffield: Sheffield Academic Press, 1995.

Strelan, Rick. *Strange Acts: Studies in the Cultural World of the Acts of the Apostles*. Beihefte zur Zeutschrift für die neutestamenliche Wissenschaft 126. Berlin: Walter de Gruyter, 2004.

———, 'Strange Stares: ATENIZEIN in Acts'. *Novum Testamentum* 41 (1999): 235–55.

———, 'Who Was Bar Jesus (Acts 13,6–12)?', *Biblica* 85 (2004): 65–81.

Stronstad, Roger. *The Charismatic Theology of St. Luke*. Peabody: Hendrickson, 1984.

———, *The Prophethood of All Believers: A Study in Luke's Charismatic Theology*. Journal of Pentecostal Theology: Supplement Series 16. Sheffield: Sheffield Academic Press, 1999.

Struthers Malbon, Elizabeth, and Adele Berlin, eds. *Characterization in Biblical Literature*. Semeia 63. Atlanta: Scholars Press, 1993.

Talbert, Charles H. *Literary Patterns, Theological Themes and the Genre of Luke-Acts*. Society of Biblical Literature Monograph Series 20. Missoula, MT: Scholars Press, 1974.

———, *Reading Acts: A Literary and Theological Commentary on the Acts of the Apostles*. New York: Crossroad Publishing Company, 1997.

Talbert, Charles H., ed. *Luke-Acts: New Perspectives from the Society of Biblical Literature Seminar*. New York: Crossroad, 1984.

Tannehill, Robert C. 'The Composition of Acts 3–5: Narrative Development and Echo Effect'. Pages 217–40 in *SBL 1984 Seminar Papers*. Edited by Kent H. Richards. Atlanta: Scholars Press, 1984. Repr. pages 185–219 in *The Shape of Luke's Story: Essays on Luke-Acts*. Eugene, OR: Cascade Books, 2005.

———, 'The Function of Peter's Mission Speeches in the Narrative of Acts'. Pages 169–84 in *The Shape of Luke's Story: Essays on Luke-Acts*. Eugene, OR: Cascade Books, 2005.

———, 'Israel in Luke-Acts: A Tragic Story'. Pages 105–24 in *The Shape of Luke's Story: Essays on Luke-Acts*. Eugene, OR: Cascade Books, 2005.

———, *The Narrative Unity of Luke-Acts: A Literary Interpretation*. 2 vols. Minneapolis / Philadelphia: Fortress, 1986, 1990.

———, 'What Kind of King? What Kind of Kingdom?' Pages 48–55 in *The Shape of Luke's Story: Essays on Luke-Acts*. Eugene, OR: Cascade Books, 2005.

Taylor, Joan E., and Philip R. Davies. 'The So-Called Therapeutai of *De Vita Contemplativa*: Identity and Character'. *Harvard Theological Review* 91 (1998): 3–24.

Taylor, Justin. 'The Community of Goods among the First Christians and among the Essenes'. Pages 147–61 in *Historical Perspectives: From the Hasmoneans to Bar Kokhba in Light of the Dead Sea Scrolls: Proceedings of the Fourth International Symposium of the Orion Center for the Study of the Dead Sea Scrolls and Associated Literature, 27–31 January, 1999*. Edited by David Goodblatt, Avital Pinnock and Daniel R. Schwartz. Studies in the Texts of the Desert of Judah, 37. Leiden: Brill, 2001.

———, *Pythagoreans and Essenes: Structural Parallels*. Paris: Peeters, 2004.

Taylor, Nicholas H. 'Luke-Acts and the Temple'. Pages 709–21 in *The Unity of Luke-Acts*. Edited by J. Verheyden. Bibliotheca Ephemeridum Theologicarum Lovaniensium 142. Leuven: Leuven University Press, 1999.

Teeple, Howard M. *The Mosaic Eschatological Prophet*. Society of Biblical Literature Monograph Series 10. Philadelphia: Society of Biblical Literature, 1957.

Theissen, Gerd. *The Miracle Stories of the Early Christian Tradition*. Edited by John Riches. Translated by Francis McDonagh. Philadelphia: Fortress, 1983.

Theodorson, George A., and Achilles G. Theodorson, eds. *A Modern Dictionary of Sociology*. London: Methuen and Co. Ltd, 1969.

Thesleff, Holger. *The Pythagorean Texts of the Hellenistic Period*. Åbo: Åbo Akademi, 1965.

———, 'The Pythagoreans in the Light and Shadows of Recent Research'. Pages 77–90 in *Mysticism: Based on Papers read at the Symposium on Mysticism held at Åbo on the 7th–9th September, 1968*. Edited by Sven S. Hartman and Carl-Martin Edsman. Stockholm: Almqvist & Wiksell, 1970.

Thiselton, Anthony C. 'Christology in Luke, Speech Act Theory, and the Problem of Dualism in Christology after Kant'. Pages 453–72 in *Jesus of Nazareth: Lord and Christ*. Edited by J. B. Green and M. Turner. Carlisle: Paternoster Press / Grand Rapids: Eerdmans, 1994.

———, 'The Logical Role of the Liar Paradox in Titus 1:12,13: A Dissent from the Commentaries in the Light of Philosophical and Logical Analysis'. *Biblical Interpretation* 2 (1994): 207–23.

———, *New Horizons in Hermeneutics: The Theory and Practice of Transforming Biblical Reading*. Grand Rapids: Zondervan Publishing House, 1992.

———, 'Reader-Response Hermeneutics, Action Models and the Parables of Jesus'. Pages 79–113 in *The Responsibility of Hermeneutics*. Edited by Roger Lundin, Anthony Clare Thiselton and C. Walhout. Grand Rapids: Eerdmans, 1985.

———, 'A Retrospective Reappraisal of Work on Speech-Act Theory'. Pages 131–49 in *Thiselton on Hermeneutics: Collected Works with New Essays*. Grand Rapids: Eerdmans, 2006.

———, 'Speech-Act Theory and the Claim that God speaks: Nicholas Wolterstorff's *Divine Discourse*'. *Scottish Journal of Theology* 50 (1997): 97–110.

———, 'The Supposed Power of Words in the Biblical Writings'. *Journal of Theological Studies* 25 (1974): 283–99. Rev. edn. Pages 53–67 in *Thiselton on Hermeneutics: Collected Works with New Essays*. Grand Rapids: Eerdmans, 2006.

Thom, Johan C. '"Don't Walk on the Highways": The Pythagorean *Akousmata* and early Christian Literature'. *Journal of Biblical Literature* 113 (1994): 93–112.

——, '"Harmonious Equality": The *Topos* of Friendship in Neopythagorean Writings'. Pages 77–103 in *Greco-Roman Perspectives on Friendship*. Edited by John T. Fitzgerald. SBL Resources for Biblical Study 34. Atlanta: Scholars Press, 1997.

Tiede, David L. 'Contending with God: The Death of Jesus and the Trial of Israel in Luke-Acts'. Pages 301–8 in *The Future of Early Christianity: Essays in Honor of Helmut Koester*. Edited by Birger A. Pearson. Minneapolis: Fortress Press, 1991.

——, '"Fighting against God": Luke's Interpretation of Jewish Rejection of the Messiah Jesus'. Pages 102–12 in *Anti-Semitism and Early Christianity: Issues of Polemic and Faith*. Edited by Craig A. Evans and Donald A. Hagner. Minneapolis: Fortress, 1993.

——, *Prophecy and History in Luke-Acts*. Philadelphia: Fortress Press, 1980.

Tovey, Derek. *Narrative Art and Act in the Fourth Gospel*. Journal for the Study of the New Testament: Supplement Series 151. Sheffield: Sheffield Academic Press, 1997.

Trompf, G. W. *Early Christian Historiography: Narratives of Retributive Justice*. London: Continuum, 2000.

Tsohatzidis, Savas L. 'The Gap Between Speech Acts and Mental States'. Pages 220–33 in *Foundations of Speech Act Theory: Philosophical and Linguistic Perspectives*. Edited by Savas L. Tsohatzidis. London: Routledge, 1994.

Tsohatzidis, Savas L., ed. *Foundations of Speech Act Theory: Philosophical and Linguistic Perspectives*. London: Routledge, 1994.

Tuckett, Christopher M., ed. *Luke's Literary Achievement: Collected Essays*. Journal for the Study of the New Testament: Supplement Series 116. Sheffield: Sheffield Academic Press, 1995.

Turner, Max. *The Holy Spirit and Spiritual Gifts in the New Testament Church and Today*. Rev. edn. Peabody: Hendrickson, 1996.

——, 'Jesus and the Spirit in Lucan Perspective'. *Tyndale Bulletin* 32 (1981): 3–42.

——, 'Luke and the Spirit: Renewing Theological Interpretation of Biblical Pneumatology'. Pages 267–93 in *Reading Luke: Interpretation, Reflection, Formation*. Edited by Craig G. Bartholomew, Joel B. Green and Anthony C. Thiselton. Scripture and Hermeneutics Series 6. Grand Rapids: Zondervan, 2005.

——, 'Luke and the Spirit: Studies in the Significance of Receiving the Spirit in Luke-Acts'. PhD diss., Cambridge, 1980.

——, *Power From on High: The Spirit in Israel's Restoration and Witness in Luke-Acts*. Journal of Pentecostal Theology: Supplement Series 9. Sheffield: Sheffield Academic Press, 1996.

——, 'The Significance of Receiving the Spirit in Luke-Acts: A Survey of Modern Scholarship'. *Trinity Journal* n.s. 2 (1981): 131–58.

——, 'The Spirit and Salvation in Luke-Acts'. Pages 103–16 in *The Holy Spirit and Christian Origins: Essays in Honor of James D.G. Dunn*. Edited by Graham N. Stanton, Bruce W. Longenecker and Stephen C. Barton. Grand Rapids: Eerdmans, 2004.

——, 'The Spirit and the Power of Jesus' Miracles in the Lucan Conception'. *Novum Testamentum* 33 (1991): 124–52.

——, 'Spirit Endowment in Luke-Acts: Some Linguistic Considerations'. *Vox Evangelica* 12 (1981): 45–63.

——, 'The Spirit of Christ and Christology'. Pages 168–90 in *Christ the Lord*. Edited by H. H. Rowdon. Leicester: InterVarsity Press, 1982.

——, 'The Spirit of Christ and "Divine" Christology'. Pages 413–36 in *Jesus of Nazareth: Lord and Christ. Essays on the Historical Jesus and New Testament Christology*. Edited by Joel B. Green and Max Turner. Carlisle: Paternoster / Grand Rapids: Eerdmans, 1994.

——, 'The Spirit of Prophecy and the Ethical / Religious Life of the Christian Community'. Pages 166–90 in *Spirit and Renewal: Essays in Honor of J. Rodman Williams*. Edited by Mark W. Wilson. Journal for Pentecostal Theology: Supplement Series 5. Sheffield: Sheffield Academic Press, 1994.

———, 'The "Spirit of Prophecy" as the Power of Israel's Restoration and Witness'. Pages 327–48 in *Witness to the Gospel: The Theology of Acts*. Edited by I. Howard Marshall and David Peterson. Grand Rapids: Eerdmans, 1998.

———, 'The Spirit of Prophecy and the Power of Authoritative Preaching in Luke-Acts: A Question of Origins'. *New Testament Studies* 38 (1992): 66–88.

———, '"Trinitarian" Pneumatology in the New Testament? – Towards an Explanation of the Worship of Jesus'. *Asbury Theological Journal* 57 (2002): 168–86.

———, 'The Work of the Holy Spirit in Luke-Acts'. *Word and World* 23 (2003): 146–53.

Turner, Terence. '"Agonistic Exchange: Homeric Reciprocity and the Heritage of Simmel and Mauss": A Commentary'. *Cultural Anthropology* 4 (1989): 260–64.

Tyson, Joseph B. 'The Gentile Mission and the Authority of Scripture in Acts'. *New Testament Studies* 33 (1987): 619–31.

Upton, Bridget Gilfillan. *Hearing Mark's Endings: Listening to Ancient Popular Texts Through Speech Act Theory*. Biblical Interpretation Series 79. Leiden: Brill, 2006.

Uspensky, Boris. *A Poetics of Composition: The Structure of the Artistic Text and Typology of a Compositional Form*. Translated by Valentina Zavarin and Susan Wittig. Berkeley: University of California Press, 1973.

VanderKam, James C. *The Dead Sea Scrolls Today*. Grand Rapids: Eerdmans, 1994.

Vanhoozer, Kevin J. 'From Speech Acts to Scripture Acts: The Covenant of Discourse and the Discourse of the Covenant'. Pages 1–49 in *After Pentecost: Language and Biblical Interpretation*. Edited by C. Bartholomew, C. Greene, K. Möller. Scripture and Hermeneutics Series 2. Grand Rapids: Zondervan, 2001. Reprinted with revisions in Kevin J. Vanhoozer, *First Theology: God, Scripture and Hermeneutics*. Downers Grove, IL: InterVarsity Press, 2002, 159–203.

———, *Is There a Meaning in This Text? The Bible, the Reader, and the Morality of Literary Knowledge*. Grand Rapids: Zondervan, 1998.

Verheyden, Joseph. 'How Many Were Sent according to Lk 10,1?' Pages 193–238 in *Luke and His Readers: Festschrift A. Denaux*. Edited by R. Bieringer, G. van Belle, and J. Verheyden. Bibliotheca Ephemeridum Theologicarum Lovaniensium 182. Leuven: Leuven University Press, 2005.

———, 'The Unity of Luke-Acts: What are We Up To?' Pages 3–56 in *The Unity of Luke Acts*. Edited by J. Verheyden. Bibliotheca Ephemeridum Theologicarum Lovaniensium 142. Leuven: Leuven University Press, 1999.

Vermes, Geza. *The Complete Dead Sea Scrolls in English*. 5th edn. New York: Penguin, 1997.

———, 'The Qumran Community, the Essenes, and Nascent Christianity'. Pages 581–6 in *The Dead Sea Scrolls: Fifty Years After their Discovery: Proceedings of the Jerusalem Congress, July 20–25, 1997*. Edited by Lawrence Schiffman, Emanuel Tov and James C. VanderKam; Jerusalem: Israel Exploration Society, 2000.

Vermes, Geza, and Martin D. Goodman, eds. *The Essenes According to the Classical Sources*. Sheffield: JSOT, 1989.

Versnel, Hendrik S. 'Beyond Cursing: The Appeal to Judice in Judicial Prayers'. Pages 60–106 in *Magika Hiera: Ancient Greek Magic and Religion*. Edited by Christopher A. Faraone and Dirk Obbink. Oxford. Oxford University Press, 1991.

———, 'Religious Mentality in Ancient Prayer'. Pages 1–64 in *Faith, Hope and Worship: Aspects of Religious Mentality in the Ancient World*. Edited by H. S. Versnel. Leiden: Brill, 1981.

Veyne, Paul. *Bread and Circuses: Historical Sociology and Political Pluralism*. Translated by Brian Pearce. London: Allen Lane / The Penguin Press, 1990.

Vogel, Cornelia Johanna de. *Pythagoras and Early Pythagoreanism: An Interpretation of Neglected Evidence on the Philosopher Pythagoras*. Assen: Van Gorcum, 1966.

Wagner, J. Ross. 'Psalm 118 in Luke-Acts: Tracing a Narrative Thread'. Pages 154–78 in *Early Christian Interpretation of the Scriptures of Israel: Investigations and Proposals*. Edited by Craig A. Evans and James A. Sanders. Journal for the Study of the New Testament: Supplement Series 148. Sheffield: Sheffield Academic Press, 1997.

Waitz, H. 'Simon Magus in der altchristlichen Literatur'. *Zeitschrift für die neuetestamentliche Wissenschaft und die Kunde der älteren Kirche* 5 (1904): 121–43.

Walker, Peter W. L. *Jesus and the Holy City: New Testament Perspectives on Jerusalem*. Grand Rapids: Eerdmans, 1996.

Walker-Ramisch, Sandra. 'Graeco-Roman Voluntary Associations and the Damascus Document'. Pages 128–45 in *Voluntary Associations in the Graeco-Roman World*. Edited by John S. Kloppenborg and Stephen Wilson. London: Routledge, 1996.

Wall, Robert W. 'The Acts of the Apostles in Canonical Context'. *Biblical Theology Bulletin* 18 (1988): 16–24. Repr. pages 110–28 in *The New Testament as Canon: A Reader in Canonical Criticism* Robert W. Wall and Eugene E. Lemcio. Journal for the Study of the New Testament: Supplement Series 76. Sheffield: JSOT Press, 1992.

Wallace-Hadrill, Andrew. 'Patronage in Roman Society: From Republic to Empire'. Pages 63–87 in *Patronage in Ancient Society*. Edited by Andrew Wallace-Hadrill. London: Routledge, 1989.

Walton, Steve. 'A Tale of Two Perspectives?: The Place of the Temple in Acts'. Pages 135–49 in *Heaven on Earth: The Temple in Biblical Theology*. Edited by T. Desmond Alexander and Simon Gathercole. Carlisle: Paternoster, 2004.

Warnock, G. J. *J.L. Austin*. Rev. edn. London: Routledge and Kegan Paul, 1991.

——, 'Some Types of Performative Utterance'. Pages 69–89 in *Essays on J.L. Austin*. I. Berlin, et al. Oxford: Clarendon Press, 1973.

Water, Rick van de. 'The Punishment of the Wicked Priest and the Death of Judas'. *Dead Sea Discoveries* 10 (2003): 395–419.

Watts, Rikki E. *Isaiah's New Exodus in Mark*. Biblical Studies Library. Grand Rapids: Baker Academic, 1997.

Weatherly, Jon A. *Jewish Responsibility for the Death of Jesus in Luke-Acts*. Journal for the Study of the New Testament: Supplement Series 106. Sheffield: Sheffield Academic Press, 1994.

Wees, Hans van. 'The Law of Gratitude: Reciprocity in Anthropological Theory'. Pages 13–49 in *Reciprocity in Ancient Greece*. Edited by Christopher Gill, Norman Postlethwaite and Richard Seaford. Oxford: Oxford University Press, 1998.

Weigand, Edda. 'The State of the Art in Speech Act Theory: Review of Savas L. Tsohatzidis, ed., *Foundations of Speech Act Theory: Philosophical and Linguistic Perspectives*'. *Pragmatics and Cognition* 4 (1996): 367–406.

Weinert, Francis D. 'Luke, Stephen and the Temple in Luke-Acts'. *Biblical Theology Bulletin* 17 (1987): 88–91.

——, 'Luke, the Temple and Jesus' Saying about Jerusalem's Abandoned House (Luke 13:34-35)'. *Catholic Biblical Quarterly* 44 (1982): 68–76.

——, 'The Meaning of the Temple in the Gospel of Luke'. PhD diss., Fordham University, 1979.

——, 'The Meaning of the Temple in Luke-Acts'. *Biblical Theology Bulletin* 11 (1981): 85–9.

Weinfeld, Moshe. 'The Covenant in Qumran'. Pages 59–69 in *The Bible and the Dead Sea Scrolls: The Princeton Symposium on the Dead Sea Scrolls. Vol 2: The Dead Sea Scrolls and the Qumran Community*. Edited by James H. Charlesworth. Waco, TX: Baylor University Press, 2006.

——, *The Organizational Pattern and the Penal Code of the Qumran Sect: A Comparison with Guilds and Religious Associations of the Hellenistic-Roman Period*. Novum Testamentum et Orbis Antiquus. 2; Fribourg: Univeritatsverlag / Göttingen: Vandenhoeck & Riprecht, 1986.

Weiser, Alfons. *Die Apostelgeschichte: Kapitel 1–12*. Ökumenishcer Taschenbuch-Kommentar 5/1. Gütersloh: Gütersloher Verlagshaus Gerd Mohn / Würzburg: Echter-Verlag, 1981.
Wenk, Matthias. *Community-Forming Power: The Socio-Ethical Role of the Spirit in Luke-Acts*. Journal of Pentecostal Theology: Supplement Series 19. Sheffield: Sheffield Academic Press, 2000.
Westphal, Merold. 'On Reading God the Author'. *Religious Studies* 37 (2001): 271–91.
White, Hayden. *The Content of the Form: Narrative Discourse and Historical Representation*. Baltimore, MD: Johns Hopkins University Press, 1987.
———, 'The Narrativization of Real Events'. *Critical Inquiry* 7 (1981): 793–8.
———, *Tropics of Discourse: Essays in Cultural Criticism*. Baltimore, MD: Johns Hopkins University Press, 1978.
White, Hugh C. 'Introduction: Speech Act Theory and Literary Criticism'. *Semeia* 41 (1988): 1–24
White, Hugh C., ed. *Speech Act Theory and Biblical Criticism*. Semeia 41. Decatur, GA: Scholars Press, 1988.
Wiarda, Timothy. 'Peter as Peter in the Gospel of Mark'. *New Testament Studies* 45 (1999): 19–37.
———, *Peter in the Gospels: Patterns, Personality and Relationship*. Wissenschaftliche Untersuchungen zum Neuen Testament 2.127. Tübingen: Mohr Siebeck, 2000.
Wilcox, Max. *The Semitisms of Acts*. Oxford: Clarendon Press, 1965.
Wilken, Robert L. *The Christians as the Romans Saw Them*. New Haven: Yale University Press, 1984.
Williams, Benjamin E. *Miracle Stories in the Biblical Book Acts of the Apostles*. Lewiston: Edwin Mellen Press, 2001.
Williams, Ronald R. *The Acts of the Apostles*. Torch Bible Commentaries. London: SCM Press, 1953.
Wilson, Scott G. 'The Ascension: A Critique and an Interpretation'. *Zeitschrift für die neuetestamentliche Wissenschaft und die Kunde der älteren Kirche* 59 (1968): 269–81.
———, 'Lukan Eschatology'. *New Testament Studies* 15 (1970): 330–47.
Winter, Bruce W. *Seek the Welfare of the City: Christians as Benefactors and Citizens. First-Century Christians in the Graeco-Roman World*. Grand Rapids: Eerdmans / Carlisle: Paternoster, 1994.
Winter, Bruce W., and Andrew Clarke, eds. *The Book of Acts in Its First Century Setting: Volume 1: Ancient Literary Setting*. Grand Rapids: Eerdmans / Carlisle: Paternoster, 1993.
Winter, Paul. *On the Trial of Jesus*. 2nd edn. Revised and edited by T. A. Burkill and Geza Vermes. Berlin: de Gruyter, 1974.
Wise, Michael O. 'Review of Todd S. Beall, *Josephus' Description of the Essenes Illustrated by the Dead Sea Scrolls*'. *JNES* 49 (1990): 202–4.
Wisse, Maarten. 'From Cover to Cover? A Critique of Wolterstorff's Theory of the Bible as Divine Discourse'. *International Journal for the Philosophy of Religion* 52 (2002): 159–73.
Witherington, III, Ben. *The Acts of the Apostles: A Socio-Rhetorical Commentary*. Grand Rapids: Eerdmans / Carlisle: Paternoster Press, 1998.
Witherington, III, Ben, ed. *History, Literature and Society in the Book of Acts*. Cambridge: Cambridge University Press, 1996.
Wittgenstein, Ludwig. *Philosophical Investigations*. 3rd edn. Translated by G. E. M. Anscombe. Oxford: Blackwell Publishing, 2001.
Wolterstorff, Nicholas. *Divine Discourse: Philosophical Reflections on the Claim that God Speaks*. Cambridge: Cambridge University Press, 1995.
———, 'The Promise of Speech Act Theory for Biblical Interpretation'. Pages 73–90 in *After Pentecost: Language and Biblical Interpretation*. Edited by C. Bartholomew, C. Greene, K. Möller. Scripture and Hermeneutics Series 2. Grand Rapids: Zondervan, 2001.

Woods, Edward J. *The 'Finger of God' and Pneumatology in Luke-Acts*. Journal for the Study of the New Testament: Supplement Series 205. Sheffield: Sheffield Academic Press, 2001.
Wright, N. T. *Jesus and the Victory of God*. Minneapolis: Fortress Press, 1996.
——, *The New Testament and the People of God*. Minneapolis: Fortress Press, 1992.
Wuthnow, Robert. *Poor Richard's Principle: Recovering the American Dream Through the Moral Dimension of Work, Business, and Money*. Princeton: Princeton University Press, 1996.
York, John O. *The Last Shall Be First: The Rhetoric of Reversal in Luke*. Journal for the Study of the New Testament: Supplement Series 46. Sheffield: JSOT Press, 1991.
Zerbre, Gordon M. 'Economic Justice and Nonretaliation in the Dead Sea Scrolls: Implications for New Testament Interpretation'. Pages 319–55 in *The Bible and the Dead Sea Scrolls: The Princeton Symposium on the Dead Sea Scrolls. Vol 3: The Scrolls and Christian Origins*. Edited by James H. Charlesworth. Waco, TX: Baylor University Press, 2006.
Zettner, Christoph. *Amt, Gemeinde und kirchliche Einheit in der Apostelgeschichte des Lukas*. Europäische Hochschulschriften. Reihe 23. Theologie 423; Frankfurt: Lang, 1991.
Zwiep, Arie W. *The Ascension of the Messiah in Lukan Christology*. Novum Testamentum Supplements 87. Leiden: Brill, 1997.
——, *Judas and the Choice of Matthias*. Wissenschaftliche Untersuchungen zum Neuen Testament 2.187. Tübingen: Mohr Siebeck, 2004.
——, 'The Text of the Ascension Narratives (Luke 24, 50–3; Acts 1, 1–2, 9–11)'. *New Testament Studies* 42 (1996): 219–44.

INDEX OF REFERENCES

BIBLE

OLD TESTAMENT

Genesis
12.1-3   169
15.1-21   169
17.7   169
22.16-18   169

Exodus
16.4-36   141

Leviticus
13.45   110
23.29   79, 183

Numbers
11.16-18   142
27.15-23   174
27.18   174

Deuteronomy
4.10-24   142
6.5   109
15.4   210
18.15   183
18.15-19   141
18.18   183
22.1   118, 212
22.3-4   118
28.28-29   158
29.17   152
31.14-23   174
31.22   174
31.23   174
34.5 6   174

Joshua
1.5   174
7   30

Job
6.16   118

Psalms
2.1-2   14, 27, 167
2.2   14
2.7   147
15.10   21, 147
17.22   16
55.2   118

Isaiah
6.9-10   28
32.15   178
37.23   126–7
39.3   127
39.4-8   127
40.3   12, 207
40.4   69
42.6   157
43.10-12   168
49.6   147, 157, 170
49.6-7   168
58.6   71, 118
58.7   118, 152
61.1   152
61.1-2   71
61.2   71, 137

Ezekiel
22.29-31   119

Zechariah
1.72-73   169
9.9-10   146

SEPTUAGINT (LXX)

Deuteronomy
34.9   174

Judges
2.15   158

1 Kingdoms
1.32-35   146
12.15   158
15.11   126
15.14   126
15.22-23   126
15.35   126

2 Kingdoms
7.6-16   147
12.10-13   126
12.19   126
15.17   126
15.19   126

4 Kingdoms
1.3   126
1.6   126
1.9-16   142
1.10   126
1.12   126
1.13-14   126
1.16   126
1.17   126
2.1-18   174
4.42-44   141
20.14   127
20.15-19   127

Psalms
15.8-11   147, 176, 180
68.26   164, 203
108.8   164, 203, 204
109.1   147, 176, 180

Joel
3.1-5   179–80

Isaiah
55.3 147

NEW TESTAMENT

Matthew
21.18-22 223
27.3-10 203

Mark
11.12-14 34, 223
11.20-21 34
11.20-25 223

Luke
1–2 132
1.1 5
1.4 147
1.19-20 127
1.20 223
1.22 127
1.27 135
1.32-33 135, 188
1.35 21
1.47 135
1.49 135
1.52 69
1.55 135, 169
1.62-54 127
1.64 223
1.69 135
1.69-72 188
1.72-73 135
1.76 207
1.76-77 135
2.1-20 135
2.11 135
2.29-32 188
2.30-32 157
2.32 147
2.34-35 70
2.38 154
2.42-47 14
2.44-45 74
2.49 135
2.52 193
3.4 12, 155, 157, 207
3.5 69
3.10-14 68
3.16-17 178
3.17 27
3.22 131, 136, 188

4 214
4.1-13 22, 26, 201, 214
4.6 152
4.18 71
4.16-30 137
4.18-19 71, 118
4.18-30 177
4.19 137
4.22 71
4.23-27 71
4.24 71, 137
4.32 154
4.34 21
4.28 71
4.37 152
4.38 194
4.38-41 194
5.5 190, 198
5.8 188, 190, 195
5.9 190
5.10 194
5.17-26 223
6.12-16 164, 194
6.13-14 189
6.16 201, 205
6.35 70
6.36 70
6.48 189
7.1-17 137
7.16 137
8.4-15 142
8.20 152
8.24 152
8.38 195
8.45 195
8.51 195
9.1 141
9.1-6 164, 188
9.2 141
9.6 141
9.7-9 137
9.7-21 142
9.8 138
9.10 164
9.11 141
9.18 195
9.19 137
9.20 141, 190, 195
9.22-24 198
9.22-27 141
9.28 195
9.28-36 142, 143, 177
9.31 142

9.32 188
9.33 190
9.35 143
9.43 154
9.46-48 142, 164, 191
9.49-50 142
9.51 144, 160
9.51–19.44 138-9
9.51-56 142
9.57-62 142
10.1-24 188
10.16 27
10.18 214
10.21 205
11.15 143
11.18 214
11.20 143
11.28 215
11.39-44 191
11.43 191
11.46-52 138
12.1 164, 191
12.1-9 192
12.8 205
12.8-12 27
12.13 191
12.13-21 68
12.16 191
12.22 191
12.22-34 191
12.36 191
12.37 191
12.38 191
12.41 191, 195
12.41-48 164
12.42 191
12.42-48 191
12.43 191
12.45 191
12.45-48 191
12.46 191
12.47 191
13.16 214
13.22 144
13.33-35 138, 197
13.34 138, 144
13.35 25, 144
14.7-11 164
14.7-24 191
14.14 70
16.1-31 164
16.30 70
17.20 143

Index of References

265

17.20-21 144
17.22-27 143
18.18-30 68
18.18-34 146
18.22 191
18.23-28 191
18.28 191, 195, 207
18.28-30 203
18.29-30 191
18.35-43 146
19.1-27 146
19.11 144
19.14 146
19.27 25, 167
19.38 146, 164
19.41 144
19.41-46 25
19.42 144
19.43-44 224
19.44 144
19.47-48 16
20.1 16
20.1-37 16
20.2 16
20.9-16 16
20.9-19 25
20.17 16
20.19 16
20.41-44 147
22.3 201
21.6 25, 145, 201, 224
21.20-54 25
21.22 145
22.2 16, 207
22.3 202, 206, 213, 214
22.4 202, 205, 206, 207
22.6 205, 207
22.8 195
22.14 195
22.14-38 146, 164
22.21 201, 205
22.21-22 127, 205
22.22 196, 201, 205, 207
22.22-47 164
22.24-27 61
22.24-30 191
22.25-27 192
22.28 195
22.28-30 164, 183, 192, 194, 204, 222
22.29 146, 206
22.29-30 165-6
22.30 164

22.31 214
22.31-32 164, 192
22.31-34 1, 192
22.32 194, 207, 222
22.33 192
22.33-34 165
22.34 195
22.47 201, 202, 207
22.48 201, 205
22.49 195
22.52 16
22.53 207
22.54 194
22.54-62 1, 165, 192, 194, 195
22.56 188, 195
22.62 153
22.64 138
22.66 16, 24
22.67-71 138, 146
22.69 25
23.1-6 9
23.2-3 146
23.10 9
23.11 146
23.13 16, 24
23.13-25 9
23.18 24
23.21 24
23.23 24
23.28-31 145
23.29 145
23.29-31 224
23.31 25, 145
23.34 141
23.35 16
23.38 146
23.39 146
23.42 146
23.46 141
24 204
24.4 193
24.12 195, 197
24.13-35 138
24.19 138
24.20 16
24.25-27 192
24.33 170, 194
24.34 197
24.36-49 168
24.44 131
24.44-49 192
24.45 131

24.45-49 164
24.46-47 131
24.46-49 183
24.47 168
24.48 18, 131, 166, 168
24.48-49 194
24.48-51 198
24.49 12, 69, 131, 168
24.50 174
24.50-51 172
24.50-53 169, 183
24.52-53 194

Acts
1–5 3, 11, 16, 148, 184, 197, 199, 219
1–7 15
1.1 5, 178, 193
1.1–8.3 9
1.1-14 172
1.2 131, 170, 178
1.3 131, 172
1.3–5.42 11, 20
1.3-11 12
1.3–8.3 11, 14, 15
1.4 168
1.4-5 12, 23, 69, 168, 169
1.4-8 198
1.4-11 222
1.5-8 169
1.8 18, 23, 53, 127, 131, 147, 150, 168, 178, 209
1.9-11 169, 177, 183
1.10 193
1.10-11 176
1.11 171
1.12 192, 194
1.12-13 194
1.12-14 17
1.12-26 12, 17, 164
1.12–4.23 17
1.12–5.42 187, 193
1.12–8.3 28, 193
1.13 194
1.14 202
1.15-22 192
1.15 26 17, 202
1.16 202, 203, 207
1.16-20 196
1.17 201, 205
1.18 202, 205, 211, 213
1.18-19 96, 202

1.18-20 127
1.19 202
1.20 193
1.21 195, 207
1.21-22 23, 53, 189
1.22 18, 167, 170, 175, 189, 209
1.22-25 205
1.25 202, 206, 207
1.26 205
2 113
2–5 18
2.1-4 69, 131, 178, 198
2.1-11 17
2.1-41 170, 183
2.1–8.3 20
2.4 17, 20, 23, 180, 188
2.5-40 11
2.6 178
2.14 23, 23, 180, 182, 188, 192
2.14-21 180
2.14-36 17
2.14-40 11, 17, 182, 187, 192, 222
2.14-41 134
2.17 179, 180
2.17-18 222
2.17-21 193
2.18 21, 69, 166, 179, 180
2.19 23, 180
2.22 23, 182, 193
2.22-23 12
2.22-28 180
2.23 180
2.25-28 193
2.27 21, 147
2.31 147
2.32 18, 167, 180, 189
2.32-33 146
2.32-36 82, 170
2.33 69, 168, 177
2.33-34 176
2.33-36 192, 198
2.34 176, 177
2.36 147, 180, 222
2.37 127, 180, 182
2.38 12, 69, 192
2.38-39 69
2.39 69
2.40 12, 139, 218
2.41 11
2.41-47 17, 20, 68, 69, 208
2.42 194
2.42-47 12, 72
2.42–5.42 18
2.43 17, 22, 23, 180, 198
2.44 93, 208
2.44-45 72, 203, 210
2.45 93, 211
2.46 24
2.47 22, 23, 209
3–4 193
3–5 197
3.1 194
3.1-5 195
3.1-10 12, 17, 127
3.1-11 17
3.1–4.22 11
3.6 192
3.7-10 193
3.12 192
3.12-26 11, 12, 182, 187, 192
3.12–5.42 16
3.13-15 13
3.14 21
3.15 18, 182, 189
3.17 182
3.19 182
3.22 183
3.22-23 79, 141, 193
3.23 22, 79, 137, 183
3.24-25 193
3.25 170
3–5 11
4 113
4–5 194
4.1 16
4.1-3 12, 16
4.1-7 17
4.1-22 9, 11, 16, 28
4.2 27
4.2-3 11
4.3 16, 192
4.4 11
4.5 16, 189
4.5-6 16, 189
4.5-22 12
4.7 16
4.8 23, 34, 187, 188, 192, 196, 222
4.8-12 11, 17
4.9 12
4.10-11 13, 197
4.10-12 16
4.11 16
4.12 12
4.13 11, 23, 165, 188, 189
4.13-17 17, 23
4.14 12
4.15-17 17
4.16 23, 180, 197
4.16-18 11
4.18 17, 165
4.19 27
4.19-20 11, 17
4.20 189
4.21 11, 16, 17, 23, 165, 197
4.21-22 196
4.21-23 17
4.22 12, 23, 180
4.23 11, 14, 16, 207, 213
4.23–5.11 11, 190
4.24 24
4.24-28 28
4.24-30 13
4.24-31 14, 15, 17
4.24–5.42 17
4.25-28 27, 167
4.25-29 9, 197
4.26-27 14
4.27 21
4.29 11, 21, 69
4.29-30 222
4.30 21, 23, 180, 193
4.31 5, 11, 17, 21, 23, 26, 34, 69, 184, 208, 211
4.32 9, 24, 69, 72, 93, 203, 208, 210
4.32-35 14, 17, 18, 69, 72, 209, 219
4.32-37 2
4.32–5.11 5, 10, 11, 13, 14, 17, 19–21, 23, 26, 28–9, 43, 59, 68, 72, 75, 97, 132, 168, 183, 208, 219
4.33 10, 18, 21, 22, 72, 78, 82, 167, 170, 199, 209, 213, 216
4.33-35 194
4.34 211, 213
4.34-35 21, 72, 93, 208, 210
4.34-37 203

Index of References

4.35 10, 210
4.36 189
4.36-37 10, 211, 219
4.37 10, 150, 208, 210
5 214
5.1 211, 212, 217
5.1-2 217
5.1-11 1, 7, 9, 10, 18, 19, 25, 30, 37, 127, 140, 161, 193, 196, 217, 219, 220
5.2 10, 210, 211, 212
5.3 2, 21, 26, 30, 76, 129, 151, 184, 192, 208, 211, 212, 213, 215
5.3-4 217
5.4 2, 9, 44, 76, 129, 211, 213, 214, 215
5.5 9, 19, 22, 39, 75, 209, 215–16, 217, 221
5.6 216–17
5.7 218
5.7-8 217
5.8 192, 208, 211, 212, 213, 217
5.9 9, 30, 33, 45, 76, 82, 139, 211, 212, 217–18
5.10 155, 210, 217, 218
5.11 19, 22, 75, 209, 217, 218, 221
5.11-12 213
5.12 11, 23, 24, 180, 193, 198, 222
5.12-16 13, 14, 17, 18, 19, 209
5.13 23, 221
5.13-14 216
5.13-16 11, 17
5.15 193
5.17 13, 21, 24, 196
5.17-18 11, 16
5.17-28 17
5.17-42 9, 11, 16, 28
5.18 16, 165, 192
5.19-28 23
5.21 11
5.26 11, 23, 196, 197
5.26-27 16
5.26-28 11
5.28 196, 197
5.29 16, 192
5.29-32 11, 13, 17
5.30 16

5.30-32 16
5.30-33 197
5.32 18, 167, 189
5.33 13, 165
5.33-39 17
5.33-40 11
5.34-39 17
5.38 22
5.39 13, 27, 28, 167, 197, 208
5.40 17
5.40-41 165
5.40-42 17
5.41 198
5.42 11
6-7 13
6.1-7 13
6.2-4 191
6.8 25, 180, 222
6.8–8.3 9, 11, 28
6.9 24
6.11 24
6.12 24
6.13 24
7.1 24
7.17-29 141
7.20-44 140
7.35-43 141
7.37 141
7.51-53 25, 197
7.52-53 197
7.54 24
7.55 222
7.56 25
7.59-60 141
8.1 150
8.4 13
8.4-25 154
8.6 149, 180
8.9-11 150
8.9-25 38, 148–53, 161
8.10 150
8.11 149
8.12 167
8.13 149, 150, 180
8.14-24 167
8.15-17 167
8.18 150
8.18-19 150
8.18-24 34
8.21 151
8.22 151
8.23 151

9.1-9 28
9.4 176
9.27 211
9.34 175
10.9-16 167, 198
10.13 198
10.13-17 191
10.14 198
10.18 26
10.25-26 150
10.28 167
10.38 26, 193, 214
10.39 18, 167
10.41 18
10.41-42 167
10.44 167
11.23-24 211
11.27-30 68
12.3 192
12.22-23 150
13.1 34
13.1-2 161
13.1-3 156
13.1-12 38, 154–8
13.2 158
13.2-3 154
13.4 158
13.4-12 127, 212
13.6 127
13.7 154, 157, 158
13.9 222
13.10 12, 26, 154, 214
13.11 155
13.11-12 34
13.12 154, 158
13.16-41 134, 147
13.17-53 147
13.31 18
13.35 21
13.38-39 147
13.40-41 147
13.46-48 147
13.47 157
14.3 180
14.11-18 150
14.26-27 154
15.11 148
15.12 180
15.13-21 134, 147
15.15-18 148
16.16-18 159
19.1-7 159
19.5 160

19.9   159
19.8-20   158-61
19.10   159
19.11-20   38
19.12   159
19.13   160
19.13-16   159
19.16   160
19.17   160
19.20   160
19.21   160
19.23-41   159, 160
20.35   68
22.3   26
23   223
23.3   223
26.13   157
26.15-18   157
26.18   26, 214
28.25-28   28, 133, 157

Romans
6.12-23   33

JEWISH SOURCES

THE SCROLLS OF THE JUDEAN DESERT

Community Rule (1QS)
1.1–4.26   112
1.10-11   113
1.11-13   109
1.18   109
2.11-19   158
2.25–3.12   112
3.5   110
5.1–7.25   112
5.7–6.1   112
5.9   112
5.10-11   112
6.13-23   73, 113, 120
6.13-24   113
6.24-25   75, 76, 114, 120, 215
6.24–7.25   114, 115
6.25   121
7.22-24   115
7.22-25   114
7.25   110, 115
8.1–9.2   112
8.20-27   115

8.22-23   115
8.23   115
9.1   115
9.3–11.22   112
9.16-17   113
9.21-23   113
10.18-20   113
11.1-2   113

Damascus Document
CD-A 4.13–5.15   117
CD-A 4.17   117
CD-A 6.15b-17a   117
CD-A 6.19   109
CD-A 7.6-9   118
CD-A 8.2b-12a   117
CD-A 8.5   117
CD-A 8.6   118
CD-A 8.7   117
CD-A 8.21   109
CD-A 9.10b-16a   118
CD-A 9.16–10.3   120
CD-A 9.16-23   122
CD-A 12.6b-11a   118
CD-A 14.12-19   119
CD-A 14-15a   119
CD-A 13   118
CD-A 13.7-10   109
CD-A 13.9-10   117
CD-A 13.11-12   109, 120, 122
CD-A 13.12b-16a   120
CD-A 13.15-18   118
CD-A 14.14-16   118
CD-A 14.19   120
CD-A 14.20-21   120
CD-A 15.5b–16.6a   120
CD-A 15.6   120
CD-A 16.10-12   118
CD-A 19.3-5   118
CD-B 19.15-24a   117
CD-B 19.17   117
CD-B 19.19   117
CD-B 19.33-34   109
CD-B 19.33–20.27a   121
CD-B 19.35   121
CD-B 20.3-10a   121-2
CD-B 20.6-10   120
CD-B 20.7   122
CD-B 20.12   109
4Q266 11.14b-16   122
4Q271 3.4-15   118
4QDa 8.1   120

4QD 10.1.11   119
4QDa 10.1.14   120
4QDd 11.1.4-5   120-1
4QDa 11.1-20   122
4QD 11.14-16   110, 120, 122

JOSEPHUS

Antiquities
15.371   86
18.18-22   100
18.20   102

Jewish War
2.119-61   100, 102
2.122   102
2.124   104
2.125   104
2.127   104
2.137-38   105
2.143-44   105
2.145   106

PHILO

Hypothetica
8.11.1-19   101
11.1   102
11.1-18   100
11.18   102

Quod omnis probus liber sit
75   102
75-91   100
76-77   103
78   104
83   103
84   103
86-87   103

De Vita Mosis
2.291   174

Index of References

GRECO-ROMAN SOURCES

DIODORUS SICULUS

Library of History
5.34.3   58, 212

DIOGENES LAERTIUS

Lives
5.25   87
8.10   91
8.54   95
8.55   96

IAMBLICHUS

De Vita Pythagorica
6.30   91–2
6.32   92
17.71-74   96
17.71-79   94
17.72   94–5
17.73   95
17.74   95
17.75   96
18.80-81   92
18.81   92
18.88   97
20   91
30.167-68   93
30.170   93
33   94
34.246-47   97
35.257   90, 94

XENOPHON

Cyrus
4.2.42   212

Index of Subjects

Abraham 135, 169
Achan 30
Aelian 87
Agrippa 157
Ahaziah, king 126
Alexander of Aphrodisias 87
Alexander Polyhistor 87
Ananias and Sapphira 30, 31, 33, 35, 36, 37, 38, 39–40, 41, 43, 45, 46, 47, 48, 54, 59, 60–1, 62–4, 67, 72, 73, 74–5, 76–7, 79, 80, 81, 82, 83, 95, 97, 106, 115, 123, 124, 125, 127, 129, 132, 140, 150, 151, 152, 153, 154, 160, 161, 167, 170, 178, 184, 193, 196, 197, 199, 219–20, 221, 222, 223, 224
    as episode in narrative of Acts 9–29
    and reopening of case 1–8
    and speech-act of divine judgement 200–18
Apollonius of Tyana 88
Aristotle 86, 87, 89
Aristoxenus 87
Ascough, Richard 3, 62–4
Austin, J. L. 31, 41, 42, 43–4, 46, 47, 48, 49, 50, 52, 53, 159, 161

Bar-Jesus 26, 38, 148, 154, 155–6, 212
Barnabas 10, 14, 29, 62, 72, 74, 147, 150, 152, 154, 170, 183, 196, 208, 210, 211, 212, 213, 216, 219
Barrett, Charles Kingsley 35–6, 151–3
Batchy, Scott 60–2, 64–5
Baumgarten, Joseph M. 119
Beyer, Robert 34–5
Borg, Marcus 145
Brawley, Robert L. 26–7, 137, 204, 207
Briggs, Richard 53, 54
Brown, Paul 2, 206, 207, 213
Burkert, Walter 89–90
Buss, Martin J. 53

Callimachus 87
Capper, Brian J. 2, 63, 72, 73, 74–5, 113, 215

Chaniotis 80–1
Cicero 88
Clement of Alexandria 39
Codex Bezae 5
Colpe, Carsten 37
community-of-goods 9–14
    and Christianity 67–76
    and friendship 56–65
Community Rule 57, 73, 75, 76, 99, 107, 108, 110, 111–16, 158, 215, 221
Conzelmann, Hans 37, 172
Cook, John G. 1
Council (Judicial) 11, 14, 16–17, 22, 23–5, 27, 29, 146, 147, 197
Croton 91
Cryer, Frederick 38

Damascus Document 57, 99, 107, 108, 110, 111, 115–23, 221
Darr, John A. 184–6, 194–5, 197, 198
David, King 126, 133, 135, 142, 143, 146–8, 177
Dawson, Doyne 65
Dead Sea Scrolls 57, 84, 98, 108, 110, 111, 116
Derrett, J. Duncan M. 3, 31–2, 35
Dicaearchus 87
Diodorus of Sicily 57–8, 212
Diogenes Laertius 85, 87, 91, 95–6
Dodd, C. H. 145
Dupont, Jacques 65–6, 70

Eco, Umberto 6
Elijah 126, 137, 138, 142, 143, 168, 170, 173, 174–5, 177, 188, 190
Elisha 137, 141, 168, 173, 175, 177
Elliot, John 68
Elymas 34, 35, 127, 154–5, 157, 158, 161, 214
Empedocles 89, 95–6
Essenes 7, 57, 65, 67, 72, 75, 76, 84, 86, 90, 94, 97–107, 110, 220, 221

Foakes-Jackson F. J. 1
Forkman, Göran 81–2, 110

Gabriel, angel 134–5
Gamaliel 13, 27, 28, 29, 197
Garrett, Susan 151, 153, 155, 158, 159–60
Geertz, Clifford 68
González, Justo 57
Gowler, David B. 187, 188
Green, Joel B. 15, 27, 68–9, 137, 145, 147, 196
Guardian/Examiner 109, 113, 118, 120
Guthrie, K. S. 88

Haenchen, Ernst 30, 41
Havelaar, Henriette 3, 76–7, 78–9, 80
Hempel, Charlotte 119
Hermippus of Smyrna 87
Herod 14, 27, 100, 137–8, 141, 150
Hezekiah, King 126–7
Hipparchus 96
Hippasus 89, 96–7
Holy Spirit 2, 9, 10, 12, 13, 20, 21–2, 24, 26, 28, 30, 31, 38–9, 41, 43, 69, 76, 80, 82, 83, 115, 124, 128–31, 134, 149, 150, 154, 155, 156, 158, 159, 161, 167, 169, 175, 178, 180, 183, 185, 188, 189, 192, 198, 205, 208, 211, 213, 214, 219, 220, 221, 222
Horbury, William 80, 81
Houston, Walter 46
Hull, John 38
Hur, Ju 21, 185–6

Iamblichus 86, 87, 90, 91–7
Iser, Wolfgang 51
Israel 9, 12, 18, 22, 28, 40, 69, 71, 81, 134, 135, 137, 138, 141, 143, 146, 147, 152, 156, 157, 170, 174, 179, 180–3, 194, 206, 216
  history of 41, 125, 139–40
  judgement of 43, 48, 110, 117, 124–5, 128, 133, 144, 161, 164–8, 188, 222
  peoples of 27, 136, 143
  restoration of 23, 25, 128, 140, 164, 176, 178, 196, 211, 222
  Scriptures of 7, 15, 41, 51, 80, 81, 107, 124, 130–1, 132, 136, 138, 141, 144, 145, 147–8, 168, 179–80, 192, 193, 198–9, 202, 203–4, 214, 221

  effective prophetic speech in 125–7
  story of 13, 14, 136, 199
  Twelve Tribes of 164–8

Jerusalem 11, 12, 73
  church in 56–83, 164, 167, 194, 221
  community-of-goods in 61, 63, 65, 69, 72, 75
  elite in 11, 12, 14, 15, 20, 23, 25, 28, 29, 51, 104, 167, 195, 196, 197, 218, 219
  indictment of by Jesus 144–5
  messianic community in 9, 13, 29, 64, 69, 71, 72, 82, 123, 219
Jerusalem Council *see* Council (Judicial)
Jervell, Jacob 22, 26
Jesus 1, 5, 8, 9, 14–15, 16, 21, 23, 24, 25, 27, 51, 127, 128, 131, 152, 156, 164, 166, 168, 169, 181, 188–9, 195, 197, 201, 204, 205–6, 207
  ascension of 170–7, 192–3
  death of 13, 15
  as Messiah 3, 81, 136, 190
  as Prophet-King 15, 43, 124–5, 132–48, 161, 164, 177, 198, 208, 221–2
  resurrection of 18, 167, 170, 176, 178, 180, 183, 209
  teaching of 70, 71, 82, 165, 191
  temptation of 22, 26, 78
Jewish War (Josephus) 100, 102, 104, 105, 106
Joel 168, 177, 179, 180
John 12, 14, 27, 69, 167, 188, 189, 194, 195, 196, 207
John the Baptist 135, 155, 157, 159, 193
Johnson, Luke Timothy 3, 23–4, 33, 79, 132, 141, 157–8, 160, 202–3, 213
Josephus 57, 76, 86, 99–100, 101, 104, 105–6, 123, 174, 212, 220
Joshua 173, 174
Jubilee motif 118
Judas 12, 26, 43, 79, 127, 152, 153, 164, 195, 196, 199, 200–8, 213, 215, 216, 218, 222

Kee, Howard Clark 37
Klauck, Hans-Josef 67, 70, 156

Ludëmann, Gerd 2, 36
Luke 1–2, 4, 6, 7, 13, 15–16, 36, 38, 41, 50, 51, 57, 60, 62–5, 67, 68, 73, 75–6, 80, 82–3, 104, 106, 125, 127, 128, 130, 132, 133, 134–5, 141, 142, 148,

149, 156, 157, 165–6, 167, 168, 169, 170, 172, 173–4, 177–8, 179, 180, 182, 183, 198–9, 202, 205, 206, 207, 208, 209, 210–11, 215–16, 217, 218, 221
Lysis 96

Marguerat, Daniel 3, 18–20, 33, 34, 69, 209
Mark 16, 187
Mary 69, 134–5, 169
Mason, Steve 24, 100, 104, 106
Matthew 16, 187
Matthias 204, 205, 206
Mealand, David 66–7
Menoud, Philippe-H. 2
Minear, Paul 179
Mitchell, Alan 64–5
Moessner, David 138–9, 142, 204
Moses 39, 43, 79, 105–6, 112, 125, 133, 136, 140–1, 142, 143, 152, 173–4, 177, 183, 188, 190, 222
Murphy, Catherine M. 111, 112, 113, 114, 116–17, 119, 121, 122

Nathan 126
Neanthes of Cyzicus 87, 96
Nicomachus of Gerasa 88, 91
Numenius of Apamea 88

O'Day, Gail 1
Origen 39
O'Toole, Robert F. 3, 33–4, 175, 217

Parsons, Mikeal 5, 176
Paul 15, 26, 28, 33, 35, 38, 127, 132–3, 134, 147, 148, 150, 154–5, 156–7, 158–9, 160, 161, 166, 167, 212, 223–4
Pentecost 13, 18, 20, 69, 176, 192, 205
  and prophetic transference and vocation 177–83
Pervo, Richard 5
Pesch, Rudolf 77–8
Peter 1, 2, 4, 7–8, 10, 13, 14, 16, 17, 18, 21, 23, 24, 25, 26, 27, 29, 30–4, 35, 36, 37–8, 44–7, 48, 51–2, 53, 55, 59, 69, 75, 76, 79–80, 81, 82, 83, 124, 125, 129, 132, 133, 134, 140, 141, 147, 148, 149–53, 154, 155, 161–2, 200, 201, 202, 203, 204, 207, 208, 211, 212, 213–14, 215–16, 219, 220, 221–2
  and apostolic-prophetic succession/ characterization 163–99

  and language as 'performative' prophetic utterance 39–43
  and Pentecost speech 12, 127, 139, 146, 170, 182, 217–18
Petrey, Sandy 42, 48, 49–50
Philip 149, 167
Philo 57, 99, 174, 220
  and Essene communities-of-goods 100–1, 102–5, 106
Pilate 14, 146
Plato 89
Plümacher, Eckhard 157–8
Plutarch 87
Polybius 212
Porphyry 1, 91, 93–4
Pratt, Mary Louise 49
Procksch, Otto 40
Pythagorean community 57, 65, 67, 72, 75, 76, 79, 100, 106, 110, 123, 220, 221
  and divine economy 84–97

Qumran covenanters/sectarians 7, 72, 75, 99, 107–23, 158

Rabin, Chaim 119
Rad, Gerhard von 40
Read-Heimerdinger, Jenny 153
Richter Reimer, Ivoni 3, 32–3, 35, 212–13, 216
Rimmon-Kenan, Shlomith 187, 190
Rius-Camps, Josep 153
Robinson, Anthony 39–40

Sadducees 21, 99
Sahlins, Marshall 58–9, 105
Samuel 125–6
Sanhedrin 15, 28, 194, 197, 207
Sapphira see Ananias and Sapphira
Satan 21–2, 26–7, 33, 35, 82, 129, 137, 143, 150, 151, 152, 153, 154, 155, 184, 192, 196, 200, 201, 206, 212, 213, 214–15, 218, 219, 220, 222
Saul 125, 126
Schiffman, Lawrence H. 115
Scriptures of Israel see Israel
Second Temple Judaism 80
Sennacherib 126
Septuagint 158, 180
Sergius Paulus 157
Simeon 157
Simon Magus 34, 148–9, 150, 153, 161
Sons of Sceva 158–61

speech-acts
    of divine judgement 200–18
    prophetic speech-acts 30–55
    unsuccessful speech-act 158–61
Speech Acts (Searle) 46
Speech-Act Theory 4, 7, 31, 40, 42, 43, 124, 199, 208, 219, 220, 222–4
    limits of 53–5
    as a socio-pragmatic tool 43–53
Spirit *see* Holy Spirit
Steck, O. H. 139
Stephen 13, 15, 23, 24–5, 29, 140, 141
Strauss, Mark L. 136–7
Strelan, Rick 81, 155–6
Stronstad, Roger 179

Talbert, Charles 17
Tannehill, Robert C. 14–17, 182–3, 192
Taylor, Justin 72–3, 74–5, 113, 210
Theissen, Gerd 34, 77, 83
Thiselton, Anthony 40–1, 48

Thom, Johan C. 90
Tiede, David L. 144
Timaeus of Tauromenium 87, 91, 94, 95
Turner, Max 130, 136
Tyrannus 159, 160

VanderKam, James C. 116

Wall, Robert 39–40
Weinfeld, Moshe 109
Wolterstorff, Nicholas 52, 53
Wuthnow, Robert 58

Xenophon 212

Zacchaeus 146
Zacharias 135, 138
Zechariah 146, 169, 223
Zerbe, Gordon 108, 110, 112, 118
Zwiep, Arie 172–3, 174, 176, 177, 207